# The Unintended Reformation

# THE UNINTENDED
# REFORMATION

*How a Religious Revolution*
*Secularized Society*

—

BRAD S. GREGORY

THE BELKNAP PRESS OF
HARVARD UNIVERSITY PRESS
Cambridge, Massachusetts, and London, England
2012

*Library of Congress Cataloging-in-Publication Data*

Gregory, Brad S. (Brad Stephan), 1963–
The unintended Reformation : how a religious revolution
secularized society / Brad S. Gregory.
p. cm.
Includes bibliographical references and index.
ISBN 978-0-674-04563-7 (alk. paper)
1. Secularism—History. 2. Reformation. I. Title.
BL2747.8.G74 2012
211'.6091821—dc22 2011016131

*For Len Rosenband, who taught me how to think
And to the memory of Helen Heider,
who showed me how to live*

# Contents

# A Note on Translations and Orthography

All translations are my own unless otherwise indicated in the notes. Biblical quotations are taken from the New Revised Standard Version (NRSV), occasionally amended slightly in favor of another translation. In the text, I have retained the original orthography of the English language sources from which I quote. In the notes, the original orthography of pre-nineteenth-century publication titles has been retained, with two exceptions: in Latin titles, "v" has replaced "u" wherever called for, and the German umlaut has been rendered in its modern form rather than reproducing the variety of ways in which it was indicated in early modern sources. A slash (/) separates page numbers from line numbers wherever the latter are indicated.

The temporal good in which the state's justice fructifies, the temporal evil in which its iniquity bears its fruit, may be and are in fact quite different from the immediate results which the human mind might have expected and which the human eyes contemplate. It is as easy to disentangle these remote causations as to tell at a river's mouth which waters come from which glaciers and which tributaries.

—JACQUES MARITAIN, "The End of Machiavellianism"

# The World We Have Lost?

T HE PLACE OF THE REFORMATION in European history seems clear. It falls between the Middle Ages and modernity as something long gone, over and done with. It seems distant from the political realities and global capitalism of the early twenty-first century, far removed from present-day moral debates and social problems. This book argues otherwise. What transpired five centuries ago continues today profoundly to influence the lives of everyone not only in Europe and North America but all around the world, whether or not they are Christians or indeed religious believers of any kind. William Faulkner famously said, "The past is never dead. It's not even past."[1] He spoke more truly than he perhaps knew, yet in ways I doubt that he suspected.

This book was unplanned. I had been working on a narrative history of Christianity in the Reformation era when it became clear that two of my scholarly preoccupations—the understanding of early modern Christians in context, and the critique of modern reductionist theories of religion— in fact concerned aspects of a single, complex history. The ideas and beliefs underpinning the modern theories were in part a response to the unresolved early modern doctrinal disagreements. That this seemed largely to have escaped scholars' notice as a single history was due partly to our customary division of labor: theorists of religion and modern European intellectual historians usually do not aspire to reconstruct the lived Christianity of the pre-Enlightenment past, and Reformation historians tend not to read the sociology or anthropology of religion as a continuation of sixteenth-century issues.[2] To try to explicate what I had seen would therefore require a different kind of history, one that did not conform to all the ways in which historians ordinarily work. Despite the implications, I would have to venture outside "my field" as conventionally defined, however central the Reformation era was to the story. In fact, conventional ways of dividing up the past—by period, type of history, and (often) country—turned out to be part of the story. They need to be analyzed rather than simply assumed. The method followed in this book is more ramifying than I suspected at the outset, encompassing much more than continuities between the Reformation era and modern explanatory theories of religion. The approach has turned out to be at once a way of studying the past, of analyzing how the past became the present, and of providing a basis for interrogating some of the assumptions that govern the pursuit of knowledge in the contemporary world. *The Unintended Reformation* is intended for anyone who wants to understand how Europe and North America today came to be as they are.

Human life is lived as a temporal succession of all the intertwined elements that comprise it. But history need not be written in just the same way, moving chronologically from A as a whole to B as a whole. This book's principal argument is that the Western world today is an extraordinarily complex, tangled product of rejections, retentions, and transformations of medieval Western Christianity, in which the Reformation era constitutes the critical watershed. Some of the ways in which this is so have been inadequately understood. Consequently we fail to understand contemporary European and North American realities as well as we might, a situation on which this study seeks to improve. On the eve of the Reformation, Latin Christianity comprised for good or ill the far from homogeneous yet institutionalized worldview within which the overwhelming majority of Europeans lived and made sense of their lives. Diversely, early twenty-first-century Westerners live in and think with and even feel through the historical results of its variegated rejections and appropriations in such knotted ways that it is difficult even to see, much less to analyze, them. In getting from the early sixteenth to the early twenty-first century, this study develops the claim from my first book that "incompatible, deeply held, concretely expressed religious convictions paved a path to a secular society."[3] As we shall see, the Reformation's influence on the eventual secularization of society was complex, largely indirect, far from immediate, and profoundly unintended. Making some progress toward understanding it in a manner greater than that afforded by ordinary narratives, and which discloses the abiding influence of the distant past in the present, calls for an unconventional way of proceeding.

This book deliberately eschews the reconstructive exhaustiveness characteristic of much professional historical scholarship as incompatible with its objective. Any attempt to "cover everything" would succeed only in producing a completely unmanageable mountain of data. Indeed, in proportion to its increase, which has been enormous in the past half century, the sheer volume of historical scholarship—what Daniel Lord Smail has recently called "the inflationary spiral of research overproduction, coupled with an abiding fear of scholarly exposure for not keeping up with one's field"—paradoxically militates against comprehension of the past in relationship to the present.[4]

A different approach is needed if we are to avoid being overwhelmed by specialized scholarship, the proliferation of which tends to reinforce ingrained assumptions about historical periodization that in turn hamper an adequate understanding of change over time. If key aspects of the distant past remain importantly influential today, then archival research limited to late medieval or early modern sources obviously will not disclose them. Reading however many monographs within chronologically delimited historical subfields will inhibit rather than increase the ability to identify them, whether one is an early modern or a modern historian. We cannot stop in 1648 or 1789, nor can we begin in 1945, 1914, 1865, 1848, or 1776. We cannot content ourselves with a concentration on ideas or institutions, culture or capitalism, philosophy or politics—*all* must be incorporated because of their *combined* explanatory power, itself a corollary of their *interrelated* historical influence. And all are explanatorily powerful and have been historically consequential precisely because late medieval Christianity in all its variety was an institutionalized worldview that influenced all domains of human life. As a matter of exposition and analysis, however, these domains must to a significant degree be *separated*, else our histories will simply tend to retrace and reflect the tangled way in which human life is lived. For analytical purposes and in the pursuit of greater insight, then, the method employed in this book presupposes a prior *dis*entangling of areas of human life that were not lived apart from one another, so as to try to see more clearly their transformations over time. Accordingly, the approach is wide-ranging, multifaceted, and genealogical. Hence the six linked narratives of this study. By distinguishing analytically among several especially consequential domains of human life through which modernity was made, we will be able to see in them, taken together, the makings of modernity in the Reformation era.

A direct comparison with genealogy might be helpful.[5] Picture the complexity of all the marital and kinship relationships in a far-flung family across many generations over several centuries. Now imagine you want to determine which present-day descendants are the offspring of which ancestors; which, among all the distant ancestors who married into the family, turned out to have produced the most living descendants; and what the relationship is of living members of the family to those most fecund ancestors. You are unlikely to make much headway by trying to grasp the entire family tree all at once—it includes hundreds of persons. Nor can you simply proceed chronologically across the whole, generation by generation from the distant past to the present, setting aside each generation as you move forward in time—that would not reveal which ancestors, including those who married into the family, have produced the most living descendants. A more promising tack is to concentrate on different familial branches, one at a time, in order to determine the relationship between living descendants and ancestors in each. Then you can compare the branches and *their* relationships, determine who is the progeny of whom, which ancestors who entered the family have the most living descendants, and how each living descendant is related to each ancestor. Such an undertaking would resemble the genealogical method employed here, although the analogy is not exact because the family tree begins not with a single couple and their offspring, but with the complex and multilayered, institutionalized worldview of late medieval Christianity that had itself been over a millennium in the unsystematic making. And of course it is not a simple matter of counting descendants and tracing them back, but is rather an interpretative endeavor throughout. Nonetheless, the basic idea is that we will misgauge the character of the Western world today—in both its extraordinary pluralism and its hegemonic institutions—unless we see that and how its differentiated branches are the progeny of the Reformation era, including those branches that might seem unrelated, such as metaphysical assumptions, ethical theories, and economic behaviors. Different progeny have different lineages and occupy different places in the family tree, with complex and diverse relationships to the late Middle Ages with which they share a common ancestry.

As a matter of deliberate intellectual strategy and not simply practical necessity, then, this book's experimental analysis of the past is highly targeted. It is self-consciously selective and, one might say, *extractive*. It seeks to apply in a particular way Nietzsche's claim that "the most valuable insights are *methods*."[6] And it rests on judgments about what in the past has been most influential in making life in Europe and North America what it is today, beginning in the late Middle Ages in what turned out to be deeply consequential ways. Such judgments are of course subject to criticism like any others. Different historians might argue for alternative aspects of the past as most influential in shaping the present, and/or for different ways of interpreting them or the ones identified here. The six intertwined historical domains selected are by no means exhaustive. A more comprehensive account would supplement them with others. "Genealogical history" or perhaps "analytical history" seem equally fitting names for the endeavor embodied in this study.

In significant respects, this book's method and its conceptualization of historical change and continuity comprise a different way of thinking about the last five or six hundred years of Western history. As such the work is indebted to scholars in different academic disciplines, such as the economist Albert Hirschman, the philosopher Alasdair MacIntyre, and the historian of science Amos Funkenstein, who have applied a similar approach to diverse historical phenomena. Until Hirschman made the case in *The Passions and the Interests* (1977), few scholars would have thought that answering questions about the current relationship between American acquisitiveness and morality requires an understanding of seventeenth- and eighteenth-century European thought in relationship to one of traditional Christianity's deadly sins.[7] He showed that explaining the present demands that we see how a particularly consequential transvaluation of avarice from the distant past continues today to animate human aspirations and to motivate human actions. So too, before MacIntyre's genealogical analysis of Western moral philosophy in *After Virtue* (1981), it would have seemed most implausible that the jettisoning of the Aristotelian moral tradition by Enlightenment thinkers, along with rightly discredited Aristotelian *natural* philosophy in the wake of Galileo and Newton, bore any significant relationship to the perpetual standoffs among consequentialists, deontologists, contractarians, pragmatists, natural law theorists, and other protagonists in contemporary analytical moral philosophy—or to the "culture wars" that have marked the United States since the 1980s.[8] Finally, until Funkenstein's *Theology and the Scientific Imagination from the Middle Ages to the Seventeenth Century* (1986), no one would have suspected any connection between late medieval metaphysics and contemporary neo-Darwinian atheism.[9] But the metaphysical and epistemological assumptions of modern science and of antireligious, scientistic ideologies are clearly indebted to the emergence of metaphysical univocity that Funkenstein identified in medieval scholasticism beginning with John Duns Scotus.[10]

The highly targeted analyses by such scholars enable us to understand more about the present than we otherwise would have.[11] They share in common the identification of seemingly minor innovations in the medieval or early modern past, which, variously transformed and appropriated in unanticipated ways, had tremendous and lasting consequences because they persisted and became embedded in subsequent changes, assumptions, and practices. In this sense, as Faulkner put it, the past remains not simply alive but "not even past," a notion perhaps akin to what Michel Foucault meant when he referred to "writing the history of the present."[12] In their respective ways, Hirschman, MacIntyre, and Funkenstein each address a particular departure from long-standing teachings of medieval Christianity, whether its condemnation of avarice as a deadly sin, its teleological view of human nature and virtue-centered morality, or its conviction that God is radically and irreducibly distinct from creation. Paradoxically, these sorts of historically consequential innovations tend to remain hidden despite their continuing influence, because of their origins in the distant past and the extent to which they have become intertwined with later developments. Once normalized, they are taken for granted; they are not looked for or questioned and thus are not seen. But a certain kind of historical analysis can discern and trace them.

What would a wide-ranging, multifaceted genealogical analysis of the Reformation era and its impact look like? The upheavals of the sixteenth and seventeenth centuries were hugely consequential for subsequent institutional and ideological developments in Europe and North America. They are part of standard narratives about how the Reformation era ushered in Western modernity, with its separation of church and state, secularization of public politics, privatization of religion, and freedom of religious belief and worship. Yet a genealogical approach can illuminate aspects of the Reformation that continue to influence the present but have remained largely unrecognized. In his own way, Max Weber influentially pursued this project in his *Protestant Ethic and the Spirit of Capitalism* (1904–1905), which sought to discern the ways in which Calvinism's transformation of medieval asceticism unintentionally laid the groundwork for the dynamism of modern Western capitalism.[13] How might familiar dimensions of the Reformation's impact—its rejection of the authority of the Roman church, its influence on the relationship between church and state, or its effects on the shaping of socially exclusive religious identities, known to historians of the period as "confessionalization"—be related to the repudiation of various aspects of medieval Christianity as studied not only by Hirschman, MacIntyre, and Funkenstein, but by other scholars as well?

A genealogical approach that emphasizes the continuing influence of the distant past in the present runs counter to the recent tendency among many historians toward "the flattening of history or the telescoping of historical time," as Smail has put it, accompanied by "a sense that history has begun to withdraw from an engagement with the deeper past" as "historicity has become confused with modernity."[14] Indeed, the ever-accelerating rate of historical change over the last century would seem to render the distant past of Peter Laslett's "world we have lost" ever less relevant to those who seek to understand the present.[15] Certainly there is no denying the enormous historical watershed that separates premodern from modern Europe and North America, with the shift from a primarily agrarian to an industrial economy between the late eighteenth and early twentieth centuries, in conjunction with the solidification of politically powerful, bureaucratic states and a demographic trend away from rural and toward urban societies. All this is incontestable.

Nevertheless, a central argument of this book is that ideological and institutional shifts that occurred five or more centuries ago remain substantively necessary to an explanation of why the Western world today is as it is. Paradoxically, the enormity *of* the transition from premodern to modern is precisely what has helped to mask the continuing influence of the distant past in the present. To be sure, the fact of the transformation is the historical reality that underlies the proper recognition of historicism as a necessary prophylactic against anachronism. There is no gainsaying this for anyone who wants to understand the past. But the radicality of the transition has also enabled the problematic elevation of historicism as the implicit guarantor of a virtually absolute separation between "us" and "them," a notion prompted especially by the wrenching upheavals in Europe during the era of the French Revolution and Napoleonic Wars—which have left modern Westerners, in Peter Fritzsche's phrase, feeling "stranded in the present."[16] Functionally, this view of historicism has since the nineteenth century created among most professional historians a barrier inhibiting the discernment and analysis of the interrelated changes and continuities traced in this study. Indeed, it has fostered the impression that there is little if anything to be thus discerned and analyzed.

Because the distant past is so obviously different and "other" in so many ways, a fact known above all to premodern historians and only intensified in proportion to their immersion in their sources, knowledge of that past is widely assumed to be largely dispensable for those who want to understand today's world. This is a mistake. A distorting, maximalist view of historicism has been institutionalized in the teaching of history and the training of historians, making of periodization virtually an intellectual prison. Graduate training tends to condition young historians to serve as new inmates in the inherited cells of periodization constructed by their forebears. Late medieval and Reformation Europe are not merely the predecessor background from which modern ideologies and institutions emerged, over against which the latter defined themselves and which they have left behind. The ideologies and institutions of modernity are also the tangled continuation, development, and extension of late medieval and early modern innovations that remain influential in the present.

The ways in which this is so have gone mostly unrecognized not only because of maximalist views of historicism, such that historians of the recent past assume that only in the most remote, indirect ways could the distant past be explanatorily relevant to an understanding of the present. Despite the increased emphasis in recent years on historically important transnational and global human interactions, the lack of recognition is also partly a product of the ways in which most professional historians continue to divide up the past—almost always by period, national or regional focus, and type of history (social, political, economic, cultural, intellectual, and so forth). Medieval English political historians, eighteenth-century German social historians, post–World War II American cultural historians, and so on, inhabit very different, largely disconnected scholarly worlds. Without a doubt, the pursuit of persuasive answers to many historical questions requires just this sort of partitioning of the past (indeed, this book's project would have been inconceivable without the fruit of such scholarship by a great many historians working over multiple generations). But research restricted to the boundaries created by such parceling cannot itself answer the question of how the Western world today came to be as it is. Instead it produces enormous quantities of specialized scholarship that tends to make the question seem unmanageably unanswerable. Many historians, in ways analogous to colleagues in other disciplines, lament the narrowness, specialization, fragmentation, and loss of any "big picture" in their discipline—in contrast to other historians who champion microhistory in place of any narratives larger than those they want to tell—but to envision intellectually responsible alternatives to these realities of scholarly life is easier said than done. Max Weber's words continue to define graduate training in history no less than in other academic disciplines, and continue to haunt historians' endeavors: "*Wissenschaft* has entered a stage of specialization unknown in the past and . . . this will remain forever so."[17]

That said, if changes that originated in the distant past remain influential today, transcend national boundaries, and are inextricable from the full range of human ambitions and actions, then the prevailing division of scholarly labor among professional historians is ill-suited even to identify them. There are few incentives to attempt to think in such terms even after academic tenure is secured, with so many sources to read, research projects to conduct, books to master, and articles to write in one's delimited field.[18] For these reasons, the very persons most intensively engaged in the study of the premodern past are conditioned to overlook in important ways its relationship to the present. As has already been mentioned and for reasons further developed below, those who study the modern era and especially the very recent past are unlikely to think that the late Middle Ages and the Reformation era remain substantively important to their concerns. Accordingly, insofar as historical processes rooted in the distant past have in crucial respects made the present what it is and continue to influence it, an inadequate understanding of the contemporary world is all but inevitable—not only among historians but also in the wider population. "Our past is sedimented in our present," as Charles Taylor has recently expressed it, "and we are doomed to misidentify ourselves, as long as we can't do justice to where we come from."[19] Historians' periodization and partitioning of the past inhibit the comprehension and thus the articulation of explanatorily compelling, integrated accounts of the makings of the modern Western world. The proliferation of historical scholarship within the prevailing division of labor only intensifies the problem. The irony could hardly be greater: history itself tends to inhibit historical understanding and hence human self-awareness.

There seems to be another, related reason why the conceptualization of the past and the historical method embodied here are likely to seem unusual, one reflected in historical periodization and assumptions about change over time. Long-term, wide-ranging, synthetic narratives that *are* attempted tend to presuppose a supersessionist model of historical change. That is, the distant past is assumed to have been left behind, explanatorily important to what immediately succeeded it but not to the present. So Reformation historians obviously need to understand the late Middle Ages, for example, in order to understand the sixteenth-century historical realities in which they are primarily interested, but twentieth-century American historians supposedly do not. Mere temporal succession—trivially true and undeniable—is insufficiently distinguished from historical explanation, as if *chronos* automatically produced *Zeitgeist*.[20] Consequently, although historians typically and rightly insist on the contingency of past historical events, most large-scale narratives of Western history over the past half millennium at least implicitly suggest otherwise: their structure tends to conflate the past's intelligibility with a quasi-inevitability conceived in holistic and supersessionist terms—as if, *all* things considered, *of course* we find ourselves where we are. And the more that we understand of the past, the better will we see why this is so. The past is conceived as a sequential series of epochal blocks: medieval realities gave way to early modern realities gave way to modern realities, leading to where we are, a succession of stages that tends to reinforce a crypto-Hegelian view of history (itself indebted to Vico and Lessing), one that dovetails with the premodern past viewed as "the world we have lost" and with Hans Blumenberg's "legitimacy of the modern age."[21] Not only have past processes made us what we are—"modern" or "postmodern" selves, rather than "medieval" or "early modern" selves—but by explaining them we both account for and implicitly justify present realities. Older ideas, values, and practices, for example, simply became untenable at certain points, it is argued or implied, and so were superseded by more adequate and/or more sophisticated ones—that is how modernization happened and how historical change continues to happen.

Originally linked to strongly positive evaluations of historical progress in the eighteenth and nineteenth centuries, this supersessionist structuring of large-scale narratives about how we supposedly came to be who we are remains prevalent today. This is so even when it is uncoupled (as now it often is) from rosy evaluations of an onward-and-upward, progressive view of Western history in the past half millennium. Regardless of its evaluative coloring, this supersessionist template continues to serve as the foundation for multiauthor Western or World civilization textbooks, for example, in which medievalists pass the baton to early modernists who in turn hand it off to modernists for the anchor leg of the relay. To the extent that the wider population has a historical sense (generally still less an issue in Europe than in the United States), this supersessionist picture is the one that is absorbed. It purports to explain who we are and how we got here. Some of the most distinguished, recent large-scale narratives by individual authors, too, proceed in the same manner regardless of how the outcome is assessed. Although Jacques Barzun's study, for example, ends on a critical note of considerable dismay about the current "demotic culture in decadence," his capacious and imaginative cultural history of the West since 1500 follows this supersessionist pattern, organized in a series of four successive chronological parts.[22] So does Andrew Delbanco's insightful essay on the character of hope in the sweep of American history: having lost a collective commitment to the sacralized nation that had superseded colonial Calvinist religiosity, "the ache for meaning goes unrelieved," he claims, in our contemporary culture of individualist consumerism marked especially by "the unslaked craving for transcendence."[23] Even the recent, magisterial account of secularization by Charles Taylor ultimately assumes much of this structure in its multifaceted exploration of transition from an enchanted late medieval era characterized by "naïve acknowledgment of the transcendent" to the modern era of multivalent "secularity" and "exclusive humanism" in which we live, a shift from the premodern, socially embedded "porous self" to the meaning-constructing "buffered self" that lives within our "immanent frame" of disenchanted modern reality that (supposedly) lacks room for the sacred.[24]

But who are "we?" *The content of the answer to this question determines what needs to be explained.* It's a very diverse group. In the Western world today "we" include, for example, Angela Merkel and Sarah Palin, skinhead racists and Mother Teresa's Missionaries of Charity, Rush Limbaugh and Michael Moore, young-earth creationists and antireligious atheists, Judith Butler and Condoleezza Rice, Juggalo and Juggalette followers of Insane Clown Posse and members of the John Birch Society, Internet pornographers and members of Morality in Media, Donald Trump and Bill Gates, MoMA devotees and NASCAR enthusiasts, Pope Benedict XVI and Hugh Hefner. The point is not that such a list enumerates typical contemporary Westerners, but that all those on it, with their respective and radical differences, are by definition equally the product of historical processes—all are early twenty-first-century North Americans or Europeans. Therefore any adequate historical explanation of the present must be able to account for all of them, and indeed for the full range of different worldviews, values, and commitments that people in fact hold, whether coherently or confusedly. It must also be able to account for the *ways* in which they hold them, from the aggressively assertive to the confessedly conflicted, as well as for the full spectrum of ways in which people modify and adapt them.

My point of departure is therefore the (banal) observation that human life in the Western world today, and perhaps most obviously in the United States, is characterized by an enormously wide range of incompatible truth claims pertaining to human values, aspirations, norms, morality, and meaning. These in turn (another banality) influence the ways in which people live and the sorts of lives to which they aspire. "Reality shows us a delightful wealth of types, the luxuriance of a lavish play and change of forms," an assertion about human life whose truth is all the more obvious now than it was when Nietzsche made it in the late 1880s, given the subsequent human interactions facilitated by technology, the movements of people, new cultural hybridities, and economic globalization.[25] Beliefs influence behavior, whether among the Old Order Amish or the New Atheists. And beliefs differ radically. A hyperpluralism of religious and secular commitments, not any shared or even convergent view about what "we" think is true or right or good, marks the early twenty-first century. This pluralistic heterogeneity generates the social, political, and cultural frictions that exercise liberal political theorists concerned rationally to legitimate the shared commitments and hegemonic institutions that make for viable democracies.[26] *Pace* Taylor, it simply is not the case that "*we all* shunt between two stances."[27] Rather, many millions of people today—devout religious believers or impassioned antireligious believers, for example—seem by all indications unperturbed by the hyperpluralism to which they themselves diversely contribute, convinced that their respective views are correct. Others indeed tend in various ways and to varying degrees toward the sort of self-conscious ambivalence or self-relativizing skepticism described by Taylor. But "we" do not, if "we" denotes Europeans and North Americans as such. Only some people do.

This book argues that the historical intelligibility of the past in no sense implies the inevitability of the present. The method employed here is *genealogical* in seeking to identify and analyze long-term historical trajectories with their origins in the distant past that happen to remain influential in the present. Yet in no respect is it *teleological*. In other words, by definition the past has made the present what it is, but things did not have to turn out this way. Institutionally and ideologically, materially and morally, we need not have ended up where we are. Human decisions were made that did not have to be made, some of which turned out to be deeply consequential. Patterns were established, aspirations justified, expectations naturalized, desires influenced, and new behaviors normalized that need not have taken hold. Within the constraints imposed and the opportunities afforded by biological realities, the human past is not a product of *any* autonomous, impersonal social, economic, ideological, or cultural "forces"—rather, such forces are themselves the cumulative, aggregate product of countless human decisions and actions, sometimes institutionalized, politically protected, and enduring and sometimes not, which in turn affect and constrain other decisions and actions. Marx was right about human beings making history but not under circumstances of their own choosing.[28] His conception was needlessly limited, however, by his atheistic and materialist metaphysical beliefs underlying his views about human beings, their aspirations, and their well-being, ideas that comprised only one set of truth claims among many others in mid-nineteenth-century Europe. Economic "forces," class formation, and class struggle represent not historical inevitabilities but rather the institutionalization and reinforcement of certain human desires, values, decisions, and behaviors rather than others.

One of this book's principal arguments is that the prevailing picture of a strong historical supersessionism between the late Middle Ages and the present is seriously misleading if not fundamentally mistaken.[29] Rejections rather than refutations—as well as selective appropriations—of ideas, commitments, norms, and aspirations have been common in the past half millennium. Inherited truth claims and values were often denounced without being disproven, just as worldviews and institutions were often *not* left behind. Rather, they frequently persisted in complex ways, in interaction with rival claims and new historical realities that differentially drew from them and influenced them in turn.

Negligence of these facts yields supersessionist history that distorts our understanding of the present, perhaps most conspicuously with respect to religion, as if religious traditions actually had been left behind either as social realities or rendered intellectually untenable as competitors to secular ideologies. Despite their rejection beginning in the Protestant Reformation, central truth claims and related practices of medieval Christianity as embodied in Roman Catholicism, for example, have never gone away. These include—in addition to the many beliefs that early modern Catholics shared with most of their Protestant contemporaries—truth claims about papal and conciliar authority, the nature of the church, the grace conferred through the church's seven sacraments, the reality of human free will despite original sin, and the necessary role of human actions in salvation, as well as practices such as participation in the Mass, sacramental confession of sins, intercessory prayer to the saints, and veneration of the Eucharist. These claims and practices have persisted to the present notwithstanding the dramatic transformations of modernity and the many influences of early modern and modern human realities on Catholicism. They today contribute to contemporary Western hyperpluralism. Also contributing to it are the myriad truth claims and practices among Protestant Christians with their roots in the sixteenth century or later, so powerfully evident a presence in the United States today, as they have been throughout the country's history and in Western Europe's Protestant countries into the twentieth century.

Ignoring such facts produces supersessionist history that cannot account for present-day human realities. Some scholars in recent years have expressed a certain wonderment that "religion is back"; the wonder is rather that it was thought ever to have departed, apart from the "scholarly wish fulfillment" or projections of those who accepted classic theories of modernization and secularization.[30] Only those writing with a confessionally secularist agenda—one that ignores not only the realities of religious belief and practice in the modern world but also intellectually sophisticated contemporary theology, biblical scholarship, and philosophy of religion—could pretend that even post-Enlightenment intellectual history, for example, might responsibly be told as a story of incremental, inexorable Weberian disenchantment and a putatively inevitable growth of post-Darwinian atheism. Kierkegaard and Newman belong to nineteenth-century intellectual history no less than do Marx and Nietzsche. One of Edmund Husserl's most brilliant philosophical students, Edith Stein, converted to Catholicism and become a Carmelite nun in the 1930s; the ardently Catholic Elizabeth

Anscombe was named in 1970 to the chair of philosophy at Cambridge previously occupied by her teacher, Ludwig Wittgenstein; Joseph Ratzinger went head to head with Jürgen Habermas over religion, philosophy, and politics in Munich in January 2004.[31] The twentieth century was marked—just as the early twenty-first continues to be—by brilliant Protestant and Catholic theologians and philosophers, from Karl Barth and Henri de Lubac to Charles Taylor and Nicholas Wolterstorff. The plausibility of the prevailing, supersessionist picture of Western history depends on overlooking such facts and prompts ongoing questions about the precise senses in which ours is "a secular age."

Professional historians—including myself—are keenly aware of the wide variety, local particularities, individual nuances, and complex realities of the human past across time and space. I have sought not to choose between J. H. Hexter's "lumpers" and "splitters," or between Emmanuel Le Roy Ladurie's "parachutists" and "truffle hunters," but rather tried to think independently from such dichotomies in keeping with my overriding objective.[32] Certainly the drawing of careful distinctions is no less important to understanding the past than is the recognition of genuine commonalities, nor is meticulous attention to concrete particularities incompatible with seeing how they fit into larger patterns. Opting for one such pole to the exclusion of the other will not suffice to explain historical changes and continuities over the *longue durée* any more than will remaining within a single historical period, country, or type of history.

BESIDES THE INTELLECTUAL DESIRE to explain better than do conventional narratives how the distant past remains influential in the present, with particular emphasis on the consequences of the Reformation era, my motivations for writing are also practical and oriented toward at least three current issues of considerable import. Even to put the matter in this way, however, is misleading—and symptomatic. One common scholarly division of labor in the academy is between historians and social scientists. The former study the past but (aside from gestures in their conclusions) do not usually concern themselves with present-day practical issues (unless they study the very recent past). Sociologists, psychologists, economists, and political scientists typically investigate current human realities but rarely advert to the past in more than background-setting, cursory ways. Historians who transgress this disciplinary divide are said to be "no longer doing history," and social scientists who trespass are allegedly "getting bogged down in the past." But this division of labor should not be as sharply drawn as it often is and clearly cannot be mutually exclusive, simply because present realities are the product of past processes. If this book's argument is near the mark, we *cannot* understand the character of contemporary realities until and unless we see how they have been *and are still being shaped* by the distant past. Seeing present-day realities in this way may well shed unexpected light on our understanding of current social, political, and economic realities, as well as on certain (mostly) taken-for-granted intellectual assumptions and the ways in which they are institutionalized in the pursuit of knowledge. Hence although I am by professional training a historian of early modern Europe, this study is as much about the present as it is about the past.

The initial strangeness of the notion that present realities are being influenced by the distant past diminishes once we are willing to question the dominant conception of historical change and periodization. Presumably no one would dispute that present-day human realities are the product of historical processes. This banality simply follows from the temporality of human life. But the tendency to regard the *distant* past as irrelevant to contemporary realities reflects the supersessionist conception of history discussed above, and its institutionalized expression in the historical profession. The widespread assumption seems to be that the Western world today is adequately explained with reference to human life since the scientific revolution, the Enlightenment, industrialization, and the advent of modern capitalism. As noted, this book seeks to show significant respects in which this presupposition is mistaken, even as the exposition incorporates these major historical developments and seeks to delineate their relationship both to the Reformation era and the present. And the analysis will suggest ways in which all three of the contemporary, practical concerns discussed below, far from being evanescent issues limited to American current affairs, belong to complex historical trajectories that have been centuries in the making and are thus unlikely to go away anytime soon.

First, along with quite a few other Americans, I am concerned about the degree to which people in the United States appear to be growing ever more politically and culturally polarized, since at least the 1980s, whether or not one thinks the phenomenon merits the designation of a "culture war."[33] Daniel Bell referred in 1996 to "a confused, angry, uneasy, and insecure America," and if anything his characterization seems even more applicable now.[34] Americans are deeply divided on many matters with major implications for their national life, including U.S. military interventions abroad, the place of religion in the public square, school vouchers and public education, abortion, race and affirmative action, gun control, the relationship between environmental protection and economic development, and the tolerability of sexually explicit and graphically violent popular culture. Whatever the issue, American national political culture as manifest in

the media is lacking in rigor and loaded with rancor. Often "our own poisoned public sphere," as Anthony Grafton has recently called it, seems little more than a shouting match of distorted and distorting slogans and
propagandistic one-liners.[35] The realities of a bumper-sticker political life
seem distant from idealizations of the well-informed, fair-minded, reasonable citizens theorized by champions of deliberative democracy, whether
in a Rawlsian, Habermasian, or some other form.[36] Add to this the empirically verified tendency of differently minded citizens to avoid face-to-face
conflict, and one arrives at Diana Mutz's sobering conclusion: "It is doubtful that an extremely activist political culture can also be a heavily deliberative one."[37] In other words, people are likely to pursue serious political
engagement only with those who are like-minded; conversely, disagreements diminish the likelihood of participation in the very venues available
for their negotiation and prospective settlement. And Americans have literally built their divides into the country: more and more people choose to
live in neighborhoods or communities with others of like views and values,
a demographic trend that has increased sharply since the late 1970s.[38]
Educational realities reinforce the same clustering by background and outlook, whether in the most exclusive prep schools, chronically neglected
urban public schools, or among the burgeoning number of homeschoolers,
some of whom are determined to shield their children from disapproved
ideas whereas others simply want to avoid subjecting them to a lousy public school education.[39]

The power of American governmental institutions and law enforcement
normally contains and controls the acrimony underlying such divisions,
despite the extent to which the polarizations increasingly influence political institutions themselves.[40] But notwithstanding repeated platitudes, neither politicians nor journalists nor academics nor celebrities appear to
have any answers about how to reverse the trajectory of polarization. Instead, the American public square seems to grow ever coarser and angrier,
its protagonists ever more outraged at each other, ever more stridently asserting their respective rights and seeking to constrain their adversaries'
actions.[41] As citizens Americans are coexisting, but it seems quite a stretch
to claim that they are flourishing. Obviously no work of history—and no
work from any other academic discipline—can do much about such a big
problem. I have no illusions about this. But seeing some of the deep historical roots of our predicament might at least enable us to understand it
better, and so to think more fruitfully about ways of addressing it.

Second, along with many others, I am concerned about global climate
change and what it portends for the earth's environmental well-being.[42]
The problem is deeper than the policies of this or that political administra-

tion, as though it were fixable through a few more environmentally responsible policies or new corporations that might literally profit from the
business of environmental cleaning and greening. Nor is the waking of
environmentalism from its post-1970s slumber in the media, popular culture, and advertising likely to have more than a marginal impact. The
poisoning of the atmosphere that has followed from increased carbon di-
oxide emissions is the result of industrial manufacturing and agriculture,
petroleum-based transportation, and energy technologies throughout the
world, which are themselves the means to the end of satisfying the cycle
of seemingly insatiable consumer desires and capitalist production. The
underlying problem is that most people seek—and through relentless advertising are encouraged to pursue—ever greater material affluence and
comfort, despite the fact that average American income, for example, rose
eightfold in real terms during the twentieth century.[43] Westerners now live
in societies without an acquisitive ceiling: a distinctly consumerist (rather
than merely industrial) economic ethos depends precisely on persuading
people to discard as quickly as possible what they were no less insistently
urged to purchase, so that another acquisitive cycle might begin. In proportion as an individual's identity is derived from consumption, the quest
to (re)construct and (re)discover oneself is inseparable from endless
acquisitions—there *can never be* "enough" if to be is to buy, if self-fashioning
depends on ever more and newer fashions for the self.[44] This sort of consumerist ethos has consequences. In the United States, "excess" has now
lost any socially significant moral meaning: there is literally no such thing
as "too much," so long as one has the economic means to do as one pleases.[45]
This remains as true now as it was before the economic downturn of 2008,
as is evident, for example, in the fact that American contractors in early
2011 were continuing to build spec homes costing tens of millions of
dollars.[46]

The models of neoclassical economists collapse any distinction between
needs and wants into demand, and construe human rationality as the most
efficient instrumental means to satisfy the desires of definitionally maximizing individuals.[47] So in microeconomic theorizing, preference-driven
individuals might rationally decide to drive by themselves in an SUV because of the pleasure it affords, as opposed to enduring the hassles of car-
pooling in a hybrid, despite the dramatically discrepant environmental
impact of the two choices. The opportunity cost of giving up the SUV is
simply greater than that of continuing to drive it. And desirous individuals
might rationally make this choice every day for years, rationally buying
another SUV to satisfy their desires when the color or condition of their current one no longer sufficiently pleases them. Millions of people apparently

believe that to enact laws that would take away SUVs—or any other available consumer goods—would be an intolerable restriction on individual freedom, not to mention an ill-advised constraint on market efficiency and economic growth.

Despite sociological evidence to the contrary, it remains to all appearances virtually axiomatic that the acquisition of consumer goods is the presumptive means to human happiness—and the more and better the goods, the better one's life and the happier one will be.[48] Or so consumers in China and India seem to think, following the lead of the United States and Europe. But absent a solution to the problem of $CO_2$ emissions and their climatic effects, an India and China consuming per capita at an American rate would almost certainly threaten the planet's ability to support life in the long term. So maybe the story won't have a happy ending. Maybe the instrumentally rational pursuit of individual consumption and enjoyment and affluence will turn out to entail a gradual, collective destruction of the earth's capacity to sustain life. Maybe steadfast faith in the market and insistence on perpetual economic growth will lead not to a better future, but to none.[49] (The financial crisis that exploded in 2008 seems highly unlikely to yield any basic reorientation of the reciprocal relationship between consumerism and capitalism, considering that international and respective national efforts alike are seeking ways to restore that relationship.) The pursuit of ever more and better *stuff* seems collectively to be making the planet dangerously warmer in ways that serve as a stark reminder of reality—not realities we "fashion" or "construct" for ourselves, but the one that biologists and ecologists, atmospheric scientists and oceanographers investigate. Attempting to understand historically the roots of the entangled attitudes, values, institutions, and practices that have contributed to the environmental dangers we now face seems like a worthwhile undertaking. In his major recent contribution to a burgeoning historiography on consumption, Jan de Vries has rightly stated that "consumer aspirations have a history."[50] Their origins long antedate the advent of modern industrial manufacturing in the late eighteenth century.

Finally, I am concerned about the blithe and incoherent denial of the category of truth in the domains of human morality, values, and meaning among many academics. It is frequently alleged that all human meaning, morality, and values can be nothing more than whatever human beings of different times and cultures subjectively and contingently construct for themselves, or at least that we cannot know whether any among them might be more than this. By no means is this attitude limited to cultural anthropologists or humanistic scholars who embrace the latest critical-theoretical trend. In the words of the Nobel Prize–winning physicist Steven Weinberg, for example, a harsh critic of postmodern attacks on science, "moral or aesthetic statements are simply not of the sort which it is appropriate to call true or false," since we are "inventing values for ourselves as we go along."[51] If this is so, then for example it is ultimately inappropriate to say: "It is true that genocide and rape are wrong for everyone." If we invent our values and morality, then there are no bases beyond preference on which to condemn torture or the selling of teenage girls into sexual slavery. We simply happen to live in a culture in which most people happen not to like such things. But in fact, "human rights" cannot serve as a stable, shared basis for morality in a society riven by fundamental disagreement about what "human" means, as is apparent from the abortion debate. Nor can "human nature," in an academic climate in which it is widely believed that such a notion is an oppressive, essentialist chimera. The natural sciences can offer no help if, as many evolutionary biologists claim, *Homo sapiens* is simply a remarkably adaptive hominid, no different in kind from other mammalian species with which it shares so much genetic material. Science neither observes any *persons* nor discovers any *rights*—for the simple reason that there are none to be found given the metaphysical postulates and empiricist assumptions of science. So-called transhumanists understand the implications. If "rights" and "persons" no less than "morality" are mere constructs without empirical grounding in the findings of science, and only science can legitimately tell us anything true about reality, then such constructs can be deconstructed and dismissed in the pursuit of alternatives— such as a calculatingly eugenicist ethical agenda that seeks to hasten the evolutionary self-transcendence of *Homo sapiens*.[52] Quite literally, the transhumanists' aim is the deliberate self-elimination of human beings through genetic manipulation.

From the undeniable fact of pluralism, it is frequently inferred that moral and cultural relativism is true, that there are no norms and values rightly applicable to people of all times and places. (Hence the incoherence of attempts to abandon truth as a category: its denial always involves at least this one truth claim. *Consistently* to abandon truth requires that one stop making assertions or arguments.) Instead of seeking to advance exclusive and particularistic and divisive truth claims, it is said, we should (note the normative imperative) promote toleration and diversity. But not all diversity. Racism, sexism, and violence, for example, are bad, and so are not to be tolerated. But "bad" is a moral category. So we need a moral criterion to distinguish good diversity and toleration from bad diversity and toleration. But morality has already been relegated to the realm of subjective and contingent constructions. Hence moral constructivists have nowhere to stand, no basis on which to make normative claims.[53] If they are correct, why should anyone accept *their* arbitrary construction of morality rather than that of a fascistic racist, an authoritarian Catholic, a fundamentalist Protestant, or a militant Islamist? Why indeed, unless it is true?

Denials of truth and of nonsubjective moral norms in the name of toleration and diversity are self-defeating and self-contradictory—unless one is prepared to go the whole way, and grant that genocide, rape, slavery, and torture are acceptable. Thankfully, only the pathological would claim as much, although why this is so is unclear if ethics lacks any objective basis. Yet how to ground truth claims about morality and values amid swarms of incompatible, shifting assertions about them remains a genuine and pressing problem. We *must* make moral arguments if the condemnation of such evils is not to be a matter of mere individual choice or lucky-for-us majoritarian preference—if we are to articulate *why,* for example, exploitative, abusive human relationships are always and everywhere *wrong.* A historical analysis of the genesis and character of our situation that at a minimum could illuminate the nature of the problem seems desirable. It so happens that any history restricted to the modern era is bound to be inadequate.

IF THE CONTINUING INFLUENCE of the distant past in the present usually goes unnoticed partly because of the complex ways in which its elements are entangled, then neither disentanglement nor genealogy are mere metaphors. Following Nietzsche's claim quoted above, they also suggest a method and a form of historical writing. Each of the following six chapters concentrates genealogically on one of the entanglement's major strands, which are analytically distinguished in an attempt to foster comprehension and *not* because the respective areas of human life on which they focus were lived separately from the others. Each chapter analyzes a consequential historical trajectory within a particular domain of human life, noting along the way some of its relationships to the other domains analyzed. As a whole the book thus constitutes an explanation about the makings of modernity as both a multifaceted rejection and a variegated appropriation of different elements of medieval Christianity. None of the chapters stands alone; the overarching argument depends on each being taken in conjunction with the others.

The six long-term narratives are simultaneously distinguished from and related to each other as parts of what is intended as a single explanatory account. So it is perhaps worth stating in the briefest terms the overall argument. This is neither a study of decline from a lost Golden Age nor a narrative of progress toward an ever brighter future, but rather an analysis of unintended historical consequences that derived from transformative responses to major, perceived human problems. Late medieval Christianity was an institutionalized worldview, but one long and deeply marked by the gulf between the faith's own prescriptions and many Christians' actual practices, between its ideals and its realities. This comprised a first set of problems. How was the gap to be narrowed and shared human life to be made more genuinely Christian? Reformation leaders thought the root problem was doctrinal, and in seeking to fix it by turning to the Bible they unintentionally introduced multiple sorts of unwanted disagreement. This constituted a new set of problems, different from the first. What was true Christianity and how was it known? Doctrinal controversy was literally endless, and religio-political conflicts between Catholics and magisterial Protestants from the early sixteenth through the mid-seventeenth century were destructive and inconclusive. The undesired nonresolution of intra-Christian contention brought with it a third set of problems, related to the second. How was human life among frequently antagonistic Christians to be rendered stable and secure? The solution eventually adopted in all modern, liberal Western states was to privatize religion and to distinguish it from public life, ideologically as well as institutionally, through politically protected rights to individual religious freedom. Not subjective faith but objective reason, in science and modern philosophy, would be the basis for public life. But modern states continued to rely on citizens' behaviors that depended on beliefs rooted in Christianity (such as individual rights) even as other cross-confessionally embraced behaviors (such as material acquisitiveness) were antithetical to its teachings. Within the liberal institutional framework of modern rights, secularization in recent decades has led to the proliferation of secular and religious truth claims along with related practices that constitute contemporary hyperpluralism. These contemporary realities present a set of problems that are an outgrowth of those of the Reformation era, but in radically altered intellectual, institutional, and material circumstances. What sort of public life or common culture is possible in societies whose members share ever fewer substantive beliefs, norms, and values save for a nearly universal embrace of consumerist acquisitiveness?

Because late medieval Christianity was an institutionalized worldview, the Reformation affected all domains of human life in ways that have led over the long term and unintentionally to the situation in which Europeans and North Americans find themselves today. That is why this book combines and endeavors to analyze across half a millennium human realities that at first sight might seem to have nothing to do with one another, such as conceptions of God, practices of consumption, and the character of universities. In so doing, the inquiry also encompasses the formation of some dominant assumptions that govern modern intellectual life. Each chapter begins by describing the situation characteristic of the contemporary Western world with respect to an important area of human life, and then offers a genealogical explanation of its historical formation with particular attention given to the Reformation era's transformative and unintended influence. The six strands in the analysis focus respectively on the relationship among religion, science, and metaphysics; the basis for truth claims related to human values and meaning; the institutional locus of the public exercise of power; moral discourse and moral behavior; human desires and capitalism; and the relationship between higher education and assumptions about knowledge.

I begin by exploring some long-term consequences of the initially subtle rejection of the long-standing Christian view of God's relationship to creation beginning in the later Middle Ages, and the extent to which this rejection tacitly and yet far from subtly continues to dominate modern intellectual life. Among the most significant consequences has been the pervasive modern spread of the view that increasingly powerful scientific explanations of natural regularities provide progressively compelling evidence against the claims of revealed religion as such. This view turns out to be the result of contingent (and often unknowingly held) metaphysical assumptions with medieval roots. The historical significance of these assumptions became unexpectedly important starting in the seventeenth century because of the ways in which doctrinal controversy in the Reformation era unintentionally marginalized theological discourse about God and the natural world.

Chapter 2 analyzes the Protestant Reformation and modern philosophy as the two most important (and related) means by which attempts were made to ground truth claims by those who rejected medieval Christianity as embodied in the Roman church, which led in divergent ways to unintended pluralisms based respectively on the Bible and reason. Doctrinal impasses in the Reformation era helped to foster a renaissance of ancient epistemological skepticism and to inspire modern philosophical foundationalism. But historically and empirically, "reason alone" since Descartes has proved no more capable than "scripture alone" since Luther of providing a basis for reaching shared answers to questions about what is true, how people should live, or what they should care about. The long-term result is the open-ended multiplication of truth claims about such issues that proliferate within modern, liberal states today and that collectively contribute to Western hyperpluralism.

Chapter 3 shows how the Reformation transformed the growing late medieval oversight of ecclesiastical institutions by nonecclesiastical authorities, leaving a lasting legacy of the modern state's control of religion and its eventual midwifery of secularization via religious toleration. Among those Christians who rejected the Roman church, only politically supported forms of Protestantism were able to have a wide, lasting influence alongside Catholic regimes in the early modern period. Inconclusive religio-political conflicts in the Reformation era prompted the eventual political protection of individual religious freedom in exchange for religion's privatization, although liberal states today control churches no less (albeit very differently) than did confessional states in early modern Europe.

In Chapter 4, the transition is traced from medieval Christianity's ethics of the good to modern liberalism's formal ethics of rights via the disagreements and disruptions *about* the Christian good during the Reformation era. Because Christian socio-ecclesial divisions reflected disputes about the good and its implications for human life, modern moral and political discourse transformed the traditional discourse on rights and left determination of the good up to individuals whose rights the state would protect. But advanced secularization has exposed the extent to which modern moral and political communities continued to rely on substantive beliefs about the good appropriated from Christianity, the growing abandonment of which has precipitated divisions among citizens today that put increasing pressure on the liberal democracies that enable those very divisions.

Chapter 5 concentrates on how consumption in conjunction with capitalism and technology, from the Middle Ages through the Renaissance to the seventeenth-century Dutch Republic and the Industrial Revolution, forged an ideology and related practices that dominate Western modernity and increasingly, through globalization, the world. Given the destructive fruitlessness of religio-political conflicts in the Reformation era, Catholics and Protestants alike built on trends that antedated the Reformation and decided to go shopping instead of continuing to fight about religion, thus permitting their self-colonization by capitalism in the industrious revolution. In combination with the exercise of power by hegemonic, liberal states, a symbiosis of capitalism and consumerism is today more than anything else the cultural glue that holds together the heterogeneity of Western hyperpluralism.

Finally, Chapter 6 analyzes the relationship among different sorts of knowledge together with the sites where new knowledge has been sought and transmitted from the Middle Ages to the present. The confessionalization of universities in the Reformation era included a privileging of theology that insulated theologians from new knowledge, the pursuit of which increasingly migrated outside universities in early modern Europe. Persistent doctrinal disagreements among Christians plus intellectual weakness born of political protection rendered most theologians diversely unable to cope with eighteenth-century intellectual innovations. In the following century, knowledge-making was centralized in research universities, theology progressively marginalized, and knowledge increasingly secularized, a process that was essentially complete by the early twentieth century except among Catholic universities, which largely followed suit in the late twentieth century.

Together the chapters constitute a whole that endeavors to explain major features of the Western world today as the unintended, long-term outcome of diverse rejections as well as variegated retentions and appropriations of medieval Christianity. The book seeks not only to study the distant past and its continuing influence on the present, but also thereby to shed new light on the character of some present problems, and to question some of the basic assumptions that frame contemporary intellectual life by understanding where those assumptions come from and what they are based on. It hopes to make good on the words of John Noonan: "Looking intently at the past can improve our present vision."[54]

# CHAPTER ONE

# Excluding God

INTELLECTUALLY, INSTITUTIONALLY, and in their concrete applications, the natural sciences have transformed the Western world and continue to exercise an enormous global influence. Especially since the eighteenth century, numerous intellectuals have thought that their cumulatively impressive explanations of natural phenomena undermine central claims of revealed religion. In research universities since the late nineteenth century, the ontological framework of the natural sciences has largely dictated the legitimate investigative boundaries for the social sciences and humanities as well. Applied scientific findings underlie the military, computer, and communications technologies of modern Western states, by means of which their leaders maintain order and wage wars. The use of science also enabled and continues to sustain engineering and manufacturing technologies that since the late eighteenth century have made possible a dramatic transformation of the built environment as well as the symbiosis of modern capitalism and consumerism. Later chapters consider the relationship of science to morality, capitalism, and higher education, respectively; this one concentrates on the relationship among science, metaphysics, and Christian theology since the Middle Ages.

Max Weber (1864–1920) was an intellectually capacious sociologist who became one of the most influential thinkers of the twentieth century. In "Science as a Vocation," a lecture written near the end of the Great War in late 1917 and published in early 1919, he expressed a view about the relationship between science and religion that summed up a central thrust of nineteenth-century Western intellectual life, a view that would become increasingly widespread in the twentieth. According to Weber, "intellectualist rationalization through science and scientifically oriented technology" means that "fundamentally no mysterious incalculable powers are present that come into play, but rather that one can—in principle—master all things by calculation. This implies the disenchantment of the world [*Entzauberung der Welt*]." Laying out the basis for his influential fact-value distinction, Weber contrasted science's disenchanting effect with medieval philosophy and the seventeenth-century investigation of the natural world, which were thought to show "the way to God."

> And today? Who today still believes—aside from certain big children whom one can indeed find in the natural sciences—that the findings of astronomy or biology or physics or chemistry have something to do with the meaning of the world or indeed could teach us something about it? By what path could one come upon the trace of such a "meaning," if any is there? If the natural sciences lead to anything and are suited to any belief along these lines, it is to make the notion that there is a "meaning" of the world die out at its roots! And to conclude: science as a way "to God"? Science, this power expressly antithetical to religion [*die spezifisch gottfremde Macht*]? No one today in his heart of hearts [*in seinem letzten Innern*] is in doubt that science is antithetical to religion, whether or not he admits it to himself.

Science and religion are incompatible, Weber thought, the one undermining and displacing the other. Scientific investigation of the natural world discloses a reality devoid of meaning, purpose, value, or God's presence, and therefore disenchanted. Insofar as science had demystified "these former illusions," latter-day affirmations of religious faith demanded a sacrifice of intellectual integrity.[1] One could coherently acknowledge scientific findings or submit to religious claims, but not both. To be a modern, educated person was necessarily to be without religious belief, because science reveals a natural world without God.

This is the dominant view today among European and North American academics at leading research universities, whether they are natural scientists, social scientists, or humanistic scholars. In the late 1990s, for example, among members of the National Academy of Sciences in the United States, only 7 percent reported belief in a personal God and 7.9 percent in human immortality.[2] The incompatibility between revealed religion and science is presupposed in modern reductionist theories of religion derived from the social sciences and cultural theory.[3] If anything, because of the stunning advances especially in the biological sciences during the past half century, the incompatibility between science and substantive religious claims is widely thought to be even stronger than it was when Weber wrote. The social correlate seems to be the steep decline in religious practice particularly in Western Europe and Canada since the 1960s. The plausibility of religious claims seems to diminish in proportion to scientific discoveries about the natural world. Even though religion persists as a sociological reality, people apparently become less religious as they become better educated and more rational. John Searle's remarks capture this perspective well. As he puts it, "the contemporary scientific world view" is "like it or not" simply "the world view we have":

> Given what we know about the details of the world—about such things as the position of elements in the periodic table, the number of chromosomes in the cells of different species, and the nature of the chemical bond—this world view is not an option. It is not simply up for grabs along with a lot of competing world views. Our problem is not that somehow we have failed to come up with a convincing proof of the existence of God or that the hypothesis of an afterlife remains in serious doubt, it is rather that in our deepest reflections we cannot take such opinions seriously. When we encounter people who claim to believe such things, we may envy them the comfort and security they claim to derive from these beliefs, but at bottom we remain convinced that either they have not heard the news or they are in the grip of faith. We remain convinced that somehow they must separate their minds into separate compartments to believe such things.[4]

Like Weber before him, Searle thinks that science and faith are incompatible, capable only of an intellectually dichotomous coexistence in someone who has failed to acknowledge our worldview as dictated by science. In ways vastly less sophisticated but which sell many more books, the same message is central to the shrill, screedy truth claims in the recent best sellers of the so-called New Atheists.[5]

Presumably by "we" Searle means others who draw from the findings of science conclusions similar to his own. He apparently does not mean—and seems unaware of—those intellectuals fully apprised of the findings of modern science who also affirm substantive religious claims with no sign in their writings of the sort of mental bifurcation he posits. A few examples include physicist-theologians such as John Polkinghorne and Robert John Russell, evolutionary biologist Kenneth Miller, human geneticist and former director of the Human Genome Project Francis Collins, philosophers such as Michael Buckley, David Burrell, Alasdair MacIntyre, Alvin Plantinga, and John Rist, and theologians such as David Bentley Hart, John Haught, Christopher Knight, Joseph Ratzinger, and Christoph Schönborn.[6] They and others like them contribute to the hyperpluralism of contemporary Western intellectual life—they do not lie outside it. They have all "heard the news" about modern physics and chemistry and biology, and unlike, for example, those biblically literalist Christians who continue to think that the earth is around six thousand years old, none can fairly or accurately be described as being unreflectively "in the grip of faith."

To see this, however, would require familiarity with their writings and arguments. But if "we cannot take such opinions seriously" precisely *because* they attempt to show the compatibility of scientific findings and (some) religious claims, including the reality of God and the possibility of an afterlife, then the effort requisite for the attainment of such familiarity is simply not made. One instead exempts oneself from the intellectual labor needed to understand their writings and remains content to beg the question about the alleged incompatibility of science and (all) religion, assuming it has been settled. But clearly it hasn't. The very existence of such scientists and scholars as a social fact, in combination with the articulated compatibility of their religious claims and the findings of science, empirically falsifies the notion that science and religion are necessarily incompatible. Accordingly, a putative historical and intellectual inevitability is shown instead to be a mere—albeit widespread and highly influential—sociological reality, institutionalized in the culture of the academy and demographically pervasive in post-Christian, Western European countries and Canada. Chapter 6 will analyze the long-term historical formation of this secularized intellectual culture and the institutions of higher education that sustain it. The present task is to investigate one of its ideological cornerstones, the ostensible incompatibility between the findings of the natural sciences and the truth claims of revealed religion, in particular the claims of the Christianity in the context of which modern Western science emerged. As we shall see, the unintended self-marginalization of theology through doctrinal controversy in the Reformation era played an indirect but critically important role in the story.

Perhaps Searle's "deepest reflections" and the convictions of those who agree with him are on these matters not deep enough. Perhaps they are based not on the findings of science, but on contrary faith commitments that are neither metaphysically neutral nor self-evidently justifiable. Rather than those "in the grip of faith" refusing to accept atheistic naturalism as an unavoidable consequence of science, perhaps those under the spell of atheistic naturalism have not heard different news: that not only all the findings of science but all *possible* scientific findings are compatible with at least one understanding of God in relationship to the natural world. Today. As it happens, in the Western world this understanding was first subtly (but by no means unanimously) rejected centuries ago, long before the emergence of modern science, its protagonists unaware of how their ideas would subsequently be transformed and where they would lead. Since then, so much has transpired—much of it unrelated to metaphysics, science, or intellectual history per se—that notwithstanding the embodied persistence and continued intellectual viability of the rejected view, it rarely appears in current considerations of the relationship between science and religion in the secular academic mainstream. Nor is *this* surprising, insofar as theology and the consideration of religious truth claims on their own terms have been banished from nearly all research universities for reasons to be analyzed in Chapter 6. Today, even when this view of the relationship between God and the natural world is known and understood, as a corollary of supersessionist conceptions of the past it is widely assumed to belong irretrievably to "the world we have lost."

In part because of a particular strand of thought from the distant past in the present, the idea has become common that the findings of science either prescribe atheism as a matter of intellectual integrity or require a schizophrenic separation of scientific findings from religious faith. Neither is true. This chapter traces the historical trajectory whereby the assumptions about God, nature, and science that dominate contemporary intellectual life have come to be taken with such uncritical matter-of-factness. They are widely regarded as ideologically neutral, obvious truths rather than seen for what they are: ideologically loaded, contestable truth claims based on unverifiable beliefs. In order to see this, however, we will have to take a rather broader conceptual and chronological perspective than is typical of most sorts of historical analysis, and to question some assumptions that are usually taken for granted.

MODERN SCIENCE INVESTIGATES the natural world, which in Christianity, as well as in Judaism and Islam, was and is said to be God's creation. The traditional Christian view of creation is distinctive in its claims about both the nature of God and the relationship of God to the natural world. Except for the account found in Judaism, on which it expands, this view of creation differs from other ancient philosophical ideas or religious creation accounts that sought to explain the existence and nature of the universe. It was developed especially from reflection on the experiences and stories of ancient Israelites and Jews (some of whose descendants became first-century Christians), as redacted and compiled in texts which by the end of the fourth century, selected from among a much wider range of writings, had been canonized by church leaders as the Old and New Testaments.[7]

The difference between Christian and other ancient views of God (or gods) is more fundamental than is often recognized, and goes far beyond a distinction between monotheism and polytheism. According to this Christian view, God is not a highest, noblest, or most powerful entity within the universe, "divine" by virtue of being comparatively greatest. Rather, God is radically distinct from the universe as a whole, which he did not fashion by ordering anything already existent but rather created entirely ex nihilo.[8] God's creative action proceeded neither by necessity nor by chance but from his deliberate love, and *as* love (cf. 1 Jn 4:8) God constantly sustains the world through his intimate, providential care. Although God is radically transcendent and altogether other than his creation, he is sovereignly present to and acts in and through it. There is no "outside" to creation, spatially or temporally, nor is any part of creation independent of God or capable of existing independently of God.

Such a God is literally unimaginable and incomprehensible, a claim rooted in numerous biblical passages, including many among the Psalms: "Great is the Lord, and greatly to be praised; his greatness is unsearchable" (Ps 145:3). Or again, "Even before a word is on my tongue, O Lord, you know it completely. You hem me in, behind and before, and lay your hand upon me. Such knowledge is too wonderful for me; it is so high that I cannot attain it" (Ps 139:4–6). Similar passages occur elsewhere in the Bible. For example, Deutero-Isaiah claims, "For as the heavens are higher than the earth, so are my ways higher than your ways and my thoughts than your thoughts" (Is 55:9), and in the first of the two letters attributed to Paul and addressed to Timothy, the author says of God that "it is he alone who has immortality and dwells in unapproachable light, whom no one has ever seen or can see" (1 Tm 6:16).[9]

Because the Bible has been from the time of its canonical compilation by far the most important collection of texts in Christianity, it is not surprising that this biblical notion of a transcendent God has been reiterated by countless Christian thinkers. Despite having ascribed to God dozens of superlatives near the outset of his *Confessions,* for example, Augustine (354–430) asked immediately afterward, "What does anyone say when he speaks about you?"[10] Anselm of Canterbury (1033–1109) was similarly struck: "You are in me and around me and I do not feel [*sentio*] you."[11] Notwithstanding her unusual visions, Hildegard of Bingen (1098–1179) repeated the merest commonplaces in saying that God was "incomprehensible in all things and above all things" and that "no one can understand or extend to holy divinity with the keenest of his senses, because it is above all things."[12] In his analogical metaphysics of creaturely participation in God, Thomas Aquinas (1225–1274) presupposed and sought to preserve a view of God so "otherly other" that God shares *no* genus in common with creatures—not even being—so utterly different is God's literally indefinable, "improperly knowable" reality from that of everything else.[13] In the late sixteenth century, the Spanish Discalced Carmelite John of the Cross (1542–1591) wrote that "God's being cannot be grasped by the intellect, appetite, imagination, or any other sense, nor can it be known in this life."[14] In the mid-nineteenth century, too, John Henry Newman (1801–1890) repeated the same idea in asserting that God "is absolutely greater than our reason, and utterly strange to our imagination."[15] Already in his influential commentary on Paul's letter to the Romans, a young Karl Barth (1886–1968) objected vehemently to natural theology and insisted that God is "entirely other" *(ganz anders)*.[16] And the American writer Flannery O'Connor (1925–1964) noted in a letter from 1962 "how incomprehensible God must *necessarily* be to be the God of heaven and earth. You can't fit the Almighty into your intellectual categories."[17] Paradoxically, then, one might say that according to this Christian view, God "exists" but does not exist, insofar as God is by definition not *like* anything else that is real.

According to traditional Christian teaching, for human beings the most remarkable fact about this incomprehensible, constantly active God is that among his chosen people and as an utterly unexpected expression of his love, he miraculously caused a young Jewish woman named Mary in ancient Palestine to become pregnant. God himself became incarnate in a human being, Jesus of Nazareth, "the image of the invisible God" (Col 1:15). What would otherwise have remained much more inaccessibly unfathomable became concretely, humanly manifest: "the Word became flesh and lived among us" (Jn 1:14). Not only is it claimed that Jesus worked miracles as an adult during his lifetime—turning water into wine at a wedding feast, multiplying loaves and fishes to feed thousands of people, and healing numerous people of debilitating illnesses—but it is also asserted that after his crucifixion by Roman authorities in Jerusalem, God raised him from the dead in some sort of strange, transformed human body. The resurrection of Jesus ratified the incarnation: this man was not merely a human prophet and admonitory preacher, it is alleged, but also God himself, the same God who had created the universe through the Logos, unfathomably become human as the definitive, divine self-revelation for human beings. According to the Gospel of John, following his resurrection Jesus promised that after his ascension to "the Father" (as he called God), the Father would send to Jesus's disciples an "advocate," the Holy Spirit (Jn 14:26). The Spirit would lead the community of Jesus's followers, the church, into the fullness of truth (Jn 16:13), God's chosen people having been the bridgehead for the salvation not only of the Jews, but of all those who are united with one another in love through Jesus in his church.

Obeying Jesus's directive to do so "in remembrance of me" (Lk 22:19), members of the church would celebrate God's victory over death and Jesus's continuing presence among them in the Eucharist, a ritual meal through which God would re-present to them Jesus's self-giving, sacrificial, saving passion and death. Christianity's sacramental worldview is rooted in God's incarnational action in and through Jesus, the most startling, particular instantiation of God's constant, intimate relationship to his creation in general. Not despite but *because* God is radically other than his creation, it is claimed, God can and does manifest himself in and through it, as he wills—ordinarily through the regularities of the natural world, of which ancient peoples were aware in the cyclical rhythms of the seasons and the movements of celestial bodies, for example, but also extraordinarily through events that diverge from natural regularities, including not only the Eucharist but also singular miracles such as those reportedly worked by Jesus and his apostles.

It is self-evident that a God who by definition is radically distinct from the natural world could never be shown to be unreal via empirical inquiry that by definition can only investigate the natural world. To posit any link between science and the unreality of God therefore presupposes that God is in some sense being conceived as part of the universe—or, in Christian categories, that God and creation have been in some way combined, conflated, or confused. Seemingly unaware that this is what he is doing, the philosopher Charles Larmore, for example, writes that "to explain something in terms of divine action or Providence always amounts to placing God among the finite causes we have already found or can imagine discovering."[18] This is not so. With the conception of God just discussed, it simply implies an assertion that the otherly other, transcendent creator is active in and through his creation. Similarly, to think that science has falsified or could falsify claims about God's presence in and through the natural world presupposes that scientific explanations about causality in the universe exclude any possible simultaneous or supervening divine presence. That is, it assumes that natural and supernatural causality (to use the categories of a terminological contrast devised in the Middle Ages) comprise a zero-sum game, a sort of competitive, either-or relationship between God and creation.[19] In short, it presupposes that Christianity's sacramental view of reality is false—that if God is real, he does not or cannot act in and through his own creation, the natural world.

Correlatively, on this antisacramental view of science and religion, if the universe as a whole were a closed system of natural causes, there would be no place for God either causally or conceptually. God would simply be superfluous, because there would be neither a place nor any evidence for him. But a genuinely transcendent God, if real, is not spatial *at all*. So such a God, if real, no more needs room to act than he needs room to exist. Both presuppositions—the assimilation of God to the natural world and the mutual exclusivity of natural causes and divine presence—are implicitly part of modern science as it is conceived and practiced, although both have long ceased to be active concerns among practicing scientists qua scientists. Both indeed repudiate central claims of Christianity as discussed thus far. Where do they come from?

They are not empirical findings of science itself. No one found or discovered them. At no time since the seventeenth-century revolution in physics or the nineteenth-century revolution in biology have they been observed, measured, or verified. Nor could they be, according to scientists' own self-understanding of their endeavor as an empirical investigation of natural phenomena and natural causality based on hypothesization, observation, experiment, prediction, confirmation, and falsification. If real, a transcendent God is by definition not subject to empirical discovery or disproof. Nor could the influence of a transcendent, nonspatial God either be detected or ruled out in any empirical investigation of ordinary natural processes. So if it is believed that science as Weber's "power expressly antithetical to religion" entails or even tends toward atheism, the God being imagined and whose reality is denied or doubted is not the God of traditional Christianity. Something else must be going on.

As we shall see, the alleged incompatibility of science and religion derives not from science but in the first instance from a seemingly arcane metaphysical presupposition of some medieval scholastic thinkers. Yet it would be misleading to attribute it exclusively to the ideas of intellectual elites. Their views reinforced what would seem to be the general influence of linguistic grammar itself on conceptions of God, regardless of the historical period in question. Few things are as difficult as keeping clear about the distinction between God and creation as understood in traditional Christianity, and hence few things are as intuitive as unself-consciously regarding God as a quasi-spatial part within the whole of reality. Despite their formal, grammatical similarity, "the book is on the table" and "God is in heaven" are not comparable statements in traditional Christian metaphysics. But beginning in the fourteenth and fifteenth centuries, influential thinkers reinforced the default tendency in discourse about God and in effect made them comparable. In combination with other influences, including the appropriation of certain ancient philosophical ideas revived in the Renaissance and the upheavals within Christianity during the Reformation era, the widespread acceptance of a new metaphysics set the stage for conceptions in modern science about the mutual exclusivity of natural causality and transcendent, divine presence. As will become clear in Chapter 6, the later institutionalization of these assumptions in modern universities underlies the common conviction today that knowledge and reason—in contrast to faith and feelings—are and must be secular.

CHRISTIANITY MAKES TRUTH claims based on God's putative actions in history. Insofar as truth cannot contradict truth, if Christianity is true these purported actions should in principle be compatible with all other truths discoverable through human observation and rational reflection— indeed they must be compatible, if God's actions actually occurred as alleged. Showing this compatibility has been since at least the third century one of the aims of Christian theology. Since then, theology has sought to enable Christians better to understand and so better to live the way of life modeled by Jesus, about which more will be said in subsequent chapters. Christian theology has also sought since the patristic era to show the rational cogency of Christianity in relationship to what else is known and knowable, and to defend it against those who reject its claims about God's ostensible, extraordinary actions. Moreover, if *something* true might be said about God based on rational reflection and observation, including some "improperly knowable," ana-logical glimpse of what God is "like" based on the natural world allegedly created through the Logos, it might be employed as part of Jesus's directive to spread the Gospel. Or so many Christian intellectuals have thought since late antiquity. They have thought that as a sort of rational bridge, this might persuade some otherwise intellectually unmoved non-Christians to inquire about Christian claims based on God's alleged actions in history, and so to come to accept the latter as true, in part because of their compatibility with what else is known. Such an endeavor would show the *sense* in which Christianity is rational, and how it could be true, whether or not particular individuals affirm it as such. That is, it would show Christianity's intellectual viability whether or not someone assents to Christian truth claims in faith.

Among patristic authors between the third and seventh centuries, the principal philosophical framework employed as a tool in this endeavor was neo-Platonism, which continued to provide the framework for medieval monastic authors. Among scholastic theologians in Latin Christendom after the twelfth century, it was Aristotelianism combined with neo-Platonism. The radical distinction between God and creation, however, and the correlative incomprehensibility of God have the strange consequence that no philosophical framework or system of thought can be adequate to theology's subject matter considered in its broadest sense, namely God in relationship to all things. This fact has some critical corollaries. If God is inconceivable and unrepresentable, then so is any *adequate* grasp of God's relationship to creation, in general *and in all its particulars*. The exact nature of such a God's relatedness to human beings, for example, or the precise mode of his presence in the sacraments, or the specific relationship of God to the subatomic particles disclosed by twentieth-century physics, could and can *only* be inexplicable as a corollary of God's own incomprehensibility. Similarly, central Christian claims about God—the reality of his providence, the fact of his grace, the compatibility of his will and power with those of each human being—are unavoidably and irreducibly mysterious. Attempts to fathom them will run up against conceptual and linguistic limits derived from the incomprehensibility of a reality that by definition is outside space and time. So too, neither the alleged humanity-cum-divinity of Jesus nor the putative incarnation of God in Jesus *can* be intellectually apprehended, precisely because God is not and cannot be thus apprehended.

Philosophical tools might show the coherence of Christian truth claims and their compatibility with what is known and knowable by rational means. They can offer categories and concepts that might be useful for trying to say *something* true about God and his activity in and through creation, including ostensible divine actions as narrated in scripture. But an incomprehensible God cannot be comprehended rationally, nor can his extraordinary actions in history be inferred from philosophical principles, any more than such a God can be empirically discovered, confirmed, or disproved. However human reason is construed or understood, it cannot fathom what is by definition unfathomable, and so despite traditional Christian theology's pervasive and variegated *use* of reason it can never finally grasp directly that with which it is chiefly concerned. This makes it a sort of intellectual endeavor different from any other.

This strange and singular character of theology is important to keep in mind, because we might well get a different impression from the use of Aristotelianism in medieval Christian theology. Once most of Aristotle's works were translated and began to come into wide use as the basis of academic subjects in university arts and theology faculties in the mid-thirteenth century, Aristotle was called simply "the Philosopher," and "the master of those who know," as for example Dante referred to him in the *Inferno*.[20] In theology, the intellectually powerful expansiveness of Aristotelian categories such as act and potency, form and matter, substance and accident—plus the scholastic method's supple adaptability in multiple contexts, its creative capacity for facilitating the relentless questioning characteristic of university disputations, and its ability to support nuanced distinctions that served analysis as well as synthesis—might seem to suggest that medieval theologians thought they possessed a philosophical medium condign to their subject matter. It might create the impression that in eucharistic theology, for example, because "transubstantiation" made use of Aristotelian categories, it described a physical process belonging to *natural philosophy,* as if an Averroistic rationalism were sufficient to express what theologians believed was going on, or as if "substance" were being conceived as matter in a modern sense. Not so—at least not in Christian thinkers up through Aquinas, whose denial that God belonged to any genus with creatures used Aristotelian categories to *preserve* the traditional distinction between God and creation.[21] Among the distinction's many implications was the obvious fact that after transubstantiation, the consecrated bread and wine looked, smelled, tasted, and seemed in every empirical respect just as they had before.[22]

John Duns Scotus (c. 1266–1308), however, had a different idea regarding what can be said about God and how it can be said, which implied a view about what Scotus thought God had to be, insofar as God was real. Although his idea was not condemned as doctrinally heterodox, it was a critical departure from the inherited Christian notion of the relationship between God and creation, and one that in combination with other developments would eventually prove enormously consequential, not least because of its aforementioned congruity with the influence of ordinary grammar on discourse about God. Insofar as Scotus was a faithful Franciscan friar who studied and taught at the universities of Oxford and Paris, whose faculties of theology comprised the very center of the church's intellectual establishment in the late thirteenth and early fourteenth centuries, it might seem odd to describe him as departing in any respect from traditional Christianity. Yet the particular way in which he did so becomes clear when we see, in conjunction with many subsequent contingencies, where his move led and what it made possible.

Starting from the traditional position of the radical distinction between God and creation, Scotus asked what could be said about God strictly on the basis of reason or philosophy. In response to the views of Henry of Ghent (c. 1240–1293), another Parisian master whose own position on theological analogy differed in important ways from that of Aquinas, Scotus argued that at least *one* predicate was and had to be common to and shared *in the same sense* by God and creatures. Were this not so, the inherited view would prevent anyone from saying anything at all directly about God on the basis of reason alone.[23] This in turn, Scotus thought, would burn every potential bridge between what observation could discover or philosophy could discern about God on the one hand, and Christianity's central claims about God's actions in history on the other. So Scotus "broke with the unanimous and traditional view."[24] He predicated of God something that he thought God *had* to share with everything else in the same sense, simply by virtue of existing, namely *being*. The eleventh-century Muslim philosopher Ibn Sīnā (Avicenna; c. 980–1037) had argued that being is conceptually prior to and common to God and creatures. Insofar as God's existence is considered in itself and in its most general sense, Scotus agreed that God's being does not differ from that of everything else that exists.[25] This is Scotus's univocal conception of being—"univocal" because it is predicated in conceptually equivalent terms of everything that exists, including God.[26] By contrast, Christian theologians who continued to hold the inherited view, before and after Scotus, denied that God belonged to the same order or type of existence as his creation. Notwithstanding the differences that, Scotus thought, continued to distinguish the reality of God from that of creatures (his infinite and perfect power, sovereignty, wisdom, and so forth), Scotus's move made God, in Robert Barron's phrase, "mappable on the same set of coordinates as creatures."[27] It had the effect of removing the ironic quotation marks implicit in the traditional conception of God—according to Scotus, God does not "exist," he exists.

In and of itself, Scotus's move need not have mattered much. It belonged to the stratosphere of high intellectual culture and was shared only among a small number of educationally privileged male clerical elites; it was written in a language that only a tiny percentage of the population could understand; and it was transmitted only by means of hand-copied manuscripts among male teachers in friars' *studia* and the three universities (Paris, Oxford, and Cambridge) with faculties of theology before the 1340s.[28] The social, political, wider cultural, and economic impact of Scotus's idea in the early fourteenth century, a tumultuous period for the church and for Scotus's Franciscan order, was nil. So why bother with it? Because history is the study of human change over time in all its dimensions, not just the assessment of short-term influence viewed in social, political, cultural, or economic terms. Partly because of its relationship to default ideas about God born of ordinary linguistic grammar, the unforeseen, long-term influences of Scotus's move have been enormous, as will become clear not only in this but also in later chapters.

By predicating being of God and creatures univocally, Scotus brought both within the same conceptual framework. However much God differs from creation, according to Scotus the fact of his existence *necessitates* that he belongs to a more encompassing reality with creatures, one defined by being, conceived in its most abstract, most general sense. This would prove to be the first step toward the eventual domestication of God's transcendence, a process in which the seventeenth-century revolutions in philosophy and science would participate—not so much by way of dramatic departures as by improvising new parts on a stage that had been unexpectedly transformed by the doctrinal disagreements among Christians in the Reformation era.

The seventeenth-century contributions were shaped not only by Scotus, but by further developments in scholastic philosophy. These developments included the appropriation and transformation of metaphysical univocity by nominalist thinkers, the most influential of whom was Scotus's younger Franciscan confrere, William of Occam (c. 1285–c. 1348). In the early fourteenth century, Occam radicalized Scotus's views on univocity and much else, rejecting more thoroughly Aquinas's way of speaking about God, for whom "ana-logical" had not meant comparable or proportional to creatures or creation.[29] According to Aquinas, God in metaphysical terms was, incomprehensibly, *esse*—not a being but the sheer act of to-be, in which all creatures participated insofar as they existed and through which all creation was mysteriously sustained. In Occamist nominalism, by contrast, insofar as God existed, "God" had to denote some *thing,* some discrete, real entity, an *ens*—however much that entity differs from everything else, a difference Occam highlighted by emphasizing the absolute sovereignty of God's power *(potentia Dei absoluta)* and the inscrutability of God's will within the dependable order of creation and salvation he had in fact established.[30] When combined with an either-or categorical distinction between natural and supernatural plus nominalism's heuristic principle of parsimony known retrospectively as Occam's razor—the idea that explanations of natural phenomena "ought not to multiply entities beyond necessity"— the intellectual pieces were in place, at least in principle, for the domestication of God's transcendence and the extrusion of his presence from the natural world.[31] Aside from some late medieval Dominican preference for Aquinas and the persistence of Scotism, the nominalist *via moderna* became and remained the principal intellectual framework for natural and moral philosophy as well as for theology in many universities after the mid-fourteenth century. The number of universities in Europe nearly doubled in the fifteenth century, while those with faculties of theology proliferated at the hands of rival papal claimants after the schism of 1378 and increased almost tenfold in the fifteenth century.[32] Metaphysical univocity and nominalism spread along with them. At the outset of the sixteenth century, the dominant scholastic view of God was not *esse* but an *ens*—not the incomprehensible act of to-be, but a highest being among other beings.

In combination with a univocal metaphysics, the Renaissance revivals of three major ancient philosophical traditions—Platonism, Stoicism, and

Epicureanism—would contribute substantially to the forging of modern science. They would also play a role in the eventual perception that science and religion are incompatible. Their intellectual challenges to scholastic Aristotelianism contested both its conceptualization of knowledge as taught and the disciplinary configuration of knowledge as institutionalized in universities.

Amos Funkenstein explained how these philosophical revivals contributed to the peculiar confluence of theology and physics in the seventeenth century.[33] From Platonism came mathematization—only mathematics would have to function as an explanatory language applicable to the motion of things in the imperfect world of appearances, rather than derive metaphysically from or depend upon the transcendent world of extra-material ideas.[34] This mathematization of natural phenomena, which began in late thirteenth-century Paris and Oxford and was preoccupied with measurement, gradation, equilibrium, and the attempt to quantify qualities, derived significantly from the influences on natural philosophy of scholastic economic analysis that sought to comprehend an increasingly monetized world of exchange characterized by market practices.[35] The revival of Stoicism contributed to modern science a view of nature as homogeneous and deterministically governed by forces—only this conception would have to be severed from the Stoic notion of mutual sympathies among all natural things teleologically informed by the pneuma, the spiritual-and-material pantheistic continuum that provided theoretical underpinnings for practices of Renaissance magic and astrology.[36] From Epicureanism came a conception of the uniformity of efficient, natural causes without final causality—only in order to contribute to the formation of modern science it would have to substitute a universal Stoic determinism in place of its physics of random collisions among atoms in the void.

In and of themselves, the revival of these ancient philosophies, and even of their aspects incompatible with Aristotelian natural philosophy and metaphysics, need not have presented insuperable problems for Christian teachings. Aristotle's own philosophy, after all, had been appropriated in the twelfth and thirteenth centuries despite initial condemnations, intense contestation, and some ideas entirely at odds with Christianity, such as the eternity of the world and the mortality of the soul, which were officially rejected despite being championed by philosophical Averroists. Institutional innovations, too—most significantly, the creation of universities—could be and were incorporated into Latin Christendom despite presenting an alternative to long-standing monastic conceptions of the ways in which faith, worship, and knowledge were related to one another. Because the central claims of Christianity were not based or dependent on *any* philosophy but rather on God's putative actions in history, inherited assumptions and practices provided a stable framework for the testing, debate, and discriminating assimilation of philosophical ideas compatible with the faith. So Petrarch, Erasmus, and Rabelais, for example, could adopt aspects of Stoic ethics, as many of the church fathers had done, without accepting the Stoics' pantheistic determinism.[37] Likewise, in the midst of the seventeenth century's intellectual ferment, the Catholic priests Pierre Gassendi (1592–1655) and Marin Mersenne (1588–1648) could adopt Epicurean atomism without embracing its hedonistic ethics or denial of teleology.[38] Aspects of Platonism, Stoicism, and Epicureanism might even have been assimilated in combination with a univocal metaphysics in the universities, so long as the church's teaching, preaching, worship, devotional practices, and prayer continued to convey and embody the faith's central truth claims. Indeed, in broad terms this was the case in the fifteenth and early sixteenth centuries, in the combination of a prevailing nominalistic theology in many universities, an unprecedentedly robust lay piety, and the Renaissance humanists' enthusiastic retrieval of non-Aristotelian ancient philosophies.

BUT IF THE very nature of God's actions, their meaning, or how they are known were contested or rejected, it might alter fundamental aspects of Christians' relationship to God and what they thought they knew. Indeed, it might call into question what Christianity *was,* and so what Christians were to believe and how they were to live. This is what happened with the Reformation. It is primarily important for the story of modern science not because Reformation theologians directly undermined the radical distinction between God and creation. On the contrary, Luther, Calvin, and other Protestant reformers, based on their respective readings of the Bible, wanted to rescue the distinction from what they took to be distortions that derived from popish superstitions and Aristotelianism as such. The Reformation chiefly matters for the emergence of modern science in quite another way: the intractable doctrinal disagreements among Protestants and especially between Catholics and Protestants, as we shall see, had the unintended effect of sidelining explicitly Christian claims about God in relationship to the natural world. This left only empirical observation and philosophical speculation as supra-confessional means of investigating and theorizing that relationship. With this unplanned marginalization of disputed Christian doctrines, widespread univocal metaphysical assumptions and the nominalist principle of parsimony became unprecedentedly important as the de facto intellectual framework within which such observation and speculation would unfold—and within which modern science would emerge. Modern philosophers since the seventeenth century have disagreed no less than have theologians about God's relationship to the natural world, and empirical investigation was obviously not going to discover something that by definition transcended the natural world. Hence metaphysical univocity in combination with Occam's razor opened a path that would lead through deism to Weberian disenchantment and modern atheism.

Although there is a complex story to be told about the relationship between late medieval metaphysical and epistemological ideas on the one hand and the respective truth claims of Protestant reformers on the other, Protestantism as such did not disenchant the world. One can hardly imagine, for example, a stronger characterization of divine providence than Calvin's: "vigilant, efficacious, busy, engaged in constant activity," such that "there is no wayward [*erraticam*] power, or action, or motion in creatures, but rather they are governed by God's hidden plan such that nothing transpires unless he knowingly and deliberately decrees it."[39] Persecuted Anabaptists, including the Swiss Brethren, the south German and Austrian Anabaptists of the late 1520s and 1530s, the Moravian Hutterites, and the Dutch Mennonites in the aftermath of the Anabaptist Kingdom of Münster (1534–1535), were thoroughly imbued with a sense of God's providential care and intimate love that sustained them in their suffering, just as they believed it had sustained Jesus, his apostles, ancient martyrs, and the martyrs' latter-day Anabaptist successors.[40] So too, in England between the Henrician Reformation of the 1530s and the religio-political upheavals of the 1640s, Protestants who spanned the spectrum of religious commitment from mere conformity to zealous Puritanism to separatist nonconformity shared a nearly universal belief in a providential, constantly active, transcendent creator-God.[41]

Protestant reformers sought to restore a proper understanding of the relationship between God and creation as they respectively understood it. Nevertheless, some of their departures from the traditional Christian view seem to have implied univocal metaphysical assumptions in ways that probably did contribute to an eventual conception of a disenchanted natural world. One such departure was their variegated rejection of sacramentality as it was understood in the Roman church, not only with respect to the church's seven sacraments, but also as a comprehensive, biblical view of reality in which the transcendent God manifests himself in and through the natural, material world.

Like many Dominican and Franciscan friars before them, humanist reformers such as Erasmus (c. 1469–1535) had been concerned to distinguish genuine from almost certainly specious claims about God's activity in the world. Far from all of the many miracle claims made in the Middle Ages, for example, were credible. Credulously to accept all alleged miracles, no less than blithely to attribute supernatural causes to natural events, corrosively worked to discredit claims of miracles as such among the unlearned and/or the undiscriminating.[42] Superstition harmed Christianity because it took and promulgated falsehoods for truths. Apart from God's extraordinary actions in individual miracles, however, the most important, recurrent point of direct contact between God and the natural world was simultaneously the center of traditional Christian worship—the allegedly supernatural, real presence of Jesus in the Eucharist despite the steady appearance of bread and wine after their consecration by a priest.

Interwoven as it was with much else in the Roman church that Protestants rejected—including a sacerdotal priesthood, prescriptions of clerical celibacy, eucharistic devotion, and scholastic theology as institutionalized in universities—transubstantiation was one of the elements of traditional Christianity to which especially Reformed and radical Protestants in their respective ways objected most vociferously (in contrast to Luther, who insisted on the real presence of Christ in the Eucharist but rejected the doctrine of transubstantiation as objectionably Aristotelian). A torrent of Protestant polemics against traditional eucharistic teachings and practices started in the early 1520s and persisted throughout the early modern period. Antoine Marcourt's anonymous and widely posted broadsheet, for example, the *True Articles on the Horrible, Enormous, and Unbearable Abuse of the Papal Mass, Directly Contrary to the Holy Supper of Jesus Christ*, sparked the Affair of the Placards (17–18 October 1534), the watershed event of the early Reformation in France.[43] Reformed and most radical Protestants, in particular, rejected as idolatrous superstition or worse the very thing that Catholics revered, adored, and consumed as the re-presentation of the same body and blood of Christ sacrificed at Calvary for the redemption and salvation of human beings.[44] The Dutch Anabaptist leader Menno Simons called the claim that the Mass was a sacrifice "an abomination above all abominations" that substituted in Christ's place "an impure [*onreyn*], blind, seductive, and fleshly idolater with a piece of bread."[45]

Whether it was explicitly recognized by its protagonists or not, the denial that Jesus could be *really* present in the Eucharist—which is particularly clear, for example, in Zwingli's spatial dichotomizing of Jesus's divine and human natures, and the claim that "he sits at the right hand of the Father, has left the world, is no longer among us"[46]—is a logical corollary of metaphysical univocity. A "spiritual" presence that is *contrasted* with a real presence presupposes an either-or dichotomy between a crypto-spatial

God and the natural world that precludes divine immanence in its desire to preserve divine transcendence. But in traditional Christian metaphysics the two attributes are correlative: it is precisely and only God's radical otherness as *nonspatial* that makes his presence in and through creation possible, just as it had made the incarnation possible. (Otherwise, Jesus would have been something like a centaur—partly human and partly divine, rather than fully human and fully divine.) The denial of the possibility of Christ's real presence in the Eucharist, by contrast, ironically implies that the "spiritual" presence of God is *itself* being conceived in spatial or quasi-spatial terms—which is why, in order to be kept pure, it must be kept separate from and uncontaminated by the materiality of the "mere bread."

As central as the Eucharist was in medieval Christianity and remains in official Roman Catholic teaching—in 1964, the Second Vatican Council called it "the source and summit of the Christian life," a claim repeated in both the recent *Catechism of the Catholic Church* and by Pope John Paul II[47]—and as divisive as eucharistic controversy was in the Reformation era, this sacramental context remained narrow in comparison to the relationship between God and the natural world as a whole. But what if the anti-Roman exclusion of divine immanence that presupposed metaphysical univocity were to be combined with Occam's razor and a conception of the natural world as an explanatorily adequate system of self-contained, efficient causes? Then there would be neither a place for the active, ever-present, biblical God of Christianity, nor a reason to refer to him except perhaps as an extraordinarily remote, first efficient cause. This would mean, of course, that the God under consideration would no longer *be* the biblical God. It would be the God of deism. As we shall see, this is what had happened by the end of the seventeenth century among some thinkers who made the same univocal metaphysical assumptions and were *au courant* with Newtonian natural philosophy. In this way, the Protestant denial of sacramentality as it was understood in the Roman church contributed unintentionally and indirectly to post-Enlightenment disenchantment.

If the Reformation's supporters had been contained and controlled like the Alpine Waldensians or English Lollards in the late Middle Ages, then Protestant repudiations of medieval Christian teachings, including those pertaining to sacramentality, might not have mattered much. But unlike medieval heresies, the Reformation spread explosively in the early 1520s. Beginning in Germany and Switzerland, many cities and rulers embraced its rejection of the Roman church and offered political protection to Lutheran or Reformed Protestantism. The Reformation endured and brought endless doctrinal controversies in its wake—about Christ, the sacraments, liturgy, sin and grace, salvation, the church, ministry, scripture, and authority. The controversies obliterated the existing, shared framework of beliefs within which new intellectual challenges and influences might be confronted, appropriated, and discriminatingly assimilated, as neo-Platonism had been in early medieval monasteries or Aristotelianism in thirteenth-century universities.

Indeed, another major intellectual sifting-out was already well under way when Luther protested against indulgences in October 1517: humanistic philological scholarship was being tried and tested despite its challenges to scholastic assumptions and the traditional curriculum in university faculties of arts and theology. This intellectual contestation became more marked in the late fifteenth and early sixteenth centuries in northern European universities than it had been in Italy, where most theological education occurred in the *studia* of the mendicant religious orders, and where with little ruckus humanists had been appointed to university positions in arts faculties since the 1420s.[48] But whatever the tensions that tend to accompany new discoveries and that characterize all genuine intellectual interactions between different ways of thinking, and whatever the disputes among academics across and within faculties, there is no reason to think that humanists' philological methods or philosophical interests posed any greater intrinsic threat to the faith than had Aristotelian philosophy. At least any number of leading intellectuals on the eve of the Reformation did not think so. Spain's most powerful prelate, Francisco Jiménez de Cisneros, founded the University of Alcalá in 1507, for example, with chairs in Hebrew and Greek as well as Thomism and Scotism; John Fisher, chancellor of the University of Cambridge and the bishop of Rochester, supported scholasticism and patronized the study of Hebrew and Greek at the university in the 1510s; and through the efforts of Gilles and Jerome de Busleyden in consultation with Erasmus, even the theologically conservative University of Louvain established a humanistic, trilingual college for studies in Hebrew as well as Greek and classical Latin in 1517.[49]

With the Reformation, however, the background beliefs about the church and its teachings that made the assimilation of new ideas possible were *themselves* thrown into dispute. This changed everything, because what the Reformation rejected was not an intellectual system narrowly confined to erudite elites in university classrooms. As we shall see in multiple ways in subsequent chapters, it was an institutionalized worldview that diversely informed the whole of human life—which, according to those who repudiated the Roman church's authority, was exactly the problem, given the church's grave corruptions born of its doctrinal waywardness.

Against the intentions of its protagonists, the Reformation ended more than a thousand years of Christianity as a framework for shared intellectual life in the Latin West. In a sustained fashion and with unprecedented consequences, Christianity itself became the central bone of contention, not only in publications and from pulpits, but also through politics and on battlefields, from the 1520s through the 1640s and beyond.[50] Instead of humanism and scholasticism continuing to push and pull at one another within a shared Christianity, as they had been doing for decades before 1520, Catholics and magisterial Protestants marshaled the intellectual tools of Renaissance humanism *against* each other in theological controversy, including methods of textual and historical criticism as well as historical writing.[51] They did likewise with the weapons of another ancient philosophical tradition revived by humanists, Pyrrhonian skepticism, popularized through Montaigne's *Essays* after the publication of Sextus Empiricus's works in the 1560s.[52] Beginning no later than 1520 and continuing throughout the early modern period, intellectual activity pertaining to nearly everything that concerned God's extraordinary actions in Jesus was implicated, if not entirely subsumed, within doctrinal controversies among confessional combatants who concentrated on the differences that divided them. In concrete terms, an unending stalemate ensued—one that, in an enormous range of expressions and subject to many subsequent influences, has endured to the present, notwithstanding the notable ecumenical thaw of the past half century.[53] As ongoing ecumenical efforts in the early twenty-first century make clear, Western Christians continue to disagree about what Christianity is and what it entails, despite a concentration in recent decades on what ecumenical dialogue partners share in common. Doctrinal disagreement—along with its multiple social, moral, and political effects—is the most fundamental and consequential fact about Western Christianity since 1520, as we shall see repeatedly in subsequent chapters.

Protestant reformers scorned medieval scholastic theology for having perverted the right understanding of the Gospel; besieged Catholic leaders defended Aristotelianism all the more, associating its repudiation with heresy and lacking anything like a comparable substitute whether intellectually or institutionally. Reformed and radical Protestant reformers in particular, as we have seen, ridiculed Catholic sacramentality as unbiblical superstition and idolatry in the service of ecclesiastical power; Catholic leaders not only defended its biblical basis with reference to specific texts—before, during, and after the Council of Trent (1545–1563)—but insisted that the categories of Aristotelian natural philosophy should continue to govern discussion of God's activity in the natural world. However understandable was this Catholic demand in the face of Protestant rejections of the Roman church's authority, it would prove hugely consequential. Not only was it integral to the anti-Copernican condemnation of 1616 and of Galileo in 1633, with their centuries-long fallout, but backed by inquisitorial censorship it associated Roman Catholicism intellectually with an increasingly untenable physics that was eventually discredited entirely. Echoing ideas articulated by Galileo himself in 1615, the leading Jesuit scientist of the eighteenth century, Roger Joseph Boscovich (1711–1787), wrote perspicaciously in a letter of 1760 that "the greatest harm that can be done to religion is to connect it with things in physics which are considered wrong even by a great number of Catholics."[54] The damage was caused because everyone self-conscious about the matter knew, through implicit recognition of the principle of noncontradiction, that truth could not contradict truth. Thus any rejections by church leaders of genuine discoveries about the natural world both risked the intellectual alienation of the educated faithful and invited ridicule from the church's detractors. More broadly, shielded by the Roman Inquisition and Index of Prohibited Books, much of post-Tridentine Catholicism would for centuries be characterized by an intellectually defensive style, extremely sensitive to any deviations from orthodoxy and obedience, and linked in early modern Europe to the exercise of power by rulers of confessional Catholic states.

Still, it was not as if God's promises could be undone or his activity halted either by a defensive insistence on Aristotelianism in natural philosophy or by Protestant denials of the natural world as the theater of God's grace. The consecrated Eucharist did not cease to be Christ's body and blood, for example, simply because heretics denied it. Conversely, as far as Protestants were concerned, the papist perpetuation of false doctrines did not make them true, regardless of whether they were venerable, widespread, or successfully imposed by political power and military might. If the postlapsarian natural world was as deeply mired in sin and as subject to Satan as most Protestants thought it was, then the Jesuits' Ignatian directive to see God in all things was a delusion. And if the age of miracles had ceased after apostolic or early Christianity, as many Protestants alleged, then all latter-day Catholic miracle reports were no more credible than the crackpot stories from the saints' lives in the *Golden Legend*, the most important hagiographical collection of the later Middle Ages.

And so it went, with enormous consequences. An unintended result of literally interminable, pervasive doctrinal controversy was a strong tendency toward the de facto elimination of substantive religious claims from any bearing on the investigation of the natural world. But it was exactly these claims, as we have seen—based on God's self-revelatory actions in history, above all in Jesus—that were the heart of Christianity as a world-view and which provided the correct understanding *of* the natural world *as* God's creation. Because creation ex nihilo is neither an intuitive nor an obvious notion, bracketing the consideration of it and its coordinate teachings was bound to have major implications. Without the traditional, biblical theology of creation and reference to God's actions in Jesus, Christianity's cupboard would look awfully bare.[55] Nevertheless, any arguments that hoped realistically to avoid the quagmire of theological controversy and fruitfully to transcend confessional boundaries—including discussion about God and his creation—would have to bracket both the content of the contested claims and the disputed bases to which antagonists appealed. The consequences were profound. Ecclesiastical authority, tradition, scripture, and religious experience were all out of bounds, despite the fact that most Protestants still shared many beliefs with Catholics. Also excluded was God's self-revelation as disclosed in his extraordinary actions in history, because Christians disagreed about the meaning and ramifications of those actions.

As a result, the still prevalent, univocal metaphysics already characteristic of late medieval conceptions of the relationship between God and the natural world assumed an unprecedented importance. It could no longer be supplemented in extra-confessional discourse by the biblically based claims of Christianity—even those that most Protestants continued to hold in common with Catholics. *Empirical investigation of the natural world had not falsified any theological claims.* Rather, incompatible Catholic and Protestant views about the meaning of God's actions created an intellectually sterile impasse because of the objections they inevitably provoked from theological opponents, and the intractable doctrinal controversies they constantly reinforced.

WHAT WAS LEFT as a means for understanding the natural world? Only reason—understood and exercised in ways that did not depend on any contested Christian doctrines. By the early seventeenth century, this meant some combination of inherited philosophical ideas, new philosophical ideas, mathematics, and/or empirical observation and controlled experiments that sought to understand the workings of nature. Controversial Christian doctrines that were still discussed—as they were, for example, by Leibniz, who worked for decades to reconcile Lutherans and Reformed Protestants with one another and both of them with Catholics—would have to be subordinated to extra-confessional rational discourse if they sought to be something more than preaching to the choir, or an attack on those outside it.[56] New institutions, too, such as the Royal Society of London, were dedicated to the Baconian investigation of "matters of fact" about the natural world in ways that could transcend the interminable fruitlessness of theological controversy. Organized in 1660 and chartered by Charles II two years later, the Royal Society reflected in its aspirations both Restoration experimentalists' distrust of religious "enthusiasm" and a forthright rejection of radical Protestantism, which had been so disruptive during the decades of the English Revolution.[57]

In approaching the natural world, different thinkers combined philosophical ideas, mathematics, empirical observation, and experimentation in a wide variety of divergent ways during the intellectual efflorescence of the seventeenth century. Galileo scorned Aristotelian natural philosophy in the face of mounting empirical counterevidence (including his famous sunspots); transgressing traditional disciplinary divides between mathematics and natural philosophy, he discovered mathematical formulas that described the mechanics of moving objects.[58] Descartes made the demonstrative certainties of mathematics the methodological foundation of his entire philosophy; reality, he argued, was a radical dualism of thinking spirit and lifeless matter, the latter consisting solely in extension and comprising the universe conceived as a vast, interlocking mechanism of efficient causes.[59] Spinoza essentially combined a Cartesian rationalism, a quasi-Epicurean causal determinism devoid of final causality, and a Stoic conception of the universe as *Deus sive Natura*: spirit and matter, he argued, are simply two modes of the one substance, whence all that occurs transpires by necessity.[60] Like Descartes and Spinoza, Hobbes in *Leviathan* (1651) took geometrical, demonstrative certainty as his model for knowledge; but rather than starting from the *cogito* or substance, he began with sense impressions and precise terminological definitions set within a deterministic materialism that combined aspects of Stoicism and Epicureanism.[61] In his *Principia* (1687), Newton applied mathematical formulas to a growing body of empirical observation and experimental results, unifying the laws that governed the movement of celestial bodies and the motion of ordinary objects.[62]

Having sidelined theology, scripture, tradition, and religious experience as sources of knowledge about God, the reason exercised by nearly all leading seventeenth-century thinkers, whatever its particular manifestations or emphases, assumed a univocal metaphysics. God existed—and thus, analogous to creatures, God was an individual *ens,* an entity within being, or God was in some way coextensive with the totality of being. The entire category of God's actions in history had been unintentionally paralyzed by doctrinal controversy. Hence reason—including observation and experiment—bore the full burden of the endeavor to understand God's relationship to the natural world. Therefore all theology that sought to avoid confessional controversy *had* to be natural theology, based on reason alone.[63] Creatures were finite, imperfect, limited, natural beings; God was an infinite, perfect, unlimited, supernatural being.

Seventeenth-century thinkers, among whom "nearly all original philosophical minds were Nominalist,"[64] showed that they could be quite loquacious when it came to talking about God based on reason. Apparently unbeknownst to some of them, it was no longer the transcendent God of traditional Christianity about whom they were speaking. Augustine had famously said in one of his sermons that "if you comprehended [*cepisti*], it is not God."[65] By contrast and despite Augustine's influence on him,[66] Descartes based his entire philosophy on the indubitability of God as an idea in his mind, ostensibly no less "clear and distinct" than Descartes's own supposedly incontrovertible self-understanding as a "thinking thing." Fortunately for Descartes—in contrast to his many contemporary and subsequent critics—his clear and distinct idea of God included undeceiving goodness, constant will, and necessary existence, which enabled Descartes to trust both his clear and distinct idea about matter as pure extension as well as his sense perceptions about the existence and features of the external world.[67] The Cambridge Platonist Henry More, however, used *his* reason *against* Descartes, arguing that not only material bodies but also spirits in general and God in particular possess extension, such that the full plenum of space is to be understood *as* God.[68] Small wonder, with so many competing notions in the air, that Hobbes scoffed at the idea of spirits as putative "thin aëreall bodies" and, convinced of the truth of materialism, ridiculed the very idea of an incorporeal spirit as a contradiction in terms.[69] Newton's physics was inseparable from his view of God, who had not *created* space and time, he argued, but whose being constitutes space and time: homogeneous, absolute, and infinite space was the "sense organ of God" *(sensorium Dei)*.[70] Spinoza, in contrast to all these thinkers, explicitly identified the universe with God's body, and said that he had as certain an idea of God as he had of the properties of a triangle.[71] Dramatically different yet again, God according to Leibniz was "the most perfect of all minds and the greatest of all beings [*les Estres*]," in an age of absolutist baroque regimes the "most enlightened and the most just of all monarchs," and as such was the principle of sufficient reason that explained why our universe *had* to be understood as the best of all possible worlds.[72] In the 1750s, Voltaire's Candide would hear it thirdhand from Dr. Pangloss.

As even these few examples suffice to show, reason alone yielded wildly divergent and incompatible ideas about God and his relationship to the natural world, notwithstanding a shared univocal metaphysics. More examples would only expand further the range of rival truth claims. Protestant and Catholic theological controversialists could not agree about the meaning of God's extraordinary actions in history; (natural) philosophers had even more discrepant views of his ordinary relationship to the universe. Nothing has changed in this respect since the seventeenth century. Was God a highest being within the whole or in some sense the whole of being? How could one tell? Later philosophers would shuttle back and forth between variations on these poles within univocal metaphysical assumptions—in the early nineteenth century Hegel would play Spinoza, as it were, in a sort of sequel to Kant's Descartes, with process philosophers such as Alfred North Whitehead (1861–1947) and Charles Hartshorne (1897–2000), among others, adding their own versions of post-Hegelian panentheism in the twentieth century.[73]

Aquinas had anticipated the problem in the thirteenth century: "Human reason is greatly deficient in things concerning God, a sign of which is that philosophers, even in searching out human affairs through natural investigation, have erred in many things and have held contrary opinions among themselves."[74] Hence the indispensable importance of God's self-revelatory actions in history. Without them, one was left with a philosophical discourse about God pullulating with the conflicting, arbitrary preferences of divergent thinkers, all allegedly based on reason as such. But the never-ending theological controversies among antagonistic Protestants and Catholics about God's extraordinary actions had forced the issue and pushed attempts at a supra-confessional solution in this direction. Pascal, resolutely Augustinian after his conversion experience in 1654, was the one first-rank, seventeenth-century thinker who both contributed to its intellectual revolution and repudiated the entire rationalist discourse about God. All of it, in his view, amounted to so much speculation *about* "the God of the philosophers" rather than relationship *to* "the God of Abraham, Isaac, and Jacob," who had become incarnate and worked miracles. "We not only know God only through Jesus Christ," Pascal wrote, "but we only know ourselves through Jesus Christ."[75] The rest was mere philosophical pretense and arbitrary speculation.

Increasingly and eventually, however, the radically divergent philosophical ideas about God would cease to matter for the empirical findings and explanatory power of science. More and more, the emergent natural sciences would become discrete and autonomous intellectual endeavors, in practice separable not only from theology but also from philosophy. After

Newton's achievement, despite the lingering preference for varieties of Cartesian mechanism on the Continent into the early eighteenth century, disagreements about God and his relationship to the natural world would become incrementally superfluous to the endeavor to understand how nature itself worked, whatever the particular views about God held by individual scientific investigators. The speculations on God and the human soul by successive generations of sixteenth-century Italian natural philosophers such as Pietro Pomponazzi (1462–1525), Girolamo Cardano (1501–1576), and Giordano Bruno (1548–1600) simply ceased to be explanatorily competitive intellectual options pertaining to natural phenomena, as did that Renaissance natural philosophy that blended neo-Platonic, Hermetic, kabbalistic, and other ideas in eclectic ways from Marsilio Ficino (1433–1499) through the Jesuit polymath Athanasius Kircher (1602–1680).[76]

By discovering mathematical formulas that described both the invariable relationships of motion and the force of gravity among all material bodies within a homogeneous space and time, Newton combined aspects of Platonic, Stoic, and Epicurean natural philosophy in a manner that made God's existence irrelevant for understanding the regularities of natural phenomena. He opened the way to methodological naturalism in the sciences, even though it would not become institutionally widespread in universities until the later nineteenth century. As his successors would recognize and despite Newton's own interests in theology, scriptural prophecy, and biblical exegesis, Newtonian physics was explanatorily powerful no matter what God might be, how he was related to the universe, or even whether or not he was real.[77] In time, it would turn out that the same thing was true, mutatis mutandis, of the explanatory power of astronomy, chemistry, biology, geology, and all other modern sciences. Through methodological naturalism the sciences worked and explained a great deal about their respective domains of inquiry, regardless of what people thought about God—or whether they thought about him at all. Science as such, in its methods of inquiry and the content of its findings, was no different for Protestants than for Catholics, for Christians than for Jews, for religious believers than for unbelievers. It could be distinguished from theology not because anyone had disproved any religious truth claims, but because science was separable from such claims as the distinctive form of knowledge that sought to explain the regularities of nature.

Newtonian physics thus marked a crucial (though far from absolute) watershed. Some cutting-edge thinkers in the late seventeenth and early eighteenth centuries saw in Newtonianism exciting prospects for natural theology, and were keen on what William Derham, a fellow of the Royal

Society, called "physico-theology," or "a demonstration of the being and attributes of God, from his works of creation." They contributed to an intellectual trajectory that led to the arguments for God's existence based on design in William Paley's *Natural Theology* (1802), and that would remain important deep into the nineteenth century.[78] But for most innovative eighteenth-century thinkers—like Newtonian natural theologians, thoroughgoing if unwitting proponents of univocal metaphysical assumptions that were simply taken for granted—the principal remaining significant question about God was whether he was an initial, remote, efficient cause of the universe's deterministic mechanism, or simply a superstitious invention of unenlightened, primitive peoples ignorant of the truth about dynamic, eternal matter. Deists such as John Toland (1670–1722) and Matthew Tindal (c. 1657–1733) in England, Henri de Boulainvilliers (1659–1722) before his conversion to Spinozism and François-Marie Arouet Voltaire (1694–1778) in France, and later Thomas Paine (1737–1809) and Thomas Jefferson (1743–1826) in the United States took the former view; atheists such as Julien Offroy de La Mettrie (1709–1751), Denis Diderot (1713–1784), and the Baron d'Holbach (1723–1789) took the latter.[79] His domestication now complete or nearly so among such thinkers, God was in both cases conceived as though he were spatial and temporal. In fact, the transcendent God had been assimilated to the natural world and then marginalized through natural causality, in sharp contrast to the way in which God was and is still regarded by Christians who reject metaphysical univocity.

To be sure, God remained important in the reflections and natural-theological theorizing of many scientists throughout much of the nineteenth century.[80] But whether individual scientists continued to insist on his integral relationship to the natural world, relegated him to a remote first cause, or denied his existence altogether, the combination of two ideas had rendered him expendable. The first was the metaphysically univocal conception of God as a highest being among others: this brought God within the same ontological and causal order as his creation. The second was Occam's razor: if God was unneeded to account for causal explanations of natural phenomena, there was no reason to invoke him. A clear corollary of this notion was methodological naturalism. God simply no longer had a place in the workings of the world, whether spatially or causally: if all natural events were adequately explained by natural causes, God was redundant. So however unrepresentative at the time was Laplace's famous quip to Napoleon in 1802 when asked about the place of God in his physics—"I have no need for that hypothesis"—the leading French physicist of his day proved to be prophetically prescient.[81] He correctly saw that scientists *qua* scientists had no need to invoke God, even though in the nineteenth century many would continue to do so in various ways because of the abiding relationship between science and natural theology.

Perhaps because it is presumed to have been left behind by successive historical layers of metaphysical univocity, ancient philosophies of nature revived in the Renaissance, the Reformation rejection of the medieval notion of sacramentality, and the obdurate early modern Catholic insistence on Aristotelian natural philosophy, the biblically based Christian conception of God within a sacramental worldview is usually thought not to have been intellectually defensible with the emergence of modern science. Indeed, its supposedly patent weakness and inevitable crumbling in the face of scientific discovery is a textbook commonplace and cornerstone claim of supersessionist Western intellectual history, taken to be a fundamental watershed between premodern and modern worldviews that laid the foundation for Weberian disenchantment. Certainly the recent triumphalistic, Spinoza-centric histories of the Enlightenment by Jonathan Israel conform to this familiar narrative.[82] Mark Lilla, too, refers exemplarily to "the recognized fact that Christian cosmology collapsed under the assaults of the new natural sciences, making it impossible to connect God and man directly through the medium of nature."[83] Well, no. Ironically and in fact, despite undermining Aristotelian cosmology, science left untouched the biblical conception of God within a sacramental worldview—despite the widespread rejection of the latter, and despite the lack of recognition by early modern Christians, whether Catholic or Protestant, about just *how* science and the traditional view were compatible.

Early modern Christian intellectuals did not or perhaps could not see how the traditional view of God was compatible with science because they were unaware of how importantly it differed from God as understood within a univocal metaphysics. They seem in general to have had little sense of the extent to which they had absorbed metaphysical univocity. Nor is this surprising, for univocity had been widely appropriated through late medieval Aristotelianism in European universities and intellectual life long before Copernicus, Kepler, or Galileo, and it was this Aristotelianism that remained adamantly the principal, reactionary idiom of Catholic intellectual life after the Reformation. Even the Thomism of sixteenth- and seventeenth-century Spanish scholasticism, following on that of Cajetan and including Suárez, had departed in important respects from the traditional conception of God: "Since [Suárez] had redefined analogy to put it closer to univocity, he remained substantively on Scotus's side against Aquinas."[84] The discovery of mathematically expressible laws of nature equally applicable to sub- and superlunary objects exploded the Aristotelian conceptualization of nature and configuration of knowledge, with which the traditional conception of God was still linked, ever more uneasily and anachronistically, in the late seventeenth- and eighteenth-century universities and post-Tridentine seminaries of Catholic Europe.

But however entrenched was Aristotelian scholasticism in early modern Catholic educational institutions, the traditional view of God and creation was neither derived from nor dependent on any philosophy, Aristotelianism included. *This* recognition was expressed not in any new, post-Aristotelian, early modern Catholic theological system, because there was none. It remained implicit, however, in the Roman church's business-as-usual liturgy and religious practices in the face of Protestant rejections: faithful Catholics continued participating in the Mass and believing in transubstantiation, praying to a God who they believed could act in history and did act in their lives, affirming that God had become incarnate in Jesus and raised him in the resurrection, invoking the saints as efficacious intercessors with God, believing that the sacraments really conveyed grace, reporting latter-day miracles, and so forth, despite the lack of any adequate conceptual replacement for Aristotelianism. Post-Tridentine Catholicism as lived religion could and did flourish from the Iberian Peninsula to Poland, and indeed in the overseas' expansion of Catholicism from New France to the Philippines, but clerical leaders' insistence on Aristotelian curricula in universities and seminaries, coupled with the Roman Index of Prohibited Books, hampered and hamstrung the relationship between the practice of the faith and the life of the mind. As both an attempt to shore up embattled authority and an expression of grave pastoral duty, the defensive measures were intended to shield students from dangerous ideas in a world swarming with deadly heresies, which is unsurprising given the stakes: the hope of eternal life versus the prospect of eternal damnation. But these measures also had major consequences in the world of learning and beyond, some of which will be explored in Chapter 6.

Despite cascades of (post-)Enlightenment propaganda to the contrary, the mathematization of ordinary natural processes could entail no exclusion of God's alleged, abiding, mysterious presence in and through them. That required metaphysical univocity plus Occam's razor: if a natural cause explained a natural event, it was thought, there was nothing supernatural about either. Therefore, as post-Newtonian deists believed, once all the regularities of nature were understood to have natural causes, God could be no more than a remote first cause. Nor, despite generations of (post-)Enlightenment polemics denouncing allegedly primitive superstitions, did the discovery of laws that explain natural regularities exclude the possibility of extraordinary actions by God. That, as we shall see, required a dogmatic, unverifiable belief that natural laws are necessarily and uniformly exceptionless, such that miracles as traditionally understood were impossible.[85] But if, having absorbed and taken for granted metaphysical univocity, one imagined that God belonged to the *same* conceptual *and causal* reality *as* his creation, and if natural regularities could be explained through natural causes without reference or recourse to God, then clearly the more that science explained, the less would God be necessary as a causal or explanatory principle. In Funkenstein's words, "it is clear why a God describable in unequivocal terms, or even given physical features and functions, eventually became all the easier to discard."[86]

This is what happened in modern science. It continues to explain why so many secular intellectuals today—most of whom have probably never heard of metaphysical univocity, and who might be as surprised to have their metaphysical beliefs pointed out to them as they would be to learn of an intellectually viable alternative—think that science and revealed religion as such are incompatible. Even a thinker as sophisticated as Ronald Dworkin does not see what is entangled in his assertion that "since astrology and orthodox religion, at least as commonly understood, purport to offer causal explanations they fall within the large intellectual domain of science, and so are subject to causal tests of reliability."[87] Not if "orthodox religion" entails a God understood in traditional Christian, Jewish, or Islamic terms. Similarly, the ingrained predominance of scientistic naturalism in contemporary analytical philosophy[88] is deeply beholden to metaphysical univocity. Indeed, as already noted, the nature of language itself, including the religious language used by believers to talk about God, veers by default in a univocal and nominalist direction, as if "God" were the name of a thing, an *ens,* an entity within the totality of being. It requires a concerted effort linked to a traditional metaphysics of creation to see that "the king reigns at court and throughout his kingdom" and "God reigns in heaven and throughout his creation" are not the same kind of statement. But if God is thought to be a "highest being" within the universe, they are.

The same assumptions with their roots in the distant past, unknowingly held and woven into ordinary experience, also explain why many religious believers today feel anxiety when pressed about where God is or how God acts or what God is like. The key point is not, as is commonly but wrongly believed, that the empirical investigation of the natural world made or makes a transcendent God's existence increasingly implausible. It is rather that this presumption depended historically and continues to depend on a conception of God as a hypothetical supernatural agent in competition with natural causality, polemically vulgarized, for example, in the rants of Richard Dawkins about the "God hypothesis" and the putative "God delusion." In diametric contrast, with the Christian conception of God as transcendent creator of the universe, it is precisely and only *because* of his radical difference from creation that God *can* be present to and through it.[89] This is the metaphysics that continues to underlie and make possible a sacramental worldview, against supersessionist conceptions of history, in combination with any and all scientific findings.[90]

WEBERIAN DISENCHANTMENT HAS often been thought and is sometimes still said to derive from science's detached, objective, disinterested perspective on nature as it really is, in contrast to ordinary, commonsensical perceptions of nature as it seems to be. Hence human beings might, for example, perceive nature as beautiful, bountiful, and well-suited to their sustenance and flourishing. But science, it is said, sets straight their self-referential, subjective wishful thinking and confronts them with a cold, indifferent reality devoid of meaning or purpose. Undeniably, beginning with Copernicus's unmaking of Ptolemaic geocentrism, science *has* shown the natural world to be vastly different in innumerable respects from how it appears in everyday human experience. This contrast underlay John Locke's distinction between primary and secondary qualities, for example, in his epistemology of perception.[91] Without question, modern science in every field from particle physics and human genetics to physical chemistry and cosmology discloses a natural world dizzyingly unlike what we perceive through ordinary sense perception, or what medieval or early modern people could have imagined. But it does not necessarily disenchant the world. Nor was the conception of nature that from the seventeenth century increasingly sought to replace the traditional Christian conception of nature as created by a transcendent, loving God in fact objective, detached, or disinterested, as recent historians and philosophers of science have recognized. In Peter Dear's apt term, the scientific revolution of the seventeenth century was driven by an "operational knowledge" in which "knowledge of nature increasingly implied knowledge of how natural things *worked* and how they could be *used*."[92] This prompts some important questions: used by whom, and for what?

Medieval Christian teachings claimed that God created the world, became incarnate for human beings' salvation, remained mysteriously present in and through his creation, made stringent moral demands, commanded human beings to deny themselves for the sake of others in pursuit of a certain kind of shared human life, and would judge for eternity all human beings after death based on how they had lived. Such claims impinged on any number of potential human plans about the use of natural things, including one's own body as expressed in one's behavior. They were restrictions on the human will, encumbrances to human self-determination. Beginning in the 1520s Catholic and Protestant controversialists had unintentionally paralyzed theological discourse based on ecclesiastical authority, tradition, scripture, and religious experience, leaving reason, however construed, as the basis for argument about God, creation, and morality. In principle, the less any view of nature was linked to restrictive religious claims, the greater would be the scope for human beings to realize their ambitions to use nature however they pleased. Here was a new opportunity. The intellectual impasse created by theological controversy provided an opening for ideas about nature based on novel beliefs. A *subjective* conception of nature as "objectively" devoid of God's presence would neatly serve a highly *interested* view of nature as "disinterested"—even for thinkers who were Christians.

Desacramentalized and denuded of God's presence via metaphysical univocity and Occam's razor, the natural world would cease to be either the Catholic theater of God's grace or the playground of Satan as Luther's *princeps mundi*. Instead, it would become so much raw material awaiting the imprint of human desires. This would come to be called an "objective" view of the world. Despite having had the great French devotional writer and churchman Pierre Bérulle (1575–1629) as a spiritual guide, and whatever his own intentions might have been, Descartes's mechanical universe devoid of God's presence is the antithesis of a Christian sacramental worldview.[93] Supplemented by subsequent scientific discoveries, it bears close comparison to the antiteleological, materialistic conceptions of the universe among twentieth-century scientistic atheists such as Bertrand Russell and Jacques Monod.[94] So too, despite his own keen attention to theology and ecclesiastical history, Francis Bacon's interest in wanting a disinterested nature seems implicit is his notion of deliberate vexation as the metaphor for scientific experiments. Inductive science involved "nature fettered and harassed [*constrictae et vexatae*], indeed when through human art and agency it is forced out of its own state, pressured and shaped," for "nature discloses itself more through the vexations of human practices than in its own proper liberty."[95] How else could nature be made to serve human desires? Bacon seems not to have held the notion widely attributed to him, namely that through experiments nature was actually to be tortured.[96] Nevertheless, forcing nature out of its natural state is no more disinterested than declarations of nature as devoid of God's presence are objective. But the first practice serves human ambitions, and the second clears the way.

Harold Cook has shown the extent to which the early modern Dutch ambition to discover, describe, and classify natural objects throughout the world was driven by commercial interests, the desire for profit, and "warm hope of material progress and gain more than otherworldly aestheticism": inquisitiveness was propelled by acquisitiveness.[97] What the Golden Age Dutch sought through commerce by building on patterns already present in the Middle Ages, the English would apply to the first wave of industrial manufacturing a century later. In his analysis of the "industrial Enlightenment," Joel Mokyr writes that "useful knowledge" focuses on "natural phenomena that potentially lend themselves to manipulation" and "technology in its widest sense is the manipulation of nature for human material gain."[98] That sounds rather undisinterested. In this sense, medieval and Renaissance alchemists and magicians had been no less concerned with useful knowledge than were their Enlightenment successors, or for that matter than are many present-day scientists. Baconians *avant la lettre,* medieval and Renaissance adepts simply tried to match much less adequate means to ends, whereas "our magic—unlike theirs—actually works."[99] In the late 1580s, Marlowe's Dr. Faustus had exclaimed:

> O, what a world of profit and delight,
> Of power, of honor, of omnipotence,
> Is promised to the studious artisan!
> All things that move between the quiet poles
> Shall be at my command. Emperors and kings
> Are but obeyed in their several provinces,
> Nor can they raise the wind or rend the clouds;
> But his dominion that exceeds in this
> Stretcheth as far as doth the mind of man.
> A sound magician is a mighty god.
> Here, Faustus, try thy brains to gain a deity.[100]

Besides its empirical and explanatory successes, modern science superseded Renaissance magic because it delivered on the human desires for greater power and control over the natural world that motivated both early modern magic and science. Beginning gradually in newly successful ways in the seventeenth century, science became the means by which to realize this ambition for control in the service of human desires, from Enlightenment *philosophes* through nineteenth-century progressive liberals to present-day eugenicist transhumanists. The greater the scientific understanding of nature, the greater is science's power, and the greater are the ambitions to which human beings can aspire—and the fewer the limits, provided God is not in the picture.

In order to clear the path for an unobstructed human liberation, in order to safeguard human interest in a disinterested nature, not only would protagonists have subjectively to insist that ordinary natural phenomena were objectively godless. "Knowing beforehand that the truth would make them free," as Carl Becker put it, eighteenth-century *philosophes* "were on the lookout for a special brand of truth, a truth that would be on their side, a truth they could make use of in their business."[101] They would have to go further than subjective assertions about the natural world's objective godlessness in general, explicitly denouncing and rejecting claims about God's extraordinary actions in history. Because if the latter were true—if, for example, as not only Catholics but almost all early modern Protestants believed, God had indeed become incarnate in Jesus and had raised him from the dead, working miracles through him and among his early followers, as the Gospels and Acts of the Apostles allege—then Jesus's rigorous morality would presumably still apply to human life and constrain human desires, even if Aristotelian scholasticism and Catholicism's sacramental worldview were rejected. Doctrinal controversy's unintended segregation of theological discourse from the rational investigation of the natural world did not mean that Protestants or Catholics went away, or stopped making their respective truth claims about God, creation, Christ, morality, and so forth. Indeed, those claims were enforced by political authorities and shaped divergent confessional identities throughout the early modern period.

But perhaps science could undermine the purported foundations of the entire worldview by showing that miracles, such as Jesus's supposed resurrection, are impossible or irredeemably superstitious and incredible. Even Paul had said, after all, that "if Christ has not been raised, your faith is futile and you are still in your sins" (1 Cor 15:17). If miracles as such could be discredited, then even if something of Christianity might be retained—Jesus as enlightened ethical sage, for example, his teachings and directives subject to modification, critique, and improvement by rationalist moral philosophy—the testimonies on which it was alleged to rest would *have* to be mistaken. They could be dismissed as either the uncritical primitivism or the deliberate con game of ancient, prescientific peoples. Christianity might dodder on among the unlearned masses, and insofar as it helped to keep them in line, that might not be the worst thing. Politically coercive Christian confessionalization had its social utility, just as pagan religion had had its social utility in the Roman Empire before Constantine's conversion. Voltaire, according to whom "the people is between man and beast," wrote that "I want my attorney, my tailor, my servants, even my wife to believe in God, and I think that I shall then be robbed and cuckolded less often."[102] But eliminating miracles would cripple Christianity as an intellectual competitor to science and philosophy among the learned, influential, and powerful. This move would weaken restrictions on human ambitions by liberating human desires from the constraints imposed by Christian morality and the fearsome prospect of eternal judgment by God. Then, at least in principle, individuals could do as they pleased, according to *their* wills. An emancipatory pathway would be cleared.

Newton's physics made possible an intellectually powerful conception of nature consisting of inviolable natural laws. Half a century earlier, Descartes's conception of the universe as a comprehensive mechanism of efficient causes was already interpretable as leaving no possibility for miracles. This is exactly how it was viewed by Spinoza in his *Tractatus Theologico-Politicus* (1670). As a Sephardic Jew cast out of the Amsterdam synagogue he was unconcerned about alleged miracles pertaining to Jesus. Because Spinoza had on the basis of his own assumptions, definitions, and axioms assimilated God to nature, "which maintains an eternal, fixed, and immutable order," a belief in miracles "would be contrary to nature and its laws, and consequently such a belief would make us doubt everything, and would lead to atheism."[103] Or it would lead at least to the subversion of Spinoza's philosophical system. He apparently did not think to cast doubt on the assumptions of his own philosophy, later disdained by Nietzsche as "the love of *his* wisdom," with its "hocus-pocus of mathematical form."[104] Spinoza's rejection of miracles depended on his uncritical self-satisfaction with his own philosophy, his idiosyncratic conception of God, univocal metaphysical assumptions, and his subjective view of the relationship between God and the natural world, a conception and view radically unlike the traditional Jewish or Christian conceptions.

Newtonianism was the intellectual backdrop to what R. M. Burns called "the great debate on miracles" in early eighteenth-century Britain.[105] The dispute's best-known contributor was David Hume, that aspirant to become the Newton of the human sciences, who argued in his *First Enquiry* (1748) that allegations of miraculous events ought never to be believed over against the uniformly observed regularities of the natural world explained by Newtonian physics.[106] On the surface, Hume's argument seems different from Spinoza's—not an a priori denial of the possibility of miracles based on the deterministic constancy of the laws of *Deus sive Natura,* but an epistemological objection to testimony concerning particular miracle claims, intended as "an everlasting check to all kinds of superstitious delusion" for "as long as the world endures."[107] Hume claimed that no ostensible miracle is credible compared to the natural world's regularities observed in ordinary life by everyone and explained by Newtonian physics, regardless of what the supposed miracle is, who reports it, in what circumstances, and with respect to what background context(s). Therefore any and all testimony about putative miracles should be dismissed as incomparably less probable than the evidentiary weight borne by the observed uniformity of natural regularities, because "a wise man," as he put it, "proportions his belief to the evidence"; and "a firm and unalterable experience" had established the laws of nature such that there must "be a uniform experience against every miraculous event."[108] Hume believed that the exceptionality of purported miracles is always sufficient reason to reject them in favor of contrary evidence about the workings of the world conceived as an autonomous, independent natural order separate from God's influence or presence.

But the post-Presbyterian Hume had already made up his mind that the natural order *was* autonomous, independent of God, and without any divine influence or presence. He begged the entire question. As Hume recognized, allegedly miraculous events are extra-ordinary by definition; otherwise, miracle claims would not contravene the experience of nature's ordinary course, and thus cause controversy. In order to get to where he wanted to go, therefore, Hume relied on a premise akin to Spinoza's about the character of the natural order, according to which claims about supposedly miraculous events should *never* be believed over against seeming evidence for nature's unexceptionally regular course. Hume rightly asserted, in a manner consistent with traditional Christian beliefs, that "it is a miracle, that a dead man should come to life," but followed this by claiming that "that has *never* been observed in any age or country."[109] This latter assertion begs the question about whether natural regularities *are* exceptionless, just as it implicitly begs the question about whether the God of traditional Christianity is real. It implies nothing more than that Hume did not believe the testimony in question.

Standing squarely in the univocal metaphysical tradition and yet apparently oblivious of the tendentiousness of his beliefs, Hume did not base his argument against miracles on a careful, critical, case-by-case evaluation of the evidentiary testimony pertaining to discrete, alleged miracles. That was how the evaluation of purported miracles in canonization proceedings was being conducted at the time in Rome, in accord with the best medical science of the day, under Benedict XIV (r. 1740–1758), fifteen years after this intellectually voracious pope, as Prospero Lambertini, had in Bologna named the experimental physicist Laura Bassi (1711–1778) as Europe's first female university professor.[110] Hume, by contrast, dogmatically rejected all alleged miracles based on his own beliefs. His scornful repudiation of Christianity was a *premise* of his argument against miracles. He did not arrive at their rejection based on science or reason; he started from it based on his own faith in a skeptical naturalism.

Some scholars today remain impressed by the arguments of Spinoza or Hume against the possibility or the believability of miracles. If they have decided already not to believe in the possibility or reality of miracles, it is understandable that they would find comforting a confirmation of their own beliefs among Enlightenment thinkers whose views concur with their own. Some true believers in skepticism seem unaware that Hume's argument has been challenged since the eighteenth century and has been subjected to devastating criticism by multiple philosophers in the past two decades.[111] Ostensibly resting on the authority and rationality of science, dismissive denunciations of miracle claims as superstitious, primitive, and credulous have been a staple of antireligious polemic from Enlightenment deists to the so-called New Atheists today. The demythologization of biblical miracles as symbolic, metaphorical, or purely "spiritual" in post-Kantian, liberal Protestantism similarly assumes that science shows the untenability of any and all alleged miracles as real events, whether in first-century Palestine or at any time or place since.[112] Some intellectuals seem to think that science confirms or supports the idea that miracles are impossible— that just as the advance of scientific knowledge has supposedly made the existence of God increasingly implausible, so has it supposedly shown ever more convincingly that the laws of nature are uniform and exceptionless. To be sure, in their endeavor to explain natural regularities, modern natural scientists deliberately and properly set aside any other questions that might be asked about reality, adopting methodological naturalism and thus entertaining only natural causes as legitimate candidates for plausible explanations of natural phenomena. The epistemological companion to this abstractive endeavor is realist empiricism: science can examine only what is observable, investigable, verifiable, and (in principle) falsifiable through empirical methods as an extension of human sense perception.[113]

Given the assumptions and endeavor of the modern natural sciences, the profound irony is that science *precludes* any possible verification of the claim that miracles worked by a transcendent God are impossible. Only a *transgression* of science understood as an empirical investigation of the natural world could rule out the possibility of miracles.[114] The *philosophical* belief that natural laws are necessarily exceptionless is not empirically verifiable in our own or any conceivable configuration of human knowledge, because verification would require the observation of all natural events in all times and places. And were a miraculous event to occur, it would neither contradict nor undermine the findings of science; it would simply mean that overwhelmingly regular natural phenomena are not equivalent to inviolable natural laws. Of course, scientists *qua* scientists—because of their deliberately restricted aims and methods—could only declare such an event inexplicable in natural terms, not pronounce it a supernaturally wrought miracle. This would in no way prevent them from believing with intellectual consistency, as scientists *qua* human beings, that the same event was a divinely worked miracle—provided they were not scientistic atheists. If such an event really were miraculous, it would obviously not be repeatable by human experiment, but only observable by those present on a subsequent occasion if God chose to act again in the same way. Otherwise, evidence for it could only be based on the testimony of alleged witnesses.[115]

It follows that regardless of the rhetoric in which the claim is couched, any assertion that miracles are impossible, far from being confirmed by science, is either a corollary of subjective theological presuppositions about what God (if real) supposedly can and cannot do, or an unconfirmable, atheistic dogma that transgresses science's own self-limitations. In the latter case, it depends on an ideological alchemy that conjures methodological restraints into unsupported and unsupportable assertions, as if methodological naturalism somehow entailed metaphysical naturalism. If the creator-God of Christianity is real and created the entire universe out of nothing, there is no reason to think he could not, provided it served his purposes, miraculously cause a virgin to become pregnant, raise a crucified man from the dead, or cure people of otherwise terminal illnesses. Events such as these on the third planet from a medium-size star in the Milky Way galaxy, if they occurred, would seem to have called for less divine exertion than creating ex nihilo a universe that includes literally billions of galaxies.

The miracle claims inextricable from traditional Christianity can obviously be denied and ridiculed, as they have been since the eighteenth century by many secular believers based on their own countervailing commitments. If such events occurred, they are certainly unfathomable and would seem wholly inexplicable in naturalist terms. But in no way could any of the *natural sciences* provide evidence that they could not have happened or that miracles cannot happen today.[116] The idea that science undermines all alleged miracle claims is based on a fundamental misunderstanding of what the natural sciences can and cannot do, as well as on ignorance of a non-univocal understanding of God. In the end, the denial of miracles amounts to no more than an autobiographical report of subjective faith claims in the manner of Spinoza or Hume: "*I* do not *believe* that miracles are possible," or "*I* do not *believe* any reports of alleged miracles." Such professions might be relevant if one is interested in the personal beliefs of those who make such pronouncements. But they are a long way from conclusions drawn from the findings of science or the exercise of putatively neutral, objective reason. Such faith commitments take their place in contemporary Western hyperpluralism alongside the rival claims of many millions of people, particularly in the United States, who believe that miracles worked by God can occur, have occurred, and still do occur.[117]

IF THE HISTORICAL ANALYSIS presented here is substantially correct, then the nineteenth and twentieth centuries appear in quite a different light. Usually they are central to narratives about modern atheism and the presumed incompatibility between science and religion. But the enormous progress and transformative impact of modern science via technology, combined with the ideas of the most influential antireligious thinkers of the past two centuries—Comte, Feuerbach, Marx, Spencer, Nietzsche, Freud, Durkheim, Weber, Heidegger, Sartre—simply contributed further to a trajectory already in place, as Funkenstein implies and Buckley argues.[118] The wide *demographic spread* of unbelief is without question a modern story that belongs especially to social and cultural history, beginning in the second half of the nineteenth century and accelerating enormously in Western Europe and somewhat in the United States since the 1960s.[119] But its *intellectual bases* remain what they were in the seventeenth century, and even more deeply, what they were in the late Middle Ages: a univocal conception of being and the use of Occam's razor in the relationship between natural causality and alleged divine presence, whether in the United States, Britain, or Europe.[120] Nothing *conceptually* original, including Darwinian evolution, has been added for many centuries.

Metaphysical univocity in conjunction with Occam's razor are the two presuppositions that govern the thought of those intellectuals whose contributions are usually taken to be so critical for the formation of modern, secular views. Kant's philosophy, for example, fits snugly into the analysis offered here: once Newtonian physics is absorbed with metaphysical univocity, the positing of something like Kant's noumenal realm, despite being undetectable among the phenomena of the desacramentalized natural world and human sense experience, is *necessary* if morality is to be defended as objective and rational. As Kant acutely saw, neither God nor moral norms are discernible in the naturalist universe of efficient causes investigated by science, a point to be revisited more broadly in Chapter 4. Kant rejected the providentially active, biblical God who acts in history, accepting instead only "religion within the limits of reason alone."[121]

In a different way, Schleiermacher's anti-Kantian "cosmic religious feeling" as the basis for religion, like various other post-Rousseauian, Romantic exaltations of sentiment as the foundation of faith, also dovetails with the presupposition that putatively objective, disinterested modern science discloses a material world of deterministic causality devoid of divine presence. According to Schleiermacher, religion is entirely distinct in its essence from metaphysics as well as from morality, and it "maintains its own domain and its own character only because it entirely abandons the domain and character of speculation as well as that of praxis." Indeed, "its essence is neither thinking nor acting, but intuition and feeling."[122] Once science has colonized the intellect, what else can faith do but flee to the emotions? The social-historical, demographically widespread correlate of such notions is the massive sentimentalization of Christianity since the early nineteenth century. Science is about objective knowledge; faith is about ineffable feelings. In intellectual terms, it is then a short step to Weberian disenchantment: all that is needed is not to feel Schleiermacher's feeling. Or to feel other things very strongly, as Nietzsche did, exalting the desire to dominate via Dionysian instinct and the will to power unbridled by reason.

Heidegger, influenced by Nietzsche and sometimes regarded as a profound thinker who had deep insights about ontology, conflated traditional Christianity's understanding of God with Western metaphysics since Plato in his critique of "onto-theology"—the conception of being in terms of a highest being.[123] Despite his early work on Scotus, Heidegger sensed but seems not to have seen that the "forgetfulness of being" *(Seinsvergessenheit)* pertained not to a Christian understanding of God per se but only to a univocal metaphysics, which, especially since the advent of medieval nominalism, has indeed tended toward a recurrence of the ancient pagan conception of god(s) as the highest being(s) *within* the universe.[124] In seeking to transcend onto-theology, Heidegger merely conformed to the post-Cartesian norm: falling into line with the expectations of modern philosophy, he thought up his own ideas and followed his own speculations, thus adding yet another variation to the same tradition of supposedly self-sufficient rationalism criticized nearly three centuries earlier by Pascal. Insofar as all modern Western philosophy brackets any consideration of God's alleged, extraordinary actions—a legacy of the way in which they were unintentionally marginalized via Reformation-era theological controversy—it is no wonder that Heidegger's *Sein,* considered as such and in its relationship to *Dasein* and the natural world, looks so unlike the Christian God and his relationship to human beings in particular and to creation in general.

Darwin and his intellectual descendants, including sociobiologists and evolutionary psychologists, are extensions of the same story, despite the recent vogue for neo-Darwinism as a comprehensive worldview. More than *The Origin of Species* (1859), Darwin's *Descent of Man* (1871) is often thought to have inaugurated an epochal shift, with the ultimate subversion of teleology and human exceptionalism. It supposedly undercut the biblical idea of deliberate design and loving creation by God, making of *Homo sapiens* just another living species that happened randomly to evolve by the blind processes of natural selection, for which Watson and Crick later supplied the mechanism in their research on DNA and its double-helix structure.[125] To be sure, from Victorian Britain to the present, Darwinism has been widely *perceived* as intellectually disruptive and religiously unsettling, as the ongoing feud over "creationism science" in the United States continues to illustrate.[126] This is unsurprising given the lack of knowledge, naïve assumptions about biblical interpretation, unawareness of metaphysical presuppositions, and dearth of intellectual sophistication among those whom it tends to unsettle—a fact itself often related to the post-Romantic tendency to base faith on feeling, and, since the late nineteenth century, a fact also linked sociologically to the exclusion of substantive religious perspectives from secularized universities, as we shall see in Chapter 6.[127] But as with Newtonianism in the eighteenth century, (neo-)Darwinism can be troubling to Christians on *scientific* grounds only if they have a univocal conception of being and reject a sacramental view of reality.[128] Hostile reactions to Darwinism since the 1860s are a symptom of the extent to which many religious believers are oblivious of their implicit univocal metaphysical beliefs and other assumptions with which they are entangled.

Along with vast amounts of mutually corroborative evidence from geology, astronomy, paleontology, and genetics, evolutionary biology certainly undermines any literalist reading of the creation accounts in Genesis. Patristic writers from the third through the sixth century already knew not to interpret them so naïvely.[129] But evolutionary biology cannot extrapolate on *scientific* grounds from microcausal mechanisms of genetic mutation, for example, to evaluative judgments about the putative lack of meaning, order, and purpose in the evolutionary process as a whole or in the universe as such. *That* move requires extrascientific interpretation and atheistic faith commitments. So does the assertion that because empirical methods cannot discern God's presence in processes of microscale genetic mutations or in the history of evolution on earth, therefore God *is* not present in and through both—as if, not having been found "intervening" to sprinkle new dinosaur species about during the Jurassic or Cretaceous periods, nor having been located between the liver and gallbladder of any members of *Homo sapiens* in abdominal surgeries, God might nevertheless have appeared in cytosine but not thymine nitrogenous bases in DNA molecules. To claim that empirical methods have "not yet" found any evidence for God's presence in and through ordinary natural processes, including the evolutionary development of *Homo sapiens,* simply reflects a category mistake symptomatic of univocal metaphysical beliefs. Like all other scientific findings, those of evolutionary biology merely reveal, according to religious believers who reject metaphysical univocity, more than we knew before about the unexpected intricacies of God's creation, including human beings.

Unless one grasps what science can and cannot discover, and is aware of the difference between the methodological self-restraint of science and ideological scientism, and understands the difference between a traditional theology of creation and a univocal metaphysics of being, and is sensitive to the nature of religious language, and avoids lumping different traditions and truth claims together in a catch-all category called "religion," and questions the adequacy of a supersessionist view of history, and sees one's subjective commitment to atheistic skepticism for what it is, one is unlikely to see how a traditional Christian, Jewish, or Muslim conception of God is compatible with all the findings of evolutionary biology. And one is likely to think that the burgeoning findings of science in general leave incrementally less room for God and lead rationally to atheism, as though God—if real—were spatial. Daniel Dennett, for example, offers a book-length demonstration of his bewitchment by his own assumptions in *Breaking the Spell.* Quoting himself from his earlier book, *Darwin's Dangerous Idea,* he presents a well-known, supersessionist historical picture in which primitive, superstitious, prescientific peoples rationally became disabused of their illusory conceptions of God through the progressive illumination of science, leading to "us brights," that is, to Dennett and other neo-Darwinian atheists who agree with him: "We began with a somewhat childish vision of an anthropomorphic, Handicrafter God, and recognized that this idea, taken literally, was well on the road to extinction.... That vision of the creative process still apparently left a role for God as Lawgiver, but this gave way in turn to the Newtonian role of Lawfinder, which also evaporated, as we have recently seen, leaving behind no Intelligent Agency in the process at all."[130] Primitive peoples once ignorantly believed in God to explain events in the world; then came science, which now separates smart atheists from stupid religious believers. Ignoring any serious theology as well as all critical but nonskeptical biblical scholarship, and avoiding as well any serious engagement with history, Dennett seems unaware of the extent to which he is held captive by his own metaphysical assumptions about God as an "intentional object." Substituting mockery for argument, he pokes fun at an apophatic conception of God and reports that "I am not at all persuaded by it."[131] Those interested in Dennett's personal views might find this disclosure informative. But they should not be confused in thinking that his individual confession has any bearing on the compatibility of the findings of science with the understanding of God that he rejects.

THE CENTRAL PARADOX of science in the past century is that the more scientists discover, the less do they comprehend in any integrated way how the natural world works. Perhaps the most striking example comes from the heart of the twentieth-century revolutions in physics, the discipline long regarded as fundamental in the explanatorily reductionist hierarchy of the modern sciences, in which physics is the basis of chemistry, chemistry the basis of biology, and so on. More than eighty years after the experiments of the 1920s that confirmed quantum theory, physicists still have no idea about how to combine it with general relativity theory. In the words of the distinguished theoretical physicist Brian Greene, "as they are currently formulated, general relativity and quantum mechanics *cannot both be right*," even though they are the "two foundational pillars upon which modern physics rests."[132] Attempts to reconcile the Standard Model of elementary particle physics with general relativity since the mid-1980s have concentrated overwhelmingly on superstring theory. Its proponents posit six or seven additional dimensions of inaccessible space-time in which experimentally unverifiable loops vastly smaller than elementary particles are vibrating. So much for empirical investigation, observation, and experimental falsifiability.

But even should some version of string theory turn out to be true—a matter about which some physicists and mathematicians have expressed grave doubts[133]—it is clear that our universe, with its dancing clusters of subatomic particles, bizarrely small cosmological constant, strange symmetries and geometrical spaces, baffling dark matter and dark energy, is orders of magnitude more complex than the universe that Newton and Laplace thought they knew. In retrospect, the greatest physicists before Einstein and Bohr seem to have been quaintly naïve. Also exposed as naïvely inadequate are the speculations by those many philosophers and theologians who during the eighteenth and nineteenth centuries regarded Newtonian physics as a firm, even inescapable, foundation for their truth claims. To be sure, the natural world is astonishingly intelligible and subject to mathematization to an extent unimaginable to Galileo or Lavoisier.

We have only to consider the biochemistry of cells, the atomic structure of matter, the simplicity-cum-complexity of the genetic code, the precise values of the physical constants, and so forth. But the intelligibility that accompanies further scientific discoveries goes hand in hand with a burgeoning mysteriousness that resists anything remotely resembling comprehensive integration. The more we learn about reality at every scale from the subatomic to the cosmological, the more unexpectedly complex and strangely bizarre does it become, with no end to this trajectory in sight.[134]

The traditional Christian conception of God asserts both his unimaginable transcendence and his surpassing wisdom manifest in the ordered beauty of his creation: "The heavens are telling the glory of God, and the firmament proclaims his handiwork" (Ps 19:1). Or with respect to oneself: "I praise you [God], for I am fearfully and wonderfully made. Wonderful are your works; that I know very well" (Ps 139:14). If an incomprehensibly *transcendent* God is real and created all things *through* divine reason— the Logos of the prologue to John's Gospel, which according to the text is identified with Jesus as the "Word made flesh" (Jn 1:1–18)—then perhaps the natural world's combined mysteriousness and intelligibility as disclosed by science, especially in the past century, is what might be expected. Perhaps it is not in any human *ability* to connect the particularities of the natural world with specific divine intentions, as Leibniz or Paley thought, but in the *in*ability to comprehend the evolutionary complexity of the universe that one sees a created reflection of the unfathomable creator. Numerous Christian intellectuals seem to think something along these lines in flatly rejecting the Weberian view of science as inherently disenchanting.[135] They would concur entirely with the observation of leading theoretical physicist Freeman Dyson, that through the natural sciences, "in the living and in the nonliving world, we see a growth of order, starting from the featureless and uniform gas of the early universe and producing the magnificent diversity of weird objects that we see in the sky and in the rain forest. Everywhere around us, wherever we look, we see evidence of increasing order and increasing information."[136] In the experience of such Christian intellectuals, the findings of science can just as well inspire wondrous awe at the character of the natural world and of the God who they believe created and sustains it. Their work thus undermines any claim that science leads logically, inherently, or ineluctably to atheism, or that science and religion must be incompatible. Otherwise the evidentiary data could not be interpreted as they in fact interpret it. The real issue is the specific religious truth claims one makes, and how they are to be understood. Without question, the findings of science falsify *some* religious truth claims, such as those of young-earth creationists. Anyone who cares about truth should reject such views as false. But none of these Christian intellectuals is a young-earth creationist, just as none is ignorant of the findings of science. Indeed, some are themselves scientists as well as theologians.

Conversely and in contrast, many scientists demonstrate a woeful ignorance of Christian theology (and indeed, of religion in general) and seem unaware of how disputable are their own philosophical assumptions. Many seem to take their own beliefs so much for granted that they are oblivious of them *as* beliefs, so obvious, normal, commonsensical, and incontestable do their convictions seem, so apparently the uncontroversial product of sound reason, proper education, and clear thinking. Consider the either-or, antisacramental, metaphysically univocal claim by Edward O. Wilson that "if humankind evolved by Darwinian natural selection, genetic chance and environmental necessity, not God, made the species," which he compounds with an inaccurate, historically supersessionist claim about the implications of modern scientific findings: "However much we embellish that stark conclusion with metaphor and imagery, it remains the philosophical legacy of the last century of scientific research."[137] The percentage of leading scientists who profess not to believe in a personal God tells us little unless we also know on what they base their profession. How much do they know about metaphysics, Christian theology, and intellectual history in relationship to their particular areas of scientific expertise? The intellectual relationship between religion and science is a two-way street. Just as one ought not to place much stock in the geological views of a religious believer who has never studied geology, so one ought not to give much credence to the religious views of a scientist who has never studied intellectual history, the philosophy of religion, and theology. The highly specialized character of contemporary academic life makes it perfectly possible to win a Nobel Prize in chemistry or physics, for example, while knowing nothing about the theology of creation, metaphysical univocity, and why they matter for questions pertaining to the reality of God and the character of God's relationship to the natural world.

As a sociological fact, most scientists and other intellectuals in the early twenty-first century are secular unbelievers or skeptics. Perhaps, so long as one avoids the asking of certain kinds of philosophical questions, the findings of modern science might be compatible with atheism. Alvin Plantinga has argued, however, that belief in evolution *contradicts* belief in naturalism, and David Bentley Hart has recently reiterated the difference in kind between empirical questions characteristic of science and philosophical questions about the fact of existence itself (a distinction lost on those who think that the universe as a whole, or matter-energy, or anything else that exists, might adequately explain its own being).[138] But the sociological fact of the prevailing skepticism and unbelief in the secularized academy, despite claims to the contrary, has nothing to do with the findings of the sciences as such, or with intellectual sophistication or advanced education per se. It is rather the result of the particular faith commitments of those who happen subjectively to embrace atheistic or skeptical beliefs, a powerful inculturation into which is now provided by secularized universities, as we shall see in Chapter 6.

Most scientists and other scholars are unfamiliar with the intellectual scaffolding that reveals the compatibility between all scientific findings and a conception of God as radically transcendent creator of all that exists. In Christianity, this is understood to be the same God who became incarnate in Jesus and worked miracles. Shielded from having to engage the issues by the specialization of academic disciplines and supersessionist conceptions of history, most secular scholars and scientists seem as well to be unfamiliar with the historical genesis of their own contrary beliefs, which are neither self-evident nor evident. Hence one reason for this chapter, which has sought to shed light on the historical genealogy of both positions and to note their presence within contemporary Western hyperpluralism. The chapter has sought to expose the widespread but mistaken assumption that modern science has rendered revealed religion untenable. What is more, it is certain that all *possible* scientific findings are compatible with the conception of a transcendent creator-God discussed in this chapter. This conclusion follows directly once one understands what the conception entails—because any and all scientific discoveries simply tell us ever more about the natural world, which throughout the history of Christianity has been understood, following scripture, as God's creation. More scientific discoveries do not leave less room for God understood in this way, because God as traditionally conceived is not spatial in any sense, which is precisely how and why, if such a God is real, he could be present to all moments of space-time and to every bit of matter-energy. As has already been suggested, all possible scientific findings would also seem to be compatible with conceptions of a transcendent creator-God in Judaism and Islam, provided one does not subscribe to metaphysical univocity. In neither of these traditions is God viewed as an "intentional object" within the universe.

The metaphysical assumptions in conjunction with which modern science historically emerged are not the only ones compatible with the findings of science. This fact is critically important today for understanding the ways in which the relationship between science and religion is conceived. Inadequate, supersessionist history that regards a traditional conception of God as a long-gone casualty of Aristotelian philosophy facilitates the uncritical perpetuation of the myth that no metaphysical views besides neo-Scotist univocity are compatible with the findings of modern science. Regardless of how widespread or taken for granted, this notion is simply false. But a willingness to question what is usually assumed, and a historical method that can discern the continuing influence of the distant past in the present, are required in order to see this.

Secular affirmations of disenchantment are subjective, autobiographical descriptions of human experience, not intellectual inevitabilities based on scientific findings. They coexist in the early twenty-first century with contrary autobiographical descriptions of joy, hope, meaning, and purpose by religious believers fully aware of the same scientific findings. Therefore the claim that scientific findings ineluctably lead to disenchantment is empirically falsified. On this point Weber was wrong; so is everyone who agrees with him. Similarly, the claim that science and religion are necessarily incompatible is empirically falsified. Their alleged incompatibility is not based on science, but on atheistic faith commitments or (paradoxically, and perhaps contradictorily) resolute skepticism.[139] The roots of this belief in the distant past of medieval scholasticism are partly what prevent it from being properly seen and understood, as does the extent of its entanglement with a host of other historical developments, as will become clearer in subsequent chapters.

To be sure, there *are* reasons to be disenchanted with the modern world. It is just that science per se is not one of them. The ways in which some human beings have applied the findings of science through technology in pursuit of their desires is another matter altogether. Plenty of room for disenchantment there. Wars and genocides, for example, understandably tend to make God seem distant if not illusory. So too, perhaps, in less dramatic and less obvious ways, do the long-term effects of industrialization, urbanization, and consumerism, and the placing of sovereign human selves as Faustian deities at the center of their respective, Cartesianized universes. If religious beliefs are integrally connected to concrete social practices, and such practices presuppose communities whose members in turn share and help to sustain substantive beliefs, then perhaps disenchantment tends to grow in proportion as communities become mere "societies." The world built both ideologically and concretely by Westerners over the past several centuries might well inspire disenchantment, among religious believers and unbelievers alike. We will see more evidence for this in the following chapters.

Within the institutional structures and political arrangements of modern Western states, the world as constructed by human beings acting in accord with their desires certainly inspired disenchantment, for diverse reasons, in thinkers such as Marx, Nietzsche, Freud, and Foucault, and in writers such as Kafka, Sartre, Beckett, and Vonnegut. Unsurprisingly, those who believe the truth claims of the disenchanted find themselves disenchanted. But why should one believe *them*—and which among their contrary views—in a world filled with so many competing secular and religious truth claims? The historical formation and character of the myriad truth claims that comprise our contemporary hyperpluralism is the focus of the following chapter.

# CHAPTER TWO

# Relativizing Doctrines

DESPITE THE PERVASIVE influence of science in our world, very few people look to it for answers to questions about the most important concerns of human life, and for good reason. "What should I live for, and why?" "What should I believe, and why should I believe it?" "What is morality, and where does it come from?" "What kind of person should I be?" "What is meaningful in life, and what should I do in order to lead a fulfilling life?" These questions and others like them are Life Questions: they are serious questions *about* life, with important implications *for* life. Although not everyone asks them explicitly, everyone answers them at least implicitly. All people think *something* is true, some things are right and others wrong, some things are meaningful or at least seem like they could be. And the ways in which people try to live are usually related to what they think they should live for, at least insofar as they have the economic means to do so in stable political circumstances. Although some sociobiologists and evolutionary psychologists seem to think otherwise, the findings of the natural sciences cannot answer the Life Questions—about the sort of person one *should* become and the sort of life one *should* lead, concerning what one *should* value and what one *should* prioritize. One must look elsewhere for answers. In the Western world, the most salient sociological fact pertaining to the Life Questions in the early twenty-first century is the overwhelming pluralism of proffered religious and secular answers to them. Radically different answers are articulated by, say, the televangelist

Pat Robertson and the philosopher Peter Singer, and lived by *Médecins sans Frontières* and hip-hop recording stars. Where does this hyperpluralism come from?

Historically, the large majority of Westerners since the Middle Ages have answered the Life Questions through some form of Christianity. Today this remains the case in the United States, much less so in Canada and Europe, even as unprecedented numbers of men and women in recent decades have been answering the Life Questions through some form of Christianity in many countries of sub-Saharan Africa and Asia.[1] Whatever else they might entail, Christian answers to the Life Questions in one way or another involve doctrinal claims. Such claims explicitly or implicitly affirm that certain things are true, which logically always implies that others are false. For example, if God is real, then atheism is false; if Jesus Christ rose bodily from the dead, then denials of his resurrection are erroneous; if dogmas are unimportant to religion, then claims of their centrality are mistaken. Doctrinal affirmations refer to matters of *content* (what one thinks, for example, about the nature of God or sacraments or prayer), how one regards the *status* of what one affirms ("an eternal, universal truth," for example, as opposed to "my personal opinion"), and the relative *importance* in one's life of what one affirms (a spectrum ranging from foundational to marginal). In all these respects, one's attitudes toward and articulations of one's truth claims can and often do vary over time, and in relationship to specific episodes and periods in one's life. Religious conversions typically involve a change in what one believes, and/or how one regards it, and/or how central it is in one's life.

Christian truth claims vary greatly across different individuals, congregations, churches, and traditions. In countless ways they conflict with one another. As the doctrinal analogue to the institutional variety apparent under the entry "Churches" in the yellow pages of American telephone books, Christian truth claims exhibit an extremely wide, open-ended range in terms of their content *and* status *and* importance among their respective proponents. What Christians believe about the Bible, God, Jesus, the Holy Spirit, church(es), collective worship, prayer, morality, social justice, ecumenism, the importance of theological doctrines, the significance of scholarship for faith, or believers' relationship to the wider society, for example, varies enormously. Somewhere, at some time, by some congregation or individual, almost anything has gone or still goes under the adjective "Christian." Combined with this vast pluralism is the widespread (but not unanimous) view that whatever its particular content, religious conviction is a highly personal, individual matter, such that only each person can determine what is right and best for her or him. In matters of religious truth claims, each person is widely thought to be his or her own sovereign authority; this is in effect what freedom of religion means. Certainly it is what the laws of Western states protect. Although they are not the focus of this chapter, other religious traditions, including Judaism, Islam, Buddhism, Hinduism, and so forth, each with its respective, divergent expressions analogous to the pluralism within Christianity, augment further the religious pluralism in the West today through their adherents' answers to the Life Questions.

Those who reject any substantive religious answers to the Life Questions—and who in the United States, as we saw in the previous chapter, are statistically overrepresented in research universities—often view this wide-ranging pluralism of incompatible religious truth claims as evidence in favor of contrary, secular truth claims of their own. The multiplicity and radically diverse content of religious truth claims, it is argued, point to religion's arbitrary, subjective character, so dramatically different from the cross-cultural universality of highly corroborated, modern scientific theories such as the theory of evolution. This contrast was the basis for Weber's sharp distinction between facts and values, the former the ostensibly objective realm of science, the latter the supposedly subjective domain in which "the diverse value spheres [*Wertordnungen*] of the world stand in irresolvable conflict with each other": "so long as life rests on itself and is interpreted from out of itself, all it knows is the unending conflict of those gods with one another."[2] Jeffrey Stout has recently expressed a skeptical corollary, imperialistically speaking for a "we" that either misrepresents or impugns the honesty of millions of religious believers: "If we are honest, we will admit that the margin of error in religious matters encompasses very nearly the entire subject. In religious pursuits, we all seem to be groping in the dark. Otherwise, how are we to explain the history of religious discord?"[3] Honest religious believers, Stout seems to imply, should confess the arbitrariness of their truth claims regardless of what they believe or why they believe it, and hence become skeptics about their own faith commitments.

Whether overtly or not, those who reject religion often make a different truth claim: that no religious claims are true, all religious beliefs are subjective, no religious doctrine is more than a human construct, and/or that all religion is to be explained exclusively in terms of its social, political, and psychological functions. God does not reveal himself (or gods do not reveal themselves) to human beings; human beings invent God (or gods). The invented, constructed character of religion explains the open-ended arbitrariness of its proponents' beliefs over time and across cultures. Such truth claims about religion have been made in various ways by the most influential, disenchanted disenchanters of the past two centuries, including Feuerbach, Marx, Nietzsche, and Freud. These sorts of claims are pervasive in universities and have been theorized in many different forms in the academic study of religion, especially since the late nineteenth century.[4] They have also become socially widespread in less formal, less explicitly intellectual ways in Western European countries and Canada, especially since the 1960s.[5]

To reject religious answers to the Life Questions, however, does not absolve one from answering them, even if only implicitly. Nonreligious answers are always based on something, too, whether or not their protagonists are aware of the fact—and again, such a ground is for good reason rarely even sought in the findings of the natural sciences. In Western society at large, the early twenty-first-century basis for most secular answers to the Life Questions seems to be some combination of personal preferences, inclinations, and desires: in principle truth is whatever is true to you, values are whatever you value, priorities are whatever you prioritize, and what you should live for is whatever you decide you should live for. In short: whatever. All human values, meanings, priorities, and morality are contingent, constructed, and subjective. In principle you are your own basis, your own authority, in all these matters, within the boundaries established by the law, whether you ground your answers in your feelings, arguments you find convincing, principles you find appealing, beliefs you like, what your parents taught you, what your favorite celebrities say, some combination of these, or anything else. You can change the basis for your answers, as well as their content, at any time, any number of times, and for any reason or without any reason. You are *free*—hence, whatever. So long as you do not infringe on others' legally and politically protected rights to do as they wish, particular answers to the Life Questions can be literally anything human beings can invent and affirm. This would seem correlative to something like the essence of the contemporary, Western freedom of the individual. As it was put in 1992 by the U.S. Supreme Court's majority decision in *Planned Parenthood v. Casey*: "At the heart of liberty is the right to define one's own concept of existence, of meaning, of the universe, and of the mystery of human life."[6] Note here the parallel to the common (though not unanimous) view among Christians that religious truth is a function of what one sovereignly and freely chooses to believe, and the importance one decides to attribute to one's truth claims.

On this view, open-ended pluralism regarding the content of or bases for truth claims, meaning, values, and priorities is not a problem. It is simply what should be expected when individuals are given the freedom to devise their own answers to the Life Questions, resulting in what Lisa

Jardine has called "our own exuberant multiculturalism."[7] Much more important than *what* one affirms is the effective protection of one's right to affirm whatever one wishes. The answers particular individuals give are paramount to the unique ways in which individuals invent and reinvent themselves, the personal manner in which they construct and reconstruct their identity. If there are no genuine answers given by God to the Life Questions—and according to secular believers there are not, either (according to atheists) because God is not real or (according to skeptics) because it is impossible to determine which among competing religious truth claims might be true—then the basis of the answers can *only* be individual human preference, and a fundamental role of the putatively neutral state is to enable and protect individual rights to divergent preferences. This would seem to belong to the essence of contemporary, Western liberal democracy, and will be explored further in Chapter 4. The general secular answer to the Life Questions in the early twenty-first century is implicit in a remark by Kwame Anthony Appiah: "I have no more reason to resent those who go to Mecca on the hajj than I have to begrudge the choices of those who go to Scotland for golf or to Milan for opera. Not what I'd do, but, hey, suit yourself."[8] Or more colloquially: whatever. A once-in-a-lifetime religious pilgrimage, taking in the links at St. Andrews, or enjoying Verdi at La Scala—it's all up to you. Ironically, this seems not too different from the attitude taken by many religious believers toward religion: whatever respective individuals believe is fine for them, so long as they keep it discreetly to themselves, are nondisruptive, and do not try to impose it on anyone else. In concrete, sociocultural terms, this attitude in combination with the state's legal and political protection of individual rights has resulted in an enormous range of divergent secular truth claims alongside the vast pluralism of divergent religious truth claims.

Most of the answers to the Life Questions given in the academy, whether among natural scientists, social scientists, or humanistic scholars, while more sophisticated and articulate, seem not to differ in kind from this secular view of the constructed, subjective character of all truth claims in the domain of human values, priorities, morality, and meaning. Some academics, whether poststructuralist literary scholars or theoretically minded network-structuralist sociologists, go further, offering (rival) explanations for how and why it is that human beings or persons are *themselves* ostensibly "constructions."[9] One does not need a Ph.D. to see that taken at face value, such claims are obviously false. The evident absurdity of Saussurean views run amok conflates the flesh-and-blood reality of members of the species *Homo sapiens* with the vast range of competing views about how human beings are to be *understood* and how human beings *regard* themselves amid the full complexity of their social lives and institutional em-beddedness, a difference related to John Searle's well-drawn distinction between "brute realities" and socially constructed "institutional realities."[10] Before his Nietzschean turn, Michel Foucault made this sort of conflation part of his historical-supersessionist enterprise in *Les mots et les choses* (1966).[11] Human beings are not "constructions"; whatever else they might also be, they are biological animals of the species *Homo sapiens* that are born, live, and die, as do other mammals. Anyone who doubts this should read a biology textbook, or look around (where they can see living human beings) and visit a hospital (where they can see human beings being born and dying). Perhaps scholars who allege that human beings are constructed are trying to say that a wide range of different truth claims *about* human beings have been and continue to be made, and that such truth claims are constructed insofar as they are articulated in language and make use of contestable concepts. Or that inherited social patterns, institutions, and customs inescapably influence individual human beings, who do not exist apart from them. If so, they should adopt a clearer idiom to make their unobjectionable points. Otherwise, media stories about what on the face of it are ludicrous ideas tend to harm higher education and the reputation of academics in general in the eyes of legislators and the wider public.

In the academy a few exceptions to the widespread view that all values, meanings, and norms are subjective and constructed run in the opposite direction. Some sociobiologists, evolutionary psychologists, and neurosci-entists seek an objective, evolutionarily grounded basis for claims about human nature or certain moral values. Yet insofar as *every* behavior and practice by individual members of *Homo sapiens* is by definition equally the product of biological evolution—competing with ferocity and cooper-ating with kindness, practicing monogamous sexual fidelity and having intercourse with many sexual partners, perpetrating genocide and cam-paigning to stop it, dedicating one's life to the poor and ignoring them completely—it is unclear what normative force or applicability to morality evolutionary theory could have. Far from "explaining" all human behav-ior, evolutionary theory is analytically impotent in accounting for its vari-ety and antitheses. It implies nothing about what one should believe or how one should live or the values one ought to adopt. And that all human be-ings are the products of biological evolution tells us nothing about why individual human beings behave as they do.[12] Evolutionarily, there was no difference between Adolf Hitler and Dietrich Bonhoeffer during World War II, or between Idi Amin of Uganda and Mother Teresa of Calcutta in the late twentieth century. So too, "survival" or "perpetuation of genes" is not an adequate, actual answer given by human beings to the question

"What should I live for?" One is alive, one is surviving—has one thereby answered any of the Life Questions? Obviously survival (though not perpetuation of genes) is a minimal precondition for any substantive answers one might give. But what comes next, and why?

Most neoclassical economists and some political scientists make universalistic claims about all human beings as self-interested agents who employ instrumental rationality in order to maximize their material well-being. But historical research and cultural anthropological findings no less than contemporary counterexamples demonstrate that such claims are mistaken. Either they are empirically falsified, because there *are* people who subordinate the maximization of their material well-being to other priorities, such as those in environmentally self-conscious "intentional communities" who radically alter their lifestyle so as not to exacerbate global warming, members of Old Order Amish communities in North America, or members of ascetic Catholic religious orders.[13] Or such claims about self-interested maximization are emptily tautological, if *whatever* an individual chooses—say, a life that combines a balance of prayer, worship, ascetic self-denial, and service to others—is by definition construed as maximizing behavior. According to this view, all people are seeking to maximize whatever matters most to them, regardless of what it is, how it is expressed, or how dramatically it might change in the course of an individual's life. On this count, both Donald Trump and Sister Helen Préjean (of *Dead Man Walking* fame) are self-interested maximizers, as are workaholic lawyers and all-day-long watchers of television reruns, zealous activists for human rights under dangerous political regimes and sun-loving surfers on Southern California beaches. We are all self-interested maximizers, and cannot help be anything but. If alleged in *this* sense, then like the invocation of evolution as a putative explanation for all human behaviors, the claim is trivial and without any analytical value in explaining the wide range of different human behaviors and priorities.

Numerous academics in various disciplines, traditionally and above all in philosophy, purportedly base their truth claims relevant to the Life Questions on reason as such. But the sheer diversity of rival, conflicting assertions ostensibly rooted in reason casts grave doubt on its viability as a ground for such claims. What prevails instead is a wide-ranging pluralism of competing truth claims among philosophers, as well as among academics in many other disciplines whose views rely in one way or another on various strands in modern philosophical thought. (The last part of this chapter will return to this point.) In other humanistic and social scientific disciplines, including history, literature, sociology, and anthropology, the study of different cultures and traditions in the past and across the world reveals a vast number of incompatible religious and secular truth claims pertaining to the Life Questions. Academic research of this sort seems most unlikely to provide any basis for arguments about which if any among the plethoric claims might actually be true in anything more than a historically and culturally contingent way—that is, certain people in certain times and places *considered* X or *regard* Y to be true. Without question, they did and do. But as everyone knows who understands the principle of noncontradiction, it is impossible that all their respective claims might actually *be* true on the points at which they are contrary to one another. Hence the widespread tendency in the academy to echo Weber and to conclude or imply that there *are* no true answers to the Life Questions, but only an enormous number of competing views—which is, of course, a (relativistic and skeptical) truth claim of its own.

Scientific inquiry, economists' claims, philosophical reflection, and the study of human cultures and traditions *augment further* the open-ended religious and secular pluralism that prevails in Western society at large with respect to the Life Questions. Through academic inquiry we learn about more than contemporary Western hyperpluralism, greatly extending the range of answers to the Life Questions across space and time. If the current academy has any persuasive, substantive answers to the Life Questions to offer, what they might be is no clearer than trying to discern which among the countless religious truth claims manifest in the Western world today might actually be true. According to the political scientist John Mearsheimer, this indeed describes and should be the academy's relationship to the Life Questions. Nor does he think this is a problem: "Universities do not have a moral agenda and do not give students moral guidance, because that would involve preaching about values, and that is an enterprise that holds hardly any attraction for modern universities. Religious institutions and families are expected to provide their members with explicit advice about moral virtue, but universities are not. Indeed, it is difficult to imagine a professor at a school like [the University of] Chicago making the case that the faculty should devise a wide-ranging code of ethics for its students. Other faculty would probably think the poor soul had lost his or her mind."[14] Natural scientists, social scientists, and humanistic scholars neither can nor should answer questions about values, meaning, purpose, or morality from among the competing claims and practices that make up our contemporary hyperpluralism. Their mandate, according to Mearsheimer and the prevailing view, is "not about telling students what to think, but how to think."[15] The secular academy is the domain of Weberian facts, not values—except, contradictorily, for the one hegemonic and *supreme* value that no judgments about competing truth claims pertaining to values or morality should or can be made. Which is itself, in fact, a normative claim that reflects certain values, despite diversionary disavowals to the contrary. And which, in fact, virtually no academics actually believe, unless they would be prepared not to give any "moral guidance" or "moral advice" if a student claimed to find nothing wrong with genocide, murder, torture, or rape. But according to Mearsheimer, it seems, an academic who not only objected to ethnic cleansing or opposed the torture of children, but sought to explain why they were morally wrong and indeed evil within a "wide-ranging code of ethics," would qualify as mentally imbalanced for promoting a "moral agenda" and "preaching about values."

Chapter 4 is devoted expressly to moral discourse and moral behavior in relationship to political ideas and political institutions. This chapter seeks more generally to explain how current Western hyperpluralism pertaining to the Life Questions came about historically. In principle, the range of particular assertions encompassed in this inquiry is vast—it includes all religious and secular truth claims made about the Life Questions between the beginning of the sixteenth century and the present. Yet as we shall see, the bases on which this vast range of claims has rested are quite limited. Only a few types of foundational moves have been made in the past half millennium; indeed, only a few types seem possible. In an effort to make explanatory headway, the analysis in this chapter deliberately concentrates on the justificatory *bases* rather than on the specific *content* of divergent answers to the Life Questions. To try actually to cover all the different views would entail a nearly endless, encyclopedic quest, the results of which— besides being impossible to obtain in a lifetime—would in fact inhibit historical explanation, overwhelming it with historical data in an ongoing work of many volumes. To risk belaboring a metaphor: without misrepresenting any of the trees, the point here is not to examine each one but to see the *kind* of forest we are in, where its trees came from, and in what sorts of soil they have grown. The aim is to discern and delineate the historically consequential strands with the explanatory power adequate to account for the situation in which Westerners find themselves today with respect to the Life Questions. We need to begin prior to the Protestant Reformation, which articulated the first important, alternative basis for Christian truth claims in opposition to important claims by the established, Roman church. To the extent that they carried out their duties— which was far from always—the church's clerical leaders had for centuries before the Reformation imparted to all of the baptized, whether explicitly or implicitly, truth claims that were held to be God's answers to the Life Questions, and thus applicable to everyone.

WESTERN CHRISTIANITY on the eve of the Reformation comprised an institutionalized worldview, a many-layered combination of beliefs, practices, and institutions built up over many centuries. Deeply embedded in social life, political relationships, and the wider culture, Christianity had as its ostensible, principal raison d'être the sanctification of the baptized through the practice of the Christian faith, such that they might be saved eternally when judged by God after death. As we saw in Chapter 1, medieval Christianity's central truth claim was that the same transcendent God of love who was metaphysically distinct from the universe he had created ex nihilo had become incarnate in Jesus of Nazareth for the salvation of human beings. The church, established by Jesus himself, was said to be the continuing instrument for the achievement of God's plan of salvation for the human race after Jesus's ascension that followed his crucifixion and resurrection.

Christianity at the outset of the sixteenth century exhibits two major paradoxes. First, it combined sharp limits on orthodoxy with a wide tolerance of diverse local beliefs and practices. Any picture of medieval Latin Christianity as a homogeneous, uniform set of rigidly prescribed, strictly enforced, and closely followed practices is deeply misleading, however much this myth survives as a vestige of nineteenth-century liberal views of the Reformation or of nostalgic, romanticizing Catholic notions of the Middle Ages. Beyond a few basic expectations and implicit affirmation of the truth claims that they presupposed, variety and voluntarism marked late medieval religious life, from minimal participation in collective practices to the spiritual athleticism of individuals such as Henry Suso or Catherine of Genoa.[16]

At the same time, however, orthodoxy conceptually and necessarily implied heterodoxy. Not only was this a demand of logic; it was also entailed by God's actions in history, especially in Jesus, all of whose teachings (if true) and actions (if they actually occurred) necessarily meant that their respective contraries and denials were false. Paul and the apostles, too, had understood this, as had the Greek and Latin church fathers. "Now if Christ is proclaimed as raised from the dead," Paul asked, for example, "how can some of you say there is no resurrection of the dead?" (1 Cor 15:12) Early church leaders, especially in the contentious fourth and fifth centuries, had decided amid theological controversy—through the guidance, they claimed, of the Holy Spirit as promised by Jesus (Mt 16:18, 28:20)—what truth claims were and were not consistent with God's self-revelation in Jesus, and therefore integral to life as a Christian in God's church. Orthodoxy was therefore simply a corollary of the fact that the church made truth claims, whether in the fifth century or the fifteenth. It was a necessary condition for shared Christian life. Consequently, crossing the wrong lines could quickly land one in serious trouble—as the late medieval Waldensians, Lollards, and Hussites knew firsthand.[17]

As a result, the church around 1500 exhibited an identifiable unity in doctrinal, liturgical, devotional, and institutional terms across Latin Christendom from Iceland to Poland, from Scandinavia to Spain. But it also manifested a cornucopia of local religious customs, voluntary devotional practices, specific ecclesiastical subgroups, particular jurisdictional privileges, divergent theological approaches, and syncretistic beliefs in a spectrum ranging from the impeccably orthodox to the edge of heresy.[18] References to medieval "Christianities" that downplay the common beliefs, practices, and institutions of Latin Christendom are as distorting as older, facile exaggerations about the Middle Ages as a homogeneous "age of faith." The combination of unity and heterogeneity can be expressed simply by seeing that late medieval Christianity was variegated and diverse. Polyphonic settings for the Mass always used the same Latin texts, for example, but composers such as Josquin des Prez (c. 1450–1521), Jakob Obrecht (1451–1505), Franchino Gaffurio (1451–1522), John Taverner (c. 1490–1545), and Cristóbal de Morales (c. 1500–1551) worked in different patronage contexts, rendered diversely the standard parts of the Mass, and varied the number and interplay of choral voices in their compositions.[19] Similarly, artists in Flanders and Italy, England and the Holy Roman Empire, France and Castile were all painting Annunciations, Nativities, Crucifixions, and other scenes from the life of Jesus, just as they were painting many of the same saints, but their compositions manifest wide-ranging variety in style and scale, from the monumental to the miniature.[20] So too, although nearly all theologians were Augustinian in their basic outlook, some more explicitly and narrowly than others, most were also Scotists or Occamist nominalists, others were Thomist realists, and still others blended nominalism and realism, while some scholastic theologians, such as John Fisher (1469–1535) and Johannes Eck (1486–1543), were also keen on humanism.[21] Exaggerating either the diversity or the unity of late medieval Christianity distorts its character. The late medieval church was a large playground, but one enclosed by forbidding fences—an almost riotous diversity held together in an overarching unity by a combination of ingrained customs, myriad institutions, varying degrees of self-conscious dedication, and the threat of punishment.

The second paradox of late medieval Christianity is its combination of long-standing, widely criticized shortcomings with unprecedented, thriving lay devotion and dedication. Notwithstanding Huizinga's influential opinions about purported spiritual decadence during the alleged "waning of the Middle Ages,"[22] the fifteenth century was arguably more devout than any preceding century in the history of Western Christianity. Never before had so many of the laity thrown themselves into their religious lives with such gusto, with so many devotions to Christ and the saints, participation in confraternities, works of charity, practices of pious reading and prayer, and monetary contributions in support of the church.[23] At the same time, criticisms of clerical corruption and greed, of lay superstition and ignorance, of manifest sinfulness by individuals in every station of life, were legion throughout the late Middle Ages.[24] Critiques of the late medieval church's many real, pervasive, and undeniable problems were paradoxically related to religious commitment: people who care about their faith tend to complain about such things. From the fourteenth-century Avignonese papacy through the decades of the Western schism and into the sixteenth century, reformers and academic administrators such as Jean Gerson (1363–1429), preachers such as Bernardino of Siena (1380–1444), and churchmen such as Antonino of Florence (1389–1459) exhorted Christians to live as Jesus and the church taught that they should live, imitating their Lord and the saints, pursuing holiness by practicing the virtues.[25] Such reforming efforts had an effect: new spiritual movements such as the *devotio moderna* enjoyed great success despite provoking suspicion; new confraternities such as the Oratory of Divine Love attracted many members even as established confraternities continued to thrive; the Observantine movement among the religious orders revitalized hundreds of male and female monasteries; and the sacred philology of the northern humanists sought through erudition and education to instruct and so morally to renew Christians.[26] But repeated calls for a systematic reform "in head and members" found no sustained response among popes and the papal curia, even when, under duress, Pope Julius II called the Fifth Lateran Council in 1512.[27] The nepotistic, wealthy cardinals at the papal court and the aristocratic prince-bishops of the Holy Roman Empire saw that any thoroughgoing, sustained reforms concerning simony, pluralism, and ecclesiastical revenues would undermine their wealth and privileges.[28] So they tended to stymie any genuinely ambitious (and therefore threatening) reforming initiatives. The gulf between the church's prescriptions and the practices of its members—from clerical avarice in high places to lay superstition among the unlearned—inspired constant calls to close the gap, from Catherine of Siena in the 1370s to Erasmus in the 1510s.[29]

But the church's prescriptions, based on its truth claims, were a given, apart from their rejection by members of minority groups such as the Bohemian Hussites and the tiny pockets of English Lollards (and of course the comparatively small numbers of Jews and Iberian Muslims, who were geographically situated within Latin Christendom but not among the baptized). The (sometimes implicit) doctrines that delimited orthodoxy were logically presupposed by practices such as the celebration of the liturgy, processions and pilgrimages, and prayers to saints, as well as by institutions such as the papacy, the sacerdotal priesthood, religious orders, and confraternities. The negotiated concordats that began in the 1410s between late medieval rulers and popes altered neither the church's truth claims nor its assertions of right religious practice.[30] Nor were its doctrines changed when some territorial princes and city councils in the Holy Roman Empire began wresting away from their respective bishops jurisdictional control over many ecclesiastical affairs.[31] For to reject the church's teachings was to reject its authority as the caretaker of God's saving truth, the means of eternal salvation legitimated with biblical reference for more than a millennium to its establishment by Jesus himself.

A REJECTION OF THE church's authority and many of its teachings is precisely what happened in the Reformation. All Protestant reformers came to believe that the established church was no longer the church established by Jesus. So they spurned many truth claims of the faith as embodied in the Roman church. Their repudiation was not based primarily on the church's rampant abuses, the sinfulness of many of its members, or entrenched obstacles to reform. All of these had been obvious to conscientious clerical reformers and other open-eyed Christians for well over a century. The Reformation's upshot was rather that Roman Catholicism, *even at its best,* was a perverted form of Christianity even if all its members had been self-consciously following all the Roman church's teachings and had been enacting all its permitted practices. Institutional abuses and immorality were seen as symptomatic signs of a flawed foundation, namely false and dangerous doctrines—that is, mistaken truth claims.[32] The established church *itself* was teaching errors and lies as if they were truths. *This* was the problem that had to be fixed. And because the church had pressed into every nook and cranny of politics, social life, economic activity, and culture—in myriad ways, according to Protestant reformers, distorting them all—it looked like the apocalypse was nigh.[33] Already in the early 1490s the Dominican friar Girolamo Savonarola had preached as much in Florence, his admonitory prophecies seemingly confirmed when Charles VIII of France invaded Italy in 1494.[34] Even as the storm of God's wrath gathered strength, the Reformation, according to its protagonists, would be Christendom's urgent, eleventh-hour rescue and recovery mission.

Once the scales fell from long-clouded eyes in the early Reformation, the errors of a stubbornly self-interested, papist church had to be rejected in light of God's truth. This meant comparing latter-day doctrines, practices, and institutions with the one genuine source for Christian faith and life, namely God's word in scripture, and cleaving to the latter. Martin Luther articulated the principle as early as July 1519 at the Leipzig Disputation, ironically citing Jean Gerson and Augustine as authorities to make his point: "No faithful Christian can be forced beyond the sacred scripture, which is nothing less than [*proprie*] divine law, unless new and approved revelation is added. On the contrary, on the basis of divine law we are prohibited to believe, unless it is approved by divine scripture or palpably obvious [*manifestam*] revelation."[35] In the German and Swiss cities that played such a crucial role in the early Reformation, other reformers who rejected the Roman church's authority agreed with Luther about the foundational importance of scripture. In 1521 the gifted young humanist Philipp Melanchthon stated in his frequently reprinted handbook of Luther's theology that "whoever seeks the nature of Christianity from any source except canonical scripture is mistaken."[36] Andreas Bodenstein von Karlstadt, at this point still the dean of the theology faculty in Luther's Wittenberg, delivered a sermon in February 1522 in which he said that "all preachers should always state that their doctrine is not their own, but God's. . . . They can discover nothing out of their own heads. If the Bible is at an end, then their competence is also at an end [*Wan die Biblien aus ist, sso ist ir kunst auch auss*]."[37] Huldrych Zwingli, the humanist reformer of Zurich, held the same view, declaring in his 1522 treatise on the clarity and certainty of scripture that "no such trust should be given to any word like that given to [the word of God]. For it is certain [*gewüß*] and may not fail. It is clear [*heiter*], and will not leave us to err in darkness. It teaches itself on its own [*es leert sich selbs*]."[38] So too, Balthasar Hubmaier stated in the Second Zurich Disputation in October 1523 that "in all divisive matters and controversies [*spänigen sachen und zwyträchten*] only scripture, canonized and made holy by God himself, should and must be the judge, no one else. . . . For sacred scripture alone is the true light and lantern through which all human argument, darkness, and objections are recognized."[39] Those responsible for drawing up the Mühlhausen Articles, one of many such lists of grievances and demands composed during the German Peasants' War, asserted in September 1524 that the proper standard of justice was given "in the Bible or holy word of God," and stated that the parishioners and craftsmen in the city who had drawn up the articles had "derived their judgments from the word of God."[40] As a final example, Argula von Grumbach, a Bavarian noblewoman partial to Luther, along with Katharina Schütz Zell of Strasbourg one of the very few women who wrote evangelical pamphlets in the 1520s, told officials at the University of Ingolstadt in 1523 that "no one has a right to exercise authority over the word of God. Yes, no human being, whoever he is, can rule over it. For only the word of God, without which nothing was made, should and must rule."[41] Referring to scripture in 1524, Karlstadt put the matter bluntly: "The naked truth alone [*Die blosse warheit allein*] . . . should be your foundation and rock."[42]

According to those who rejected it, the Roman church had selfishly twisted or ignored the word of God to suit the church's own interests, from the bogus Donation of Constantine to the revenue streams that poured into papal coffers from the sale of church offices. Their Lord commanded Christians to return to him in fidelity and holiness, in word and deed, beginning with God's own truth claims taught in the Bible, uncluttered by human traditions and clerical manipulations. Emphatically, this was not a matter of individual opinion—the point was not what readers wanted or listeners thought, but simply and only what God taught.

Hence the reformers who rejected the Roman church distinguished sharply between God's word and merely human writings and opinions. They insisted that Christians not presumptuously proffer their own views or impose their own ideas on the Bible, but rather submit themselves to God's unadorned teachings. Zwingli criticized anyone who comes to scripture with his "own opinion and forwardness [*sinn und fürwitz*] and forces scripture to agree with it. Do you think he has something? No—from him will be taken away the opinion and understanding that he thinks he has."[43] Luther concurred, in a treatise defending the adoration of the Eucharist from 1523: "This is not Christian teaching, when I bring an opinion to scripture and compel scripture to follow it, but rather, on the contrary, when I first have got straight what scripture teaches [*tzuvor die schrifft klar habe*] and then compel my opinion to accord with it."[44] According to Karlstadt, writing in 1524, "We are bound to scripture, . . . [and] no one is permitted to judge according to the arbitrary opinion of his heart [*seines hertzen gutduncken*]."[45] In September of the same year, Conrad Grebel, like Zwingli a learned reformer from Zurich, wrote a letter to Thomas Müntzer, telling him, "I do not want to concoct, teach, or establish a single thing based on personal opinion [*eignem gütduncken*]."[46] Another Anabaptist leader, Hans Hut, an heir to Müntzer's legacy in Germany, stated in 1527 that "God has forbidden us to do as we think fit [*was uns guet dunkt*]; rather, we should do what he has commanded and hold to it and not deviate to the left or to the right."[47] All these reformers, along with others who rejected the Roman church's authority, were on board with *sola scriptura*. Their shared goal was to discern and to follow what God had revealed in scripture. The idea that biblical interpretation was in principle a matter of individual opinion or preference was utter anathema to the early evangelical reformers.

So much the more disconcerting, then, was the undesired result of their shared commitment. From the early 1520s, those who rejected Rome disagreed about what God's word said. Therefore they disagreed about what God's truth was, and so about what Christians were to believe and do. "Yet you might ask," Luther wrote in 1520, "'What then is this word, or in what manner is it to be used, since there are so many words of God?' "[48] These were great questions. Indeed, they were the most fundamental questions of the Reformation, given the anti-Roman implications of the shared insistence on scripture as the sole authority for Christian faith and life. By March 1522, Karlstadt disputed Luther's marginalization of the book of James, plus his views on the character of the Old Testament, eucharistic practice, the oral confession of sins, and the permissibility of religious images.[49] Luther and Melanchthon disagreed with Zwingli and the latter's reforming allies about the nature of Christ's presence in the Lord's Supper. Between 1525 and 1527, at least nine different evangelical reformers—including Zwingli, Martin Bucer, Johannes Oecolampadius, Wolfgang Capito, Leo Jud, and Johan Landtsperger—published no fewer than twenty-eight treatises, in Latin as well as German, against Luther's views on the Lord's Supper, before the dramatic, face-to-face standoff and nonresolution between the two sides at the Marburg Colloquy in early October 1529.[50] This became the doctrinal—and therefore also the ecclesial and social—headwaters of the division between Lutheran and Reformed Protestantism, notwithstanding how much they continued to share in common with one another, and indeed, with Christianity as embodied in the Roman church.[51] That the theologians at Marburg agreed on fourteen of fifteen disputed points only underscores how important was the disagreement about this one issue, which, through centuries of variegated relations between Lutherans and Reformed Protestants, has had enormous political and social consequences down to the present.

Zwingli also disagreed with his former Zurich colleagues Hubmaier and Grebel about the biblical basis for infant baptism, with its dramatic ecclesiological implications for the nature of the Christian community. This conflict precipitated the first adult baptisms by early 1525, a year before the Zurich city council, with whose members Zwingli worked to dismantle inherited ecclesiastical institutions and practices, enacted capital legislation against local Anabaptists.[52] In their denunciations of infant baptism, early German-speaking Anabaptists were following the same insistence on scripture and rejection of merely human teachings that they shared with their Protestant opponents. According to Anabaptists, the issue went to the essence of being a Christian—hence their vehemence. In Grebel's words, "the baptism of children is a senseless, blasphemous abomination [*grewel*], against all scripture"; his colleague in Zurich, Feliz Mantz, pronounced it "against God, an insult to Christ, and a trampling under foot of his own true, eternal word"; Hans Hut, in his unpublished treatise on baptism from 1527, denounced it as "a pure human invention, without God's word and commandment. It is a defrauding of simple people, a cunning trick on all Christendom, and an arch-rogue's cover for all the godless"; and Michael Sattler, a former Benedictine monk and the author of the Schleitheim Articles, an important articulation of Swiss Brethren teachings from February 1527, condemned "all infant baptism, the pope's greatest and first abomination."[53] Zwingli disagreed. His treatise on baptism from May 1525 (one of several he wrote on the subject) defended infant baptism based on its nonprohibition in scripture and by analogy to Jewish circumcision. Zwingli's work also repudiated the entire patristic and medieval theology of the sacrament: "I can conclude nothing else but that all the doctors have greatly erred [vil geirret habend] from the time of the apostles. . . . Therefore we want to see what baptism actually is, at many points indeed taking a different path against that which ancient, more recent, and contemporary authors have taken, not according to our own whim [nitt mit unserem tandt] but rather according to God's word."[54] Just like his Anabaptist opponents, Zwingli was following God's word.

By 1525 the German Peasants' War was raging, with leaders such as Thomas Müntzer flatly repudiating Luther's sharp distinction between "the Gospel" and social, economic, and political concerns. This will be explored in Chapters 3 and 5. Other anti-Roman reformers, such as the Nuremberg printer Hans Hergot and Michael Gaismair, previously the secretary to the prince-bishop of Brixen, shared Müntzer's appreciation for the Gospel's socioeconomic implications, but rejected his apocalyptic exhortations to violence. Instead, they envisioned in their respective ways communitarian Christian societies predicated on a dismantling of feudal institutions.[55] Withdrawing from dreams of remaking Christendom after the utter defeat of the "common man" in the Peasants' War, Anabaptists proved a highly fissiparous lot, disagreeing among themselves in a host of doctrinally and therefore socially divisive ways, beginning already in the late 1520s.[56] For example, the early Swiss Brethren included not only pacifist leaders such as Grebel and Mantz, but also Hubmaier, who sanctioned the coercive use of political power.[57] By the time of the Anabaptist Kingdom of Münster in 1534–1535, harsh persecution of the south German and Austrian Anabaptists under Ferdinand I had helped to precipitate the formation of the Austerlitz Brethren (including the young Pilgram Marpeck), Gabrielites, Philipites, and Hutterites, themselves distinct from the central German Anabaptists.[58]

These controversies and the divergent groups that were their social outcome reflect only a few major disagreements about the meaning, implications, and application of God's word from central Europe in the 1520s and 1530s. Expanding the geographical scope and chronological range to encompass Europe as such during the entire Reformation era, up to the mid-seventeenth century, discloses many more disagreements and correlative socio-ecclesial divisions, whether for example among German Lutherans between so-called Philippists and Gnesio-Lutherans in the decades after Luther's death in 1546, among Dutch Anabaptists beginning in the 1530s and continuing throughout the era, or between Reformed Protestants and Arminians in the Low Countries and England in the early seventeenth century.[59] Christians who rejected the authority of the Roman church and its truth claims, notwithstanding certain alliances and reconciliations (such as the Lutheran Formula of Concord) among some of the constituent groups, never exhibited anything remotely resembling agreement about their own, alternative truth claims. It is thus misleading to say that "Protestantism itself splintered into rival denominations, or 'confessions,'" as if there ever was some point in the early Reformation when anti-Roman Christians had agreed among themselves about what scripture said and God taught.[60] There wasn't.

Nor was this simply a feature of the tumultuous years of the early German Reformation, when, it might be thought, such contestation was only to have been expected, but after which there was some movement toward agreement about the Bible's meaning, once things "settled down." That is not what happened. It was not as if, say, once John Calvin rejected the Roman church in late 1533, or at any time between the first publication of his *Institutes* in 1536 and his death in 1564, Protestants tended toward a consensus around his exegetical claims and theological assertions.[61] On the contrary, like Luther, Calvin was involved in doctrinal controversies with other Protestants throughout his reforming career.[62] Seeing the historical consequences of the commitment to *sola scriptura* does not depend on examining all the myriad, biblically based truth claims made by those Christian groups and individuals who rejected the authority of the Roman church between the early 1520s and the mid-seventeenth century. The important point is that every anti-Roman, Reformation-era Christian truth claim based on scripture fits into this pattern of fissiparous disagreement among those who agreed that Christian truth should be based solely on scripture.

"The Bible, I say, the Bible only, is the religion of Protestants!" the English theologian William Chillingworth famously declared in 1638.[63] This is indeed what Chillingworth and many other Protestants said—but what did the Bible say? *That* was the question, to which so many incompatible answers were given—and with so many ramifying consequences, precisely because Christianity in the early sixteenth century was not a discrete set of beliefs and practices called "religion" separated off from the rest of human life, but an institutionalized worldview that shaped all its domains. As will be analyzed further in Chapter 3, scripture *officially interpreted by hermeneutic authorities and backed by political authorities* led to confessional Protestant cities, territories, and states, whether Lutheran or Reformed Protestant (including the Church of England), which stipulated, imposed, and policed their respective versions of what the Bible said in a manner analogous to Catholic political regimes. Scripture *"alone,"* on the other hand, *without* an alliance between anti-Roman reformers supported by political authorities, resulted in a vast range of conflicting and irreconcilable Christian truth claims.

Commitment to the authority of scripture led neither obviously nor necessarily to justification by faith alone or to salvation through grace alone as the cornerstone doctrines of Christianity. Radical Protestants made abundantly clear that the Bible did not "interpret itself" in this way, whatever protagonists claimed to the contrary. Unfettered and unconstrained, the Reformation simply yielded the full, historically manifest range of truth claims made about what the Bible said. We see a latter-day outcome of this today in the United States—but very importantly, in a political setting that *protects all* rather than *suppresses any* religious views, so long as its adherents observe the state's laws, which facilitates the open-ended proliferation of truth claims in the "religious marketplace." The relationship between modern, liberal states and the expansiveness of religious pluralism will be considered further in Chapters 3 and 4. From the very outset of the Reformation, the shared commitment to *sola scriptura* entailed a hermeneutical heterogeneity that proved doctrinally contentious, socially divisive, and sometimes (in the German Peasants' War, the Anabaptist Kingdom of Münster, and the English Revolution) politically subversive. In Benjamin Kaplan's apt phrase, "Protestantism itself was irrepressibly fissile."[64] Adamant claims that "the Bible is the religion of Protestants" did not arrest the fissility—they caused it.

This matters today because the most important, distant historical source of Western hyperpluralism pertaining to the Life Questions is the Reformation insistence on scripture as the sole source for Christian faith and life, combined with the vast range of countervailing ways in which the Bible was interpreted and applied. For the sorts of disagreements about answers to the Life Questions characteristic of the early Reformation have never gone away—they have only been transformed, modified, and expanded in terms of content even as efforts have been made to contain and manage their unintended and undeniably enormous effects. As we saw in the previous chapter, one unanticipated consequence was the unplanned self-marginalization of theology (via doctrinal controversy) with respect to modern philosophical and scientific discourse about God and the natural world. And as we shall see, the disagreements precipitated by *sola scriptura* prompted in turn novel *kinds* of attempts to answer the Life Questions. Both Roman Catholicism and the many varieties of Protestantism provided in the early modern period and continue today to provide their respective answers to the Life Questions, as constituent elements within contemporary Western hyperpluralism. At no point between the 1520s and the present have either Protestants' divergent truth claims or those promulgated by the Roman Catholic Church ceased to find adherents or stopped competing with varied, rival, secular views that have become more prevalent in surges since the later seventeenth century. Dominant, supersessionist narratives of the modern Western world, however, with their notion that revealed religion was somehow left behind or ceased to be intellectually viable as a result of the rise of modern science and philosophy, give a different (and mistaken) impression.

In addition to the tendency of historians of modernity not to think about the abiding influence of the distant past in the present, the Reformation's relevance for contemporary hyperpluralism has not been seen because "Protestantism" is so often paired in misleading ways with "Catholicism" in discussions of early modern, modern, and contemporary Western Christianity. The history of the Reformation and very probably of Western modernity as well would have looked dramatically different if those who insisted on *sola scriptura* and abominated interpretative individualism had agreed among themselves about what the Bible taught and thus about what Christians were to believe and do. Then there would be some evidence for the endlessly repeated maxim that scripture "interprets itself." Or there would be some evidentiary indication that comparing biblical passages with one another tends toward antagonists' interpretative agreement about the meaning and implications of the Bible, rather than simply auguring additional rounds of exegetical disputes. Then "Protestantism," whatever the sorts of diversity it presumably would also have exhibited, would have designated something with discernibly coherent doctrines, worship, institutions, and devotions, analogous to the combination of wide-ranging variety and multidimensional coherence in early modern, modern, and contemporary Roman Catholicism. The latter combination of diversity and unity can be seen in comparing, say, Polish, French, and Mexican Catholicism in the eighteenth century, or Italian, Quebecois, and

Brazilian Catholicism in the early twentieth.[65] This historically long-standing combination of unity and diversity has been sociologically less true since the Second Vatican Council in the early 1960s, with many Catholics rejecting the claims to authority by their church's magisterium when they disagree with it.

Nevertheless, with respect to the relationship between unity and diversity since the Reformation, Protestantism is dramatically different from Catholicism. They are not meaningfully comparable. As a historical and empirical reality between the early Reformation and the present, "Protestantism" is an umbrella designation of groups, churches, movements, and individuals whose only common feature is a rejection of the authority of the Roman Catholic Church.[66] Despite the desires and intentions of anti-Roman Christian protagonists, but as a result of their actions, beginning in the early 1520s Protestant pluralism derived directly from the Reformation's foundational truth claim. The assertion that scripture alone was a self-sufficient basis for Christian faith and life—independent in principle of papal, conciliar, patristic, canon-legal, and/or any other traditional authorities in conjunction with which scripture was understood in the Roman church—produced not even rough agreement, but an open-ended welter of competing and incompatible interpretations of Luther's "one certain rule" *(ein gewisz regel)* or Karlstadt's "naked truth."[67]

Moreover, Reformation scholars tend analytically and in their division of labor to hive off the magisterial Reformation—Lutheranism, Reformed Protestantism, and the Church of England—from the radical Reformation. Consequently, whether oriented primarily toward theology or toward social history, they have overlooked the significance of the principle of *sola scriptura* for contemporary hyperpluralism. Unless radical and magisterial Protestants are studied together, historically and comparatively, this significance cannot be seen. No radical Protestant reformer had a theological influence nearly as great as did Luther or Calvin, Zwingli or Bucer, Theodore Beza or Heinrich Bullinger, Thomas Cranmer or Melanchthon. And because with very few exceptions radical Protestants rejected alliances between religious bodies and political authorities, they were not engaged in confessionalization in the demographically ambitious manner characteristic of Catholics, Lutherans, or Reformed Protestants.[68] Schwenckfelders shaped gender roles as little as the Swiss Brethren affected state-building; Familists wielded no coercive power; and the Davidite influence on wider cultural trends was nil. Because since the 1960s most Reformation scholars have concentrated on the state and society, politics and power, culture and confessionalization, they have relegated radical Protestants to a handful of scholarly specialists. For good reason, it might be thought: as with

Scotus's univocal metaphysics in the early fourteenth century, how much real impact did sixteenth-century radical Protestants have on society at large? To treat the radical Reformation as a curious theological sideshow with little social influence, however, is to miss its critical importance. Historically reintegrated with the magisterial Reformation, it reveals how the Reformation *as a whole* is crucial to understanding the distant past in the present because of the wide range of incompatible truth claims that a shared commitment to *sola scriptura* produced. Regardless of subsequent changes in the content of the claims, they created an unanticipated and (to its Reformation-era protagonists) undesired reality that has never gone away. The latter fact becomes clear once we get beyond the assumptions of a supersessionist view of history.

Some theologically minded Reformation scholars are likely to dispute this reintegration of magisterial and radical Protestant reformers based on the reformers' shared appeal to the authority of scripture. Whereas radical Protestants, it is sometimes alleged, indeed favored scripture *alone* (or *scriptura nuda*, "naked scripture") and opened the way to an individualistic, hermeneutical anarchy, magisterial reformers such as Luther, Zwingli, Bucer, and Calvin maintained the importance of many aspects of tradition, such as the writings of the church fathers or the decrees of the early ecumenical councils, in addition to scripture.[69] But this distinction is untenable, because despite the undeniable influence of the church fathers (especially some aspects of the later Augustine) on the magisterial Protestant reformers, and notwithstanding their acceptance of early conciliar decrees, the magisterial reformers rejected patristic theological claims and interpretations of scripture, just as they rejected medieval exegesis, papal decrees, canon law, conciliar decrees, and ecclesiastical practices, precisely wherever any of these contradicted their own interpretations of the Bible. In no sense therefore was "tradition" for magisterial Protestant reformers an authority to which they deferred relative to their respective readings of scripture, as it was for their Catholic counterparts. This was the whole point and part of the power of "scripture alone."

Neither magisterial nor radical Protestant reformers modified their hermeneutical judgments when these were at odds with traditional authorities; instead, they rejected the latter at each point of disagreement. In principle and as a corollary of *sola scriptura*, tradition thus retained for them *no independent* authority. Luther was clear by the Leipzig Disputation in 1519 that the church fathers belonged on the same side as popes, councils, and canon law in contrast to the authority of scripture: "Even if Augustine and all the Fathers were to see in Peter the Rock of the church," he said, "I will nevertheless oppose them—even as an isolated individual—supported by the authority of Paul and therefore by divine law."[70] We have already seen that Zwingli cast aside the entire patristic and medieval theology of baptism because it conflicted with his biblical interpretation relative to the sacrament. Like Zwingli, both Bucer and Calvin followed suit more generally in their respective ways: the fathers and ecclesiastical tradition were criticized and rejected or simply ignored wherever they failed to corroborate a given reformer's interpretation of scripture.[71] Radical reformers proceeded in the same way—but did so based on their *different* interpretations of scripture, despite the *shared* commitment of both groups, radical and magisterial, to the principle of *sola scriptura*. The difference between magisterial and radical reformers was therefore not that the former accepted some patristic writers, conciliar decrees, and ecclesiastical tradition as authoritative and the latter none. Rather, they *all* rejected *every* putative "authority" whenever the latter diverged from what each regarded as God's truth, based on scripture as they respectively and contrarily understood it. Their respective distinctions between what in the church's tradition was acceptable and unacceptable were *themselves* a function of their respective understandings of the Bible, which was of course the underlying bone of contention in the first place.

We should remember two things about both radical and magisterial Protestant reformers in the Reformation era. First, along with their Catholic contemporaries they knew that orthodoxy necessarily implied heterodoxy, because they understood that the principle of noncontradiction was required for the pursuit and assertion of truth in any domain of human life—including, most importantly, the domain of God's revealed truth. So they knew that it was impossible for their respective, competing assertions all to be true in fact. Rival claims *had* to be mistaken if their own were true, a logical necessity that helps to explain the massive production of doctrinal controversy in literally tens of thousands of publications throughout the era—not only between Protestants and Catholics, but also among Protestants.[72] What logic demanded, Paul well understood and reinforced as a prerequisite for shared life in Christ, here in William Tyndale's translation from the mid-1520s: "I beseech you brethren in the name of our Lord Jesus Christ, that ye all speak one thing and that there be no dissension among you: but be ye knit together in one mind and in one meaning" (1 Cor 1:10).[73] Contentious controversy was incompatible with Christian community. "Is Christ divided?" (1 Cor 1:13)

Second, Protestant reformers were not secular philologists merely seeking accurate interpretations of ancient texts from the distant past. They were Christians seeking eternal salvation in the precarious present. So they all thought that beyond scholarship, a *correct* understanding of the Bible, a *genuine* comprehension and grasp of God's word, depended upon some sort of direct enlightenment or inspiration by God. Expressions of this supplementary but necessary interpretative principle took different forms, whether it was an insistence on the work of the Holy Spirit in the heart of the believer, for example, a distinction between the internal and external word, or a contrast between God's living word and the mere letter of scripture. Simply reading the Bible, whether in translation or in the original languages, was not enough. "If we are to receive and to understand anything," Zwingli wrote in 1522, adapting the words of John the Baptist from John 3:27, "it must be given from above."[74]

Accordingly, the Reformation era is filled not only with Protestant professions about the foundational importance of scripture coupled with discrepant views about what it meant, but also with pervasive claims about illumination by the Holy Spirit, God's action in the heart of the believer, Tyndale's contrast between "an historicall faith and a felynge faith," and so forth.[75] Argula von Grumbach exclaimed, "Oh, how wonderfully the spirit of God teaches and gives understanding, and jumps from one [text] to another—praise be to God, that I saw the real, true light shining forth."[76] Hubmaier noted in his *Catechism* (1526/7) that "undoubtedly, many people hear the word of God outwardly but do not understand it inwardly"; he advised his readers (as did Zwingli) "to pray and in faith desire wisdom from God."[77] Hans Denck, a south German Anabaptist and colleague of Hut's, distinguished between scripture and God's word along similar lines: "Holy scripture I hold above all human treasure, but not as high as the word of God, which is living, powerful, and eternal, and which is unencumbered [*ledig*] and free from all the elements of this world."[78] A distinction between those who were enlightened and those who were not, whatever specific form it took, helped respective protagonists to explain why others stubbornly refused to see the truth. Whoever they were, and whatever they claimed, they manifestly had not been taught authentically by God. The Holy Spirit had obviously not enlightened them, for, as Calvin put it, "the only true faith is that which the spirit of God seals in our hearts."[79] The way out of darkness and confusion, contention and wrangling, was to open oneself to the light of the Spirit, which suggested a means of overcoming the disagreements about God's teachings. For in Paul's endlessly quoted words (here again as translated by Tyndale), "the natural man perceiveth not the things of the spirit of God," but "he that is spiritual discusseth all things: yet he himself is judged of no one" (1 Cor 2:14, 15). By following the truly enlightened, spiritual interpreter, then, the champions of the restored Gospel might overcome the divisions so patently at odds with "the unity of the spirit in the bond of peace," so that "there be but one Lord, one faith, one baptism: one God and father of all" (Eph 4:3, 4).[80]

But however satisfactory such criteria were in explaining *seriatim* to each interpreter how so many other biblical readers could be wrong, they proved utterly useless for resolving the doctrinal disagreements in which the respective parties were embroiled. As with the principle of *sola scriptura* itself, claims of the Spirit's authenticating, illuminating influence were voiced by those on all sides of every dispute.[81] Such appeals compounded competing claims about the understanding of scripture with competing claims to genuine inspiration by the Holy Spirit. "What am I to do," Erasmus asked in 1524, "when many persons allege different interpretations, each one of whom swears to have the Spirit?"[82] Indeed. Rarely if ever in the course of doctrinal controversy did anyone say something like this: "You're right—I lack the Holy Spirit's guidance in my reading of scripture, and I see that you have it in yours. I admit I was mistaken, so I'll trust you instead."

Exchanges between exegetical and doctrinal rivals tended to proceed rather differently, more like this: whereas Zwingli wrote, "I know for certain that God teaches me, because I have experienced it," Luther countered, "Beware of Zwingli and avoid his books as the hellish poison of Satan [*hellischen Satans gifft*], for the man is completely perverted [*gantz verkeret*] and has completely lost Christ."[83] With controversialists transposing the sometimes contentious discourse between scholastic theologians and humanists from the 1510s, rebuffs tended to trigger rhetorical rants: angry insults often replaced textual evidence or even assertions based on experience when antagonists dared to resist and reject one's own claims, as is known to anyone familiar with the era's doctrinal controversies.[84] Such frustration is readily intelligible, because neither dueling biblical interpretations nor competing allegations about God's direct influence *could* resolve disputes among determined adversaries. Hence the repeated recourse to vituperation and name-calling. Or, if one was in a position of sufficient power against a vulnerable opponent—say, Zwinglians against Anabaptists in Zurich—there was always recourse to execution, a time-tested medieval practice (of Catholic authorities with unrepentant heretics) that persisted in the sixteenth century. That never failed to shut them up. But it frequently strengthened those whom it sought to cow and silence: fellow believers of the slain victims memorialized them as heroic martyrs, with social and political consequences that would endure for centuries and indeed persist in the present.[85]

Unlike exegetical disagreements about the "external Word"—in which texts could be cited and weighed, compared and debated—disagreements about whom the Spirit had "taught from above" "in the heart" were insurmountably problematic because of their inaccessible interiority. Nothing has changed in this respect between the early Reformation and the early twenty-first century. This is apparent when one considers the contrary claims about the work of the Spirit today among the hundreds of Pentecostal denominations, for example, the latter-day legacy of the schisms between Trinitarian and Oneness, "First Work" and "Second Work," Pentecostals in the 1910s.[86] Erasmus's question remains as pertinent today as it was in 1524, especially if coupled with the stunning contrast between appearance and reality implicit in Paul's warning about false apostles: "Even Satan disguises himself as an angel of light" (2 Cor 11:14).[87] Apparently, this meant that sixteenth-century people who seemed to be devout Christians leading upright lives inspired by the Holy Spirit might in fact be just the opposite. This is what Reformed Protestant critics of the Anabaptists such as Guy de Brès argued in sharply distinguishing between the appearance and reality of a holy life, the former including the Anabaptists' willingness to die with seeming tranquility for their beliefs.[88] At the very least, Paul's warning problematized Jesus's seemingly straightforward criterion for telling true from false prophets, and by extension, those whom the Spirit had enlightened or failed to enlighten: "You will know them by their fruits" (Mt 7:16, 20).

Yet Jesus's maxim was not straightforward. Even had all concurred that "by their fruits ye shall know them," the disagreements evident from the outset of the Reformation would have rendered impossible any consensus about the content of this criterion. Because Christians disagreed about what they were to believe and do, they disagreed about what the fruits of a Christian life *were*. For example, was the Anabaptist withdrawal from political participation after the Peasants' War—save for the debacle of Münster—a fruit of their holy rejection of a sinful world, or a sinful shirking of their duty to participate in its public life? Did Hutterite communitarian life in the mid-sixteenth century manifest the fruits by which Christians were known, in accord with the community of goods practiced by first-century Christians and mentioned in Acts 2 and 4, or was it an aberrant distortion of the nuclear families living in separate households with private property that constituted the basic units of any viable Christian society? Were Calvinists manifesting the fruits of the Spirit in seeking to shape political and social institutions in accord with the Gospel as they understood it, or were they backsliding on justification by faith alone and violating the proper distinction between the "two kingdoms" of the Gospel and the world as stipulated by Luther? Such questions could be extended almost indefinitely. "By their fruits ye shall know them" was an impotent principle because "fruits" was disputed. Disagreements about what Christianity is entail divergences about what Christians should believe and do. Inevitably and proportionally, disagreements follow about whether the alleged fruits of Christian life are ripe or rotten. So it was in the sixteenth century, and so it is today.

Protestant appeals to scripture alone produced an unwelcome pluralism of competing Christian truth claims; supplementary appeals to the Holy Spirit reinforced it. A small minority of radical Protestants, beginning already in the 1520s, saw the problem: evangelicals had foundered on their own foundation. Ironically, on this point these radical Protestants agreed with Catholic critics of the Reformation. Both recognized that *sola scriptura,* even when supplemented by an insistence on the illuminating influence of the Holy Spirit, had created an unintended jungle of incompatible truth claims among those who rejected the Roman church, with no foreseeable likelihood of resolution. Beginning already in the early summer of 1523, when two Augustinian friars who followed Luther were put to death in Brussels, the executions of Protestants for rival truth claims further diminished hopes for doctrinal reconciliation or compromise.[89] *Sola scriptura* led to an open-ended proliferation of contested, competing doctrines among exegetical rivals, some of whom were demonstrating their willingness to die for their respective beliefs. Objectionably papist, merely human ecclesiastical tradition had simply been supplanted by objectionably subjective, merely human biblical interpreters. Something else was needed.

The proposed solution was to make the Holy Spirit (or some analogue) the direct source of truth rather than just a necessary exegetical supplement. Among those who in diverse ways made this move in response to Protestant pluralism were Caspar Schwenckfeld and Sebastian Franck in the early German Reformation, Dirck Coornheert and Valentin Weigel in the later sixteenth century, Collegiants in the seventeenth-century Dutch Republic, and English Quakers such as George Fox and James Nayler in the mid-seventeenth century (with their emphasis on the "inner light").[90] By making the Holy Spirit more than a necessary supplement to and supposed guarantor of proper exegesis, spiritualist Protestants were in effect proposing a new foundation for answers to the Life Questions. The biblical text itself had to be transcended, they thought, since it obviously caused interminable interpretative disagreements without any realistic prospects for resolution. Not scripture but a radical, selfless, genuine openness to the Spirit alone was the authentic basis for Christian truth claims. God would illumine those who sought him humbly, with the right intention and a pure heart—as Jesus had said, "Ask, and it will be given to you;

seek, and you will find; knock, and the door will be opened to you" (Mt 7:7; cf. Lk 11:9).

But it turned out to be much easier to rail against the flaws of existing churches, disdain rival sacramental doctrines, disparage competing readings of scripture, and condemn rancorous theological disputes than it was to convince others that one had discerned Christian truth through God's unmediated inspiration. No more than *sola scriptura* Protestants did spiritualist Protestants remotely agree about Christian truth, and thus about what Christians were to believe and do. By relativizing the importance of biblical exegesis in an effort to transcend doctrinal controversies, spiritualists actually exacerbated the problem they sought to resolve. Mistakenly thinking that they had found an escape from Protestant pluralism by opening themselves directly to God, they in fact added *more* rival truth claims and forms of Protestantism to those they sought to surmount. They were drawn into the controversies they wanted to stand above, pilloried by Protestant, Catholic, and Anabaptist adversaries who seized on spiritualists' own contrary assertions. Competing claims about the genuine understanding of scripture were compounded by rival reports of authentic inspiration by God.

It was entirely unclear then—and remains entirely unclear today—who among those claiming to have "the Spirit" actually might have been (or might today be) right. Shared criteria for adjudication are neither clear nor, it would seem, even conceivable. Countervailing claims that one *really* has the Spirit over against rival claimants, no matter how strident, only demonstrate the problem—as sixteenth-century Catholic and Protestant critics of spiritualists already recognized, as English Restoration disdainers of religious "enthusiasm" would reiterate, and as secular adversaries of Christianity continue to point out today. Various New Age philosophies and self-realization programs today, depending on the content and bases of their claims, might be seen as a latter-day analogue to Reformation-era spiritualism, in their own ways secularized successors to nineteenth-century British and American spiritism and occultism that sought concourse with the dead.

In no sense did spiritualists manage to transcend doctrinal controversy, as they alleged, by downplaying the importance of doctrines, sacraments, or formal worship. Rather, their assertions to this end were *themselves* merely new truth claims about the putative, relative unimportance of traditionally central aspects of Christian faith and life that the large majority of early modern Protestants continued to share with Catholics. So in fact, *these* spiritualist claims only added a novel *type* of rival truth claim to those already in play. A new axis entered intra-Christian doctrinal controversy, one that sought to diminish the importance of scripture, dogmas, and religious practices altogether, in ways that virtually all sixteenth-century Catholics, magisterial Protestants, and Anabaptists rejected—but which many early twenty-first-century Christians endorse.[91] Derived from doctrinal pluralism plus the principle of noncontradiction, the relativization of doctrines would turn out to have a powerfully influential future. It would pass through Enlightenment attacks on revealed religion and continues today to find expression not only in arguments against religious truth claims as such, but also among many millions of Christians who seem to regard matters of biblical interpretation, doctrine, worship, and religious practice as much less important than a sort of conformist moral civility toward others. Implicitly, they seem to have settled for themselves the meaning of "by their fruits ye shall know them."

During the Leipzig Disputation in 1519, Luther said that scripture was the sole authority for Christians "unless new and approved revelation is added." Of course, he did not himself offer any additions to scripture (although questions of canonicity are related to the same issue with respect to alleged, past revelation). Others, however, not only disagreed, but implied that new revelation from God was precisely the means to overcome the immovable impasses in exegetical and thus doctrinal disagreements. Such claims might be understood as extending convictions about illumination by the Holy Spirit, representing a further point along the same spectrum; they might also be seen as a new move regarding the basis for truth claims. If the living God was real and could reveal himself to human beings, as all early modern Christians believed, it seemed rash—and indeed, would have been metaphysically absurd—to insist that he *could* not do so, dramatically and decisively, in sixteenth-century Europe just as he had in ancient Israel.

This possibility had been acknowledged for centuries. It led to wide-ranging and long-standing concerns about individual, extrabiblical religious experiences within the Roman church, from medieval Rhineland mystics through Spanish *alumbrados* to would-be visionary saints in seventeenth-century Italy and beyond. In Catholic settings, the possibility of such "private revelation" was taken for granted; the principal conundrum lay in determining whether its origin in individual cases was divine or diabolical. As with the interpretation of scripture and the guardianship of doctrine, these judgments were the duty of duly delegated ecclesiastical authorities. For example, the inquisitors who in 1526 imprisoned the disturbing lay Basque visionary and street catechist Ignatius Loyola, also interrogated, admonished, and released him, a process repeated the following year by the Dominicans in Salamanca.[92] Apart from the challenges posed by putative private revelations to individuals, Catholic leaders affirmed the long-standing notion that the Holy Spirit guided the church and its truth claims in accordance with Jesus's promises: "the gates of hell will not prevail against it" and "I am with you always, to the end of the age" (Mt 16:18, 28:20).

Among Christians who rejected Rome, extrabiblical revelation had different implications. Analogous to the spiritualists' emphasis on God's unmediated influence, it offered the prospect of resolving the problem created by *sola scriptura*. For what could be more authoritative in a context of conflicting claims by merely human biblical interpreters, or dueling assertions about the testimony of the Holy Spirit, than direct, fresh declarations by God himself about what Christians were to believe and do?

From the very beginning of the Reformation era, starting with Thomas Müntzer and the Zwickau prophets, direct revelation from God was regarded by various Christians not merely as supplementary to the Bible, but as the necessary key to its meaning and in some cases as superseding it altogether. Müntzer coupled it with radical skepticism about the reliability of the biblical text per se. "What kind of assurance of faith is this which comes from books?" he asked already in 1521. "Perhaps [the authors of scripture] have lied in what they have written? How can one know whether it is true [*Wobei kann man das wissen, ab es war sey*]?"[93] The apocalyptic prophets Lienhard and Ursula Jost, along with Barbara Rebstock, also made robust claims of direct revelation from God in Strasbourg in the late 1520s. They influenced another purported prophet, Melchior Hoffman, a formative influence on Dutch Anabaptists, including the best-known of all such prophetic figures in the sixteenth century, the polygamous Second David of the New Jerusalem, King Jan van Leiden of Münster.[94] David Joris, too, the most important Dutch Anabaptist leader in the immediate aftermath of Münster, was regarded by his followers as a Spirit-filled prophet, as was Hendrik Niclaes, the founder of the Family of Love in the 1540s.[95] Numerous individuals in England, from Elizabeth's reign through the Revolution, claimed to be prophets or messianic figures, including William Hacket (executed in 1591), John Traske (who blended elements of Familism with radical Puritanism in the 1610s), and Lady Eleanor Davis (whose career as a prophetess lasted from 1625 until her death in 1652).[96] The de facto breakdown of both ecclesiastical oversight and censorship in England during the 1640s and 1650s, combined with the dislocation of the two civil wars, proved to be fertile ground for numerous claims of prophecy and assertions of new revelations from God amid an efflorescence of socially and politically subversive religious radicalism unseen since the first decade of the Reformation in central Europe.[97]

Nor was this phenomenon restricted to early modern Europe. Various alleged prophets and messiahs have continued to make their respective claims down to the present day. Conditioned by supersessionist assumptions about change over time, historians do not normally think in this category across the divide between early modern and modern—but they should, in order to see continuities that are normally overlooked. The best known and most successful modern example is probably the American polygamist and putative prophet Joseph Smith, the founder of the Church of Jesus Christ of Latter-Day Saints in early nineteenth-century upstate New York.[98] Smith's assertions about the significance of the revelatory vision he claimed to receive in 1820 are strikingly similar to claims made by the Quaker George Fox: the confusing cacophony of competing Christian groups and their countervailing claims characterized New York's "burned-over district" during the Second Great Awakening no less than it had England's "world turned upside down," in which Fox started preaching in 1647.[99] Whereas Fox claimed the "openings" of the "inner Light," Smith claimed a vision of divine "personages" and the discovery of golden plates containing the original text of the Book of Mormon, plus his own ongoing, prophetic revelations. Each purported to transcend the competing truth claims of the Christian groups by which he was surrounded. More recent manifestations of analogous claims include those of Jim Jones and his Peoples Temple, which came to its highly publicized end with hundreds of deaths in Guyana in 1978, as well as David Koresh and his Branch Davidians in Texas, who perished in a conflagration during a showdown with U.S. federal officials in 1993.[100] Obviously, all these individuals and the movements they inspired differ from one another in crucial respects and arose in very different contexts. But they also share, explicitly or implicitly, a fundamental truth claim: that substantive, extrabiblical revelation provides a means of answering Life Questions and transcending the Protestant pluralism that has derived historically and empirically from a commitment to *sola scriptura*. This pluralism is especially obvious in modern democratic states, with their legally enforced absence of doctrinal policing by any confessional political authorities, a point to be revisited in Chapters 3 and 4.

No more than spiritualism, however, did or do claims of new extrabiblical revelation overcome religious pluralism. Instead, they contributed to it in the Reformation era and have continued to do so ever since, right up to the present. Even cursory familiarity with the claims of Müntzer, Hoffman, Jan van Leiden, Niclaes, Traske, and the others during the sixteenth and seventeenth centuries shows that they claimed wildly disparate and contrary things as divinely revealed by God, from the necessity of proactive apocalyptic violence to pacifist withdrawal from political engagement, from the necessity of new rituals and liturgies to the unimportance of all externals in religious worship. The principle of noncontradiction makes it certain that not all could have been correct, as their critics have always seen and rightly noted. Moreover, how the respective, rival truth claims involved might be convincingly evaluated, whether among early modern Europeans or now, remains no less intractable than are would-be criteria for evaluating spiritualists' competing claims, or indeed divergent claims among Protestants concerning whose biblical interpretations have been ratified by the Holy Spirit.

Empirically and historically, rival assertions of direct revelation from God only intensify the condition they are intended to settle. Ever since Joseph Smith first began making his claims in the 1820s, for example, the overwhelming majority of Christians and other non-Mormons have regarded them not as clarifying interventions that supplement and fulfill Christian truth claims, but as bizarre and deeply objectionable departures from them.[101] Accordingly, Mormonism has become one more element within the religionscape of the contemporary United States and the world, in the analysis of Jan Shipps a new religious tradition as different from historical Christianity as ancient Christianity proved to be different from Judaism.[102] Some central Latter-Day Saints' (LDS) assertions were or are rejected in different, sharply divisive ways by the dozens of historically related groups that derive from the LDS church. At odds with it and with one another, they include the Community of Christ (from 1872 until 2001 known as the Reorganized Church of Jesus Christ of Latter-Day Saints) and the Fundamentalist Church of Jesus Christ of Latter-Day Saints, the largest group that continues to practice plural marriage.[103]

Whether as a supplementary hermeneutical principle, an insistence on the reality of the Spirit's action in the believer's heart, or a claim of substantively new divine revelation, recourse to the authority of God's direct influence intensified the problem it was meant to resolve. But these were not the only moves possible in the face of the unwanted disagreements that stemmed from *sola scriptura*. What about reason? From the very beginning of the Reformation, all Protestant reformers used discursive rationality in some way or other in articulating their respective claims and in doctrinal controversy—how particular biblical texts were related to specific prescriptions about the sacraments, for example, or how to understand texts from the Bible's prophetic books in relationship to the Gospels. Even the downplaying of reason in relationship to the power of the Spirit depended and depends on a rational distinction between the two. The consequential questions were exactly how, in what manner, and with what scope reason was to be applied in both the determination of Christian truth and in its directives for Christian life.

The problem immediately apparent from the 1520s was that those who rejected the Roman church disagreed about reason's role in all these respects, just as they disagreed among themselves about the influence of the Holy Spirit. Zwingli used reason in his exegesis, for example, to argue against the doctrine of the real presence of Christ in the Eucharist defended by Luther.[104] Their contemporary the Spaniard Michael Servetus (1511–1553) used reason to revisit and reject as unbiblical, illogical, and incomprehensible the traditional understanding of the doctrine of the Trinity.[105] Through his influence on Italian reformers such as Fausto Sozzini (1539–1604), Servetus and his convictions became part of a stream of antitrinitarian Christianity that in the seventeenth century shaped hundreds of Polish Brethren communities as well as Socinianism in the Dutch Republic and England, which in turn nourished modern Unitarianism.[106] But at the same time, in Restoration England, Latitudinarian theologians including Edward Stillingfleet (1635–1699) and John Tillotson (1630–1694) sharply *opposed* Socinian denials of the Trinity, defending as rational their *own* theological views over against the claims of Puritans, Quakers, and other dissenters who had so unsettled England during the 1640s and 1650s and who still posed problems once Charles II returned to the throne.[107]

Whereas Latitudinarians emphasized reason in vindicating the Bible as God's word and in establishing basic biblical truths, spiritualists employed reason against the reliability of scripture itself. The more suspect the biblical text, they reasoned, the stronger the case for seeking the truth inwardly, through the Spirit speaking in the heart. Already in the early decades of the Reformation, Sebastian Franck, in *The Book Closed with the Seven Seals* (1539), compiled countervailing scriptural texts as an argument against the Bible's coherence.[108] The same strategy was employed in 1660 at much greater length and with more sophistication by the Quaker exegete Samuel Fisher (1604–1665), a former Baptist who coupled his massive assault on the reliability of "the bare *External Text of Scripture*" with a defense of "the *Holy Truth* and *inward Light and Spirit*" as the necessary foundation of Christian faith and life.[109] In this combination, Fisher resembled certain of the Dutch Collegiants, rationalizing spiritualists in Holland, some of whom were friends with Spinoza—a better-known seventeenth-century biblical critic and one who was influenced by Fisher. Collegiants such as Pieter Balling and Jarig Jelles claimed in the 1660s and 1670s that the dictates of reason and of God's inner light were one and the same. Protestant spiritualism was thus a bridge to modern rationalism and naturalism in biblical exegesis.[110]

As even these few examples demonstrate, reason's role was as controversial and contested as the Holy Spirit's in the determination and expression of Christian truth. In 1660 the erudite English divine Jeremy Taylor (1613–1667) averred that "every mans reason is not right, and every mans reason is not to be trusted."[111] No one would have disagreed. But whose *was* to be trusted? The impotence of reason in resolving Protestant doctrinal disputes made it not the polar opposite of appeals to the Spirit, but rather its non-

identical twin. Both augmented rather than ameliorated, complicated rather than clarified, the doctrinal pluralism they were intended to surmount. Discursive rationality could not stand above the fray of doctrinal controversy as a neutral means to determine Christian truth, because the disputants disagreed radically about its character, compass, and application. So it became yet another means by which Protestant pluralism was exacerbated rather than overcome. Luther accused Zwingli of rashly placing limits on God's omnipotence and of contradicting the plain meaning of scripture: *"Hoc est corpus meum"* meant what it said, namely "This is my body." "For if we allow such violence to be done in one passage," Luther reasoned, "that without any ground in scripture one can say the word 'is' is equivalent to the word 'signifies,' then it would be impossible to stop it in any other passage. All of scripture would be brought to nothing [*wurde die gantze schrifft zu nichte*], since there would be no good reason why such violence would be valid in one passage but not in all passages."[112] Calvin and many others attacked antitrinitarian assertions as an outrageous insistence that the transcendent, biblical God's self-revelation conform to the finitude of the fallen human mind. Calvin warned that "if at any point in the hidden [*reconditis*] mysteries of scripture we ought to philosophize with sobriety and great moderation," it was with respect to the Trinity. "For how can the human mind according to its measure determine the immeasurable essence of God?"[113] As if God's revealed truths *had* to be humanly comprehensible!

Such standoffs implied in turn that divergent claims about true Christianity were inseparable from controversies about the character of human capacities—which was itself deeply contested among Christians as a result of the Reformation. Just *how* fallen was man as a result of original sin? Was human reason entirely corrupted, the human will completely vitiated, with respect to Christian life and matters of salvation? If not, what might they accomplish, to what should they aspire? Answers to such questions had profound implications for morality and its relationship to politics, too, as we shall see in Chapter 4. Because the character of human faculties was contested, appeals to them could not resolve disagreements about Christian doctrine. Instead, their character became and remained yet another arena for dispute, adding further to the doctrinal pluralism that had characterized the Reformation since the early 1520s.

An impasse about human capacities analogous to that between Calvin and Servetus was thus replayed at the end of the seventeenth century between English Latitudinarians on the one hand and deists such as Charles Blount (1654–1693) and John Toland (1670–1722) on the other. "We hold that *Reason* is the only Foundation of all Certitude," Toland wrote, "and that nothing reveal'd, whether as to its *Manner* or *Existence,* is more exempted from its Disquisitions, than the ordinary Phenomena of Nature."[114] Ironically, in defending the presence of suprarational mysteries in the faith against deistic denials, Latitudinarian writers insisted on the primacy of scripture as God's authoritative word—and thus were plunged back into the maelstrom of exegetical controversy born of *sola scriptura,* which appeals to reason were supposed to surmount.[115] Instead of offering a broad, restorative synthesis of faith and reason for the Restoration church, as they intended, the Latitudinarians found themselves inhabiting yet another new, self-constructed niche in the open-ended spectrum of English Protestants.

The rejection of both original sin and Christ's atonement accompanied the deists' stronger claims about the ability of human reason to determine religious truth.[116] They could point to many experimental triumphs and much theoretical progress in explaining natural regularities since the days of Galileo and Bacon, which had culminated in discoveries by members of London's Royal Society and in Newton's stunning achievement. If reason was so demonstrably powerful when applied to nature, why not apply it also to controverted Christian doctrine? "The universal disposition of this *Age* is bent upon a rational religion," wrote Thomas Sprat, the historian of the Royal Society, in 1667.[117] Exegetical controversy was permanently deadlocked, as were rival assertions about alleged inspiration by the Spirit, which had resulted in the English Revolution's gangrenous cancer of doctrinal pluralism and disruptiveness deplored by the Presbyterian preacher Thomas Edwards in 1646.[118] Why not let a more robust application of reason have a go? Already in 1563 Sebastian Castellio had argued in his posthumously published work, *On the Art of Doubting and Believing,* that reason alone could and must arbitrate among disputed Christian doctrines. "Reason, I say, is a certain eternal word of God," he wrote, "far more ancient and certain than writings and ceremonies, according to which God taught his own before there were any ceremonies and writings, and according to which he will teach when ceremonies and writings no longer exist, so that men may truly be taught by God."[119] By the later seventeenth century, some exegetes had decided to make new philosophical ideas their foundational framework for biblical interpretation[120]—commitments that, adopted and adapted, were also presupposed in Enlightenment attacks on allegedly primitive superstitions such as the belief in miracles. Following Spinoza's rejection in his *Tractatus Theologico-Politicus* (1670), Blount repudiated biblical miracles altogether: "Whatever is against Nature, is against *Reason;* and whatever is against Reason is *absurd,* and therefore also to be rejected and refuted," because *"all events happen according to the Eternal Order of Nature."*[121]

This rationalist move in biblical exegesis, and the conviction that theology was both intellectually dependent on the claims of modern philosophy and forced to retreat ever further as the findings of the natural sciences progressed, would have a powerful subsequent influence in both Europe and North America on what would eventually be called liberal Protestantism. Institutionally, such commitments would help to constitute the assumptions that defined what counted as knowledge in modern research universities, beginning in nineteenth-century Germany. Although their theology was much more sophisticated, Albrecht Ritschl (1822–1889), Ernst Troeltsch (1865–1923), and Rudolf Bultmann (1884–1976) shared critical rationalist assumptions with Hermann Samuel Reimarus (1694–1768), Gotthold Ephraim Lessing (1729–1781), and the Thomas Jefferson who confidently cut and pasted "The Life and Morals of Jesus of Nazareth."[122] As Chapter 1 showed, such assumptions relied on a univocal metaphysics that had departed from a traditional Christian understanding of God as radically distinct from creation. These theological forays were therefore not the product of a metaphysically neutral historicism and *Wissenschaft* born strictly of biblical textual criticism, matters to be taken up further in Chapter 6.

HAD PROTESTANTS SIMPLY DISAGREED about the interpretation of scripture as such, their disputes would have remained much more circumscribed than they became. But more was sought—and needed—because the principle of *sola scriptura* itself did not yield the desired result. The would-be solution for reforming the late medieval church immediately became an unintended, enormous problem of its own, one different in kind from the problem of how to close the gap between the Roman church's prescriptions and late medieval Christians' practices. Had the widely anticipated apocalypse in fact come, the problem of intra-Protestant disagreement obviously would not have mattered for long. But it did not come. Instead, in addition to their continuous doctrinal disagreements with defenders of the Roman church before and after the Council of Trent, Protestants disagreed among themselves on multiple fronts. They disagreed about the meaning and prioritization of biblical texts, and the relationship of those texts to doctrines regarding the sacraments, worship, grace, the church, and so forth. They disagreed about the broad interpretative principles that ought to guide the understanding of scripture, such as the relationship between the Old and New Testaments or the permissibility of religious practices not explicitly prohibited or enjoined in the Bible. They disagreed about the relationship among the interpretation of scripture, the exercise of reason, and God's influence in the hearts of individual Christians. And they disagreed about whether (and if so, to what extent) explicit, substantive truth claims were even *important* to being a

Christian, with some spiritualists and alleged prophets radically relativizing the place of doctrines in Christian life.

The net result was an unintended Protestant doctrinal and social pluralism, as the number, range, and character of the truth claims asserted and lived by protagonists within communities of belief remained indefinitely open-ended. Religious disagreement persisted, however frustrating was its proliferation. The political, social, and moral ramifications of this disagreement will be explored in Chapters 3 and 4. All the contending protagonists were well aware of the principle of noncontradiction: if their own truth claims were right, then everyone else's had to be wrong on the points of disagreement. This remains no less the case in the early twenty-first century than it was in the early sixteenth, even though now millions of people apparently believe that in the special case of religious truth claims, logic is abrogated to accord with politically protected religious individualism and desires for social civility among fellow citizens—as if, say, Jesus really was and really was not God incarnate, depending on what one believes.

Leaving aside considerations of how specific claims bear up under scientific and historical scrutiny, it is obvious that enduring forms of meaningful, shared human life have been developed in conjunction with the truth claims, devotional sensibilities, and worship particular to many different Protestant churches and traditions, as well as in conjunction with Mormonism. In their respective ways, they simply *are* and have been since the sixteenth century the answers to the Life Questions given and lived by hundreds of millions of people. It is similarly obvious that individually appropriated and self-consciously held convictions by members of these churches and traditions have inspired and continue to motivate great religious zeal and impressive service to others. It is entirely possible that some of their competing truth claims based on interpretations of scripture, claims of the Holy Spirit's inspiration, allegations of direct revelation from God, or reason combined with scripture might be what they purport to be—namely, true. But it is equally clear that their respective bases have empirically and historically led and continue to lead to an open-ended proliferation of irreconcilable truth claims, with neither any shared criteria by means of which to adjudicate among the rival views, nor any shared means of adjudicating among second-order, rival criteria of adjudication.

It is possible that Hutterite Anabaptism or Wisconsin Synod Lutheranism or liberal Methodism or Unitarianism or double-predestination Presbyterianism or James Nayler's Quakerism might be the fullest expression of Christian truth. Justification by faith alone might or might not be true; the sacraments might or might not be important; specific dogmas might or might not be essential; some sort of formal liturgy, or waiting for the Spirit to speak, might be the way in which God wants to be worshipped. But how would or could it be sorted out? Attempts to settle such questions *can* only unfold based on rival criteria that are themselves in dispute, and all proposals of new criteria only compound the problem. Nor are there any shared institutional mechanisms for resolving Protestant disagreements. The evidence is plain to see, spread across nearly five centuries. Consequently, there are no foreseeable prospects for determining which among all the competing views might actually be true based on the foundations or criteria put forward, no matter what they might be, or how deeply their protagonists might feel about their respective views or experiences. No one's sincerity is in doubt.

It is easy to see the influence of this historical trajectory and present-day reality on the relativization of religious truth claims in general. Extrapolating from the fact of Protestant pluralism, by the end of the twentieth century increasing numbers of people, especially in Western Europe and Canada, had made either an atheistic inference that *no* religious claims are true, or drawn a skeptical conclusion that it cannot be known which among them might be, even as they continued to embrace values rooted historically in Christianity or Judaism. In the same cultural milieu, many Western Catholics have especially since the Second Vatican Council deliberately eschewed some of the truth claims of their own church's magisterium, including most fundamentally its claims of authority, claims that had expanded during the nineteenth century amid ultramontanist papal antimodernism. Instead, taking ecclesiastical *aggiornamento* to imply a sanction of modern individual autonomy, Catholics who have made this move have made themselves their own de facto authorities about doctrinal and moral truth claims—which is what John Henry Newman criticized in the nineteenth century as "the right of private judgment."[123] These Catholic departures from the magisterium's truth claims blend seamlessly into the wider culture, because the political and legal protection of religious belief afforded by modern Western states is the institutional incubator of contemporary hyperpluralism, as will become clearer by the end of Chapter 3. The pullulating pluralism reinforces the relativizing impression that *all* religion can only be a matter of individual, subjective, and irrational personal preference, a theater of Feuerbachian and Freudian projection, despite the fact that many religious believers continue to regard their respective beliefs as true.

Yet large numbers of religious believers, themselves influenced by these cultural currents and the desire to be inoffensive, in effect relativize and subjectivize their own truth claims, making clear that they speak only for themselves, base their opinions only on their own experience, or choose their religious community based ultimately on what they like and what makes them comfortable.[124] Thus does modern, individual religious preference mesh readily with what Philip Rieff analyzed as "therapeutic culture," in which life's overriding concern is to feel good, because there is "nothing at stake beyond a manipulatable sense of well-being."[125] Religious believers who act in this way implicitly do Jeffrey Stout's bidding: functionally they concede that they are "groping in the dark" and dutifully thus look elsewhere, such as to Stout's own skeptical pragmatism, for supplementary light.[126]

Today, within the limits of the law, literally anything goes as far as truth claims and religious practices are concerned—an extension and latter-day manifestation of the full range of views produced by the Reformation unfettered. In the public sphere are protected not only all Protestant views derived from the principle of *sola scriptura* and its adjuncts, but any and all religions, religious claims, and post-religious claims that fill a similar niche. Hence whatever the particular country in which they happen to reside, all Westerners now live in the Kingdom of Whatever. For a great many people, subjective, individual preference seems to be the extent of any foundation for answers to the Life Questions amid our hyperpluralism. For them, the basis for such answers in Western society today is literally *arbitrary*, in the etymological sense: it is a function of the *arbitrium*, the individual human will. Modern liberal states protect exactly this arbitrariness, as the following two chapters will make clear. The prospect was already polemically intimated in the mid-1520s: "Whoever has gone astray in the faith may thereafter believe whatever he wants to, everything is equally valid."[127] These were the words not of a defender of the Roman church denouncing the dangers of Protestant individualism, but of Luther railing against Zwingli.

Thank goodness, then, for reason alone, the real basis for truth claims that are actually true. Without the sober, dispassionate rationality that has transcended the arbitrary, ever-proliferating assertions made on the basis of the Bible, the inspiration of the Holy Spirit, new divine revelation, or reason still tethered to scripture, we might never have emancipated ourselves from the pre-Enlightenment labyrinth. Or so one might think, and so many champions of secular reason have argued in one way or another, from the seventeenth century up to and including the present. The real way out of the early modern Christian controversies concerning answers to the Life Questions, it was and by some is still alleged, was not a Band-Aid, but an amputation: an unblinking, uncompromising application of reason alone by modern philosophy and science. Not God but Nature, not enthusiasm but empiricism, not revelation but reason would liberate human beings from the primitive practices and senseless stupidities of Christian conflicts—

written in the blood of religious wars no less than in the ink of theological polemics.

Seventeenth-century pioneers such as Hobbes and Spinoza were joined by more intellectuals in the eighteenth century who asserted in various ways that not only Roman Catholicism and Protestant Christianity, but all revealed religion, was irrational superstition fueled by fearful imaginations exploited by power-hungry priests and pastors. The root problem was the assumption shared by Protestants and Catholics alike, namely that questions about truth, morality, purpose, and meaning were to be answered in ways that depended on claims of supernatural revelation by a transcendent God who had become incarnate for the salvation of sinful humanity. Did any of this make any sense? Was it comprehensible and useful? Could it endure the scrutiny of critical rationality, whether in ancient forms revivified by late Renaissance thinkers or as developed in new, early modern philosophies? The credo of modern philosophy, the various expressions of the Enlightenment, and nineteenth-century notions of progress would be that *sola ratio* could achieve what *sola scriptura* manifestly could not. A clean break with the past was necessary, rejecting Christianity's interminable doctrinal controversies and destructive religious wars. Thus would the way be cleared to a brighter, more rational, more prosperous future for humanity.

Among the ancient philosophies revived in the Renaissance was Pyrrhonian skepticism. After the first publication of Sextus Empiricus in 1562 greatly augmented its influence, which had been very limited in later fifteenth-century Italy, skepticism spread especially through Montaigne's popular *Essays* (1580). Above all in what was much the longest essay in the work, his "Apology for Raymond Sebond," Montaigne explored cultural relativism, skepticism about knowledge of the natural world, and the problem of adjudication among rival religious claims.[128] As Richard Popkin first showed fifty years ago, modern philosophy's foundationalist aspirations, beginning with Descartes, emerged in an intellectual milieu pervaded by Pyrrhonism. Hence "first philosophy" in the modern period, from Descartes through Edmund Husserl and arguably beyond, would be not metaphysics but epistemology. In a specifically epistemological context, the chief objective was to transcend skeptical doubt about the possibility of certainty regarding moral principles, human nature, metaphysics (including God), and the natural world. In the context of competing views about Christian truth, the aim was to secure a rational foundation for the domains of human life covered by Christianity, and so to provide a means of superseding intractable doctrinal controversies and destructive conflicts. Seventeenth-century intellectual innovators were affected firsthand by religio-political disruptions: Descartes served as a soldier in the early years of the Thirty Years War, for example, and Hobbes lived in exile in Paris from late 1640 until early 1652 because of the unrest in his native England.[129]

Because reliance on ecclesiastical authorities and biblical interpreters had led to so many competing Christian truth claims, some protagonists understandably surmised that only reason divorced from religion could hope to establish a neutral, solid foundation for truth. We saw in Chapter 1 the same aspiration at work in the emergence of a seventeenth-century rationalist discourse about God and the natural world, which was part of the same broader, anti-skeptical ambition of modern philosophy. An analogous objective animated early modern political theorists, too, as we shall see in Chapter 4. Whatever God might have revealed in the past was mired in theological controversy; supra-confessional truth would have to be discovered by man in the present and validated in the future based on his own rational faculties. Armed only with reason, the philosopher would have to reject all inherited traditions and defer to no alleged authorities in order to transcend them all and to exorcise the Pyrrhonian demon, so that Europeans might enter a better, less belligerent future.

Descartes led the way in the seventeenth century, establishing an ideal that would endure for centuries: that of the autonomous, self-sufficient, individual philosopher who demonstrates the truth based on reason alone, without relying on anyone else. In this respect, as far as their methods and pursuit of truth were concerned, the pioneers of modern philosophy paradoxically turned their backs on the inherently social, deeply collaborative character of the learned circles to which they themselves almost always belonged. Because the erudite correspondents who had peopled the Republic of Letters since at least the early sixteenth century were buzzing with all manner of conflicting truth claims pertinent to the Life Questions, the philosopher could not risk a mere trusting of any of their opinions.[130] Reason demanded more than agreeing with the views of one's learned friends, just as it demanded more than assenting to any alleged authorities, whether Christian or non-Christian, dead or living. The desired payoff was undeniably attractive: success would mean that everyone, if properly educated according to reason and stripped of prejudices and superstitions, might acknowledge the truths discovered by the philosopher. This would enable the wide establishment of a shared, supra-confessional basis for morality, social life, politics, and human happiness, uncontentious because uncontroversially and universally rational. Conflicts based on arbitrary religious assertions no less than on preferred ancient philosophies would be transcended. Others had already shared the same aspiration to rational autonomy, albeit with very different intellectual bearings. Half a century before Descartes, for example, the philosophically eclectic Giordano Bruno (1548–1600) stated that "I would be ungrateful and insane, unworthy of that participation in light, if I were to act as agent and champion for someone else, seeing, perceiving, and judging by another's lights."[131]

Distraught by the recurrent religio-political violence in his native France, Montaigne professed the value of scholarly solitude in "a back room, entirely our own" (or in his case, on the top floor of a tower on his estate near Bordeaux).[132] It allowed him not only to converse with a wide range of classical and contemporary authors in puzzling over himself via a pragmatic skepticism tempered by neo-Stoicism, but also to seek to forge a workable politics and an ethics of coexistence amid the French Wars of Religion.[133] His was a richly humanistic—and hence derivatively social—self-seclusion that reverberated with hundreds of voices through which he essayed himself amid the on-and-off troubles of religio-political conflict. Descartes's solitude was very different, more like that of the young George Fox before his "openings" began. The early Quaker leader was disenchanted with the vanity of the world and the behavior of others, so "at the Command of God," Fox later wrote, "on the *Ninth Day* of the *Seventh Month,* 1643[,] I left my relations, and brake off all Familiarity or Fellowship with Young or Old."[134] Similarly, in 1641 Descartes related how he had sought in his own meditative solitude to sever the distracting influence of other people, whether past or present, in order to discover the foundations for truth. Having recognized how many false opinions he had regarded as true in his youth, and so how dubious was everything he had inferred on their basis, he realized he had to start over: "Everything had to be torn down to the ground and I had to begin anew from the first foundations, if I ever wanted to establish anything firm and enduring in the sciences."[135] Stepping methodologically out of the Republic of Letters, he wrote that "therefore today I have fittingly freed my mind from every care, procured untroubled tranquility for myself, and am withdrawing into solitude [*solus secedo*]."[136] Despite Descartes's hope that the members of the Paris faculty of theology would support his ideas, the contrast with the Roman Catholic Church to which he belonged—in which the most important, saving works of a God acting in history are claimed to be authoritatively transmitted over many centuries by innumerable others in the living community through shared liturgy, other practices, scripture, and teachings—could hardly be greater. In a milieu filled with deadlocked theological disputes, the truth claims of Descartes and other modern philosophers would be self-consciously antitraditional and methodologically scornful of putative authorities, as a corollary of truth pursued, grounded, and articulated *sola ratio*. Hence the deep antipathy of so much modern philosophy to claims of divine revelation in general, and to those of Roman Catholicism in particular.

In Paris throughout the 1640s, Hobbes no less than Descartes was enamored of geometry as a model of rational certainty, although his empiricist epistemology and materialism belonged to a philosophy very different from Descartes's rationalistic, metaphysical dualism. Geometry's indubitability had inspired Descartes's clear and distinct ideas; it also inspired Hobbes's attempt to define every word precisely and according to his own conceptions as a means of avoiding error. As he put it in *Leviathan*, "a man that seeketh precise *truth*, had need to remember what every name he uses stands for; and to place it accordingly; or else he will find himselfe entangled in words, as a bird in lime-twiggs; the more he struggles, the more belimed." Accordingly, "it appears how necessary it is for any man that aspires to true Knowledge, to examine the Definitions of former Authors; and either to correct them, where they are negligently set down; or to make them himselfe." Despite his great divergences from Descartes, Hobbes likewise insisted on the pursuit of truth apart from received opinions, texts, and authorities: "Those men that take their instruction from the authority of books, and not from their own meditation," he wrote, are "as much below the condition of ignorant men, as men endued with true Science are above it. For between true Science, and erroneous Doctrines, Ignorance is in the middle." One's own ideas alone were reliable; better to remain ignorant than to trust those of someone else, if that someone were "but a man."[137] Although he was himself but a man, Hobbes reposed in his own assumptions, axioms, and definitions.

So did Spinoza, mutatis mutandis. Notwithstanding his own relentlessly geometrical method and indebtedness to Descartes, Spinoza developed his philosophy along dramatically different, deterministic and pantheistic lines, and with bravura confidence: "I do not presume that I have found the best philosophy, but I know that I comprehend the true one [*sed veram me intelligere scio*]."[138] Epitomizing the austere project of detached, autonomous, rational reflection that defers to no received opinions or alleged authorities, Spinoza contended that "the intellect, by its innate power, makes for itself intellectual tools through which it acquires other powers for other intellectual works, and from these works other tools or the power of investigating further, and thus continues step by step until it reaches the summit of wisdom"[139]—that is, presumably Spinoza's own philosophy as "the true one," most systematically expressed in his posthumously published *Ethics* (1677). Already by 1662, Spinoza was sure not only that the intellect could have a "true idea" of "the objective essence" of things, but that among the true ideas and therefore the certainty enjoyed by his intellect was the awareness "that everything that happens transpires according to the eternal order, and according to fixed laws of nature."[140] Hence in the *Ethics* Spinoza started with his definitions and axioms about reality's one substance, *Deus sive Natura.* He claimed to know with certainty the essence of its two humanly knowable modes, immaterial thought and material extension.[141]

At the outset of his *Treatise of Human Nature* in 1739, a twenty-eight-year-old David Hume lamented the "ignorance" that still prevailed "in the most important questions, that can come before the tribunal of human reason," in no small part due to "principles taken upon trust, consequences lamely deduced from them, want of coherence in the parts, and of evidence in the whole."[142] A century after Descartes's *Discourse on Method* and *Meditations,* the same root problem remained of trusting unexamined opinions. The same corrective ideal persisted, too, that of the individual philosopher deferring to no one and seeking the truth based on reason alone. In diametric contrast to Spinoza, Hume wrote that "it seems evident, that the essence of the mind being equally *unknown* to us with that of external bodies, it must be equally *impossible* to form any notion of its powers and qualities otherwise than from careful and exact experiments." Spinoza's philosophy led into "gloomy and obscure regions" with "this hideous hypothesis" of one substance, "almost the same with that of the immateriality of the soul, which has become so popular."[143] Instead, Hume proposed what had hitherto eluded philosophers, as "the only expedient, from which we can hope for success in our philosophical researches, to leave the tedious lingring method, which we have hitherto followed, and instead of taking now and then a castle or village on the frontier, to march up directly to the capital or center of these sciences, to human nature itself; which being once masters of, we may every where else hope for an easy victory.... There is no question of importance, whose decision is not compriz'd in the science of man; and there is none, which can be decided with any certainty, before we become acquainted with that science." The martial metaphor of conquest and mastery is perhaps not trivial. With no less confidence than Spinoza, Hobbes, or Descartes, but with conclusions very different from any of them, Hume wrote that "we in effect propose a compleat system of the sciences, built on a foundation almost entirely new, and the only one upon which they can stand with any security." What Newton was to the natural sciences, Hume would become to the science of man, beginning with "the perceptions of the human mind," a foundation which, in the tradition of Hobbes and Locke, he called "impressions and ideas."[144]

Buffeted by the divergent claims of different philosophers forty years later, Rousseau did not draw from this evidence the inference that the ideal of autonomous rational reflection and individual introspection might itself be suspect. Rather, he stressed all the more the necessity of independent thought: "Their philosophy is for others; I need one for myself. Let me seek it with all my strength while there is still time, so as to have a steady rule of conduct for the rest of my days."[145] Deeply concerned with answers to the Life Questions that presented themselves to him in the mid-eighteenth century, Rousseau saw that "what we ought to do depends heavily on what we ought to believe; and in everything that does not pertain to our basic natural needs, our opinions are the rule of our actions." He recalled that by the time he was forty he was "without any evil inclinations of the heart, living at random without principles well-determined [*bien décidés*] by my reason," and thus "set about a strict self-examination which was to order my inner life for the rest of my days as I would wish it to be at the time of my death." Like Montaigne and Descartes in their respective ways, Rousseau was convinced that "the work I had undertaken could only be carried out in complete isolation [*dans une retraite absolue*]; it would require lengthy and peaceful meditations that are incompatible with the commotion of life in society." The more alone and undistracted one was, the better. Despite at first finding himself "in such a labyrinth of obstacles, difficulties, objections, convolutions, and obscurities that twenty times" he was "tempted to abandon everything," Rousseau persisted and pursued "what were perhaps the most ardent and the most sincere investigations ever made by any mortal," admitting that "the prejudices of childhood and the secret wishes of my heart tipped the scales to the side most comforting to me." He concluded that individual sincerity was its own unimpeachable, blameless criterion for answering the Life Questions: "It is important to have an opinion of our own, and to choose it with all the maturity of judgment that we can muster. If despite this we fall into error we cannot justly be held responsible, because we are not culpable." The outcome of these "difficult investigations" was "more or less" Rousseau's "Profession of Faith of the Savoyard Vicar" included in book four of *Émile* (1762), an articulation of his religious and other beliefs. For it Rousseau had exalted hopes: it "could effect a revolution among men one day, if there is ever a revival of good sense and good faith."[146]

For Kant, independence from received authorities plus the exercise of reason was the very essence of *Aufklärung* and autonomy: "Enlightenment is the exodus of human beings from their self-imposed immaturity. Immaturity is the inability to make use of one's own reason without guidance from someone else. . . . *Sapere aude!* Have courage to make use of your own reason! That is the watchword of Enlightenment."[147] But "your own reason" did not mean anything like the acceptance of Rousseau's individualistic, self-satisfied sincerity, but rather the discovery of the universal possibility-conditions for and categories of rational knowledge, and of the universal nature and character of rational morality—in short, it meant reaching Kant's conclusions in his *Critique of Pure Reason* (1781) and *Critique of Practical Reason* (1788). "Our age is the true age of criticism," Kant wrote in the preface to the first edition of the first critique, "to which everything must submit"—including religion, lest it "arouse just suspicion and cannot claim that genuine respect that reason grants only to those who have been able to endure its free and open examination." Submitting to criticism meant submitting to reason, and submitting to reason meant submitting to Kant (recall once again Hume's martial metaphor). Over against the "battlefield of these endless disputes" about reason and knowledge "under the dogmatists' dominion," Kant had dispassionately shouldered the "summons to reason to take up anew the most difficult of all its occupations, namely that of self-knowledge, and to establish a court of adjudication in which its own just claims might be dispatched against all groundless presumptions, not through decrees imposed by authority [*Machtsprüche*], but rather according to reason's eternal and unchangeable laws; and this court is nothing other than the critique of pure reason itself." He was scarcely less confident than Spinoza had been: "I make bold to say [*erkühne mich zu sagen*] that there is bound to be not a single metaphysical problem that has not been solved here, or for the solution to which at least the key has not been provided."[148] Kant was equally sure about his deontological ethics, because the difference between a merely subjective ethical maxim and the universal, objective categorical imperative was precisely the claim that the latter was determined by reason alone—it was ostensibly a correlative, practical application to morality of the pure reason explored by Kant in the first critique.[149]

Many of the most influential nineteenth- and twentieth-century philosophers carried on in the same fashion. Sometimes, like Kant, they were more willing to acknowledge their indebtedness to predecessors—even if only to note the mistaken ideas of the latter that they had purportedly transcended. Writing in 1807, for example, Hegel disdained those contented with Romantic sentimentalism and thought that "it is time for the elevation of philosophy to the level of a science," an aspiration he had accomplished in his own thought, fully aware that his ideas were "different from and indeed entirely opposed to current conceptions of the nature and the form of truth."[150] In the midst of Europe's Napoleonic upheavals, Hegel wrote that "it is not hard to see that our era is one of birth and of transition to a new age" in which "Spirit has broken with the world of its previous instantiations and representations"—his philosophy being nothing less than the historically manifest, Absolute Spirit becoming conscious of itself in an objective, scientific form, surpassing even as it incorporated all its previous artistic, religious, and philosophical expressions.[151] Hegel utterly repudiated Kant's epistemological attempt to corral metaphysics. So too, at the outset of his *Philosophy of Right* (1820), he belittled the superficial, so-called philosophy of his contemporaries and recent predecessors, particularly those who believed "that that alone is true concerning ethical matters which each individual permits to arise out of his heart, feeling, and inspiration, especially concerning the state, government, and constitution." He lamented that in place of the truth, "the same old gruel [literally "cabbage," *Kohl*] is always reheated, divvied up, and distributed on all sides," such that "now the sophistry of arbitrariness has seized the name 'philosophy' and has been able to establish in a large public the opinion that such activities *are* philosophy [*als ob dergleichen Treiben Philosophie sey*]," as a result of which "the concepts of what is true [and] the laws of ethics also become nothing but opinions and subjective convictions." By this point, in the early 1820s, Hegel could presuppose the truth of his method and assumptions, since, as he put it, "I have comprehensively developed the nature of speculative knowing in my *Science of Logic*."[152] There he displayed the same aspiration to universal truth based on rationalist autonomy that had captured his predecessors since Descartes: "The necessity of once again starting from scratch [*von vorne anzufangen*] with this science" derived from "the very nature of the subject matter and the lack of previous works that might have been used in the reconstruction [of logic] at hand," because "what is involved is an altogether new concept of what it means to treat something scientifically [*Begriff wissenschaftlicher Behandlung*]."[153]

Across the Atlantic, placing more emphasis on intuition as the foundation for right reason and taking it in directions Hegel would have deplored, Ralph Waldo Emerson extended the same tradition of breaking with tradition: "When good is near you, when you have life in yourself, it is not by any known or accustomed way; you shall not discern the foot-prints of any other; you shall not see the face of man; you shall not hear any name;—the way, the thought, the good, shall be wholly strange and new. It shall exclude example and experience." As if trying to outdo Rousseau, and appropriating the categories of revealed religion to himself, Emerson baldly asserted that "nothing is at last sacred but the integrity of your own mind" and "no law can be sacred to me but that of my own nature. Good and bad are but names very readily transferable to that or this; the only right is what is after my constitution, the only wrong what is against it." Individual "Spontaneity or Instinct" were what counted, the self's immediacy and outspokenness, and not "a foolish consistency" or coherence: "Speak what you think now in hard words, and to-morrow speak what to-morrow thinks in hard words again, though it contradict everything you said to-day." Emerson had little use for revealed religion or religious dogmas, regardless of their content, claiming that "as men's prayers are a disease of the will, so are their creeds a disease of the intellect." Not God but the self-reliant, self-assertive individual was "the centre of things. Where he is, there is nature. He measures you, and all men, and all events." Indeed, "every new mind is a new classification" and if "of uncommon activity and power . . . it imposes its classification on other men."[154] Prophetic words, those.

Having digested and transformed Hegel's dialectic of *Geist* in history, Marx wanted nothing more than to impose what he took to be the objectively true philosophy of historical materialism on other men, women, and children, emancipating them for their own good. As he famously put it in 1845, "The philosophers have only *interpreted* the world in different ways; the point is to *change* it."[155] Marx's philosophy and its concretely applied adaptations would have extraordinary consequences especially in the short twentieth century, from the outbreak of World War I through the fall of the Soviet Union.[156] His activist philosophy of class struggle demanded an unprecedented *"ruthless criticism of all that exists,"* for "reason has always existed, only not in the reasonable form," and so "we only show them why they are really fighting, and consciousness is something that they *must* acquire, even if they do not want to."[157] Marx's call for proletarian revolution entirely rejected and subverted Hegel's effort "to grasp and depict the state as something inherently rational," the political expression of the historical unfolding of Absolute Spirit itself.[158] According to Marx, the real was not rational; the real was ideological and oppressive and self-justificatory. Like so many other philosophers before him and since Descartes, Marx imagined himself discovering the truth that had eluded all his predecessors, whom he scorned. Celebrated, bourgeois professors such as Hegel disgusted him: "Up to now the philosophers had the solution of all mysteries lying on their desks, and the stupid, exoteric world only had to open its mouth wide and the roasted pigeons of absolute science flew into its mouth."[159] Until and unless philosophers and others faced up to the truth discovered by Marx, and saw dominant ideologies as the mystifying superstructure that legitimated the fundamental economic realities of the means of production, they would remain ignorant of class struggle as the motor of history and the veiled source of their stupefying speculations.

John Stuart Mill began his *Utilitarianism* (1861) with an echo of Hume, pronouncing on "the backward state in which speculation on the most important subjects still lingers," including "the little progress which has been made in the decision of the controversy respecting the criterion of right and wrong," a problem linked to the lack of a well-articulated "one first principle, or common ground of obligation" underlying "a science of morals." Mill noted how "from the dawn of philosophy" the question "concerning the foundation of morality" had "occupied the most gifted intellects, and divided them into sects and schools, carrying on a vigorous warfare against one another. And after more than two thousand years the same discussions continue, philosophers are still ranged under the same contending banners, and neither thinkers nor mankind at large seem nearer to being unanimous on the subject." Indeed, they were nowhere near even a rough agreement. Like his disputatious predecessors, Mill sought to end the quarrels with a breakthrough. Concerned about "to what extent the moral beliefs of mankind have been vitiated or made uncertain by the absence of any distinct recognition of an ultimate standard," Mill found it in a modified version of Bentham's utilitarian "Greatest Happiness Principle," which "holds that actions are right in proportion as they tend to promote happiness, wrong as they tend to produce the reverse of happiness. By happiness is intended pleasure, and the absence of pain; by unhappiness, pain, and the privation of pleasure." So much for Kant's categorical imperative. Against the critics of his version of utilitarianism, with its distinction between higher and lower pleasures overlooked by Bentham, Mill wondered "what recommendation possessed by any other morality they could possibly affirm to be wanting to it," not least because "the corollaries from the principle of utility, like the precepts of every practical art, admit of indefinite improvement, and, in a progressive state of human mind, their improvement is perpetually going on."[160] Thus *Utilitarianism* would link arms with *On Liberty* (1859). Analogous to Rousseau's hopes for "a revolution among men" based on his beliefs, Mill thought that if people saw the light of his utilitarianism, the prospects for progress were bright.

In 1904 Edmund Husserl wrote to his teacher Franz Brentano that although he was "always inclined to acknowledge the superiority of others and to let them lead me upward, again and again I find myself compelled to part company with them and to seek my own way." In other words, despite his inclinations, he did not in fact let others lead him. "Instead of continuing to build on the foundations laid by others as I would so gladly do, I have to build, while despairing of the solidity of their work, new foundations of my own."[161] The founder of phenomenology was a neo-Cartesian not only regarding the foundational place of human subjectivity and consciousness in his philosophy, but in thinking that philosophical truth was to be found through the individual, independent exercise of his reason. Husserl's student, Martin Heidegger, would charge his teacher with insufficient attentiveness to the existential concreteness of the knowing subject as *Dasein*, the place where the forgotten, fundamental question of *Sein*—

being—is asked, or at least can be.[162] But another student of Husserl's, Emmanuel Levinas, would in the wake of the Holocaust criticize Heidegger's critique of "onto-theology" and his attempt to revive metaphysics as a fundamental failure to attend to what matters most. According to Levinas neither metaphysics nor epistemology, but rather ethics, is first philosophy.[163]

THIS BRIEF TREATMENT of a few major modern philosophers could have been extended, but it would only have lengthened the exposition, not affected the analysis or its conclusions. As with Protestantism since the early 1520s, one need not investigate every instance in order to see the shared assumptions that had major historical consequences and therefore have explanatory power in understanding the makings of modernity. Indeed, to seek comprehensiveness would militate against comprehension. Since the seventeenth century, modern philosophers with universal, foundationalist ambitions have sought to offer post-religious, rational answers to the Life Questions. Had they either agreed among themselves, or were they discernibly engaged in an intellectually cumulative enterprise such as modern physics, chemistry, or biology, there would be evidence for a claim that reason has replaced revealed religion, or at least a basis to hope that it might eventually do so. But neither is even remotely the case. This is apparent from a cursory familiarity with the history of modern philosophy since the early seventeenth century, and with the realities of academic philosophy today.

The last chapter noted a few examples of how seventeenth- and eighteenth-century philosophers disagreed dramatically among themselves about God despite the shared assumptions of a univocal metaphysics. Chapter 4 will note analogous disagreements in modern moral philosophy. Here it can simply be observed that in no domain of philosophy since the seventeenth century has there ever been even general agreement about what reason dictates, discloses, or prescribes, whether in terms of metaphysics, epistemology, philosophical anthropology, or morality. To see this does not demand mastery of abstruse postmodern thought; it requires only a competent survey course in the history of modern philosophy. The reason is straightforward: reason "alone" is never without assumptions and a starting point, which are always vulnerable to critique and subversion because they are never self-evident. This applies to Descartes's *cogito*, Spinoza's conviction that the human intellect is adequate to reality, and Kant's Newtonian views underlying his sharp separation between phenomena and noumena. It applies as well to Marx's atheism and materialism, Husserl's account of subjectivity, and Heidegger's assumption that metaphysics rather than ethics is *philosophia prima*. Like all modern philosophers in this tradition, Hume believed he was laying hitherto unrecognized foundations for truth based on reason (or in his case, showing what was left of them after his skeptical critique). In fact, he not only characterized philosophy in his own day, but, like Luther *contra* Zwingli, proved uncannily prophetic despite himself: "There is nothing which is not the subject of debate, and in which men of learning are not of contrary opinions."[164] Looking to reason as a "regulative idea" rather than as an apodictic foundation, in the manner of certain German Idealist thinkers of the late eighteenth and early nineteenth centuries,[165] alters this reality not at all—on the contrary, it introduces a new issue about which "men [and women] of learning" can and do disagree.

Although modern philosophers have self-consciously and explicitly aspired to truth about the Life Questions based on reason, it might seem unfair to point out their radical disagreements and to hold them accountable to their own stated ambitions. After all, the problems are difficult and complex; thinking clearly and well is hard; perhaps their reach has exceeded their grasp. Although they manifestly have not come close to agreeing about the dictates of reason, perhaps they have at least made some progress in their endeavor. Perhaps we are closer now to answering at least some of the Life Questions based on reason than we were four or two or one hundred years ago. Perhaps we are. But how would or could one know, based on reason? How, among rival views, would we recognize a truer, more rational answer to the question, "What should I believe, and why should I believe it?" or "What should I live for, and why?"

In dramatic contrast to the modern natural sciences, which notwithstanding Kuhnian and other protestations have revealed a strongly cumulative explanatory character and variously demonstrated their predictive power,[166] contemporary philosophy offers no rational way of deciding among its practitioners' contrary claims, nor any reason to think that their labors are plausibly converging toward truth. All that is evident are ever more, shifting truth claims and endless disagreements. "Reason is such a boxe of Quicksilver that it abides no where," Jeremy Taylor said three and a half centuries ago. "It dwells in no setled mansion; it is like a doves neck, or a changeable Taffata; it looks to me otherwise then to you who doe not stand in the same light that I doe." In his own way, Taylor's remarks implied a relativizing skepticism as radical as that which Luther or Müntzer deployed, depending on the context, in the 1520s: "We cannot tell what is true and what is good and what is evil; and every man makes his own opinions to be laws of nature, if his persuasion be strong and violent."[167] Taylor wrote this in 1660. It applies no less in the early twenty-first century than it did then.

Try this thought experiment: Put in the same room Remi Brague, Daniel Dennett, Jürgen Habermas, Vittorio Hösle, Saul Kripke, Julia Kristeva, Jean-Luc Marion, Martha Nussbaum, Alvin Plantinga, Hilary Putnam, John

Searle, and Peter Singer. Tell them they will be fed and housed, but that they cannot leave until they have reached an agreement about answers to the Life Questions on the basis of reason. How long will they take? I wouldn't hold my breath. Now, in their attempts to answer these questions, let them draw in addition on any and all of the natural sciences, social sciences, and humanistic disciplines besides philosophy. Same result.

In their respective ways, analytical and Continental philosophers today simply contribute to hyperpluralism in the academy. As such, they are the contemporary heirs to nineteenth-century neo-Kantians, Hegelian idealists, Marxist materialists, Millian liberals, Comtean positivists, and so forth. As Alasdair MacIntyre has observed, modern philosophers have themselves long been susceptible to the same critique leveled by late nineteenth-century philosophers against theologians in seeking to discredit theology as a rational discourse with a rightful place in the modern university: there is no consensus at all among them about the most important questions in their discipline, what methods are best for trying to answer them, or how disagreements about such second-order issues could conceivably be resolved.[168] As far as the Life Questions are concerned, then, modern philosophers are analogous to Protestants who claim the correct interpretation of the Bible based on the inspiration of the Holy Spirit. Of course, different philosophers powerfully and sometimes passionately criticize competitors, defending their respective assumptions, approaches, and answers. Just like the clash of exegetical and prophetic adversaries working within or seeking to transcend Protestantism. Sometimes with considerable insight and clarity, working within one (or more rarely, across both) of the two broad traditions of analytical and Continental philosophy, professional philosophers address problems and issues they respectively regard as important and interesting. Just like learned, articulate Protestants tackling issues of concern to them. But given the manifest vulnerability of their respective assumptions and starting points, the preferences of both are ultimately and literally arbitrary—that is, a function of the will.

MacIntyre's analogy between philosophy and late nineteenth-century Protestant theology is apt. Modern philosophy sought to provide what Protestantism could not, via reason rather than scripture. Not only has it failed thus far, but judging from the last four centuries as well as from contemporary philosophy, there is no reason to think that it might ever succeed. Already in the late eighteenth century and with uncanny prescience, the Lutheran Johann Georg Hamann (1730–1788) saw this in his critique of Kant's allegedly autonomous, secular reason.[169] With respect to the Life Questions, the history of modern philosophy offers no evidence at all for Mill's claim that "wrong opinions and practices gradually yield to fact and argument."[170]

Near the outset of his *Philosophy of Right*, Hegel noted "the supposed [*vermeynte*] difficulty of how to distinguish and discern from among an infinite number of different opinions what among them is universally acknowledged and valid."[171] He missed that there is nothing *vermeinte* about the problem within modern philosophy; that whatever its influence and his own self-satisfaction, his philosophy was and remains, like others, susceptible to devastating criticisms; and that despite himself he was simply contributing further to the philosophical pluralism he sought to overcome. Historically and empirically, modern philosophy, like Protestantism, has produced and continues to yield an ever-proliferating number of truth *claims*, the institutional incubators of which are modern, liberal states. *Sola ratio* has not overcome the problem that stemmed from *sola scriptura*, but rather replicated it in a secular, rationalist register.

This realization should not be construed as an indictment of reason per se, without which any rational endeavor would be impossible—a point lost on those postmodern irrationalists who self-contradictorily use reason in attacking reason as such. Nor does it dim the analytical light that philosophers can and do shed on a wide range of issues. But it *does* strongly suggest that reason *alone* is as unlikely a candidate for *answering the Life Questions* as is scripture alone, claims about the inspiration of the Holy Spirit, or assertions of new divine revelation. Attempts to salvage modern philosophy by claiming that it is concerned with asking questions *rather than* either finding or getting closer to finding answers might make sense—if one just happens to like asking questions in the same way that thirsty people just happen to like seeking water *rather than* locating a drinking fountain, or indeed having any idea whether they are getting closer to one. Appeals to philosophy as a "quest" or "journey" toward the truth about morality, meaning, or metaphysics by means of reason presuppose a promising path to follow. Neither the history of modern philosophy nor the state of contemporary philosophy suggests any reason to think that reason alone offers one. The evidence of nearly four hundred years suggests that those who persist nonetheless are as Pollyannaish as those who doggedly continue to maintain the sufficiency and perspicuity of scripture as a basis for Christian truth despite a half-millennium of irreconcilable biblical interpretations, and a lack of any consensual means for deciding among them. The reasonable conclusion is that it is irrational to go on thinking that reason alone might yield truth about human values, priorities, meaning, or purpose. The foundationalist ambitions of modern philosophy sprang from the challenges of Pyrrhonian skepticism. Based on the evidence, the rational conclusion is that they have failed, and should end amid the skepticism whence they came.

The first influential, heavy blows against the ambitions of modern philosophy were of course delivered by Nietzsche in the 1870s and 1880s, with his scathing attacks on revealed religion *and* philosophy. With relentless rhetoric, he ridiculed Spinoza's views, for example, as "the cobweb-spinning of concepts by a hermit" absorbed in "the love of *his* wisdom," and denounced Kant as "an *insidious* [*hinterlistigen*] Christian" and "the most deformed conceptual cripple who has ever existed."[172] But precisely *in* his self-admiring and self-absorbed self-understanding as an intrepid trailblazer breaking with authority and tradition, Nietzsche merely followed faithfully in the well-worn footsteps of those whom he belittled. Despite fancying himself the first thinker beyond post-Socratic philosophy, Nietzsche simply and dutifully added more competing truth claims to already existing philosophical options. It is not surprising that subsequent, similarly disenchanted academics find Nietzsche enchanting, or think that his nihilism can somehow be avoided even as his philosophy is marshaled to serve the post-Enlightenment individualist agenda of self-determining self-construction that runs from Rousseau through Emerson and Mill to Sartre and Rorty and on to the present.

One who took up the Nietzschean option was Michel Foucault, for whom it prompted his shift in emphasis from "archaeology" to "genealogy" beginning in 1971.[173] After the dissolution of the New Left in the 1970s and 1980s followed by the fall of the Berlin Wall and the disintegration of the Soviet Union, it is no accident that Foucault's neo-Nietzschean thought has become popular among those American academics in multiple disciplines who, understandably disgusted with the exercise of power by and for the powerful, have coupled their disaffection with a carefully calibrated sort of moral relativism (to be explored further in Chapter 4) inferred from the fact of hyperpluralism. The shift from neo-Marxist to Foucauldian ideas permits the migration of a rhetoric of resistance previously invested in anticapitalist class struggle, and the survival of a secular sense of purpose that it afforded.[174] Properly politicized in the approved ways, scholarship can remain meaningful even if one studies obscure people who lived centuries ago, so long as it obeys the one-note analytical paradigm of power imposed and resisted. The recovery of the agency and discontented voices of the oppressed, by prefiguring the emancipatory narrative of modernity, can at least partially redeem the otherwise dismal premodern human past. In a worldview premised on individual autonomy as the teleological apotheosis of human history, locating the agency of resistance becomes a secular substitute for the salvation of scholars who reconstruct its redemptive exercise by their premodern subjects and thereby, through fashioning a suitably usable past, stand in vicarious solidarity with them. Scholars thereby make their subjects' voices heard instead of merely publishing articles or monographs that only a handful of scholarly specialists will read.

But Foucault's philosophy is just as vulnerable to subversion as any other, however much it *does* help to illuminate the particularly self-serving expressions of post-Enlightenment, instrumentalist rationality deployed in modern European colonialism or the modern state's domination of human life. Foucault's thought is not a successful philosophical foundationalism, succeeding at last where thinkers from Descartes through Husserl or Heidegger failed. It is a product of late twentieth-century hyperpluralism combined with anger at the self-serving manifestations of power in Western society. It is one more philosophical option among many. Despite Foucault's critique of disciplinary regimes that seek to produce "docile bodies" through the deployment of "biopower," his underlying objective coincided with and perpetuated the Enlightenment ideology that in other respects he excoriated: to liberate individuals to think and do and live as they please. To exercise their wills as they will—the *summum bonum*. No wonder his appeal persists. Explaining Foucault and the popularity of his ideas requires an analysis of the past that reaches back further than the eighteenth century or even the seventeenth, and recognizes how the modern philosophies that informed the Enlightenment in all its varieties, whether in Scotland or Germany, England or France, belong to the same historical trajectory and endeavor as Protestantism: the attempt to offer answers to the Life Questions on bases different from those on which they rested and continue to rest in Roman Catholicism.

The proliferation of unintended pluralisms based respectively on scripture alone and reason alone cannot be understood on the basis of intellectual history alone. Religious and secular answers to the Life Questions have unfolded within institutional settings over the past five centuries. Western modernity is unintelligible apart from sovereign states, which began to exercise a public monopoly of power in the Reformation era. But the consequential genealogy for understanding the contemporary Western relationship between politics and religion has its roots in the Middle Ages. The actions of medieval ecclesiastical leaders in wielding power set in motion changes that have been no less important than metaphysical univocity or *sola scriptura* for the makings of present-day human realities in the Western world. They provide the crucial headwaters for the historical trajectory analyzed in the following chapter, which shifts from ideas to institutions, from truth claims to the exercise of power, and is devoted to states' domestication and control of the church(es) since the late Middle Ages.

# CHAPTER THREE

# Controlling the Churches

Freedom of religion is regarded as a fundamental civil right in contemporary liberal democracies and is legally protected as such. It contrasts sharply with the brutal suppression of religion in some of the twentieth century's most tyrannical regimes, including the Soviet Union, which was so hostile toward Russian Orthodoxy and minority religions, as well as Nazi Germany, which was bent on the extermination of the Jews and domineering in its control of Christian churches. Contemporary freedom of religion also contrasts sharply with the confessional regimes of early modern Europe, in which allied political and ecclesiastical authorities prescribed specific forms of Christian worship and prohibited others. The principal narrative line of modern Western religious toleration, a story usually focused on the incremental recognition of religious freedom for individuals, is a familiar one: the problems that derived from the hostilities among Christians in the Reformation era, including the persecution of religious dissenters and destructive wars of religion, were eventually solved by separating religion from politics, privatizing religion, and permitting individuals to believe and worship as they wished. What Mark Lilla has aptly called "the Great Separation" is widely regarded as having been a great success. Echoing James Madison and speaking of the United States, John Noonan, for example, has extolled the free exercise of religion rooted in individual conscience as "the lustre of our country" that "has been reflected round the world" and "has lighted up the skies."[1] Based on European and American experience, this solution is today widely touted to the Islamic world by Western scholars, political commentators, and politicians, who hold it up as the model for extricating religion from politics, where it does not belong, and for recognizing individual religious freedom as a core human right beyond the legitimate reach of political coercion. If Islam would have had a Reformation like Western Christianity, so the thinking goes—or at least enough religio-political disruption within their tradition—Muslims too might have avoided the unmodern perpetuation of religion in politics and the public sphere where it is bound to cause such trouble. The sequestration of sectarianism is essential to societal stability and salvation.

Because individual freedom of religion contrasts so radically with religion's suppression in twentieth-century dictatorships and its politically enforced prescription in early modern Europe, it would seem strange, on the face of it, to identify all three realities as part of a shared historical phenomenon. Yet this chapter endeavors to show a crucial sense in which they are. Because they are *also* so obviously different—religion as freely permitted, overtly suppressed, or officially mandated, respectively—their common roots in the distant past have usually been overlooked. This hiddenness is compounded if our attention is held captive by modern religious toleration and the free exercise of religion for individuals, which indeed constitutes a major caesura between early modern confessional states and modern liberal ones. Yet if we shift our analytical focus from individuals to institutions and from the recognition of rights to the exercise of power, things appear differently. Whether in Western confessional, liberal, or totalitarian regimes, states control churches: whether they prescribe, permit, or proscribe religion, they do so entirely on their terms, exercising an institutional monopoly of power in the public sphere. Whatever the particularities involved, nonecclesiastical—that is, secular—authorities and the state's laws are the sovereign arbiters of permissible religious practice and of public morality.[2] No modern Western state lies outside this pattern, which characterizes every polity in Europe and North America today. Historically, the control of the church in ways continuous with contemporary realities began in the late Middle Ages, was transformed and hastened by the Reformation, when the church became the churches, and was essentially accomplished by the second half of the sixteenth century. Late eighteenth-century measures granting limited religious toleration in various European countries, as well as subsequent legal enactments and political developments, extended in diverse ways the states' control over the churches that already marked Philip II's Spain and Elizabeth I's England.

This chapter focuses not on individual rights, a subject broached in Chapter 4, but on the public exercise of institutional power. It concentrates on the most consequential historical changes that enable us to explain the situation in which we find ourselves today, whatever the contemporary legal specificities pertaining to religion in respective Western countries and regardless of the historical path by which each country arrived at them. The historical particularities of the relationships between states and churches in individual countries or local settings are unquestionably important and worthy of focused investigation. Indeed, many historical questions about these relationships can only be answered by attending to highly specific primary sources, and a chapter such as this one could never have been attempted apart from the outstanding scholarship of many historians. But insofar as such inquiries are limited to individual countries or more-restricted geographical contexts within them, they cannot show the sense in which all Westerners today also find themselves in the *same* situation: whether in Europe or North America, our respective sovereign states dictate what individuals and institutions can and cannot do in exercising religious faith. That this seems so self-evidently obvious and normal is exactly why it merits analysis, because such institutional arrangements and the assumptions behind them have not always existed, and neither their emergence nor their eventual dominance was inevitable. Institutionally and with respect to the public exercise of power, ours is both a historically contingent and a quasi-Kantian reality: religion and unbelief within the limits of the state alone.

In order to see the explanatorily powerful historical trajectory that has led to the situation in which Westerners find themselves today, we must start before the fifteenth century and the beginnings of what turned out to be a permanent shift in the control of the church by secular authorities. Already long before the Reformation, secular authorities were diversely gaining at the expense of ecclesiastical authorities in the exercise of public power. Reacting to and capitalizing on the self-inflicted fiascos and pervasive problems of the late medieval church, the Reformation altered and accelerated this process in dramatic ways. Against all the Protestant reformers' intentions but as a result of their actions, the church became the churches: doctrinal differences derived from exegetical disagreements were embodied in rival ecclesiastical institutions composed of mutually exclusive bodies of Christian believers. What previously had been a jurisdictional matter negotiated between frequently contentious secular and ecclesiastical authorities thereby acquired a new character: ecclesiastical leaders, whether Lutheran, Reformed Protestant, or Roman Catholic, were compelled to rely on secular authorities both to promote their rival views of Christian truth and to protect themselves against religio-political enemies. For their part, sovereigns had to control religion lest the revolutionary potential of *sola scriptura,* so disturbingly manifest already in the German Peasants' War of 1524–1526, threaten political hierarchy and social order.

Institutionalized in magisterial Protestant and Catholic confessional regimes, churches' divergent doctrines as sanctioned by sovereigns became templates for the inculcation of religious values, moral behavior, and political obedience in their subjects. Heterodox men and women were identified and punished; antagonistic regimes, inspired partly by their respective Christian commitments, fought wars from the 1520s to the 1640s, with publicly expressed hostilities enduring much longer. The destabilizing destruction that accompanied the wars and the political cost of suppressing dissenters led rulers to experiment with limited forms of religious toleration, beginning already in the sixteenth century.[3] In addition, Sebastian Castellio, Dirck Coornheert, Roger Williams, Pierre Bayle, John Locke, and other innovative Christian thinkers theorized religious tolerance; Thomas Hobbes theorized not only an Erastian control but the de facto absorption of the church by the secular sovereign.[4] Later, depending on what their increasingly nationalist leaders thought would serve their purposes, nineteenth- and twentieth-century states either divergently persisted in maintaining confessional alliances with ecclesiastical authorities while granting some measure of toleration to religious minorities, or permitted individuals to believe and worship as they pleased within legal limits, or harshly suppressed religion in keeping with one or another antireligious ideology. Regardless of their leaders' decisions, *nation*-states—their bureaucratic reach augmented by the increasingly centralized orchestration of tax revenues, industrial and communications technologies, military power, and police forces—controlled the churches and all expressions of religion with greater effectiveness than had ever been possible during the Reformation era. During the Cold War, this was no less true of the United States than it was of the Soviet Union, despite the radically different ways in which these two nations regarded religion and treated religious believers.

The remainder of this chapter expands upon this sketch. I take it as obvious that the state's control of churches as expressed in the legally and politically protected individual freedom of religion is vastly preferable to its control in the forms of violent suppression or heavy-handed coercion. This protection solved intractable problems that derived from the religio-political conflicts of the Reformation era and the mistreatment of religious dissenters within confessional regimes in early modern Europe, some of whom theorized religious tolerance based on Christian assumptions, as Perez Zagorin has shown.[5] Less obvious are some further consequences that, in combination with intertwined historical developments, either followed from or are related to what is now all but self-evidently regarded in the West as the only legitimate way in which religion and politics can coexist: religion is privatized and removed from politics and the public sphere, a right to religious belief and worship (or none) is guaranteed for all individuals, and the limits of religious expression are set and policed by the sovereign state. This chapter not only traces the control of the churches by states since the late Middle Ages, but also explores some of the attendant—and, it seems, largely unrecognized—consequences of this process that continue profoundly to affect present-day human realities in both Europe and North America.

As an institutionalized worldview in the Middle Ages, Western Christianity included politics. It had to: fallen human beings remained ineradicably the apple of God's eye and the object of his boundless love, and postlapsarian human life inescapably included the exercise of power. Lest sheer power prevail, *caritas* was supposed to inform and motivate coercion just as it was supposed to inform all of human life. Politics would have been superfluous in medieval Christendom only if the "kingdom of God" *(basileia tou theou; regnum Dei),* the central referent in the preaching and teaching of Jesus of Nazareth, had been not only in some embryonic way present in and through him, but fully realized already.[6] The sordid realities of human life, however, reflected the gulf between the proclamation and the fulfillment of God's kingdom in medieval Europe despite centuries of Christianization. Overwhelmingly and obviously, human beings tended to be selfish and self-righteous; they wanted their own way; left to their own devices, they were driven by their passions and desires. According to the Gospel accounts that were canonized as part of what Christians came to call the "New Testament," however, Jesus heralded the kingdom of God and called others to it. If Jesus really was divine as well as human, as church leaders at Chalcedon would assert officially in 451, then by doing what he told them to do human beings would submit their wills to God's and presumably participate in some mysterious way in the promotion of his kingdom: "Thy kingdom come, thy will be done, on earth as it is in heaven" (Mt 6:10).

Jesus's central imperatives were disarmingly straightforward as reported in what became the scriptures of Latin Christendom. They were impossible to miss but very difficult to enact, because they grated so uncomfortably against ordinary human inclinations. They included loving God as obedient Jews did, with all one's heart, soul, mind, and strength, and one's neighbor as oneself; extending even to one's enemies the same kind of love with which Jesus had loved his followers, being "perfect as your heavenly Father is perfect" (Mt 5:48); and actively practicing virtues such as forgiveness, compassion, kindness, patience, and mercy in one's relationships with others, with particular solicitude for sinners, the poor, the marginalized, and the outcast. This sort of life entailed not the pursuit of wealth, familial security, or power, but their renunciation. Self-fulfillment lay paradoxically in self-denial, genuine freedom in binding oneself to God and subjugating oneself to others in service: "whoever wishes to be first among you must be slave of all" (Mk 10:44). Salvation lay in putting oneself not first but last, willing to wash others' feet, even to lay down one's life for them: "For whoever wishes to save his life will lose it, but whoever loses his life for my sake and the gospel's will save it" (Mk 8:35).[7] In no sense did Jesus exhort his followers to seek the exercise of power—just the opposite.

Like the Hebrew prophets before him, Jesus did not invite or suggest—he commanded and rebuked: "Why do you call me 'Lord, Lord,' and not do what I tell you?" (Lk 6:46) All the imperative force of the jealous God of the Israelites, whose covenant required obedience to his commandments, had been concentrated in the incarnate Word and focused decisively on his listeners—and by extension, on all human beings, insofar as according to medieval Christians Jesus was the definitive self-revelation of the one creator-God.[8] They knew of the terrifying, eventual consequences for those who disobeyed him and therefore God "the Father" by neglecting to feed the hungry, welcome strangers, clothe the naked, care for the sick, and visit the imprisoned: "You that are accursed," Jesus would say when he returned in judgment, "Depart from me into the eternal fire prepared for the devil and his angels" (Mt 25:41). Those who obeyed Jesus's commands as mediated by his church, on the other hand, had reason to hope that they would be welcomed by him into eternal joy when he came again as judge: "Come, you that are blessed by my Father, inherit the kingdom prepared for you from the foundation of the world" (Mt 25:34). None of this had anything to do with seeking or exercising power; as John's Gospel put it, Jesus said, "My kingdom is not of this world" (Jn 18:36).

Christian morality was irreducibly communal and social.[9] According to the Gospels, Jesus did not tell his listeners to believe whatever they wished to believe as individuals, or to follow him only in their private thoughts and interior sentiments but not in concrete, public, shared human life. On the contrary, a shared, social life of faith, hope, love, humility, patience, self-sacrifice, forgiveness, compassion, service, and generosity simply *was* Christianity. It was the Gospel concretized and enacted. It was not something called "religion" distinguished from the rest of life, but rather all of life lived in a certain way. As we shall see further in the following chapter, this common life was meant reciprocally to model and to inspire the behaviors through which it was constituted. Being a Christian therefore necessarily entailed the fostering of certain kinds of social relationships and not others.

It necessarily meant acting in certain ways and not others. Implicitly, it required as well some means by which, until Jesus's second coming, that shared way of life might be sustained, a concern already evident in the writings that were copied, redacted, circulated, and eventually chosen by early church leaders for inclusion in the "New Testament." Indeed, according to Matthew's Gospel as understood by patristic writers and medieval theologians, Jesus had himself in part provided for this means by telling Peter that he would build his "congregation" or "church" *(ekklesia)* on him as his "rock," against which the "gates of hell" would not prevail: "I will give you the keys of the kingdom of heaven, and whatever you bind on earth will be bound in heaven, and whatever you loose on earth will be loosed in heaven" (Mt 16:18–19).

Although first-century Christians had expected the imminent return of their resurrected Lord, they were disappointed. Jesus tarried, complicating their eschatological expectations. So they made do, seeking insofar as they obeyed Jesus's commands to live in the kingdom that he had heralded and modeled for them, as diverse communities of believers in "the world." They celebrated the thanksgiving—the Eucharist—as he had commanded ("do this in remembrance of me" [Lk 22:19]): by re-presenting himself to them anew, Jesus renewed and strengthened their shared way of life, because, as he disarmingly asserted, "those who eat my flesh and drink my blood have eternal life" (Jn 6:54). To an unprecedented extent in the ancient world and in keeping with Jesus's example, Christian bishops and clergy singled out the poor and cared for them in the post-Constantinian Roman Empire, whether or not they were Christians, impressively enough that the Emperor Julian recognized the importance of competing with them after he renounced Christianity in 361.[10]

What about power? Until Jesus's deferred second coming, human actions contrary to his directives—so pervasive in the stubbornly sinful world—were not only to be avoided but actively resisted insofar as one loved others. Just what this entailed would depend on the local and wider circumstances in which Christians found themselves, as indeed was true of all the virtues commanded by Jesus. It could not but differ according to whether they were seeking to survive imperial mistreatment or to transform the Roman Empire from a position of authority. The latter must have seemed most unlikely at the outset of the fourth century during the Diocletian persecution just before Christianity's approval by Constantine, whose conversion Eusebius of Caesarea interpreted in fulsomely providential terms in the final book of his *History of the Church*.[11] But the emperor's approval of the faith hardly transfigured overnight the sinful world into the realized kingdom of God. Sin and suffering, callousness and cruelty still abounded.

Precisely because of this fact, and considering the alternative of political passivity, the virtuous exercise of power came to be regarded as a Christian duty. *Caritas* itself was the bridge. As especially Augustine contended and so influentially theorized in *The City of God* in the early fifth century, the practice of Christian love in obedience to Jesus in a far from fully redeemed world would require as a moral responsibility the proper exercise of power, over oneself and over others, lest selfish sinfulness rush in and default wickedness be given free rein. To wash one's hands of politics and refuse to exercise public power justly and virtuously was in effect to relinquish the "city of man" to the frightening *libido dominandi* on which Augustine trained his unsparing analytical gaze. Absent resistance via rightly informed politics, power and pride would still have their way and continue to crush human lives. Instead, motivated by *caritas* and tempered by clemency, some measure of coercion that sought the salvation of sinners via Christian community was unavoidable lest a hydra-headed *cupiditas* receive unrestrained sanction by default. This essentially became the Western Christian political ideal for more than a millennium. In Peter Brown's apt words, "power was redeemed, by becoming power over souls. It was a trust, wielded to advance the common good—the salvation of all believers."[12] But who would exercise it, and how? And to what extent would the ideal be realized?

By THE LATE FIFTEENTH CENTURY, Christianity in the Latin West had existed under a very wide range of political conditions. Sometimes it thrived; sometimes it merely survived. At different times and successively, the church had been persecuted as an outlawed sect under Roman emperors, permitted by Constantine and then prescribed by Theodosius, allied with Frankish kings and Carolingian emperors, dominated by aristocratic Roman families and Ottonian emperors, dominant through the efforts of zealous reformers and papal leaders, based administratively in Avignon rather than Rome for nearly seventy years, divided between rival popes for almost four decades, and reconstituted in the mid-quattrocento Renaissance among rival monarchies and city-states. In order to understand the late medieval shift that is historically continuous with Western states' control of religion today, we must heed the relationship among three major, long-term historical realities amid these radically disparate political conditions from the pre-Constantinian Roman Empire through the high Italian Renaissance: the jurisdictional distinction between ecclesiastical and nonecclesiastical institutions, the increased influence and power of the church beginning in the eleventh century, and the gulf between the church's teachings and the behaviors of many medieval Christians.

First, never was the Latin church either coextensive with or absorbed by any secular political entity, both because of historical contingencies and out of fidelity to Jesus's own words: "Render unto Caesar the things that are Caesar's, and unto God the things that are God's" (Mt 22:21, Mk 12:17, Lk 20:25). Jesus's early followers lived not in an institutional vacuum, but within the Roman Empire's complex world of multilevel politics and patronage, especially in port cities along eastern Mediterranean coasts.[13] Following his conversion, Constantine moved the imperial capital from Rome to Constantinople in 324, which led the church to develop differently in the Latin West than in the Greek East. The decline and fall and further decline of the Western Empire, for example, left the bishops of Rome as de facto political rulers of the decrepit city by the pontificate of Gregory the Great (590–604) and as sovereigns of an independent political republic from the 730s, their view of themselves and their conception of authority influenced by imperial precedent as well as by biblical images and imperatives.[14]

A millennium and more after Constantine, from the papacy to the parishes into which Christendom was parceled, the church remained institutionally and jurisdictionally distinct from secular political entities, including the Holy Roman Empire and medieval kingdoms, principalities, duchies, and independent cities and city-states. In diverse local expressions and countless particular arrangements, *sacerdotium* and *imperium* coexisted as political authorities. Each had its own laws, courts, and organizational structures, even though disproportionately literate and educated clergy often served also in secular institutions, as administrators, secretaries, and advisers.[15] Ecclesiastical authorities exercised public power in certain domains of life, and secular authorities exercised it in others; in principle and ideally both worked for the salvation of embodied souls.[16] Just like clerical leaders, secular authorities subscribed to, promoted, and defended Christian truth claims, whether explicitly or implicitly, in the domains of life in which they exercised power. Most of the considerable friction between ecclesiastical and secular authorities during the Middle Ages concerned who would exercise control over which areas and activities of human life, and who, in the end, rightly wielded ultimate authority and power. Theirs was a jurisdictional contestation. Along the way, the church bolstered its case for priority with monastic forgeries, most importantly the eighth-century Donation of Constantine, which elaborated upon claims dating back to the fifth century.[17]

Again, according to the synoptic Gospels, Jesus had said, "Render unto Caesar the things that are Caesar's, and unto God the things that are God's." This made clear that the two were not coextensive, yet left conspicuously unspecified what things belonged in each category and how their relationship was to be understood. Open-ended indeterminacy was inevitable insofar as human beings were embodied souls and therefore unified wholes. No simple, dichotomous demarcation—body versus soul, public versus private, outer versus inner, or even temporal versus spiritual—*could* provide a formulaic answer to the question of how ecclesiastical and secular authorities were to divide their responsibilities in the exercise of power, because Christianity entailed creatures seeking body-and-soul to live a certain kind of shared life in fidelity to Jesus's commands. The result was prodigious commentary and argument, endless negotiation, ongoing contestation, and frequent conflicts between ecclesiastical and secular authorities at every scale, from local disputes over privileges regarding land use and taxation to centuries-long power struggles between popes and emperors.[18] It could hardly have been otherwise, unless *either* the kingdom of God had been fully realized, which presumably would have made coercion and therefore politics unnecessary; *or* the church had left "the world" to itself, which would have meant renouncing Jesus's commands to love others and thus to resist evil in pursuit of the kingdom of God; *or* human beings had been crypto-Cartesian creatures of neatly separable souls and bodies, in which case ecclesiastical authorities might somehow have tried to content themselves with the governance of human souls while secular authorities governed human bodies.[19]

The second important medieval historical reality for understanding the trajectory traced in this chapter is that beginning in the mid-eleventh century, the church progressively and increasingly extended its bureaucracy, power, and influence, both in absolute terms and relative to secular authorities. This process continued throughout the thirteenth century and in some respects up to the schism of 1378, despite the ways in which King Philip IV of France curtailed the aggressive political exertions of Pope Boniface VIII at the outset of the fourteenth century.[20] Notwithstanding modern, Weberian views that tend to regard bureaucratization per se in a negative light, this extension of ecclesiastical influence need not have been a problem, if Christian ideals had been largely realized. To have expanded the scope of an institution that helped more people live in communities more nearly as Jesus taught they should live—worshipping God, practicing the spiritual and corporal works of mercy, cultivating the virtues, receiving the sacraments, exercising religious devotion, and in general furthering the kingdom of God by following Jesus's commands as stipulated through the church—would have been a desirable thing in the judgment of nearly all medieval Christians, clergy and laity alike. No one had any illusions, given the refractory selfishness of sinful human beings, that this was achievable without some exercise of power. The real question was how far the power exercised could manage to be genuinely charitable and persuasive as opposed to merely coercive, for coercion without *caritas* would render the church itself unchristian in this respect on Jesus's own terms. To the extent that the Gregorian reforms, elaboration of canon law, patronage of universities, support of new religious orders, deputizing of inquisitors to combat dangerous doctrinal errors, approval of popular devotions, more frequent celebration of the liturgy, and supervision of episcopal and abbatial appointments promoted Christian life in the kingdom of God, there was not a problem. There was rather an extension and expansion of Jesus's command to preach and to live the good news.

But—and this is the third and by far the most consequential point—the church as a whole and in practice never closely resembled the kingdom of God proclaimed by Jesus, despite the way in which late medieval theologians self-flatteringly tended to identify the two. In fact, by the fourteenth century, the *more* the church lengthened its bureaucratic reach and influence, the *less* did it look like the kingdom. This caused serious trouble, because by then the church's very pervasiveness, "religious in coloration, but political, social, and cultural in expression,"[21] in effect proclaimed not the good but the bad news always, everywhere, and among everyone, as it were—in papal and prelatic simony and nepotism, clerical greed and other forms of immorality, lay indifference and ignorance, and in any number of other ways. Whatever the church's preservation, proclamation, and celebration of God's actions in history, above all in the incarnation and resurrection of Jesus, the gap between the church's truth claims and the actions of many Christians was in general readily apparent and sometimes enormous.

The church's hierarchical structure and the *plenitudo potestatis* claimed by medieval popes provided an effective, authoritative court of appeal in disputed doctrinal and disciplinary matters within the church. But it also thrust the *vicarius Christi* into a singular spotlight. If St. Peter's successor flouted the very virtues and values he was supposed to promote, if the one "set above nations" blatantly failed to live like a participant in the kingdom of God, if the "servant of the servants of God" was serving himself and fleecing the flock he was supposed to be shepherding, then the consequences were bound to be damaging in proportion to the exaltation of papal claims. And they were. In such a boldly asserted and jealously guarded hierarchy, adverse papal example at the font of authority could not but affect others ecclesiastically downstream: worldly cardinals at the papal court; nonresident bishops who had purchased their frequently plural sees; secular and regular clergy who sought to work the system to their advantage; and those in minor orders who endeavored, like Lazarus, to eat the scraps that fell from the rich men's tables. Flouting the faith might also prompt criticism, anger, cynicism, indifference, or all of the above. Could parish priests be expected to desist from keeping concubines if privileged prelates had courtesans? And could the laity be expected to keep marital fidelity if priests contravened their clerical vows of celibacy?

According to the Gospels, Jesus had been a carpenter's son among simple fishermen and Palestinian peasants who warned that "it is easier for a camel to go through the eye of a needle than for a rich man to enter the kingdom of God" (Mt 19:24, Mk 10:25, Lk 18:25). In a preindustrial economy of relative scarcity, a contextually wealthy institution such as the medieval church was courting critique if ostentatiously well-off prelates seemed not only avaricious but also self-righteously self-justificatory about it. And often they did, usually in proportion to their rank in the ecclesiastical hierarchy. From Hildegard of Bingen (1098–1179) to Catherine of Genoa (1447–1510) and after, the gulf between prescriptions and practices, between the kingdom of God and the actual church, was obvious to everyone who was serious about living as Jesus had commanded. The sinfulness of Christians, including its leaders, inspired apocalyptic warnings by holy men and women, from Joachim of Fiore (1135–1202) to Girolamo Savonarola (1452–1498) and beyond. No wonder some fourteenth-century Italian thinkers, such as Dante and Marsilius of Padua, argued for an end to political *sacerdotium*: all the church's public power, they said, should be ceded to nonecclesiastical Christian rulers.[22] John Wyclif and John Hus radicalized Augustine's ecclesiological reflections and juxtaposed the sordid realities of the all-too-visible, Roman church under the pope to an invisible, true church of the elect directly under Christ.[23]

If the efficacy of the church's sacraments had depended on its clergy's holiness rather than on God's power and Jesus's actions, there might well have been cause for despair. It was perhaps consoling that even Jesus had been denied three times in his direst hour by the very man, the Petrine rock, on whom he had established his church. Fortunately for the church's leaders and so many other Christians, Jesus had told his followers to forgive those who wronged them as many times as they sinned, for "if there is repentance, you must forgive" (cf. Mt 18:21–22, Lk 17:3–4). In the sacrament of penance, he had mercifully provided a structured means for the forgiveness of sins, having told his disciples after his resurrection, "If you forgive the sins of any, they are forgiven them" (Jn 20:23). And it was a *very* good thing that the once-for-all sacrifice of the Lamb of God in his passion and death, represented in the Mass, was one that "takes away the sins of the world": *Agnus Dei, qui tollis peccata mundi, miserere nobis.* In the Middle Ages there were ample reasons to pray, "Have mercy on us."

The chasm between ideals and realities provided the wellspring for the recurrent waves of Christian reform between the eleventh and the early sixteenth centuries, from popular movements and an effusion of new monastic foundations, to the explosive urban and university success of the Dominicans and Franciscans, to the austere piety of the *devotio moderna,* the Observantine revitalization of religious orders, and the humanists' scholarship in the service of moral reform. Sometimes—and only in some respects— exceptional popes such as Innocent III (r. 1198–1216) led the way by example, in the tradition of Leo IX (r. 1049–1054) and Gregory VII (r. 1073–1085). More often popes defended the status quo or exacerbated the very problems that reforms sought to address, at most sanctioning minor alterations rather than seeking to effect any major changes *in capite et membris.* For the latter would have meant stripping themselves of pride and pretense, nakedly facing themselves and the call to conversion, as did those men and women genuinely seeking to imitate Jesus as vowed religious—or who, depending on circumstances, deliberately *declined* professed religious life *in order* to pursue holiness, as did the Brothers and Sisters of the Common Life in the late fourteenth and fifteenth centuries.[24] Earnest popes who acted on their faith—as to an extent was true of Benedict XII (r. 1334– 1342), the Cistercian pope at Avignon—threatened an ever-burgeoning ecclesiastical money-making machine and an ever more lavish papal court, which at Avignon became resident in the imposing papal palace financed by none other than the personally austere Benedict.[25] The popes of the tenth and early eleventh centuries had on the whole been a sorrier, more debauched, and more politically manipulated lot than were those who ruled the church from Avignon[26]—but by the fourteenth century, popes were much more influential and the church's institutions much more pervasive than either had been four centuries before. Clerical sins were therefore proportionally more consequential because more visible, at the curial source and in all the streams that flowed from it. More was seen and became fodder for gossip, too, because Avignon was much more accessible than Rome had been for the large majority of traveling Christians, including those seeking favors and deals from papal patrons.

By the 1450s the papacy was securely back in Rome. However ably Renaissance popes such as Alexander VI (r. 1492–1503) and Julius II (r. 1503– 1513) did some things at the outset of the sixteenth century, they also perpetuated long-standing traditions. Aside from the continuing venality, luxury, and blatant violations of Christian morality at the papal court, it was impossible to misread Alexander VI's penchant for granting nepotistic favors, including the multiple episcopal sees bestowed on one of his illegitimate children, Cesare, a ruthlessly violent instrument of Borgia expansionist ambitions much admired by Machiavelli as a model to be imitated.[27] Nor could anyone misinterpret the spectacular self-aggrandizement on display when Julius II, arrayed in full armor, led his own mercenary troops into battle on horseback. Was this political *caritas* in action? Erasmus satirized Julius posthumously as having been barred from heaven by St. Peter himself.[28] Machiavelli blended cynicism with commendation, whereas Erasmus was shocked; but *Il principe* was written by a hardened veteran of Italian political machinations, whereas *Julius exclusus* was the work of the morally earnest proponent of a humanistic *philosophia Christi*. In their respective ways, each comprehended the papacy in the early sixteenth century.

After 1378 the crisis of the schism had made a bad situation worse. It set in motion changes that prompted secular authorities increasingly to take matters of ecclesiastical reform and control of the church into their own hands, in keeping with their duty to preserve and promote the faith. The French crown's influence on the Avignonese papacy (1309–1377) rankled many, but in some respects it simply installed a steadier French (and Languedocian) influence on the papacy in exchange for rough competition among aristocratic Roman families. And however much clergy and laity alike complained about the explosive expansion in the sale of indulgences and benefices in what Petrarch, a third-order Franciscan, called "the Babylon on the Rhone," many of them (including Petrarch) availed themselves—demand exceeded supply.[29] Small wonder that the Spiritual Franciscans, champions of their *poverello* founder's radical poverty in the *usus pauper* controversy, were finally condemned in the late 1310s, or that the indulgence of the papal court at Avignon—had it also provoked God's wrath in the Black Death?—inspired apocalyptic warnings.[30] But the schism that began in 1378 was a different *kind* of crisis, a conflict about authority and power between elected, rival claimants to the see of St. Peter. It divided Christendom into two mutually exclusive, mutually excommunicated religio-political allegiances. It inspired novel developments in the canon-legal ecclesiological theory of conciliarism in order to address an emergency situation.[31] At first the new conciliarism exacerbated the problem, when in 1409 the Council of Pisa's efforts to end the schism inadvertently led to a third rival pope. The Council of Constance successfully addressed the situation, however, deposing the contenders and electing Martin V in 1417. In the decree *Haec sancta* (1415), the council departed strikingly from long-standing Christian church governance and the ecclesiological emergency at hand in formally declaring that councils were jurisdictionally superior in authority to popes. Two years later, in another unprecedented departure from traditional ecclesiological theory and practice, the decree *Frequens* called for regularly convoked councils as a permanent feature of church governance.

The tug-of-war between Eugenius IV (r. 1431–1447) and conciliarists during the 1430s at the Council of Basel provided a new opportunity for secular rulers.[32] Whatever the mix of motives in particular cases, lay rulers capitalized on the clash within the church both to strengthen their power and to assume greater control of ecclesiastical reform in the regions under their authority. Forced by political conditions out of Rome and into exile in 1434, Eugenius was doubly desperate because papal income had plummeted by almost two-thirds from 1427 to 1436.[33] By exploiting the strife between papalists and conciliarists to their advantage, secular rulers followed the pattern of the concordats previously negotiated with Martin V in 1418, gaining further at the expense of the church through the Pragmatic Sanction of Bourges in 1438, the Acceptation of Mainz in 1439, an arrangement with Aragon in 1443, and the Concordat of Vienna in 1448. Ultimately, rulers backed the papacy against conciliarism and Basel's implosions, but only after having exacted major tax reductions and much greater control over ecclesiastical affairs. The Renaissance papacy, restored to Rome by the 1450s, had triumphed over conciliarism, but with its political wings clipped— which, insofar as popes sought to live as princely cultural patrons among their quattrocento peers on the Italian peninsula, placed enormous pressure on them to find new sources of income. Which they did—hence the actions of Alexander VI and Julius II, for example, as well as of Leo X (r. 1513–1521), who more than doubled the number of papal venal offices, to over 2,200.[34] Secular leaders had to a large extent regained the control over the church that had been wrested from their predecessors by the clerical authorities who devised and implemented the Gregorian reforms beginning in the second half of the eleventh century. As it happened, the pendulum would never swing back again.

Tired of prelates making the church worse instead of better, significant numbers of secular authorities at every level used their new power to oversee ecclesiastical reforms in their respective regions, "anxious to have churchmen perform their religious duties and religious houses uphold their reputations."[35] Kings appointed bishops and abbots within the territories they governed, and some, such as Ferdinand and Isabella of Spain, founders of the Spanish Inquisition, were major patrons of Observant religious houses.[36] Territorial princes in the Holy Roman Empire, including the Emperor Sigismund (r. 1433–1437) himself, began reforming the church on their terms, because so few aristocratic prince-bishops evinced significant interest or initiative.[37] City councils of the free imperial cities took charge of ecclesiastical life in their towns: they self-consciously regarded them as sacral communities, fully in keeping with the responsible Christian exercise of power over embodied souls.[38] They increasingly excluded bishops from the very cities in which their sees were located, thereby diminishing episcopal influence over urban religious life. Civic authorities themselves regularly funded preacherships, and they appointed pastors to vacancies and regulated monastic houses within the walls of their cities to the extent that they could.[39] Although far from all secular authorities were diligent and devout, to an unprecedented degree they were controlling the church. They were simultaneously promoting piety and increasing their own power, a development that would continue and intensify after 1520 in an unexpectedly altered context.

Viewed in comparison to the Reformation, what is most striking about this fifteenth-century process is the extent to which it presupposed and sought to promote inherited Christian teachings and practices. Indeed, greater secular control over the church coincided with the efflorescence of demand-driven devotion noted in Chapter 2.[40] With the exception of Bohemia, in their desire for ecclesiastical *reformatio* within their respective cities or regions, secular authorities did not seek to alter the content of the church's truth claims, their bases, or the practices that presupposed them.[41] They did not seek to change the church's teachings or worship. For *these* claims and practices, they believed, went back to Jesus himself, to God's actions in history through the incarnation and resurrection, having been passed down through God's word in scripture as interpreted within the church's tradition, re-presented in its liturgy, and embodied most nearly in the lives of its saints. Secular authorities seem to have agreed with the general of the Augustinian order, Giles of Viterbo, who preached the sermon to open the Fifth Lateran Council in 1512, that the root problem in the church was not what it taught but how appallingly so many Christians lived. In Giles's dictum, "human beings must be changed by the dictates of religion, not religion by human beings."[42] However sinful were the behaviors of the clergy or laity, of popes or peasants, they could not undo God's actions, nor revoke Jesus's promises to Peter and the apostles; nor could they nullify papal or episcopal authority, take back the coming of the Holy Spirit, disempower the efficacy of the sacraments, empty the Eucharist of Jesus's real presence, or get round the church's necessary unicity as a corollary of the impossibility of truth contradicting truth. So no matter how grave the practical problems, no matter how deep the chasm between the kingdom of God and the actual church, no matter how intense the "normative centering" of fifteenth-century theological and devotional emphases,[43] the only recourse for secular authorities no less than for souls on fire was to pursue *renovatio* and holiness within the one body of Christ.

Whatever its problems, it was the only church there was, or could be: "one, holy, catholic, and apostolic." This recognition was presupposed by every attempt to overcome the eleventh-century schism between Latin West and Greek East, including the negotiations at Ferrara and then Florence that resulted in the ephemeral reunion of 1439.[44] The necessary indivisibility of the necessarily visible church (an extension of God's incarnation in Jesus and a parallel to human beings as embodied souls) explains why the medieval conflicts between secular and ecclesiastical authorities in Western Christendom were almost exclusively about jurisdiction, not about doctrines. Those who *did* reject the church's truth claims in the Middle Ages sometimes found political patrons, at least for a time—the Cathars in Languedoc in the early thirteenth century, for example, the Lollard knights under John Oldcastle in 1415, or the Utraquists and various other Hussite groups in Bohemia before and after Hus's execution in the same year.[45] But overwhelmingly, even when secular authorities' revulsion at sinfulness in the church matched that of zealous saints, they poured themselves into efforts of reform within the framework of its practices and the teachings those practices presupposed. They did not reject the church's truth claims, including its claim to be the visible, concrete instrument of God's salvation, which, until Jesus came again, alone made eternal life possible: *extra ecclesiam nulla salus.*

THIS IS JUST how Martin Luther started out, too. The intensely devout Observant Augustinian friar did not seek to establish a "different" church, as if there could have been such a thing. He knew full well what the letter to the Ephesians said: "There is one body and one Spirit, just as you were called to the one hope of your calling, one Lord, one faith, one baptism, one God and Father of all, who is above all and through all and in all" (Eph 4:5–6). Luther was no less aware of Paul's concern "that all of you be in agreement and that there be no divisions among you, but that you be united in the same mind and the same purpose" (1 Cor 1:10). But when Luther's initially implicit and then explicit challenge to papal authority via his objection to indulgences was rebuked and he was threatened, he came to draw the same shocking conclusion as had some medieval heretics: that the Roman church was now ruled by the Antichrist. And he invoked as symptomatic evidence Leo X's curia, "such an entangled, swarming mass and mess" that was "more wicked and disgraceful than any Sodom, Gomorrah, or Babylon ever was," as Luther informed the pope in a published letter addressed to the pontiff, which had made "the Roman church, previously the holiest of all, . . . a den of thieves above all dens of thieves, a whorehouse above all whorehouses, a head and a kingdom of all sins of death and damnation."[46]

By the time of the Leipzig Disputation in the summer of 1519 Luther had come to believe that scripture alone was the foundation for Christian faith and life, for in it, and not through his intensely introspective examination of conscience and penitential practices, he had found the living waters of God's saving word. His experience of justification by faith alone convinced him that the dialectic between Law and Gospel as he understood it comprised the cornerstone for correctly understanding God's word. It followed that the Roman church's teachings were mistaken wherever they contradicted his reading of the Bible, linked to his transformative experience of God's gratuitously given grace. Hence a Christian should be "courageous and free," Luther wrote in August 1520, "and not let the spirit of freedom (as Paul calls it) be frightened off by the contrived words of the pope, but rather move right through everything and judge what [the Romanists] do and leave undone according to our faithful interpretation [*gleubigen vorstand*] of scripture, and compel them to follow the better interpretation and not their own."[47] As we saw in Chapter 2, all other Christians did likewise who not only denounced the sinful shortcomings of the Roman church, as so many medieval reformers before them had done, but in addition rejected its authority based on their respective interpretations of the Bible. This meant rejecting in various ways many inherited Christian truth claims— often *not* in accord with Luther, as it happened and as we have seen, but in an open-ended plethora of rival views about "the better interpretation." The endemic, manifest sins of Catholic clergy and laity alike seemed to provide evidence for anti-Roman claims that unbiblical doctrine was Christendom's base problem. Reforming the church meant getting the truth claims straight, the source for which had to be scripture alone, God's liberating word itself liberated from the self-servingly sinful prelates and oppressive ecclesiastical structures that for so many centuries had held it captive.

Historians frequently regard the Reformation as a natural extension of secular authorities' increasing control of the church in the fifteenth century. Such a view distorts more than it discloses, because the doctrinal disagreements introduced by the Reformation radically altered the nature of the long-standing jurisdictional conflicts between ecclesiastical and secular rulers. If we are to understand the Reformation's impact on the subsequent history of the relationship between secular and ecclesiastical authorities, we must grasp what a difference the divisive contestation over Christian truth made for the exercise of power. In the summer of 1520, reversing the *Kirchlichkeit* of fifteenth-century secular authorities, Luther urged German nobles to reform the church *against* many inherited Christian teachings and practices. He exhorted them, for example, to reject papal authority, eliminate perpetual monastic vows, permit clergy to marry, "tear down to the ground the whole of canon law [*das gantz geystlich recht zu poden gehen*]," abolish or at least severely curtail all saints' feast days, raze pilgrimage chapels and churches, endow no more Masses and eliminate most of those already endowed, and do away with confraternities.[48] This was not a continuation of the ecclesiastical reforms pursued by secular authorities during the preceding century, but its antithesis—despite the fact that even in subsequent years Luther himself also retained other teachings and practices in common with the church whose authority he came to reject. Other reformers who rejected Rome (and disagreed with Luther) would retain less.

The relationship of post-Reformation secular authorities to the *churches* would differ critically from that of medieval secular authorities to the *church*. The pervasive problems of late medieval Christendom had opened the door. Struggles over the public exercise of power *within* the framework of the faith's teachings, practices, and institutions became public struggles over what the faith *was*, in print, from pulpits, and on battlefields. And as the remainder of this chapter will endeavor to show, the multifaceted conflicts among the confessional regimes of the sixteenth and seventeenth centuries would stimulate experiments in states' control of churches, which, combined in complex ways with other ideological and institutional developments, would eventually make almost impossible the pursuit of the kingdom of God as preached by Jesus, not despite but *because* modern, liberal states permitted individuals to believe and worship and pray—or none of the above—as they pleased.

In Luther's estimation, the Gospel as such had nothing to do with the remaking of the hierarchical political structures or the altering of the inequitable socioeconomic relationships characteristic of late medieval Europe. Whether the apocalypse was imminent or not, the Gospel was not a mandate for changing secular institutions in the world, dominated more than ever in the Last Days by Satan, the *princeps mundi*.[49] According to Luther, justification by faith through grace transformed human lives by obliterating the anxiety of consciences overwhelmed by their inevitable inability to follow Jesus's commands, thus liberating them for the loving service to others that flowed from faith.[50] Related to the clarity of his own experience, Luther modified the understanding of human beings as embodied souls in relationship to the exercise of secular power. In his treatise of 1523, *On Secular Authority: How Far Obedience Is Owed to It*, Luther hoped "to make so clear" the legitimate extent of secular authority that a path would be opened for the elimination of all abusive exercise of ecclesiastical power by the Roman church. Luther thus interpreted Jesus's dictum ("Render unto Caesar . . .") to mean that all human beings belonged to two entirely different kingdoms *(Reiche)*, each with discrete and respective jurisdiction over bodies and souls: "Secular government has laws that extend no further than the body, goods and whatever is external on earth. But God cannot and will not allow anyone but himself alone to rule over the soul."[51] Ecclesiastical authorities, too, even among the ministers of the restored Gospel in Jesus's one church, could have jurisdiction only over the public, visible externals of religion, never over the hidden interiority of faith and intimacy of the soul that belonged only and always to God. The heart, the soul, the "inner man" was free, and faith could not be coerced.

Viewed retrospectively, Luther's move anticipated Descartes's philosophical anthropology, with crucial political implications. For there were no disembodied human souls on earth. Even souls justified by faith, liberated by grace, and among the Lord's elect were always still enfleshed. So although Luther sought to curtail tyrannical domination by either secular or ecclesiastical authorities over souls, in fact his solution implicitly theorized the control of human bodies *and thus human beings* by secular authorities. In effect and as Luther elaborated the matter, a corollary to justification by faith alone was power exercised by secular rulers alone.[52] Members of the "priesthood of all believers" were interiorly as free as could be, their hearts governed only by God and his gratuitous grace, but secular rulers were the sole stewards of the public sphere within which *alone* the flesh-and-blood social relationships of Christian life unfolded. Or failed to unfold. And because according to Luther salvation and the soul had nothing to do with worldly power, all men and women were bound to remain in their social locations, obliged, following Paul, to obey political authorities as ordained by God: "Let every person be subject to the governing authorities; for there is no authority except from God, and those authorities that exist have been instituted by God" (Rom 13:1).

According to others, Luther was gravely mistaken about these issues. Indeed, the Gospel was inseparable from social, economic, and political realities that trampled on human beings, soul *and therefore body*, contravening Jesus's unmistakable, concrete concern for the poor and downtrodden. The medieval church had recognized this in its insistence that concrete actions in obedience to Jesus's commands were necessary for salvation, above and beyond the anti-Pelagian necessity of God's grace. This recognition was paradigmatically expressed in the biblically based spiritual *and corporal* works of mercy: "For just as the body without the spirit is dead, so faith without works is also dead" (Jas 2:26), a text emphasized repeatedly by late fifteenth- and early sixteenth-century Catholic preachers in France, for example.[53] Some anti-Roman Christians in the mid-1520s went much further, seeking the abolition of existing social and political relationships and their reconfiguration along egalitarian, fraternal lines inspired by scripture. The point of the Gospel was not to soothe neurotically scrupulous consciences through a hyper-Pauline demotion of the book of James, but to rouse sinfully complacent Christians actually to heed Jesus's proclamation of the kingdom of God: "Do not think that I have come to bring peace to the earth; I have not come to bring peace, but a sword" (Mt 10:34). Those who drew up the Mühlhausen Articles in September 1524, for example, took "action for themselves [daselbst gehandelt]" and "based their decision on God's word [ir urtell aus Gots wort beschloßen]": according to scripture, they maintained, rich and poor should be treated alike.[54] The most widespread of the commoners' reform grievances in the early German Reformation, the Twelve Articles, denounced in February 1525 the feudal rights of lords over serfs, "insofar as Christ redeemed and purchased all of us with the precious shedding of his blood, shepherds as well as those of the highest rank, without exception [kain außgenommen]. Therefore with the scripture it is established that we are and shall be free."[55] Thomas Müntzer, a former ally turned hostile opponent of Luther, elaborated on such notions in ways that went well beyond these and other lists of grievances, as did the Nuremberg printer Hans Hergot, and the onetime secretary to the prince-bishop of Brixen, Michael Gaismair.[56]

Had it been a mere exchange of ideas, the Reformation might today warrant a few footnotes in a history of theology understood as a subdivision of intellectual history. But Christianity remained in the sixteenth century what it had always been—a shared way of life, not simply as an ideal but in practice, inescapably social because of Jesus's central command: "Love one another as I have loved you" (Jn 15:12). And the Bible was God's word, his saving truth for embodied human beings with implications for that life understood as a comprehensive whole, including politics and the right ordering of society. Preached to laypeople of widely varying social locations and educational backgrounds in the early 1520s, "the Gospel" ignited a firestorm of anticlericalism in the towns and villages of the Holy Roman Empire and Switzerland.[57] Christian women and men were only too familiar with the shortcomings of their omnipresent church whose clergy and religious, they were now told, had twisted scripture and concealed God's truth from them. No wonder privileged priests were so self-serving and sinful! Sparked at least partly by such ideas, the German Peasants' War of 1524–1526 was the largest series of popular uprisings in Western Europe before the French Revolution, involving hundreds of thousands of ordinary villagers and small-town dwellers before it was forcibly suppressed.[58] It simply was the Reformation in its most widespread, visibly manifest, earnest early form.

Secular leaders drew the obvious conclusion: biblical ideas could be dangerously subversive. So their appropriation would have to be carefully monitored and policed. Reformers such as Luther, Philipp Melanchthon, Huldrych Zwingli, and Martin Bucer agreed—the "freedom of a Christian" was not a license to disobey secular authorities, for "whoever resists authority resists what God has appointed" (Rom 13:2). But Christian freedom also demanded a principled *dis*obedience and the cutting of all ties to the Italian, interventionist, money-sucking papacy and its usurpatious Roman minions. Predictably, secular authorities convinced by the reformers' truth claims liked the distinction drawn between the necessity of obedience to them and of disobedience to Rome. They liked hearing "the Gospel" accompanied by such "good news"—it would allow them, for starters, to appropriate for themselves all ecclesiastical property, including the many buildings and lands that belonged to religious orders, and to use it or the money from its sale in whatever ways they saw fit.[59] In two stages during the late 1530s, seizing for himself the vast holdings of all the hundreds of English monasteries and friaries, Henry VIII would demonstrate how thoroughly a ruler could learn this lesson without even having to accept Lutheran or Reformed Protestant doctrines about grace, faith, salvation, or worship.[60] Assertions of royal authority over the church were enough, provided they were backed by enough force. By the time Henry was demonstrating that his will was up to the task, a frightening, polygamist, and communitarian "New Jerusalem" in Münster led by the prophet-king Jan van Leiden had removed any lingering doubts among secular authorities anywhere in Europe about the dangers of religious radicalism and dissent.[61] Lest rulers' negligence permit another Peasants' War or Kingdom of Münster, rebellion under pretense of religion had to be suppressed in accord with the divinely given duty to "execute wrath on the wrongdoer" (Rom 13:5). Thus was forged the confessionalizing alliance between those Protestants who supported and worked with secular political authorities, and those who did not—in short, the difference between magisterial and radical Protestants. Throughout the sixteenth and seventeenth centuries, only a carefully controlled and domesticated Reformation would be permitted to exert a widespread influence.

As a result, Lutheranism and Reformed Protestantism became the great exceptions of the Reformation—precisely the opposite of how they usually have been and are still regarded. In light of the full range of anti-Roman Christians who made truth claims based on *sola scriptura* and its supplements, the vast majority of whom were proscribed, prosecuted, and punished, Lutheran and Reformed Protestant leaders were abnormal and atypical in garnering the political support of secular authorities. Andreas Bodenstein von Karlstadt (before he settled in Zurich in 1530), all the leaders involved in the Peasants' War, the Swiss Brethren, the South German and Austrian Anabaptists who later contributed to the Austerlitz Brethren (including Pilgram Marpeck), Gabrielites, Philipites, and Hutterites, plus the Melchiorites, Münsterites, Batenburgers, Davidites, Mennonites, central

German Anabaptists after the Peasants' War, spiritualizing Anabaptists such as Johannes Bünderlin and Christian Entfelder, as well as Caspar Schwenckfeld, Sebastian Franck, and Michael Servetus constitute an incomplete list of anti-Roman Christians who sufficiently disagreed with Luther, Zwingli, Bucer, John Calvin, and every other Lutheran or Reformed Protestant leader about God's truth to refuse to worship or have fellowship with them.[62] With the few, short-lived exceptions of "civic Anabaptism" in the mid-1520s and the Münster regime of 1534–1535, none of these Christians were allied with secular authorities.[63] And all this had happened by the late 1530s—never mind all of the many other anti-Roman Christian reformers, theologians, and communities that similarly rejected Lutheranism and Reformed Protestantism (including the Church of England's Reformed Protestantism after Henry VIII's death with the exception of Mary's reign in the 1550s) throughout the remainder of the sixteenth and seventeenth centuries.[64]

The very success of confessional regimes, magisterial Protestant as well as Catholic, in suppressing radical Protestants between Münster in 1535 and England in the 1640s kept the number of Protestant radicals small and their sociopolitical influence minimal. Thus the fact of *political approval and support*, essential to long-term success in forging Lutheran or Reformed Protestant confessional identities across a wide swath of the population, has for centuries been conflated with *doctrinally and theologically normative Protestantism* in the Reformation era. This is analytically unfortunate, because there is no intrinsic, necessary, or logical connection between enjoying political support and rightly interpreting God's word. No Anabaptist agreed in the sixteenth century that Lutheran or Reformed Protestantism was true Christianity, just as no Mennonite, for example, agrees today. Ironically, little has changed historiographically in recent decades with the shift in emphasis from traditional political and theological history to the social and cultural history of the Reformation. The same streams of scholarly attention long devoted to Lutherans and Reformed Protestants by confessional historians continue among post-confessional historians to flow in the same channels—not because of Luther's or Calvin's putative theological genius or the supposed sublimity of magisterial Protestant piety, but because secular power gave magisterial Protestant confessionalization a broad, deep, and enduring impact across large populations. As a result, because of their influence on the lives of millions of ordinary men, women, and children over centuries, Lutheran and Reformed Protestantism continue to merit the attention of post-confessional historians, whether or not they are interested in religion or theology. Radical Protestants do not warrant the same scholarly interest because their social impact was minimal. Chapter 2 showed, however, how negligence of the radical Reformation has distorted our understanding of the Reformation as a whole and obscured its relationship to contemporary hyperpluralism.

THE DOCTRINAL DISAGREEMENTS of the Reformation era both strengthened and changed the character of secular authorities' control over churches and thus importantly affected the churches and the experience of their respective members. For different reasons, Protestant reformers and popes found themselves severely constrained. The reformers' rejection of the Roman church left them entirely dependent on secular authorities for protection, beginning with Friedrich of Saxony's sheltering of Luther after the latter's excommunication by Leo X and imperial condemnation by Charles V in early 1521. Simply put, no Protestant regime was even possible save through dependence on secular rulers, without which those who rejected the Roman church would presumably have been crushed by Counter-Reformation ecclesiastical or secular authorities, just as medieval heretics (except for those in fifteenth-century Bohemia) had been. Protestant reformers and ecclesiastical leaders could seek to persuade and might sometimes secure significant political influence through their moral *auctoritas* and alliances (as Calvin did in Geneva, for example, from 1555 until his death in 1564), but never were they in a position to force the political hand that fed them.[65]

Nor were popes, as it turned out. For them, the Reformation entailed a much stronger and more threatening return of the conundrum faced in the fifteenth century by Eugenius IV with respect to conciliarism. If popes unduly antagonized Catholic rulers, they risked defiance ranging from polite inaction to the specter of full-scale withdrawal in the manner of Henry VIII in England. The latter prospect lay not far beneath the surface of French Gallicanism throughout the sixteenth and seventeenth centuries, and partly explains why the decrees of the Council of Trent were never officially sanctioned by the French crown despite the extraordinary dynamism of seventeenth-century French Catholicism.[66] Philip II of Spain, by contrast, in 1564 eagerly became the first sovereign to approve the Tridentine decrees, just weeks after their papal promulgation—"without prejudice to the rights of the crown."[67] And they were not infringed, in Spain or anywhere in the vast expanse of the Spanish colonial empire, prompting Pius IV to complain that Philip "meant to be pope as well as king."[68] But Philip knew who held the cards in the Spanish church—and every other secular ruler, Catholic or Protestant, was similarly self-conscious throughout a Christendom now deeply divided. Popes had no choice but to negotiate and play along if they hoped to retain some influence in regions whose rulers had not embraced Lutheranism or Reformed Protestantism.[69] The papacy's political subordination would likewise be evident when Catholic rulers ignored Innocent

X's juridical objections to the Peace of Westphalia at the end of the Thirty Years War, or when in 1773 they successfully pressured Clement XIV to suppress the Jesuits, despite the wide-ranging service to the church for more than two centuries by the papally loyal Society of Jesus.[70]

Whether they were Lutheran, Reformed Protestant, or Catholic, secular rulers controlled churches everywhere in Western Europe by the late sixteenth century and arguably even earlier. To be sure, they were not able to impose their wills to the extent they would have liked: their states remained bureaucratically scanty by comparison to modern states, and they were constrained by distances, forms of communication, modes of travel, and entrenched local customs. (This basic fact is sometimes forgotten by historians who, mistaking absolutist political rhetoric for reality, think that Foucault's ideas are meaningfully applicable to medieval or early modern European regimes.)[71] Depending on circumstances, Christians acting for religious reasons could be socially and politically disruptive in Europe into the eighteenth century and beyond. But in the centuries-long, back-and-forth struggle for the public exercise of power between secular and ecclesiastical authorities, the former had won a monopoly. When in 1577 Edmund Grindal declined Elizabeth I's directive to dampen puritanizing activities within her Church of England, the queen did not hesitate: she suspended her Archbishop of Canterbury for the final six years of his life, and after 1588 she saw to it that England's Presbyterian movement was crushed.[72] On her watch, England would be institutionally no godlier than she allowed. Always and only on the terms of sovereign secular rulers, churches in general would exert only as much public power and authority as they were permitted. In the confessionalizing sixteenth and seventeenth centuries, that was usually quite a lot. In the nineteenth and twentieth centuries, as nationalist and imperialist states not only controlled churches but also diverted to themselves the primary, deepest devotional allegiance and mandatory obedience of their citizens in what John Bossy called a "migration of the holy" from church to state, it was usually much less.[73] And in the early twenty-first century, when sovereign states rule together with the market, it is almost none.

In the early seventeenth century, Christian minorities could still cause serious political trouble. English lay Catholics sheltered missionary priests during the latter decades of Elizabeth's reign, for example, and shortly after James I came to the throne they concocted the Gunpowder Plot in 1605.[74] French Huguenots clung to the fortified towns granted them along with circumscribed privileges of worship by the Edict of Nantes in 1598, then became embroiled anew in military conflicts during the 1620s that ended with the loss of their last fortified town, La Rochelle, in 1629.[75] Religiously motivated subjects might still risk *rebellion* against secular authorities, as happened in the English Revolution when Puritans cast off Archbishop Laud's hated "Beauty of Holiness" and resisted Charles I's centralizing pretensions, temporarily unsettling royal control of the Church of England.[76] Lessons learned, instability was swiftly steadied as soon as Charles II was restored to the throne in 1660. Nowhere, however, did or could leaders in institutional churches dictate to secular sovereigns either the terms of the public exercise of power, or the terms of the relationship between secular and ecclesiastical authorities. Churches were entirely subordinate and dependent institutions. This reality was already apparent, for example, in England's seesaw shifts in religious polity between 1530 and 1565, from Henry's repudiation of Rome to the two-stage Reformed Protestant measures of the "Tudor church militant" under Edward VI to the Marian restoration of Roman Catholicism to the Reformed Protestant Elizabethan settlement, just as it was apparent in the Holy Roman Empire's implicit principle and actual practice after 1555: *cuius regio, eius religio*—"whose kingdom, his religion."[77] Consequently, one had to persuade a ruler to adopt one's version of Christian truth in order to pursue any ambitious religious initiatives, a fact well understood by the Jesuits, for example.[78]

Western states' control of religion in the early twenty-first century is a latter-day extension of the sixteenth-century control of churches by states. Secular authorities have exercised this control in many different ways in the interim, with divergent historical trajectories in individual countries and regions. But every one of these trajectories derives from sixteenth-century states' control of the churches. With the exception of the Papal States in central Italy before 1870 and some small Catholic ecclesiastical principalities before the Napoleonic era, never since the Reformation era has a church exercised sovereignty over a state. Only a long-term, comparative perspective can bring the distant past's continuing influence into focus as far as the public exercise of power is concerned. We cannot see it if we concentrate only on individual countries and particular narratives, with all their contingent twists and turns over time. Nor can it appear if our purview is internationally comparative but limited to early modern Europe to the exclusion of the modern era, or focuses on religious toleration for individuals but neglects the institutional exercise of power. Analogously, we cannot see the nature and implications of rival answers to the Life Questions since the Reformation if we concentrate on the vast range of specific answers that have been given, rather than identifying the small number of bases on which they rest and analyzing how the answers have unfolded historically.

WHAT DID EARLY modern secular authorities influenced by, committed to, and in control of their respective churches do with their increased power?

In addition to the many problems of late medieval Christendom, the fifteenth century had been an era of unprecedented devotion as growing numbers of lay people, whether acting on their own initiative or encouraged by the secular and regular clergy, willingly embraced a wide range of voluntary, discretionary religious practices. By contrast, Protestants made the sixteenth century an era of unprecedented emphasis on doctrine. In their divergent ways, all Protestants thought that the most fundamental problem with the Roman church was its mistaken truth claims, that is, its false doctrines. As we saw in the previous chapter, they offered their respective corrections based on scripture, variously supplemented by the inspiration of the Holy Spirit and the exercise of reason. Because Lutherans and Reformed Protestants were supported rather than suppressed by political authorities, theirs were the particular Protestant truth claims institutionalized in cities, territories, and countries whose leaders rejected Rome.

Catholic churchmen responded in turn with institutional gravity at the Council of Trent (1545–1563). They had no choice but to answer anti-Roman denunciations of "works righteousness" and to make more explicit—with a doctrine of justification that had never before required official formulation—the relationship between faith and action, God's grace and human exertion, that had implicitly characterized the practices and understanding of these issues in medieval Christianity. According to the Council of Trent, no Christian could save himself or herself without God's grace; but without a genuine response of the human will to divine grace, expressed in actions in accord with God's will, neither grace alone nor "faith" alone could save any Christian. So too, most Protestants rejected five of the seven Catholic sacraments, prompting Trent's reaffirmations of both the supposed dominical origins of all seven sacraments in Jesus's actions and their ostensible, divinely warranted efficacy.[79]

And so forth: the Tridentine counter-flood of Counter-Reformation anathemas raged against the torrent of Reformation denunciations of papist errors. There is nothing odd or mysterious about this. It simply reflected a clear understanding on all sides of the logical necessity that contrary truth claims cannot all be true. But it also had the cross-confessional effect of placing unprecedented emphasis on interior assent to the propositional content of doctrinal truth claims, whatever they were. It risked making Christianity seem more a matter of what one believed than of how one lived—of making the faith a crypto-Cartesian matter of one's soul and mind, *rather than* a matter of what one does with one's body. Still, early modern Catholics and nearly all Protestants clearly saw and rightly agreed that in order to live out the faith, someone had to articulate what it was. Only spiritualistic Protestants (mistakenly and naïvely) thought that by eschewing the emphasis on doctrine they could somehow solve the problem of what it was to follow Jesus and promote the kingdom of God—as if the truth claim that dogma was unimportant were not *itself* a critically important and contestable truth claim, and as if Christian piety and morality could make any sense apart from knowing what they entailed.[80] Unless there literally were no guidelines at all—in which case it is hard to see what the adjective "Christian" could mean, or what the point of its retention would be—someone had to determine what counted as Christian piety and morality, which unavoidably involved making truth claims that were necessarily based on something. No doctrines, no Christianity.

With so many thousands of commoners slaughtered in the suppression of the Peasants' War, Anabaptists, save for the equally ill-fated, revolutionary Münsterites in 1534–1535, left the wicked world to itself. Separating themselves from it in the decades after 1525, they miniaturized their efforts to follow Jesus—but did not relinquish the idea that Christianity ought to inform the whole of human life.[81] The Bible offered ample resources for opposition to Romans 13:1–5, the Pauline exhortation to obey constituted authorities that loomed so large in Lutheran and Reformed Protestant political thought in the early sixteenth century. Resisting Catholic and magisterial Protestant pressures to conform and comply, Anabaptists quoted the words of Jesus's disciples against attempted coercion by Jerusalem's first-century Jewish elders: "We must obey God rather than men" (Acts 5:29). In their estimation, oppressive practices wielded by authorities through dominant social and political structures made impossible the sorts of human relationships on which shared Christian life depended, although in the later sixteenth and seventeenth centuries, to a large extent, they made various accommodations with confessional regimes.[82] Today, Old Order Amish communities in North America make accommodations of their own, yet fundamentally agree in their negative estimate of prevailing political, social, and cultural realities.[83]

By contrast, magisterial Protestants, like medieval and early modern Catholics, saw in hierarchy God's providential structuring of society and a potential instrument through which redemptive power might be exercised to further the kingdom of God. With their increased emphases on doctrine, especially Reformed Protestant and Catholic leaders sought in their respective ways to advance it through right Christian faith, worship, morality, and practice. Viewing the past in the retrospective light cast by the Reformation, post-Tridentine Catholic leaders largely agreed with magisterial Protestants that too much had been tolerated for too long in the Bad Old Days, when implicit faith had been good enough for a largely illiterate laity and too many clergy had flouted their vows. Christians were supposed to walk the walk, and far too many had not done so. They had failed to pursue holiness by following their Lord. Hence the Tridentine fathers devoted themselves diligently to disciplinary as well as to doctrinal measures, expanding on precedents stipulated by the Fifth Lateran Council in the 1510s and the *Consilium de emendanda ecclesia,* the unvarnished recommendations of an elite group of cardinals to Pope Paul III in 1537.[84] The Tridentine representatives focused especially on the reform of the parish clergy, whose formation newly resident, non-pluralist bishops would oversee in their respective dioceses. Each diocese was to build and staff its own *seminarium,* a "seedbed" for the growing of educated, committed parish priests. Seminary-trained, New Model clergy would catechize and minister to and create a self-aware, devout New Model laity. Too much had been left up to uninformed, whimsical lay preference, with discretionary devotions running helter-skelter in divergent directions. More instruction, education, catechesis, preaching, exhortation, supervision, warnings, and focus were needed, because living the faith well required conversion of heart and profound amendment of life—this much was incontestable from Jesus's teaching. About all of this, magisterial Protestant and post-Tridentine Catholic leaders agreed entirely. "For such is the inclination of human weakness toward all vices," Martin Bucer wrote in *De regno Christi* (1551) during his English exile near the end of his life, "that no one is without need of a caretaker, monitor, and overseer of piety and virtue."[85] In large measure it was Augustine's vision, still—but now in the context of a divided Christendom whose magisterial Protestant and Catholic antagonists each claimed Augustine.

It turned out that these concerted efforts at Christianization would require the exercise of more consistent, surveillant, coercive power than had characterized medieval Christendom. As we shall see, this would have major, enduring consequences. Secular, lay authorities obliged, in what looked like a win-win scenario for them and the clergy. Not only would rulers discharge their God-given duties conscientiously; they would also get subjects who were more obedient, more disciplined, and less immoral. What city council, territorial prince, or royal sovereign could object to that? For their part, members of a better educated, more austere, more diligent clergy would have unprecedented, committed secular power at their backs in their efforts to instill orthodox beliefs and behaviors. Broadly speaking, thus were efforts made to create self-conscious confessional identities across wide swaths of Europe's population between the sixteenth and the eighteenth centuries, whether among Spanish Catholics, Swedish Lutherans, or Scottish Presbyterians. Post-Tridentine Catholic leaders were partially successful in trying to corral and supervise popular piety, but the local variety and devotional voluntarism that had characterized medieval Christianity persisted. In various ways it was not only permitted but encouraged, both in regions that remained Catholic and among Catholic minorities under Protestant regimes, such as England and the Dutch Republic.[86] By contrast, in keeping with their denunciations of most late medieval Christian practices as unbiblical superstition and idolatry, Lutheran and especially Reformed Protestant leaders drastically curtailed the range of acceptable Christian practice. They prescribed much more narrowly both mandatory worship and a voluntary devotion usually centered on the doctrinally guided reading of scripture. Protestant pastors did their duty and bid good riddance to the discretionary, lay-initiated character of so many late medieval religious practices, making sure that over the long term it became a thing of the superstitious, papist past. Well-trained, biblically educated clergy would be the arbiters of piety, worship, and everything else pertaining to Lutheran and Reformed Protestant religious life.

Truth and error are polar concepts: one cannot exist without the other. Because Jesus was "the way, the truth, and the life" without whom "no one comes to the Father" (Jn 14:6) and who told his followers that "apart from me you can do nothing" (Jn 15:5), the gravest obligation of ecclesiastical and secular authorities alike was to safeguard Christian truth and prevent the spread of error as baseline prerequisites for the salvation of their subjects. Unless *this* were maintained, any prospects for Christianity as a shared way of life would dissolve, for salvation did not consist in concocting one's own ideas that contradicted Jesus's teachings, or in following one's own inclinations rather than obeying his commands. In ways continuous with medieval authorities since late antiquity, no conscientious Catholic or magisterial Protestant leader in the Reformation era, whether secular or ecclesiastical, disputed the self-evident obviousness of this notion. Even when their own sins had been egregious, and no matter how spottily they had lived up to this responsibility, medieval rulers and prelates had assumed it since late antiquity. Adapting Augustine, Gregory the Great had theorized it in his enduringly influential *Regula pastoralis* in the late sixth century.[87] But with the Reformation, bitter disagreement about Christian truth found lasting, institutional expression. This changed everything, raising the bar for both vigilance and urgency, with the eternal salvation of souls now at stake in newly perilous circumstances. Fortunately, so it seemed, secular authorities were now stronger than ever and more self-consciously on board with their duty and mission than they often had been in the Middle Ages.

Catholics and Protestants were anything but "knit together in one mind and in one meaning" (1 Cor 1:10), as William Tyndale rendered Paul's words, so they could not build the social relationships required for Christian life in common.[88] They did not and manifestly could not agree on what Christianity was, despite all the convictions that the large majority of Protestants continued to share with Catholics—about the reality of the Trinitarian creator-God, the Father's incarnation in Jesus, the power of the Holy Spirit, the fact of divine providence, the inspired character of God's word in scripture, the necessity of grace for salvation, and much else. From the very beginning of the Reformation in the early 1520s, concrete experience confirmed conventional wisdom: nothing was more unsettling to a city or territory than heterodox men and women. They refused to help create and sustain shared Christian life. Indeed, they outrageously claimed that the doctrines and practices stipulated by authorities were not even Christian.

The first prerequisite for a viable community, then, was getting people to come to their senses—*metanoia,* conversion—and thus to acknowledge their socially and spiritually subversive errors so that they might resume their place within the community. Should even repeated efforts regrettably fail, as they did in a minority of cases, then in the absence of facilities for long-term incarceration (which would have been beyond the fiscal means of early modern European regimes, just as they are enormously expensive today) the only logical alternative was coercive expulsion, whether by exile or execution. That is what ecclesiastical and secular authorities had been doing with considerable success since the twelfth century, with late-antique precedents rooted in the Old Testament books of Leviticus and Deuteronomy. Catholics and magisterial Protestants continued it with variable diligence in the sixteenth century. How ludicrous would it have been to threaten and punish with death mere counterfeiters, arsonists, thieves, or murderers, but not resolute subverters of God's truth?[89] Authorities thought that not to have taken action would have implied either an indifference to Jesus's commands, or—*per impossibile*—some notion that Christianity might be lived and the kingdom of God advanced apart from the social relationships that both fed and flowed from *caritas.*

Secular and ecclesiastical authorities had made war and violence an endemic feature of medieval European life for a host of reasons, including dynastic claims, expansionist ambitions, affronts to honor, and opposition to Islam. Except for the Crusades, including the Spanish *reconquista* on the Iberian Peninsula and the Albigensian Crusade, these seem to have been motivated more by secular rulers' selfish ambitions, desires, and pride than by zeal for the faith. The Reformation era created opportunities for a new martial motivation in the eyes of devout rulers: the clear defense of God's truth and opposition to his enemies within a divided Christendom. If a ruler was willing to levy taxes, hire troops, and marshal force of arms for his own sake, or that of his familial dynasty, how much more ought he to have done so out of love for his creator and obedience to his savior? Which was the nobler motivation: to wage war for oneself or for God? Such questions seemed to answer themselves. Catholic and Protestant forces clashed in Switzerland in the late 1520s and early 1530s; Charles V defeated the Schmalkaldic League in 1547 only to have his gains reversed before the stalemate of the Peace of Augsburg in 1555; French Huguenots and Catholics fought a bloody series of eight civil wars interspersed with religious riots between 1562 and 1598, with further hostilities lasting until 1629; the Dutch resisted Philip II's suppression of heresy beginning with the *Wonderjaar* of 1566, their revolt becoming, against William of Orange's wishes, a confessionalized struggle that endured off and on until 1648; the Thirty Years War, its battles and sieges situated mostly in central Europe, involved nearly all European countries at some point between 1618 and 1648; and in England, Puritan resistance to Charles I's "personal rule" led in the 1640s to two civil wars and widespread disruptions from which religion was inextricable.[90] Never before had Europe seen such committed, extended, multifarious military sacrifice, at least in part for Christian truth—wars waged and lives lost "for the greater glory of God," as some Jesuits might have put it.

THE COERCIVE, PROSECUTORY, and violent actions of early modern confessional regimes are all lucidly intelligible on the terms of their protagonists. They all make perfect sense. That is why they are so shocking. In contrast to the relative success of similar actions in containing heresy during the Middle Ages, they also proved catastrophically destructive to the ambitions of their proponents and apologists. As things turned out, not only did no one win in early modern Europe, but Catholics, Lutherans, Reformed Protestants, and Western Christianity in general all lost. Collectively, their conflicts amounted to an unintended disaster that has fundamentally shaped the subsequent course of Western history in ways they could not have foreseen and which nearly all of them would have deplored. Not only did they create a poisoned legacy that has endured into the early twenty-first century. Early modern Christians themselves also unwittingly provided a firm launching pad for ideological and institutional secularization.

However eagerly English Puritans gadded to sermons and however enthusiastically so many post-Tridentine Catholics embraced Marian and eucharistic piety, authorities' breaches of *caritas* via confessional coercion created a reservoir of resentment sufficient to spring and sustain the secularizing, antireligious, liberationist ideology pervasive in the modern era down to the present. They made religion as such memorably associable with coercion, oppression, and violence, and thus provided ballast for the still widespread conviction that emancipation, autonomy, freedom, and modernity as such imply the supersessionist rejection of religion. Faithful Christians try to behave morally, because Jesus's commands are ethically strenuous. But as the next chapter will suggest, obedience to laws per se cannot replace the practice of virtues regardless of how thoroughly early modern rulers might have succeeded in ensuring the behavioral compliance of their subjects. The *mere* securing of social control by coercive laws and practices worked *against* the kingdom of God, because grudging conformity simply is not a joyful life of shared faith, hope, and love. As Pascal put it, "to attempt to implant [religion] into the mind and heart with force and threats is to implant not religion but terror."[91] "You know that the rulers of the Gentiles lord it over them," Jesus had said, "and their great ones are tyrants over them" (Mt 20:25, Mk 10:42). The same was true for the rulers of the Christians who, understandably *but disastrously* given the dangerous circumstances of a divided Christendom that followed from the Reformation, flubbed the extraordinarily delicate task of exercising power in the service of *caritas* as understood by Augustine and Gregory the Great.[92] The consequences were diversely manifest in early modern Europe. Given the opportunity, large numbers of people in the Golden Age Dutch Republic, for example, chose no church affiliation over any.[93] And not fortuitously did the eighteenth century see both France's furthest demographic penetration of confessionalization and the Enlightenment's most strident critiques of Christianity.[94]

With similarly disastrous consequences did the practice of executing unrepentant heretics and religious traitors backfire on confessional authorities and their respective churches. Eamon Duffy has recently referred to the burning of the more than 280 Protestants in Marian England from 1555 through 1558 as "a horrifying moral blot on any regime purporting to be Christian," noting with dry-as-dust understatement that executions for religion appear to "any civilised twenty-first-century person" as "both obviously and profoundly 'the wrong weapon' in a struggle for religious reconstruction."[95] Without question executions were profoundly influential in the formation of mutually exclusive Christian identities. Among magisterial Protestants, Anabaptists, and Catholics alike, angrier and more intransigent coreligionists celebrated those killed as heroic martyrs who had defended doctrines rendered ever less negotiable by their deaths, a fact that continues negatively to influence Christian ecumenical efforts today.[96] Already in the 1520s, protests were raised that killing others in Jesus's name for *whatever* reason contravened his parable of the tares (Mt 13:24–30) and egregiously contradicted his command to love.[97] Executions for heterodoxy inspired a discourse of toleration critical of Christian persecution that ran from Balthasar Hubmaier and Sebastian Castellio through Dirk Coornheert and Roger Williams to Locke, Bayle, and Voltaire, and has remained central to modern Western ideas about religion and politics, and even to official Roman Catholicism since the Second Vatican Council in the early 1960s.[98]

Intelligibly given the early modern circumstances, but in seemingly direct opposition to Jesus's commands, some protagonists even began to claim that toleration—allowing people to believe as they wished and to act accordingly—was itself an expression of *caritas*. How different that was from Jesus's intolerant treatment of the attitudes and actions of the Pharisees, who according to the Gospels he repeatedly called "hypocrites," "blind fools," and a "brood of vipers," or his treatment of the money changers in Jerusalem: "Making a whip of cords, he drove all of them out of the temple" and "he also poured out the coins of the money changers and overturned their tables" (Jn 2:15).[99]

Much more damaging than five thousand or so judicial executions for religious heterodoxy, though, were the millions of lives lost and the destruction wrought through the wars of the Reformation era in which religion played an important role.[100] Confessional identities were stronger by the late seventeenth century than they had been in the mid-sixteenth, partly because so many Catholics and Protestants hated one another more than ever. And frankly they had reason to. The historical impact of "moderate voices" in the Reformation era, however ecumenically edifying today, was minimal in comparison to the influence of the era's religio-political violence.[101] The era's polemical severity and ferocious intolerance are still routinely invoked by antireligious secularists as evidence for the putatively inherent character of Christianity,[102] just as Protestant reformers had invoked the failings of late medieval Christians as evidence for the Roman church's allegedly mistaken truth claims.

The "wars of religion" prompted dramatic innovations in political thought that, beginning most clearly with Hobbes, rejected the idea that had been at the heart of politics for well over a millennium—that a ruler's principal obligation was to protect and promote God's truth as the foundation that made possible shared Christian life in fidelity to Jesus's commands. Whereas Machiavelli had been cynical and pragmatic in *The Prince*, Hobbes was principled and systematic in *Leviathan*. The sovereign's role, Hobbes argued, was not to safeguard and submit to God's independently revealed truth, but to determine, define, and dominate it as a tool for exercising power, punishing anyone who defied the state in the name of religion. Small wonder: in January 1649, just this sort of defiant and rebellious zealotry had led to the beheading of Charles I. The entire tradition of modern liberal political thought remains Hobbesian in its insistence that "mixing" religion and politics, church and state, is an awful idea and an even worse practice to be avoided at all costs, the Reformation era's violence being the principal historical body of evidence, augmented in recent years by allegations of Islam's failure to see the light. The inseparability of Christianity from the exercise of power by secular authorities in the Reformation era does not diminish the continuing ideological utility of singling out "religion" as a supposedly discrete domain of human life particularly prone to violence.[103] The modern Leviathan must have and exercise a public monopoly of legal and political power and the exclusive right to punish those who break its laws. Its violence is legitimate; its violence is justified.

But theories aside, after the mid-seventeenth century, rulers still had to maintain order in their respective states within a no less religiously divided (though increasingly exhausted) Western Europe.[104] Their divergent choices presupposed the continuing control of churches by states. The greater intellectual diversity and toleration of the eighteenth-century Anglican Church, for example, contrasts in important ways with the staunch French alliance of church and crown against proscribed religious and Enlightened dissent right up to 1789, which in turn differs from the appropriation of Enlightened ideas in Spain under the devoutly Catholic Carlos III, a third-order Franciscan whose counter-papal Febronianism followed in the footsteps of Philip II.[105] In all these instances and others, however, ecclesiastical leaders were in no position to impose their will on secular authorities, who regulated religious affairs in ways they thought would best reinforce the state's "sinews of power."[106] The decisions of England's leaders had consequences different from those of leaders in France. For example, John Wesley, sensing little evangelical vitality in the Anglican Church during the early decades of the eighteenth century, sought to inspire those whom he regarded as complacent Anglicans with what he regarded as Christian truth after his conversion in 1738. Methodism subsequently succeeded in adding to both the vigor and the heterogeneity of English Protestantism.[107] Meanwhile, between 1740 and 1790, Wesley's French Catholic contemporaries published some six hundred titles explicitly defending the Roman church's teachings against the *philosophes'* antireligious (and especially anti-Catholic) polemics.[108] Had France's final two ancien régime monarchs showed Carlos III's openness to certain Enlightened and judicially Jansenist ideas, the Revolution almost surely would have been less catastrophic for Catholicism in France. Counterfactuals aside, however, the broader point is that Christians everywhere in late seventeenth- and eighteenth-century Europe risked secular sanction and punishment unless they remained within the limits of religious practice as defined and however defined by the state.[109]

THE DUTCH REDEFINITIONS were the most innovative, especially in Holland's commercially successful (and therefore influential) Golden Age cities. Reformed Protestantism had been the "public church" of the United Provinces since the 1580s but never became the established church. In contrast to contemporary confessional regimes elsewhere in Western Europe, attendance at Reformed Protestant worship services was not compulsory. Alongside this religiously dominant minority, ruling urban regents practiced a significant de facto toleration of most Protestants, a sizable Catholic minority, and even Sephardic Jews, which turned on a carefully monitored distinction between public and private space.[110]

The results struck the English ambassador William Temple in 1673: "It is hardly to be imagined how all the violence and sharpness, which accompanies the differences of Religion in other Countreys, seems to be appeased or softened here, by the general freedom which all men enjoy, either by allowance or connivence."[111] Dutch magistrates oversaw and regulated religion no less than did Charles II in England or Louis XIV in France.[112] But they did so very differently. They broke with more than a millennium of Christianity—as well as with Jesus's commands to his followers, about which Christians were so consequentially divided—in making the faith a private matter of individual preference. Temple described the effects: "The power of Religion among them, where it is, lies in every man's heart; The appearance of it, is but like a piece of Humanity, by which every one falls most into the company or conversation of those whose Customs and Humours, whose Talk and Disposition they like best: And as in other places, 'tis in every man's choice, With whom he will eat or lodg[e], with whom go to Market, or to Court; So it seems to be here, with whom he will pray or go to Church, or associate in the Service or Worship of God; Nor is any more notice taken, of what every one chuses in these cases, than in the other."[113] Christianity—or to use Temple's more abstract term, "Religion"—here has been interiorized, subjectivized, and compartmentalized.[114] Prayer and worship are compared to eating and shopping. Christianity in this instance is no longer even a worldview—or what John Rawls calls a "fully comprehensive doctrine"—much less an institutionalized worldview.[115] It is conceived as one wedge in the pie of an *individual* life, a matter not of shared obedience to the Word incarnate with eternal life in the balance, but of preferred inclination toward the "company or conversation of those whose Customs and Humours, whose Talk and Disposition they like best." In effect, this amounted to a subjectively sovereign Cartesian *cogito* breaking radically with tradition and making itself the creator of its own religious universe. Between this conception and religion as a matter of individual consumer preference in the late twentieth century there is an unmistakable connection.[116]

Indisputably, it *was* better in the seventeenth century to be able to worship together unmolested with one's coreligionists than to be persecuted for one's faith. Who could deny it? Beleaguered believers were understandably willing to relinquish hopes of promoting the kingdom of God at large in exchange for permission to attend Mass or to hear a Mennonite preacher behind the closed doors of *schuilkerken* (semi-clandestine churches), discreetly concealed in private homes.[117] As Temple indicated, *what* people believed and *how* they worshipped was simply a matter of indifference to others. This made sense in a setting in which shared religious beliefs and worship *already* were ceasing to inform the human interactions of political and social life at large, and in which many people were opting for different priorities. Across the Atlantic a little more than a century later, Thomas Jefferson would articulate a corollary: "It does me no injury for my neighbour to say there are twenty gods, or no god. It neither picks my pocket nor breaks my leg."[118] Or more colloquially, in an early twenty-first-century idiom: "Whatever." For what did beliefs about the nature of God, the incarnation, or the Eucharist have to do with "real life"?

Nothing, apparently. Or so argued Temple's contemporary, John Locke (1632–1704). Already in 1667, prior to spending several years in Holland during the tense 1680s, Locke asserted that "purely speculative opinions" such as "the belief of the Trinity, purgatory, transubstantiation" and the like give "no bias to my conversation with men" and are without "any influence on my actions as I am a member of any society." What seventeenth-century Catholics continued to regard as authoritative truth claims based on God's actions in history as promulgated by the church established by Jesus, Locke demoted to "purely speculative opinions." That was quite a reclassification. Then again, Locke was a rationalizing Protestant who believed that such Catholic claims were false; he was one of those numerous seventeenth-century philosophers who, notwithstanding their myriad disagreements, had great faith in his reason. He sharply separated doctrinal claims and forms of worship from "opinions and actions" that were neither good nor bad "but yet concern society and men's conversations one with another." These in turn he severed from opinions and actions that were "good or bad in their own nature," namely "moral virtues and vices."[119] In other words, by implication, society and ethics were separable from religion. So too were politics and religion, state and church, entirely distinct, as Locke put it in his famous and influential *Letter Concerning Toleration* (1689): "The Commonwealth seems to me to be a Society of Men constituted only for the procuring, preserving, and advancing of their own Civil Interests," that is, "Life, Liberty, Health, and Indolency of Body; and the possession of outward things, such as Money, Lands, Houses, Furniture, and the like," whereas "a Church then I take to be a voluntary Society of Men, joining themselves together of their own accord, in order to the publick worshipping of God, in such a manner as they judge acceptable to him, and effectual to the Salvation of their Souls."[120] Despite his very different epistemology, Locke's conception of politics presupposed no less a dichotomy between the human body and soul (or mind) than was true of Descartes, or indeed of Luther before him. On one side of the divide, human bodies, material things, politics, the sovereign state, and the exercise of all public power; on the other side, human souls, spiritual things, religion, the subordinated churches, and the ceding of all public power to the state. Thus were the things belonging to Caesar distinguished from and made to control the things belonging to God.

In the late seventeenth century the future was far from realized, but the seeming solution for taming a disruptive, divided Christendom was beginning to be articulated. In the aftermath of religio-political violence and amid the continuing suppression of religious dissenters in one way or another in most countries, a bargain was struck. "Freedom of religion" would triumph, whereas Christianity as an institutionalized worldview would be abandoned like the wake left behind a Dutch merchant ship in the North Sea. By offering satisfaction to individuals who were understandably content to believe as they pleased and worship as they wished, given the track record and character of confessional regimes since the 1520s, "society"—the public life of power, politics, capitalism, nonecclesiastical institutions, and "normal," "nonsectarian" social interactions—had in principle, at least embryonically, found its way free of "religion," which had simultaneously become something definable and separable from the rest of human life. Such a society would doubtless be quite different from the forms of human life it was displacing, because Christianity itself was being so radically redefined as a private and highly circumscribed matter of individual preference.

Whether or not one agrees with Jan de Vries and Ad van der Woude that the Golden Age Dutch Republic should be considered "the first modern economy," its commercial success is much to the point, as we shall see at greater length in Chapter 5.[121] For as it happened, many more people understandably preferred to shop for wares along the wharfs of Amsterdam than to weary themselves further with endless doctrinal controversies, to say nothing of more violence in which religion was implicated. In addition, as we saw in Chapter 2, the very fact of persistent Christian pluralism in the wake of the Reformation seemed to suggest to certain observers that religion itself was unavoidably subjective, the domain of "purely speculative opinions." This continued contestation stood in sharp contrast to burgeoning knowledge about material objects in the natural world, which not only was the same for everyone across confessional divides, but could be usefully applied according to human desires regardless of one's religious beliefs.

If, even *after* the Thirty Years War and the English Revolution and not-withstanding reservoirs of confessional ill-will, private individuals would not *only* be content to believe and worship as they pleased but *also* remain publicly obedient to the state's laws as productive and acquisitive citizens, then the state had a chance to salvage the societal wreckage wrought by religio-political violence. It could turn inside out all the confessional assumptions about how best to control churches and manage religion. Not by coercing confessional uniformity through one established church, but by permitting all individuals to worship within the respective churches of their choice, the state would maximize the obedience of citizens in a manner that reinforced its power and stability. The circle of conventional—but now increasingly discredited—wisdom would be squared. The disaster of the Reformation era might be redeemed by elevating into a principle the individualism implicit in Luther's "Here I stand." Might not *all* be permitted to stand where they pleased? Indeed, it was to be hoped that individuals would be *more* obedient to the state and its laws *because* grateful *because* free to believe and worship according to their own inclinations or consciences. Then everyone could also share in the hope of material prosperity, perhaps even the "embarrassment of riches" that the Dutch demonstrated was the fruit of some measure of religious toleration linked with commercial initiative, scientific discovery, and Baconian ambitions to improve human life.[122] Although such acquisitive aspirations were antithetical to Jesus's commands as an alternative to the ways of the world—"one's life does not consist in the abundance of possessions" (Lk 12:15)—they seemed obviously preferable to further fruitless rounds of confessional violence. As we shall see further in Chapter 5, not only in the Dutch Republic did most people of all socioeconomic ranks apparently like consumer goods in the seventeenth and eighteenth centuries. Most people of all socioeconomic classes seem to like them now, too, heirs of the early modern industrious revolution and of post-Romantic ideologies of consumerist self-fashioning.[123]

Institutionally, the circle was first and most influentially squared in the United States, with Thomas Jefferson and especially James Madison as its chief theoreticians.[124] Several years after Jefferson drafted his "Bill for Establishing Religious Freedom" (1777), Madison grounded the "free exercise" of religion in the "individual conscience" during the debate over Virginia's prospective church establishment in 1784–1785, and then again in his work on the First Amendment to the Constitution in 1789 (the final version of which was so different from what he had originally proposed).[125] In practical as well as in intellectual terms, doctrinal disagreement and its correlative socioreligious pluralism were the principal obstacles to the establishment and public support of any church, including the Anglican Church that had been institutionalized in Virginia during the colonial period. As Madison wrote in his notes in December 1784:

3. What is Xty [Christianity]? Courts of law to Judge
4. What edition, Hebrew, Septuagint, or vulgate? What copy—what translation?
5. What books canonical, what apocryphal? the papists holding to be the former what protestants the latter, the Lutherans the latter what other protestants & papists the former
6. In what light are they to be viewed, as dictated every letter by inspiration, or the essential parts only? or the matter in generall not the words?
7. What sense the true one, for if some doctrines be essential to *Xnty*, those who reject these, whatever name they take are no *Xn* Society?
8. Is it Trinitarianism, arianism, Socinianism? Is it salvation by faith or works also—by free grace, or free will—&c, &c, &c
9. What clue is to guide Judge thro' this labyrinth? When the question comes before them whether any particular Society is a Xn Society?
10. End in what is orthodoxy, what heresy?[126]

These same questions and others like them—"&c, &c, &c"—had been constantly present in Western Europe since the 1520s. They lay behind the profound ambivalence about the meaning and scope of "religious liberty" debated by individual states in the years after the American Declaration of Independence.[127] In 1789 the unintended, open-ended Christian pluralism that resulted from *sola scriptura*, institutionalized by confessional regimes and cemented by more than a century of European conflicts in the Reformation era, would also be the deep historical context for the First Amendment to the U.S. Constitution: "Congress shall make no law respecting an establishment of religion, or prohibiting the free exercise thereof."

Whatever this implied about Congress, it plainly did not entail the institutionalization of the metaphor used by Jefferson in 1802, that of a "wall of separation between church and state." This much is evident from the continuing public provisions for churches and subsidies for particular religious practices in states such as Connecticut (until 1818) and Massachusetts (until 1833), a legacy of colonial-era Puritanism.[128] The important and paradoxical point, however, is that the fledgling United States could disestablish religion federally *because* the country remained "awash in a sea of faith" and was deeply shaped by Christian assumptions despite the unsettling effects on religious practice of the upheavals of the 1770s and 1780s.

Consequently, especially once the surge of American Protestant evangelization began in the 1790s, "the churches went about constructing civilization with little assistance from government or the social hierarchies that
had been mainstays of religion in establishmentarian Europe."[129] Moreover,
this American ecclesiastical disestablishment and the activities of disparate
(and overwhelmingly Protestant) churches were possible because the effects
of Christianity on the life of the nation were widely considered to be no less
positive than the influence of republican political ideas in the late eighteenth and early nineteenth centuries—despite the reality of chattel slavery,
still biblically legitimated, in the South.[130] After his presidency, in 1819 and
again in 1823, Madison expressed his contentment at how things had
worked out despite the form of the First Amendment itself: "the number,
the industry and the morality of the Priesthood, & the devotion of the people
have been manifestly increased."[131]

Not merely in theory but to a significant extent in practice, an open-ended
religious pluralism and a toleration more lenient than Locke's (it even included papists, despite widespread anti-Catholic discrimination) were contributing to the American state's strength and the vitality of its slavery-
sanctioning, Indian-displacing, democratic government. This amazed the
young Alexis de Tocqueville (1805–1859)—accustomed to French animosity
between post-Napoleonic royalist Catholics and antireligious republicans—
during his visit to the United States in 1831. "There is an innumerable
multitude of sects in the United States," he rightly noted four years later,
in the first volume of *Democracy in America*. "They are all different in the
worship they offer to the Creator, but all agree concerning the duties of men
to one another" and "all preach the same morality in the name of God."
Note here the distinction between Americans' diverse religious worship (in
turn a reflection of discrepant truth claims) and a collective, shared sense of
secular, public duties underwritten by a common morality. Consequently,
Tocqueville wrote, even though religion "never intervenes directly in the government of American society," it "should therefore be considered as the first
of their political institutions."[132] This was magic: the substantive similarities
among American Christians from different churches *with respect to public
life* rather than *relative to their doctrinal disagreements* were doing the work
that early modern European confessional regimes had sought to achieve
through frequently coercive, established churches, and which had resulted
so catastrophically in persecution and had contributed to multiple wars.
Through its control of disestablished churches the American state was simultaneously buttressing public political life—which in fact, as David Sehat
as recently argued, remained deeply under the sway of a Protestant "moral
establishment" backed by force of law into the early twentieth century.[133]

In contrast to highbrow philosophical disputes and theological controversies in Europe, Tocqueville was struck by American anti-intellectualism, which included its Christianity: "Americans have accepted the main dogmas of the Christian religion without examination," it being for them "a religion believed in without discussion."[134] Tocqueville underestimated the intellectual importance of Baconianism and Scottish Common Sense philosophy among well-educated American Protestants in what Henry May called the "didactic Enlightenment."[135] Nevertheless, building on the flattering fusion of sentiment and sincerity championed by Rousseau, influenced by the Romantic cult of *Gefühl* in its various national colorations, and seeing in human feelings not only a sharp contrast but also a balancing complementarity to the hard edges of scientific objectivity, the nineteenth century on both sides of the Atlantic inaugurated an age in which religion not only encompassed human affectivity but was for large numbers of people rooted in emotion. (This age persists.) We saw in Chapter 1 how metaphysical univocity also contributed indirectly to the sentimentalization of Christianity by prompting a flight of faith to feelings, driven by the widespread (but mistaken) belief that modern science unavoidably discloses a disenchanted natural world.

Beyond this, however, and aside from that American propensity for pragmatism over abstraction on which Tocqueville also impressively trained his analytical eye, perhaps discussion of divergent dogmas was largely avoided because the European experience showed so plainly that it might breed divisive disputes and hostility. Despite the most elementary demands of logic, better to be polite and not to raise discomfiting questions concerning important matters about which people were known to disagree. Better to keep "belief" and "opinion" entirely separate from "knowledge" and "science," to let people contentedly believe that their respective beliefs—whether "twenty gods, or no god," trinitarian or Unitarian, obligation to or condescension toward the poor—could be true for them, and to make believe that flatly contrary truth claims might each be true for their respective adherents. Indeed, this was only to be expected of convictions derived from irreducibly personal, subjective sentiments and intimately interior, individual experiences. How could a sincerely felt feeling be false?

We see here the deep cultural roots of the individualism presupposed by the "Moralistic Therapeutic Deism" identified by the sociologist Christian Smith as "the actual dominant religion among U.S. teenagers" and many of their parents in the early twenty-first century, regardless of the particular religious tradition to which they belong. Extensive interviews in 2002–2003 revealed "the core underlying ideas constituting American religious individualism: that each individual is uniquely distinct from all others and deserves a faith that fits his or her singular self; that individuals must freely choose their own religion; that the individual is the authority over religion and not vice versa; that religion need not be practiced in and by a community; that no person may exercise judgments about or attempt to change the faith of other people; and that religious beliefs are ultimately interchangeable insofar as what matters is not the integrity of a belief system but the comfortability of the individual holding specific religious beliefs." In Moralistic Therapeutic Deism, religion is conceived instrumentally, its central purpose being to make one "feel good and happy about oneself and one's life." Hence one should believe whatever conduces to this end. God's "job is to solve our problems and make people feel good," God being "something like a combination Divine Butler and Cosmic Therapist: he is always on call, takes care of any problems that arise, professionally helps his people to feel better about themselves, and does not become too personally involved in the process."[136] All of this is certainly far from Madison's concern for religious freedom. Yet whatever his own conception or intentions, such an eventual outcome was enabled by his construal of individual conscience as an autonomous and inviolable court; it is what American laws permitted and protected, initially in principle and eventually in practice; and it is what the state's control of the churches made possible.

The practices that William Temple had observed among the seventeenth-century Dutch were upgraded by Madison into a principle for Americans: "It is the duty of every man to render to the Creator such homage and such only as he believes to be acceptable to him."[137] The laws guarding this principle meant that notwithstanding their social relationships in self-chosen communities of faith, the ideological scaffolding and political framework beneath the energetic, mostly Protestant churches and effervescent evangelization in the United States between the ratification of the Constitution and the Civil War was religion of the individual, by the individual, and for the individual. Thomas Paine understood one of the implications already in 1794: "My own mind is my own church."[138] Tocqueville observed more broadly that "in most mental operations each American relies on individual effort and judgment. So, of all countries in the world, America is the one in which the precepts of Descartes are least studied and best followed."[139]

At the same time, as Tocqueville saw, the Cartesianized congregants who peopled early nineteenth-century, disestablished American churches in all their diversity were indispensable to the nation's political life. Their faith was real, active, earnest, and transformative, socially important and culturally influential.[140] The workability of the disestablishment clause *depended* paradoxically upon vibrant churches and movements such as the Second Great Awakening that provided for their respective members substantive answers to the Life Questions. In addition to families, churches were the principal means through which were instilled the shared virtues, mores, and sense of civic responsibility essential for the robust functioning of a society animated by republican ideals. The prescriptive content of the country's foundational political documents was so thin and abstract as to be virtually nonexistent: "life, liberty, and the pursuit of happiness," but nothing about how to live, how to exercise one's liberty, or in what happiness consists. The sustainability of this deliberate ideological vacuity was possible because such questions were being answered by individuals in churches in ways that strengthened rather than strained the new polity. As Tocqueville rightly discerned, disestablishment's success turned on substantial Protestant (and much less numerously, Catholic) agreement about the *content* of truth claims pertaining to matters of human meaning, purpose, morality, and values; a distinction between public and private life and where the proper line between them lay; and the nature of religion itself.

The privatization of religious belief and practice pioneered in the Dutch Republic and institutionalized in the United States rejected confessional Christianity as a publicly shared way of life. With supreme irony and as a result of understandable pragmatic decisions, it repudiated Jesus's uncompromising, anti-subjectivist, anti-individualist commands precisely because disagreement about them had proven so costly in the Reformation era and in the enduring confessional antagonisms it left in its wake. Doubly ironically, however, by pointing the way to the emancipation of politics from any and all religious institutions, the American founders unwittingly laid the groundwork for the potential erosion of the church-nurtured, virtuous behaviors *of* the nation's citizens, and so for the eventual endangerment of the nation's own public, political well-being that *depended* on citizens who exhibited certain behaviors rather than others. Controlling the churches by disestablishing them freed not only political institutions from churches but also established the institutional framework for the eventual liberation of society from religion. It left public culture, political life, economic activity, and social relationships dependent on the individual behaviors that informed them, whatever those behaviors happened to be. The politically protected, ideological framework undergirding the socially and culturally efficacious, antebellum churches was radically individualist. What would happen if individuals started behaving differently?

Left free to choose, Americans might decide *not* to clothe the naked, for example, or not to feed the hungry, care for the sick, visit the imprisoned, or comfort the afflicted. They might choose not to engage in the many social outreach and charitable actions characteristic of so many nineteenth-century Protestant churches. It was their legally protected freedom, if they so chose, to live for their own enjoyments and pleasures and the acquisition of material things, to pursue the fulfillment of their desires while ignoring whomever they chose to ignore. It was constitutional. Each American citizen had a right to it. Such a life would bear scant resemblance to the teachings of Jesus, who preached the opposite: "If anyone wants to follow me, he must deny himself, take up his cross, and follow me" (Mk 8:34, Mt 16:24, Lk 9:23), warning his followers that whatever they did to the least well-off among their fellow human beings, they did to him (Mt 25:34), and that they would be judged by him accordingly. By contrast, lives geared toward the pursuit of individual, self-determined enjoyments would look more like the embodiment of Hobbes's ideas about the insatiability of human desires in *Leviathan,* or of David Hume's views about the power of avarice in his *Treatise of Human Nature,* or perhaps akin to Adam Smith's proto-Goffmanesque notions in *The Theory of Moral Sentiments* about the yearning "to be observed, to be attended to, to be taken notice of with sympathy, complacency, and approbation."[141] The collective impact of individual human decisions taken according to one's affective religious preferences and in pursuit of one's own desires would in time transform the nature of social relations in society at large. This was especially so once the entrepreneurs behind the manufacturing processes of industrial capitalism began producing material objects of desire in vastly greater abundance and variety than had been the case in early modern Europe. Thus was the freedom of a Christian and a crypto-Lutheran distinction between the two kingdoms, like Locke's sharp distinction between obligatory membership in the commonwealth and voluntary participation in churches, adapted and institutionalized in the United States.

But in some measure a concrete human *community*—not merely a de facto "society" of autonomous individuals who kept their private views to themselves and lived as they pleased within the state's laws—was not only the social product but also the social producer of embodied Christian faith. It always had been. Without it, beyond the micro-social context of one's family, it is unclear how one might learn to *live* as a Christian, as opposed simply to learning what to believe and how one should spend an hour or two each Sunday. Such Sunday mornings might satisfy people who had reimagined Christian churches as social clubs that could help them to feel certain ways or could offer personal consolations. *Of course* freedom of religion was a blessing compared to state-supported coercion or persecution. Individuals worshipping as they pleased in their chosen churches on Sundays could rightly thank God for it. But like devout late medieval Christians keen to follow their Lord despite being surrounded by so many manifest sins and shortcomings, American Christians also could read the Gospels with a clear eye—as distinct from the rosy lenses afforded by nineteenth- and twentieth-century ideologies of progress—and see how their society diverged from Jesus's exhortations. They could see the unplanned, cumulative, collective product of Americans exercising their freedom. They could see the costs of having construed religion as narrowly and interiorly as the free exercise of the individual conscience, whether in the increasingly pervasive effects of market capitalism in the nineteenth century, the deliberate flouting of Christian sexual and social morality in the 1920s, or the idolatry of the nation "under God" especially since the early years of the Cold War.[142] Controlling the churches by granting individual freedom of religion unintentionally created institutional structures that in principle left "the world" to itself. But what would happen if churches and families, precisely because awash no longer in a sea of faith but plunged into an ocean of capitalism, consumerism, advertising, self-interest, and popular culture, failed any longer to generate virtues conducive to the flourishing of a democratic society? It would become unclear where those virtues might come from. And it would become obscure why people whose emotional and social needs were being met by secular substitutes for religion would bother with churches or religious groups—especially if such people cared about making concrete changes in American society that churches neither sought to pursue any longer, nor apparently could bring about even had they wanted to.

This is the unintended situation in which Americans find themselves today. Freedom *of* religion protected society *from* religion and so has secularized society *and* religion. In *this* sense we are living, it would seem, whether or not one happens to be a religious believer and regardless of one's particular beliefs, in what Charles Taylor has called "a secular age."[143] Free human decisions and actions have progressively eroded any socially efficacious, symbiotic separation of church and state, most obviously since the 1960s, reversing the reality analyzed by Tocqueville: far from "all agree[ing] concerning the duties of men to one another," American Christians today simply mirror the increasingly rancorous secular political division between liberals and conservatives, with negligible numbers of politically independent, publicly impotent outliers at each extreme.[144] American Christians are divided about every significant, disputed moral and political issue, from divorce and abortion to health care and the environment. As a result, socially and politically conservative Christians manifest their concern by increasingly striving to shore up "family values" in their "Christian nation" amid an ever more secularized public culture, whereas secular citizens and many liberal Christians resent and resist their efforts as objectionable attempts to impose "sectarian" values in the public sphere.

The American judiciary is caught in the middle. Inescapably, it is forced to do just what Madison wanted Congress to avoid, namely to pronounce on substantive matters in the "free exercise" of religion. Judges determine what privileges and exemptions specific religions will or will not enjoy, which religious holidays will receive state approbation, what public expressions of religion are permissible and in which contexts, which branch of a church gets the ecclesiastical property following a schism, and indeed, even what constitutes a religion, "subordinating every particular religion to the supreme interests of the nation."[145] Unsurprisingly, reflecting a dissolution of truth claims once much more widely shared, the courts' decisions since the landmark cases of the 1940s—*Cantwell v. Connecticut* (1940), *Everson v. Board of Education* (1947), and *McCollum v. Board of Education* (1948)—have evinced nothing close to a coherent principle of either the "free exercise of religion" or the "separation of church and state." Indeed, Steven Smith has convincingly referred to the search for the latter principle as a "foreordained failure," while Winnifred Fallers Sullivan has argued that religious freedom is literally impossible in the United States insofar as the state determines what is and is not legitimate religious practice (in contrast to religious *belief,* which is left as untouchably free as Luther envisioned it).[146]

More and more, as once-shared values yield progressively to contested identity politics and rival assertions of entitlement, Tocqueville passes the *baton,* as it were, to another influential French thinker—Michel Foucault— whose thought, considered as an analysis of advanced capitalist democracies, is much more applicable to present American realities. Christianity in the United States remains superficially strong by comparison with Western Europe, but it is a mile wide and an inch deep.[147] As already mentioned, in the analysis of Christian Smith, "another popular religious faith, Moralistic Therapeutic Deism, is colonizing many historical religious traditions and, almost without anyone noticing, converting believers in the old faiths to its alternative religious vision of divinely underwritten personal happiness and interpersonal niceness."[148] To be sure, American Christianity remains socially vigorous among many of its adherents and continues to motivate acts of charity and generosity that help millions of people, without which the inadequacies of federal and state social services in the United States would be even more egregiously exposed. But the sovereign state wields all public power and legally permits, protects, and indeed indirectly promotes a thriving, dominant ethos of individualist consumerism flatly contrary to the heart of Jesus's message: you are your own authority, so choose what to believe, pursue your own interests, and satisfy your own desires.

So long as they obey the laws, Americans are all free to believe or not to believe whatever they want to, no matter how bizarre or demonstrably false their convictions.[149] The resulting heterogeneity and confusing religious hyperpluralism tends to reinforce the widespread perception of religion per se as irreducibly subjective and arbitrary, as we saw in Chapter 2. The freedom of each American citizen to make doctrinal claims has always greatly exceeded that of any pope. In contrast to the constraints imposed on popes by the Roman Catholic Church's tradition, all Americans can say what they think God's truth is, appeal to their individual consciences, express their unique opinions and make their voices heard, indeed start their very own churches. But this simply means that an anything-goes religious hyperpluralism is protected, incubated, enabled, and perpetuated by the state. (Look under "Churches" in the yellow pages of any American phone book.) The state's laws and institutions provide the framework permitting the arbitrary exercise of the will in answering the Life Questions, based on scripture, reason, feeling, or whim. The supreme value is individual choice per se, regardless of what is chosen.[150] The American social and political reality today is that churches *cannot* serve as indirect, Tocquevillian support for the state as they once did, because, with religion secularized via freedom of religion and subsumed by politics, churches promote so many countervailing values and virtues as a reflection of their members' individual preferences and desires. Submerged in the Western symbiosis of capitalism and consumerism, they have no influence on—and indeed, are almost always co-opted by—the acquisitive ethos and practices that dominate public life, except insofar as they contribute to and strengthen them.

Families, too—along with churches the long-standing seedbed of citizens' virtues, values, habits, and mores, on which the American nation's political health relied so heavily—can only diminishingly serve this support function in a manner that still informs society at large. Widespread challenges to the very meaning of family and marriage have been added to the many millions of divorces which, for decades, have exacted vast human costs. All this, too, is the product of individuals exercising their legally protected liberty, guided by the dominant ethos of a therapeutic society based on feelings. Lacking the indirect support once rendered by socially and politically efficacious churches and families, the state's new symbiotic partner is an all-pervasive consumerism wedded to a staunch faith in market capitalism, as we shall see in Chapter 5.

EVER SINCE THE French Revolution—at once the cataclysmic demise of the confessionalized ancien régime and the springboard apart from which subsequent European politics are incomprehensible—Western European states have controlled religion no less than has the United States. But none has done so with political institutions so deliberately free of substance and with such unprescribed, free exercise of religion for individuals. By American standards, the anticlerical ideology of *laïcité* regnant in France for the past century, for example, which restricts the public wearing of jewelry with prominent crosses no less than the wearing of a Muslim *hijab,* blatantly infringes on free exercise.[151] The recent, aggressively secularizing measures of states in once-Catholic countries such as Belgium and Spain (same-sex marriage in both, euthanasia in Belgium) seem driven at least as much by overtly antireligious, bigoted vindictiveness as by principle. The Church of England needs emergency life support more than it needs controlling, so total has its collapse been since the 1960s; the German state continues to keep its Catholic and federated *Evangelische* churches nominally alive with traditional subsidies and regulation.[152] Since the 1960s, church membership and activities have plummeted everywhere in Western Europe, even though opinion polls reflect a large percentage of people who in some sense or other "believe without belonging."[153] On the other hand, certain aspects of European welfare states since World War II—universal health care, for example, or access to quality education for all children—would seem to reflect Christian *caritas* more nearly than did either the American lack of provision for health care that reigned for so long (and is still far from altered), or the still abiding, tolerant neglect of the United States' neediest public-school children.

Millions of Americans seem still to believe the Wilsonian notion that the United States has a divine destiny and providential mission to accomplish in the world, that of "spreading freedom and democracy." Adapting Rousseau, the aim is apparently to force (at least certain strategically selected) others to be free,[154] if necessary through proactive military intervention, even if it means killing tens of thousands of the would-have-been-liberated and unsettling the lives of millions more. Early modern wars fought in part over conflicting hopes for eternal joy with God and the shaping of a Christian society were ostensibly absurd, but apparently, to judge from the Iraq War, preemptive, secular killing for the sake of the American Empire and its way of life is supposed to make sense. Having had quite their fill of the nation-state between 1914 and 1945, Europeans since the end of World War II have tended to be critical of such cocksure nationalist ideologies and the self-justificatory, violent actions they are liable to inspire. The astonishing demilitarization of Western Europe in recent decades not only has been a luxury afforded by a substantial American military presence; it is also a reaction against two world wars and their incalculable devastation in human terms.[155] In Europe, at least, the Great War demolished the peculiar nineteenth-century Western fantasies concocted of faith in scientific discovery, technological advance, material and moral progress, and nationalism, all anchored by competitive nation-states as the putative guarantors of goodness and the civilizing colonizers of backward, dark-skinned peoples on other continents. In their respective ways, Europe's confessional churches had been embedded in these competing nationalisms. When the latter collided in unprecedentedly destructive violence, the churches' days were numbered in part because of the nationalist-cum-imperialist realities with which they were complicit if not overtly supportive. Whatever the causal complexities, in the decades after World War II, the striking about-face in European attitudes toward their own colonialisms coincided with the precipitous decline in church membership and Christian worship. Decolonization and moral reckonings accompanied disclosures of the human realities characteristic, for example, of the ruthless "scramble for Africa" after 1870, such as the brutalization of indigenous peoples by Catholic Belgians in the Congo.[156]

Yet 1918 was not another 1648: unlike bellicose confessionalism at the end of the Thirty Years War, European nationalism was far from spent at the end of the Great War. By the late 1940s, Europeans had also reaped the horrors of extremist regimes bent on controlling churches and everything else with a murderous iron fist. In the case of Hitler's anti-Semitic *Reich,* a racist state's resources were marshaled to serve the industrial killing of millions of Jews not because of their religious beliefs and practices, but because of who they were.[157] In Spain, Franco's fascism with a different face cynically used *nacionalcatolicismo* as a tool in the service of oppressive rule.[158] Meanwhile, the twisted political religion of Stalin's Soviet Union, a nationalist atheism built on Marxism's immanentized eschatology, demanded the brutal oppression of the Russian Orthodox Church and its clerical "parasites," along with any other religious believers who dared to oppose its pseudo-scientific certainties.[159] It is hard to imagine that Europe's horror show in the first half of the twentieth century had nothing to do with the voluntary dissipation of its churches in the second half. Short of emigrating, citizens could not opt out of obedience to their respective nation-states, which continued to hold a monopoly of public power over churches. But they could stop attending church, and since the 1960s they largely have.

The actions of men such as Hitler, Franco, and Stalin—at once so powerful, deluded, and evil—understandably fostered disenchantment and disillusionment, which have cast a pall over much of twentieth-century European culture. Where was God in the Gulag and the gas chambers, in the "bloodlands" in which Hitler and Stalin oversaw the mass murder by deliberate starvation, shooting, and gassing of *fourteen million noncombatants* from 1933 through 1945?[160] Yet as dramatically as they have waned, neither Catholicism nor Protestantism has disappeared in Europe. After the Catholic Church in France had endured the Revolution's frontal assault and violent suppression, Pius VII's Concordat with Napoleon in 1801 ensured its institutional stability, while especially after 1848 popes set themselves defiantly against nearly everything associated with the Enlightenment and political liberalism, adopting an ultramontane siege mentality.[161] Ironically, this partially shielded the Roman Catholic Church institutionally and intellectually from some of the most potent secularizing realities of the nineteenth and twentieth centuries. Only with the pontificate of Leo XIII (r. 1878–1903) did Catholic ecclesiastical leaders seriously begin to engage the industrializing world, and only with the Second Vatican Council in the early 1960s did Roman Catholicism officially and cautiously appropriate some substantive aspects of post-Enlightenment modernity.

Vatican II did not prevent (and in some ways might inadvertently have contributed to) the demographic collapse of European Catholicism in the last third of the twentieth century. Among its participants were two men who had lived through Europe's midcentury traumas and who later, through their travels, writings, and media publicity, became for good or ill the church's first two celebrity popes. The first, John Paul II, apologized numerous times (if in the eyes of some commentators, still inadequately) for the countless sins committed by Catholics over the paining course of the church's history—although evil once enacted cannot be undone, only forgiven. The second pope, Benedict XVI, used his first encyclical to reassert and reflect on one of Christianity's central truth claims: *Deus caritas est*—"God is love."[162]

In ancient Greece and Rome, as well as in late antique, medieval, and early modern Christianity, politics and morality were inseparable. As an institutionalized worldview, Christianity had been before the Reformation the principal bearer of moral norms, virtues, and behaviors in Europe. The control of the churches by sovereign states and the subsequent separation of politics from religion also meant the separation of politics from morality—or rather, a transition from a Christian ethics of the good to a secular ethics of rights in combination with a distinction between public and private spheres in conjunction with the privatization of religion. The historical analysis of this process and its consequences is the subject of Chapter 4.

CHAPTER FOUR

# Subjectivizing Morality

I N CONTEMPORARY Western societies, religious beliefs and practices are
optional; moral beliefs and practices are not. Distinctions between right
and wrong, between acceptable and unacceptable behavior, are indispensable for living a meaningful individual life as well as for societal stability.
Whether one's beliefs are religious or secular, human beings are inescapably, in Christian Smith's phrase, "moral, believing animals."[1] But *what*
morality, given so many countervailing claims about right and wrong, good
and evil, what human beings should care about, and the ways in which
people ought to live? And why these rather than those moral claims—on
what are they based, in what are they grounded?

An unanticipated feature of academic moral philosophy in recent decades
has been the revival of Aristotelian virtue ethics, due especially to the work
of Alasdair MacIntyre. His point of departure is an observation that per-
tains to Western society at large as much as it does to contemporary moral
philosophy: ethical disagreements are pervasive, and there are no shared
means to resolve them rationally.[2] Appeals to reason denote not a common
method of argument or shared standard of adjudication—a point lost on
moral philosophers and political theorists who continue to employ a
question-begging "we" in their arguments—but rather open additional, vexing questions about different traditions of practical rationality and respective, related conceptions of justice. Because the protagonists of moral arguments do not agree about human nature (if indeed they think there is

such a thing), the human good, or indeed what ethics itself is or should be, they do not—and, MacIntyre argues, *cannot*—reach or even move toward consensus on the sorts of divisive issues characteristic of moral disputes in our era. Nothing that has transpired since the appearance of MacIntyre's *After Virtue* in 1981, whether among professional moral philosophers or in the public sphere of day-to-day human life, offers evidence to the contrary. Deontologists, consequentialists, contractarians, pragmatists, and natural law theorists continue to argue with the same interminable inconclusiveness in their respective articles and books. Perhaps most obviously in the United States there has been no movement toward a resolution of major moral disagreements concerning abortion, fetal stem cell research, responsibility for the poor, the support of public schools, the treatment of illegal immigrants, military interventionism, and other similarly contested issues. Nor can there be any resolution, according to MacIntyre, because even when rival protagonists present internally coherent arguments, they rely on incompatible assumptions that cannot but yield disagreement. Dialogue and rational discussion are themselves destined to be frustratingly fruitless so long as antagonists maintain their respective, underlying presuppositions.

MacIntyre argues that this situation is the latter-day outcome of the abandonment during the Enlightenment of the long-standing tradition of Aristotelian virtue ethics. Antagonists in moral philosophy and ethical debates today are and will remain at irresolvable impasses if they continue to ignore the history that explains the character of their disagreements. In seventeenth- and eighteenth-century natural philosophy, Aristotelian final causes were rejected and replaced by a conception of nature as a universal mechanism of efficient causes that encompassed human beings, and thus subsumed morality. Yet the elimination of any natural teleology from human life rendered not just problematic but incoherent the related notion of moral virtues as precisely those acquired human qualities and concrete practices whose rational exercise enables the disciplined reorientation of human passions and impulses, and thus the realization of the human good.[3] If there are no final causes in nature, and human beings are no more than a part of nature like everything else, then there *is* no such thing as human nature conceived teleologically in Aristotelian terms. Hence there is no natural human good thus conceived, and therefore no characteristic activities that human beings intrinsically must practice in order to realize an alleged *telos* and so to flourish. The rejection of Aristotelian teleology thus left the moral virtues marooned; they looked to some who rejected the tradition like outdated annoyances that objectionably constrained human desires. Whether moral philosophers have turned instead to post-Aristotelian conceptions of nature, or reason, or sentiment, or intuitions, from the seventeenth century to the present, MacIntyre argues, they have been proposing different conceptions of human beings, ethics, the purpose of human life, and the relationship between morality and politics, without settling or even beginning to converge on any shared framework to take the place of the Aristotelian moral tradition.

It is hardly surprising, then, that neither do ordinary men and women in the Western world today concur among themselves about right and wrong, good and evil, how human beings ought to live, or the relationship between morality and politics. Nor is it surprising, with so many competing claims and related behaviors and changing assertions over time and across cultures, that confusion is widespread, or that some people, whether ordinary persons or academic moral philosophers, argue for or imply that moral relativism and/or skepticism seems to be the only conclusion justifiably entailed by the fact of moral pluralism. In 1977, for example, the self-proclaimed moral skeptic J. L. Mackie opened his book *Ethics: Inventing Right and Wrong* with the confidently unskeptical claim that "there are no objective values," and in 1986 David Gauthier appealed to reason (as other moral philosophers also continue to do) as the basis for devising a "morals by agreement."[4] But no evidence offers any reason to think that agreements might be forthcoming, including among those who champion reason as the basis for their moral claims.

As MacIntyre notes, the widespread default in Western societies at large is emotivism, an ethics of subjective, feelings-based, personal preference, which only exacerbates the unresolved and irresolvable disagreements.[5] The de facto guideline for the living of human life in the Western world today seems simply to be "whatever makes you happy"—"so long as you're not hurting anyone else"—in which the criteria for happiness, too, are self-determined, self-reported, and therefore immune to critique, and in which the meaning of "hurting anyone else" is assumed to be self-evident, unproblematic, or both.[6] Because there is no shared framework within which such disagreements might rationally be debated and perhaps overcome, and yet life goes on, moral disagreements are translated socially into political contestation within an emotivist culture—one that is closely related to if not largely identical with the individualistic "therapeutic culture" diagnosed by Philip Rieff.[7] Protests, the exertion of power, and manipulation, whether overt or disguised, displace rational moral discourse, as has become ever more apparent, for example, in American public life and the media in recent decades. Everything becomes "political" because once morality has been subjectivized no *arguments* can succeed, since there is no shared set of assumptions from which they can proceed. Hence the applicability of Foucauldian notions of power to analyses of contemporary Western society.

According to most contemporary moral philosophers and liberal political theorists, the so-called problem that MacIntyre describes simply reflects the difference between premodern, traditional societies and modern, pluralistic ones. Modern people within modern societies realize that individuals within them reckon different things as good, and different moral claims as true; and individuals can do so because a typical modern democracy, unlike its premodern predecessors, recognizes their rights and protects their freedom to do so. There are no shared ways of rationally ordering or organizing the divergent, various goods that individuals happen to prefer, whether across individuals or within an individual life, because such ordering and organization, too, are matters of individual discretion.[8] On this view, the Aristotelian moral tradition was neither natural, nor rational, nor just, but rather a culturally contingent, imposed morality implicated in a false, misogynist philosophy that legitimated an oppressive social order sustained by hierarchical, inegalitarian political regimes. The overthrow of Aristotelian assumptions permitted the rational, just, democratizing liberation of modern individuals and the progressive, emancipatory "invention of autonomy."[9] As a brute sociological fact, human goods simply *are* heterogeneous when human beings are granted the politically protected freedom—the right—to live as they please within shared laws and this fact simply constitutes a foundational baseline for "deliberative democracy" in some form or other.[10] Moral pluralism is an unavoidable political challenge to be managed, a corollary of what Mill called "the only freedom which deserves the name," namely "pursuing our own good in our own way."[11]

In Aristotelian (and Platonic) conceptions, ethics and politics are inseparable from one another and necessarily part of the same discourse, because the good for individual human beings as social, rational animals depends on the common good that they acknowledge, build, share, maintain, and police. Only in a community made possible by a shared common good can human beings realize as well their individual good. In political liberalism, by contrast, ethics and politics are distinguished—or put more precisely, the particular, substantive moral views that individuals happen to hold and are free to hold according to their preferences are distinguished from and subordinated to the universal, formal and foundational ethical imperatives of individual liberty and equality, with politics and laws arranged accordingly. From Locke through Mill to Rawls and his contemporary followers, this distinction and its political institutionalization is the heart of modern liberalism. The overriding social imperative and the principal objective of politics is not the pursuit of a chimerical, substantive common good based on shared values—none exists—but the empowerment of individuals who desire heterogeneous goods and who affirm incompatible values to coexist in peaceful stability, which is itself conceived as the de facto common good. In this respect, modern liberalism remains Hobbesian (or perhaps Grotian) in its animating objective.

The way in which this is achieved, both in theory and in practice, is through a formal ethics of rights rather than a substantive ethics of the good: combining liberty with equality, an ostensibly neutral state (save for its absolutist, normative commitments to individual liberty and equality) recognizes individuals' rights to hold their respective conceptions of the good, whatever they might be, and to lead their lives as they please, however they might wish, within the laws that it stipulates and enforces, in a manner consistent with the same recognition for everyone else. In Rieff's words, "all governments will be just, so long as they secure that consoling plenitude of option in which modern satisfaction really consists."[12] As it has turned out, the highest political good is the maximization of individual choice, and the greatest social virtue is toleration of others' choices and actions. The only Western alternatives since the early twentieth century have been oppressive, Marxist or fascist totalitarian regimes that seek to impose by force a particular version of the "good," with catastrophic results. Hence there are no genuine competitors to democratic liberalism. Arguments such as MacIntyre's, it is alleged, amount to nostalgia for an ancient moral theory mismatched to the highly differentiated, diverse societies characteristic of modern liberal democracies.[13] In keeping with supersessionist views of history, (post-)modernity is thought to have left behind the premodern past and moved beyond its assumptions and truth claims. As Alan Wolfe has recently stated, "Modern citizens all too often forget that the liberal way of life is a good way of life, indeed, under the political conditions in which they live, the best way of life."[14]

That may be true, given "the political conditions in which [we] live." But what of the historical emergence of those political conditions and their implications for ethics? Note what Wolfe implies: "the liberal way of life" has *itself* become the governing good, indeed "the best way of life." This certainly was not always so. How did it come about? This chapter argues that a transformation from a substantive morality of the good to a formal morality of rights constitutes the central change in Western ethics over the past half millennium, in terms of theory, practice, laws, and institutions. Moreover, there is a historical relationship between the creation of an ethics of rights and the antecedent ethics of the good that it displaced, a shift that involves much more than the institutionalized triumph of putatively superior ethical and political ideas. Whatever the particularities of the process of its adoption (which included resistance and reversals) as it played out in different Western countries, the modern ethics of rights characteristic of liberalism has proven paradoxical: its makers relied on substantive, shared beliefs about human goods but unwittingly fashioned an institutional framework for their subversion. Today, the consequences of this ongoing process are manifestly placing increasing pressure on the concrete, everyday human relationships within the framework. Contemporary disagreements about ethical values and human priorities reflect a subjectivization of morality that has been centuries in the making and remains under way. This chapter's principal concern is to explain how and why this transition occurred, and to consider some of its implications.

The fundamental historical realities that drove the central change were the religious disagreements and related sociopolitical disruptions of the Reformation era, because in the late Middle Ages, Christianity—with all its problems—was Western Europe's dominant, socially pervasive embodiment of a morality of the good. As we have seen, Protestant rejections of the authority of the Roman church produced an open-ended range of rival truth claims about what the Bible meant. Correlatively, they yielded rival claims about what the Christian good was and how it was to be lived in community. Those who repudiated the Roman church uncoupled the medieval discourse on natural rights from the teleological Christian ethics within which it had been embedded. That discourse was transformed and the consequential trajectory to a modern ethics of rights established as a result of Christian contestation about the good, the violence of the Reformation era, and subsequent demands for religious freedom. In its reference to the importance of the Reformation era's religio-political violence—although not in its implication that "religion" in that era is analytically separable from "politics"—the liberal narrative of the emergence of modern rights is nearer the mark than MacIntyre's overly internalist account of the reconfiguration between ethics and politics.[15] Despite his proper insistence on the relationship of moral philosophy to social relationships and politics, MacIntyre ignores almost entirely the concrete disruptions of the Reformation era. Aristotelian virtue ethics was not rejected in the first instance or primarily because of a direct assault by Enlightenment thinkers, as a corollary of post-Aristotelian natural philosophy, because of the increasingly specialized character of academic inquiry in late medieval universities, or even through its repudiation by early modern Lutherans, Reformed Protestants, and/or Jansenists—even though all of these played a role.[16] Rather, its repudiation stemmed more fundamentally from its continuing association with Roman Catholicism in an era of deadlocked doctrinal controversy and religio-political violence.

Although many liberal political theorists and moral philosophers point to Reformation-era violence to justify the exclusion of religion from present-day politics, they almost always ignore other historical realities that were intertwined with the emergence of an ethics of rights—including the state-building processes that antedated the Reformation, through which nonecclesiastical authorities increased their control of the churches after the Reformation began, and by means of which these authorities were the most important agents in the "wars of religion."[17] As a result, nearly all liberal political theorists and moral philosophers tend to overlook the ways in which an ethics of rights, linked to liberal political ideas, laws, institutions, and the exercise of power, itself contributed to the construction of human realities that extend far beyond what is normally regarded as the domain of moral philosophy or political theory as such. Something cannot be seen if it is not looked for, and it need not be sought if it is thought adequately to be studied in a different academic discipline, such as economics, sociology, environmental science, or the history of science and technology. But if we want to understand human life in North America and Europe today, it makes as little sense to think about morality and politics apart from one another as it does to separate moral philosophy from political thought, or to sequester either of these from other academic disciplines and their respective domains of inquiry.[18]

Moral discourse and moral practice never exist in a vacuum. This sounds banal; everyone knows it. But its implications remain unrecognized unless we question two assumptions widely taken for granted: that we can adequately comprehend the character of either moral disagreements or citizens' political conflicts today without understanding their relationship to the past half millennium of Western history; and that there *are* discretely delineable, "private" areas of human life that neither affect nor are affected by the behavior of others and the public exercise of power. Regardless of the ways in which liberal thinkers and moral philosophers theorize the distinction between private individuals and the public sphere, concrete human beings are always the ones who interact in social and political life. Consequently, "what we do in private will almost certainly have a gradual and subtle, but very real, influence on the sort of community all of us experience."[19] In a reciprocal manner, public interactions affect the attitudes, values, aspirations, and behaviors of the same human beings in their particular, personal relationships. Private life and public life are inseparable in real life.

However open-ended the pluralism that it permits, a modern ethics of rights requires that those whose rights it protects share certain values and commitments—certain goods—among their preferences. Otherwise the state would have to be crushingly oppressive in order to insure social stability.[20] The more heterogeneous the preferred goods of flesh-and-blood human beings in democratic civil society, the more difficult does the achievement of a Rawlsian "overlapping consensus" among those with different "comprehensive theories"—or simply preferred desires—become, and the more difficult is the task of the state in ensuring peace and civility, let alone something resembling a justice widely reckoned as legitimate by its citizens. When political institutions and laws that enshrined a formal ethics of rights began to be created in the late eighteenth century, the shared beliefs drawn upon were overwhelmingly derived from Christianity despite intra-Christian doctrinal antagonisms and social exclusivities, and notwithstanding the non-confessional language in which the articulation of rights was couched. As we saw in the previous chapter with respect to the role of churches, for most Western Europeans and North Americans throughout the nineteenth century and into the twentieth, those largely shared beliefs and related goods continued to provide the moral content that rendered socially and concretely viable the formal commitments to the goods of liberty and equality.

Advanced secularization in recent decades, however, has profoundly affected the historical consequences of the ethics of rights institutionalized in modern Western states. In society at large, aside from the ever-burgeoning dominance of consumerism and capitalism, nothing has replaced Christianity in providing for shared goods. The result is a de facto reliance on emotivist, individual preference to determine the good as such and a seemingly inexorable trend toward increasing permissiveness necessarily coupled with ever more insistent calls for toleration. (Consider the transformation of traditional sexual morality and its consequences over the past half century.) But the more the limits of the tolerable are legally extended and politically protected via rights, the more do those citizens object who, because of their *different* conceptions of the good, find *in*tolerable precisely the novel goods that are being newly protected through the assertion of rights under the aegis of liberty. The result tends to be friction, faction, and anger. Mill's progressivist prognostication has proven naïve and thoroughly mistaken: "As mankind improve, the number of doctrines which are no longer disputed or doubted will be constantly on the increase." He added that "the well-being of mankind may almost be measured by the number and gravity of the truths which have reached the point of being uncontested."[21] It would seem, then, that we are neither improving nor doing too well—for as the issue of abortion shows, there is deep disagreement even about who is a human being and so is to be counted among "mankind" in the first place. Even liberalism's staunchest advocates today would shrink from touting liberalism as the path to a progressive consensus or a substantive common good, in the manner of its nineteenth-century champions. For good reason, since there appear to be no grounds to think we are headed in such a direction.

Perhaps especially in the United States, a Rawlsian "overlapping consensus" sounds Pollyannaish, despite the fact that "deliberative democracy" and assumptions about what is "reasonable" continue to be pressed into service to perpetuate a liberal vision of progress now reconceived as the maximization of individual choice for all, regardless of the problems that this ideology produces. But given the divisions "in a society as pluralistic as ours" and the lack of any agreed means of adjudicating disagreement, what alternative is there to Wolfe's alleged "best way of life"?[22] And whatever its drawbacks, how could the dominant, liberationist narrative of Western modernity—the supersessionist historical transition from premodern restrictiveness to modern individual freedom—possibly be construed as anything but progress?[23]

This chapter's exposition will show how ironies and unexpected consequences abound in this story. The bitter disagreements among early modern Christians about the objective morality of the good led *through* the *right* of religious freedom itself to the secular, open-ended expansiveness of rights today as "deified preferences" or "an unchecked wish list . . . of conflicting subjective wants."[24] And the expansion of rights inaugurated by the right to religious liberty would eventually include the right to religious unbelief and the right to live in ways antithetical to Christian morality.[25] Conversely but no less ironically and despite wishful protestations to the contrary, the proponents of modern secular views of rights, having rejected the metaphysical foundations from which they derived historically, are reduced to "convictions from which we will not budge" that enable "the way of life expressed in these convictions."[26] Mutatis mutandis, no militant religious believer or committed racist would disagree: they will not budge, either, from *their* convictions and *their* ways of life. Absent defensible foundations, it is unclear how or why any such resolute preferences, including those favored by secular believers, amount to anything more than stubbornness among the like-minded.

Who are "we" given the realities of Western life in the early twenty-first century? More fundamentally, what would be best for human beings as such as a way of life? Such questions become progressively more problematic as pluralism proliferates within the very institutions that enable it, and without any persuasive arguments to contain it based on "public reason." For as so many historical examples make plain, once social practices are widely established they are either normalized as "natural," or the same end is contrarily sought by dismissing "nature" as a subjective, oppressive construct, lest any constraints inhibit the highest good of individual choice. The sovereign state threatens with punishment those who object to legal changes that safeguard newly protected preferences, thus compelling their toleration by any and all recalcitrant citizens. The normalization of once-novel practices in turn affects social relationships and cultural norms, as well as the sorts of arguments likely to find traction within an analogously altered intellectual culture and its institutional settings (as we shall see in Chapter 6).

Once the metaphysical basis of an ethics of the good has been jettisoned, nothing remains in principle but the human will and its desires protected by the state.[27] In practice, whether self-consciously or not, even highly secularized Westerners today continue in variegated ways to rely upon a reservoir of beliefs and values derived from ancient and medieval Christianity, as well as upon the almost infinitely complex, tangled permutations of Protestant, Catholic, and secular adaptations of them, in addition to similar beliefs and values from peoples of other religious traditions and parts of the world. Were this not so, human life in Europe and North America would be either unbearably oppressive, unbearably chaotic, or both. But enough water has passed under the bridge in the past few centuries for us to discern clearly the direction and character of the dominant current. Morality is being progressively subjectivized within the West's liberal institutional channels. In order to ameliorate the resulting clash of commitments to divergent, incompatible preferences and pursuits, political leaders and other elites rely heavily and increasingly on platitudinous rhetoric and consumerism, the latter involving citizens' widespread conformity to a seemingly insatiable acquisitiveness regardless of their income level. Were the flow of prosperity's spigot seriously to wane, however, citizens' clashes would likely intensify, reversing the dominant trajectory through which Westerners have willingly permitted their self-colonization by capitalism since the seventeenth century. Hence the *necessary* ideological commitment of modern Western states to unending economic growth, which perpetuates "the notion of the state as a vast bureaucracy in the service of appetite, aimed above all at the promotion of economic life and comfort."[28] Chapter 5 examines the relationship between the emergence of an ethics of rights and the goods life characteristic of capitalism and consumerism. This chapter analyzes the historical process by which an ethics of rights displaced and marginalized a substantive Christian ethics of the good even as it continued to draw on it, and thus fostered the subjectivization of morality.

AT THE OUTSET of the sixteenth century the institutionalized worldview of medieval Christianity in all its variety, not Aristotelian moral philosophy as such, was Western Europe's bearer of a teleological ethics of the good, even though Aristotelian scholasticism remained the dominant idiom of ethical discourse in universities and among university-educated elites.[29]

Based on logically antecedent truth claims about reality and history, late medieval Christian ideals were laden with other truth claims about how human beings should act so that they might pursue the common good in this life and be saved eternally by God in the next. In other words, Christianity on the eve of the Reformation entailed an eternally ramifying ethical discourse based on a metaphysics that was disclosed through a history and embedded within a politics. With its teleological ethics rooted in God's self-revelation through his creation and his covenant with Israel, above all in the life, death, and resurrection of Jesus of Nazareth, medieval Christianity involved reciprocally related moral rules, the practice of moral virtues, and a moral community—the church—all of which were supposed to foster the common good and the salvation of souls.

It would seem that some moral rules are necessary for the existence of any sort of human community, and thus for any sustained practice of moral virtues. Without a prohibition of murder and theft, for example, any human community risks radical destabilization. Medieval Christian authorities, whether ecclesiastical or secular, understood this well. But however indispensable it is to the securing of order, the following of moral rules alone, such as those in the Ten Commandments or in Jesus's uncompromising radicalizations, was regarded in medieval Christianity as insufficient for the realization of the individual good or the common good. The flourishing of individuals and communities depended on the shared practice of moral virtues and avoidance of vices, which in their best-known (but not exhaustive) expressions in the late Middle Ages were respectively categorized and pervasively taught, preached, and painted as the seven holy virtues and the seven deadly sins.[30] Human beings could not flourish or promote the common good unless, for example, they were to a significant degree habitually diligent rather than slothful, generous rather than greedy, and kind rather than cruel. Peter Lombard's substantial treatment of the virtues in book 3 of his *Sentences* (c. 1150) insured not only that all university-trained theologians were exposed to reflection on the virtues, their interrelationships, and their place in Christian life. It also meant that they lectured and often wrote commentaries on the virtues, because lecturing on the *Sentences* was required to become a master of theology.[31] The rational application of each of the virtues to specific circumstances amid the complexities of human life required at least implicitly the virtue of prudence *(phronesis; prudentia)*, which is the acquired ability to exercise each moral virtue in particular circumstances such that it objectively conduces to individual and common flourishing.

Given the medieval recognition of the human propensity for self-deception and prideful overestimation of one's own capacities, the necessity of prudence implied the importance of counsel, which in turn implied the trust-worthy social relationships characteristic of a moral community.[32] "Keep counsel with a wise and conscientious man," Thomas à Kempis wrote, paraphrasing Tobit 4:18 in one of the fifteenth century's most influential works of exhortative piety, "and seek rather to be taught by someone who is better than to follow your own devices."[33] Without a stable moral com-munity, neither the rules requisite for its very existence nor the virtues con-ducive to its vitality and the common good were possible—there would be neither model practitioners to imitate in one's acquisition of the virtues, nor experienced, virtuous counselors to consult in one's prudential delibera-tions. Hence the church, as the temporal extension of the community of Jesus's followers after his ascension, interpreted and enforced what it un-derstood to be God's rules, just as its clergy preached and exhorted one another and the laity to the practice of virtues and the avoidance of sins. To the extent that Christians practiced what they preached, they tended to overcome individually and together their predisposition toward sinful self-regard in a movement toward the imperfect *eudaimonia* in this life that prefigured perfect *beatitudo* among the communion of saints with God in heaven—the final human good and *telos* of human existence willed by God, "who desires everyone to be saved and to come to the knowledge of the truth" (1 Tim 2:4). Such was the ideal.

What human beings are if left to their own devices is not all that they can be, nor what they should be, nor what God wants them to be: this was a basic truth claim about the reality of the fallen human condition and the purpose of human life implicit in medieval Christianity. Even after baptism conferred the grace that effaced original sin, that sin's pervasive effects con-tinued to incline human beings to think and act in ways objectively detri-mental to their well-being and to the common good. Pride rather than hu-mility corroded human relationships through overestimation of one's worth; wrath rather than patience damaged through violent words or actions the bonds of friendship and therefore of community; lust rather than chastity risked the unleashing of sexual desire in ways harmful to persons and fami-lies; and so on. To pretend otherwise was to misread human nature and to delude oneself about human relationships. Unconstrained by moral rules or undisciplined by the virtues, whatever natural inclination toward the good that human beings might have possessed was bound to be dissipated in de-sires, passions, and impulses that tended away from flourishing and to-ward individual self-absorption (if not self-destruction) and the erosion of community, all of which, even apart from divine judgment after death, were part of God's condemnation of sins in and through his created order. As à Kempis asked rhetorically, in effect echoing Augustine and the entire medieval Christian tradition, "What hinders or afflicts you more than the uncontrolled passions of your heart?"[34]

In their respective ways, many ancient Greek and Roman philosophers had understood that moral virtues are indispensable in the pursuit of the individual good and the common good within political communities. Their teleological conception of ethics made many of their ideas appropriable by Christian theorists, whether with the grudging suspicion of Augustine, for example, so attuned to the self-congratulatory pride woven deeply into the fabric of Roman imperial culture in late antiquity, or with the austere confidence of Aquinas, who saw how Paul's "three things that last, faith, hope, and love" (1 Cor 13:13)—conceptualized as the theological virtues and properly understood—permitted the Christian use and transformation of Aristotle's *Nicomachean Ethics* beginning in the later 1240s with Robert Grosseteste's Latin translation.[35] The ancient pagan sages, however, despite their understanding of the virtues as indispensable to human flourishing, had, according to Western Christian thinkers, misgauged human nature: flattering themselves, they overestimated its baseline goodness, underestimated its recalcitrance, and could not have imagined its true *telos*. Hence they misjudged the difficulties of realizing one's individual good, the virtues requisite for the enterprise and their proper ordering in the endeavor, the insufficiency of human exertion without divine grace, the sort of moral community that the practice of the virtues sought to create, and the universally inclusive scope of that community in principle. Nor, according to Christian theorists, were these oversights surprising. Ancient pagan thinkers had not known the one, true God of Israel who had created the universe and had made them, like all human beings, in his image and likeness, and whose actions in history among his chosen people and above all in Jesus had revealed so much more than common sense supposed, ordinary experience disclosed, or rational reflection could demonstrate. Consequently and notwithstanding their insights, pagan philosophers were bound to exaggerate human capacities and self-sufficiency in the ways diagnosed and analyzed by Western Christian thinkers from the early Latin church fathers through medieval scholastic theologians to Renaissance humanists and beyond. Hence the importance of both faith and the grace conveyed in and through the church's sacraments and sacramentals. Especially central were the liturgy and its adjuncts: the Eucharist re-presented the body of Christ in one sense even as it promoted it—the common good and the kingdom of God—in another.

Without the virtues there could be no sustained community, which meant no common good and thus no individual good and no salvation: this was the moral logic of medieval Christianity. Virtuous actions were rational because they simultaneously fostered individual and communal flourishing;

they were also actions consonant with God's natural law, if it were understood to mean that good must always be sought and evil avoided. No wonder that late medieval Christianity so strongly emphasized the acquisition of the virtues via behaviors through which men and women were habituated to them, such as the seven spiritual and seven corporal works of mercy. Their depiction was common in late medieval Europe, as in the panel painting of the seven corporal works of mercy rendered by an unknown Netherlandish master from Alkmaar for the city's St. Lawrence Church in 1504.[36] Moral virtues were sermonized in preachers' *exempla,* narrated in ubiquitous stories about the saints, enacted through morality plays, and depicted in personified images. All these derived from and focused in turn on the incarnate Word as the faith's center and its model for mimesis. "Be imitators of me, as I am of Christ" (1 Cor 11:1)—Paul's exhortation pointed to the source and standard of the virtues for Christians, whether in the first century or for their early sixteenth-century successors who read the pithy *dicta* assembled in à Kempis's *Imitation of Christ* in one of its more than 120 editions in seven languages published between 1470 and 1520.[37] As for the Brothers and Sisters of the Common Life, "a never-ending progress in virtue that would open out into everlasting gain" was "truly the *leitmotif* of their program."[38] Scripture supported and reinforced the church's teleological, Christocentric ethics: do certain things and avoid others, cultivate these habits and attitudes and shun those, become this kind of person and not another kind, become *holy*—"as he who called you is holy, be holy yourselves in all your conduct; for it is written, 'You shall be holy, for I am holy'" (1 Pt 1:15–16; cf. Lv 19:2).

There was no doubt about the governing virtue at the center. In his popular collection of feast-day sermons that was printed twenty-three times from 1483 to 1532, the early fifteenth-century English priest John Mirk elaborated on the ways in which Jesus's command to "doo to a nother as thou wold be done unto" fulfilled and worked together with the Ten Commandments because it "includeth all the lawes and prophetes of god" (Mt 7:12). As Mirk put it, "That lyke as in all the body is but one hede, of the whiche procedeth all the governaunce of man, as his reason, his vnderstondyng, and other. So all the rule of vertuous lyfe groweth and procedeth only of love and charyte, whiche is God hymselfe."[39] Indeed scripture says (1 Jn 4:8) that God is love *(agape; caritas)* and the church taught that God had become incarnate in Jesus, who out of love suffered and died on the cross to redeem sinful humanity. The incarnation ennobled human nature and (like Christ's passion) underscored God's love for human beings, a theme emphasized by Christian thinkers from late antiquity into the Renaissance.[40] Jesus's central directive implied practices that fostered a particular sort of moral community: "This is my commandment, that you love one another as I have loved you" (Jn 15:12). Hence the exhortations in the first epistle of Peter: "love one another deeply from the heart," and "above all, maintain constant love for one another, for love covers a multitude of sins" (1 Pt 1:22, 4:8). And in the first letter of John: "this is the message you have heard from the beginning, that we should love one another," and "let us love, not in word and speech, but in truth and action" (1 Jn 3:11, 18). Thus Augustine, for example, by far the most influential church father throughout the Middle Ages in the West, had distilled his minimalist maxim for Christian life in commenting on 1 John 4: "Love, and do what you will."[41] The early thirteenth-century beguine Hadewijch of Brabant was more expansive in one of her letters: "May you at all times be urged to true love [ghewaregher Minnen], that you may live to the truth and to perfection in order to do all that you should for God, and love and honor him and [show him] justice, in himself first, and then in the good people who are loved by him and he by them; and may you give them everything they need in whatever condition [in welken manieren] they may be."[42] Her contemporary, Aquinas, thought that *caritas* had to be Christianity's controlling super-virtue or "form of the virtues," as he put it, just as Paul had said that among faith, hope, and love, "the greatest of these is love" (1 Cor 13:13).[43]

Paul thought that *agape* was the hub from which all the other virtues radiated and that the imitation of Christ provided the standard for living a certain kind of life within "communities of mutual admonition."[44] Throughout the Middle Ages Paul was regarded as the author of the letter to the Ephesians, which urged its recipients to practice particular virtues geared toward the common good whose outcome *was* Christian community: "I therefore, the prisoner in the Lord, beg you to lead a life worthy of the calling to which you have been called, with all humility and gentleness, with patience, bearing with one another in love, making every effort to maintain the unity of the Spirit in the bond of peace. There is one body and one Spirit, just as you were called to the one hope of your calling, one Lord, one faith, one baptism, one God and Father of all, who is above all and through all and in all" (Eph 4:1–6).[45] Similar passages denouncing vices and extolling virtues are found throughout Paul's letters and elsewhere in the New Testament.[46] Despite their very different circumstances, it was the same charge for late medieval Christians. Thomas à Kempis was characteristically straightforward: "Love everyone for Jesus's sake and Jesus for his own sake."[47] To live as a Christian meant practicing certain virtues in a community in part constituted by them and coordinately bounded by moral rules based on God's commandments. Whether late medieval Christians sought to imitate Christ directly or took their cue from the saints as his exemplary imitators, the end was the same: to live as part of the body of Christ extended in space and time—the moral community of the church, including its deceased members militant and triumphant—through the shared practice of the virtues constitutive of that community as the *via* to salvation.

Such was the ideal and the mandate. As we saw in Chapter 3, in practice and by its own standards Latin Christendom left a great deal to be desired, a fact acknowledged and deplored by waves of reformers from the eleventh century into the sixteenth. As a whole, medieval Christians' concrete relationships never approached the unity and community about which, according to John's Gospel, Jesus prayed for his disciples to God: "that they may be one, as we are one, I in them and you in me, that they may become completely one, so that the world may know that you have sent me and have loved them even as you have loved me" (Jn 17:22–23). Anyone familiar with the social and political history of late medieval Europe knows how sharply such a hope contrasts with the character of so many of its human relationships, apparent in the wars fought by rival rulers no less than in the endemic violence and crimes among ordinary folk attested by surviving legal records. Theirs was a frequently harsh human world embedded within a constantly harsh material one. In the early fifth century, Augustine, in his *City of God,* had cautioned against expecting too much. To be sure, there were many holy men and women in late medieval Europe, and by the late fifteenth century lay devotion was booming, encouraged by the clergy and aided by the invention of printing and rising literacy. But paradoxically, self-conscious individuals and subgroups within the wider mass of the merely conformist or indifferent might unsettle, through the microsocial character of their cultivation of holiness, the wider communities for which they sought to model the Christian common good. In one way or another, this had been a conundrum for Latin Christianity from the fourth century, when its leaders almost overnight found themselves unexpectedly tasked with transforming rather than merely enduring the Roman Empire. Ironically, suffering persecution by pagans was in important respects easier—or at least less complicated—than was trying to remake the glaring injustices and harsh human realities of the late antique Mediterranean world that had been centuries or even millennia in the making.

During the millennium in which Western Christianity was forged into an institutionalized worldview, nearly all its leaders came largely to accept the vast disparities in social status, political influence, and economic standing among human beings in the world they had inherited. They tended to regard these differences either as among the consequences of original sin or as deliberately willed by God in his hierarchical ordering of creation.

This interpretation of inequalities had profound implications for authorities' conception and administration of justice, because what it meant to receive one's due was heavily influenced and sometimes determined by one's social and political location, a point to be considered further in Chapter 5. Tension was thus created between de facto inequalities and Christian ethics, a tension that would prove problematic and potentially unsettling for centuries (and indeed, continues to remain significant today). Just as its ecclesiastical and secular leaders never succeeded in consistently combining *caritas* with coercion in the exercise of power, so the medieval church influenced but never managed thoroughly to transform, according to its own ethics of the good, the moral behavior, social relationships, and political life of the baptized.

With its leaders forced by circumstances to improvise beginning in the fourth century, a Christendom was created that included all the baptized. But not everyone was expected to practice all the virtues in the same ways, or to the same degree. Distinctions were drawn. Picking up on practices pioneered by the Egyptian desert fathers, those who embraced monasticism sought to build in miniature the moral communities envisioned by Jesus. Benedict's sixth-century *regula* provided the model in the Latin church for men and women self-consciously dedicated to practicing the faith's highest virtues, including voluntary poverty, chastity, and obedience, in vowed *stabilitas* with others. By extending to the point of renunciation the disciplining of the strongest human passions—*concupiscentia* for wealth, sexual pleasure, and power—these virtues, to the extent that they were realized, maximized promotion of the common *and* individual good, presaging the joy of heaven as a self-offering to God that fulfilled Christ's command of *caritas*: "those who lose their life for my sake will find it" (Mt 10:39). Female and male religious genuinely living their vows discovered paradoxically that their self-renunciation in shared practices of prayer, worship, and work rooted in love was precisely what overcame self-interest. It fortified love and therefore the community to which they belonged. The sustenance and increase of Christian love presupposed the community through which it was strengthened: this was the chicken-and-egg social paradox of vowed medieval religious life.

But far from all late medieval religious were living such lives. In the fourteenth and fifteenth centuries, vices were rampant even among the friars and contemplative orders, vices that the Observantine movement tried, with some success, to rectify (even as such efforts also provoked a backlash from religious that remained loyal to established ways).[48] Meanwhile, bishops in their dioceses and their clerical deputies in the parishes—when they or their vicars were resident and doing their jobs—sought to coax and cajole the laity from the ways of the ever-recalcitrant *mundus,* hopeful that they might at least get them to practice what was minimally expected of all Christians. That the clergy often seem to have flouted the commandments and virtues they were teaching could not have helped. Partly for this reason, it would appear, many laypeople seemed simply not to get it, despite all the exhortations and models to which they were exposed. Many of them apparently thought, for example, that saints were no more than powerful intercessors from whom to curry favors, and that the church was just a reservoir of power (and money) exploitable for their own gain—as indeed some members of the clergy seem to have regarded it in their rivalries among themselves.

Brian Tierney has shown how a discourse of natural human rights *(ius naturale)* first emerged in the twelfth century among canonist commentators on Gratian's *Decretum* (c. 1140) in a context of contestation between popes and emperors, regular and secular clergy, and feudal lords and their subjects.[49] Intellectually indebted as they were to the recent revival of Roman law, the canonists nevertheless claimed something unknown to the ancient Romans or Greeks: that not simply certain categories of persons but all human beings as such have subjective natural rights, an inherent freedom and power, the violation of which is unjust. The implicit foundation for this notion was the ancient Jewish claim, taken up in Christianity as well, that all human beings are created in the image and likeness of God (Gn 1:26–27): the *ius naturale* of men and women was part of the fabric of the natural world as God had created it.

Ironically, it would seem that the pervasive shortcomings of Christians in enacting the virtues occasioned this medieval discourse on natural rights as a sort of complementary compensation, a protection against others' sinful exercise of their vices. If the rich and powerful had been generally and habitually generous, for example, in sharing from their surplus with the desperately poor, the canonists would not have had to discuss and to affirm the right of those in situations of life-threatening hunger to steal from them.[50] Of course, the canonists envisioned the exercise of individual subjective rights *within* Christianity's teleological ethics, not as an alternative moral system or in opposition to it. Properly to exercise one's rights was to exercise one's freedom and to pursue one's individual good with an eye toward the common good and eternal salvation as a member of the church's moral community, not to do as one pleased as the sovereign possessor of "an expansive list of basic entitlements."[51] When others sinfully sought their own advantage at the expense of others, thus both preventing them from flourishing and damaging the common good, rights provided a way of signaling the injustice of their actions, theorizing the wrong that was done, and providing for legal redress, at least in principle. Accordingly, the same widespread problems that inspired repeated calls for reform and exhortations to holiness within the late medieval church also stimulated the development of the discourse on individual rights, from the early canonists through thinkers such as Henry of Ghent and William of Occam to later nominalists such as Jean Gerson and Jacques Almain.[52] In the late 1530s, in the context of Spanish colonization in the New World, Francisco de Vitoria would extend and apply the same discourse to the rights of American Indians against theologians who argued that they were properly seen as Aristotelian "natural slaves."[53] But discourse is one thing and concrete human realities are another. At the outset of the sixteenth century, no one in Western Europe with open eyes would have disagreed: despite many conspicuous exceptions, in general the Augustinian *civitas terrena* remained part and parcel of the social realities, political life, and moral behavior of Christians high and low, clerical and lay, male and female.

Although they had little use for nuanced scholastic discussions of rights, devout and reform-minded humanists had their eyes open. The polemics and genuine intellectual differences between them and their scholastic contemporaries can obscure the fact that the erudite lovers of ancient Latin and Greek literature stood squarely within the tradition of the church's teleological ethics.[54] They simply wanted more people, more consistently, to live by it, and so to move a still inadequately Christianized *society* toward the demographically inclusive Christian *community* willed by God. Hence the value of and enthusiasm for hagiography among dozens of German humanists in the late fifteenth and early sixteenth centuries, their saints' lives devoted especially to virtuous medieval bishops as latter-day models for reform in the church.[55] Between 1420 and 1520 more than ninety Italian humanists were similarly eager hagiographers, concerned that the *vitae* of holy bishops and members of (especially mendicant) religious orders, as well as the *passiones* of early Christian martyrs, not remain trapped in sub-classical Latin.[56] No less than Augustine or Gregory the Great, Anselm or Bernard of Clairvaux, Aquinas or Bonaventure, did Erasmus, John Colet, Thomas More, or their humanist colleagues think that Christianity was something else than practicing in community the virtues ordered to Christian *caritas* as the means to realizing the individual good and aspiring to eternal salvation as members of the "common corps of Christendom."[57] Moreover, despite the disdain among some humanists for scholasticism, others (beginning already with Leonardo Bruni in the 1410s) admired Aristotle's *Nicomachean Ethics* for its affinity with Christian morality, and so wanted it made available in the best texts and translations: the introduction to it by Jacques Lefèvre d'Étaples, for example, first published in 1494, became his most frequently reprinted work, and in 1497 he produced his own edition with a laudatory commentary.[58]

Thrilled with the recent recovery of so much long-forgotten classical literature, humanist reformers generally evaluated more positively than had many of their medieval Christian predecessors the value of the virtues as theorized and taught by ancient Greek and Roman writers. And they had their own ideas about the best means, through curricular reform, revisionist pedagogy, classical rhetoric, and the use of print, for trying to inculcate what Erasmus called the *philosophia Christi*, given their circumstances and opportunities at the outset of the sixteenth century. But when it came to which virtues were most important, the necessity of instilling them, and the possibility of doing so, Erasmus and his humanist colleagues were thoroughly unoriginal. The same message of disciplining the passions and practicing the virtues with Christ as one's model and salvation as one's goal constituted the core of the spiritual warfare that Erasmus enjoined, when in his popular *Handbook of the Christian Soldier* (1503), for example, he expanded upon pugilistic imagery for Christian life (Eph 6:10–17), or when he laid out a program of formation for the future Charles V in his *Education of a Christian Prince* (1516).

In the prefatory remarks to his own Latin translation of the New Testament in 1516, Erasmus echoed Paul no less than à Kempis: "If we seek a model for living, why is another pattern more important for us than Christ himself?" Education and direct lay exposure to the font of the virtues—scripture itself—were the key, through which Christians could move from knowledge to practice: "The first thing, however, is to know what he taught, [and] the next is to carry it out," so that Christians might "be transformed in [the literature of Christ], as studies are changed into morals."[59] Except for in England, where the condemnation of the Lollard Bible in 1409 had made vernacular translations suspect, Erasmus was unoriginal as well in his enthusiasm for the lay reading of scripture—despite the theologians' toes on which he was otherwise stepping—considering all the complete, partial, and adapted editions of the Bible in various vernaculars that had been published in the preceding half century.[60]

Erasmus's close contemporary, Machiavelli, was also a moralist steeped in ancient Latin literature. Involved in Italian politics beginning in 1498 on behalf of his native Florence, he too had his eyes open and so was keenly aware of the difference between the church's teachings and the behavior of so many of its members, or as he put it, "the gap between how people actually behave and how they ought to behave."[61] The same gap inspired the moral fury and fiery sermons of the most influential Florentine of the 1490s, the Dominican friar Girolamo Savonarola.[62] Erasmus and

Savonarola as well as à Kempis and Augustine would have found little to contest in Machiavelli's conventional view of human beings: "men are wicked" and "by nature inconstant," he wrote in *The Prince*, "simple-minded and so preoccupied with their immediate concerns," as well as generally "ungrateful, fickle, deceptive and deceiving, avoiders of danger, eager to gain."[63] This was standard fare, a staple description of sinful human beings unhabituated in the moral virtues. But unlike the northern humanists concerned, in a traditional Christian fashion, with the infixion of the virtues oriented toward eternal salvation, Machiavelli's different view of the collective human good—the political liberty and glory of the (preferably republican) state—signaled a neo-Ciceronian renunciation of the enterprise that linked moral rules, the practice of the virtues, and the pursuit of the common good as understood in inherited Christian terms.

Machiavelli was not a Florentine Nietzsche *avant la lettre*, espousing a Renaissance vision of human life "beyond good and evil." He did not deny that traditional morality correctly taught right and wrong. He simply claimed that the successful exercise of power frequently and necessarily required the abrogation of that morality: "a ruler is often obliged, in order to hold on to power, to break his word, to be uncharitable, inhumane, and irreligious."[64] To be sure, those in power should as much as possible *seem* to have the virtues and *appear* to be good, lest they render themselves noxious in the eyes of their subjects and thereby weaken their control. But if they wanted to exercise dominion in any sustained fashion, expedient *virtù* had to trump traditional Christian virtues, some of which, such as humility and self-abnegation, were incompatible with the martial vigor and boldness necessary for political success.[65] Machiavelli was all too familiar with the brutality of peninsular politics, especially after Charles VIII of France invaded Italy in 1494. Erasmian humanists articulated their version of teleological Christian ethics with the same aim as their medieval reforming predecessors, seeking to narrow the gulf between moral prescription and practice. Machiavelli saw the gulf, shrugged, and re-paganized the exercise of power. In multiple ways and with supreme irony, the ecclesiastical prelates with whom he rubbed shoulders had themselves in fact modeled the separation of morality from politics, led by Popes Alexander VI (r. 1492–1503) and Julius II (r. 1503–1513): "Owing to the bad example set by the Court of Rome," Machiavelli wrote in his *Discorsi*, "Italy has lost all devotion and all religion."[66] Machiavelli reversed Augustine: by extolling republican civic virtues the *civitas Dei* faded from view, or perhaps, in light of Machiavelli's idiosyncratic theology, it was seen as subordinate to and contingent on the actions of rulers who successfully managed the vagaries of *fortuna* in pursuit of worldly honor.[67]

As it happened, Machiavelli's ideas about human nature would influence subsequent rejections of the Christian (and Aristotelian, and Platonic) claim about the inseparability of morality and politics. Whoever believed that human beings simply *are* wicked, deceptive, acquisitive, and/or self-interested, regardless of how they are educated or socialized, would have to regard Christianity's teleological view of human nature as mistakenly utopian. Efforts expended in trying to live virtuously could only seem quixotically futile, aspirations to create a correlative moral community unrealistic. For such believers, the exercise of power would instead primarily seek to control inevitably self-interested, typically immoral subjects, not misguidedly endeavor to instill *caritas* among other virtues in pursuit of a putatively objective individual or common good conducive to "true" human flourishing. In his views about human nature, Machiavelli would find successors in Hobbes, Hume, and many other thinkers.

In theory, at least, Machiavelli's practical distinction between the demands of political life and moral norms severed the exercise of power from teleological virtue ethics in public affairs, the "realism" of the former contrasted with the "idealism" of the latter. Successful and therefore good politics was unavoidably immoral, and immoral politics was the norm.[68] No longer *aspiring* to encompass traditional morality, politics becomes instead "the art of the possible"—and as people grow accustomed to new human realities, their views change concerning what is and is not possible. What his contemporaries and Reformation-era successors who offered advice to princes continued to regard as the *telos* of human nature within an inherited Christian worldview, Machiavelli consequentially disdained as the "imaginary world."[69] In so doing, he took the historically contingent human realities he knew, plus his knowledge of the ancient political dealings that so captivated him, as evidence for how things simply were, and had to be. Human beings are what they are; the world is as it is; the effective exercise of power requires the abrogation of morality; successful rulers override the virtues with *virtù*. One could exercise power or be moral, but not both. Thus were theorized important elements of modern Realpolitik—and in combination with the unrest set in train by the Reformation, of the subjectivization of morality in part through its separation from the successful exercise of power.

MACHIAVELLI DIED IN 1527. His *Discourses* and *Prince* had circulated in manuscript but were not published until 1531 and 1532, respectively.[70] What the influence of these and his other writings might have been had the Reformation never occurred is obviously an unknowable counterfactual. Together with the frequently bitter and recurrently violent contestation over the Christian good in the Reformation era, however, Machiavelli's uncoupling of politics from morality contributed to novel transformations. The unanticipated, eventual result was a new kind of ethics in the Western world, one that would eventually be policed and enforced by sovereign states that protected individual rights and, as we saw in the previous chapter, controlled all expressions of religion in the public exercise of power. Despite the many convictions shared by sixteenth-century Catholics and most Protestants, their disagreements and concomitant disruptions would be the unintended springboard for ideological and institutional innovations they would certainly have found inimical.

None of this was foreseen at the outset of the Reformation. Many observers then thought the world's end was imminent. Those who rejected the authority of the Roman church beginning around 1520 were concerned about the same gap between Christian prescription and practice to which Erasmian humanists and Machiavelli were responding, even as they regarded Christendom's problems as a symptom of deeper doctrinal errors. But unlike Machiavelli, they were not prepared to unhitch the exercise of power from Christian ethics. On the contrary: if anything, politics needed much more—and more strictly biblical—Christian morality, not less. Those Christians who repudiated the Roman church therefore sought remedy not in reflection on personal political experience or ancient pagan histories, but in scripture. For who knew better than God himself what the good was for human beings, how they were to live, and what they should pursue as well as avoid? And how was God's will to be known save through his word, stripped clean of diluting and distorting accretions, unbiblical inventions, and pagan philosophical speculations?

We have seen what happened more generally when those who repudiated the Roman church turned instead to scripture for answers to the Life Questions. Beginning in the early 1520s, they disagreed about the meaning of God's word in socially and politically divisive ways. Unavoidably, this divisiveness was also morally disruptive precisely because of morality's inseparability from politics, and the deeply ingrained ways in which both had for centuries sought to shape social relationships and human behavior within the moral community of the church. Protestants claimed that the sinful behaviors of Catholic clergy and laity were not merely the result of failures to exemplify Christian virtues, as medieval and Renaissance reformers had thought. Much more disturbingly, they were the product of false doctrines explicitly contrary to God's revealed will. This claim provided an alternative explanation for the sorry state of Christian practices: what else was to be expected when even the "holy" behaviors of "saints" had been based on erroneous teachings in the first place? And shocking as it was, insofar as one understood the stakes, such a conviction meant that (at least in principle) one had to leave the Roman church, which in its self-serving self-defense all but proclaimed itself the abode of the Antichrist now unleashed in the End Times. Unlike the much more limited impact of medieval rejections of the Roman church's authority, the Reformation's much greater success ended more than a thousand years of efforts in the Latin West to create a unified moral community through Christianity. As the Reformation played out, the Roman church's virtual monopoly on Christendom was over. Even as dedicated a fourteenth-century critic of papal claims as William of Occam had relied heavily on canon law for his arguments; by contrast, Luther burned the books of canon law along with the papal bull *Exsurge Domine* in Wittenberg on 10 December 1520, just months after he had urged German nobles to reject canon law entirely in reforming the church.[71] Fleeing the scripturally unmasked Whore of Babylon, anti-Roman Christians would have to constitute a moral community afresh, based on the Bible.

Yet no such alternative moral community emerged. There were only rival moral communi*ties*, because social divisions were an immediate, direct outcome of Protestants' discrepant exegetical and doctrinal claims. Fortified by their respective interpretations of scripture ostensibly ratified by the Holy Spirit, sixteenth-century magisterial and radical Protestants continued to believe in eternal salvation as the final *telos* and ultimate good for human beings. In this respect, theirs remained, like traditional Christianity, a teleological ethics of the good that extended beyond death. But they diverged greatly about how that ultimate end was related to what else God said in the Bible, from the character of fallen human nature and ecclesiology to the proper function of ministry, exercise of discipline, and celebration of the sacraments. How should Christians live this side of death? What did God command, what did he commend, what did he prohibit, and what did he permit? Christians who cast off the Roman church disagreed dramatically about the good as a direct result of their incompatible readings of scripture, which in turn determined their divergent appropriations of tradition, as we saw in Chapter 2.

Here again we see the cost of the scholarly tendency to cordon off the radical Reformation from the magisterial Reformation. For in exactly the same way that conscientious Protestants in general were at least in principle obliged to leave the Roman church once they grasped the implications of their convictions, conscientious radical Protestants were obliged to reject moral communities such as Luther's Wittenberg or Zwingli's Zurich. As Michael Sattler, the former Benedictine monk turned Swiss Anabaptist leader, summed it up in 1527, "everything that is not united with our God and Christ is nothing other than the abomination [*dy grewel*] which we should shun and flee."[72] In their heterogeneous ways, radical Protestants were simply following the lead of the politically more secure Protestant antagonists who opposed them. Radical Protestants were doing exactly what the former Dominican Martin Bucer, Luther's humanist colleague Philipp Melanchthon, Andreas Osiander, Wolfgang Capito, Johannes Oecolampadius, Johannes Bugenhagen, and every other politically protected Protestant reformer did: they rejected objectionable moral communities whose claims they would not abide, convinced that the leaders of such communities taught falsehoods in place of God's truth. As we saw in Chapter 2, all Protestants based their flight on the same foundation: their interpretation of scripture, its adjuncts, and their experience. Because they read differently, they fled differently.

In 1524, for example, Thomas Müntzer excoriated Luther as "doctor lügner" (liar) and ridiculed the "unspiritual [*gaistloße*], soft-living flesh at Wittenberg" for insulating his soteriological self-absorption from radically unjust social relationships and political practices. Müntzer urged instead the moral imperative of divinely sanctioned revolution.[73] In Balthasar Hubmaier's estimation, the insistence on justification by faith alone and rejection of free will in matters of salvation were at best "only half-truths from which one may infer no more than half-judgments," and if taken as the whole truth were "more harmful than a whole lie [*vil schedlicher, denn ein gar gantze lugen*]."[74] So much for Luther's cornerstone Reformation "discovery." Caspar Schwenckfeld's eucharistic theology led him not only to reject Luther and his moral community but also indefinitely to suspend the celebration of the Lord's Supper for all his followers in 1526, whereas Sebastian Franck's very different sort of spiritualism dispensed altogether with religious "externals" and reconceived faith itself in experiential, noncognitive terms.[75] Hutterites insisted on communal ownership of property as essential to the Christian common good, which divided them not only from magisterial Protestants but also from the Swiss Brethren and other Anabaptist groups.[76] One could multiply examples at length, not only from the 1520s and 1530s but throughout the Reformation era and beyond.

Like the rival answers to the Life Questions based on scripture as the distant and unintended origin of contemporary hyperpluralism, the social divisions derived from divergent readings of the Bible make up a crucial part in the story of the unplanned, modern subjectivization of morality. Because the exercise of the virtues and the maintenance of moral rules *depended* on social relationships in moral communities, disruptions of those communities were bound to jeopardize the practice of the virtues. Which among the rival communities ought one to belong to, and why? The constitution of mutually exclusive moral communities would eventually suggest to some people that morality itself is contingent and constructed, or at least that its basis and precepts are separable from religion. From the outset of the Reformation to the present day, the insistence on *sola scriptura* and its adjuncts has produced and continues to yield an open-ended range of incompatible interpretations of the Bible, with centrifugal social and wide-ranging substantive implications for morality.[77]

Because moral communities are inescapably social, it is an analytical mistake to seek to separate sixteenth-century Protestants' ethical commitments from their doctrinal disagreements or concrete communities of faith. Although nearly all Anabaptists, for example, along with Lutherans and Reformed Protestants, affirmed the truth of the Ten Commandments plus many of the same ethical teachings from the Gospels, they did not belong with Lutherans or Reformed Protestants to a shared Christian moral community. Disagreements about infant baptism and other issues divided them socially, and therefore rendered any shared moral community impossible—a fact starkly underscored already in the late 1520s and early 1530s, when Lutheran, Zwinglian, and Catholic authorities in central Europe, taken together, put several hundred unrepentant Anabaptists to death.[78]

Analogously, if one wants to understand the Reformation's historical influence, it is an analytical mistake to substitute one's own theological views for those of sixteenth-century Protestants in an endeavor to distinguish "central Reformation principles" from "secondary issues."[79] To be sure, Luther and Zwingli agreed on fourteen of fifteen articles discussed at the Marburg Colloquy in early October 1529, but their abiding disagreement on eucharistic doctrine was not therefore a matter of secondary significance.[80] On the contrary, because their standoff on the Lord's Supper divided Lutheran from Reformed Protestantism in social terms, it also divided them as moral communities. They neither worshiped together nor pursued a shared common good *because* they disagreed about the Eucharist, which constituted, as G. R. Potter put it, "an unbridgeable gap of highest import for the future."[81] Insofar as the difference between Lutheran and Reformed Protestantism persisted throughout the Reformation era, and has remained socially significant to the present day, this doctrinal disagreement between Luther and Zwingli can no more be regarded as a matter of secondary importance in the history of Protestantism than it was to them. Individual opinions and ecumenical yearnings today are beside the point. *Whatever* divided Christians from one another doctrinally was of cardinal moral significance *because* of its social implications. The modern tendency and temptation not to see this is itself a symptomatic consequence of the history analyzed in this chapter, reflected in the widespread view that the determination of right and wrong, good and evil, is a matter of the discretion and discernment of autonomous individuals apart from substantive moral communities—what J. B. Schneewind calls "a distinctively modern way of understanding ourselves as moral agents."[82]

Notwithstanding the fact that Protestantism's more numerous modern expressions are an outgrowth of the heterogeneity that has characterized it since the early 1520s, its social, political, and cultural influence during the early modern period, especially in Europe, was overwhelmingly a function of Lutheran and Reformed Protestant churches (including the Church of England). Only confessionalizing magisterial Protestant regimes had the political means to seek to establish moral communities coextensive with their respective political communities. Their efforts presupposed a traditional, anti-Machiavellian commitment to the idea that a Christian morality of the good and the exercise of politics were and should be integrally connected and mutually reinforcing, however ecclesiastical and secular authorities might divide their respective responsibilities. This was especially true of Reformed Protestant regimes in geographically restricted areas, such as the walled cities of Heinrich Bullinger's Zurich or Theodore Beza's Geneva. There, magistrates were expected to foster the zealous preaching of the Gospel, the diligent promotion of Christian morality, and the steadfast maintenance of the discipline that John Calvin called the "sinews" *(nervis)* of the church.[83] Deploring the chasm between actual practice and true Christian teaching in 1523, Zwingli argued "that rulers should, above all else, bring their people under the right, true knowledge of God" and that "all laws be made to conform to the law of God [*alle gsatzt stellen by dem gsatzt gottes hin*]."[84] Any contrast with Luther's "two kingdoms" and his distinction between them was less significant in practice than might be imagined, because Lutheran authorities similarly sought to create a Christian moral community through political authorities' oversight of subordinate, cooperative pastors, whether in German territories or the Scandinavian countries.[85]

Despite retaining an orientation toward eternal salvation, the morality that magisterial Protestant regimes sought to inculcate differed from inherited Christian virtue ethics in crucial ways. The differences derived especially from the magisterial reformers' theological anthropology and soteriology, which was in turn contingent on their biblical exegesis. In sixteenth-century Lutheran and Reformed Protestant theology, salvation had nothing to do with the virtues because it had nothing to do with human freedom or the human will. Virtuous Christian behavior did not contribute to one's eternal salvation but was a sanctifying *consequence of* salvation by faith through grace, effected wholly by God. Magisterial Protestant reformers rejected the Roman church's view of human nature, convinced that it was based on a misreading of scripture adulterated by pagan philosophy. According to them, even after baptism human beings apart from God could do nothing but sin and could contribute nothing to their own salvation. As Calvin put it, "whatever our nature conceives, incites, constructs, and sets in motion is always evil."[86] Had not Jesus said plainly, "apart from me you can do nothing"? (Jn 15:5)

There was no positive remnant of the *imago Dei* in the human will, no "there" there onto which God's grace could be grafted, but only a bottomless cauldron gushing forth sin, "just as a raging furnace blows forth flame and sparks, or a bubbling spring pours out water without end."[87] This was simply a corollary to and the very point of justification by faith *alone* and salvation by grace *alone*. Predictably, sinful human beings rebelled against the humiliating implications of Christianity's foundational truths. But God's Law decimated every self-justificatory human pretense, for no one could fulfill the standard that Jesus set in his Sermon on the Mount. Only thus drained of self-satisfied pride could desperate sinners, like desiccated sponges, be readied to receive the waterfall of God's saving grace that produced justifying faith, then sanctifying works. A gradual process of habituation and rational disciplining of the passions by incrementally more competent practitioners of the moral virtues, whether theorized by scholastic theologians or Erasmian humanists, risibly misgauged the depravity of fallen human nature and radically misunderstood how God works. A gratuitous gift divinely guaranteed, God's grace came all at once, not in sacramentally dispensed dribs and drabs or through the "free" exercise of acquired virtues. Indeed, exhortations to practice the virtues as part of the process of salvation were blasphemous: they amounted to covert calls for human beings to try to save themselves, to resist, in Calvin's phrase, being "broken and crushed by consciousness of our poverty."[88] God smashed through his Law and saved through his Gospel. Human beings contributed exactly nothing. Small wonder, then, that Luther railed against Aristotle in 1520 as "a damned, arrogant, roguish heathen" and specifically lambasted his *Nicomachean Ethics* as "worse than any other book, completely opposed to the grace of God and Christian virtues."[89]

In these ways, the magisterial Protestant reformers, despite creating their own versions of a Christian ethics of the good, not only separated themselves from the moral community of the Roman church but rejected its version of teleological Christian morality. They denied the free, rational exercise of the virtues in pursuit of the good any place in disciplining the passions and redirecting untutored human desires. Twisted human wills retained no orientation toward the good, so there was nothing to tutor—no "*Voluntas*" but only a "*Noluntas,*" in Luther's neologism. Morality's natural law as traditionally conceived was therefore a category mistake, because sinful human beings were *not* free to pursue good and avoid evil. As Luther said, the human will was like a beast of burden *(iumentum)*, ridden either by Satan or by God, and utterly unable itself to choose between them.[90] It was clear to Melanchthon which rider sat astride the wills of Anabaptists no less than of the "common man" in 1524–1526: his visitation to sites in Thuringia in the summer of 1527 was followed promptly by a much more positive reassessment of Aristotle's *Nicomachean Ethics* and a decision to reintroduce it into the university curriculum in Wittenberg.[91] Precisely because Law and Gospel were radically distinct, Melanchthon could entirely separate morality from theology, "in effect applying Luther's doctrine of the two kingdoms to ethics."[92] Self-exonerating papists remained oblivious of morality's foundation: movement toward the Christian good could only begin when human beings realized just how shockingly bad they are. But this was exactly what Romanists resisted. Far from being the universal Christian moral community, the Roman church *could* only be a satanic institutionalization of self-deception.

Promoted from its traditional subordination to *caritas* among the three theological virtues, faith was redefined by Lutheran and Reformed Protestant theologians as the all-or-nothing cornerstone of Christian life, the result of no human merit, goodness, effort, or cooperation with God. God's elect, however, whom he mercifully chose to justify by his gift of faith through grace—in contrast to the reprobate whom he mysteriously chose to damn eternally—would *as a result* of God's saving action bear good fruit out of divinely worked, zealous gratitude to their savior, doing his will by loving others and meeting their needs in biblically sanctioned ways. Freed from the anxiety of trying to be good enough for God, joyful Christians, certain of their salvation, would become good-works dynamos for the sake of the common good. Seventeenth-century Arminian protestations notwithstanding, the reprobate were by contrast deprived of God's saving grace and thus by definition lacked any genuine exercise of *caritas* regardless of appearances, just as they were unalterably destined for eternal damnation after death. But so long as the reprobate lived and listed toward wickedness, divinely established magistrates (Rom 13:1–4) assisted by pastors could at least try to make them conform to laws consistent with the Gospel, and were obliged to punish their transgressions. Authorities were to seek dutifully to create the concrete political conditions within which the moral community of the church could flourish. Though it had nothing to do with salvation, ethics could still regulate the external behavior of the outer man. And it had to, considering the squalor of sin in which the Johannine world was mired. "Let no one dare think," Luther wrote in 1524, "that the world can be ruled without blood. The secular [*welltlich*] sword should and must be red and bloody [*blutrustig*], for the world will and must be evil. Thus is the sword God's rod and vengeance on it."[93]

Accordingly, and consistent with their coordinated concerns to secure political control as they promoted the Gospel, conscientious Protestant rulers oversaw ethical regimes that were dominated not by habituation in Christian virtues but by the following of moral rules. These rules were based on God's biblically revealed laws, above all the Ten Commandments. This was little burden for the godly elect, keen as they were not merely to observe God's laws but divinely empowered to love others with gratitude. But insofar as such tirelessly virtuous, zealously loving magisterial Protestants seem to have remained distressingly few and far between—a fact deplored by many of the reformers themselves, lamented by Elizabethan and Jacobean Puritans, and criticized by radical Protestants as well as Catholics— conscientious authorities needed a clear-eyed strategy to maintain order commensurate with the depravity of human nature. Through biblical moralism Protestant reformers and rulers sought to close the pre-Reformation gap between Christian prescription and practice. Hence the centrality of covenant theology in Reformed Protestantism, whether in late sixteenth-century Heidelberg or seventeenth-century New England.[94] Public morality simply *was* following the rules stipulated by the restored church's leaders working with the political authorities established by God. Small wonder that scripturally ignorant medieval Christians had been so immoral. The most important social virtue among early modern Lutherans and Reformed Protestants, at every social level from disciplined individuals through patriarchal households to well-ordered regimes as a whole, was therefore not *caritas* but obedience—newly important given the sobering truth about human nature and the reality of a divided Christendom. Interiorly freed Christians were to be publicly obedient Christians in magisterial Protestant regimes. Leniency was an unaffordable luxury considering the constant threat posed by radical Protestants and papists, whose pluriform waywardness and stubborn resistance to self-knowledge only confirmed for knowledgeable magisterial Protestants the depths of human sinfulness. The Peasants' War of 1524–1526 and Anabaptist Kingdom of Münster of 1534–1535 remained permanent reminders of the cost of nonchalance, while the post-Tridentine reinvigoration of Antichrist's kingdom permitted no easing of vigilance. Soteriological convictions and external threats thus reciprocally influenced the moralistic character of magisterial Protestantism throughout the early modern period.

The dangers posed by distressingly persistent heresies and their disruptive successes fostered an increased emphasis on obedience in post-Reformation Catholic regimes as well—not that it had been lacking alongside the emphasis on the virtues in late medieval Christianity. Early modern Catholic monarchs viewed loyalty to Rome, the use of baroque art's emotive power, and the formation of devoutly dutiful clergy and laity as the best bulwark against religiously deadly, socially divisive, and politically subversive errors. This was as true in regions where heresy was largely suppressed, such as Spain and Italy, as it was in those where the faith was violently contested, such as France and the Low Countries. Indeed, insofar as disobedience was the sine qua non of the entire Reformation, nothing was more important than obedience to the precepts of Christ's universal church led by his vicar, the pope. What else could hold anything together? More weight placed on obedience meant that Catholic leaders also stressed laws, obligations, and rule-following more than their medieval predecessors had, which was related to the transformation of post-Tridentine Catholic moral theology into a discrete expertise. Focused more on the natural moral law and the Ten Commandments than on the exercise of the virtues, it emphasized the fulfillment of obligations in particular human acts according to legal requirements consonant with the dictates of the informed individual conscience conceived in juridical terms, an emphasis that largely displaced the traditional virtue of prudence.[95] This transformation fueled the boom in Catholic moral casuistry from the late sixteenth century, especially among the Jesuits, and essentially created what would become known as the "manualist" tradition in Catholic moral theology.[96] Closely related to the sacrament of penance and to the evaluation of "cases of conscience," this tradition persisted into the second half of the twentieth century in Roman Catholicism. Just as the practice of moral virtues demands the exercise of prudence, so do moral rules and obligations always require interpretation and application to specific cases, a complex task for which the Roman church's continuing commitment to scholasticism remained well-suited despite the implications of its transformed moral theology for seminary-trained clergy and the laity whom they taught, pastored, and counseled.[97]

Indeed, the moralistic character of early modern Catholic and magisterial Protestant regimes carried over into the nineteenth and twentieth centuries. It helps to explain why in the early twenty-first century many Christians understand ethics less as the pursuit of holiness linked to human flourishing as part of the imitation of Christ, than in legalistic terms as "following the rules" lest punishment ensue. It also helps to account for the strength of the dominant secular narrative of Western modernity as an emancipatory drive for ever-greater individual liberation from resented impositions, with religion interpreted primarily as a form of oppressive social control.

Yet formal moral theology and its applications were far from the whole of Roman Catholicism as it was lived in early modern Europe. Despite their increased moralism and legalism, post-Reformation Catholic leaders and writers maintained a commitment to teleological virtue ethics, just as they insisted on an Aristotelian framework for natural philosophy throughout the early modern period. Post-Tridentine Catholicism was therefore not as exclusively moralistic as early modern Lutheranism or Reformed Protestantism because the virtues remained centrally important to the pursuit of holiness and salvation, a fact reflected in Catholic homilies, catechisms, saints' lives, plays, and works of piety. François de Sales, for example, devoted by far the lengthiest part in his *Introduction to the Devout Life* (1609), one of the most popular Catholic devotional treatises of the seventeenth century, to "many counsels pertaining to the practice of the virtues" and filled his work with references to episodes from the lives of the saints as examples to be imitated.[98] Even Pascal, deeply influenced by Jansenism, claimed at the end of his famous wager that transcending religious doubt required overcoming the passions through habituation to practices for which others provided the example: "Follow the way by which they began. That is, in acting entirely as if they did believe, in taking holy water, in having masses said, and so forth. Naturally enough that will make you believe and will derationalize you [*vous abêtira*]."[99] One did not wait until God flooded one's soul with the grace to believe and thus to act. Rather, one came to understand what grace and faith *were* by engaging in the right practices, as centuries of ancient and medieval Christianity had maintained about the liturgy and the virtues. That was why implicit faith had been and remained sufficient for salvation, however desirable was the formal catechesis that fostered an understanding of doctrine. Logically, orthodoxy preceded orthopraxis, but in life it was almost always the other way round.

THE REFORMATION'S INFLUENCE on teleological Christian virtue ethics is apparent in the doctrinal disagreements that precipitated a multiplicity of mutually exclusive Protestant moral communities, in magisterial Protestant soteriology and theological anthropology, and in the increased moralism of early modern Christianity across confessional lines. But much more directly consequential for the displacement of a substantive ethics of the good by a formal ethics of rights, both ideologically and institutionally, were the persistent disagreements *between* magisterial Protestants and Catholics, and especially the recurrent recourse to wars by rulers from different Christian moral communities (however often they found it politically expedient to ignore religious solidarities). Destruction and death of the sort that characterized central Europe during the Thirty Years War, for example, including the famine and disease that war brought in its wake, were incompatible with sustained social and political life, and thus with the maintenance of any meaningful common good.[100] Such unrest damaged whatever church was established, whatever form of Christian life was sanctioned. Unless confessionalization could successfully exclude religious minorities as well as dissent—which would require ever greater surveillance, coercion, and moralism, as for example Louis XIV sought for his France[101]—Europeans seemed to face a grim future with more conflict and violence in which religion was implicated.

We have already seen how the eventual Western solution, pioneered in the Golden Age Dutch Republic and the explicit institutionalization of which began in the United States, addressed this problem in terms of the public exercise of power. Drawing on a long-standing discourse of religious toleration, James Madison's theorization of the free exercise of religion by the individual conscience received institutional sanction and political protection within an American Protestant moral establishment.[102] The same solution was also part of the transformation of morality, for the discourse of religious toleration was simultaneously a discourse of individual rights—one that continued to rely on some Christian claims while rejecting others, whether Catholic, Lutheran, or Reformed Protestant. Although at the end of the eighteenth century few Americans (as opposed to some French revolutionaries) seem to have imagined such an eventuality, the institutional framework of the modern liberal state and its ethics of rights provided the political protection for individuals to reject religion altogether. Combined with the failure of modern attempts to discover or fashion a persuasive secular ground for morality, the liberal state and its correlative ethics of rights have thus facilitated the subjectivization of morality and, in the ways analyzed by MacIntyre, insured the insolubility of moral disagreements for the foreseeable future. Hence the character of contemporary moral disputes and the history of modern moral philosophy cannot be separated from the history of the Reformation, the history of liberal political thought, or the exercise of power by modern states—not to mention the expansive growth of capitalism, the development of modern science, and the explosive growth of technology and its applications, all of which have been facilitated by the institutional framework of modern states and have in turn affected ethical discourse and practice by influencing claims about what is true, what is good, and what is desirable.

In 1789 the disestablishment clause of the First Amendment to the U.S. Constitution would address the relationship between the fledgling American nation and religion, but its underlying notion of individual, subjective rights already animated the Declaration of Independence. In the Declaration's preamble, the young Thomas Jefferson asserted in a phrase only lightly edited by his congressional colleagues that "we hold these truths to be self-evident: that all men are created equal; that they are endowed by their creator with certain inalienable rights; that among these are life, liberty, and the pursuit of happiness."[103] Given that there had never been anything self-evident about such claims, however common they had become by the late eighteenth century, one might admire the strategic moxie that in pressured circumstances sought preemptively to stifle all would-be criticism and debate. That is what claims of self-evident truths try to do, by offering assertions in place of arguments. But as Jefferson and his colleagues must have known, and as subsequent intellectual history has also shown, such claims—the createdness of all people, their equality, the reality of a creator-God, and the existence of individual rights in general as well as those stipulated in particular—are neither evident nor self-evident. All ancient Greek and Roman, some Renaissance, and some Enlightenment thinkers had either not recognized or rejected some or all of these claims in different ways, based on their respective observations and arguments (and as critics at the time recognized, the American practice of slaveholding itself contradicted the claim about equality and the creator-endowed rights of slaves). Where then did such anything-but-evident truth claims come from, and why did the American founding fathers not argue for them?

They could assert without arguing because of their shared assumptions about God, nature, and human beings, which seemed to place the matters beyond question. They did not argue about the *basis* for rights because they did not have to: in the midst of their crisis with the British, inherited beliefs functioned as needed among the Anglicans, Congregationalists, Presbyterians, Baptists, Lutherans, Quakers, Methodists, Dutch Reformed, deists, and Catholic (Charles Carroll of Maryland) who belonged to the Second Continental Congress.[104] It was critically important for their assertions, however, that despite their doctrinal pluralism the congressional representatives and their respective constituents were *not* divided among themselves—nor, for that matter, with Jews—about the belief that human beings were created by God in his image and likeness. Early modern Christians overwhelmingly had not disputed this point. Had the American founding fathers disagreed about this and drawn out its implications, arguments would have been both as necessary and as interminably inconclusive as they were in doctrinal disputes about grace, sacraments, or ecclesiology. *Because* the congressional representatives and the vast majority of their audience at least implicitly believed what the Western church had always taught and virtually all Protestants continued to share with Catholics, *therefore* their language implied that all human beings were equal before the God who had created them and that they had an inherent dignity and freedom, the violation of which was morally wrong. *Therefore* they believed that rights were real. *Therefore* they condemned King George III's tyrannical violation of their rights; and *therefore* the free male colonists legitimately exercised their rights and made emancipatory war on the British, buoyed by a republican ideology that dovetailed with their beliefs about rights. The colonists' exertion of power, their accusations of tyranny, their declaration of independence, and their ultimately successful war depended for legitimacy on a shared belief that human beings were what Christianity said they were. Otherwise their actions would have been criminally rebellious and indefensibly treasonous. Because the traditional Christian view of human beings as created by God was part and parcel of the wider culture that had survived the Reformation era's religious divisions and their transplantation to North America, it could be and was taken for granted in both the Declaration of Independence and the Bill of Rights.[105] In this respect, given the eventual, subsequent influence of the United States in the spread of individual rights especially since the international human rights movement burgeoned in the mid-1970s, the moral foundations of the modern liberal state in general are inextricable from central Christian truth claims.[106]

At the same time, however, the founding documents of the United States enshrined not a substantive ethics of the good but a formal ethics of rights, one that departed in critical ways from the conception of rights both in medieval Christianity and in magisterial Protestantism during the Reformation era. In the sixteenth century, Lutherans and Reformed Protestants had transformed the medieval discourse on rights, turning it *against* the Christianity taught and practiced in the Roman church. They claimed that the established church tyrannically oppressed the Gospel and was a corrupt, (im)moral community. Basing their resistance on (divergent) biblical counterclaims about true Christianity, the Lutheran leaders who composed the Magdeburg Confession (1550), for example, and the Reformed Protestant leaders who articulated political resistance theories beginning in the 1550s, argued for the rights of true Christianity and the true church in the face of oppression by the Romish Antichrist.[107] But this simply begged the Reformation era's central questions about what true Christianity and the true church were. Beginning in the early 1520s and never disappearing thereafter, it was obvious that *individuals* who rejected the authority of the Roman church disagreed about the meaning of scripture. As far as many radical Protestants were concerned, attaching rights to Lutheran or Reformed churches merely replicated, in a magisterial Protestant idiom, the traditional corporate rights and oppressiveness of the Roman church. What about all the other Protestant truth claims, present from the outset of the Reformation but largely held in check after the Anabaptist Kingdom of Münster was suppressed in 1535 and before the English Revolution exploded in 1640?

Radical Protestants neither went away nor ceased to reject magisterial Protestant moral communities, regardless of the dissembling to which they were frequently driven and the accommodations they reached with political authorities.[108] The vastly greater influence of Lutheran and Reformed regimes, a function of their political power, had obscured the preferentiality of the particular versions of Protestantism that anti-Roman political authorities had institutionalized, whether in Europe or in Puritan New England. But increasingly, especially in the seventeenth century, radical Protestants such as John Milton and Roger Williams exposed it. They claimed that an individual Christian was no more bound to institutions, traditions, authorities, or the opinions of others than was an individual philosopher as construed by Descartes, Spinoza, or Hobbes, their contemporaries. In Milton's view, "the scripture only can be the final judge or rule in matters of religion, and that only in the conscience of every Christian to himself," for "every true Christian, able to give a reason of his faith, hath the word of God before him, the promis[e]d Holy Spirit, and the minde of Christ within him."[109] Milton, Williams, and others simply spelled out what was implicit in Luther, Calvin, and every other sixteenth-century Protestant reformer. In principle, this undermined the importance of counsel that shaped one's formation in a moral community and the exercise of prudence within it—in the end one was one's own sovereign authority, answerable only to God. Indeed, in principle this pointed to the end of Christian moral communities as such, except among those individual Christians who happened to agree with one another, for as long as they happened to agree, and thus formed a Lockean "voluntary Society of Men, joining themselves together of their own accord"—that is, a church.[110] Those who disagreed simply found or founded another community, as William Temple observed admiringly in the early 1670s about Holland, where "almost all Sects that are known among Christians, have their publique Meeting-places," and yet "the differences in Opinion make none in Affections, and little in Conversation, where it serves but for entertainment and variety."[111]

Because *individuals* disagreed about the meaning of God's word, *individuals* and not politically favored churches were and had to be the bearers of rights, beginning with the right to religious liberty. After all, individual human beings, not institutional churches, were the ones created in the image and likeness of God, and it was thus individuals who had to be protected from persecutory depredation. Correlatively, this meant that individuals had simultaneously been conceived—in principle—as their own arbiters of the good, because the good is exactly what was at stake in the disagreements among Christians. Leaving each person free to determine the good based on "the word of God before him" and "the mind of Christ within him" would prove to be *at one and the same time* the modern basis for protecting individual human beings against certain forms of coercion by the state, and the unintended road to the elimination of any shared notion of the good. It was both the means to safeguard the integrity of individual human consciences and human bodies, and the principal ideological foundation for the eventual subjectivization of morality. Beginning in the late eighteenth century, the state's political protection of an ethics of rights provided the principal institutional framework.

The drastic transformation of the discourse of natural, universal subjective rights as articulated in medieval canon law—first used against the Roman church by magisterial Protestants, then applied by radical Protestants against magisterial Protestant churches as well—accompanied a rejection of the idea that a ruler's foremost duty was to promote a moral community and a substantive common good. The new ethics of rights reflected the identification of "religion" as a domain of life *separate* from "secular" concerns, as discussed in Chapter 3, as well as the construction of new distinctions between public and private affairs, politics and ethics. Characteristic of such conceptualizations, for example, were the opening words of the 1757 edition of Montesquieu's *Spirit of the Laws:* "What I call *virtue* in a republic is love of the homeland, that is, love of equality. It is not a moral virtue or a Christian virtue; it is a *political* virtue."[112] The wars of the Reformation era and the prosecution of religious dissenters had revealed the deleterious practical costs of rulers' aspirations to promote a substantive moral community. The sanction of an individual right to freedom of religion signaled the renunciation of this aspiration, at least in principle. No more would—or could, it seemed—rulers persist in the long-standing Platonic, Aristotelian, and Christian conviction that politics and ethics formed an integral whole. Ironically, it was the intensification of this ideal by confessionalizing Christian authorities, and the concretely destructive ways in which they acted on their commitments, that helped to precipitate its demise. And no less ironically, it was the deliberate separation of church and state in the United States that helped eventually to ensure a much wider protection of individuals from political coercion in ways that relied both on teachings about nature as God's creation and about human beings as created in God's image.

The sixteenth-century fact of recurrent violence and its consequences prompted increased appreciation for Machiavelli's bracketing of ethics from the public exercise of power. Not fortuitously was the combination of a revived Pyrrhonian skepticism and neo-Stoicism, which persisted well into the seventeenth century, first articulated in the 1570s at the height of the French Wars of Religion and the Dutch war with Spain. Indeed, those who forged the "new humanist" Tacitean ideology of raison d'état in the late sixteenth century had a still darker view of rulers and ruled than did Machiavelli, and certainly sought less from politics.[113] Republican glory and honor were out; simply securing peace was in. Machiavelli had not denied the rectitude of traditional morality. By contrast, the anti-Aristotelian moral skepticism common in the early seventeenth century separated the self-interested desires of individual subjects more decisively from the bottom-line duty of self-interested rulers to preserve peace and maintain public order. It was this distinction between the interests of individual subjects and the interests of rulers that major seventeenth-century thinkers in their respective ways wanted to extricate from its skeptical origins, seeking to set both ethics and political theory on stable, supra-confessional foundations that could avoid the problems derived from Christian doctrinal disagreements.[114] In his *Rights of War and Peace* (1625), Grotius thus sought to overcome skepticism about shared moral and political norms, just as Descartes sought in the 1630s to transcend epistemological skepticism.[115] As the Thirty Years War and English Revolution plainly showed, neither neo-Stoicism nor skepticism had tamed the militantly Catholic ambitions of the Jesuit advisers to Emperor Ferdinand II or Duke Maximilian I of Bavaria in the 1620s, for example, or persuaded anti-Laudian Puritans in England to conform to Charles I's crypto-papist Protestantism in the early 1640s.[116] Subsequent political and moral theorists would seek to offer stronger remedies.

Beginning formally in the United States, individuals, their rights secured by the state, would choose their own goods as they chose their own beliefs—so long as they obeyed the state's laws, which because of the new way in which politics was distinguished from ethics defined public *but not individual* morality. Something new was created: a "private sphere" within which individuals could do as they pleased based on their own beliefs and preferred goods, provided they were publicly obedient. As we saw in the previous chapter, too, this was widely welcomed. The enthusiastic, patriotic republicans of the new nation would be doing no more than obeying the laws of free men, self-legislated through their elected representatives. And legislators could afford to give American citizens such freedom in their private lives in part because capitalist production and consumption practices were providing new goods to stimulate and satisfy the desires of politically

obedient individuals, heirs to the industrious revolution that had penetrated even the rural areas of the American colonies-become-states by the
later eighteenth century.[117]

The unprecedentedly formal, substantively empty, and baldly asserted
claims about self-evident truths and inalienable rights in the founding documents of the United States were socially viable because American Christians
continued to hold so much in common despite their differences.[118] Prior to
the Civil War, too, Americans filled in the blanks of their constitutionally
guaranteed rights through their participation in their respective moral communities: the (mostly Protestant) churches (and in much smaller numbers,
the synagogues) to which they belonged. Overwhelmingly, through them
and their families they learned their moral values and behaviors. Tocqueville
saw this clearly in the early 1830s, and the most prominent nineteenth-
century American Catholic intellectual, too, the convert Orestes Brownson,
was from the mid-1850s keen on the way in which such remarkably empty
rights could be filled with Catholic content.[119] The American founding fathers intuited, for their own time, how a novel ethics of rights could assume
without having to spell out or justify the widespread beliefs that socially
divided Christians continued to share notwithstanding their divergent convictions. *What they could not have foreseen was what would happen to an
ethics of rights when large numbers of people came to reject the shared
beliefs that made it intellectually viable and socially workable.* They could
not have imagined what would happen when instead, intertwined with new
historical realities and related behaviors, millions of people exercised their
rights to convert to substantially different beliefs, choosing different goods
and living accordingly. Only then, especially after World War II and even
more since the 1960s, would the emptiness of the United States' formal ethics of rights start to become visible, the fragility of its citizens' social relationships begin to be exposed, and its lack of any substantive moral
community be gradually revealed through the sociological reality of its
subjectivized ethics. Civil society and democratic government depended on
more than deliberately contentless formal rights. But what would or could
that "more" be, and where would it come from, if religion no longer provided shared moral content as it had during much of the nineteenth century? Temporarily, the Cold War helped. Some high-profile expressions in
the 1950s symptomatically linked lowest-common-denominator religious
phrases to anticommunist American nationalism. In late 1952, for example,
President-elect Eisenhower famously remarked of the United States that
in contrast to Soviet ideology, "our form of government has no sense unless
it is founded in a deeply felt religious faith, and I don't care what it is."[120]
In 1954 the phrase "under God" was added by Congress to the American

Pledge of Allegiance, followed in 1955 by the addition of "In God We Trust" to American currency, the same phrase that in 1956 replaced "E Pluribus Unum" as the nation's official motto.[121]

The creation of modern, liberal states as the institutional guarantors of individual rights might have avoided the subjectivization of morality if modern moral philosophy had succeeded in its principal objective: to discover or create a convincing secular foundation for ethics and thus for a shared moral community independent of inherited Christian or other religious beliefs. But this did not happen, whether with respect to the good, human priorities, or right and wrong. Or at least it has not happened thus far, and to judge from the last four centuries and current state of Western moral philosophy, there are no realistic prospects for its success. The attempt was obviously an urgent enterprise of the greatest "real-life" significance: as Albert Hirschman put it, "particularly as a result of the increasing frequency of war and civil war in the seventeenth and eighteenth centuries, the search was on for a behavioral equivalent for religious precept, for new rules of conduct and devices that would impose much needed discipline and constraints on both rulers and ruled."[122] How were indispensable distinctions between good and evil, right and wrong to be justified, how were assertions about the ways in which human beings ought to live to be grounded, if the religious tradition through which the vast majority answered these questions was itself an intractable part of the problem?

Insofar as contentious Reformation-era Christians based their rival truth claims on scripture, ecclesiastical authority, tradition, the witness of the Holy Spirit, and so forth, any moral theory that hoped to transcend confessional antagonisms would have to find a different basis. In this respect, the challenge facing early modern and modern ethical theorists paralleled the challenge besetting post-Reformation metaphysicians who sought to rethink the relationship between God and the natural world. Like metaphysics, morality would have to be based on something else—nature or natural law, reason itself, intuitions, or emotions—and it would have to make persuasive arguments without recourse to contested matters of God's revelation. Proto-Rawlsian "public reason" was born.

Persistent Christian doctrinal disagreements and mutually exclusive moral communities launched modern moral philosophy as an autonomous discipline, deliberately separate from Christian theology—even though most seventeenth- and eighteenth-century moral philosophers were Christians of one sort or another. Almost all of them unconsciously carried Christian assumptions into what they took to be strictly rational philosophizing that stood above mere "beliefs" or "opinions," including into the discourse on individual rights.[123] Chapter 2 argued that modern philosophy has failed in its objective to provide answers to the Life Questions based on reason alone. As part of modern philosophy, modern ethics has failed in the same ways and for the same reasons: there is nothing approaching even rough agreement about what reason discloses or demands with respect to normative claims about human life, the good, human nature, or the scope of ethics itself. Nor are there any neutral means for the adjudication of such disagreements. The same applies even more obviously to attempts to ground morality in intuitions or emotions, which are analogous to spiritualistic Protestants' endeavors to transcend exegetical disputes via recourse to the extrabiblical witness of the Holy Spirit.

Those who reject MacIntyre's analysis of irreconcilable moral disagreements must explain why sophisticated moral philosophers today continue to argue in trajectories that are now more than two centuries old without approaching any nearer to a resolution of their disagreements, and how anyone could possibly devise a rational, consensual means to resolve their differences. Question-begging reassertions such as this one have all the persuasive force of Pentecostal claims concerning the testimony of the Holy Spirit: "A rational approach to ethics becomes possible once we realize [sic] that questions of right and wrong are really questions about the happiness and suffering of sentient creatures."[124] Not according to Kant and the entire anti-eudaimonistic tradition of modern ethics that follows him, in which moral right and wrong have nothing to do with happiness or suffering. Consequentialists, contractarians, and deontologists are all capable of making internally consistent arguments, but they neither share the same assumptions nor start in the same places. They disagree about the nature of human beings and about what ethics is and should be. So they disagree even about the basic principles that should govern the morality of, say, lying or torture. Nor will they ever agree unless they alter their respective assumptions. The rational conclusion, based on the evidence, is the one MacIntyre draws: modern moral philosophy has miscarried in its central objective. Not only has it failed to stem the subjectivization of morality rooted in the Reformation; it has augmented it in a secular, rationalist register. This failure has quite properly marginalized professional moral philosophy, at least as currently institutionalized, as a realistic resource for resolving any ethical disagreements, because it gives no indication of being able to do anything but perpetuate them. In the words of the analytical philosopher C. A. J. Coady, "I, for one, would no sooner think of consulting your average moral philosopher over a genuine moral problem than of consulting a philosopher of perception about an eye complaint."[125]

Because God's revealed will in the Bible was such a bitter bone of contention among Reformation-era Christians, it is unsurprising that many seventeenth- and eighteenth-century Christian as well as deistic moral philosophers turned to God's "other book"—the Book of Nature—in the hopes of discovering a foundation for human morality that could transcend confessional strife. Besides the urgent push born of religio-political conflict, at the time there was also a strong pull: beginning especially with Galileo, exciting discoveries in multiple domains of natural philosophy had overturned mistaken Aristotelian conceptions and revealed the predictive power of careful observation linked to the early mathematical modeling of natural phenomena. Why not apply the same methods to human nature? Many seventeenth- and eighteenth-century thinkers, from Grotius through the philosophers of the Scottish Enlightenment and beyond, sought to ground moral philosophy and political thought in "natural law" or "natural rights."[126] The Newtonian, largely deistic Jefferson in the preamble to the Declaration of Independence referred in seemingly innocuous fashion to "the laws of nature and of nature's God" as the basis for ideas that legitimated the rejection of Britain's continued control of the American colonies. The following year, in the "Bill for Establishing Religious Freedom" that became the Virginia Statute for Religious Freedom in 1786, he wrote that liberty of religion belonged among "the natural rights of mankind," for "Almighty God hath created the mind free."[127]

But as had long been apparent by the late eighteenth century, despite the enthusiasm among Enlightenment philosophers for natural law or natural rights as the basis for morality and politics whether in France, Germany, Scotland, or England, both notions had stimulated a welter of rival truth claims that replicated the open-ended indeterminacy of the Protestant appeal to scripture, without any impartial means of adjudicating among them. The wildly different claims made about the human "state of nature" by Hobbes, Locke, and Rousseau, for example, suggest how arbitrary such a notion became once it was detached from its original medieval context.[128] (The same sorts of enormous discrepancies are observable today in the claims made by sociobiologists and evolutionary psychologists about which human norms and behaviors [selfishness? altruism? competition? cooperation?] are allegedly, *as opposed to others,* rooted in evolution—a latter-day extension of attempts to ground morality in nature. In fact, as noted in Chapter 2, all human behaviors are by definition equally the product of evolution.) Natural laws or natural rights were supposed to provide a consensual and uncontroversial basis to settle disputes. Instead, like appeals to reason, recourse to them created new disputes and new things about which to disagree, without prospects of rational resolution. But without other promising paths to pursue, those who had cast off the Roman church and abandoned the contentiousness of Protestant pluralism kept at it. In the

meantime, it was important to keep the rationalist faith, and to keep re-
peating claims about the divisive arbitrariness of subjective religious opinions as opposed to the lucidity putatively shed by the objective light of
reason.

In the mid-seventeenth century anti-Aristotelian thinkers such as Hobbes
and Spinoza observed human beings, unburdened by Christian teleological
assumptions. They did not see sinners awaiting the justification by faith
through grace that would produce good works; nor did they see sinners
with unhabituated passions as yet untutored by the moral virtues, which,
once acquired and exercised, would tend toward the imperfect happiness
and the common good that pointed toward heaven. Rather, they shared beliefs with skeptics and neo-Stoics about the necessarily self-interested character of all human motivation, and the inability of traditionally conceived
moral virtues rationally to control and reorient the passions. They sought to
maintain these commitments, but to replace skepticism with certainty: not
the traditional moral virtues but autonomously exercised philosophical
reason would provide the means to address the passions. Having rejected
final ends in nature and therefore in human nature, Hobbes observed
nothing in human behavior but universal, efficient causality that produced heterogeneous desires without any *telos*, highest good, or prospect
of fulfillment beyond mechanistically determined self-interest propelled by
self-preservation, nothing but "a generall inclination of all mankind, a per-
petuall and restlesse desire of Power after power, that ceaseth only in
Death."[129] Pushed by passions and driven by desires, Hobbes's human beings were recognizably the same as Augustine's—but the latter recounted
how he had been turned toward God, of whom he famously said that "our
hearts are restless until they rest in you."[130] According to Hobbes, there was
no "until," but rather only unceasing restlessness. There was no conversion,
and there were no objective moral values. "Good" was simply the name
given by individuals to the subjective objects of their desire, "evil" the name
attributed to the subjective objects of their aversion.[131] Considering Hobbes's
metaphysical beliefs, good and evil could be nothing else. How diametrically
this differed from the prophetic, biblical warning: "Woe to those who call
evil good, and good evil!" (Is 5:20)

Having rejected the Aristotelianism that he mocked repeatedly in *Leviathan*, Hobbes drew the inference of relativism from pluralism and regarded
any morality of the good as a necessarily subjective, constructivist enterprise. These and similar notions were far from confined to elite discourse
divorced from the rest of human life. The social consequences of those who
believed and acted on such ideas, regardless of where they got them, were
evident no less in the Golden Age Dutch Republic or Louis XIV's France

than in Restoration England. In Lawrence Stone's words, "Man was now freed to seek his own personal pleasure here and now, no longer hedged in by the narrow boundaries laid down by moral theology or traditional custom. *This new attitude could lead to anything,* from the experimental breeding of specialized dogs and horses and cattle, to the use of sex for pleasure rather than procreation by taking contraceptive measures, and to challenging the wishes of one's parents over the choice of a spouse."[132] But such actions were restrained compared to behaviors among those who began to see more clearly the implications of the subjectivization of morality and the fully liberated pursuit of pleasure, as did the Marquis de Sade (1740–1814) a century later.[133]

Reason's role in morality, too, was radically transformed by those who rejected teleological ethics. No longer integral to the exercise of moral virtues that no longer tutored the passions that were no longer oriented toward a *telos* that was no longer believed to exist, reason became Hume's "slave of the passions"—the instrumental means applied by desirous human beings to facilitate their self-interested pursuit of whatever it was they happened to want.[134] The good was by definition simply the Hobbesian object of their subjective desires. More than two centuries later John Rawls clearly understood the implication: if there is "someone whose only pleasure is to count blades of grass in various geometrically shaped areas such as park squares and well-trimmed lawns," then "the good for this man is indeed counting blades of grass, or more accurately, his good is determined by a plan that gives an especially prominent place to this activity" and "surely a rational plan for him will center around this activity."[135] The rejection of moral teleology entailed a radically untraditional notion of reason accompanied by a radically untraditional notion of freedom. It is these notions of reason and freedom that have tended to accompany the modern proliferation of individual rights, most recently with the sharply increased influence of an international discourse and movement focused on human rights that began in the mid-1970s.[136] As we shall see in the following chapter, these notions of rationality and freedom have become integral as well to modern capitalism and consumerism. Indeed, the same instrumental understandings of reason and human motivation are now so deeply embedded in regnant neoclassical economics—and not fortuitously, presupposed by Europeans and North Americans at large—that many people simply assume them to be intrinsic features of human nature. As Hume astutely noted, "when a passion has once become a settled principle of action, and is the predominant inclination of the soul, it commonly produces no longer any sensible agitation. As repeated custom and its own force have made every thing yield to it, it directs the actions and conduct without that opposition and emotion, which so naturally attend every momentary gust of passion."[137]

WHEN THE FOUNDATIONAL documents of the United States were written, the vast majority of Westerners were Catholics or Protestants who believed (drawing on convictions shared also with Jews) that human beings were created in the image and likeness of God and that the natural world was God's creation. These were not beliefs that had divided Christians in the Reformation era. Hence in the late eighteenth century a constitutionally guaranteed ethics of rights could be unproblematically rooted in nature. But things have changed. Hundreds of millions of people, especially in Europe, seem no longer to believe such things. Most of them, along with many secular intellectuals, apparently conflating a belief in metaphysical naturalism with the empirical findings of modern science, seem (erroneously) to think that scientific findings make such religious beliefs untenable, as we saw in Chapter 1. And yet most seem unaware of or nonchalant about the fact that their convictions have eliminated any basis for human rights in nature—which means, given their metaphysical views, any basis for human rights in reality. Construed in secular terms, the dominant modern discourse of Western morality has thus been left without any warranted foundation even as strident advocacy for human rights—and the critically important protection of human beings via rights over against brutal political regimes—proceeds apace.[138]

Not only has the good been subjectivized via the political protection of individual rights. Not only has the character and scope of morality become the subject of irreconcilable differences among moral philosophers. In addition, shorn of its justificatory basis, the nakedness of the modern ethics of rights has itself been exposed. Jeremy Bentham famously wrote, in response to the French Declaration of the Rights of Man and of the Citizen: "*Natural rights* is simple nonsense: natural and imprescriptible rights, rhetorical nonsense—nonsense upon stilts."[139] But the situation is more problematic than Bentham surmised, confident as he was that his utilitarianism had at last laid the solid foundations for human morality after millennia of superstitious, pre-Enlightened bumbling. The commitments to metaphysical naturalism and ideological scientism that today govern "public reason" dictate a conception of reality that prevents the grounding of any morality at all. Whatever most eighteenth-century philosophers might have thought, having absorbed in various ways from Christianity a belief in the natural world as creation, if metaphysical naturalism is true then human rights are not and cannot be real, natural, or discovered. They are at most constructed conventions or useful fictions, but intellectually they are unwarranted remnants from a rejected conception of reality.[140] Once metaphysical naturalism and scientism are assumed, "taking rights seriously" is beside the point. All the seriousness in the world cannot conjure them into existence.[141] One cannot *have* them, because there *is* simply nothing of the sort to be had. If human beings are no different in principle from any other living organism—or indeed, to adopt the more fundamental perspective afforded by physics, insofar as no living or nonliving system of matter-energy is ultimately different from any other—then there simply is no basis for any rights, human or otherwise. What empirical inquiry could reveal them? By what methods could they be recognized? One might as well join Descartes in his search for the incorporeal *res cogitans* in or near the pineal gland.[142] Those who think one can both defend an objective basis for rights and reject a belief in the reality of the soul or its equivalent should think harder.[143]

It is not uncommon to hear people insist on the constructed arbitrariness of moral values and yet denounce certain human actions as wrong because they violate human rights. That such a self-contradictory absurdity seems to be widespread and tends to escape the notice of its protagonists suggests both that it is deeply rooted and that it fulfills an important function. Its latter half depends on what Steven Smith aptly calls "smuggling": the importation of unacknowledged premises and convictions from normative religious worldviews that its protagonists have ostensibly discarded, and which are inadmissible on the protagonists' own naturalist terms.[144] If rape or murder is *wrong*, then all moral values are not arbitrary, and therefore there must be a reason why they are not; and if all moral values are arbitrary, then there is and can be nothing wrong with rape, murder, or anything else, regardless of what laws happen to be in place. Similarly, either human rights are real and therefore there is something to violate; or they are constructed fictions based on false beliefs, and therefore no wrong is or can be done when they are allegedly violated.

The incoherence of such a pervasive sensibility—moral values are arbitrary but some actions are wrong—derives from unawareness of the historical genealogy of two desires that are contradictorily combined. The first seeks to maximize individual autonomy to determine the good according to one's preferences (hence the advocacy for arbitrariness). But the second endeavors to uphold human rights as a safeguard against the horrific things human beings can do to one another depending on their preferences (hence the insistence on nonarbitrariness). The first desire is the long-term product of a rejection of teleological virtue ethics, the second a residue of the belief that human beings are created in God's image and likeness. Their combination depends for its appeal on a skepticism that goes only so far but no further. One needs to get rid of a God who acts in history, who makes moral demands and renders eternal judgments consonant with a teleological and divinely created human nature. Otherwise human beings would no longer be the neo-Protagorean measure of all things, and the ideologically foundational modern commitment to the autonomous, unencumbered self would be threatened. But one equally cannot permit human actions that are consistent with the scientific finding that human beings are nothing more than biological matter-energy. Otherwise human beings would be ultimately no different from amoebae or algae, in Stephen Hawking's words "just a chemical scum on a moderate-sized planet," and one could act accordingly depending on one's preferences and desires.[145] So souls must go, but rights must stay; skepticism must be embraced with a carefully calibrated and catechetically inculturated arbitrariness.[146] It must be frozen where it unstably stood after the Enlightenment's supposed supersession of the Reformation era in the late eighteenth century: in just the rights place. As Carl Becker saw decades ago, in order to sustain their moral visions eighteenth-century *philosophes* in different national contexts relied on unacknowledged (and perhaps unknowingly held) commitments about nature and morality derived from Christianity.[147]

In an attempt to address the unintended problems derived from doctrinal disagreements in the Reformation era, Christian contestation about the good was eventually contained by the sovereign liberal state through individual rights. The political protection of rights has in turn unintentionally fostered the subjectivization of morality by legalizing the self-determined good as a matter of preference. But any intellectually warranted defense of rights requires a view of human beings that transcends what can be disclosed through the methods of science. It is difficult to see how such a defense could be mounted today within the confines of "public reason" as institutionalized in the secular academy or permitted in the public square of secularized Western societies. One can of course *insist* on rights, which along with their political enforcement is a very good thing compared to the abusive treatment of human beings under oppressive regimes. But there is no reason to think that rights are more than useful fictions if one believes that metaphysical naturalism is true. In this case there are no grounds for believing there is anything to violate, whatever might happen to be illegal.

Unless one views modern Western moral philosophy in relationship to Christian virtue ethics with a chronological scope that encompasses the Middle Ages, and brackets one's own metaphysical commitments, and questions the adequacy of a supersessionist view of modern Western history, and sees the connectedness of morality to religion, the state, capitalism, and secular ideologies, then one's assessment of morality in the contemporary Western world is likely to be distorted. For example, despite the encyclopedic erudition of his intellectual history of the Enlightenment, the antireligious metaphysical beliefs that Jonathan Israel apparently shares with his favorite historical protagonists lead him both to mistaken supersessionist views about the relationship between religion and reason in early modern and modern Europe, and to misunderstandings about the origins and status of modern human rights. Israel claims that the "systematic, moral, political, and social naturalism" of specifically radical Enlightenment thinkers such as Spinoza, Diderot, and d'Holbach was not only rationally justified (as opposed to preferentially arbitrary) in its repudiation of the still more radical and skeptical claims of thinkers such as La Mettrie, but also secured a foundation for modern, liberal human rights that "clearly constitutes a package of rationally validated values which not only were, but remain today, inherently superior morally, politically, and intellectually not only to Postmodernist claims but to *all* actual or possible alternatives, no matter how *different*, national, and Postcolonial and no matter how illiberal, nonwestern, and traditional."[148] Israel's preference masquerades as reason, and one particular strand in modern rationalism is championed as though it had rationally and clearly vanquished its rivals. Neither the last two centuries of Western intellectual history nor the current state of moral philosophy offers evidence to support his claim.

The antireligious, metaphysical naturalism of radical Enlightenment thinkers neither did nor could do anything of the sort that Israel alleges, given what empirical investigation by the natural sciences has disclosed since the eighteenth century. Assertions such as Israel's ignore the lack of any connection whatsoever between normative moral claims, whatever they are, and the empirical investigation of natural regularities based on the assumptions of the natural sciences. As Christian Smith rightly puts it, "Matter and energy are not a moral source. They just exist and do what they do."[149] That includes the matter and energy that happen to be doing what they are doing, regardless of what they are doing, in the bodies of members of the species *Homo sapiens* that happen to exist today. If we restrict ourselves to the findings of the natural sciences, then feeding the poor, buying one's fifth Lamborghini, and selling girls into sexual slavery are morally equivalent. By design and necessarily, the natural sciences per se are definitionally amoral and disclose no values, whether secular or religious—they are nihilistic in the etymological sense. Their practitioners discover no "dignity" or "goodness," just as they discover no rights to "equality" or "liberty" or "autonomy" or anything else. Nor does anyone else who understands the demands of knowledge as dictated in the academy by the metaphysical naturalism and epistemological empiricism of the natural sciences. In their modern, secular forms in the Western world, all such rights are derived and adapted from Christianity and Judaism, religions in which it makes sense to say that rights are real because it is believed that all human beings are created in the image and likeness of God.

Given the findings of science plus the assumptions of naturalism, any intellectual justifiability for an ethics of rights vanishes. There is simply no empirically verifiable basis for them *at all*. Because of contestation among Christians in the Reformation era about God's revealed will, early modern thinkers understandably turned to God's Book of Nature. But whatever the assertions of Enlightenment thinkers about natural law or natural rights, the findings of modern science in combination with naturalism guarantee that the book can say nothing about ethics. This fact is well understood by those postmodern moralists who, heirs to Emerson's exaltations of nonconformity and Mill's exhortations to ethical experimentation, champion moral "transgressivity" per se as a good.[150] Often with impassioned enthusiasm or even adamant advocacy, people continue to use the language of rights—indeed, considering the subjectivization of the good and the dissipation of any shared sense of duty toward any common good, virtually all moral discourse in contemporary Western society takes the form of assertive and confrontational "rights talk"[151]—but without any warrant for doing so based on the assumptions that govern "public reason." If metaphysical naturalism is true, it is false to claim that human beings are created in the image and likeness of God, because God is a fiction. The human soul as traditionally understood is likewise a fiction.[152] Secular believers delighted to cast off such alleged superstitions will perhaps find less attractive the corollary that exactly the same assumptions leave no basis for regarding individual members of the species *Homo sapiens* as persons. Or for treating them in certain ways rather than others.[153] For by the same assumptions, "persons" are just as illusory and superstitious as souls, as a recent blogger has recognized in claiming that human beings are "all just little pieces of meat walking around this floating rock in space anyways."[154]

In this as in so many other respects, the great modern unmasker was Nietzsche. Deeply influenced by the advances of nineteenth-century science and deeply beholden to metaphysical univocity, Nietzsche understood what it meant to look out on a genuinely indifferent and autonomous natural world, "such that there is no God, or that he takes no Care of human affairs," in Grotius's famous phrase.[155] It meant that *"there are no moral facts whatsoever. Moral judgment has this in common with religious judgment, that it believes in realities of which there are none. Morality is only an interpretation of certain phenomena, or more properly put a mis*interpretation. Like religious judgment, moral judgment belongs to a level of ignorance at which the concept of the real itself, the distinction between the real and the imaginary, is lacking: so that 'truth' at such a level designates nothing but things that we today call 'imaginings.'"[156] But far from rejecting ethics, Nietzsche was all about how to live. His alternative morality of "we immoralists" looking down from the Zarathustrian heights was a hyper-Hobbesian valorization of the passions, of pitilessly strong "ascending life" that despised the weak and loathed Christian compassion for the downtrodden, reviling as well the moral-philosophical residue of Christianity in Kantian ethics and English liberalism. Nietzsche rightly saw that the belief in natural rights that sustained modern rationalist ethics was dependent on Christianity (and on the Judaism he likewise hated); hence atheism entailed nihilism, which cleared the way for Dionysian instinct. To which in recent decades especially, many Westerners have in effect added the expansive coda—"or whatever"— that has become increasingly apparent in the prevailing ethos. It is a point still lost on all moral philosophers who ignore or brush aside Nietzsche's challenge and who continue to argue as if human rights were real despite subscribing to views of reality that afford no such warrant.[157]

Nothing said here should be confused with an alarmist prediction that secularization leads atheists liberated from the threat of eternal judgment by God to rush headlong into all manner of raucous debauchery and blatant immorality. That is generally not what happens. Largely enforced laws and the threat of punishment by increasingly surveillant states contain much of what most Westerners continue to regard as immoral. And as we shall see in the next chapter, capitalism has colonized the desires of the vast majority of modern Europeans and North Americans, regardless of their metaphysical beliefs, in ways that conduce to self-interested conformity. Moreover, as has been mentioned, even highly secularized Westerners continue atavistically to affirm beliefs and values derived and adapted from religious traditions whose logically prior, foundational truth claims they reject. The subjectivization of morality is usually a gradual, piecemeal process that combines new truth claims, behavioral novelties, political decisions, the exercise of power, legal stipulations, institutional innovations, and social accommodations. Societal sea changes typically come through slow, long-term shifts in cultural ocean currents, not because revolutionary surf pounds the shore.

That for now many secular believers still happen to act in ways recognizably consistent with traditional Christian morality is not the issue. It is rather that the subjectivization of the good within a formal ethics of rights whose intellectual foundations have in turn been undermined by ideological naturalism and scientism leaves no basis for grounding any moral values or sustaining any moral arguments. Hence reason is impotent when faced with those who choose to act in ways antithetical to morality *however* defined. "Who are you to tell me what to do or how to live?" Q. E. D. Consequently, rival antagonists can and understandably do dispense with counterarguments in favor of mere (if sometimes sophisticated) counterassertions—as MacIntyre has seen, politics subsumes ethics and power displaces reason once morality is subjectivized.[158] If there is no foundation for the good besides preference, then the lyrics of "Love is a Battlefield" as sung by eighties rocker Pat Benatar trump any and all moral philosophy: "No one can tell us we're wrong." The song is right—because if morality is subjective, no one has or can have any supra-subjective basis for doing so. This view was simply one among countless pop-culture echoes of Nietzsche in the late twentieth century, which continue to proliferate unabated. Another was Woody Allen's emotivist maxim: "The heart wants what it wants"—the implication being that human desires as such justify whatever behaviors they prompt.[159] Goethe's Werther had suggested as much a century before Nietzsche: "And I mock at my heart—and do what it demands."[160] The eighteenth-century Humean slave of the passions is thus indistinguishable from the liberated, twentieth-century Sartrean individual living authentically. The rejection of a teleological Christian conception of human passions, moral virtues, and the good renders them one and the same.

Some biogenetic engineers and so-called transhumanists here see exciting new opportunities, based on their preferences and eager to cater to potential future consumers.[161] Only in self-deceived fantasies could science and technology, and the possibilities they present, be divorced from a history or contemporary assessment of ethics. Nikolas Rose grasps this clearly: "It is now at the molecular level that human life is understood, at the molecular level that its processes can be anatomized, and at the molecular level that life can now be engineered. At this level, it seems, there is nothing mystical or incomprehensible about our vitality—anything and everything appears, in principle, to be intelligible, and *hence* to be open to calculated interventions in the service of our desires about the kinds of people we want ourselves and our children to be."[162] Note here how the "hence" presupposes the subjectivization of the good that leaves nothing but "our desires" in its wake: *because* we now understand human life on the molecular level, Rose implies, *therefore* it is morally permissible to do as we wish. Only the complex history of the relationship among Christianity, metaphysics, science, morality, and politics in the West in the past half millennium could account for such a peculiar logic: if we understand X, we can do as we please with X. Rose's inference is three and a half centuries removed from Milton's insistence that "only in the conscience of every

Christian to himself" can the meaning of scripture be ascertained, but the trajectory from the one to the other is unmistakable: what I affirm and how I will act is a function of my sovereign will. Just as Descartes failed to locate the mind in the strictly material mechanism of the human body, contemporary biogeneticists have found "nothing mystical or incomprehensible" about the biological structures or processes that sustain human life. Of course they haven't. Nor will they ever. What did they expect to find—a soul, or perhaps some rights?

If morality, like all religion, is simply a function of subjective preference, and there are neither intrinsic human goods nor such a thing as human nature, then there can be no *moral* impediments to the deliberate genetic manipulation of human beings so as to accelerate the evolutionary self-transcendence of the species, whatever *legal* prohibitions might happen to remain in place.[163] Why not try to overcome humanity's many problems by making human beings obsolete? Perhaps a biogenetically engineered, higher, better, newer, more advanced post-human species will succeed where *Homo sapiens* is failing. Upbeat transhumanists simply want to enact *their* choices, to pursue their own good in their own way, rather than to sulk in Weberian disenchantment or uptight hand-wringing. Scoffing at "bio-Luddites" inhibited by their "sciphobia," Simon Young declares that "the human adventure is just beginning, and there are no limits to what we might achieve once we embrace the Will to Evolve beyond our human-all-too-human condition."[164] In Ray Kurzweil's expansive vision, "we can imagine the possibility of our future intelligence spreading into other universes. Such a scenario is conceivable given our current understanding of cosmology, although speculative. This could potentially allow our future intelligence to go beyond any limits."[165] With such transhumanists we meet a particularly ambitious, latter-day extension of Marlowe's Dr. Faustus, who proclaimed that "a sound magician is a mighty god."[166] In keeping with the dominant, liberationist ideology of modernity, more choices equals more progress. Technological advances provide the means to move forward. Why let mere biology hold us back? Perhaps transhumanists will eventually garner enough support to protest effectively enough to have their desires enshrined in law as a right, which others will then be exhorted—indeed compelled by the state—to tolerate. As Mill asked, "why then should tolerance, as far as the public sentiment is concerned, extend only to taste and modes of life which extort acquiescence by the multitude of their adherents?"[167] Why indeed, if morality is subjective?

The central social virtue in medieval Christianity was *caritas,* the obviously inadequate instantiation of which was thought by Protestant reformers to imply false teachings that required a rejection of the Roman church. The threat of subversion and fears of heterodoxy in the conflicts between confessionalizing Catholic and magisterial Protestant rulers made *obedience* the central social virtue of early modern Europe. And the central social virtue of Western modernity, within the institutions of the liberal state, is *toleration*—as it must be. The subjectivization of morality demands it, because of the open-ended way in which individuals choose their respective goods and act accordingly, the result of which is contemporary Western hyperplualism. But obviously not everything can or should be tolerated, as is minimally attested by the masses of laws enforced by sovereign states in Europe and North America today. No one is calling for more sexism, racism, or violence in American universities, for example, even though they would obviously make campuses more diverse than they currently are.

Despite rhetorical exhortations to toleration as such, no one except the confused, unreflective, or pathological actually advocates that *everything* should be tolerated, as a moment's consideration makes clear. The real question is thus never whether one should be tolerant or intolerant in general, but whether one ought to tolerate a specific measure or a particular behavior, and why. About this, disagreements are destined to be insoluble in the same way as every other significant moral issue, because of the incompatible, conflicting views of what is good and right that have resulted from the subjectivization of morality as one of the many unintended outcomes of the Reformation. At the same time, the institutional framework of liberal states today *depends* on toleration if they are to avoid becoming more oppressive. The increasing hostility and incivility that characterizes moral disagreements in the early twenty-first century, such as in the American feud over same-sex marriage, in part reflects the extent to which proposed innovations depart from and offend others' countervailing conceptions of the good. It would seem that there can be no rational resolutions to any such disagreements within the institutions and assumptions that govern Western societies today. There can only be political outcomes based on the exertion of power by those who succeed in getting the laws and judicial decisions they want, and thus secure the strength of the state in accord with their desires. The friction and faction produced by an ever more pluralistic subjectivization of morality is bound therefore to lead to states whose character is increasingly surveillant and invasive, coupled with an ever-reiterated rhetoric of freedom and the persistence of formally democratic institutions. Absent convincing arguments for resolving moral conflicts, we are likely to be told ever more about how free we are, and reminded repeatedly about Mill's "greater good of human freedom" that sustains Wolfe's "best way of life."[168] To the extent that citizens do not willingly tolerate what the state sanctions, they will be threatened into doing so or suffer the consequences, for "the nation-state is not a generous agent and its law does not deal in persuasion."[169]

Without question, the protection of human beings via individual rights in modern, liberal regimes is incomparably preferable to the appalling brutalization of men, women, and children in modern dictatorships, whether fascist or Marxist. Nothing could be clearer. And modern, liberal states have in important respects used their political power, which is so much greater than that of early modern states, to permit the potential for genuine flourishing by vastly more people than was true of hierarchical early modern confessional regimes premised on privileges for small minorities. At the same time, if one wants to understand the Western world today, one should not let enthusiasm for the post-Enlightenment triumph of individual rights as the putative apex of the emancipatory narrative of Western modernity blind one to its consequences and the larger processes in which it was and remains embedded. This chapter has sought to encompass more aspects of what was in fact a more complicated past, and thus to tell a less sanguine story that better explains the situation in which Europeans and North Americans find themselves today. In keeping with the critique of historical supersessionism, however, the account would be incomplete without noting the persistence of teleological Christian morality. Intertwined with the lingering influence of post-Tridentine moralistic legalism, the Roman Catholic Church continues to espouse it amid contemporary Western hyperpluralism, notwithstanding the dramatic attenuation of Catholic Christianity in socially significant communal expressions even in many once predominantly Catholic European countries, such as Belgium, France, Italy, Ireland, Austria, and Spain.[170] Officially since the Second Vatican Council the church has also defended universal human rights, but not in the anti-teleological forms typical of the defense of individual rights in modern Western liberalism or the promotion of universal human rights in secular discourse since the 1970s. As was the case in the Middle Ages, the church's defense is based on natural law understood theologically, with the natural world viewed as God's creation, and on the biblical claim that human beings are created in the image and likeness of God.

In medieval Christianity, not only politics but also economics was inseparable from ethics. Just as politics and ethics were radically reconfigured in the makings of modernity, so was economic behavior severed from traditional morality. Avarice in medieval Christendom was one of the seven deadly sins, a vice seen to damage both individuals and the common good. But after the Reformation era, acquisitiveness regarded as virtuous self-interest provided ideological legitimation for the triumph of the industrious and industrial revolutions. Unable to agree about the Christian good, contentious Catholics and Protestants would demonstrate their supra-confessional eagerness to pursue material goods. Chapter 5 analyzes the most consequential way in which increasingly autonomous individuals sought to exercise their politically protected rights within sovereign states keen to promote capitalism and consumption.

CHAPTER FIVE

# Manufacturing the Goods Life

CAPITALISM AND CONSUMERISM have deeply shaped and continue to transform the Western world. Markets make them symbiotic and mutually reinforcing. The engineering applications of scientific discoveries in manufacturing technologies by corporations continue to yield an ongoing stream of salable commodities with no end in sight. Within the legal frameworks of contemporary Western states one can buy whatever one wishes according to one's preferences, one can buy as much as one likes within one's means (including the means extended by credit), and when shopping and buying one is not obliged to heed the needs of anyone else. One is not free to live in a different kind of country in North America or Europe, because only this kind exists. Every Westerner lives in a society pervaded by consumerism and its twin, post-Fordist capitalism,[1] in which the vast majority of the manufactured items for sale are made by poor laborers working for low wages in faraway countries. To be sure, individuals are not compelled to make central to their lives the prevailing consumerist cycle of acquire, discard, repeat. Mutually reinforcing individual desires, institutional structures, cultural attitudes, and pervasive practices have proven sufficiently influential in the aggregate to make coercion unnecessary. The consumerist cycle of acquire, discard, repeat now makes up the default fabric of Western life in the early twenty-first century, regardless of how one assesses it and whether or not one resists it, because "the conditions under which choices are made are not themselves a matter of choice."[2]

Whether in the United States, where professions of Christian belief and practices of worship remain widespread, or in more secularized Western Europe and Canada, the overwhelming majority of people are profoundly influenced by ideologies, practices, and institutions geared toward the consumption of an ever-expanding array of goods to satisfy their wants, whatever they want. Amid the hyperpluralism of divergent truth claims, metaphysical beliefs, moral values, and life priorities, ubiquitous practices of consumerism are more than anything else the cultural glue that holds Western societies together. Hegemonic, liberal states protect and promote these practices. Whatever our differences, acquisitiveness unites us (or is supposed to). Judging from people's behaviors reflected in statistics for consumer spending and economic growth, it is correctly assumed by corporate executives, marketing specialists, politicians, and economists that most people in the early twenty-first century will want more and better stuff whatever their beliefs about the Life Questions or their income level.

Scholarly laments are legion of the advanced capitalist, consumerist reality in which Westerners live and move and have their being. Traditionally such complaints have come from the political left and have often been indebted to Karl Marx. Classic moral critiques of capitalism's exploitative (and often brutally gendered) effects on industrial workers have lost none of their relevance amid the scramble to outsource labor since the 1970s, notwithstanding the precipitous decline of Marxism as a political option in the West since the late 1980s. Only now Western consumers are spared having to see the workers who make their stuff and the factory conditions in which they toil.[3] Preeminently in the United States, outsourcing is directly related to the marked waning of a living-wage working class and of organized labor, a trend that in recent decades has augmented social polarization, opening a greater gulf between (disproportionately white and suburban) white-collar professionals and the (disproportionately black and urban) women and men who, when they can find even minimum-wage work, people the burgeoning American "service industry."[4]

Contemporary criticisms of consumerism elaborate on Marx and Engels's famous line that with industrial capitalism, "everything that is established and permanent evaporates," or more lyrically put, "all that is solid melts into air." But in the early twenty-first century this vaporizing of human life reaches much further than the traditional social relationships and cultural customs of an exploited nineteenth-century proletariat.[5] Zygmunt Bauman, for example, observes in a Levinasian vein that consumers of whatever class increasingly eschew moral responsibility for others unless it happens to suit their lifestyle choices (an observation consistent with the subjectivization of morality analyzed in the previous chapter). Consumerist ideology succeeds through the inculcation of a manipulative, contradictory message: endless acquisition is the highway to human happiness, *and* one should be *un*happy with whatever one has just been persuaded to purchase, no matter what it is.[6] Arlie Hochschild places consumerist capitalism at the center of the decline in the American culture of care, and the deleterious impact of this slide on women, families, and human intimacy in recent decades. In the later nineteenth century "female homemakers formed a moral brake on capitalism. Now American women are its latest recruits, offered membership in the public side of market society on the same harsh terms as those offered to American men. The result makes for a harshness of life that seems so normal to us we don't see it."[7] Marx's "commodity fetishism" has passed through Veblen's conspicuous consumption and Galbraith's affluent society to become a wall-to-wall commodification of everything, exempting neither religion, nor weddings, nor women's ova, nor men's sperm, nor the human body itself, in a milieu into which children are inculturated literally from infancy.[8] Intensified consumerism has also been linked to a waning of political engagement and diminished concern with social justice since the 1960s, whether among the self-regarding Bobo (bourgeois bohemian) baby boomers analyzed in David Brooks's "comic sociology," or among their self-absorbed, twenty-something "Generation Me" children.[9] Why get all worked up about people you don't know when you can go to the mall instead? Combine this attitude with a therapeutic culture's emphasis on feeling good at all costs, and one has a recipe for ignoring politics—because sustained attention to capitalist and consumerist realities might not make one feel good. And feeling bad might prompt recourse to another round of "retail therapy."[10] Considering the effects of consumerism in the world of post-Fordist capitalism, it seems clear enough that one-dimensional man has not generally spawned well-rounded individuals since Herbert Marcuse published his well-known work in 1964.[11] Even the sharpest critiques of the prevailing culture, however, whether in books by astute intellectuals or songs by angry pop artists, are rendered innocuous precisely by being so successfully marketed and sold. Capitalism liquefies all because it can incorporate all.

Many contemporary Westerners, however, swim with articulate enthusiasm in the current of the prevailing culture. They celebrate the triumph of capitalism, extol the ways in which it has transformed the Western world, encourage its proliferation via globalization, and view the export of American consumerist practices as a liberating and democratizing force. Traditionally such views have come from the political right, and often they invoke Adam Smith as their patron saint. The followers of free-market theorists such as Milton Friedman and Friedrich Hayek view modern capitalism as a triumph of individual freedom that has incalculably improved the living conditions and quality of life of billions of people.[12] In David Landes's words, with the Industrial Revolution, "for richer and better, mankind was now set on a path of persistent innovation and development": led in the eighteenth century by Britain and thereafter emulated on the Continent, "those economies grew fastest that were freest" because "the private sector was in a better position to judge economic opportunity and allocate resources efficiently."[13] Markets freed from governmental interference stimulated and continue to stimulate economic growth, it is argued, creating the jobs and generating the wealth that improve individuals' lives and thus contribute to human happiness. Incontestably, what Landes called the "unbound Prometheus" of capitalist entrepreneurship wedded to technological innovation, industrial manufacturing, and practices of consumption has alleviated much of the material impoverishment associated with the lives of most people in preindustrial Europe. It has made possible human comforts and conveniences, experiences and aspirations that were hitherto inconceivable. And whatever the shortcomings of capitalism, few critics would judge it more pernicious than its twentieth-century, state-sponsored alternatives, such as the Soviet Union's centralized economy steered by a political dictatorship, which, especially under Stalin, killed millions of people and destroyed the lives of many millions more.

The very aspects of capitalism and consumerism criticized by those on the political left are lauded by its supporters on the right. Attacks on the dehumanizing effects of outsourced labor, whether skilled or unskilled, have had no discernible impact on the raft of recent authors who encourage entrepreneurs to seize the cost-reducing, profit-making opportunities it represents.[14] From China and Indonesia to Brazil and Mexico, to be sure, many millions of workers are at least to some extent materially better off because of it than they otherwise would have been. Some advertising theorists claim that marketing to children from infants through teens is not only acceptable but praiseworthy, so long as it aims at "kid empowerment."[15] As for consumerism's deadening impact on citizenship and political engagement, James Twitchell notes the changing meaning *of* politics for young Americans: "Ask any group of teenagers what democracy means to them. You will hear an extraordinary response. Democracy is the right to buy anything you want. Freedom's just another word for lots of things to buy. Appalling, perhaps, but there is something to their answer. Being able to buy what you want when and where you want it was, after all, the right that made 1989 a watershed year in Eastern Europe." In the end, despite "the banalities of an ever-increasing worldwide consumerist culture," the fact is that "human beings *love* things. In fact, to a considerable extent we live for things. . . . We live through things. We create ourselves through things. And we change ourselves by changing our things."[16] Certainly (as Bauman and other critics deplore) this is a message reinforced endlessly by advertisers eager to convince human beings that they construct their identity through a never-ending series of acts of self-creation and re-creation mediated by the things they consume. To be is to buy. There is no point, it is claimed, in trying to resist human nature: people want stuff in order to fulfill the natural and normal desires that neoclassical economists claim are insatiable. The fundamental difference between ourselves and all previous periods and cultures, the result of creative entrepreneurship and manufacturing technology, is simply that we have more and better stuff from which to choose—that is, we are vastly freer than our impoverished forebears. As Stanley Lebergott puts it, "the industrialized society is not morally superior. But its members are no less moral, or happy, because their choices are wider."[17] On this count, the acquisitiveness that stems from justified-because-natural desires is at worst morally neutral, fueling what Twitchell calls our "amoral consumerama."[18]

Diverse ethical evaluations of capitalism-cum-consumerism reflect the subjectivized morality characteristic of contemporary Western hyperpluralism. But there is no disputing its empirical consequences. One may think Chinese or Mexican factories in which workers earn less than a dollar an hour and work ten or more hours a day morally justified or not. But their existence and place in the production of goods sold in North America and Europe are undeniable. That is why those on the political right often tend to explain away or minimize the fact—such workers are better off than they would be otherwise, no one is forcing them to labor, conditions in the factories are not really so bad, and so forth. Similarly, one may think the endless proliferation of consumer goods a boon or blight. But that modern capitalism has enormously alleviated poverty and its allied hardships in the Western world is incontestable. That is why since the late nineteenth century only a few nostalgic romantics on the political left (or right) have ever advocated a return to preindustrial life. Whether as political radicals or liberals, they have instead usually argued in one way or another for a less lopsided distribution of the wealth generated by capitalism.

So too, one may regard the *extent* of recent concern about climate change as unwarranted, a politically motivated scare tactic of eco-maniacal liberals desperate to corral galloping globalization. But a large number of different types of empirical studies have confirmed the fact and rate of increase in the earth's average temperature in recent decades and what it might portend for the sustainability of human (and other) life over the long term. Collectively, these studies strongly suggest the likelihood that the increases are related to the industrial processes associated with the production and use of ever more stuff. This renders increasingly untenable any claim that the empirical basis for concern about climate change is *itself* a deceptive political plot cooked up by left-leaning scientists and politicians.[19] To the contrary, it seems more likely that the *denial* of global warming and its relationship to human activities is a politically motivated fantasy of those unwilling to consider the prospect that the globalization of the American dream might be leading the planet in the direction of an environmental nightmare.[20] If the latter were true, it would call into question some fundamental cultural assumptions: that if we have the money or the credit, we are entitled to have as much as we want of whatever we want, when we want it and without obstruction or delay. We construct ourselves, and we make the world in our image. It is, after all, the American dream, and because at a minimum benign if not providentially sanctioned, is supposed to end happily ever after.

What do all these contemporary concerns have to do with the distant past? The relationship between the development of modern capitalism and the Reformation has been debated for more than a hundred years, in large measure because of Max Weber's *Protestant Ethic and the Spirit of Capitalism* (1904–1905), one of the twentieth century's most influential works of historical sociology. Working backward from sociocultural divergences between Catholics and Protestants in various regions of central Europe in the late nineteenth century, Weber argued that Reformed Protestantism in particular unintentionally and indirectly precipitated the takeoff of Western capitalism. Radicalizing the notion of the "calling" *(Beruf)* that Luther had expanded from vowed religious life to encompass all Christians, Calvin emphasized double predestination, which prompted psychological anxiety and a desperate quest to discern in one's own behavior the signs of God's election. Anxious self-scrutiny about one's status in God's eyes thus generated the Reformed Protestant "innerworldly asceticism" characterized by self-conscious hard work, diligence, self-discipline, and frugality that seemed to betoken elect status in proportion as such virtues were consistently practiced. The behaviors driven by this Protestant ethic also generated wealth and profits, especially among English Puritans, which in turn contributed to a sense of God's individually tailored providential favor. Once the original religious impulse about the discernment of one's election was secularized (and here Weber's notion of *Entzauberung* is relevant), the established behavioral patterns remained as a residue: hence the acquisitive, entrepreneurial zeal of modern capitalists, those "specialists without spirit, hedonists without heart" who fashioned the inescapable "steel-hard casing" *(stahlhartes Gehäuse)* of modern society that Weber excoriated at the end of his work. Thus did the migration and transformation of traditional Christian asceticism "out of the monastic cells and into the life of work" through

Reformed Protestantism help "to build the powerful cosmos of the modern economic order . . . that today determines with overwhelming force the way of life [*Lebensstil*] of all individuals who are born into this mechanism, *not* only of those explicitly employed in business, and perhaps will continue to determine it until the last ton of fossil fuel is consumed."[21]

The Weber thesis has generated an enormous amount of scholarly debate and discussion, some of which will be relevant to this chapter.[22] As we shall see, especially concerning the indirect, unintentional effects of the Reformation, there is something to Weber's argument, although probably not quite for the reasons he supposed. Yet his pioneering work has long made modern capitalism's relationship to the Reformation an issue in multiple academic disciplines. Their presumptive relationship is part of the intellectual furniture of educated persons in the early twenty-first century, if only in the vague association of Protestantism with economic progress in contrast to the putative traditionalist backwardness of medieval Catholicism. Despite his major divergences from Marx on matters of economics, politics, and culture, Weber was hardly less appalled by the effects of modern capitalism on human beings.

Very different is the assessment of Lisa Jardine, who has sought and found the deep historical roots of present-day Western consumerism in the Renaissance, antedating by a century or more the Reformed Protestantism emphasized by Weber. She sounds more like Twitchell than Bauman in the conclusion to her history of material culture among the wealthiest Renaissance elites: "The world we inhabit today, with its ruthless competitiveness, fierce consumerism, restless desire for ever wider horizons, for travel, for discovery and innovation, a world hemmed in by the small-mindedness of petty nationalism and religious bigotry but refusing to bow to it, is a world which was made in the Renaissance."[23] Like Weber, Jardine too is partly right. The Western world of all-pervasive capitalism and consumerism indeed has its roots in the distant past and cannot be understood apart from the complex historical processes that have produced it. But in neo-Burckhardtian fashion, Jardine says next to nothing about the continuity between medieval practices and the supposedly "new Renaissance mind" manifest in the acquisitiveness she sympathetically reconstructs: in smaller numbers, powerful lay and clerical elites had been engaging in similar behaviors since at least the twelfth century, when the significant monetization of the European economy began.[24] Jardine also ignores the profound *dis*continuity in the dominant moral attitude toward material acquisitiveness before and after the Reformation era. As we shall see, only through a combination of unintended consequences and deliberate, novel ideology did Renaissance consumption develop into contemporary consumerism.[25]

Friedman, Hayek, and their respective followers are quite right: modern capitalism and consumerism cannot be understood apart from the formal ethics of rights and the individual freedom politically protected by modern liberal states. Modern liberalism, individualism, and capitalism are profoundly intertwined. By and large, liberal democracy really *has* come to mean the right to buy whatever you want—hence the many recent laments about politically disengaged citizens and the impassioned calls for the reinvigoration of public political life.[26] But neoclassical economists no less than the champions of consumerist self-fashioning are quite wrong in thinking that the practices of never-ending, material acquisitiveness are an unavoidable given of human nature, a cross-cultural and transhistorical constant. Such a claim naturalizes acquired, contingent human behaviors in order to justify them and to preempt analysis. Most human cultures have not exhibited such practices, nor have they believed what most modern Westerners believe about material things and their acquisition; rather, "consumer aspirations have a history."[27] The goods life has been manufactured in a double sense: it has been concocted ideologically, and stuff has been fabricated in ever-expanding ways in tandem with the extraordinary malleability and manipulability of human desires. Practices once regarded as dangerous and immoral because detrimental to human flourishing and to the common good have in a dramatic reversal been redubbed the very means to human happiness and to the best sort of society. This is the Western world's fundamental shift from the distant past with respect to capitalism and consumerism. It affects politics, morality, religion, education, marriage, families, and every other domain of human life in what Joyce Appleby has aptly called a "relentless revolution" characterized by ceaseless change.[28] Now more than ever it moves the whole world.

As we shall see, expanding on Albert Hirschman's classic analysis, seventeenth- and eighteenth-century ideologies of acquisitiveness were not based on discoveries of previously unrecognized, timeless truths about human nature.[29] Rather, they relied on particular, historically emergent, tendentious truth claims about human beings and the natural world. Their protagonists rejected competing claims by Reformation-era Catholics *and* Protestants about the ways in which Christians ought to relate to material things, money, and God's creation. Yet ironically, Christians' supra-confessional adoption of practices *consistent* with the new ideology of acquisitiveness was a sine qua non for the transformation of late medieval capitalist practices into modern capitalist societies, heralded above all by the Dutch Republic.[30] The concrete religio-political disruptions of the Reformation era came between the "bravura consumerism" of Jardine's Renaissance elites and the "New Luxury" commodities first sought by members of Jan de Vries's Golden Age Dutch households across a broad socioeconomic swath of Holland's urban population.[31]

As we have seen, religious persecution understandably led most Catholics and Protestants alike eventually to welcome the free exercise of individual conscience with respect to religious belief and worship. By privatizing religion and separating it *from* society, individual religious freedom unintentionally precipitated the secularization of religion *and* society. In an analogous way, this chapter shows how especially from the mid-seventeenth century, Christians willingly permitted their self-colonization by capitalism and consumption whether as an adjunct of a providentially conceived national imperialism, or simply as preferable to the apparent alternative of further religio-political conflicts. Increasingly they preferred to agree to disagree, eschewing theological controversy in order to go shopping—"household management," which in the ancient world was the meaning of economics as such, had come to mean something quite different in the industrious revolution of the long eighteenth century analyzed by de Vries.[32] With a newly acquisitive culture having prepared the ground especially in northwestern Europe, the "gifts of Athena" in what Joel Mokyr has dubbed the "industrial Enlightenment" made more and more stuff available for purchase regardless of what Protestants or Catholics believed.[33] Eventually, markets would function to allocate industrially manufactured, desired goods efficiently among men and women whose religious beliefs no longer mattered at all in the pursuit of the goods life, however they divergently defined the moral good within the state-sanctioned, formal ethics of rights that contained the subjectivization of morality. We saw in Chapter 1 that scientists' particular beliefs about God have long ceased to influence the investigation of regularities in the natural world. Similarly, Westerners' privatized and personal religious beliefs have long ceased to influence the market—except on the margin, as expressed in their preferences of the religious commodities and services they might choose to buy.

Understanding how the goods life has been manufactured demands more than attention to the modern histories of economics, technology, labor, and business. It requires that we attend to the Reformation era, and see how the intensification and demographic spread of capitalist behavior and acquisitive practices in the wake of its disruptions precipitated the progressive disembedding of economics from any public morality except that dictated and reinforced by the market and the competitive self-interest of autonomous individuals.[34] This chapter tells a story of Schumpeterian creative destruction, regardless of how one assesses what was created and what was destroyed.[35] Or what one thinks about the creative destruction still under way.

ECONOMICS CONCERNS ISSUES more fundamental than the allocation of scarce resources or the relationship between supply and demand. It is about the relationship of human beings to the natural world of which they are a part, and to both the naturally occurring and humanly made material things in it. The latter are obviously dependent on the former: what human beings make is necessarily derived from the material resources of the natural world, which in medieval Christianity was understood as God's creation. Hence economics was never independent of theology in medieval Christianity, nor could it be, any more than material things could be outside of creation. What human beings do with material things depends on how they exercise their wills in relationship to their desires and aspirations. Thus economics also fell within the domain of medieval Christianity's teleological ethics and its concern that human beings become the creatures God intends them to be through the social relationships and shared practices of the moral virtues, which, oriented toward the hope of eternal salvation, tend toward reciprocally related individual flourishing and the common good as discussed in Chapter 4, and the promotion of the kingdom of God as discussed in Chapter 3. Some practices that were related to material things conduced to the human good, and others did not; rationally, the former were to be fostered and the latter avoided insofar as one cared about human flourishing. The story of Christianity with respect to economics, throughout the Latin Middle Ages and into the early sixteenth century, parallels the medieval histories of morality and the exercise of public political power: a complex relationship between prescriptions and practices, with so many Christians' manifest failures to live by their church's teachings as a precipitant of new human realities and problems within Christendom that lent strength to Reformation attacks on the Roman church.

Consistent with Christianity's anti-dualist theology of creation and its teleological virtue ethics, late medieval theologians as well as Renaissance humanists argued that money was not evil in itself. The material world was fallen, not evil; nothing in God's creation was evil per se. The medieval Cathars were as mistaken about this as the late antique Manichees had been before them. But money was unquestionably dangerous, capable of dire consequences unless handled with the greatest care, like a deceptively potent substance in an apothecary's shop. After his conversion in the early thirteenth century, Francis of Assisi did not want his companions even to touch it. Unless human beings self-consciously acted in ways that made money serve individual human flourishing and the common good, experience showed how easily it tended to undermine both. If fallen human beings' self-regarding passions were undisciplined by virtues such as humility, self-denial, generosity, and *caritas,* money would function as a poisonous accelerant that transformed baseline selfishness into the deadly sin of avarice, against which so many medieval preachers railed, from Peter Damian in the mid-eleventh century to John Colet in the early sixteenth.

Because according to medieval Christianity human beings were *embodied* souls, material things played an indispensable albeit subordinate role in the pursuit of human flourishing, the common good, and salvation. According to medieval Christian moralists, who drew ideas and fashioned their ideals from scripture as well as the church fathers, avarice perverted this role.[36] It was nearly impossible to thrive when one was hungry, without shelter, and/or without clothing, yet avaricious men and women selfishly sought to augment their superfluous wants at the expense of meeting others' most basic needs. "If a brother or sister is naked and lacks daily food, and one of you says to them, 'Go in peace; keep warm and eat your fill,' and yet you do not supply their bodily needs, what is the good of that? So faith by itself, if it has no works, is dead" (Jas 2:15–17). The wealthy who neglected the needy sinned not only against justice, as Ambrose and others had maintained, but also against Christianity's central commandment of *caritas.*[37] In the twelfth century Bernard of Clairvaux said in one of his sermons on the Song of Songs: "Scripture likewise says: 'If your enemy is hungry, feed him; if he is thirsty, give him drink' [Rom 12:20]. And here you have a matter of action, not of feeling [*non de affectu*]. But listen as well to the commandment of the Lord about love of himself: 'If you love me,' he says, 'keep my words' [Jn 14:15]. And here too he sends us forth to action by enjoining observance of the commandments. For it would have been superfluous for him to admonish us concerning action, if in feelings love were already present."[38] Some material things were a necessary prerequisite for human flourishing because they were indispensable to survival. They were needs, not wants.

An implicit corollary of Christian love, then, was ascetic self-denial: voluntarily declining to seek more than one needed left more things for others still in need, as the actions of many male and female saints had demonstrated, perhaps most dramatically those of Francis of Assisi. "How does God's love abide in anyone who has the world's goods and sees a brother in need and yet refuses to help?" (1 Jn 3:17) According to Matthew's Gospel, Jesus had said that when he came again as eternal judge, he would welcome into his kingdom those who had succored him by feeding the poor, sheltering the homeless, and clothing the naked, whereas he would condemn to eternal punishment those who had ignored him by neglecting them (Mt

25:31–46). Painted and sculpted depictions of the Last Judgment inspired by the same biblical passage were seen by Christians throughout Western Europe in the late Middle Ages. Peter Damian said in the eleventh century that when Paul flatly equated avarice with idolatry (Col 3:5, Eph 5:5), he taught "in a clearer light that the *avarus* is a servant not of God, but of coins."[39] "You cannot serve both God and Mammon," Jesus had said, again according to Matthew's Gospel, making clear in the same utterance that a person could no more ally with both than a slave could belong to two rival masters (Mt 6:24).

The analogy was apt, at least according to virtually all patristic and medieval commentators. Given free rein, avarice tended toward free reign: like a virus that bred adjunct vices, it fed on itself as human desires were twisted to serve the insatiable, unredirected selfishness that Augustine had analyzed with such unsparing insight. A fourteenth-century preachers' manual said of avarice that "when it has gained the whole earth, it wants the sea; and after that, it soon craves for what is in the air. And by rising thus it knows no limit."[40] In barter economies, avarice finds little purchase. *Money* was so dangerous because by powerfully inflating greed it sinfully subverted the good, and *itself* insidiously doubled as the emptily general object of human desire, precisely because with it one could buy whatever one wanted. On its own good for nothing that fostered human flourishing because in itself it served no natural end—what good was a heap of small metal disks?—money was a path to everything and anything, whether good or evil. It was nothing but an amoral means, and therefore potentially deadly. Again, according to the synoptic Gospels Jesus seemingly shocked his own disciples ("Then who can be saved?") with an apparent awareness of the danger that cut to the chase: "It is easier for a camel to pass through the eye of a needle than for a rich man to enter the kingdom of God" (Mk 10:25; cf. Mt 19:24, Lk 18:25). Or again: "Be on your guard against all kinds of greed; for one's life does not consist in the abundance of possessions" (Lk 12:15). The author of the first letter to Timothy, regarded as Paul throughout the Middle Ages, was no less adamant: "those who want to be rich fall into temptation and are trapped by many senseless and harmful desires that plunge people into ruin and destruction. For the love of money is the root of all kinds of evil" (1 Tm 6:9–10). Steeped in the scriptures, the Greek and Latin church fathers reiterated in their respective ways the same concerns about the dangers of money, wealth, and greed—even as they accepted imperial favors and protection beginning especially in the late fourth century, in both respects establishing a foundation for later medieval churchmen in the Latin West.[41]

More than three centuries before Jesus and Paul, Aristotle had analyzed economic realities with unprecedented acuity in his consideration of commerce in Athens and the wider Aegean world. This ancient Mediterranean economy was overwhelmingly based on agriculture and focused on sufficiency. Although it included artisanal manufacture, trade, money, and price fluctuations, it was not a market or capitalist economy.[42] Aristotle saw how the use of money constituted a natural development beyond barter in facilitating the exchange of commodities. This was acceptable, even laudable, insofar as it contributed to the acquisition of material things that aided the human flourishing (of male citizens) within the polis. But he also saw that if the acquisitiveness inherent in wealth-getting *(chrêmatistikê)* was detached from the use value of commodities—once shoes (to use Aristotle's example) were produced for the purpose of exchange rather than for the purpose of being worn on one's feet and thus contributing their minor part in the pursuit of *eudaimonia*—then acquisitiveness could in principle become limitless by becoming an end in itself. Exchange value could overwhelm the use value of material things. *Money* was dangerous precisely because of the ease with which the monetarily mediated, legitimate trade of commodities oriented toward the human good could become the mere buying and selling of commodities for the purpose of making money—or worse still, the usurious use of money for the sake of making more money, by lending money at interest and bypassing material things and natural moral teleology altogether.[43] Like Jesus, other ancient Jews, first-century Christians, and the church fathers, Aristotle regarded economic activity as inseparable from and subordinate to ethics and its objective of human flourishing—which of course in medieval Christianity included not only shared political life but also the hope of eternal salvation for all baptized men and women with God in the communion of saints.[44] Hence Aristotle's terse but penetrating and integral economic analysis in the *Nicomachean Ethics* and *Politics* was taken over enthusiastically by scholastic theologians beginning in the mid-thirteenth century, once Latin translations of works by "the Philosopher" became available.[45] Theologians expanded upon and applied this analysis productively to a European economy that by this time was much more monetized and profit-oriented than the ancient Mediterranean economy had been.[46]

Consistent with the Christian theology of creation and notwithstanding their embrace of voluntary poverty, Franciscan and Dominican university masters in the thirteenth century understood that although money was indeed dangerous it was not diabolical. The humanists with whom they competed for academic chairs and influence from the 1420s, beginning in Italy and spreading north of the Alps later in the fifteenth century, thought likewise—which is unsurprising to the extent that humanists shared with their scholastic predecessors and contemporaries the teleological ethics of medieval Christianity. Indeed, just as Renaissance humanists such as Leon

Battista Alberti (1404–1472) tended to esteem classical virtues more highly than did scholastic theologians, so they tended to rate money's positive potential more highly if not unambiguously, provided it was used in accord with what Alberti called the "holy virtue of thrift [*santa masserizia*]."[47] Both humanists and scholastic theologians thought that if harnessed by the moral virtues rather than perverted by avarice and other vices, money could aid one's own salvation, others' well-being, and thus the common good by making more material resources and related opportunities available for the right ends. Examples such as the twelfth-century merchant-saint Omobono of Cremona demonstrated that nothing at the outset of the sixteenth century compelled a wealthy Venetian, South German, or Flemish merchant to reinvest his profits rather than give them to destitute men and women, for example—even if harsher attitudes toward the poor had become more common by then, and even though civic authorities were increasingly overseeing provisions for urban charity just as they were assuming greater jurisdictional control of other aspects of religious life.[48] On the eve of the Reformation, nothing forced the aristocratic or mercantile well-to-do to buy the latest fashions in fine clothing or to acquire expensive jewelry. They could as well donate the money they would have spent on luxuries to a local house of Observant Augustinians, or to a Dominican community such as San Marco in Florence, the renovation of whose cloister and construction of whose church had been financed in the late 1430s and early 1440s by Cosimo de' Medici.[49]

Among the biblically based, seven corporal acts of mercy so emphasized in the late Middle Ages, at least four—feeding the hungry, giving drink to the thirsty, clothing the naked, and burying the dead—ordinarily involved some financial expenditure, at least in the urban settings where merchants lived and where money circulated year round.[50] The fruitful exercise of the spiritual works of mercy, too, indirectly presupposed the virtuous expenditure of money: the ability to practice these works normally implied that one's own basic bodily needs had been met, just as other people were more likely to be comforted when afflicted, or well counseled when doubtful, or profitably instructed when ignorant, if they were not hungry, thirsty, homeless, and/or naked. There was no doubt that according to the Gospels Jesus had commended if not commanded such behavior, from singling out the widow whose paltry copper coins given "out of her poverty" amounted to more than the donations by the wealthy (Mk 12:41–44, Lk 21:1–4), to his praise of the tax collector Zacchaeus for volunteering to give half his possessions to the poor (Lk 19:1–9), to the chilling story of Lazarus at the rich man's table and their respective destinies after death (Lk 16:19–31), to the haunting admonition to the rich young man who had unimpeachably yet *merely* kept God's commandments: "sell all that you possess and distribute it to the poor, and you shall have treasure in heaven; then come, follow me" (Lk 18:22; cf. Mk 10:21, Mt 19:21). As we saw in the last chapter, ethics in medieval Christianity entailed the pursuit and practice of holiness in imitation of Christ, not simply obedience to moral rules.

The intellectual achievement of scholastic theologians in seeing how money, despite its dangers, fit within Christianity's theology of creation and teleological ethics addressed an imperative of the greatest practical importance. The collective impact of Christians' actions in Western Europe since the eleventh century had made the matter increasingly urgent. Michael Mc-Cormick's magisterial research shows that the upturn in east-west Mediterranean trade expanded already in the last quarter of the eighth century in ways that affected the movement of people and goods on the European continent from Italy and southern France to England and Scandinavia.[51] Yet this commerce occurred in what remained fundamentally a rural world of regional or subregional economies deeply rooted in local subsistence agriculture.[52] Only after Magyar, Viking, and Arab disruptions were controlled did medieval Europe become progressively more morally dangerous with respect to money, however one assesses the relationship among the increase in economic exchange during the tenth century, the "commercial revolution" of the eleventh that was led initially by merchants in the port cities of the Italian peninsula, and the influx of new German silver from the 1160s, which so profoundly influenced the monetization of the European economy.[53]

Eleventh- and twelfth-century commerce entailed human interactions for the purpose of exchanging material things. Buying and selling required physical proximity, so those involved in commerce had to know where to meet. Whereas already existing towns served this function in Italy, in northern Europe the commercial revolution made headway through mercantile fairs such as those in Flanders and Champagne, which in turn fostered the creation of towns as meeting places for buying and selling—functionally speaking, towns were permanent fairs.[54] Like the markets they hosted and the money that changed hands in them, towns in and of themselves were not evil. If integrated with a public exercise of power that promoted the common good through the shared practice of the moral virtues, they expanded considerably the prospects for human flourishing.[55] Around 1260 the learned Dominican Albert the Great delivered a cycle of sermons in Augsburg on Matthew 5:14—"a city on a hill cannot be hidden"—which extolled the German mercantile city and the importance of wealth to its vibrant life long before fifteenth-century Renaissance humanists such as Leonardo Bruni echoed similar views in their effusive urban encomia.[56]

But parallel to the case with money, to the extent that civic power instead served selfishness and sinful vices, towns disclosed their morally dangerous character.

Not only did towns present a much wider range of objects for the potential exercise of avarice, but money facilitated interactions between complete strangers and thus affected the character of social relationships. It depersonalized them. In contrast to face-to-face exchanges of goods in kind among familiar local villagers, urban markets and money made possible the production and consumption of material things by human beings who had never met and likely never would.[57] An absent maker or merchant did not have to look a buyer in the eyes—only a seller did. And even for exchanges transacted in person, unless one acted in a manner consistent with *caritas*, understanding that the unfamiliar persons with whom one did business were created in God's image and likeness no less than were one's family members and friends, one might see them merely as a means to securing a profit, satisfying one's own desires, or both. One might seek to maximize one's own gain at their expense, violating the Christian commandment to love one's neighbor. Such temptations would be all the greater if one was just passing through a town and mistakenly thought that a lack of extra-commercial social ties to its inhabitants somehow exempted one from moral responsibility to them. And one would be more likely to act on such temptations to the extent that one was not well habituated in the moral virtues—which, as we have seen in previous chapters, large numbers of medieval Christians seem not to have been.

Paradoxically, the advent of the European profit economy took Christians by surprise—even though unbeknownst to them, at least at first, some of them were incrementally contributing to its creation through their individual actions. Some of the most committed Christians of the eleventh and twelfth centuries fled from the growing towns when they saw in them the moral effects of money and the social effects of commerce: inspired by the late antique Egyptian desert fathers, voluntarily poor hermits sought Christian perfection in remote mountains and forests, for example, and the leaders of the reform-minded monastic orders—the Cistercians, Carthusians, and Premonstratensians—deliberately established their monasteries far from cities. But the astonishing success and rapid growth of especially the Cistercians revealed the extent to which the monetized economy was already penetrating the northern European countryside in the twelfth century. Indeed, the lay support of Cistercian monasteries and the monks' efficient (and sometimes ruthless) administration of their material resources contributed to its spread. The Cistercians ended up replicating in more compressed chronological compass the trajectory of Cluniac Benedictines over against whose wealth and elaborate worship they had originally sought austerity of life and liturgy.[58]

In what would remain a problematic paradox for holy men and women in subsequent centuries, the renunciation of money attracted money: like bees to nectar, wealthy donors eager to have the prayers of vowed religious were drawn to those who lived the voluntary poverty characteristic of the holiness exhorted by Jesus. Small wonder: even in a world of relative dearth and whatever their level of explicit awareness, lay donors knew how powerful was the concupiscent pull of acquisitiveness and thus how hard it was to overcome. So they admired and sought out those in whom God's power was visibly manifest in voluntary poverty. Holy self-denial thus bred a prosperity that constantly re-presented, especially to the most self-consciously devout in religious communities, the challenge of what to do with material things and how best to use money such that human behavior would serve the pursuit of salvation and the common good.

The monetizing economy and cities were not going away; nor were the Gospel's injunctions about the dangers of money or the counterintuitive rewards of voluntary self-denial. Lay members of the Humiliati pioneered attempts to combine the two as cloth workers in northern Italian cities in the late twelfth and early thirteenth centuries, as did the women who became beguines in parts of France, the Rhineland, and later especially in the Low Countries.[59] But the articulation of Christian moral theology for an increasingly urban, commercial economy was preeminently the achievement of Franciscan and Dominican friars beginning in the mid-thirteenth century. Drawing on the parable of the rich young man and other biblical passages together with patristic and monastic commentaries on them, they fashioned in combination with Aristotle's ideas a solution consistent with the two-tier structure of the Latin Christianity that they inherited. The embrace of voluntary poverty and ascetic self-renunciation belonged to those who "would be perfect" (Mt 19:21) as part of the "counsels of perfection" derived from the beatitudes in Jesus's Sermon on the Mount, but keeping the commandments required only an attitudinal detachment from possessions and money, plus a demonstrated willingness to use them for the common good. After all, about the salvation of the wealthy, Jesus himself had said that "nothing is impossible for God" (Mt 19:26; cf. Mk 10:27, Lk 18:27), so the eye of the needle had to provide a legitimate loophole. The distinction between commandments and counsels of perfection, between mere detachment and voluntary poverty, provided the basic structure for Christian economic thought and the template for Christian economic behavior throughout the later Middle Ages (and beyond in Roman Catholicism). It furnished the framework for *Dives and Pauper*, for example, an anonymous English treatise written around 1410, perhaps by a Franciscan, and printed twice in the 1490s.[60] This distinction also made paramount the determination of what it meant, in one's actions and way of life as an embodied soul guided by the hope of eternal salvation and living in social relationships with others, to be detached from one's possessions rather than possessed by them, such that they might be made to serve one's well-being and that of others. This underscored the critical importance of the moral and intellectual virtue of *prudentia*.

Throughout the later Middle Ages, Christian morality continued to inform a monetized, profit economy centered on cities and increasingly characterized by market practices. Jesus's admonition to "lend, expecting nothing in return" (Lk 6:35) was intellectually reinforced by Aristotle's critique of usury. So usury was still condemned for the way in which it preyed upon those whose circumstances compelled them to borrow money, although scholastic thinkers in their sophisticated analyses of commercial exchange increasingly came to a deeper appreciation of what business loans entailed, and thus argued that repayment for more than the amount of the principal was not necessarily usurious.[61] Debate about the character of the just price for respective goods presupposed that there was such a thing, which was obvious no less from the many biblical injunctions against grinding the poor than from Aristotle's consideration of economic exchange in book five of his *Nicomachean Ethics,* the book devoted to justice. To exact unjust profits in selling was an expression of avarice, a violation of the Golden Rule to treat others as one would want to be treated (Mt 7:12, Lk 6:31).[62] Hence oversight of the market and of prices was a moral imperative incumbent on political authorities lest sellers take unfair advantage of buyers.[63] Whether the private ownership of property was thought to have been originally intended by God or was viewed as a consequence of the fall from Eden's divinely willed community of goods, it lacked the importance later imputed to it by John Locke and was justifiable only insofar as it conduced to the common good.[64] Whatever the mechanism and means, materially to support the poor and otherwise vulnerable remained the biblical injunction it had always been, and avarice was no less a deadly sin than it had been when Jesus and Paul condemned it. In the late fourteenth century, the Paris-trained theologian Henry of Langenstein (c. 1325–1397) argued that the only justifiable reasons to seek more than was needed for sustenance were to secure money to perform religious acts (see Omobono of Cremona above), to make provision for future emergencies, or to support one's children. "Whoever has enough for these things but still works incessantly to gain riches or a higher social status," he wrote, "or so that later he may live without working, or so that his sons may be rich and great—all such are driven by a damnable avarice, physical pleasure and pride."⁶⁵

THE LATE MEDIEVAL GAP between the prescription and practice of the moral virtues in general, as discussed in Chapter 4, is also the key to understanding the relationship between Christianity and economic realities from the eleventh into the early sixteenth century. What the church taught was one thing; what Christians often did was another. This was hardly a matter of poorly catechized, sinfully grasping merchants leading Christendom astray. Those who exercised ecclesiastical authority, safeguarded doctrinal orthodoxy, led the church's worship, and administered its sacraments appeared to many people, clerical as well as lay, as though they were the pioneering, principal violators of the church's own condemnations of avarice—men who, in Tawney's phrase, "preached renunciation and gave a lesson in greed."⁶⁶ Most conspicuous among them were the highest-ranking members of the clergy—the popes and cardinals at the papal court, along with wealthy bishops in their respective dioceses—who, already long before the Avignonese popes and their courtiers intensified all these trends in the fourteenth century, so often sought to augment their incomes through simony, pluralism, and a deep participation in the monetized economy through the purchase of luxurious material things and the borrowing of large sums of money.⁶⁷ Their actions went well beyond paying for beautiful objects and beautiful buildings for beautiful liturgies in which God made Christ present in the Eucharist. The members of religious orders, too, whose holiness attracted wealth, rendered themselves targets of criticism insofar as their expenditures seemed disproportionately to benefit themselves at the expense of the common good. The Spiritual Franciscans found themselves increasingly—and by the late 1310s heretically—on the other side of papally approved, Conventual Franciscan and Dominican arguments about the relationship between the possession and use of material things, even as they sought to adhere to Francis's uncompromising embrace of poverty and contempt for money.⁶⁸ Francis was so displeased at his confreres' purchase of a "brothers' house" in Bologna in 1219—it must have seemed to him a contradiction in terms—that he ordered (mandat) them all to leave it immediately, even those who were sick. Had he been alive to see the magnificent Franciscan church of Santa Croce in Florence, for example, the construction of which began in 1294, it seems clear what his reaction would have been.⁶⁹

But lay crowds flocked to hear the friars preach, and the shepherds dared not neglect them; holiness attracted sinners, and poverty bred wealth. In a church so self-consciously and pervasively hierarchical, the lower clergy learned from and imitated the higher. By the eve of the Reformation, the greediness of the clergy and religious high and low was the most common, long-standing complaint made against them. It is hardly surprising that so many of the laity also behaved avariciously. In January 1510 the humanist and ardently neo-Platonic priest John Colet addressed the Convocation of gathered clergy from the Canterbury Province in St. Paul's Cathedral in London. He enumerated the multiple ways in which priests pursued money and the adjunct vices thereby bred, asserting that "every corruption, every ruin of the Church, every scandal of the world comes from the avarice of priests, following Paul's words which again I repeat and impress upon your ears, 'Avarice is the root of all evil!' "[70]

Besides the condemnation and simultaneous indulgence of avarice among many of the clergy, the medieval Christian acceptance and assumption of *socioeconomic* hierarchy profoundly affected its clerical and lay leaders' conception of the common good, and relatedly of justice, as we saw in the previous chapter. Deference to social superiors was explicitly exhorted in some biblical passages, just as the pervasive ancient institution of slavery was assumed: "Slaves, accept the authority of your masters with all deference, not only those who are kind and gentle but those who are harsh" (1 Pt 2:18). According to the prevailing view in medieval Christendom, God did not intend that those born poor should starve. But neither, apparently, did he intend for them anything more than illiterate poverty. As the poor man is made to say in *Dives and Pauper,* noting that "nothyng in erthe is made without cause" (Jb 5), "I suppose within my selfe, that by ye prevy domes [judgments] of god that be to me unknowen, it is to me prouffytable to be poore. For well I wote [know] that god is no nygarde of his gyftes[.] But as the apostle sayth Rom. viii[:28]. To them that ben chosen of god alle thynges werken to gydre in to good. And soo sythen I truste thorugh the goodness of god to be one of his chosen I can not deme but [that] to me it is good to be poore."[71] However relatively limited was upward social mobility in medieval Europe, it was an observable and known reality, especially in cities. Nevertheless, those whose material means improved through opportunities afforded by patronage, marriage, education, hard work, or their own wits did not unsettle the deeper assumption inherited from the ancient world that socioeconomic hierarchy was a basic template for human life, whether it was thought to be willed directly by God or was seen as an unalterable result of Adam's fall.

Most medieval Europeans probably understood better than do nearly all Westerners today that acquisitive affluence is not a prerequisite for human flourishing—even though they also knew, in times of famine, for example, that utter material *destitution* made flourishing nearly impossible.

But neither could or can human beings flourish fully without education, the ideal end of which in medieval Christianity was integrated understanding, love of God, and contemplation. The illiterate poor who for centuries had tilled the soil and continued to do so on the eve of the Reformation had few if any prospects for such learning. But in a world so dependent on labor-absorbing agriculture, rarely if ever did it occur to elites that everyone might be educated as an expression of *caritas* and a desire for their well-being, which, to the extent that it might have been realized, would also have enhanced the common good. The same applied a fortiori to slaves in the West, whose presence increased, mostly after the mid-fourteenth century and largely in Mediterranean cities, and who were owned, bought, and sold not only by affluent laypeople but also by religious orders and churchmen, including popes.[72] The deeply ingrained, concretely reinforced assumption of socioeconomic hierarchy along with entrenched practices of social deference overwhelmed any socially significant recognition of what Christianity's central ethical claims implied: that insofar as *all* persons are created in the image and likeness of God, a genuinely common good entails the full flourishing of *all* human beings in a given community.

The misgauging of the (allegedly unchangeable) character of human institutions, which in turn was linked to the central moral blindness in Western Christianity throughout the Middle Ages and beyond, would prove extremely consequential. In 1524 it would turn the early German Reformation from a theological protest with political implications into an enormous albeit short-lived mass movement. Especially from the eighteenth century it would become a major target of egalitarian political ideas fused with the revivified republican ideologies that were transformed as they passed from Renaissance Italy through seventeenth-century England to the North American English colonies.[73] The Catholic Church would be a primary target in the French Revolution, too, its leaders insulated by privileges that protected their thoroughgoing acceptance of socioeconomic hierarchy allied with royal absolutism. And from the 1840s, the contempt by Marx and his followers for religion would derive partly from traditional Christianity's self-justificatory naturalization of socioeconomic hierarchy.

Before the Reformation, this Christian misperception and blindness—perhaps partly explicable not only by the need for agricultural laborers, but also by the uncertainties of life and authorities' limited ability to provide security—militated against any deliberate attempts to redistribute wealth in ways that might affect the basic structure of socioeconomic hierarchy. Alms for the poor were an imperative; enough alms to alleviate poverty were a perversion. Some people were impoverished and others rich, even if God in his mysterious providence—to which the ancient pagan category of *fortuna* was assimilated—raised some up and cast others down. The example of numerous affluent men in scripture made clear, *Dives and Pauper* noted, that God opposed not wealth per se but rather avarice: "For ye riche men be not lacked [reproached] in holy wryte for theyr richesses, but for [t]her wicked covetyse and myswyll of richesse."[74] Correlatively, detachment from material possessions meant something different for Italian cloth merchants than for cloth workers, something different for Hanseatic timber traders than for the lumbermen who logged the trees and lugged them to barges and boats for transport, something different for central European nobles who visited Augsburg or Nuremberg than for the peasants whom they taxed with labor obligations and fiscal duties. Clothes that fit the one misfit the other; prosperity suited the powerful, poverty the powerless, and the beautiful material things that belonged on the bodies and in the magnificent homes of the former were scandalously out of place when sought by the latter. By the late Middle Ages, Christians in Western Europe's economically most dynamic cities did not need the theories of Erving Goffman, Thorsten Veblen, or even Adam Smith to understand the relationship among public self-presentation, conspicuous consumption, and the social esteem of others. They had only to look around the streets of Florence or Paris, London or Bruges. The astute words of Thomas à Kempis applied to lay Christians in urban settings no less than to the professed female canonesses and male canons associated with the *devotio moderna*: "Just as you regard other people with your eyes, so in the same way you are observed by others."[75]

As it happened, an unanticipated turn of God's providence in the mid-fourteenth century gave the European artisans, urban wage laborers, and agricultural workers who survived it something of a temporary respite. Between 1348 and 1350 the unprecedented demographic disaster of the Black Death killed at least a quarter of Europe's population, which continued in the aggregate to decline until the mid-fifteenth century. But although the epidemic delivered an exogenous shock to the European economy, the net long-term result was a social spread and reinforcement of acquisitive behaviors already in place.

With the Black Death, harvests were disrupted, fields were abandoned, and labor was suddenly scarce, which led agricultural laborers as well as urban workers to demand—and receive—higher wages. More money enabled them to buy more and better things, which they did. Resenting this encroachment by their perceived social inferiors, urban elites throughout much of Europe stepped up their sumptuary legislation and policing of fashion that sought to preserve clear sartorial markers of social status and restrain the demographic spread of public displays of vanity to which women seemed especially prone.[76] At the same time and grating against this legislation, elites upped the consumption ante, seeking to reestablish through a more ostentatious acquisition of material things the cultural distance between themselves and their putative inferiors—a desire that lies behind the allegedly novel, fifteenth-century consumption of the very wealthiest among them as described by Jardine.[77] So too, the higher cost of labor for many decades after the Black Death may have prompted labor-saving technological innovations, one of which—Gutenberg's movable type and printing press in the 1450s—would come to transform intellectual culture and the dissemination of ideas. The printing press also could be and was used to create beautiful objects whose ownership distinguished cultural elites from pretenders as surely as did the knowledge of the Greek and classical Latin on the pages of their printed books.[78] A demographic shock from the plague opened to ordinary folk unprecedented opportunities for acquisitiveness, which many of them seized, prompting in turn higher aspirations by elites who sought to maintain their cultural distance from social climbers in a manner that matched their sense of self-importance, "a creeping wave of taste to feed the tastes of the powerful in all the European capitals."[79] In their sermons, friars called this avarice in thrall to vanity and pride.

In cities above all, fifteenth-century Christians high and low were buying, selling, trading, lending, borrowing, and financing in a European economy more profit-seeking than ever, one marked by innovative credit mechanisms, new banking institutions, and time-tested accounting procedures.[80] Were they remaining detached from their more plentiful possessions and avoiding the unprecedentedly great dangers of money by making it serve others and the common good through the practice of the moral virtues? To some extent—although as most of them probably would have acknowledged if they were honest, not as well as they might have. Following much recent research, Chapter 2 argued that fifteenth-century Christians were impressively devout when measured by lay enthusiasm for and participation in voluntary religious practices. Many such practices among well-to-do laity in the cities of Flanders, northern and central Italy, and southern Germany, for example, the leading economic centers of Europe, fostered both their practitioners' salvation and that of others. They included not only the corporal and spiritual works of mercy, but also charitable contributions to the poor, donations to religious orders, the endowment of Masses for oneself and one's family members, the purchase of indulgences, participation in confraternities, the confession of sins and reception of Communion more than once a year, and the patronage of religious art and architecture. Indeed, elites poured money into religious paintings as never before—some intended for secluded display and private devotion in ostentatious family chapels, to be sure, but others commissioned as public aids to meditative prayer and worship available to everyone in a given city, including visitors.[81] The poor certainly had not gone away. In fact, much to the chagrin of urban magistrates, their numbers were increasing with the return of demographic growth and the fall of real wages in the late fifteenth and early sixteenth centuries.[82] Yet they could worship and pray and hear sermons in churches as beautiful as Santa Croce in Florence, consecrated in 1443,[83] a structure without which their lives no less than those who belonged to the city's wealthiest families would have been poorer. Depending on how it was spent, money could and did beautify the built environment for everyone as part of the common good.

Manifestations of greed, self-regarding vanity, and puffed-up pride were everywhere among fifteenth-century Christians. But insofar as more of them were more self-consciously devout than ever before, they also understood that avarice was a grave sin, a message that constantly recurs in the late medieval penitential manuals whose views on acquisitiveness into the early sixteenth century remained what they had been in the thirteenth.[84] Indeed, there might even have been a connection between Christians' economic vices and their increased religious devotion: the instructed knew not only that greed was a deadly sin, but also that if one properly confessed one's avaricious actions and intentions, and made proper restitution for them through clerically stipulated acts of penitential satisfaction, the gracious God forgave those sins through the sacrament he had mercifully provided for this purpose.[85] The well catechized also knew that a generously exercised *caritas* was God's compensatory compass that could reorient their waywardness: "Above all, maintain constant love for one another, for love covers a multitude of sins" (1 Pt 4:8). Including avarice. No one would have mistaken the elder Giovanni Rucellai of Florence (1403–1481) for a Christian pursuing perfection through self-renunciation, any more than one would have thought that members of the similarly mega-wealthy Strozzi or Medici families were on the same path. But neither had Rucellai acted out of a secular self-interest at the expense of his faith or the common good when, like Cosimo de' Medici and so many others before him, he financed public religious projects that afforded him "the greatest satisfaction and the greatest pleasure, because it serves the glory of God, the honour of Florence, and my own memory."[86]

None of this discussion should obscure the fact that on the eve of the Reformation, most of Europe from Portugal to Poland remained a rural world inhabited by householders who lived in villages and owned very few possessions. Many of them were legally bound in one way or another to work the land in an agricultural capacity, and their cultural and commercial horizons were primarily local and to some extent regional. But few if any localities remained untouched by markets or money. Gradually, since the eleventh century, Christians' actions had been without any central institutional planning or oversight, creating a complex, overlapping series of monetized, profit-oriented economic networks that increasingly affected them regardless of their individual intentions.[87] More in cities than in villages, this system-in-the-making strained traditional Christian ethics no less than it influenced social relationships. In towns, it exerted general sociological downward causation,[88] yet without *forcing* any individual to buy into it. Hence thousands of fifteenth-century men and women voluntarily pursued lives of Christian self-renunciation—even though the ecclesiastical institutions to which they belonged, such as Observantine religious houses, participated thoroughly in the buying and selling, borrowing and lending mediated by the money that depersonalized relationships and threatened the teleology of traditional Christian morality. So too, although the Netherlandish Modern Devout sought to avoid the traps and the trappings of religious orders, the communal houses in which they pooled their resources, practiced the virtues, and pursued lives of prayerful interiority and personal austerity were situated in highly monetized towns. The Sisters of the Common Life wove textiles, and the Brothers copied religious books, on demand for a consumer market.[89] Disturbingly to contemporaries, already by the early fourteenth century the market for the necessities of human life was beyond the control of even the most powerful: in both France and England, for example, royal edicts setting maximum grain prices in years of agricultural scarcity, including during the great famine of the later 1310s, had no effect.[90] When prices for a given commodity were not set and overseen, producers and procurers, regardless of their individual intentions, already had to play by the mysterious rules of their wares' bafflingly independent market if they wanted to play successfully at all.

In effect, outside the price protection afforded by guilds, capitalist practices compelled mercantile competitors to act as if they were driven by acquisitive desires even when they were not.[91] Not to do so was to be undersold, outmaneuvered, outworked, short on salable-because-desired commodities, or in other ways to fall behind and before long to risk losing one's livelihood. Social relationships among immediate and extended family members, friends, neighbors, and confraternities were crucial as a partial counterweight, because unregulated markets intrinsically fostered competitive human relationships. To the extent that laws and social solidarities failed to constrain the demands of the market, if devout merchants wanted to stay afloat even they *had* to act—at least in their business dealings per se—in ways behaviorally akin to their more religiously indifferent, avaricious competitors. In this respect, the former contributed no less than the latter to the strengthening and extension of economic realities in which competitive participation was the price of mere survival. *An unplanned system-in-the-making was itself pressuring Christian merchants to act in ways indistinguishable from avarice.* Here was a long-term consequence of money's use and its dangers that Aristotle could not have foreseen, one that lent a new dimension to Jesus's and Paul's stark warnings about greed and where it could lead.

Nevertheless, because late medieval economic behaviors remained embedded in the ethical framework of Christianity as an institutionalized worldview, even in cities such behaviors remained market activities in what had not yet become a market society. Speaking of England in the early sixteenth century, Keith Wrightson notes that "if this was an economic culture familiar with markets, it was also one which lacked the concept of a market order as a self-regulating system of economic relationships. . . . Contemporaries regarded economic activity as being subordinated to ethical ends. They assessed its legitimacy in terms of moral imperatives and their attitudes were both enshrined in their economic institutions and expressed in practice."[92] In this sense, because moral constraints inimical to acquisitiveness and the maximization of profit remained in place, backed by force of law and (at least sometimes) by punishment, late medieval Europe was not a capitalist society despite the increasing pervasiveness of capitalist practices.[93] However dangerous the monetization of life that was emerging as a result of Christians' cumulative, collective actions, both in theory and practice—even when vices were enacted and sins committed—economics remained enmeshed in the morality and social relationships that were inseparable in medieval Christianity. Even among the families of the fifteenth-century Florentine mercantile elite, social relationships restrained economic individualism because "however much their business practices anticipate modern capitalism," they "were still strongly tied into the medieval tradition of guild corporatism."[94]

In his 1429 dialogue *De avaritia,* the humanist scholar and papal secretary Poggio Bracciolini (1380–1459) put into the mouth of his colleague, Antonio Loschi, heterodox ideas about greed as a virtue, the supposedly universal, natural source of all human motivation and the putative wellspring of civic prosperity and stable government. In the following decade Alberti was more cautious about such ideas in the third book of his unpublished *Libri della famiglia,* but centuries later, as we shall see, such views would gain wide currency. Yet the thrust and culmination of Poggio's dialogue is a searing condemnation of avarice drawn especially from the fourth-century Greek church father John Chrysostom.[95] Meanwhile

Poggio's exact contemporary, the saintly Observant Franciscan and virtuoso preacher Bernardino of Siena (1380–1444), tended plague victims, cared for the sick, reconciled hostile urban factions, championed *caritas* for the poor, and condemned usury and avarice while maintaining a traditional understanding of how commerce should serve the common good in the bustling Italian cities whose economic practices he analyzed with subtlety.[96] By the mid-fifteenth century, some prominent Florentine families held a stunning 40 percent of their wealth in fashionable clothing. This proportion subsequently *increased* as the rich and powerful continued to pour money into the meticulously tailored showy silks, expensively dyed fine woolens, and carefully trimmed sumptuous furs that were woven into the civic culture of their sartorial self-presentation.[97] Eschewing anything like Bernardino's analytical nuance, at century's end Girolamo Savonarola fiercely attacked the city's avaricious "lukewarms" *(tiepidi),* whose sinful vices not only damaged the common good, but had summoned God's peninsular scourge in the person of Charles VIII of France. The impact of the Dominican's preaching was most dramatically manifest at Carnival in 1497 and 1498, when so many Florentines consigned huge quantities of their consumer goods to the giant public conflagrations that consumed them in the Piazza della Signoria, where the friar was himself burned as a heretic on 23 May 1498.[98] But however much well-to-do urban Christians by the early sixteenth century continued to indulge their desires in the service of pride, vanity, and the desire for influence—whether in long-standing commercial centers such as Florence and Venice or in new entrepôts such as Antwerp—they "had not learned to persuade themselves that greed was enterprise and avarice economy."[99]

That would come later. As Albert Hirschman and before him R. H. Tawney recognized, a capitalist *society* required an *ideological* about-face, one that upended the Gospel's clear condemnation of greed and—reversing Jesus's words in Luke 12:15—in effect took the side of Poggio's Loschi: "One's life—or at least the good life—*does* consist in the abundance of possessions." A capitalist society required not just capitalist practices among urban elites, but a demographically widespread social acceptance among Christians of the counter-biblical notion that the good life was the goods life. Like Aquinas and Albert the Great before them, civic humanists such as Bruni had argued that the proper exercise of an Aristotelian virtue such as magnificence could make money serve the common good, but even Italian humanists "justified wealth without, however, introducing any new cultural values that informed and reshaped economic behavior."[100] So long as enough acquisitive men and women acknowledged their avarice and vanity as sins, and not only sought God's forgiveness but engaged in countervailing practices in subordination to the common good, an ethical brake remained on the formation of a market-based, capitalist society. But it would disappear if avarice were reconceived as self-interest and acquisitive desire reckoned as desirable, or supposedly unavoidable.

THIS IDEOLOGICAL SHIFT was not the direct consequence of the Reformation. On the contrary, both radical and magisterial Protestant reformers thought that economic behavior, like politics, needed a massive overhaul through an infusion of biblical morality. They deplored greed and adjunct sins as socially destructive and morally gangrenous, even as they disagreed dramatically among themselves concerning what was to be done about them. Protestant reformers also repudiated, albeit in discrepant ways, the traditional distinction between mere commandments and counsels of perfection. No more winking at the Fuggers and the Medici while a (wrongheaded) minority pursued "sanctity": regardless of how different reformers understood the Gospel, they thought all Christians were bound by it equally—even as they rejected, as had many humanists, the traditional notion that the pursuit of Christian perfection should include the practice of voluntary poverty. Saints as traditionally understood—the nearest imitators of Christ and ascetic models of extraordinary material self-denial, as well as efficacious heavenly intercessors for Christians before God—would disappear in Protestant Europe.

Not Reformation teachings as such, but rather the doctrinal disagreements and concrete religio-political disruptions between magisterial Protestants and Catholics, would create the conditions for an ideological *volte-face* concerning acquisitiveness. And while controlling their respective churches, monarchical territories and states would provide the chief institutional framework within which Christians' investment in acquisitive practices would be protected and could grow, a development that facilitated in turn the growth, reach, and power of European states' commercial and colonizing endeavors during the early modern period and beyond. At the same time, correlative to the ways in which Lutheran and Reformed Protestantism departed from medieval Christian ethics, by separating salvation from morality these traditions indirectly influenced the long-term development of economic behavior in ways that their sixteenth-century leaders would have deplored. In this broad sense, Weber was right—although almost certainly not because of the alleged psychological effects on English Puritans of Calvinist predestination that was subsequently secularized.

In the autumn of 1517 the perceived commodification of the faith itself was the catalyst for what became the Reformation, manifest in Luther's worry about lay misunderstandings of the papal indulgences that had become so popular in preceding decades. As we saw in the previous chapter, those reformers who rejected the authority of the Roman church beginning around 1520 were deeply concerned about Christians' sinful moral behavior. This included anxiety about Christians' relationship to material things, and attention paid to the desires and actions of central Europeans who were trying to cope with demographic growth, rising prices, and falling wages. Convinced that Christendom's root problem was false doctrines, anti-Roman reformers turned to God's word, where none of them could miss the many scriptural denunciations of greed, insistence on care for the poor, and concern for the material well-being of others. Just what the avaricious Antichrist had neglected! The grasping papacy was situated in indulgent Italy, Europe's most commercialized region, whence acquisitiveness spread over the Alps to poison the otherwise virtuous towns of the Empire and Switzerland. In their respective ways, Protestant reformers wanted not to liberate but to *restrict* the runaway greed and sinful selfishness that they associated with the predatory papacy and its covetous clergy, its corruptions of Christian doctrine, and the corrosive reach of Rome that burdened every domain of human life. To this extent, as H. M. Robertson argued long ago, the notion of any direct connection between Protestantism and modern capitalism is mistaken and misguided.[101] Sixteenth-century magisterial and radical Protestant reformers were far too familiar with scripture to dream of trying to dislodge its clear condemnation of greed from the biblical commandments that grounded Christian ethics. Their aim was just the opposite: to get men and women to live according to God's will as expressed in his word and guaranteed in believers' hearts by the Holy Spirit. What did this mean with respect to economic behavior and material things?

Here as in so many other matters, anti-Roman protagonists disagreed among themselves from the outset of the Reformation. Up through the mid-1520s, the movement's most socially conspicuous and unsettling expressions—those of the German Peasants' War—came from Christians who radicalized the traditional conviction that the Gospel as well as salvation itself was inseparable from human desires and behavior in relationship to material things. So they took aim at the existing socioeconomic hierarchy as unjust and denounced widespread economic practices as unchristian.[102] "To accept and to pay out usury is manifestly against [*offenbar wider*] the Gospel of Jesus Christ," Jakob Strauss baldly asserted in a pamphlet published first in Eisenach in 1523 and afterward reprinted at least twice.[103] "It is the greatest atrocity on earth that no one wants to take up the plight of the poor," Thomas Müntzer wrote in September 1524.[104] The anonymous author of the preamble to twenty-four articles from Salzburg, written in the spring of 1525, excoriated "the unchristian seduction, the cruel thievery, usury, and tyranny through which godly truth and justice has been criminally, contemptuously, mockingly, and forcibly despised, rejected, and trampled underfoot."[105] Also from the spring of 1525, the author of an anonymous pamphlet from Upper Swabia cried, "God help us, where has such misery ever been heard of? They tax the poor and rip out the marrow from their bones, and we have to pay interest on it! . . . Where are the tyrants and the bloodthirsty, who take taxes, customs, and fees, so shamefully and sinfully wasting and dissipating what should go into the common chest or purse to serve the territory's needs. . . . Damn the unchristian, pagan way that they torture [*marter treybent*] us poor people! We are the clergy's possessions in soul but the secular authorities' possessions in body [*des weltlichen gewalts leyb aygen*]."[106] Expressing hopes that outlived the suppression of the peasants, Hans Hergot wrote in his *New Transformation of the Christian Life* that "for the advancement of God's honor and the common good, do I, a poor man, know those things that are to come, that God will humble all social estates [*stenden*], villages, castles, church foundations and cloisters, and will establish a new way of life [*wandlung*] in which no one will say, 'That is mine.' The cities will be humbled, their houses will be reduced to rubble, and their people and crafts will leave them; the villages will become rich in goods and people, and will be delivered of all their burdens; those born noble will pass away, and the commoners will occupy their houses."[107]

Such examples from the mid-1520s could be multiplied at great length. Similar ideas would be articulated by some Protestants during the English Revolution, such as Gerrard Winstanley (1609–1676) in the late 1640s.[108] In the most extensive concrete expressions of the early German Reformation, made manifest in the uprisings of 1524–1526, protagonists agreed with the medieval Christian teaching that material things and economic behaviors could not be separated from salvation itself. But because present-day realities diverged so grievously from God's word, the Gospel itself demanded opposition to the socioeconomic injustices built by the long-standing alliance between political and ecclesiastical authorities, which Müntzer called simply "the abomination" [*den grewel*].[109]

In their respective ways, Anabaptists agreed that salvation was inseparable from economic realities. Concerned about socioeconomic injustices, numerous Anabaptists and those who subsequently became Anabaptists participated in the Peasants' War. And despite their many differences, early Anabaptists, beginning with the first Swiss Brethren in and around Zurich, were animated by a vision of the communal sharing of material possessions based directly on chapters 2, 4, and 5 in the Acts of the Apostles.[110] What medieval Christianity had applied only to vowed religious was intended by God to inform the shared life of all believers as a *Nachfolge Christi*. After the peasants and their supporters were crushed in 1525, Anabaptists modified their interpretation of community of goods: it ranged from an attenuated expression in voluntary mutual aid among the Swiss Brethren and (beginning in the later 1530s) Mennonites, to "a legislated community of goods," whether in the short-lived Anabaptist Kingdom of Münster or among the Moravian Hutterites. The latter became for several decades the most successful—because politically protected—Anabaptist group of the sixteenth century.[111] Despite the many disagreements that made Anabaptists so doctrinally and therefore socially fissiparous, in the sixteenth century all Anabaptist groups were hostile to mercantile life and acquisitiveness, prizing manual labor and a materially humble way of life (as the Old Order Amish in North America continue to do today). Menno Simons, for example, contrasted Zacchaeus, the tax collector who climbed a sycamore tree in his desire to hear Jesus and who volunteered to give half his possessions to the poor (Lk 19:1–9), with "our rich people [who] seek still more and more how they might increase their money and possessions, build their houses expensively, and add one field to others," who "are so fixed on accursed, shameful avarice and unseemly profits [*onbehoorlicke gewin*], and act so bluntly and flatly contrary to love."[112] As Arnold Snyder puts it, "there were to be no Swiss Brethren, Hutterite, or Mennonite financiers or entrepreneurs."[113] At least not until the Dutch Golden Age—in the 1630s, for example, some of those deeply involved in the runaway tulip speculation were Mennonites from the extended De Clercq family, including wealthy merchants from Amsterdam, Haarlem, Rotterdam, and Utrecht.[114]

Aside from the Peasants' War, the Münsterites of 1534–1535, and the English Revolution, the political suppression and therefore small numbers of radical Protestants insured that in the Reformation era their influence on economic matters would be as minimal as their impact on wider European culture. As we have seen, only those reformers who allied themselves with political authorities in the formation of magisterial Protestant confessional regimes—that is, Lutherans and Reformed Protestants (including the Church of England)—had a chance for sustained and demographically widespread influence. Magisterial reformers rejected radical Protestant efforts to remake existing socioeconomic realities through political rebellion or separatism, even though they *agreed* that avaricious acquisitiveness was a socially destructive, sinful blight that conscientious Christian authorities should correct and control as part of their obligation to police morality. But because of their repudiation of teleological virtue ethics, magisterial reformers *rejected* the medieval Christian claim, adopted and adapted by Anabaptists, that one's actions pertaining to material things affected or indeed *could* affect one's eternal salvation. We must grasp both of these aspects of Lutheran and Reformed Protestantism in order to understand, respectively, their intended aims with respect to economic realities and their unintentional influences on the development of capitalism and consumption.

Magisterial Protestant reformers regarded economic behavior as part of Christian morality, condemned avarice as sinful, preached detachment from material possessions, insisted on care and concern for the poor, and excoriated those who selfishly prioritized their individual desires above the common good. The freedom of a Christian in no wise entailed an entrepreneurial liberation to do as one pleased as an autonomous individual. It was rather, as Luther said, a paradoxical realization that the emancipation from anxiety about one's salvation wrought by God was precisely what bound one to serve others out of love. Seeking simply to fulfill one's own desires was its antithesis. Hence from his first sermon against usury in 1519 through his lengthy admonition to pastors to preach against it in 1540, Luther regarded Christian economic behavior as entirely subject to the Gospel. He disdained "the gaping maw of greed" *(schlund und rachen des geytzs)*, condemned the vanity of exotic goods procured through foreign trade, and rejected merchants' desire to maximize profits as "making room for avarice and opening every door and window to hell." He also conceived explicitly Christian social relationships with respect to material things in radical terms. In 1524, Luther reiterated in *On Commerce and Usury* what he had said four years before: Christians were not to resist others who seized their temporal goods, they were to give freely to everyone (including enemies) who asked for help or was in need, and they were to lend money interest-free to others (or else by definition they were not lending at all). Mere buying and selling— which Luther treated with much less indulgence than had protagonists in the scholastic theological tradition he rejected—did not distinguish Christians from pagans, Turks, or Jews.[115]

Other reformers agreed with Luther on the complete embeddedness of economic behavior within Christian morality, regardless of where they stood on the doctrinal issues that divided them. Echoing medieval (and biblical) ideas about detachment from possessions, for example, Zwingli argued in 1523 that "we absolutely must realize that riches belong to God, and in all ways be prepared to put them at the will and in the service of God; they must be [for us] as if we did not possess them [*glych sam wir sy nit habend*], else I cannot understand how a rich person can be a believer if he sets his heart by worldly treasure."[116] Martin Bucer, tutor to England's boy-king Edward VI after leaving Strasbourg in 1549, offered him in *De regno Christi* (1551) a blueprint for a godly Reformed Protestant commonwealth. Writing a decade after the seizure of monastic lands and possessions by Henry VIII and their sale by the king to eager purchasers among the gentry and aristocracy, Bucer wrote that it was "clear also that one of the chief causes of civil discord and disturbances in the commonwealth is greed [πλεονεξίαν], that sickness [*morbum*] by which everyone strives to surpass others in wealth," adding that "rich men are powerfully occupied with their possessions."[117] Three years before, Robert Crowley, one of those Edwardian divines referred to as the "Commonwealthsmen," had said that "if ther were no god, then would I think it leafull [lawfull] for men to use their possessions as thei lyste[.] Or if God woulde not requitre an accompt of us for the bestoweynge of them." But this was sheer fantasy, "forasmuch as we have a God, and he hath declared unto us by ye scripturs yt [that] he hath made the possessioners but Stuardes of his ryches and that he wyl holde a streyght accompt with them for the occupiynge and bestoweynge of them: I thynke no christian ears can abyde to heare that more then Turkysh opinion."[118]

Calvin, too, who is often contrasted with Luther for his supposedly forward-looking acceptance of commercial realities as the economic framework for living out the restored Gospel, nevertheless insisted in traditional terms on the strict subordination of material things to "that end for which the author himself created and intended them for us, inasmuch as he created them for our good," which included one's integral participation in social life geared toward the common good. Christian life simply had no place for self-indulgence, avarice, or individualistic autonomy: "We are not ours [*Nostri non sumus;* cf. 1 Cor 6:19]: therefore let neither our reason nor our will rule over our intentions and actions. We are not ours: therefore let us not fix as a goal for ourselves the pursuit of what is advantageous for us according to the flesh. We are not ours: therefore as far as is allowed, let us forget ourselves and everything that is ours." Thus the human necessity of clothing, for example, did not legitimize an idolatrous, sartorial ostentation among the wealthy: "Where is our recognition of God if our minds are obsessed [*defixae*] with the splendor of our clothes?"[119] Inspired by the New Testament and concerned about the plight of impoverished Christians, doubly so in a city flooded with Huguenot refugees from France in the 1540s and 1550s, Calvin reconceived and institutionalized the diaconate as an ecclesiastical ministry dedicated specifically to care of the poor.[120] Despite his "realistic" acceptance of interest on loans (Geneva's maximum on which was raised from a low 5 percent to a still-low 6.67 percent in 1557), Calvin insured that the Consistory policed and punished "commercial practices such as fraud, usury, price gouging, or hoarding," which annually constituted between fifty and two hundred of its cases from 1542 through 1564.[121] The use of money motivated by *caritas* was supposed to facilitate the circulation of material things for the sake of the common good, but greed, selfishness, vanity, and pride had made it the idol that ruled the world.[122]

Even on the question of usury, once thought and sometimes still argued to constitute a significant economic caesura between supposedly backward Catholicism and putatively progressive Protestantism, the differences between magisterial Protestant reformers and their Catholic contemporaries were more apparent than real. Calvin distinguished objectionable, usurious loans (sought by those in material distress) from unobjectionable, nonusurious production loans (sought by entrepreneurs), which might seem like a major conceptual breakthrough in comparison to the traditional prohibition of usury. But Calvin was not seeking to liberate individual economic enterprise. Rather, he sought through such distinctions to establish clear limits that might contain and control the otherwise rampant human propensity "to long for wealth and honors, to strive for power, to accumulate riches, to bring together all those absurdities which seem to make for grandeur and display," for which "our passion is mad, our desire infinite."[123] Decades earlier, Johannes Eck, in the years just before he became Luther's theological adversary, had been shopping among university colleagues his idea for acceptance of a 5 percent interest rate on business loans that had been for decades the de facto practice in South German commercial cities such as Augsburg and Nuremberg.[124] And medieval scholastic thinkers had long since arrived at distinctions similar to Calvin's by emphasizing the importance of intentions in morality, and had found ways theologically to legitimate the repayment of loans for more than the amount of the principal. In this matter, late medieval theologians such as the Franciscan Bernardino of Siena and the Dominican bishop Antonino of Florence (1389–1459), passed the baton, as it were, to members of the new Society of Jesus in the second half of the sixteenth century, who worked through similar questions in a radically changed political and religious context.[125] Fundamentally and for all practical purposes, Catholic theologians and canon lawyers long before Calvin had already arrived differently and less directly at his supposedly novel position regarding usury. Conversely, Elizabethan and Jacobean Puritans remained preoccupied with usury understood in expansive terms as uncharitable and selfish economic practices, a concern that early New England Puritans brought with them across the Atlantic in the 1630s and that informed both discourse and discipline in the early years of the Massachusetts Bay Colony.[126]

The bottom line is clear: like radical Protestants, the magisterial reformers, including Calvin, unambiguously condemned avarice, acquisitive individualism, and any separation of economic behavior from biblical morality or the common good. Despite their rejection of voluntary poverty as a means to and expression of Christian holiness, their attitudes about the proper human relationship to material things and acquisitiveness are much closer to those of medieval Christianity than to the central assumptions of modern Western capitalism and consumerism. Although magisterial reformers repudiated the Roman church's authority and its interpretations of scripture in many respects, they were well aware that the Bible's pervasive themes pertaining to the pursuit, acquisition, possession, and use of material things could not be denied without rejecting God's word.

Yet as we saw in the last chapter, Lutheran and Reformed Protestants disagreed with their Catholic contemporaries about teleological virtue ethics, and its relationship to human flourishing and eternal salvation. One's actions—including buying, selling, acquiring, borrowing, lending, and financing—did *not* contribute to one's salvation, which was entirely and exclusively God's free gift by faith alone through grace alone to his elect alone. The extraordinary experience of passively being plucked from the depths of depravity was precisely what produced (or was supposed to produce) the overwhelming gratitude, clarity, and zeal to act in ways sanctifyingly consonant with God's will, which of course implied the shared building and social sustenance of moral communities. To claim that one's actions influenced one's status with God was the self-regarding error of "works righteousness," the popish lie that Christians cooperated with God or somehow otherwise contributed to their salvation, arrogating to themselves what was strictly God's achievement. Correlatively, even though into the seventeenth century magisterial Protestant theologians remained markedly biblical and largely traditional in the content of their economic thought, despite their repudiation of voluntary poverty, their rejection of virtue ethics would have indirect effects on the development of modern capitalism.

Here the Weber thesis might be relevant for early modern Reformed Protestantism, at least to some extent, but not because of the putative anxiety about one's elect status for which feverish work yielded psychological reassurance. Although this might have been the case for some of the godly, something close to the opposite seems more likely nearer the mark: according to Reformed Protestants, disciplined, efficient, zealous work in one's worldly calling was the proper, grateful response to God's irrevocable gift of salvation. Depending on one's vocation this might indeed tend to translate into material success to the extent that it was embraced and enacted. It could mean more goods and more money among merchants to redistribute for the relief of the poor and the sake of the common good in accord with biblical teaching and the demands of Christian love, as Omobono of Cremona had shown four centuries earlier. If many people acted similarly— and with the possible exception of early Puritan New England and perhaps

seventeenth-century Scotland, it seems unlikely that Reformed Protestantism per se anywhere had this sort of socially expansive, transformative
effect[127]—their collective behavior could have changed work culture as Weber posited, in the direction of greater industriousness and self-discipline.
Even in the absence of societal transformation, however, if given individuals
were eventually to reject the motivating beliefs and directed purpose of their
labor as Reformed Protestants, then their inculturated work discipline, despite its original rootedness in religious gratitude, might indeed be redirected
to whatever they happened to desire rather than to the common good as
construed by Reformed Protestant theologians.

Unless, of course, all acquisitive efforts were redefined as contributing to
a redefined common good. Putting historical meat on the bones of Weber's
speculations, Mark Valeri has recently analyzed the process whereby English Protestants generally and New England Puritans in particular incrementally came to reject inherited Reformed Protestant economic views between the 1630s and the early eighteenth century, through "the accretion of
daily practices and regular religious reflection made over a very long period
of time."[128] Midwifed by novel conceptions of prosperity as providentially
sanctioned and reflecting John Bossy's "migration of the holy" from church
to state,[129] this was a long-term, internal development within Reformed
Protestantism in which once-devout, shared busyness would eventually yield
to individuals' self-appointed secular business in a disenchanted "public
sphere," within which the descendants of Reformation-era Protestants had
learned to segregate economic behavior from interior dispositions. Then
when asked about one's decisions or priorities, from a complementary and
politically protected "private sphere" one could utter a quintessential, modern Western imperative that would have appalled sixteenth-century Reformed Protestant leaders: "Mind your own business."

An analogous but somewhat different process seems to have been at work
in early modern Lutheranism. Given the control of churches by states, Luther's sharp two-kingdom distinctions between faith and politics, the inner
man and the outer man, the freedom of a Christian and obedience to secular
authorities, were probably more important than a zealous work ethic as an
indirect influence on the development of modern capitalism. By deliberately
leaving the public exercise of power exclusively to political authorities, the
latter had legitimate charge of policies and practices pertaining to material
things as well as control over their subjects' bodies. On Luther's terms, that
was fine for Christians. For however much Satan might rage in a world
overrun with greed and ambition and power, the *princeps mundi* could not
ruffle the inner certainty in the heart of the believer of the salvation won by
Christ. As Luther told Erasmus in no uncertain terms, the Gospel "ought to

be asserted and defended unto death, even if the entire world were consequently not only thrown into fighting and uproar, but actually to collapse into a chaos and be reduced to nothing."[130] From the haven of God's invincible and invisible church, Christians could disregard the world's anti-Christian embrace of self-regarding acquisitiveness and yet still keep the faith. The imperturbable interiority of the saved Christian, *simul justus et peccator*, was a safe refuge and a secure retreat, even if the world went to hell—whether in the sixteenth century, during the Thirty Years War, or much later, in the working conditions during aggressive German industrialization in the decades before and after 1871, during the Great War, amid the Weimar Republic's hyperinflation, or during a two-front bid for European domination in Hitler's Reich.[131]

Lutherans and Reformed Protestants shared with seventeenth-century Jansenists a final important, indirect influence on the subsequent development of capitalism and consumerism in their rejection of medieval Christianity's virtue ethics. Their hyper-Augustinian claims about the depravity of fallen human nature—the lack of any "there" there onto which grace could be grafted so that habituation in the moral virtues and the exercise of reason might lead incrementally toward human flourishing—included ideas about the insuperable force of the passions or affections, and the helplessness of human beings to master them. For example, in his *Loci communes,* first published in 1521 and often reprinted in the sixteenth century, Philipp Melanchthon had echoed Luther's view that "internal passions [*adfectus*] are not in our power. For by practice and experience we discover that the will cannot by itself put down love, hate, or similar passions, but rather passions are overcome by passions." Indeed, "I deny that there is any force in man that can seriously resist the passions [*adfectibus adversari*] and hold that those acts alleged are nothing but the invented thought of the intellect."[132] This conviction was related to justification by faith alone through grace alone: only if God drove the will like a rider on a stubborn mule (to use Luther's image) might human beings live, at least to some extent, as if they (but actually God) had mastered their inevitably self-regarding, sinful passions. Not only eternal salvation but any real control of selfish desires in this life depended on God's all-or-nothing intervention. If one retained this view of human beings but dropped the Christian worldview and theology of grace, then having *already* jettisoned Christian virtue ethics, one would be left with inescapably passion-driven human beings invariably seeking to fulfill their own selfish desires. But such aspirations would not necessarily be sinful—indeed, they might even be virtuous and rational, provided one also redefined virtue and reconceived the aim of human life, as Machiavelli in his own fashion and context had already done.

Contemporaneously with the transformation of the morality of acquisitiveness in Anglophone Protestantism as analyzed by Valeri, this is also what Hobbes and Hume would do in their respective ways. So would Adam Smith.

EVEN THE INDIRECT influence of magisterial Protestantism on the emergence of modern capitalism and consumption was probably less important than many scholars have thought. More consequential was the concrete, religio-political violence between magisterial Protestant and Catholic regimes, from the conflicts between the Swiss cantons in the late 1520s through the Thirty Years War and England's civil wars during the 1640s, plus the antagonisms among the rival Spanish, French, and English confessional empires that endured much longer. There seems little reason to imagine that without the Reformation, any socially widespread embrace of ascetic self-restraint and a repudiation of socioeconomic hierarchy would have arisen and reversed in any fundamental way Christendom's overall economic trajectory between the eleventh and sixteenth centuries. But neither is there much reason to doubt that desires and behaviors related to material things would have remained part of publicly shared Christian ethical discourse and moral practices, notwithstanding their strained relationship. With the Reformation and as things actually transpired, however, the opposite occurred: the market and inherited Christian morality were increasingly divorced, which removed the ethical restraints inhibiting the eventual formation of a full-blown capitalist and consumerist society.

The great irony of the Reformation era with respect to economics is the fact that despite themselves, Catholics, magisterial Protestants, and radical Protestants collectively forged the very things that they condemned. Their doctrinal disagreements, confessional intransigence, and mutual hostility *understandably* contributed to a reactive proliferation of social behaviors, the formation of institutions, and an articulation of ideologies that together created modern Western capitalism and consumption. Discord about the Bible subverted biblical teachings about human desires and material things. Antagonisms between Christian moral communities liberated market practices from traditional Christian morality and produced a market society. Competing confessional empires prompted countervailing nationalist assimilations of providence that viewed wealth, power, and prosperity as signs of God's favor, thus recasting mercantile avarice as politically and religiously sanctioned duty. Doctrinal impasses led to the demographically widespread, cross-confessional acceptance by Christians of practices and values that had been antithetical to Christian teaching since Jesus and Paul. Disruptions born of doctrinal disagreements among Christians launched the legitimation of acquisitiveness and the strange—although now all but naturalized—Western notion that a "standard of living" refers neither to a normative human model nor even to ethical precepts, but to the quantity and quality of one's material possessions and the wealth that accompanies them. And disagreements about the substantive Christian good unintentionally hastened an acceptance of the goods life *as* the good life within the formal ethics of rights characteristic of hegemonic, modern Western states. In Thomas Hobbes's words, "Desire of Ease, and sensuall Delight, disposeth men to obey a common Power."[133]

The beliefs, priorities, decisions, and actions of rulers indeed played a critical part in this complex process. We have seen that their control of churches, whether Lutheran, Reformed Protestant (including the Church of England), or Catholic, put them in a position to foster the implementation of theologians' ambitions to create moral communities coextensive with a regime's political reach. Also integral to effective confessionalization was the suppression of religious dissenters, who doctrinally and therefore socially rejected the sovereign's moral community. Rulers' exercise of public power also enabled them to wage war for God against his enemies, a cause (as many theologians reminded them) incomparably nobler than mere personal ambition or worldly glory. Just as God in his old covenant had sustained and made the ancient Israelites triumph in their battles against their enemies, so would he sustain and make prosper in the embattled present his beloved children of the new covenant. For it was beyond question that God was on the side of what was right, good, just, and true—who could deny that? Hence rulers and other Christians who decided to fight for God and his truth, as many did between the 1520s and 1640s, had good reason to think that they would prevail, and that the Lord would reward them for their fidelity by (among other things) providing materially for their prosperity. Spanish commitment to the Roman church, for example, seemed to explain why shiploads of silver accompanied their dedicated evangelization of the New World. Having built a colonial empire that included baptized Indian laborers and turned back the Ottomans in the Mediterranean at Lepanto in 1571, the mercenary armies of the *Rey más católico* were bound to subdue the heretical rebels in the Dutch Revolt. Whether among Spanish Catholics or English Protestants, material prosperity accompanied Christian commitment as the reward of God's goodness and sign of his approval. As the motto beneath a depiction of the Spanish military captain Bernardo de Vargas Machuca put it in 1599: "By compasses and by the sword / More and more and more and more."[134]

Early modern Christians who reasoned thus were by the mid-seventeenth century sharply and doubly reminded of the mysteriousness of God's providence. First, God did not follow the script; he did not fulfill their hopes. None of the antagonists in the major religio-political conflicts from the Schmalkaldic War and Peace of Augsburg (1555) through the Thirty Years War and the Peace of Westphalia (1648) achieved their principal objectives. In whatever proportions, in the Holy Roman Empire, France, England, Switzerland, Bohemia, and the Low Countries, heretics persisted and papists endured. Even more puzzling, Europe's newest, self-declared country—the Dutch Republic—deliberately eschewed confessional uniformity, and it was prospering the most in material terms, in wild disproportion to its puniness and paltry natural resources. Remarkably, in an era of baroque monarchs with absolutist pretensions, this decentralized "constitutional monstrosity" and "political freak" had not merely held off once-mighty Spain for eighty years but brilliantly financed its war while its urban *regenten* and merchants simultaneously grew rich.[135] How had this happened?

The answer confounded committed Catholics and magisterial Protestants alike: by bracketing questions of Christian truth rather than letting doctrine dictate political decision-making. Instead, the Dutch Republic's leaders yoked the de facto embrace of a standard antithetical to the Gospel— the avaricious pursuit of profit—to the defense of particularist, traditional political liberties against Spanish rule. Dutch regents saw the effects of unyielding Catholicism, militant Calvinism, and war on commerce in the southern provinces (once again under Spanish control after 1585) and in France. So they experimented in the opposite direction. Persecuted and beleaguered textile workers from Flanders were offered refuge in Leiden, for example, and by 1600 had transformed their adoptive city from a manufacturing nonentity into a European powerhouse of cloth production rivaled in the seventeenth century only by Lyon. Antwerp's economic difficulties began before the Dutch Revolt but were greatly exacerbated by its disruptions, precipitating a "veritable merchant diaspora" to other northern European cities, especially Amsterdam by the late 1590s.[136] Well aware of Reformed Protestant militancy (which had played a crucial role in the success of the Dutch Revolt in the 1570s), the Republic's urban regents reckoned that installing Reformed ministers directly in place of ousted Catholic clergy was likely to hamper trade and the acquisitiveness that drove it. So with commercial rather than confessional priorities, they sanctioned the support of a privileged, Reformed Protestant public church, but without making it the compulsory state religion in a manner analogous to confessional regimes elsewhere.

A broad buy-in and material benefits reached sufficiently far down the socioeconomic hierarchy to permit the Dutch to weather without significant economic cost their most serious religio-political crisis, the conflicts between Arminian Remonstrants and Calvinist Counter-Remonstrants in the 1610s. Hundreds of polemical pamphlets had no effect on the Dutch East India Company's spice-laden ships returning from the South Pacific, nor did street violence among religiously politicized and economically disaffected men and women in Holland's cities obstruct the operations of Amsterdam's new bourse (finished in 1608) or exchange bank (1609).[137] The Counter-Remonstrant triumph at the Synod of Dort (1618–1619) did not hinder the market. It was business as usual. In Harold Cook's words, "by the 1630s, Dutch merchants had virtually created a state resembling an aggressive commercial firm, the 'Republic, Inc.' "[138] Across the channel, in sharp contrast, England was about to enter more than a decade of severe religio-political turmoil, including two civil wars, the execution of a king, and a proliferation of radical Protestant groups unseen in Europe since the 1520s. How different were the Dutch: the identically attired syndics of Amsterdam's clothmakers' guild who sat for Rembrandt's famous group portrait in 1662 included a Calvinist, a Remonstrant, two Catholics, and an Old Frisian Mennonite. The image dovetails with William Temple's remarks a decade later about the way in which the Dutch individualization of religious preference, and the partitioning of religion from the rest of life, had paved the way for what Simon Schama called "the embarrassment of riches."[139]

However they assessed it, contemporaries were well aware that the transformations wrought by commerce and consumption did *not* amount to business as usual. Or to life as their ancestors had known it. Attentive Dutch Christians of whatever church could hardly fail to notice that more and more, their world's de facto values and priorities contradicted Jesus's teachings about self-denial and material things. Socially accepted acquisitiveness was advancing as quickly as land reclamation in Holland and Zeeland, as those Mennonites who maintained their forebears' hostility to commerce could well discern. Thieleman Jans van Braght, a Flemish Mennonite minister from Dordrecht, expressed in 1660 the counterintuitive but cogent view that the flood of material things pouring into the United Provinces made the present "certainly more dangerous" than the overt persecution of Anabaptists had been in the sixteenth century. Then the devil had raged openly; now he seduced sweetly. Which harmed souls more? Van Braght singled out expansive commerce, expensive houses, exotic clothing, and extensive feasting as part of the way in which Satan enticed even "such city people [*Borgerlijke lieden*] who are not entirely unacquainted with religion or the worship of God and who also, so they say, earnestly would be saved [*geerne saligh waren*]; and even though with their mouths they acclaim, glorify, and praise God and his Word . . . nevertheless many of them show (by means of which the simple are seduced) that the world is their dear friend, indeed guides their hearts, since most of their actions aim at its service, that thereby they may share in its seemingly beautiful [*schoon-schijnenden*] but deceptive reward."[140] Such widespread, dangerous behaviors "come constantly before our eyes, and are more damaging and dangerous insofar as some worldly-minded people [*aerdtsch-gesinde*] proclaim them to be allowable because neutral, neither good nor evil."[141] Or indeed more than merely allowable. Kaspar van Baerle (Casparus Barlaeus), for example, in his inaugural address for Amsterdam's new Athenaeum in 1632, had gone well beyond mere permissibility and moral neutrality, praising commerce as the key to the good life in both material and intellectual terms.[142]

Yet although the regents who upheld the governing Dutch ideology prized commerce above any Christian group's truth claims, including those of the politically privileged *Gereformeerde Kerk*, Dutch Christians did not suddenly abandon the practice of their faith, whatever its content, for unbelief and self-indulgent individualism, any more than Protestants in England and New England would in the later seventeenth and early eighteenth centuries. In their religiously heterogeneous society with its divergent ecclesial moral communities, and with large numbers of men and women who exercised religious choice by opting for no church affiliation, the Dutch retained a concern to make money serve others in ways reminiscent of fifteenth-century Italian merchants.[143] At the peak of tulipmania, for example, Christian *caritas* and fevered financial speculation were combined at an estate auction held in Alkmaar on 5 February 1637. A single flower bulb sold for 5,200 guilders, more than twenty times the average annual wages of an urban laborer—but the auction as a whole netted a staggering 90,000 guilders for Alkmaar's civic orphanage.[144] Within a week the speculative bubble had burst.[145] In Maarten Prak's estimation, "the tulip craze of 1636–7 was the logical outcome of the flourishing Dutch economy, which had experienced huge growth in the previous fifty years, growth which had left the province of Holland with an abundance of ready money."[146] With that money Hollanders did as they pleased. As medieval theologians had understood, it was the means to anything and everything, including the purchase of flower bulbs for enormous sums in the pursuit of more money.

The Mennonite minister van Braght, born in 1625, was only a boy when the tulip market collapsed, too young to have thought about the phenomenon in Aristotelian terms even had he later been schooled in them. But there could hardly have been a more dramatic example of the way in which a market economy fueled the insatiability of avarice, once the use value of things was entirely detached from their exchange value. Tulips were beautiful, even very beautiful. Gazing on them delighted the eye, and their blossoms in April might also delight and impress one's neighbors, contributing to their perception of one's "good taste," that culturally contrived, social byproduct of affluence that Italian Renaissance elites had also imputed to and admired in themselves.[147] But unless one had entirely jettisoned any and all teleology linked to human flourishing as understood in medieval Christian terms, a single tulip bulb was not more valuable than a year's food, clothing, and shelter for twenty working families, no matter what people proved willing to pay for it. To have drawn such a conclusion would have been madness. It would have required an obliteration of any distinction between human needs and wants in favor of an undiscriminating, catch-all category: "demand." Although some tulip speculators let their acquisitive desires run wild and dictate their actions, very few seventeenth-century Europeans had yet begun to think in the terms that neoclassical economists today take for granted. But a few had started to move in that direction—in which the value of anything and everything is by definition what people are willing to pay for it, everything has its price, and all values are therefore commensurable. As Hobbes put it with characteristic bluntness, "The value of all things contracted for, is measured by the Appetite of the Contractors," including "the *Value,* or WORTH of a man" which "is as of all other things, his Price; that is to say, so much as would be given for the use of his Power." Human beings were no different from any other commodity: "As in other things, so in men, not the seller, but the buyer determines the Price. For let a man (as most men do,) rate themselves at the highest Value they can; yet their true Value is no more than it is esteemed by others."[148] As van Braght astutely discerned, those who had begun to think in this way were prompted to do so in part because of the social practices around them, which affected them whether they liked it or not, and which taken together were forging a full-blown market society regardless of individuals' intentions or disapproval. The English ambassador William Temple saw the same phenomenon but assessed it more positively, not only for its fostering of economic prosperity but also for its social effects on religious toleration: "I believe the force of Commerce, Alliances, and Acquaintance, spreading so far as they do in small circuits (such as the Province of *Holland*) may contribute much to make conversation, and all the offices of common life, so easie, among so different Opinions, Of which so many several persons are often in every man's eye; And no man checks or takes offence at Faces, or Customs, or Ceremonies he sees every day. . . . Religion may possibly do more good in other places, But it does less hurt here."[149]

Especially in northwestern Europe, other rulers and their subjects, Protestants and Catholics alike, heeded what was afoot in the United Provinces. Led by Dutch precedent and before it was theorized, European Christians began more deliberately to create what would become a capitalist society out of late medieval capitalist practices midwifed by Reformation-era religio-political disruptions born of disagreements about God's truth. Indeed, throughout the Reformation era itself, numerous Christians in Europe's religiously divided countries had been in various ways contributing to this same process, in what Benjamin Kaplan has analyzed as the social history of toleration.[150] Then as now, except for arms manufacturers and munitions suppliers (some of whom made enormous fortunes in the sixteenth and seventeenth centuries), war was disastrous for business and in general among those whose lives it destroyed.[151] Even more by the end of the Thirty Years War and English civil wars, frustrated with failed goals and fed up with the catastrophic financial, military, and human costs of waging war for God, in religiously divided areas Christians across confessional boundaries increasingly drew the unsurprising conclusion that they would rather learn somehow to live alongside, if not in harmony with, those with whom they disagreed. In this way, early modern Christian rulers and their subjects paradoxically became the agents of their self-colonization by capitalism and consumption. By their actions, they essentially turned their backs on biblical teachings about material things, teachings that had largely been shared across confessional lines. As it turned out, and comprehensibly, some sort of religious toleration came to seem to increasing numbers of people in the later seventeenth and eighteenth centuries like the lesser of two evils, and according to some people, desirable in principle and in its own right.[152]

The material payoff, it was hoped, would be more and better stuff for all regardless of their beliefs—the goods life. The related social payoff, many hoped, would be at least toleration and perhaps even some neighborliness across confessional lines—if affluence could work the magic of softening hardened confessional antagonisms. The price would be the de facto repudiation of traditional Christian teachings about and practices related to material things—the service of Mammon rather than God. The mechanism would be the privatization and individualization of religious belief and practice, and the political insulation of economic life from religion—the disembedding of economics from traditional moral constraints. The bridge would be a legitimation of acquisitiveness centered on families rather than individuals, and a shift in the social referent of the common good to the state and away from the sub-common good of mutually exclusive, separate churches—a precondition for modern nationalism. Aside from theological transformations such as the one analyzed by Valeri, the supra-confessional intellectual justification would be the articulation of truth claims about human beings, rationality, and reality that increasing numbers of people would come to believe, and in accord with which many more would act—the secular ideologies of Western modernity. The applied intellectual means would be the adaptation of scientific findings to technologies that could procure and manufacture material things that consumers wanted, a trajectory that would reach a first culmination in the contributions of Mokyr's industrial Enlightenment to the Industrial Revolution—and which is still thriving today in global capitalism.[153] One cost would be wars fought and empires imposed out of apparently insatiable desires for material prosperity and profits, whether linked to convictions about divine providence or without reference to God—which from the mid-seventeenth century up to the present has remained a motive for nations to kill people. The eventual result would be the Western world of all-pervasive capitalism and consumerism as we know it today.

As we saw in the previous chapter, seventeenth-century thinkers such as Hobbes and Spinoza, whose truth claims departed most dramatically from Catholic, Lutheran, and Reformed Protestant Christianity, conceived human beings as passion-driven individuals, social atoms moved most fundamentally by a natural desire for self-preservation. But that is not how seventeenth-century Christians lived, nor does it capture the way in which they sought, bought, worked, shopped, desired, and consumed during what Jan de Vries has called the industrious revolution, which stretched from the mid-seventeenth to the mid-nineteenth century. Rather, the large majority lived as members of nuclear families within households, as Western Europeans had done since at least the late Middle Ages. Households as centers of production and consumption were the social site for the legitimation of the family as the locus of acquisitiveness, the desires of its individual members stimulated rather than sated by the increased income and greater purchasing power born of longer working hours and more specialized, intensive labor.[154] Whether among the religiously mixed Dutch, the Anglican gentry in Restoration England, or Catholic bourgeois in northern France, the ethos of monetary and material gain was focused on the family rather than on individuals conceived as socially autonomous agents.

This could make acquisitiveness seem like self-sacrifice rather than a serious sin: one was not piling up unnecessary consumer goods for oneself, but providing for the material well-being and "comfort"—in no way to be confused with the prodigal luxury—of one's wife, husband, father, mother, sons, daughters. But how large a house, with how many things, of what quality, were *needed* for human flourishing, as opposed to *wanted* by family members whose acquisitive desires somehow always seemed proportional to their self-estimation as persons of "taste," "fashion," "civility," and "respectability?"[155] Old-fashioned Christians such as van Braght—or members of the Congregation of the Mission, the new Catholic religious order founded in the 1620s by Vincent de Paul (1581–1660) to minister to France's rural poor—would have discerned in this dynamic a fig leaf of familial duty covering vanity and pride fueled by avarice.[156] Just like scholastic theologians had done, mutatis mutandis, in the late Middle Ages (recall Henry of Langenstein's remark), or like leading English Puritans continued to do in the early seventeenth century. Meanwhile, this focus on the family persisted throughout the nineteenth century, domestic space becoming among all social classes even more intensely a refuge from rough-and-tumble public life, and by the later twentieth century almost entirely a site of consumption to the exclusion of production. In Joyce Appleby's words, "It is tempting to claim that the family was sentimentalized in order to supply the safe avenues for what otherwise might be riotous broadways of spending."[157]

What did family members want? If the distinction between use value and exchange value were eliminated along with a traditional teleology of human flourishing, and the nuclear family prioritized to the relative exclusion of concrete ethical responsibility for others, then the sky was the limit. As the Dutch-educated Londoner Nicholas Barbon asserted in 1690, echoing Hobbes in a proto-Humean fashion, "The Wants of the Mind are infinite, Man naturally Aspires, and as his Mind is elevated, his Senses grow more refined, and more capable of Delight; his Desires are inlarged, and his Wants increase with his Wishes, which is for every thing that is rare, can gratifie his Senses, adorn his Body, and promote the Ease, Pleasure, and Pomp of Life." Producers catered accordingly. Barbon observed that whereas the trades that provided for food, defense, and even sensual and mental gratification were relatively limited, *"those Trades that are imploy'd to express the Pomp of Life, are Infinite;* for, besides those that adorn Mans Body, as the Glover, Hosier, Hatter, Semstriss, Taylor, and many more, with those that make the Materials to Deck it; as Clothier, Silk-Weaver, Lace-Maker, Ribbon-Weaver, with their Assistance of Drapers, Mercers, and Milliners, and a Thousand more: Those Trades that make the Equipage for Servants, Trappings for Horses; and those that Build, Furnish, and Adorn Houses, *are innumerable."*[158] By the end of the seventeenth century, after the Glorious Revolution, a mercantilist discourse that conceived economic life as independent of religion was being increasingly accepted by ministers no less than merchants in England and New England as the framework for understanding how God's anti-papist providence propelled a supra-sectarian English Protestant prosperity. In a reversal of earlier Protestant (and biblical) views of acquisitiveness, increase of wealth betokened God's simultaneous benevolence toward heroic merchants, their families, and his imperial nation.[159] At the same time, as with the increased consumption by wage-earning town dwellers in the wake of the Black Death, the lower sorts always seemed to clamber after the trendsetters of taste, arbiters of fashion, and guardians of respectability. No matter—a preferential option for the rich and the infinite arbitrariness of fashion proved effective cultural counterweights to the demographic spread of consumption and kept the Hogarthian dregs at a distance, down where they belonged.[160] Hence Adam Smith, writing in 1759: "The fortunate and the proud wonder at the insolence of human wretchedness, that it should dare to present itself before them, and with the loathsome aspect of its misery presume to disturb the serenity of their happiness."[161] Who did these unwashed, unkempt poor people think they were, besmirching the sight lines of the cultured and affluent with such brazen insensitivity?

Growing consumption was intertwined with varieties of social othering. In Golden Age Holland, urban mercantile elites across confessional lines had justified their onward-and-upward acquisitive affluence by denigrating the fiscally irresponsible, conspicuous consumption of landed aristocrats as a manifestation of the contemptible vices of a decadent other.[162] *They* were not like *them*. At least Holland's refined urbanites had the restraint and modesty to enjoy themselves in a cultivated domestic space behind the discreet residential façades of canal houses that were five or six times as deep as they were wide.[163] "There they might collectively indulge in oceans of good drink and mountains of fine food, cultivating a discriminating taste for wines, spices, and tobacco."[164] Although not as cavernous as the imposing mansions built by the mercantile moguls of Renaissance Florence, the depth of these Dutch dwellings provided plenty of rooms for the conspicuous *interior* display of silk tapestries, exotic-wood furniture, Turkish rugs, gold-embossed leather wall hangings, ebony-framed mirrors, lavish curtains, birdcages, elaborate ceramics and tableware, and musical instruments. There too the affluent Dutch showed off many dozens of paintings—portraits, still lifes, landscapes, historical subjects, domestic interiors—produced in vast quantities for an art market with a much broader social base, and depicting proportionally far fewer religious subjects, than had been true of fifteenth-century Italy.[165] Among the wealthy in Golden Age Amsterdam, "neither the degree nor, for that matter, the kind of religious commitment seemed to affect this patrician life-style," although regardless of their beliefs they "all competed with each other in dynastic splendor."[166]

Whatever their rationales, the practices of mercantile nouveaux riches departed from traditional Christian teachings about avarice no less than established or arriviste aristocrats flouted it. The entrepreneurial elite profited from stories they told themselves about *le doux commerce*: that in marked contrast to the violent passions of the honor-obsessed aristocracy and the bitter destructiveness of war, trade and industry were benign, peaceful, and sweetly beneficial to everyone's betterment. Except when violence and the desire for gain were partners, of course—as they were in overseas colonies and trading companies throughout the early modern period, in which European "merchant-warriors" across confessional lines compensated for the shortcomings of trade's putative gentleness with force of arms, piracy, slavery, and lethal working conditions.[167] Thus were goods "extracted" while non-European peoples were simultaneously "civilized." Back in Europe, the principal beneficiaries did not have to see how it was done. As Albert Hirschman put it, "the persistent use of the term *le doux commerce* strikes us as a strange aberration for an age when the slave trade was at its peak and when trade in general was still a hazardous, adventurous, and often violent business."[168] Indeed. But perhaps it was neither an aberration, nor strange, but self-deceived wishful thinking by acquisitive Christians who sought to justify how more of them were now living notwithstanding what scripture said.

In the cities and at the courts of late medieval Europe, too, the desires of the rich and the desires of the powerful had never been far apart, usually because they were the desires of the same persons. But once early modern rulers who controlled their churches started promoting for their own ends the symbiosis between acquisitiveness and commerce, they began to cement what would become the fundamental alliance between the state and capitalism to which every Western nation eventually conformed.[169] Confessional churches might be thought helpful in this process. Or not, as the Dutch showed to the amazement of observers across Europe, above all their English commercial rivals. Just as London superseded Amsterdam as the European center for world trade, so the English adopted and adapted Dutch ways. By the mid-seventeenth century, wars motivated at least partly by faith—having been politically stymied, financially wasteful, and appallingly costly in human terms—had largely run their course. Unable to achieve their protagonists' goals, they had become irrational. By contrast, wars fought for providentially sanctioned commercial gain and political advantage—because they served the expansive desires of rulers and subjects for more and better stuff, plus rulers' related desires for the power and money to secure it—now made new sense. With prospects of success, and avarice rendered benign because of its service to the micro-common good of the family and the macro-common good of the state still conceived in providential terms, such wars had become rational.

Despite the religio-political complexities of their relationship, Europe's two leading commercial powers and Protestant republics of the 1650s, the English and Dutch, demonstrated their cutting-edge, progressive reasonableness by fighting the first of three naval wars in three successive decades.[170] The past remained alive in the present: in the late 1530s Henry VIII had seized the vast landholdings of the English monasteries, the sales of which to gentry and aristocratic families provided the royal cash that funded in turn a significant expansion of the kingdom's fleet, which laid the foundations for further seventeenth-century naval growth and the centrality of England's navy to its fiscal-military state during the eighteenth century.[171] By then, in its coalition with England after 1688, the Dutch Republic was in decline, hurt not only by the wars, English and French trade restrictions, and the highest wages in Europe, but also by the lack of strong central political institutions, the very absence of which had earlier served it so well.[172] But the bellicose logic of the North Atlantic rivals in the 1650s, and the conjoined logic of the acquisitiveness it affirmed, would prove to have a long future. Indeed, both remain with us in the early twenty-first century. Some defenders of the United States' multiple recent wars, for example, claim or imply that they were and are being fought not for objectionable ideologies, but for "our way of life"—that is, the goods life, allegedly beyond ideology and rational because it *really is* the good life.

Beginning with England, practices pioneered in the political settings of medieval Italian, south German, and Flemish cities, then transformed in the politically and religiously anomalous Dutch Republic, would be adapted later for much more ambitious ends by the imperial rulers of modern nation-states.[173] A new institution—the market as a whole—would gradually displace confessional churches as the junior partner alongside states in the public exercise of power. Scottish Enlightenment thinkers such as David Hume, James Steuart, John Millar, and Adam Smith observed that the behavioral constancy of political subjects devoted to material acquisitiveness made them more predictable and less prone to being moved by other disruptive passions, which in turn made the state internally more stable.[174] Subjects' desire for stuff governed by the market produced more governable subjects than did the heavy-handed efforts of established churches seeking to inculcate resented obedience and discipline. Given political leeway, acquisitive individuals would discipline *themselves,* obeying their own desires in their pursuit of the goods life. They conformed to the social practices of others whose behavior legitimated their own, and from whom they sought sympathetic approval, for as Smith put it, "the end of avarice and ambition, of the pursuit of wealth, of power, and preheminence" was "to be observed, to be attended to, to be taken notice of with sympathy, complacency, and approbation."[175] Of course, such a dynamic portended a very different kind of society from the one it was displacing, in which the newly felt desire for sympathy was perhaps a corollary of the increasingly impersonal, competitive social relationships characteristic of human exchanges fashioned through market practices.

From the end of the eighteenth century in the new United States, which deliberately eschewed any established church, predominantly Protestant Christians of English descent—imbued with the acquisitiveness of the industrious revolution and filled with republican pride—showed themselves eager participants in the market, whatever the misgivings of some about the corrupting potential of commerce and luxury.[176] Having thrown off the very empire in which their colonial predecessors had seen God's guiding hand, it turned out that *they* had been the ones providentially delivered by God from a British yoke grown tyrannical, and that God would make *them* prosper as his chosen nation. Viewed in the aggregate, Americans have never ceased to demonstrate their devotion to ever greater levels of consumption.[177] The same is true of Western Europeans, especially with the Americanization of European consumption in the twentieth century.[178] Eventually, a thoroughly globalized market, driven by neoliberalism's deregulated profit-seeking and supercharged with computer technologies running investment algorithms, would demonstrate in significant respects its resistance to the control of the nation-states that had nurtured it—in October 2008, trillions of dollars of wealth disappeared despite the efforts of world governmental leaders to stop the hemorrhaging. The junior partner and supposed servant of the nations had become their controlling master.

We have already seen how insofar as they wanted to stay in business, late medieval entrepreneurs, wherever guild regulations were lacking, were pressured to act in ways indistinguishable from avarice. Additionally, the gradual spread of capitalist practices and consumer habits, through the Reformation era and the industrious revolution, influenced others to behave in the very ways for which the pervasiveness became its own justification ("everyone is doing it"). Contemporaneously with providentialist sanctions of commerce and consumption, this spread also helps to account for the baldly assertive, self-confident quality of so many eighteenth-century philosophical claims about human nature, desires, passions, acquisitiveness, and the things that make for human happiness. Despite so many other disagreements among the thinkers who espoused such claims, some of which we have seen in previous chapters, the growing prevalence of acquisitive practices led some of them to believe that they had discovered, through dispassionate description and rational analysis, a hitherto undisclosed aspect of universal human nature—as if the unending pursuit of more and better things were not only perfectly natural and normal, but the obvious route to human happiness via comfort, pleasure, and the enjoyment of life mediated by possessions. Hence Montesquieu: "One commerce leads to another, the small to the middling, the middling to the great, and he who earlier desired to gain little arrives at a position where he has no less of a desire to gain a great deal."[179]

Aristotle and his medieval commentators had understood as much in analyzing the insatiability of avarice. But what they had condemned, Montesquieu and others extolled.[180] Where they saw money's danger to embodied souls and the common good once it was divorced from use values within a teleological virtue ethics, the Enlighteners saw money's universal utility in the pursuit of profits and pleasures determined by individual preferences that benefited state, "sociability," and "society." By 1750, the economic behavior of merchants who warmed to New England's Great Awakening was indistinguishable from the economic behavior of post-Newtonian rationalist Protestants, notwithstanding their divergent interior feelings and self-chosen beliefs.[181] Here, for all practical purposes and in public life, religion had become irrelevant to economic realities because it no longer influenced them. Increasingly the "common good" now meant simply the state-controlled sum total of all pleasures by all individuals pursuing ever more plentiful material goods, as produced by the market's benevolent Invisible Hand.[182] It was the birth of modern utilitarianism, in which "utility" is not a *synonym* for use value, but its opposite.[183] No longer beholden to a mercantilism construed in providential terms, as in late seventeenth-century England and New England, the new views and related practices were even further from Jesus's words: "If any want to become my followers, let them deny themselves and take up their cross daily and follow me" (Lk 9:23; cf. Mt 16:24, Mk 8:34). Or again: "woe to you who are rich, for you have received your consolation. Woe to you who are full now, for you will be hungry" (Lk 6:24–25).

As a dogmatically anti-Christian moralist steadfast in his skepticism and beholden to metaphysical univocity, Hume scoffed. Having rejected all revealed religion along with the Scottish Presbyterianism in which he was reared, he subtracted God and grace from a hyper-Augustinian view of concupiscent desires. The remainder would become the de facto dominant Western ideology of "self-interest" that underpins and is taken to legitimate modern capitalism and consumerism. Hume claimed that "avarice, or the desire of gain, is an universal passion, which operates at all times, in all places, and upon all persons." And since "reason is, and ought only to be the slave of the passions, and can never pretend to any other office than to serve and obey them," it followed that all persons, at all times, and in all places could not help but rationally pursue the increase of more and better stuff. Else by definition they were irrational (just as today's social-scientific proponents of rational choice theory claim in their views of human beings as self-interested, instrumentally rational maximizers). As a powerful yet calmly sustainable passion, avarice was unlike any other: "This avidity alone, of acquiring goods and possessions for ourselves and our nearest friends, is insatiable, perpetual, universal, and directly destructive of society." So strong was avarice that only the hope of greater gain could restrain it. Hence avarice paradoxically led its captive rational slaves to a hyper-acquisitive self-restraint, for "by preserving society, we make much greater advances in the acquiring [of] possessions, than by running into the solitary and forlorn condition, which must follow upon violence and an universal licence."[184] It followed that not only voluntary poverty and the pursuit of holiness in imitation of Christ—which were very much alive in the mid-eighteenth century—but any self-denial for any reason other than longer-term, this-worldly self-interest driven by avarice was a perverse denial of universal human nature based on irrational superstition. As indeed Hume believed. Ironically, like Jesus no less than Calvin, he also understood that avarice made slaves of those bound to the pursuit of Mammon. He just thought the bondage was unavoidable, and that there was nothing wrong with it.

Although Hume and other Enlighteners thought they were finally discovering "man as he really is" through neutral observation and right reason, in fact something quite different was going on. No more than Machiavelli in the early sixteenth century were they laying bare man as he is; rather, they were describing (many) northwestern Europeans, including themselves, as they had become. Then they pronounced it good. We have already seen in previous chapters how such thinkers were trying to overcome through reason alone the intellectual challenges of a revived Pyrrhonian skepticism, and attempting to discover a rationally demonstrable foundation for morality and politics in the wake of the Reformation-era debacle. Having rejected Aristotelian moral teleology in general and medieval Christian ethics more specifically, they took as an expression of universal truths about human nature the historically emergent, increasingly common, culturally contingent practices that they observed in others, in which they also participated, and of which they approved. Whether in Holland, England, France, or Scotland, they mistook a sort of descriptive sociology and autobiographical introspection for philosophical truths arrived at by neutral, objective, universal reason. They theorized as "human nature" the human behaviors they saw around them and the desires they discerned in themselves. Hence they justified avarice as at worst a public virtue despite being a private vice (Mandeville), for example, or an invariably civilizing influence on the customs and laws of peoples (Montesquieu), or the very means by which competitive, self-interested individuals unwittingly promoted human happiness through material prosperity (Smith). Such desires and behaviors have become much more deeply ingrained since the Industrial Revolution and the far greater demographic spread of consumption within the institutions of modern, liberal states that promote the goods life. This helps to explain why so many people today (including most neoclassical economists) continue not only to believe similar truth claims about human nature, but often do so with such axiomatic and ahistorical insouciance. The more uncritically one accepts what eighteenth-century Enlightened protagonists said about themselves, reason, reality, religion, riches, and human nature, the more likely one is apt to be left in the dark.

Like intellectual history, economic history is particularly prone to a self-justificatory supersessionist historicism that overlooks the continuing influence of the distant past in the present. Undeniably, there have been enormous transformations in manufacturing technologies, consumption practices, consumer goods, material culture, the built environment, and the character of urban life in the Western world since the Industrial Revolution. These transformations make some scholars, in this respect following in Marx's footsteps, liable to bedazzlement by late eighteenth-century Britain and its early mechanization of cotton textiles, as though new manufacturing technologies and greater scales of production betokened a fundamental watershed and a new beginning. They didn't. This bubble has been burst by the voluminous scholarship on preindustrial consumption and production in early modern Europe and colonial America. The British merely wedded the lessons they had learned from their Golden Age Dutch apprenticeship to a stronger, more centralized, protectionist state and a more aggressive world empire, whether understood in providentialist terms or under the secularized category of "progress."[185] Both the technological and entrepreneurial innovators of the Industrial Revolution simply invented new means to manufacture more stuff wanted by acquisitive men and women who had been conditioned through the industrious revolution to justify desires that they also saw in their neighbors, and that influential thinkers assured them were natural and insatiable. Small wonder that some economic historians today recognize themselves reflected in an eighteenth-century British mirror, considering their admiration for the outcome of the same fundamental trajectory on which the West has remained ever since (even though in some manufacturing sectors, such as papermaking, the eighteenth-century British were laggards in manufacturing technology as well as in the transformation of labor discipline[186]). Any celebration of overwhelmingly British origins for an industrial Enlightenment that propelled the unbound Prometheus which in turn became and remains a relentless revolution is bound to misapprehend that trajectory's character, because it distorts its history.[187] Friedrich Hayek opened *The Road to Serfdom* with an epigraph from Lord Acton: "Few discoveries are more irritating than those which expose the pedigree of ideas."[188] Or the pedigree of ideas, practices, and institutions, for that matter. Economic historians bewitched by the Industrial Revolution and Britain start in medias res.

The earlier and more fundamental change was the disembedding of economics from the ethics of late medieval Christianity's institutionalized worldview, in conjunction with the disruptions of the Reformation era. What needs explanation is how Western European Christians, whose leaders in the Reformation era condemned avarice across confessional lines, *themselves created modern capitalism and consumption practices antithetical to biblical teachings even as confessionalization was creating better informed, more self-conscious Reformed Protestants, Lutherans, and Catholics.*[189] Conflating prosperity with providence and opting for acquisitiveness as the lesser of two evils until greed was rechristened as benign self-interest, modern Christians have in effect been engaged in a centuries-long attempt to prove Jesus wrong. "You cannot serve both God and Mammon." *Yes we can.* Or so most participants in world history's most insatiably consumerist society, the United States, continue implicitly to claim through their actions, considering the number of self-identified American Christians in the early twenty-first century who seem bent on acquiring ever more and better stuff, including those who espouse the "prosperity Gospel" within American religious hyperpluralism.[190] Tocqueville's summary description of Americans in the early 1830s has proven a prophetic understatement: "people want to do as well as possible in this world without giving up their chances in the next."[191]

Increasingly since the 1960s, ever more prosperous Western Europeans have wondered what God has to do with anything, and have instead opted more consistently for the enjoyments that material things afford. In contrast to the American combination of Christianity and consumerism, more Europeans have divested themselves of God in apparent proportion to greater affluence and comfort with the promise of ever more stuff on the way. In the twentieth century and especially since World War II they have largely exchanged the older solidarities of their local cultures and their commercial and bourgeois national traditions for the individualistic, mass consumerism of the American "Market Empire," thus reversing the dominant transatlantic direction in which practices of Western acquisitiveness had flowed since the seventeenth century.[192] Even for today's European Christians, less time is left for religion among autonomous individuals devoted to the pursuit of consumer goods and the enjoyment of their private lives as a refuge from increasingly impersonal, detached human interactions in public life. By definition, each human decision has its opportunity cost: one isn't feeding the hungry when dining in a fine restaurant, one isn't giving drink to the thirsty when partying with friends (unless friends' desire for alcohol counts), one isn't sheltering the homeless when relaxing in a second home, and one isn't clothing those who need it when shopping for the season's fashions. A life centered on moneymaking that serves enjoyments is time consuming. Millions of Europeans apparently believe that affluence makes religion superfluous; moreover, religion's trespass in the public sphere might threaten the goods life, which since the 1970s has "had as its most conspicuous feature the striving for the satisfaction of consumers' every desire." Just like in the United States—which, as Victoria de Grazia has shown, has in this respect thoroughly conquered the European continent.[193] But ironically, more than is true of federal or state institutions in the churchgoing United States, secularized Europeans' welfare states since World War II have more in common with the social concerns and the moral commitments of the Christianity that made the Continent and Britain, because they at least seek to meet the most basic needs of every citizen.

The radical transformations wrought by industrialization are obvious and undeniable. But unless acquisitive consumers had sought more and better stuff, industrial production would have yielded warehouses full of unwanted merchandise. Technology does not drive history; rather, since the Middle Ages human desires have driven technological innovations, which in turn influence human desires.[194] Acquisitiveness has expanded socially from its narrow medieval scope that included popes and kings, wealthy bishops and aristocrats, through late medieval mercantile and Renaissance financial entrepreneurs to middling sorts and (to a lesser extent) the laboring poor in the industrious revolution. The Industrial Revolution and nineteenth-century industrialization simply continued a process already centuries in the making. They expanded still further the social base of acquisitiveness and solidified both acquisitive practices and aspirations by making much greater quantities of many more consumer goods available much more cheaply.

But this expanded consumption wrought by industrialization presupposed the productive labor of the very people whom in the absence of Malthusian and Ricardian assumptions about population and wages it might have been supposed to benefit: the women and men of the industrial working class that it forged out of migrants from rural areas to burgeoning urban centers of manufacturing. The prospect and price of enjoying more stuff at home would be paid through the brutalization of the shop floor that included so many subsistence-waged women and children workers. This in turn affected domestic life, because public life and private life have never been mutually exclusive in real life. The gradual democratization of consumption was wrought by factory laborers who worked crushing hours in abysmal conditions for entrepreneurs who prioritized the rational maximization of profit—"utility"—above the well-being of their workers and workers' families.[195] Thus did enterprising nineteenth-century capitalists exercise freedom, seize opportunities, employ reason, make Progress, and promote the common good. Or at least increase their own wealth. Protestant ministers such as Thomas Chalmers (1780–1847) in Britain as well as Francis Wayland (1796–1865) and other "clerical economists" in the antebellum United States assured them that industrial capitalism was providentially ordained.[196] Charles Dickens saw the human costs, and conveyed them through the lives of the Gradgrinds in *Hard Times* (1854), just as Émile Zola would later in *Germinal* (1885) through the travails of French miners, and Upton Sinclair through turn-of-the-century Chicago meatpackers in *The Jungle* (1906).

Like other nineteenth-century social reformers, Marx also saw clearly the human costs of industrialization. But despite his acute analysis of industrial capitalism, he shared with the bourgeoisie whom he attacked the assumption that the good life was the goods life. Because the greedy alliance between capitalists and politicians deliberately obstructed the just return to the proletariat of the value of their labor, workers whose consciousness had been properly raised and who were apprised of their ostensibly objective— that is, material and economic—interests would have to take back by force what was rightfully theirs, seizing control of the means of industrial production. Hence Marx's solution: violent revolution was the only remedy for the injustices of capitalism, a deliberate hastening of the supposedly inexorable processes of class conflict rooted in the allegedly objective truth of historical materialism. Revolutionary violence was supposed to usher in the communist utopia and the goods life for all. Things turned out rather differently. Not only have Marxist dreams gone unrealized, but actions inspired by his ideas led in the nightmarish twentieth century to the deaths of many millions of people.

No less appalled by the human consequences of socioeconomic hierarchy than Thomas Müntzer had been three centuries before, Marx was no less mistaken about the inevitable triumph of the proletarian revolution than Müntzer had been about God's impending judgment. But aside from the small number of Anabaptists such as Hans Hut whom he inspired, Müntzer was excoriated when he was not forgotten.[197] By contrast, Marx, his followers, and his sympathizers helped to define the central, binary structure of Western politics in the later nineteenth and twentieth centuries, and its inseparability from economic concerns: on the right, the (classical) liberal defenders of Lockean private property and Millian individual freedoms (now usually known as "conservatives"), and on the left, *marxisant* critics of the unprecedented disparities of wealth and deleterious human effects produced by industrial capitalism. Both tend to take for granted that the good life is the goods life. We have returned to where this chapter began.

ANOTHER LATE EIGHTEENTH-CENTURY outcome of the Reformation era's religious disagreements was no less important than the Industrial Revolution for the making of present-day capitalism and consumerism. We saw in the previous chapter how the American political sanction of a formal ethics of rights contained the post-Reformation subjectivization of morality, permitting citizens to pursue the good however they pleased within the state's laws. They were pleased to acquire stuff, not only in thriving port cities such as Philadelphia and Boston, but even in the backcountry of late eighteenth-century Virginia.[198] The substantive emptiness of the nation's founding documents was possible not only because Americans were strongly shaped by Christian moral assumptions, but also because so many of them had simultaneously departed in practice from the traditional Christian condemnation of avarice. Despite their socially exclusive churches and divergent religious truth claims, late eighteenth-century free Americans not only shared beliefs about nature as creation and human beings made in God's image. They had also been formed by the industrious revolution. So acquisitiveness united them, too, and provided throughout the nineteenth century an all-but-axiomatic answer to what they would do with their lives, how they would exercise their liberty, and what the pursuit of happiness entailed, *whatever else* they might believe or aspire to. "Love of comfort has become the dominant national taste," Tocqueville noted about Americans in the 1830s, adding that "the main current of human passions running in that direction sweeps everything along with it."[199]

Acquisitiveness would work to contain Americans' differences. The common good of the nation would be strengthened by their consumption, just as the aggressive commerce of their colonial predecessors had strengthened the British Empire in the late seventeenth and early eighteenth centuries. More and better stuff was always a good thing, as inevitable as Manifest Destiny, despite being bound up with chattel slavery as well as the killing and coercive displacement of Indian peoples. Notwithstanding the cataclysm of the Civil War, Adam Smith's Invisible Hand—and the culturally pervasive acquisitiveness that moved it—was at once the instrument of God's Providence and the means of the Progress that connoted divine favor. The tyrannical, papist Spanish had been wrong about their sixteenth-century shiploads of New World silver. By contrast, divine blessing—that is, more and better stuff—in fact rewarded "the land of the free and the home of the brave."[200] Given to self-flattery about their unprecedented experiment in democracy, freedom, and individualism, Americans tended—and indeed, many still tend—to be confident of their ability to discern God's providence, in contrast to the benighted views of their early modern European predecessors. Even the progressive, eighteenth-century British had still been mired in hierarchy, privilege, and tyranny. History had not yet reached its apogee. Of course God blesses America—how else could it have become the world's wealthiest, most powerful country?

The legal guarantee of individual, subjective rights, pioneered in the United States, provided the political protection for what would later become the most important transformation *within* modern Western capitalism: the gradual shift from an industrial to a distinctly consumerist society. This transformation was linked to the strengthening of overtly *individual* acquisitiveness, notwithstanding the formation of households organized around a clear division of labor between male breadwinning and female homemaking from the mid-nineteenth through the mid-twentieth century.[201] The democratization of consumption linked to industrialized manufacturing, despite its harsh impact on so many female and male workers, was not all bad. Despite its many victims, industrialization eventually alleviated for many millions of people in working-class and rural families the sort of persistent poverty in human lives lived close to subsistence level that had for many centuries inhibited human flourishing. The creation of a *consumerist* society, however, combined acquisitiveness with secular ideologies about the autonomous individual linked to the dominant emancipatory narrative of modernity. As Colin Campbell has argued, the formation of consumerism as we know it today depended on a widely embraced Romantic and post-Romantic conception of the individual—not an embodied soul called by God to flourish in a family within a community through the exercise of the virtues, but an emotive "self" that constructs itself as it pleases in the self-chosen relationships it makes and breaks, by exercising its right to do so through the desire for and acquisition of material things and their contribution to its self-construction of identity.[202]

The widespread inculturation of this notion, especially since the 1960s, has contributed to the current character of capitalism and consumerism: "enough" was headed for obsolescence once acquisition was subjected to the never-ending project of self-construction and its social effects lauded by Twitchell and excoriated by Bauman.[203] There can never *be* enough, because the self is functionally a bottomless pit of arbitrary acquisitiveness served by unending technological innovation, manufacturing inventiveness, and marketing strategies. Acquisition is characterized not by a mere accumulation of more and more per se, but by an endless shopping cycle of acquire, discard, repeat, as an extension of individual identity mediated by material things and the self's preferences, without any restraint beyond the will in combination with one's credit limit. This explains why John Maynard Keynes's famous prognostication of 1930 has proven so spectacularly mistaken: "When the accumulation of wealth is no longer of high social importance, there will be great changes in the code of morals," he imagined, for we "shall be able to rid ourselves of many of the pseudo-moral principles which have hag-ridden us for two hundred years, by which we have exalted some of the most distasteful of human qualities"—such as "the love of money"—"into the position of the highest virtues." Keynes failed to see that "the love of money as a means to the enjoyments and realities of life" was not *different* from "the love of money as a possession," but rather precisely what would keep it functioning as it had for so long: in Keynes's view, as "a somewhat disgusting morbidity, one of those semi-criminal, semi-pathological propensities which one hands over with a shudder to the specialists in mental disease."[204] We see in Keynes's characterization of money-making as pathological a latter-day continuation of a traditional Christian condemnation of avarice as sinful—Martin Bucer, too, had called greed a "disease" in the mid-sixteenth century. By contrast, distinctly consumerist acquisitiveness, post-Fordist capitalism, postmodern conceptions of the self as endlessly malleable and constructed, and economists' denial of any meaningful distinction between needs and wants in favor of demand are not four different things, but rather four aspects of the same thing.

The impressive improvements in sanitation, hygiene, diet, and health in the late nineteenth century on both sides of the northern Atlantic could clearly be fit within a traditional Christian conception of human flourishing. So too could industrialization per se, if its effects on the poor were bracketed and it was regarded specifically in terms of the ways in which it eventually worked to alleviate poverty, even as it exposed a centuries-long Christian blindness to the human price paid by embodied souls for the legitimation of socioeconomic hierarchy. (The voluntary embrace of poverty in imitation of Christ should not be conflated with the toleration by the affluent of material destitution among the poor that prevents human flourishing.) But the consumerist ethos of Bauman's "liquid modernity" cannot be squared with the Christianity of the medieval church or of modern Roman Catholic social teaching any more than it can with the views of sixteenth-century Protestant reformers, whom it would have horrified.[205] A shared life of human flourishing understood in Christian terms does not depend on acquiring a smaller iPod with more memory, a bigger flat-screen TV with a sharper display, a sixteenth or twenty-fifth or thirty-third pair of shoes, or hundreds of shirts, sweaters, and scarves in all manner of colors, prints, and patterns. Yet in the early twenty-first century consumerist acquisitiveness is the default ethos and ethic of the Western world's most self-professedly Christian nation. If Christianity is among other things a discipline of self-lessness in charitable service to others, then the United States' legally protected ethos of self-regarding acquisitiveness, culturally reinforced at every turn, would seem to be its antithesis. The latter says "satisfy your own desires"; the former, "you must deny your very self." But if one thinks religion is about the life of the spirit *rather than* about the material world; that faith is about what one feels inside *rather than* what one does with one's body; that detachment from material things implies an inner attitude *rather than* actually giving things away; and that one has already "got saved" by one's "personal Lord and Savior" in the self-chosen congregation that makes one feel most comfortable, then one perhaps doesn't see much of a conflict.

Nothing in this chapter's analysis should be taken to imply that contemporary Americans and Europeans have forsaken their families, relinquished concern for others, stopped making (sometimes unprecedentedly enormous) philanthropic contributions, or thrown off all self-restraint in order to devote themselves single-mindedly to feeding their acquisitive desires. Obviously this is not the case, and thank goodness. So too, it is obvious that the advent of modern capitalism and market-governed societies has facilitated the potential for human flourishing and the possibility of living meaningful human lives for hundreds of millions of people, which considered as such is also a very good thing. But those who are devoted to their families, demonstrate care for others, make charitable donations, and practice self-restraint do so within a world dominated by wall-to-Walmart capitalism and consumerism, with all that this implies. The individual rights protected by Western nations permit citizens to practice ascetic self-denial if they wish; no one is compelled to pursue ever more and better stuff. But within the law, citizens can buy as much of whatever they want, when they want it, and without heeding anyone else's needs or concerns. Acquisitive self-interest is taken for granted, legally protected, and constantly reinforced. The law sanctions and protects the goods life, which is restricted only by one's credit limit. In the United States, the subjectivization of morality within a formal ethics of rights permits individuals to construct themselves through acquisitiveness, obsess over their identities, indulge their desires, and follow their fantasies as they please, without—if it pleases them—so much as a thought, much less an action, for millions who are homeless, hungry, persecuted, or otherwise marginalized. They are free to turn on QVC or the Home Shopping Network instead, or to go online and pull out the credit card.

The broadest material framework for economics is the relationship of human beings to the natural world of which they are a part. For some centuries now, imbued with univocal metaphysical assumptions, most Westerners have grown increasingly accustomed to conceiving of nature in post-sacramental terms within what Charles Taylor has called the "immanent frame."[206] With "creation" construed as an allegedly superstitious and superseded cultural construction, the natural world has instead come to be seen predominantly as an enormous Baconian mine of disinterested matter waiting to be made into the material things that serve human desires for self-determined "betterment." To this end the findings of science, widely (but mistakenly) thought by many intellectuals to have shown the untenability of traditional religious truth claims, have been applied via "useful knowledge" in ever more sophisticated manufacturing technologies with ever more extraordinary results to serve ever expanding desires and ever higher aspirations of affluence. Thus are scarce resources fashioned into supply to meet demand that serves progress.

But now nature seems to be biting back. We are now apparently seeing the cumulative effect of acquisitive human desires on the natural world itself. If global climate change is real, as the Keeling Curve and so much other evidence has suggested for some time, and if it is substantially caused by the industrial manufacturing and agricultural technologies devised to fuel the acquisitiveness sanctioned for centuries as the high road to human happiness, as may very well be the case, it would turn out to be the ultimate subversion of some of the most pervasive modern claims about reason and morality. Unless, of course, one defends the moral right of individuals gradually to destroy the biosphere that makes all of life possible, and regards this exercise of individual liberty as a rational and good thing. If global climate change is real and the result of human behaviors, it would call radically into question the dominant, post-Reformation, secular rationale for meaningful human action and the principal cultural glue that functions to hold together societies composed of ideologically divided individuals. It would mean that the manufactured goods life has turned out to be an unwitting chimera in painfully slow motion, built of rationalized passions and greed for gain, imperialist *libido dominandi* and complacent conformism, regardless of how much the affluent have enjoyed themselves since the seventeenth century. It would imply that we really have been unintentionally and gradually but collectively and quite literally "amusing ourselves to death."[207] It would subvert the progressive narrative of Western modernity as an inspiring story of the triumphal liberation of individual freedom and autonomy and self-determination from hidebound authority and oppressive tradition, suggesting instead that wishful thinking and self-deceptive illusions have long been posing as progressive rationality and Enlightenment truth. Perhaps this is partly why some politically conservative defenders of individual rights and free enterprise, in particular, are keen to dismiss concerns about global warming as so much politically motivated hot air—for its truth would seem to devastate values central to their answers to the Life Questions. Let's all hope they're right, and that so many teams of scientists in different disciplines throughout the world are wrong.

In the late nineteenth century, when during Leo XIII's pontificate the ultramontane papacy reemerged from its defensive retrenchment after the French Revolution, popes began to articulate for an industrial era traditional Christian teachings about human nature, human desires, material things, and the common good. They reiterated the claim that the natural world is God's creation, intended by God for the flourishing of all human beings; repeated that economics and the market are not independent of morality; reasserted that the right to private property is not absolute, but is rather subordinate to the common good; restated that unrestrained acquisitiveness does not serve but rather impedes genuine human flourishing and eternal salvation; confirmed the biblical view that the pursuit of affluence above love for God and service to others is idolatry; argued that minimizing workers' wages in order to maximize profits is exploitative and immoral; and insisted that the poor and marginalized, as a matter of justice, have a moral claim on the more affluent to share with and care for them. These and other claims run throughout modern Catholic social teaching in papal and conciliar texts from Leo XIII's *Rerum novarum* (1891) through the documents of Vatican II to John Paul II's *Centesimus annus* (1991) and Benedict XVI's *Caritas in veritate* (2009).[208]

Billions of people, including most Western Catholics, by their actions effectively prioritize above such assertions the never-ending acquisition of newer and better laptops and cell phones, iPads and iPods, and still more clothes and shoes and baubles, despite the fact that so many of the world's people live in a material misery that prevents them from flourishing. Moneymaking mesmerizes, affluence anesthetizes, and comfort conduces to conformist complacency. How ironic it is that modern popes, who champion Catholic social teaching against human life governed by unregulated markets, were preceded by medieval and Renaissance pontiffs in Avignon and Rome who, by their own acquisitive practices and example, contributed to the long-term formation of the capitalism and consumerism now criticized by their papal successors. In Western countries, everyone is free to choose self-absorbed, consumerist self-construction as one's good, buying stuff made by poor people in faraway countries—whose sweaty toil one will never have to witness, into whose eyes one will never have to look—because governments protect everyone's right to do so. Indeed, it is crucially important that in the aggregate, people *continue* to conform to consumerism. No matter what, individuals must be left free to be selfish, because the manufactured goods life is needed to hold Western hyperpluralism together. In a world pullulating with so many incompatible truth claims, values, priorities, and aspirations, what else could do the trick?

Modern science not only has facilitated the manufacturing technologies that feed the acquisitive desires of the goods life. Its presuppositions also provide the ideological foundations for what counts and does not count as modern knowledge. The doctrinal disagreements of the Reformation era precipitated the confessionalization of universities and thus comprised a critical shift in higher education that led to the eventual secularization of knowledge, and to the modern exclusion of all religious truth claims not only from the natural sciences, but also from the social sciences and humanities. A separation of religion from academic disciplines in secularized universities was constructed that now parallels the institutional separation of church and state. An analysis of the ideological and institutional secularization of knowledge, from the late Middle Ages to the present, is the subject of Chapter 6.

# CHAPTER SIX

# Secularizing Knowledge

IN THE WESTERN WORLD today, research universities are the only institutions dedicated to making and transmitting knowledge across the full range of human inquiry. This has made them profoundly influential institutions for more than a century. Especially since World War II, governmental and corporate research laboratories have increasingly contributed to the explosion of scientific knowledge as well, often with an eye to its potential military, manufacturing, and other technological applications. But such labs are not in the business of higher education.[1] Liberal arts colleges, a form of higher educational institution much more common in the United States than in Europe, span a much wider range of knowledge than do research laboratories unaffiliated with universities, but they seek primarily to transmit knowledge to undergraduate students rather than to create it. Only research universities seek both to teach what is already known and to create new knowledge, through the respective methods of each academic discipline and the ever burgeoning number of interdisciplinary research endeavors. University scientists and scholars do this in every subject area within every discipline from econometrics, ancient Greek art history, and neurophysiology to modern Japanese literature, social psychology, and biochemistry. Accordingly, research universities have been the centrally important Western institution in the definition, pursuit, and transmission of knowledge since the later nineteenth century. Indeed, "the university's invisible product, knowledge, may be the most powerful single element in our culture, affecting the rise and fall of professions and even of social classes, of regions and even of nations."[2] In the twentieth century, the many new universities established throughout the rest of the world have overwhelmingly institutionalized the structures, priorities, agenda, and assumptions of Western research universities.[3] For all practical purposes, leading scientists and scholars at research universities are the societal and indeed the global arbiters of what counts as knowledge and what does not in the early twenty-first century. It is what they say it is: secular, specialized, and universal, independent of the social circumstances and personal beliefs of those who pursue, acquire, and purvey it.

Regardless of the academic discipline, knowledge in the Western world today is considered secular by definition. Its assumptions, methods, content, and truth claims are and can only be secular, framed not only by the logical demand of rational coherence, but also by the methodological postulate of naturalism and its epistemological correlate, evidentiary empiricism. Knowledge must be based on evidence, it must make sense, and (aside from purely conceptual abstractions) it can neither assume nor conclude that anything which putatively transcends the universe is real, else it ceases to count as knowledge. What these stipulations entail differs enormously in practice among, say, applied mathematicians, historians, field-based anthropologists, and human geneticists, but in no discipline can the claims of revealed truth characteristic of religious traditions such as Judaism, Christianity, or Islam be candidates for knowledge. For this reason, the religious truth claims made by billions of people are excluded from consideration on their own terms in nearly all research universities.[4] Because all religious truth claims are based on faith, so the argument goes, they are a matter of subjective opinion and personal preference; therefore it is not surprising that they proliferate in such pluralistic and contrary ways; hence they are not and cannot be candidates for claims of objective truth confirmable by shared epistemological standards. Those who wish to pursue them in academic settings might do so in institutions whose instructors and students *already believe* such claims to be true, such as seminaries, theology institutes, or schools of divinity—institutions that, in turn, often tend not to concern themselves with the relationship between their respective religious truth claims and the findings of the natural sciences, social sciences, and humanities. But such doctrinally circumscribed institutions thereby exclude themselves from the critical inquiry characteristic of the pursuit of knowledge, it is usually thought, and they are therefore properly ignored by scholars and scientists who are dedicated to the pursuit and transmission of value-neutral knowledge.

In research universities, the beliefs, practices, sacred texts, and worship of any and all religious traditions can be and are the objects of study according to the secular assumptions of the social sciences or humanities. But religion is not and cannot be considered a potential source of knowledge, just as theology—as opposed to religious studies—cannot be an academic discipline on par with other academic disciplines if it includes claims of divine revelation. Regardless of the intellectual rigor or sophistication with which they are articulated, examined, or studied, no religious tradition's claims of divine revelation are or can be admitted in the research university for consideration on their own terms, and thus potentially contribute to knowledge that is otherwise inaccessible or unattainable: in James Turner's formulation, "the decidedly nontheistic, secular understanding of knowledge characteristic of modern universities will not accommodate belief in God as a working principle."[5] One consequence of the character of knowledge thus construed, more socially significant today in the United States than in Canada or Europe, is that the most widespread and influential ways in which most Western people answer (and historically, have since ancient times answered) the Life Questions are excluded from the principal institution where knowledge is made and transmitted, and where ideas are discussed and debated, because "the irrelevance of theology to the secular disciplines is a taken-for-granted dogma."[6] The pursuit of knowledge is ideologically secular and is institutionalized as such; academic freedom in universities precludes the freedom to consider any religious truth claims as candidates for knowledge. The ideological exclusion of religion from research universities parallels the political separation of church and state in the public sphere.

A second major feature of knowledge, whether in the natural sciences, social sciences, or humanities, is twofold. First, the pursuit and discovery of new knowledge is almost always a highly specialized affair that requires years of advanced, highly focused graduate training. Second, there is almost no attempt by anyone to see how the *kinds* of knowledge thereby gained in different disciplines might fit together, or whether the disciplines' respective, contrary claims and incompatible assumptions might be resolved. In every discipline, those who aspire to contribute to new knowledge are obliged to master an enormous quantity of already existing specialized knowledge in a narrow field before embarking on an original project in an even more circumscribed subfield. Anyone who doubts this should listen to the titles of Ph.D. dissertations as the respective degree recipients are recognized during a university graduation ceremony, or peruse even the titles of journals (to say nothing of the titles of the journal articles themselves) in electronic databases such as JSTOR or Project Muse. Since the nineteenth century, when the modern research university was constituted, the trend has been unmistakable: the growth of knowledge entails the proliferation of ever more specialized research in an ever greater number of discrete, increasingly divergent academic disciplines. They comprise "the really modern university—the multiversity," which already half a century ago Clark Kerr characterized as "a city of infinite variety."[7] Apparently infinity can be increased, considering the dramatic expansion and transformation of research universities since the early 1960s.

In part, this undeniable growth of knowledge as a result of specialized research simply reflects the previously unimagined complexity of reality in combination with the potentially infinite number of questions that scientists and scholars can ask and seek to answer. New discoveries prompt new and more research. So it has been for well over a century, and so in all likelihood it will ever be, provided that the financial and institutional resources for academic research persist in conditions of political stability and open inquiry. In this respect, research specialization is necessary, inevitable, and innocuous. What is less satisfactory—although it is not surprising, given the intensive, specialized nature of advanced academic training—is the dearth of efforts by intellectuals in whatever field even to try to understand where and how the sorts of inquiry by, say, astrophysicists, comparative political scientists, and ethnomusicologists fit within the pursuit of knowledge as a whole.[8]

It will not do to say they bear no relationship at all to one another. All these disciplines study some aspect of reality. All produce knowledge that purports to be true, unless and until it is shown to be inadequate on the basis of new research. Nor will it do to keep the human world of meanings, beliefs, symbols, and cultures entirely separate from the natural world of subatomic particles, chemical reactions, biological organisms, and diverse ecosystems. The human world is incontestably embedded in the natural world, and the natural world, if it is studied at all, is inescapably studied (at least on our planet) by human beings for certain ends via particular methods and on the basis of specific assumptions and beliefs rather than others. The recent academic vogue for interdisciplinarity reflects the perceived problem, but as Louis Menand has rightly argued, interdisciplinarity is "the ratification of the logic of disciplinarity" and paradoxically tends to reinforce the disciplinary divides it seeks to transcend.[9] It is a symptom, not a solution. Interdisciplinarity is different from an attempt to see how, if all types of knowledge are really knowledge, they cohere—which is a question not about interdisciplinarity, but about the interrelatedness of knowledge about reality. Clearly such an endeavor could not hope to encompass the actual content of everything known, which is constantly being expanded and revised. That would be impossible. But it should be possible to do more than shrug, or insist that there is no real question to be pursued, or pretend that knowledge produced in all other disciplines is reducible to that produced in one's own—as if evolutionary biology, for example, could explain the striking differences in behavior and beliefs among human beings who coexist in the same city within the same culture at the same moment of evolutionary development, or as if economics had the conceptual tools to understand a Mozart symphony.

More immediately problematic than the lack of efforts to try to integrate widely disparate kinds of knowledge, however, is the fact that some of the most basic assumptions and truth claims of divergent disciplines are incompatible. Their clashes are perhaps most starkly seen with respect to human beings, at once the most extensively and intensively investigated objects of knowledge and the epistemological agents of all human knowing. Whereas some sociobiologists, for example, claim that all human behavior is determined by and explicable in terms of evolutionary processes, humanistic scholars constantly use intellectual categories that presuppose individual freedom and creativity. Economists sometimes posit the stability of individual preferences and usually assume the universality of rationally self-interested, maximizing behavior, but cultural anthropologists tend to assert the mutability of all human behaviors, norms, and customs. Not all these things can be true. Yet all supposedly constitute part of knowledge or are assumed in its pursuit. But no academics are trained to inquire about the incompatible assumptions and claims made by scholars and scientists in various disciplines, what they are based on, where they come from, and how one might try to sort out the conflicts among them. So the incompatibilities simply sit there.

These incompatible assumptions and claims are taught to undergraduates, who might be told in a biology class that universal moral norms such as (survival-minded) cooperation or (gene-perpetuating) altruism are the product of evolutionary natural selection, only to hear in an anthropology or philosophy class the next hour, based on the empirical heterogeneity of moral practices across space and time or the obvious inconclusiveness of arguments among moral philosophers, that there are no universal moral norms. What are they to infer? No undergraduate courses teach students how they might even begin to evaluate contrary claims in disparate disciplines. (Nor do any graduate courses, which are almost invariably much more specialized.) No wonder so many students, at least intuitively aware of the principle of noncontradiction, are confused, and conclude that there is nothing intellectually coherent to be made of their education—that in the end, like consumer choice in the marketplace, knowledge of "truth" in the marketplace of ideas is a matter of whatever they want to buy on the basis of individual preference. Indeed, why should they think otherwise? By and large, their professors in their respective departments, institutes, and research specialties are *themselves* apparently unconcerned with the manifest incompatibilities that their respective disciplines generate. So it is unsurprising that most American students, including those at elite (and very expensive) institutions of higher education, tend to be nonchalant if not cynical about the pursuit of truth, and view undergraduate education primarily as grade-getting, preprofessional training en route to gaining admission to professional schools on the path to becoming doctors, lawyers, businesspeople—or the next generation of academics. That way they at least get something useful out of their education, setting themselves up advantageously for an affluent run in the goods life. For their part, most scholars and scientists simply ignore the problem by remaining burrowed in their dens of specialization, continuing to pursue what is rewarded most highly in the academy: the creation of new—highly specialized—knowledge within one's own discipline.

In addition to its definitional secularity and its highly specialized character, a third major feature of knowledge in the Western world today is its separateness and separability both from the uses to which it is put, and from the personal lives, particular beliefs, social practices, and specific commitments of those who create and transmit it. Whatever is to count as knowledge must be universal and objective: if something is known or knowable, its content is not contingent on who discovers it, who transmits it, or who applies it and for what purposes. Thus knowledge as such is distinct from morality and from concrete human relationships. Regardless of whether nuclear fission is employed in electrical power plants or weapons of mass destruction or neither, for example, contemporary atomic theory is rightly regarded as true unless shown to be inadequate based on the investigative methods of physics. Its truth does not depend on the moral behaviors of physicists, the social relationships of physics professors, or the ways in which physics students happen to answer any of the Life Questions. The same is true, mutatis mutandis, of all other academic disciplines. For example, unless new, relevant research suggests otherwise, the molecular bonds studied in organic chemistry are what they are, the kinship patterns of aboriginal tribes are what they are, and the character of economic transactions in seventeenth-century Holland were what they are said to have been, regardless of the moral commitments, social practices, or metaphysical beliefs of those who study them. In this sense, research and education across the entire domain of knowledge is separable from and independent of the rest of human life. Conversely, any truth claims about reality that are dependent on the concrete circumstances, relationships, or experiences of individuals or groups, and thus are not independently accessible to or confirmable by others in different circumstances, cannot count as a source of knowledge about reality in general. Such claims can only serve as data for knowledge *about* such individuals or groups and their particular circumstances.

The central argument of this chapter is that these three features of knowledge—its secularity, its specialized and segmented character, and its intrinsic separability from the rest of life—are related, and derive in complex and unintended ways from the doctrinal disagreements of the Reformation era. Circa 1510, knowledge in Europe was not secular but rather included Christian truth claims (except among small numbers of Jews and Muslims, whose respective religious truth claims occupied a similar niche, mutatis mutandis); qualitatively different kinds of knowledge were interrelated within the diverse, vibrant intellectual culture of Western Christendom; and neither social practices, nor morality, nor the uses to which knowledge was put were separated from knowledge as such. This chapter endeavors to show that the long-term process of the secularization of knowledge is inextricable from the Reformation era's doctrinal controversies and the ideological and institutional responses that they engendered.

We have already seen in Chapter 1, contrary to what is widely believed, that the findings of modern science as such neither demand the intellectual repudiation of a sacramental view of reality, nor logically entail a reclassification of all religious truth claims as subjective opinions. Nor, as this chapter will suggest and contrary to what is widely believed, did the advent and development of humanist philology, historical scholarship, and/or modern biblical criticism as such lead inexorably to the repudiation of Christian truth claims about God's actions in history (which most early modern Protestants continued to share with Catholics). The historical processes through which knowledge was eventually secularized were more convoluted and more paradoxical. The first major seed was planted by unsought doctrinal disagreement and pursuant Western Christian pluralism. On the doctrinal issues about which Reformation-era Christians disagreed, it was logically impossible for all of them actually to have had the knowledge of God's teachings that they claimed to have. As we have seen, early modern theological controversialists of every stripe understood this, well aware of the principle of noncontradiction (in contrast to some protagonists of Christian ecumenism today). That is why they engaged in ongoing doctrinal controversy. It is also why in the late nineteenth century, as we shall see, moves were made that led to the exclusion of all substantive religious truth claims from research universities. For how could one arbitrate among them?

In combination with unresolved doctrinal disagreements, another—deeply ironic—factor that laid the foundation for the eventual secularization of knowledge derived from states' control of churches: the triumph of theology in the confessionalized universities of the Reformation era among

Roman Catholics, Lutherans, and Reformed Protestants (including the Church of England). In contrast to the treatment of the many marginalized radical Protestant groups, only Catholic and magisterial Protestant churches were protected—and overseen—by secular authorities in confessional regimes. By privileging theology in universities, protecting orthodoxy from scholarly challenges, and policing intellectual inquiry, authorities curtailed the interactions between a regime's religious truth claims and other domains of human knowledge. Whether intentionally or not, most early modern universities thus tended to foster complacency among those who taught in their theology and arts faculties by prohibiting the pursuit of doctrinally sensitive sorts of inquiry. Meanwhile, intellectual inquiry did not stand still in the early modern period; increasingly, it simply migrated outside universities. Even when theologians scored impressive achievements within their respective confessional arenas, as some of them did, theology's place on its pedestal was precisely what rendered it vulnerable. What if rulers, on whose will its privileged perch depended, started changing their minds? In Catholic Europe, the Jesuits would find out in the third quarter of the eighteenth century.

As new knowledge of the natural world, the historical past, and other human cultures was exploding in the seventeenth and eighteenth centuries, confessional restrictions had pushed many of the most consequential avenues for its pursuit outside universities, Protestant academies, and post-Tridentine Catholic seminaries. New institutions such as the scientific academies augmented the continuing vitality of the correspondence networks and personal contacts that held together the Republic of Letters, with its intellectually voracious and irrepressibly curious members. Their knowledge-making, which deliberately bracketed contested matters of Christian doctrine, aimed at Baconian utility and supra-confessional civility and was increasingly demonstrating its worth amid the industrious revolution—in stark contrast to theology at the end of the inconclusively destructive Thirty Years War and English Revolution. Moreover, the theological protagonists of long-insulated confessional orthodoxies, in their respective ways, lacked the intellectual wherewithal to discern how their respective doctrinal claims might fit with the profusion of new knowledge. (As we shall see, it was not a matter of new findings *being* incompatible with central Christian truth claims, but of an inculturated incapacity to see how they could be.) Revealingly, the universities that fared best in accommodating new knowledge were those with the fewest confessional strictures: Leiden in the seventeenth century, Edinburgh, Glasgow, Halle, and Göttingen in the eighteenth. The consequential trajectory would lead through nineteenth-century, professorial *Lehrfreiheit* and student *Lernfreiheit* to the broader, modern association of religious dogma per se with reactionary anti-intellectualism, and of academic freedom with the insistence that genuine knowledge can only be secular.

After the disruptions of the French Revolution and Napoleonic era, rulers started to rein in the far-flung, fissiparous sites of early modern knowledge-making. They began to centralize the pursuit and transmission of knowledge in the reinvented university and to make it serve the nation-state, beginning most influentially in Prussia with the University of Berlin in 1810. As Berlin's ambitions were imitated across Protestant Germany, theology was subordinated to post-Kantian philosophy and to the multiple disciplines emergent from classical philology.[10] After the devastating attacks on Roman Catholicism during the French Revolution, Catholic universities in the late nineteenth and early twentieth centuries inhabited an intellectual subculture scaffolded by neo-Thomism that remained suspicious of a great deal of new knowledge. In contrast, in the 1820s the German Protestant research universities began to add the natural sciences alongside their humanistic lectures and seminars; the success of this approach was increasingly apparent by the later nineteenth century in universities on both sides of the Atlantic. Unlike knowledge made in humanistic disciplines, natural-scientific knowledge was technologically applicable, its practical utility demonstrated repeatedly in industrializing nation-states whose rulers dreamed of ever-increasing material prosperity in Europe's colonizing and civilizing march around the globe.

Because of the demonstrated success of the natural sciences, the nascent social sciences, most of which were professionalized as academic disciplines in the last third of the nineteenth century, wanted to be like them. Liberal Protestant theologians and skeptical biblical scholars, having hitched their wagon to post-Kantian philosophy beholden to univocal metaphysical assumptions, found that wagon's payload progressively lightened until it was unclear how Christianity could consist of anything more than post-Schleiermacherian pious sentiments. If natural scientists studied the material world from which miracles had been extruded, history covered the ancient Near East along with the rest of the human past, psychology analyzed human interiority and behavior, and anthropology explained ritual and its functions, what was left for theologians to do? Meanwhile, in both England and the United States, Darwinism provoked a reactionary biblicist literalism among some of the Protestants intellectually ill-equipped to assimilate the theory of evolution. They created what Mark Noll has called "the intellectual disaster of fundamentalism" that has since contributed to "the scandal of the evangelical mind."[11] By the 1920s, via a bridge of liberal Protestantism on both sides of the Atlantic, the knowledge-making of all academic disciplines was bounded by the metaphysical naturalism and ideological secularism that has been progressively institutionalized in Western universities since the early twentieth century. This secularization of knowledge in research universities has been imitated all around the world—including in Catholic universities, most of which have followed suit, accepting the allegedly unavoidable demands of "modernity" only since the 1960s.

As we shall see in filling out this story, the secularization of knowledge in the West was not inevitable. It was not a matter of obvious inferences based on scientific findings or of indubitable insights gleaned from neutral textual interpretation or historical research. Rather, it was a thoroughly contingent process derived from human interactions that involved assumptions, institutions, metaphysical beliefs, the exercise of power, and human desires besides the desire to discover and to learn. The dominant narrative of modern Western intellectual history, of course, suggests otherwise. This is not surprising, since this narrative is itself a latter-day descendant of the story told by early modern Enlightened protagonists about their progress in triumphing over the prescientific, superstitious credulity and the precritical, dogmatic ignorance of peoples in the superseded past. The transition from premodern religious belief to modern secular knowledge is the virtual heart of the story, nearly synonymous with the Enlightenment that ushered in modernity.[12] Seeing matters differently requires a willingness to question some fundamental assumptions that are commonly taken for granted, and to see the secularization of knowledge as embedded in historical processes whose reach extends beyond matters of inquiry, perception, evidence, reason, inference, and epistemology considered in themselves. It also requires a conceptual framework capacious enough to accommodate the different types and subjects of knowledge as they were regarded on the eve of the Reformation, and a chronological perspective sufficient to encompass their historical formation—one that stretches back through the Middle Ages to the ancient world and the texts, authorities, experiences, and alleged events at the heart of the medieval Christian worldview.

AT THE OUTSET of the sixteenth century, even the most learned intellectuals in Western Christendom knew a great deal less about the natural order, the historical past, and the peoples of the world than moderately educated people everywhere know today. But what could be and was known had a wider compass, an interconnectedness, and an interrelatedness to the rest of life that is lacking in knowledge as construed today in research universities. These features of knowledge in Christianity on the eve of the Reformation derived from reality understood as creation with its beginning and end in God. Learned Christians around 1500 had knowledge of all these things: the intelligible regularities of the natural world as God's creation; the human past, including the account of God's extraordinary actions in history as reported in the Bible and interpreted by the church's leaders over the preceding millennium and a half; and (varying widely depending on their individual circumstances) the goodness—or prospective goodness—of the Gospel's shared way of life as embodied in Christian practices. What they did not know and could not have known—although they often imagined they did—was how extraordinarily complex, in their respective ways, each of the first two kinds of knowledge would turn out to be, as modern science, history, archaeology, and biblical scholarship have made clear and continue to make clear, with no end in sight.[13]

To be sure, this lack of awareness about the complexity of the natural world and the human past did not affect what mattered most, namely the third sort of knowledge. It turned not at all on erudition or formal education, but on participatory experience and related holiness rooted in shared Christian life. This was knowledge of human flourishing, the common good, and imperfect happiness as a harbinger of eternal salvation with God and the communion of saints among those who "have the mind of Christ" (1 Cor 2:16). It was no less accessible to uneducated peasants than to the most erudite Christians, because salvation did not depend on knowledge of the natural world as understood through Aristotelian categories at the universities of Paris or Oxford any more than it depended on mastery of beautifully wrought, Ciceronian Latin among Italian humanists. According to the Gospels, Jesus had not established an educational program of formal schooling—he called followers and commanded them to live a certain way. Hence medieval Christianity was resolutely anti-Gnostic. Knowledge of God's saving truth was not complicated or esoteric; yet it was difficult *to live* and therefore hard to come to know well. The better that one lived it—the holier one was—the clearer did its truth become, a *sapientia* beyond mere *scientia*. The lived holy wisdom of the saints, quite apart from whether they were erudite or brilliant, embodied most conspicuously this sort of knowledge, in keeping with Paul's claim that "God chose what is foolishness in the world to shame the wise" (1 Cor 2:27). This participatory knowledge was no less real, and hence no less objective, than the experience of hunger or melancholy, anger or sexual desire. Ignoring or neglecting it tended demonstrably to foster interior inquietude, social strife, and competitive conflict in this life as a prelude—based on what God had revealed and the church taught—to divine punishment after death.

At the same time, because truth could not be self-contradictory, knowledge of the natural world, and of the ancient past with its sacred and pagan texts, was *in principle* related and relatable to the knowledge of God's self-revelation in Jesus that anchored Christians' shared way of life. All truth, if it was what it purported to be, contributed somehow to knowledge of God's intelligible creation in space and time. Conversely, none of these three forms of knowing alone could encompass all there was to know about God's creation, including the human beings within it. The methods of and prerequisites for each were different: interpreting texts was not *like* tracking the movement of the planets, for example, and *neither* was like the experience of forgiving and being forgiven. Therefore none of these three ways of knowing *could* monopolize all potential knowledge. But nothing guaranteed that this would be seen or acknowledged. So there was bound to be friction among learned Christians to the extent that they were invested in one of these ways of knowing to the exclusion of the others. With this in mind we can understand the character of Christendom's vibrant, varied, and sometimes contentious intellectual culture on the eve of the Reformation, with its monastic, scholastic, scientific, and humanistic strands.[14] This will in turn enable us to see how this culture and its institutional settings were affected by the Reformation.

AT THE OUTSET of the sixteenth century, monastic life had been for a millennium the institution *par excellence* within which the salvific, participatory knowledge of traditional Christianity was cultivated and transmitted, "a school for the service of the Lord" *(dominici schola servitii)* as Benedict of Nursia had called the monastery in the prologue of his sixth-century *Rule*.[15] Words were the handmaiden to the silence in which God spoke, Latin literacy the gateway both to the scriptures that contained God's words of everlasting life and to the writings of the (mostly Latin) church fathers who were considered its greatest interpreters and commentators. Erudition was a means that served Christian life as an ordered integration of *ora et labora*, prayer and work. "Seven times a day I praise you for your righteous ordinances," the psalmist had said (Ps 119:164). So that is what Benedictine monks and nuns did, too, rising in the middle of the night to pray together the first of the seven canonical hours of the divine office that structured every day of their shared life as an *opus Dei*, a work of God. In the sixth and seventh centuries, secular clergy began practicing their own version of the divine office, initially inspired by monks who staffed churches in Rome.[16]

Freed as much as possible from the distractions of the weary-making world—which was differently vexing but no less problematic after the crumbling of Roman imperial institutions—monastic life sought to embody what Christian life as such was supposed to be: a disciplined reorientation of one's desires and actions away from baseline selfishness and toward the selfless love of God and others, a deliberate endeavor to uproot default sinfulness through shared practices that habituated to virtuous life. In the monks' instance, this included ruminative *lectio divina*, the weekly chanting of all 150 psalms in the divine office, focused labor, daily celebration of the Mass, a vigilant watchfulness over one's soul, and an openness to the constant presence of the transcendent, providentially active God who had become incarnate in Jesus and whose Holy Spirit guided the church, in accord with Jesus's promise as written in John's Gospel: "I still have many things to say to you, but you cannot bear them now. When the Spirit of truth comes, he will guide you into all the truth" (Jn 16:12–13).[17] In the fourth chapter of his *Rule*, Benedict tersely enumerated seventy-two, thoroughly biblical "tools of our spiritual craft." They include, for example, "In the first place, to love the Lord God with all one's heart, soul, and strength," "To love one's neighbor as oneself," "To respect all human beings [*homines*]," "To deny oneself in order to follow Christ," "Not to embrace pleasures," "To relieve the poor," "To set nothing above loving Christ," "To speak the truth from the heart and mouth," "To love enemies," "To credit God, not oneself, with whatever good one might see in oneself," "To know with certainty that God sees everything," "Often to devote oneself to prayer," and "To fulfill God's commandments [*praecepta*] every day in one's actions."[18] Derived from God's revelation and actions in Jesus, these practices and others like them conduced to the knowledge lived in community that presaged eternal life.

One of Benedict's tools was "to listen with pleasure to holy readings," a prerequisite for which was knowledge of the Latin language. Otherwise one could not understand the words of the divine office and liturgy. Without one's own knowledge of the Latin one could not read manuscripts of the Vulgate Bible and the fathers, whether directly or in redacted *florilegia*. As Augustine had argued in his influential *De doctrina Christiana*, one could not profit fully from the riches of the word of God without knowledge of the rhetorical, grammatical, and logical elements in and through which the words of God were written—even Jesus himself had made particular rhetorical choices, used figures of speech, and employed arguments.[19] To the extent that the ancient trivium of the liberal arts, and any other sorts of knowledge, for that matter, served the tools of the monastic spiritual craft geared toward eternal life, they were not only legitimate but invaluable. On the other hand, the pursuit of knowledge for some other end, or as an end in itself, was literally vain in the sense of purposeless— indeed, it was potentially worse than useless, and unequivocally dangerous, prone to puff up its pursuers with pride or to serve sinful desires restricted only by human inventiveness, if it did not somehow contribute to the knowledge that conduced to salvation. Hence the monastic interest in astronomy (one of the four mathematically related liberal arts in the ancient quadrivium) was driven by the intellectually difficult task of calculating the annually variable, movable feast of Easter, the central celebration in the Christian liturgical calendar. Related, similarly useful calculative techniques pertaining to time and periodicity in the service of Christian life were known collectively as *computus*, a body of knowledge that received its most influential early culmination in *The Reckoning of Time*, an early eighth-century treatise by the Anglo-Saxon monastic scholar Bede (673–735).[20] Christianity's salvific, participatory knowledge as epitomized in monasticism was not anti-intellectual, but it was resolutely teleological and therefore deliberately selective: knowledge of the natural world was good, just as literacy and knowledge of rhetoric, grammar, and logic were good, if they served the common good of the virtuous, shared life and participatory knowledge of the faith oriented toward the final good of eternal salvation. Like politics and economic behavior, knowledge was embedded within a teleological ethics that had a supernatural end.

Experiential Christian knowledge was by no means limited to vowed religious, even if they remained its principal cultivators from the time of the Egyptian desert fathers of the fourth century through the twelfth-century resurgence of Western European monastic life that produced the Carthusians, the Premonstratensians, and the Cistercians.[21] It was abundantly clear that institutional structures and rules (in both the ordinary and the monastic senses of *regulae*) did not of themselves generate men and women who lived holy lives. As we have seen, whether for professed religious, secular clergy, or laity, Christian holiness required not simply obedience to moral laws but the actual practice of the virtues. Hence the history of cloistered religious life was inseparable from repeated calls for its reform, whether in the Carolingian renaissance, the twelfth-century efflorescence of monasticism, or the Observantine movement of the late fourteenth and fifteenth centuries. A negative judgment on the character of monastic institutions in any given time and place was not tantamount to a rejection of Christian experiential knowledge. Nor did it mean that one would necessarily spurn a deliberate, communal Christian life that sought it, as the Netherlandish Brothers and Sisters of the Common Life showed beginning in the late fourteenth century.[22] But as the Augustinian canons and canonesses of Windesheim demonstrated, vowed religious life was *also* a fruitful setting for the *devotio moderna*: Thomas à Kempis, for example, the author-compiler of the *Imitation of Christ,* was formed among the Brothers in Deventer but spent the last sixty-five years of his long life as a professed canon in the Mount St. Agnes monastery northeast of Zwolle, beginning in 1406.[23] His pithy maxims for Christian practice in the *Imitation* are deeply biblical, and thus unsurprisingly echo Benedict's "tools of our spiritual craft."

At the same time, the fact that at least fifty-six printed editions of the *Imitation of Christ* were published in Dutch, German, English, French, Italian, or Spanish between 1470 and 1520 strongly suggests the desire of increasing numbers of literate laypeople for Christianity's experiential, participatory knowledge.[24] So too does the production of vernacular translations of works by à Kempis, Augustine, Bernard of Clairvaux, Jean Gerson, Johannes Nider, and other writers in the scriptorium of the Benedictine monks at Salzburg beginning around the mid-fifteenth century, to give one localized example.[25] And the many editions of printed vernacular Psalters, Gospels and Epistles, and complete bibles by the beginning of the sixteenth century, often in paraphrases, moralizations, and rhymed versions, in High and Low German, Dutch, French, Provençal, Italian, Spanish, Catalan, and Valencian, point in the same direction, building as they did on long-standing medieval traditions of vernacular biblical translation and adaptation.[26]

Long before the Reformation, experiential Christian knowledge was neither locked up in Latin nor limited to cloistered religious life. The virtues could be practiced and prayers said by laywomen and laymen no less than by nuns and monks, even if in bustling, market-minded towns it was likely more difficult to do so as wholeheartedly or single-mindedly. Both Books of Hours (the most widespread genre of printed book in the decades before the Reformation) and the rosary were many-stranded transformations and appropriations of the divine office that had become extremely popular by the fifteenth century.[27] Promoted by both the regular and the secular clergy, the rosary combined Marian devotion, meditation on episodes from Jesus's life, and a reinforcement of Christian doctrines in a manner well suited to life in the world.[28] Every human being was created in the image and likeness of God, including the laity who made up the large majority of Western Christians, and therefore all could come to God's saving knowledge through the practice of the faith.

THE MENDICANT FRIARS understood this well. The aspirations of the two most influential orders among them, the Franciscans and the Dominicans, at first could only have seemed a parody of religious life to the cloistered whose vows included a commitment to *stabilitas*. The mendicants' very aim was to be on the move, active in ministry to the laity; not fleeing from the world but plunging into its midst, they (especially the Franciscans) ministered to the poor in burgeoning cities and (especially the Dominicans) preached against Albigensian heretics in Italy and southern France. The wider world, for all its fallenness and manifest dangers, was incontestably part of God's creation, after all, and it was where the large majority of Christians peregrinated from baptism to burial. Notwithstanding the protestations of monastic critics, nothing in the mendicant *vita activa* conflicted with single-minded commitment to the love of God and others, the practice of the virtues, and the sort of shared life that sustained Christianity's experiential knowledge. The followers of Francis and Dominic simply endeavored to live it out differently, especially in urban settings generally eschewed by the members of monastic orders. The friars sought to address concerns that outstripped the capacities of secular clergy to provide for the laity, as was implied by their papal approval in the early thirteenth century.[29]

Unless they knew how to articulate the faith, the mendicants could neither teach it to the laity nor exhort them in it. Nor could they preach against heresy unless they understood clearly just how it diverged from Christian truth. Hence they needed not only Christianity's participatory knowledge, but a rational comprehension that could both grasp the interrelatedness of the faith's truth claims and distinguish its tenets readily from their erroneous repudiations by heretics. This required precisely chosen words and carefully exercised reason. Knowledge of *this* kind, and the unavoidable imperative of distinguishing truth from error that eventuated in the ongoing articulation of doctrine, had implicitly been part of Christianity since the first century, when Paul had warned against "false apostles, deceitful workers, disguising themselves as apostles of Christ" (2 Cor 11:13) and Jesus himself had in the Gospels cautioned against "false Christs and false prophets" who would seek to lead God's chosen astray (Mk 13:22, Mt 24:24). Not everything that claimed to be Christian was, or indeed could be. This enterprise of knowledge-making had been explicit from the second through the fifth century, as church leaders simultaneously defined orthodoxy and determined the canon amid intense doctrinal debates. The collection of texts eventually canonized as scripture had from the earliest acknowledgments of its authority provoked countless questions, presented obscurities, and manifested apparent contradictions to attentive readers. The closely related challenges of understanding the faith's truth claims and interpreting the Bible had been central to the Latin and Greek church fathers, and were carried on by monastic commentators from Alcuin of York (c. 735–804) through Anselm of Canterbury (c. 1033–1109) to Bernard of Clairvaux (1090–1153) and beyond.

How did the church's truth claims, scripture, patristic exegesis, and monastic commentaries fit together? This was the implicit, daunting question posed by masters of dialectic in the twelfth century, one taken up in the cathedral schools of northern France in cities such as Chartres and Paris.[30]

An extension of Anselm of Canterbury's *fides quaerens intellectum,* the question arose out of Christianity's participatory knowledge, which in turn derived from communities of faith that affirmed the authority of the tradition that had transmitted the testimony about God's actions in Jesus. Abelard (1079–1142) famously left the question hanging in his *Sic et non,* juxtaposing without resolving the apparently incompatible assertions and difficult passages that he compiled from the church fathers, probably as an intellectual exercise for his students.[31] Around 1150, Peter Lombard (c. 1100–1160) provided a quarry to mine in his *Sentences,* a topically arranged compilation of biblical and patristic statements about the faith.[32] Bernard of Clairvaux's attempts to derail Abelard's intellectual efforts neither answered questions about the faith's truth claims and their interrelationships, nor made the questions disappear.[33] Neither contemplative prayer nor saintly holiness as such *could* answer them. They could only be answered by a kind of knowledge *qualitatively different* from—but not opposed to—Christianity's experiential knowledge. This different kind of knowledge required many words, rational comprehension, diverse distinctions, disciplined intellectual training, and careful arguments. Abelard called it by a neologism: "theology."[34] Many of its leading thirteenth-century practitioners were Franciscans and Dominicans laboring in Western Europe's new institution devoted to the integration and transmission of knowledge: the university.

Like monasteries, universities were intellectually selective, teleological institutions whose purposes presupposed the faith's truth claims and participatory knowledge. Even though they were not "schools for the service of the Lord" in Benedict's sense, they were Christian moral communities that sought to contribute to the wider common good amid the bewildering, commercially driven transformations afoot in the cities of Latin Europe.[35] A university master's "authority was not only intellectual, but moral also. Science was indissociable, especially where teaching was concerned, from the uses to which it was put in the social world, and the teacher was eminently responsible for such uses."[36] Because academic study was not divorced from the faith's truth claims and Christian experiential knowledge, masters were "supposed to practise all the Christian virtues," and students could fail their exams because of immoral behavior (of which there seems to have been no shortage).[37] Beginning around 1200 with the first two universities, Bologna and Paris, nearly all universities had a faculty of arts, in which masters taught the subjects of the trivium and quadrivium, and generally, from the mid-thirteenth century, also moral philosophy, natural philosophy, and metaphysics.[38] Whether they tended to follow the Bologna or the Paris model in their organization and governance, before the mid-fourteenth century only three universities (Paris, Oxford, and Cambridge) had all three of the other faculties—medicine, law, and theology—whose masters fostered the common good by training physicians to aid the sick, jurists and lawyers to help administer justice, and preachers and masters of theology to care for souls and teach the faith.[39]

Indeed, until the University of Prague was founded in 1347, only Paris, Oxford, and Cambridge had degree-conferring faculties of theology,[40] Christendom's centrally important intellectual subject because of the comprehensive and integrative character of its inquiry: God in relationship to all things, and correlatively the relationship of all things with one another, based on everything known about God's creation including God's extraordinary actions in history. More than simply the integrated understanding of the church's truth claims, theology encompassed literally everything: the creator plus all of creation. Hence the concerns of theology masters were not and could not in principle be independent of the inquiries pursued by masters in the faculties of arts, medicine, and law (where the relationship between canon law and theology was especially close). Nothing studied in any faculty was outside God's creation, hence nothing was outside theology's compass and its inalienable concern with truth and error.

During the first half of the thirteenth century—despite initial suspicions and blanket condemnations from the 1210s into the 1230s reminiscent of Bernard's disdain for Abelard—the increasing availability of Aristotle's writings (in Latin translations from the Greek) gave masters in arts and theology faculties an unprecedentedly powerful intellectual tool in their pursuit of truth.[41] As Muslim intellectuals such as Ibn Rushd (Averroës; 1126–1198) and Jewish thinkers such as Maimonides (c. 1137–1204) had also recognized, "The Philosopher" displayed an astonishing breadth and depth of integrated, rationally demonstrated knowledge in every domain from cosmology to logic, ethics to physics, and metaphysics to politics. Long central to the worlds of Byzantine and Islamic erudition, Aristotle's works far surpassed in their power anything known among the learned in Latin Christendom since the dissolution of the Roman Empire. Besides their extraordinary contributions to knowledge, however, some of Aristotle's ideas were incompatible with Christian faith—perhaps most important, he lacked any notion of creation.[42] If the faith was true, then *these* Aristotelian truth claims, such as the eternity of the world, had to be false. Hence Aristotle's ideas could not simply be absorbed uncritically, as was recognized by those who condemned his works wholesale in the early thirteenth century. Yet as theologians such as Albert the Great, Thomas Aquinas, and (less pervasively and robustly) Bonaventure began to demonstrate in the 1240s and 1250s, Aristotelian ideas could be adopted, adapted, and made to serve Christian truth claims.[43] When the number of universities expanded especially after the schism of 1378, and individual institutions came increasingly under the oversight of their respective secular rulers, Aristotle's works remained in arts faculties the primary basis for knowledge about human beings and the natural world. By the time the University of Wittenberg was established in 1502, there were over sixty universities in Europe, more than four times the number there had been in 1300.[44] On the eve of the Reformation, Aristotelian ideas and categories had constituted for over two and a half centuries the dominant, manifestly flexible and fruitful idiom of knowledge in the dominant European institutions responsible for its pursuit and transmission.

Medieval Christianity was based on claims about God's actions in the distant past as recorded in the translated collection of texts that early church leaders had selected and redacted, fourth-century leaders had canonized, and patristic and monastic writers had interpreted. In this respect, the faith was inextricably based on authority, just as it was inextricably based on testimony. Not only the church's theology but the biblical texts themselves were the product of the lived tradition that had transmitted and continued to transmit them. Hence Aquinas wrote, near the beginning of his *Summa Theologiae,* that "to argue from authority is entirely appropriate [*maxime proprium*] to this doctrine insofar as its principles are held through revelation, and so it is necessary to believe the authority of those to whom the revelation was made."[45] In contrast to God's extraordinary revelation in the past, however, knowledge of other subjects in medieval universities, such as natural philosophy and medicine, was said to be based on truths accessible to rational demonstration and confirmable by observation in the present. But very significantly, this sort of knowledge was *treated and taught* in a manner analogous to theology, with ancient, authoritative texts as its foundation. Just as theology was based on the grammatical and logical analysis of the Bible and Lombard's *Sentences,* so the study of the natural world was based on the analysis of ancient authorities such as Aristotle and Galen, together with the analysis of Islamic commentators on their writings.

University pedagogy followed suit. In all faculties it was grounded in lectures, which transmitted knowledge of authoritative texts, glosses, and commentaries to students by means of masters' careful, line-by-line, oral reading and exposition. Pedagogy was extended in disputations, which doubled as "research" insofar as they sought to refine knowledge through the constant raising of questions and the debate that inevitably ensued— about the conflicting answers proposed, and about divergent interpretations and difficult issues encountered in the authoritative texts and commentaries.[46] The aim was not to discover entirely new knowledge—in this respect, university pedagogy extended Augustine's cautionary ideas in *De doctrina Christiana*—but to clarify, integrate, and transmit what was already known.[47] Quodlibetal theological disputations, however, provided a forum within which anyone could raise any question at all.[48] Logic was a severe master: because it was impossible for flatly contrary claims both to be true, disputations were liable to bruise the (male) egos of those protagonists insufficiently grounded in humility and less concerned to pursue truth than to defeat opponents. By definition, disputations presupposed disagreements, and thus always harbored the potential to provoke discord. If theological disputants lacked the virtues, their verbal jousting could socially damage the shared life in the faith and its participatory knowledge for which their intellectual efforts were supposed to provide support.

TAKEN TOGETHER, a strong recognition of the principle of noncontradiction, the demand of logical coherence, relentless questioning, and a keen ability to make distinctions at multiple levels constituted the heart of the scholastic method. These elements remain fundamental to the pursuit and articulation of knowledge in the West today. But despite the method's strengths in logic, analysis, and synthesis, its reliance on textual authorities and deduction rendered it hugely vulnerable to new knowledge about the natural world, a fact that showed strain already in the fourteenth century and would reach a breaking point in the seventeenth. Contemplative delight in the natural world understood as God's creation—Francis of Assisi's "Brother Sun and Sister Moon"—was one thing; the close observation, careful measurement, and rational comprehension of natural regularities were another, not necessarily opposed to the first. Medieval Christian university masters for the most part did not grasp the fact that knowledge of the natural world is *in principle* not like the knowledge gained from texts, but can only be acquired through empirical observation and experiment susceptible to constant revision—even though this eventual realization came partly by wrestling with problems posed by ancient texts and new ways of reading them.[49] Scientific knowledge is irreducibly and inherently a *distinct* way of knowing. Ironically, the pursuers and practitioners of medieval and Renaissance magic, astrology, and alchemy, attuned to observation and attentive to the manipulability of the natural world, were on this point nearer the mark than were those who cleaved to textual authorities per se.[50]

The Aristotelian model of knowledge in universities influenced where and how knowledge of the natural world was pursued. In the fifteenth century, the methodological constraints on astronomy in the University of Vienna's cutting-edge arts faculty, for example, led Johannes Regiomontanus

(1426–1476) to leave. After stays in Italy and Hungary, he established an observatory and printing press in commercially prosperous Nuremberg in 1471, where the wealthy Bernard Walther and then the priest Johannes Werner continued the enterprise into the early sixteenth century. "The institution in Nuremberg represented something completely new in Latin Europe—a centre for scientific research and publication, undisturbed by teaching, independent of a university, and sponsored by an influential local patron. As such it was a sign of things to come."[51] The example of Regiomontanus showed that if those who sought knowledge could not find a place to pursue it within the university, they would go elsewhere. Throughout the early modern period and particularly as a result of changes prompted by the Reformation, as we shall see, there would be much going elsewhere.

Late medieval scholastic theology was far from the caricature made of it by propagandistic humanists in the fifteenth and early sixteenth centuries, whatever the entertainment value of the satirical depictions in Erasmus's *Praise of Folly* (1511) or the *Letters of Obscure Men* (1515).[52] Not sterility but mastery, not unthinking repetition but discerning subtlety, characterized the wide-ranging nominalist thought of Gabriel Biel (c. 1420–1495) at the University of Tübingen, for example, in the last quarter of the fifteenth century, just as it did that of the Scotsman John Mair (c. 1467–1550) at Paris or Johannes Eck (1486–1543) at Ingolstadt in the early sixteenth.[53] Similarly, the remarkable oeuvre of a theologian such as the Dominican Tommaso Gaeta de Vio (Cajetan; 1469–1534) demonstrates the continuing vitality of the *via antiqua* tradition on the eve of the Reformation.[54] So too, more generally, the faculty of theology in the University of Paris retained its standing, vigor, and influence in the early decades of the sixteenth century.[55] What had happened in the fourteenth and fifteenth centuries, however—a change already apparent in Scotus when compared with Aquinas—was the marked tendency, especially among Occam and his nominalist followers, to pursue theology as well as metaphysics and moral philosophy through specific, particular questions without regard for the interrelatedness of knowledge.[56] Despite the historical distance of more than half a millennium, late medieval scholastic philosophers and theologians thus prefigured in some respects the research specialization of scientists and scholars in universities today.[57] There is no doubting the subtlety and sophistication of late medieval logic, for example, or the impressive achievements in natural philosophy of the fourteenth-century *calculatores* at Oxford's Merton College and their influence on Parisian masters such as Jean Buridan and Nicolas Oresme.[58] But how did these endeavors and their findings fit with everything else that was known? To be sure, some of the best late medieval thinkers were beset by more-pressing concerns—such as how to fit Christendom itself back together during the difficult decades of the schism (1378–1415), a practical imperative that preoccupied Jean Gerson (1363–1429), chancellor of the University of Paris, and other ecclesiological conciliarists at the outset of the fifteenth century.[59] Nevertheless, in principle issues remained regarding the coherence and purpose of knowledge: how, for example, were late medieval scholastic pyrotechnics related to the shared practice of the virtues that was the prerequisite for what really counted, namely Christianity's experiential knowledge derived from the faith and hopeful of eternal salvation?

This question lay behind Thomas à Kempis's swipes at early fifteenth-century scholasticism, beginning on the very first page of the *Imitation of Christ:* "What is the point of learned disputation on the Trinity if you lack humility and consequently displease the Trinity? Indeed, sophisticated words do not make us holy or righteous, but a virtuous life makes us beloved by God. I would choose rather to experience compunction than to know its definition." Or again, only a few lines later, echoing but immediately interrogating Aristotle's opening sentence from the *Metaphysics:* "Everyone by nature desires to know, but without the fear of God what good is knowledge? Indeed a humble peasant [*humilis rusticus*] who serves God is better than a proud philosopher who neglects himself but contemplates the course of the heavenly bodies."[60] The point was not that anti-intellectual piety was preferable to erudite holiness—à Kempis himself was far from unlearned—but that intellectual sophistication per se was vacuously vain apart from shared life in Christ and its participatory form of knowledge. What mattered was the end to which knowledge was put, just as had been the case, respectively, for Augustine, Benedict, Anselm, Bonaventure, or Aquinas. The example of brilliant saints showed that however great a temptation to pride was learning, nothing in principle prevented erudite theologians or astronomers from rightly fearing and serving God, from possessing self-knowledge and practicing the virtues, including humility.

RENAISSANCE HUMANISTS SHARED with their scholastic contemporaries an exposure to the dangers of self-satisfied pride and condescension that accompanied advanced learning. And despite their barbs against scholastics for nitpicking narrowness and real-life aloofness, they would display for centuries their own susceptibility to distinctive species of intellectual pedantry. Many of them, beginning with Petrarch (1304–1374) and including Erasmus (c. 1466–1536), shared with à Kempis the criticism of the scholastic tendency to make the pursuit of sophisticated knowledge an end in itself, divorced from the participatory knowledge of the faith and the practice of the virtues. Despite the tendency of many of its late medieval practitioners toward segmented specialization, theology remained in principle both integrative and comprehensive because of its all-encompassing subject matter. Renaissance humanism was less intellectually ambitious in its scope, focusing more on language and human life than on reality as a whole or even as such. But in the hands of Erasmus and his fellow travelers in the first two decades of the sixteenth century, it sought more directly than contemporary scholastic theology the end of serving the participatory knowledge of Christians in the faith. Christian humanists thought they could do a better job than scholastic theologians by eschewing Aristotle for Cicero, the *Sentences* for scripture, metaphysics for morality, logic for literature, and demonstrations for dialogues plus other literary forms inspired by classical antiquity.

Whether they were making political speeches, corresponding as diplomatic secretaries, exhorting citizens to virtue, or writing treatises, humanists in general sought to convince readers and move hearers through rhetorical eloquence and well-chosen words, not to demonstrate to students or defeat disputants through dialectic.[61] They did so through a kind of knowledge that was not sought and could not be obtained through the scholastic method: the mastery of classical Latin and often Greek (and sometimes Hebrew), which entailed a host of adjunct intellectual preoccupations alien to Aristotle and the scholastic curriculum. These related interests included classical philology; the rediscovery of long-lost works and collations of multiple manuscripts to establish texts closest to their respective originals; the recovery and disentangling of complex traditions of learned commentary; the determination of forgeries and authorial misattributions; and (after Gutenberg's invention in the 1450s) the printed production of scholarly textual editions of works by ancient pagan and patristic authors.[62] Scholastic knowledge-making across the curriculum had tended blithely to assume the trustworthy character and unproblematic provenance of the authoritative texts on which it was based. Many centuries of copying manuscripts by hand had multiplied scribal errors and emendations, awareness of which grew during the second half of the fifteenth century in tandem with the proliferation of printed texts and the spread of humanism north of the Alps and west of the Pyrenees. Humanists were passionately interested in the Roman world of Cicero and Quintilian as well as the Athenian world of Aristotle and Plato (many of whose dialogues were rediscovered and sparked an important fifteenth-century revival of Platonism, beginning in Italy).[63] Admiration for and attention to classical antiquity fostered a sense of historical distance that brought the "Middle Ages" into being—whether humanists thought they were thereby making the ancient past appropriable or rendering it newly inaccessible in its alterity.[64] Unlike God's creation, classical texts had not appeared ex nihilo. They had been written in specific circumstances for particular reasons in a three-dimensional, historically distant human world.

Institutionally, humanists had their cake and ate it, too: they pursued their philological and historical knowledge both inside and outside universities. In Italy, they began obtaining chairs in arts faculties around 1425, and north of the Alps during the second half of the fifteenth century.[65] But they also worked outside universities, at the courts of princes who employed them as secretaries and diplomats, in the like-minded circles or "academies" in cities such as Rome, Naples, or Florence, or as correctors and consultants among colleagues in and around the printing houses—such as the Aldine press in Venice and Froben press in Basel—that produced scholarly texts in classical Latin and Greek.[66] Paul Grendler has argued that the absence of major university theology faculties in Italy, where most theological instruction occurred in the friars' *studia,* meant that the introduction of humanist chairs in rhetoric, Greek, and other subjects in Italian arts faculties proceeded without much fuss.[67] As is well known, it was sometimes otherwise in northern European universities with strong theology faculties, such as Paris, Cologne, and Louvain, where theologians had long been wary of arts masters trespassing on their turf. In the twelfth and early thirteenth centuries, the perceived threat of nascent scholastic theology to the long-established monastic cultivation of Christianity's participatory knowledge had sparked opposition, and initially a blanket condemnation of Aristotle. So too, in the late fifteenth century, depending on the specific issues and individuals involved, the challenge of humanist methods and discoveries to deeply ingrained scholastic ways of knowing sometimes precipitated heated exchanges and mutual vituperation.[68] Quite a few humanists sought to avoid contentious disputations in favor of epideictic dialogues that left room for the open-ended, unresolved expression of multiple perspectives. Ironically, this move *itself* engendered contention between them and scholastics, who accused humanists of being nonchalant and skeptical about the pursuit of truth.[69] In addition to their presence at courts and around print shops, humanists imitated Cicero (and Jerome) by writing letters to one another, sharing news and scholarly discoveries about history as well as natural history, about ancient texts no less than the New World.[70] By the turn of the sixteenth century their sustained interactions had created an unplanned, new institution that mirrored the spread of printing and of humanism itself across Europe: the Republic of Letters. For three centuries it would coexist alongside universities as a major institution in the transmission of knowledge.[71]

In the early years of the sixteenth century, Erasmus was at the center of the nodes and news of the *respublica litterarum.* Partly because of his stature and influence, Christian renewal and experiential knowledge was one of the Republic's central preoccupations, both north and south of the Alps.[72] Keenly aware of Christendom's problems as so many reformers had been for so long, Erasmus combined a humanist passion for the classical Greek and Latin of the ancient world, the adjunct narrative of medieval decline, a disdain for scholastic theology, a love for scripture and the church fathers (especially Jerome and Origen), and a teleological emphasis on the practice of the virtues as the key to Christian life. These concerns coalesced in his provocatively titled *Novum Instrumentum,* his edition of the New Testament published by Froben in March 1516.[73] A work years in the making despite the hastiness with which Erasmus prepared the first edition, it built on pioneering philological work on the New Testament by Lorenzo Valla (1406–1457) and Jacques Lefèvre d'Étaples (c. 1455–1536) and included a Greek text based on the collation of several Byzantine manuscripts, Erasmus's facing-page Latin translation, and a substantial scholarly apparatus. The impressively learned layman Giannozzo Manetti (1396–1459) had done a New Testament translation in Rome at the request of his pontifical patron Nicholas V (r. 1447–1455), "the first Latin version made from the Greek since Jerome's day," but it was never published. By contrast, the widely publicized printed edition by Christendom's most visible humanist scholar, with its many divergences from the Vulgate (and numerous printers' errors), caused a firestorm of controversy.[74] Medieval Christian biblical exegetes such as Nicolas Maniacoria and the Victorines in the twelfth century, as well as Nicholas of Lyra in the early fourteenth, had used their knowledge of Hebrew not only to interpret but to compile variant readings and correct errors in the Old Testament Vulgate.[75] But a new published Latin translation of the New Testament was different, not least because of the very different circumstances of the early sixteenth century. And because the Vulgate's words and phrases were by then even more pervasively embedded in Christendom's liturgical, devotional, and academic life, a different Latin translation of scripture was bound to be jarring. More fundamentally, Erasmus's printed edition implicitly challenged nonchalance about the reliability in general of the authoritative texts at the basis of university education and intertwined with Christianity's institutionalized worldview. Authorities could pressure and/or punish, as had long been considered necessary in cases of heresy. But despite the fulminations of his detractors, Erasmus was no heretic; he was northern Europe's leading Christian scholar with friends in high places. He had dedicated his edition to Leo X, only one of several popes who had been major patrons of humanist scholarship—including biblical scholarship—in Rome since the pontificate of Nicholas V.[76] And whatever the reactions to his particular translation, no claims to authority or displays of power could alter the empirical evidence of discrepancies in the biblical manuscripts, nor undo the humanists' more general, textual evidence for changes in the Latin and Greek languages over time.

Erasmus's biblical scholarship was anything but academic—it was meant to help restore the health of an ailing Christendom as diagnosed by Dr. Desiderius. No wonder things had gotten so bad, he thought, with greedy clerics exploiting superstitious laypeople once logic had sidelined rhetoric and scholasticism had stymied scripture. Erasmus believed that Christians' direct exposure to the New Testament, whether through the original Greek, his Latin translation, or accurate vernacular translations, was the key to the renewal of Christian faith and life, for "the sun is not as common and open to all as is Christ's teaching." Folk just needed to know what Christ's plain teaching was, as articulated in scripture. Unlike scholastic theology, sacred philology and scholarship would dispel ignorance and inspire sanctity. Like his reform-minded contemporaries, Erasmus judged that most Christians' participatory knowledge in the faith left much to be desired. But he also assumed a tight fit between the direct reading of scripture and improved participatory knowledge through the practice of the virtues in shared Christian life: "Therefore let all of us thirst for this [sacred literature] with all our heart, let us embrace it, let us ceaselessly attend to it, let us kiss it, let us at last die in it, let us be transformed in it, as studies are changed into morals. . . . These writings deliver to you the living image of his holy mind and of Christ himself speaking, healing, dying, and rising, and finally make [reddunt] the whole so present that you would see him less if you personally beheld him with your eyes."[77] To read was to learn was to be transformed in just this way. How different this was from Augustine's position in De doctrina Christiana: "A person strengthened by faith, hope, and love, and who steadfastly [inconcusse] holds on to them, has no need of the scriptures except to instruct others."[78] But as Erasmus and others saw it, the very problem in 1516 was that so many Christians lacked these virtues. How different Erasmus's view seemed to be, too, from the long-standing notion of implicit faith, which rendered holiness as accessible to the illiterate as it was to the learned. But Erasmus and his reforming colleagues could see for themselves that the unlettered had equally ready access to ignorance, superstition, and sinful immorality.

SOME SCHOLASTIC THEOLOGIANS toward whom Erasmus was so antipathetic returned the favor, but much evidence suggests that neither stance was necessary—however useful their either-or juxtaposition has seemed in textbook setups for the Reformation that pit forward-looking humanists against reactionary scholastics (for how else can a narrative of emancipatory progess be told?). But in fact, Western Christendom did not have an either-or intellectual culture. In the decades before the Reformation, it was diverse, robust, and reform-minded, a multilayered combination of distinct kinds of knowledge that intersected in complex ways within and across multiple institutions and individuals.

The monastic, scholastic, scientific, and humanistic strands of late medieval knowledge-making were not sequestered from one another. They coexisted and interacted among many of the church's intellectuals, all of whom, regardless of their individual preferences and proclivities, participated in "religious practices that were taken for granted as an integral part of everyone's life."[79] The master of arts degree that Denis the Carthusian (1402–1471) received from the University of Cologne, for example, did not prevent him from becoming one of the leading fifteenth-century monastic writers on Christian participatory knowledge, which in his case extended to ecstatic mystical experience.[80] Nor—unlike Erasmus—did the early formation of Jan Standonck (1453–1504) among the Brothers of the Common Life prevent him from maintaining connections with them and with the Carthusians after he earned his master's and doctoral degrees in theology at the University of Paris. From 1483 to 1499 he headed the Collège de Montaigu (the ascetic rigors of which made Erasmus an unhappy student in 1495–1496) and played a multifaceted reforming role in the city's religious life until his death.[81] Johannes Heynlin von Stein (1430–1496) also obtained his doctorate in theology from the University of Paris before teaching in the same faculty. In 1470 he helped to establish in the city France's first printing press, before moving on to teach theology at the universities of Basel and Tübingen. After entering Basel's Carthusian monastery in 1487, he aided in the publication of patristic texts and wrote a commentary on the Mass that saw thirty-nine editions from 1492 to 1519.[82] Monks studied in universities: throughout the fifteenth and early sixteenth centuries taken together, for example, hundreds of Cistercian students were enrolled in several important central European universities, including Heidelberg, Cologne, Freiburg, Prague, and Leipzig, while most monasteries in England regularly supported two to four members of their respective communities in studies at Oxford or Cambridge, with greater numbers of English Benedictines completing degrees after 1500.[83]

Moreover, monastic humanism was a widespread phenomenon, which, like humanism itself, began in Italy and spread north of the Alps during the course of the fifteenth century, where it influenced female as well as male houses—a fact well illustrated by the example of Caritas Pirckheimer (1467–1532), the Franciscan prioress of Nuremberg's Sisters of St. Clare from 1503 until her death.[84] We should not believe the humanist diatribe of Erasmus about the intellectual aridity of monastic life as such.[85] Many monastic libraries of the thriving Observant Benedictine Congregation of Santa Giustina in Italy, for example, were well stocked with sources for the study of Greek and Hebrew, as well as with manuscripts of the Greek church fathers, whose theology was influencing the Congregation's writers decades before the Reformation.[86] The intellectually omnivorous Johannes Trithemius (1462–1516), a Benedictine abbot who had studied at the University of Heidelberg, was only one among dozens of humanist Benedictines and Cistercians in monastic houses throughout the Holy Roman Empire on the eve of the Reformation.[87] Indeed, "the monasteries were the single-most important avenue for humanist education in Germany."[88]

Neither Erasmus's disdain for scholastic theology nor well-known episodes such as the Reuchlin Affair in the 1510s come close to telling the whole story about the relationship between scholastic and humanistic knowledge on the eve of the Reformation.[89] Otherwise, the combination of the two in leading preachers, church leaders, and intellectuals such as Johann Geiler von Kaisersberg, Jakob Wimpfeling, John Fisher, Cajetan, Eck, Thomas Murner, Jerome Emser, Johannes Cochlaeus, and others would be unintelligible.[90] So would the deliberate combination of scholasticism and humanism in the new University of Alcalá in Spain under the patronage of the Observant Franciscan prelate Francisco Jiménez de Cisneros, who assembled the scholarly team that produced the most impressive work of biblical scholarship from the early sixteenth century, the Complutensian Polyglot Bible.[91] Shared allegiance to the established church and Christian participatory knowledge enabled the coexistence of this cross-cutting intellectual diversity—and the sparks it provoked, just as it had among fifteenth-century adherents of the *via antiqua* and *via moderna* in university arts and theology faculties, or among Dominican Thomists and Franciscan Scotists a century before.

How were these sorts of knowledge related to each other? When Erasmus's *Novum Instrumentum* appeared in 1516, this question was as alive and unanswered as three centuries earlier had been the question of the relationship among Aristotle's newly available writings, Christian truth claims, and the faith's participatory knowledge. But as the examples above suggest, Christian intellectuals did not consider it unanswerable. The kinds of knowledge in question were undeniably different, and irreducible to one another: the individually differentiated, participatory knowledge of the faith and its shared way of life, based ultimately and above all on God's actions in Jesus; the observable knowledge of the natural world understood as God's creation, whether pursued in university arts faculties or outside them, as in the Nuremberg observatory established by Regiomontanus; the humanist knowledge of classical languages and texts, including the growing historical knowledge of the ancient world whence they came; and theology's structured knowledge of the faith's truth claims, and (in principle) of the interrelatedness of all things as elements of God's creation in space and time. With so much new data, too much was fresh and in ferment—and too many heels dug in—for any integrative synthesis to have been forged in the early sixteenth century. But there is no a priori reason to think that these types of knowledge were themselves incompatible, despite the uncomprehending intransigence of some antischolastic humanists or antihumanist scholastics.[92]

Neither the text-based study of the natural world nor scholastic curricula and categories could have survived unchanged in the face of scientific and humanist discoveries. But neither could the humanists' commitment to eloquence and rhetoric, growing historical consciousness, dedication to textual accuracy, and/or impressive erudition answer questions about the nature of reality, the basis for or content of morality, or how all knowledge might fit together.[93] Despite the naïveté of some humanists to the contrary, erudition and eloquence per se could not answer questions about how to live; for more than a millennium those answers had come from Christianity, irrespective of one's learning or linguistic prowess.[94] One might decide to suspend judgment about a given intellectual issue in dispute—and indeed prudence often dictated the advisability of such a course—for the sake of preserving concord in accordance with Christian *caritas*, for example, so that all that needed weighing could be weighed. But neither prudence nor the suspension of judgment nor the yearning for civility could get round the principle of noncontradiction: although two contrary claims might both be false, even the everlasting suspension of judgment could not make them both true. If the different sorts of knowledge might be fit together, it would depend on intellectual give-and-take within a shared framework—just as it had in the thirteenth century, when medieval Christianity's institutionalized worldview had enabled the enormous expansion of knowledge with the scholastic absorption of the Aristotelian corpus.

THE SIXTEENTH CENTURY would be different. By rejecting the authority of the Roman church, the Reformation eliminated any shared framework for the integration of knowledge. We will never know what might have become of the interactions among humanism, scholasticism, the continuing investigation of the natural world, and the participatory knowledge of Christianity in the absence of the Reformation. Because the Reformation contested the Christian doctrinal claims that underlay theology, it problematized in dramatically new and (as it happened) enduring ways the relationship of theology to other kinds of knowledge. These were the first paving stones of what would turn out to be a twisting path that led to the secularization of knowledge. Especially as the demonstrated power of applied scientific knowledge grew, the unresolved doctrinal disagreements within Western Christianity would eventually be marshaled alongside religious pluralism in general as evidence for the reclassification of all religion as a matter of belief and opinion, not as knowledge; as subjective, not objective; and as particular, not universal. In the midst of nineteenth-century positivism and naturalism in the sciences, theology would be deliberately exiled from research universities, with the study of religion installed in its stead as just one (increasingly marginal) discipline among all the rest that constituted secular knowledge-making. Christian doctrinal pluralism set the Western world on an unintended trajectory in which knowledge was secularized as faith was subjectivized. But in the sixteenth century this lay far in the future. At first, incompatible Christian doctrinal claims were made the cornerstone of rival, confessionalized universities and thus greatly affected the nature of knowledge-making in early modern Europe.

The Reformation repudiated the authority of the Roman church and much of Christian experiential knowledge that the church had sustained and continued to foster. This experiential knowledge was simply the first-hand participation in the inherited, shared practice of the virtues (including practices of prayer and worship) and avoidance of vices—a participation that comprised the faith's substantive notion of the good. In effect, the Reformation's protagonists claimed that what for centuries had been regarded as the most important sort of knowledge—incalculably more valuable than scholastic, humanistic, or scientific knowledge per se, because it conduced to flourishing in this life and presaged eternal life with God and the saints—was nothing of the sort, its alleged goodness a prideful delusion of self-justificatory sinners given to self-flattery. According to magisterial and radical Protestant reformers, much of traditional Christian experiential "knowledge" was really a diabolically deadly symbiosis of clerical con game and lay gullibility fed by self-serving additions to and distortions of scripture. The Bible was the real and only source for God's teachings and for genuine Christian experiential knowledge based on them, and thus scripture alone was the criterion for determining what in the church's tradition ought to be retained and what had to be rejected.

The interpretation of scripture had been centrally important in Christianity from the time of the church fathers, and subsequently through monastic *lectio divina,* scholastic *summae* and *quaestiones,* and humanistic attention to the Greek and Hebrew texts. The Reformation's fundamental claim of *sola scriptura* upped the ante considerably. According to those who rejected the Roman church, Christian experiential knowledge and the prospects for eternal salvation now turned directly and entirely on the correct understanding of the Bible (including, as we have seen, the insistence on the supplementary exegetical role of the Holy Spirit, which spiritualist Protestants extended). The Bible was now sharply contrasted with the "human additions" and mere "traditions of men" that had muddied the clear waters of God's word historically downstream from its scriptural source. According to Protestants, anyone who looked anywhere else for this knowledge, including the "holy" example of the church's saints, was self-deceived. Papal pronouncements, canon law, conciliar decrees, saints' lives, patristic writings, and even creedal affirmations were *in principle* acceptable only insofar as they were consonant with God's holy word in scripture.

Erasmus thought that earnest Christians who turned sincerely to scripture would see its clear meaning and be morally transformed. The Reformation exposed his hopes as wishful thinking and demolished his dreams as naïveté. Despite claims of biblical perspicuity, rival anti-Roman Christians quickly and collectively demonstrated how separable was the reading of scripture as such from *any* given set of Christian doctrines or related practices. As we have seen in previous chapters, beginning in the early 1520s those who rejected Rome disagreed about what the Bible said in socially divisive and enduring ways. Protestants correspondingly made radically divergent claims about Christian experiential knowledge. What it was to be a Christian differed drastically according to Conrad Grebel, Thomas Müntzer, Martin Luther, and Sebastian Franck, for example—to give only four central European examples from the 1520s. Champions of *sola scriptura* thought they would set Christian theology and experiential knowledge on firm ground by liberating the rock of God's word from papal tyranny. In fact, despite themselves they precipitated literally endless contestation about the Bible's meaning, entangled faith with biblical scholarship in new ways, and unavoidably had respective and rival recourse to their own preferred, putative hermeneutic authorities amid competing claims about the meaning of God's word.

With respect to the pursuit and transmission of knowledge in universities, however, the implications of Protestant heterogeneity would long remain muted, because so few Reformation-era forms of anti-Roman Christianity won political backing from secular authorities. There were no Swiss Brethren, Hutterite, Mennonite, Spiritualist, Familist, Socinian, or Quaker universities in the Reformation era. In fact, until the establishment of the dissenter academies in Restoration England, no European institutions of higher education were affiliated with radical Protestants.[95] Hence *most* of the many sorts of early modern Protestant experiential knowledge found no formal institutional intersection with scholastic, humanistic, or scientific knowledge. Only magisterial Protestants—Lutherans and Reformed Protestants, including the Church of England—had institutions of higher education before the mid-seventeenth century, because among anti-Roman Christians only they received political support from secular authorities. As it happened, the presence of these institutions alongside Catholic universities, Jesuit colleges, and post-Tridentine seminaries would prove more than sufficient to alter the character of knowledge-making in ways that contributed to the secularization of knowledge.

In multiple respects, the Reformation affected the pursuit and transmission of knowledge in early modern Europe. It changed the character of the existing *institutions* in which knowledge was made and taught, including the Republic of Letters and universities; it changed *where* knowledge was pursued, most significantly by increasing the importance of courts, scientific academies, and other locations as sites of knowledge-making; it problematized in novel ways the nature of Christian truth claims and experiential knowledge in *relationship* to other sorts of knowledge; and the era's religio-political violence prompted a shift in the primary *purpose* of knowledge-making in conjunction with other major historical processes. None of these changes can be understood apart from the exercise of power by secular rulers, whose decisions and desires—including their respective confessional choices and relationship to higher education—set the key transformations in motion.

WE SAW IN Chapter 3 how Reformation-era secular rulers held fast to the long-standing duty to maintain Christian truth and to provide for good order that promoted the temporal well-being and eternal salvation of their subjects. God would hold them responsible for their efforts no less than he had medieval magistrates and ancient Israelite kings. Just as the Peasants' War of 1524–1526 showed dramatically what could happen when "the Gospel" was let loose among the "common man," so the origins of the Reformation itself—in a seemingly innocuous proposal for academic theologians in a provincial university to debate ninety-five propositions about the misunderstanding of indulgences—demonstrated that universities could be explosive places. Higher education was dangerous because some ideas could inspire the subversion of political order, God's truth, or both, on which the salvation of subjects and God's providential favor depended. Yet universities and similar institutions that proliferated in the sixteenth century were indispensable to rulers. What alternative was there for training the lawyers, jurists, secretaries, diplomats, physicians, pastors, and educators needed to staff growing bureaucracies and dutifully to maintain good order? All the more disturbing, then, was the precipitous decline in the number of German university students in the wake of the early Reformation: a collective enrollment of about 4,200 students in the Holy Roman Empire at the beginning of the century had plunged to 650 or so by the later 1520s.[96] This would not do; recovery was imperative.

The only way forward was clear: just as biblical interpretation had to be corralled and churches had to be controlled, universities, academies, and colleges had to be regulated. Higher education had to be enlisted to serve God's truth. Fifteenth-century rulers had already begun to oversee more closely their respective universities. Both Catholic and Protestant secular authorities in the Reformation era would be much more sensitized to their importance in the imparting of knowledge and the training of elites, given the (respectively) frightening persistence of new heresies and the resilience of the pope's minions. Despite the privileges still enjoyed by universities whose origins antedated the Reformation, the making and transmission of knowledge had to be overseen no less vigilantly than the educational and catechetical efforts by confessionalizing authorities in general.[97] Loyalty oaths and professions of confessional orthodoxy for students and teachers became the norm in a divided Christendom.[98] Just as sovereigns relied on ecclesiastical authorities as partners in confessionalization, so they relied on theologians to articulate Christian truth and to establish parameters for the pursuit of knowledge in other university faculties. Accordingly, in concert with the desires of secular authorities, theology, although it was seldom the largest faculty, remained in the sixteenth century the preeminent and privileged subject in universities no less than it had been before the Reformation. Indeed, it tended to color even more the character of higher education, which included as much as ever the moral formation of students. Whether in Lutheran, Reformed Protestant, or Catholic settings, students in university residences, colleges, and academies were monitored in regular routines that combined daily lectures and study with worship, prayers, and devotional readings.[99] Rulers' concern with doctrine and the social virtue of obedience in an era of religious division dictated that universities had to be socially, morally, and intellectually stabilizing and conservative institutions.

Accordingly, the curricula in the faculties of most Reformation-era universities were circumscribed by confessional criteria and directed principally toward teaching rather than "research."[100] Although universities were far from intellectually moribund, the resources of various sorts of knowledge—humanistic, scholastic, and scientific—were employed in targeted ways in the service of doctrinal truth claims and consistent with confessionalization. Facile associations of humanism with Protestantism *rather than* Catholicism are erroneous: not only had humanism flourished for many decades prior to the Reformation, but classical languages (whose range expanded in the six-teenth century to include Arabic) served the study of scripture, and rhetoric aided the demand for preaching no less in Jesuit colleges than in Lutheran universities and Calvinist academies.[101] Likewise, simplistic associations of scholasticism with Catholicism *rather than* Protestantism are no less mistaken: despite their first flush of antischolastic fervor, Protestant theologians (including even ardent humanists such as Melanchthon, so important for Lutheran universities as the *praeceptor Germaniae*) found that they could not do without scholasticism's analytical tools—or without Aristotle, even if Lutheran and Reformed pedagogues tended to be warier of Aristotelian metaphysics in theology than were their Catholic counterparts, at least before the late sixteenth century.[102]

Throughout the entire Reformation era there was no viable substitute for the Aristotelian corpus, although beginning in the 1570s Ramist logic was substituted for Aristotelian dialectic and for several decades enjoyed a vogue in many Reformed Protestant institutions, especially in Germany.[103] Catholic university professors continued to demonstrate scholasticism's versatility and vitality, not only in the flourishing of theology and metaphysics at Salamanca and Coimbra from the mid-sixteenth into the seventeenth century, but also, for example, in the ways in which Christopher Clavius (1538–1612) and his Jesuit successors for decades fit the applied mathematization of motion within a scheme of Aristotelian science.[104] Missionaries in the Society of Jesus, which within a decade of its papal approval in 1540 was starting to become the Roman church's first de facto teaching order, were crucial contributors to the flood of new natural-historical and ethnographic knowledge that poured back into Europe from Asia and the Americas especially via Spanish and Portuguese ships.[105] In some areas, such as ecclesiastical history, confessional controversy stimulated the pursuit of knowledge through the desire to legitimate the claims of one's own church and undermine those of one's opponents. This happened both with the Lutherans around Matthias Flacius Illyricus at his Institutum Historicum that grew out of the University of Magdeburg, and the scholarly counter-team in Rome that the Oratorian Cesare Baronio assembled in composing his *Ecclesiastical Annals*.[106] Similarly, Isaac Casaubon's masterly exposure of the Hermetic corpus as an early Greco-Christian forgery posing as ancient Egyptian wisdom was motivated partly by the desire to embarrass Baronio, who along with nearly all *érudits* had accepted its authenticity from the time that Marsilio Ficino's translation and enthusiasm revived the Hermetic texts in the 1470s.[107] As even these few examples of the intellectual vitality of Reformation-era universities suggest, it would be a mistake to regard their confessional strictures as a straitjacket on the pursuit of new knowledge.

But they were a constraint, and in ways that would prove deeply consequential. The interwoven objectives of pastoral concern and political control meant that certain domains of inquiry were in effect off-limits. Very significantly, important questions about fundamental issues pertaining to the politically privileged discipline, theology, could not be pursued in universities. Ultimately, what kept theology insulated in institutions of higher education was confessional rulers' exercise of power—and understandably so, considering what had followed from a mere proposal to debate misconceptions about indulgences in late 1517.[108] As a result, the sorts of issues raised in previous generations by Valla, Lefèvre, and Erasmus were not confronted. They were deferred. Nor were there structured, curricular interfaces in universities for systematic inquiry about the relationship between Christian truth (however defined) and the human past or the natural world, even as new knowledge literally from all over the globe accumulated exponentially during the sixteenth and seventeenth centuries. In a divided Christendom, most theologians indeed had more important things to worry about: knowledge of God's truth and the salvation of souls. Hundreds of them thus devoted tremendous energy during their careers to doctrinal controversy, seeking to confute stubborn opponents—the oral disputations in medieval theological faculties within the Roman church were now transmuted into ongoing polemical print across confessional divides. Like all human decisions, this one had its opportunity cost: time spent on doctrinal controversy was time not spent on keeping up with new knowledge, or time spent in seeking to understand God in relation to all things.

Yet in expounding orthodoxy, safeguarding souls, battling opponents, and essentially abandoning theology's aspiration to integrate any and all truth about God and creation, Lutheran, Reformed, and Catholic theologians were living in an ever more vulnerable refuge. Its protective walls allowed them to ignore unbroached questions, for example, that lay behind their claims about the truth of the Bible as the divinely revealed word of God. What exactly did this mean, with respect to burgeoning humanistic and scientific knowledge? Because Lutherans and Reformed Protestants had made scripture alone their foundation for purified Christian truth, they made themselves particularly susceptible to historical and philological questions about its provenance and reliability. Protestant theologians were essentially content with the Greek text of the New Testament once Robert Estienne published his *Editio Regia* in 1550, itself an only slightly emended version of Erasmus's text as well as the close textual ancestor of the Elzevir *textus receptus* of 1633. Like the tendency of some Protestants to imagine that theology would prove intellectually sustainable without metaphysics, this contentment did not last: in hopes of restoring the original text, John

Mill (1645–1707) republished the unedited *Editio Regia* in 1707 in a massive work of Latin erudition, but he included 30,000 textual variants based on meticulous scholarship with nearly 100 Greek and Latin manuscripts. Erasmus had used six Greek manuscripts, none earlier than the tenth century; Estienne had used fourteen.[109] The Vulgate was a Latin translation, but none of the manuscripts on which it was based had postdated the fourth century. By the time Mill's scholarly milestone appeared, England's intellectual milieu included Newtonians, deists, and all manner of Protestants in the wake of the Toleration Act of 1689. What was the relationship of the word of God to the (nonoriginal) biblical manuscripts, (rival) doctrinal truth claims, and (divergent) claims of Protestant experiential knowledge?

These issues were less vexing for early modern Catholic intellectuals because their Christianity was not based on scripture alone apart from the church's tradition, before or after the Reformation.[110] Hence there was never the same threat of Catholicism being *subsumed* by critical biblical scholarship, however much some church leaders and theologians might have thought (or wished) that they could sidestep it and the issues it raised. After vigorous debate that evinced considerable support for humanistic biblical studies in clerical formation, the bishops at the Council of Trent handled this specific concern in minimalist fashion in 1546. Recognizing that there were legitimate scholarly questions about the Vulgate, they pronounced it, in exquisitely ambivalent classical Latin, "*to be regarded* as authentic [*pro authentica habenda*]" and "in public lectures, disputations, sermons, and expositions *treated as* authentic [*pro authentica habeatur*]."[111] Humanistic scholarship had shown that it was not without problems, but the Vulgate had demonstrably sustained the practice of the faith "for so many centuries" within a tradition that now explicitly anathematized *sola scriptura* and whose leaders had more than a millennium earlier compiled the canon of scripture in the first place. Hence the Vulgate as it was would suffice for these stipulated purposes, despite ongoing Protestant denunciations, until additional scholarship could yield an emended version, which followed decades later with the textually botched Sixtine and bettered Clementine editions of 1590 and 1592, respectively.[112]

In the meantime, Catholics kept practicing the faith, which thrived in seventeenth-century Italy, Spain, the Spanish Netherlands, and Catholic Germany no less than in France after the Edict of Nantes (1598). As it had been prior to the Reformation, Christianity remained a shared way of life based on Jesus's teachings, ratified by his resurrection, transmitted through testimony, and embodied in his church. Short of truly revolutionary discoveries—say, conclusive, widely corroborated first- and second-century evidence that all the texts of the New Testament were deliberate fabrications—its central teachings were not likely to be overturned by the scholarly findings of biblical philologists, despite the hair-trigger sensitivity of post-Tridentine Catholic *érudits* to scholarly Protestant attacks or the suspicions of ecclesiastical censors about heterodox scholarship within the church. And the firsthand, participatory knowledge of human flourishing in the shared practice of the virtues was certain not to be subverted, based as it was on direct experience. As Augustine had said notwithstanding his immersion in the Bible, a person rooted in faith, hope, and love would need scripture only for teaching others, something well understood in the late seventeenth century, for example, by Nicholas Herman, the kitchen servant of the Discalced Carmelites in Paris better known as Brother Lawrence.[113] Besides the shared practice of the virtues, the center of Christian *life* was not the Bible or Bible reading per se, but the liturgy of the word and the Eucharist in the re-presentation of Christ's self-sacrificing love, as seventeenth-century Catholic biblical scholars such as Jean Morin (1591–1659) and Richard Simon (1638–1712) presumably knew when as French Oratorians they celebrated the Mass.[114] For the liturgy one needed not a whole bible, still less biblical scholarship, but a priest and scripture liturgically arranged in a missal.

At the same time, other early modern Catholic assumptions about the Bible in relationship to different sorts of knowledge proved deeply consequential and vulnerable to subversion. Above all, Catholic leaders failed to recognize that the knowledge of natural regularities was not a deductive science based on authoritative texts. Their insistence on Aristotle as the basis for academic natural philosophy was still intellectually viable at the outset of the seventeenth century, but mortally crippled by its end. In 1615, the devout layman Galileo had in effect shown an intellectual alternative—one which, in distinguishing between the divergent character and purposes of scripture on the one hand and the empirical investigation of nature on the other, ironically adumbrated the position that the Roman church would centuries later adopt, and which it essentially holds today. But Galileo's argument, despite being unthreatening in its aim to show in traditional fashion that "two truths cannot contradict one another," touched on issues central to biblical interpretation—the preserve of professional theologians at a time when the Reformation had made Catholic authorities hyper-alert to the dangers of exegetical individualism for nearly a century.[115] Accordingly, the Jesuit Robert Bellarmine and his inquisitor colleagues shut the door that Galileo had tried to open, although at first only through the Congregation of the Index and without mentioning him. They condemned Copernicanism in 1616, although Bellarmine, in accord with Galileo and Augustine, acknowledged that if conclusive evidence were found to support heliocentrism, "then one would have to proceed with great care in explaining the Scriptures that appear contrary, and say rather that we do not understand them than that what is demonstrated is false."[116]

THE RELIGIOUS DIVISIONS among Catholics, Lutherans, and Reformed Protestants made rival truth claims crucial in their respective universities, thus setting up intellectually insulated and politically privileged theology for different sorts of falls. It was weakened by being protected. In addition, the Reformation radically changed the character of Europe's other important learned institution of the early sixteenth century, the *respublica litterarum*. As we have seen, important members of the "religious Republic of Letters" in the years before the Reformation were preoccupied with the renewal of Christian faith and life.[117] By rejecting the Roman church's authority and much of medieval Christianity, the Reformation pushed the Republic of Letters in a secularizing direction: instead of being a network focused *on* the renewal of Christendom, it became a refuge *from* divisive, disruptive, and embattled religious affairs.[118] For good reason was Casaubon apprehensive in the first decade of the seventeenth century "that the vicious religious controversies of his time endangered the Republic of Letters and the fabric of Christendom itself."[119] Indeed, socially, politically, and culturally the fabric of Christendom was by then already rent and had been for many decades. The Republic of Letters endured, but no longer *could* it continue with its Erasmian raison d'être, even though its members discussed many things and could and did continue to learn much from one another despite their confessional disagreements. The controverted theological issues involved in those disagreements simply were not among the topics on the table. Because Christian doctrine and experiential knowledge were constantly contested beginning in the early 1520s, the Republic of Letters could accommodate all manner of intellectual exchange *except* those concerning disputed matters in theology and countervailing claims to Christian experiential knowledge, which highlighted their distinctiveness—and problematic character—in comparison with other sorts of knowing.

On the other hand, if one considers the original thrust of the Erasmian Republic of Letters—the renewal of Christian faith and life within the Roman church—then not the subsequent incarnations of the *respublica litterarum* but rather the worldwide network of Jesuit correspondents from the mid-sixteenth into the eighteenth century, whose members shared so many new discoveries plus a commitment to Rome, might well be more accurately regarded as its successor.[120] Nor despite the rejection of the Roman church among learned Reformed Protestants and Lutherans were religious matters any less important in the international correspondence network that took shape among them—in which Melanchthon, Heinrich

Bullinger, and Theodore Beza, for example, played centrally important roles in the sixteenth century, writing thousands of letters each.[121] But when participants from the Jesuit or the magisterial Protestant networks pursued inquiries in the wider Republic of Letters, they had to bracket contested matters of Christian doctrine and participatory knowledge. Cross-confessional communication and knowledge-making required a civility that not only precluded polemics, but in effect helped to marginalize theology and Christian experiential knowledge. It started to become impolite to talk about such things in certain contexts, and the Republic of Letters thrived on civility.[122] With the persistence of the Reformation, the Republic of Letters thus became a far-flung and culturally influential arena in which religious disagreement unintentionally fostered the secularization of knowledge, by implicitly separating religious from nonreligious concerns.

In addition to the transformation of the Republic of Letters, the Reformation era saw a wide-ranging proliferation of additional sites devoted to the pursuit of knowledge, apart from the universities in which the privileging of theology constrained it. Local civic academies and societies dedicated to philosophy, vernacular poetry, or literature emerged first in Italian cities, then spread elsewhere, including Spain and the Holy Roman Empire.[123] Private homes became places where scholarly interactions were pursued intensively, as on the provincial estate of the cosmopolitan antiquary Nicolas-Claude Fabri de Peiresc (1580–1637) in Provence; or where human cadavers were dissected, as the anatomist from Brussels, Andreas Vesalius (1514–1564), was known to do; or where natural-historical collectors displayed their exotica, as the intellectually omnivorous physician Ulisse Aldrovandi (1522–1605) did in Bologna; or where astronomers built observatories on their rooftops, as Johannes Hevelius (1611–1687) did in the Baltic port city of Danzig.[124] Alchemical laboratories sprouted on noble estates especially in the Holy Roman Empire, where adepts included women as well as men, while in England certain noblewomen, such as Lady Grace Mildmay (1552–1620), turned rooms in their homes into de facto pharmaceutical distilleries.[125] On the "supply side" of knowledge-making, then, when universities offered no prospects other venues were found, as Regiomontanus had already demonstrated with his Nuremberg observatory and print shop in 1471. With their limited resources, early modern rulers could not oversee all of this centrifugal pursuit of knowledge within their respective territories.

Nevertheless, they could try to attract it like metal filings to a magnet. On the "demand side" of Reformation-era knowledge-making, rulers provided its most important sites outside universities at the same time that they relied on universities to transmit knowledge and train professionals in ways that would conduce to order within their confessionalizing regimes. This was no contradiction; it simply meant that universities did not meet all the ambitions of early modern rulers. So those in power fashioned a knowledge-making symbiosis between themselves and intellectually inquisitive, socially striving men who could make new knowledge and were drawn to the rewards of patronage. The ruling patrons, for their part, gained the new knowledge from their intellectual clients to serve their desires in running their lives and their confessional states. It was hardly the late twentieth-century's military-industrial complex, but we can see here a distant ancestor of the modern relationship between knowledge-making and state power. In early modern Europe the most important sites for this symbiosis were rulers' (and on a smaller scale, nobles') courts, and, especially from the second half of the seventeenth century, scientific academies. Both courts and academies took their place alongside universities and the Republic of Letters as crucial institutions in early modern Europe's world of learning.

The courts of sovereigns and nobles were nothing new in the Reformation era, of course, having existed throughout the Middle Ages. In the fifteenth century, Italian Renaissance princes had set the European style at court as in so much else, luring brilliant artists and humanists. But the sixteenth century brought new responsibilities and opportunities. The religious divisions opened by the Reformation entailed new necessities for military defense and new prospects for war, as we have seen. The stakes were anything but academic: the concrete application of matters as seemingly ethereal as neo-Stoic philosophy and the mathematization of kinetic motion, for example, could influence the prosperity of states in the form of better disciplined armies and more accurate ballistics.[126] The discovery of the New World heralded a constantly increasing flow of new knowledge to early modern courts about hitherto unknown peoples, fauna, and flora from hitherto unknown continents.[127] Indeed, in the sixteenth century, rulers' money funded commercial and missionary expeditions that brought back the new data and physical specimens—and the prospects of exploitable mineral resources, medicinally valuable plants, and slave labor.[128] With the production of useful professionals and the conservative transmission of knowledge being met by confessionalized universities, Reformation-era rulers made their respective courts the preferred site for the production of new knowledge that could serve differently their desires for prestige, power, and obedience to God. Why could not the stabilizing function of higher education, safeguarded by orthodoxy, coexist with the creation of new knowledge loosened from curricular constraints and authoritative texts? For the latter, rulers could assemble and monitor the intellectual talent, libraries, botanical gardens, observatories, natural-historical collections, and laboratory facilities right in their own palace complexes. And they did.[129]

Small wonder, then, that "technical expertise, novel procedures, and the critique of ancient traditions stand out prominently within court environments, in contrast with universities, as means appropriate for acquiring knowledge of nature."[130] Small wonder, too, that early modern courts figured importantly in the careers of numerous figures central to the emergent new science, including Galileo, for example, who left a position teaching mathematics at the University of Padua for a plum post as the Medici court philosopher and mathematician in Florence in 1610, and the astronomers Tycho Brahe (1546–1601) and Johannes Kepler (1571–1630), who worked at Rudolf II's dazzling court in Prague.[131] Perhaps more telling is the pantheon of major contributors to the new science who never taught as university professors: not only Brahe and Kepler, but also Copernicus, Descartes, Bacon, Mersenne, Hobbes, Pascal, Boyle, Leibniz, Christiaan Huygens, and Leeuwenhoek. Indeed, Descartes, Pascal, Boyle, and Leeuwenhoek never formally *attended* a university.[132] The new, mechanistic model of nature arose almost entirely outside of universities; Gassendi was its only first-generation advocate who held a university professorship (at Aix-en-Provence), before Cartesianism spread.[133] Aristotelian natural philosophy in universities did not generate new knowledge that rulers could use, in contrast to the hands-on, descriptive, experimental methods and information-gathering at their courts. Unsurprisingly, when in his *New Atlantis* Francis Bacon articulated his vision of Salomon's House, a utopian temple of knowledge-making on the imaginary Pacific island of Bensalem, it bore scant resemblance to any contemporary university.[134]

Yet not all seventeenth-century universities were alike. The one most influential for the eventual secularization of knowledge was the University of Leiden in the Dutch Republic, "the most innovative institution of higher learning in early modern Europe."[135] Founded in 1575 in the midst of war against Philip II's Spain, it bucked the prevailing pattern of confessional universities and attracted leading scholars, just as the Dutch Republic itself confounded state-sponsored confessionalization in ways that conduced to commercial prosperity. Within twenty years, Leiden became the second northern European university (after Basel) with both a botanical garden and an anatomy theater, those sixteenth-century indicators of cutting-edge medical faculties, and soon it overtook Padua as Europe's leading university for medical instruction.[136] Despite the proportionally small number of theology students and the high turnover of theology professors before 1587, theology was hardly unimportant at Leiden—it was, after all, where Jakob Arminius provoked opposition after his appointment in 1603 with his anti-Calvinist, biblical views about grace and free will, and the university's theologians were at the intellectual epicenter in the sociopolitically expansive controversy between Remonstrants and Counter-Remonstrants through the time of the Synod of Dort in 1618–1619.[137] But in a move that adumbrated the later segmentation and secularization of knowledge, Reformed orthodoxy was not allowed to dominate the rest of the university's curriculum, just as the *regenten* never permitted the state-supported, Reformed Protestant public church to become a politically enforced state religion. From the very start Leiden's professors were made to profess no oaths except political loyalty, and beginning in 1578 students were also released from any confessional oath. Even some Catholics taught outside the theology faculty, which further implied the irrelevance of theology for non-theological subjects.[138] Except for the theology students, who lived in two small residential colleges, Leiden's students lived in rented lodgings throughout the town and thus lacked the shared social experience of the religious regimens typical in many other universities.[139] This implied the separability of Christian experiential knowledge, cultivated and reinforced through prayer and worship, from other sorts of knowledge. With its less confessional character and more restrictive role for theology, Leiden would be accompanied in the eighteenth century by universities that contributed even more robustly to the secularization of knowledge: Halle, Göttingen, Edinburgh, and Glasgow.[140] Indeed, these universities were among those in eighteenth-century Europe that most substantively embraced and integrated diverse Enlightenment ideas rather than resisting them.

THE LONGER THAT rulers championed rival doctrines in their universities and shielded theologians, the less prepared would the latter eventually be to answer questions about how their respective Christian truth claims might fit together with the ever-growing mass of new knowledge being made elsewhere. By the mid-seventeenth century, things looked inauspicious for the epistemological status of theology and Christian experiential knowledge. Well over a century of ongoing controversies among university-trained protagonists had brought doctrinal disagreements not a whit closer to resolution than they had been in the 1520s. On the contrary, unfettered anew during the English Revolution, Protestantism demonstrated its open-endedness and the astonishing range of adjunct claims about the character of Christian experiential knowledge among, say, the Reformed Protestant framers of the Westminster Confession of Faith (1646), the General Baptist (and thus soteriologically Arminian) leader Henry Denne, the Digger Gerrard Winstanley, and the Quaker James Nayler.[141] As their respective protagonists were well aware, the principle of noncontradiction meant that not all of the competing claims could be correct. Therefore not all of them could belong to knowledge. Nor was it apparent how the disagreements could be resolved so long as each protagonist functioned as a de facto hermeneutic authority. It is little wonder, then, that enduring Christian pluralism prompted some observers to draw skeptical conclusions about religion per se, which meshed with the robust revival of Pyrrhonism and related relativistic intellectual currents in the late sixteenth and early seventeenth centuries.[142] Nor is it surprising that thinkers such as Thomas Hobbes, John Wilkins, and John Locke began in diverse ways to distinguish what was merely *believed* as a matter of faith and opinion from what could be *known* on the basis of observation and reason.[143] Such distinctions remain common today. Regardless of its protagonists or provenance, its content or basis, Christian experiential knowledge *as such* was being downgraded to subjective opinion by such thinkers in a way that paralleled the relativization of doctrine and the individualization of religious belief. John Milton, a radical in this respect as in so many others, asserted that if a person "beleeve things only because his Pastor sayes so, or the Assembly so determins, without knowing other reason, *though his belief be true,* yet the very truth he holds, becomes his heresie."[144]

Moreover, by the mid-seventeenth century it was apparent that in contrast to the character of endlessly contested Christian doctrines and experiential knowledge, the knowledge gained through observations in botanical gardens, dissections in anatomy theaters, and experiments in alchemical laboratories was different. It did not depend on one's theology of the Lord's Supper or interpretation of Paul's letter to the Romans. It looked to be the same in Protestant Scotland as in Catholic Italy. It was universal, and it was useful. It could be concretely applied to serve the desires of rulers and subjects alike, "able," in Bacon's words, "to produce worthy effects, and to endow the life of man with infinite new commodities."[145] And there were prospects for resolving disagreements about it through shared, empirical attention to the matters at hand, regardless of one's religious views. Although it went well beyond a restrictive Augustinian teleology about the purpose of knowledge, a Baconian emphasis on increased mastery over nature and the reduction of human suffering was compatible with basic assumptions of medieval Christianity if the knowledge gained were subordinated to the common good and to individuals' flourishing within it through the shared practice of the moral virtues. However, as we have seen, by rejecting the Roman church as a moral community, the Reformation precipitated lasting disagreements about what the good was. It thus indirectly prompted supra-confessional philosophical attempts to answer the question—attempts that, similarly unresolved, would eventually find their place alongside competing religious views within the formal ethics of individual rights protected by modern, liberal states. However, a Baconian desire to master nature, when combined with a Hobbesian (or in the eighteenth century, Humean) belief in the anti-teleological insatiability of human desires, was antithetical to traditional Christian ideas about how all other types of knowledge were supposed to serve experiential knowledge in the faith. But this combination would be well suited to serve the increasingly pervasive, socially sanctioned acquisitiveness of Protestants and Catholics participating in the industrious revolution.[146]

Finally, as we have seen in previous chapters, by the end of the Thirty Years War and English Revolution the religio-political conflicts of the Reformation era had proven hugely expensive, massively destructive, and conspicuously inconclusive. What had they accomplished? God's providence had frustrated ruler after ruler, all of whom had failed to achieve their principal objectives regardless of conviction or devotion. Commitment to God's truth, however understood, had proven enormously costly on multiple levels. The concrete devastation and disruption understandably dampened enthusiasm for further rounds of military engagement motivated to whatever extent by religious commitments and the competing claims about Christian experiential knowledge with which they were associated. Unrest unsurprisingly fostered interest in types of knowledge that would be less troublesome, ones geared toward goals that antagonistic Christians were more likely to share, such as the pleasures and comforts that accompanied the acquisition of more and better possessions. Although theology would remain firmly ensconced in most universities, which rulers still needed for the training of clergy and other officials to serve their confessional states, its privileged position was no longer obvious. In the mid-seventeenth century, what had theologians done for rulers lately? Meanwhile, their continuing shelter rendered most of them ever less likely to be able to cope in intellectual terms with the knowledge-making that proceeded ever more outside universities.

The most important new institutions for knowledge-making in the later seventeenth century, the Royal Society of London (chartered in 1662) and the Académie Royale des Sciences of Paris (1666), presupposed a self-conscious distinction between theology and scientific knowledge. As "the new concept of nature became the area which was undisputed between the confessions," the academies deliberately prohibited the discussion of disruptive religious matters and concentrated on the discovery of concrete, verifiable, experimental knowledge.[147] More collaborative in character and less dependent on personal patronage than either courts or earlier scientific academies, the Paris Académie in particular, with its close connection to the crown, became the model for the many national and regional scientific academies established in the later seventeenth and eighteenth centuries, including those in Berlin (1700), St. Petersburg (1724), Stockholm (1739), and Göttingen (1751).[148] The new scientific academies—and to an extent as well, the many literary and humanistic academies that were established and flourished alongside them in the eighteenth century—reinforced the contrast between sites for knowledge-making and universities. A university was all about teaching as "an agent of cultural transmission," a scientific academy all about research that could serve human desires.[149] The academies made and disseminated new knowledge (especially through their innovation of the regular scholarly journal, beginning in the 1660s), whereas universities continued to train civil servants.[150] With relatively few exceptions, approved theology continued to remain comfortably insulated from the intellectual challenges presented by new knowledge.

The two most influential new German universities of the eighteenth century, Halle (established in 1694) and Göttingen (established in 1737), illustrate in different ways the powerful consequences when Protestant rulers extended what Leiden had pioneered, and decided to downplay rather than to emphasize theological orthodoxy. Friedrich III Hohenzollern, keenly aware of intra-Protestant strife as a Reformed Protestant ruler of a Lutheran territory whose orthodox Lutheran universities (Frankfurt an der Oder, Königsberg, and Duisberg) had caused problems in the past, sought to forge an alternative at the University of Halle through an anti-orthodox alliance of Lutheran Pietism and rationalism. But the alliance broke down, partly because of Pietism's theological weakness. In the early eighteenth century the tireless pastor, biblical scholar, and theologian August Hermann Francke (1663–1727) indeed made Halle into a thriving, Pietist alternative to Germany's generally small, backward, and poor Protestant and Catholic universities. Halle's Pietism made it much keener on Christian experiential knowledge than were most universities, with leaders such as Francke far from indifferent to doctrinal truth claims whatever their ostensible attempts to transcend confessional conflict. Having separated the warm faith of the heart and a strong commitment to philology from other domains of knowledge, however, Francke and his colleagues could not rebut rationalist challenges in philosophical terms. Hence in Reformation-era fashion, power was their only recourse. When Christian Wolff (1679–1754), Germany's leading rationalist philosopher, waxed too enthusiastic at Halle about Confucian morality and the autonomy of natural reason in 1721, Francke and his colleagues protested to Elector Friedrich Wilhelm I, who expelled Wolff from his chair in 1723. As soon as Friedrich the Great succeeded his father in 1740, however, he brought Wolff back, and under the oversight of this long-lived, central European Enlightened monarch, Halle's Pietism was increasingly attenuated as both biblical exegesis and theology were subjected to rationalist philosophical assumptions in the latter half of the century.[151]

One of Halle's early alumni was the Hanoverian privy counselor Gerhard Adolf von Münchhausen, who in 1737 established the University of Göttingen with the approval of the Hanoverian king of England, George II. In the wake of the Wolff affair and in contrast to Halle, Göttingen from the very start "thrust theology into the lowest position that the discipline, to that point, had ever occupied at a European university." It emphasized instead its philosophy (no longer arts) and law faculties, to which leading professors were lured through high salaries and a deliberate commitment to an irenic, minimally Lutheran Christianity that eschewed theological conflict no less than antireligious rationalism. The institution's overriding aim was useful service to the state.[152] Because religion had been problematic in this respect, it had to be domesticated, as was well seen by Münchhausen's close adviser, the theologian and church historian Johann Lorenz Mosheim (1693–1755), and the biblical scholar whom he strongly influenced, Johann David Michaelis (1717–1791)—who taught in the philosophy rather than the theology faculty.[153]

Having rejected Roman Catholicism's truth claims based on a supposedly authoritative tradition, and recognizing that divisive, intra-Protestant doctrinal disputes were irresolvable among rival adherents to the principle of *sola scriptura,* Mosheim, Michaelis, and others at Göttingen thought they saw in scholarship itself a way to overcome the impasses. The university deliberately (and successfully) courted students from the nobility—including Reformed Protestants and even Catholics—with an innovative curriculum that included not only history, politics, physics, natural history, psychology, and modern languages, but also fencing, riding, and dancing. Pedagogically, Göttingen's famous classical philology seminar was devoted to the presentation and discussion of *research*—an innovation that, in a discipline distinct from pursuits with Baconian aspirations in the scientific academies, ran counter to the long-standing separation between the pursuit and the transmission of knowledge in early modern Europe. At Göttingen, their combination was cross-fertilized by the scholarly journal (established in 1739) that came under the direction of the city's supplementary Society of Sciences (1751). New knowledge was being sought *in a university* to serve the Hanoverian state, but without relinquishing the objective of training useful civil servants. One of the philology seminar's leading graduates, Wilhelm von Humboldt, would together with influential colleagues take the idea in decidedly non-Baconian directions when he got his chance in 1810 at Prussia's new University of Berlin. There, the secularization of knowledge would be pressed further.

Their predecessors having been protected by an institutional and ideological carapace since the early sixteenth century, long shielded in confessional universities from the wider world of knowledge-making, few eighteenth-century theologians were in a position to respond to rationalist criticisms of their respective assertions or of revealed religion in general. Most lacked the intellectual wherewithal to see how, for example, their doctrinal truth claims might cohere with Newtonian physics, the burgeoning evidence for an earth much older than Archbishop James Ussher's, or the existence of peoples who long antedated the creation accounts in Genesis.[154] Nor were many university theologians in a position to distinguish the indisputable empirical gains of the new knowledge from the tendentious metaphysical, moral, and historical beliefs with which Enlightened protagonists almost always combined and advanced them, under the ideologically conflationary banner of "reason." Later in the century, Johann Georg Hamann's critique would call out Kant's *Critique of Pure Reason* on this score, and the learned Benedictine abbot of St. Blasien, Martin Gerbert (1720–1793), would recognize the need for a self-critical renewal of Catholic scholastic theology in relationship to the gains of new knowledge—which did not include the Lockean, Wolffian, or Kantian philosophical ideas that some of his German Benedictine contemporaries enthusiastically embraced.[155] Another erudite German Benedictine, Anselm Desing (1699–1772), took direct aim against post-Grotian, Pufendorfian and Wolffian natural law theories and the rationalist assumptions and methods that they presupposed, in contrast to Catholicism's natural law tradition.[156] But such insight among contemporaries was rare, just as Pascal had been rare among first-rate intellectuals in his repudiation of the rationalist God of the philosophers in the mid-seventeenth century.

Still less were most theologians intellectually attuned to recognize the assumptions embedded in domestications of inherited Christian truth claims by scholars seeking to fashion new alternatives. One had to know a great deal even to engage, much less resist, leading intellectuals on their turf, and few theologians in their universities, academies, or seminaries—indeed, few confessional Protestants or Catholics—knew enough, despite exceptions such as New England's tireless Jonathan Edwards (1703–1758), for example, or the polymathic historian and Italian priest Ludovico Antonio Muratori (1672–1750), or the imaginative Jesuit scientist Roger Joseph Boscovich (1711–1787).[157] More commonly, eighteenth-century Catholic theologians who engaged with novel philosophical ideas—whether those of Malebranche or Locke, Wolff or Kant—tended to make theology subservient to them, whether among French Jesuits in the 1730s and 1740s or German Benedictines in the 1770s and 1780s.[158] The Protestant Mosheim wanted theologians "to be able to draw on all fields of knowledge to safe-guard religion itself"—only what he meant by "religion" over against deism or atheism only thinly resembled Luther's theology, let alone medieval Christian truth claims.[159] Not only was such an exhortation to theologians in general far too little and too late, but the knowledge thus procured was being used in tandem with new commitments, for new purposes, and with new social ideals in mind. When biblical scholars such as Johann Salomo Semler (1725–1791), Michaelis, and Johann Gottfried Eichhorn (1753–1827) published provocative new ideas about the complex formation and character of the biblical text as the cultural product of "a deep and dead past," very few theologians had the learning necessary to distinguish philological achievement from philosophical assumption.[160]

Discomfort alone could not suffice to discern what was intertwined with the new, unprecedentedly contextualized, "higher criticism" of scripture: an ideological commitment to the construction of a black-hole historicism of the biblical past. Scholars would be the arbiters of what would be permitted to escape, and on whose terms. Certainly nothing that could fundamentally challenge human desires in the present—including God's alleged actions in history recorded in a cobbled-together collection of texts written and assembled by fallible human beings within their particular national culture at a primitive stage of human development.[161] Not only would Lessing *happen* to be unable to leap across the "broad and ugly ditch" between historical claims on the one hand and moral and metaphysical truths on the other. No one would be permitted to cross the chasm between modern present and ancient past except on the terms of the guardians of the science of antiquity *(Altertumswissenschaft)*.[162] Functionally, this was just what Spinoza had sought to accomplish in his *Tractatus Theologico-Politicus* (1670), only by different means.[163] Like the widespread conflation of pluralism with relativism, the assumption that critical historicism inexorably leads to corrosive skepticism would become central to the secularization of knowledge, and the related experience of "losing one's faith" a virtual *rite de passage* among many nineteenth-century students and intellectuals. Indeed, despite abundant counterevidence, the allegedly inherent connection between historicism and desacralizing skepticism is still widely believed today.[164]

In part, most theologians could not see how the construction of the "academic Bible" and the "Enlightenment Bible" was displacing scripture in the service of novel ideologies of self, society, and state because nearly all of them unself-consciously held univocal metaphysical beliefs in common with the rationalizing biblical scholars.[165] As science advanced, it was widely thought, God retreated. And science was definitely advancing, although at nothing like the rate it would in the nineteenth and still more the twentieth century. Newton himself was no deist, but with metaphysical univocity taken for granted his physics provided deism with a plausible foundation, just as it provided the background for Hume's question-begging skepticism about any and all miracles. The vast majority of theologians seem simply to have been unaware of the implications of their own metaphysical assumptions for the ways in which the relationship between the natural and the supernatural was being construed. Even Catholic theologians were unlikely to see how deeply the Enlightened rejection of the biblical God, whether in aggressive or subtle forms, impinged on their sacramental worldview—indeed some late eighteenth-century German Benedictines, understandably frustrated by the inflexible impositions of an intellectually brittle and unresponive scholasticism, were self-consciouly keen to embrace Wolff or Kant as the virtual intellectual saviors of the faith.[166] Or so it appeared to them.

Structurally homologous to the relationship between creator and creation in Catholic Christianity is the relationship between the divine and human natures of Jesus; between grace conveyed in the sacraments and the material signs that convey it; between the real presence of Christ and the eucharistic elements after consecration; and between the human soul and human body.[167] If one rejects the traditional, non-univocal Christian conception of the relationship between God and creation, these other aspects of Christianity are bound sooner or later to topple like dominoes. So it is no surprise that neo-Arian denials of the divinity of Christ, the construal of sacraments as nothing but social rituals and cultural symbols, and modern materialist conceptions of human beings (as well as conceptions of human beings that substitute the "self" or "mind" for the soul) have been so common since the eighteenth century, and remain widespread today.[168] Reject the traditional Christian conception of God as creator, and creation disappears as well, leaving eventually a disenchanted natural world in its stead. But it is a world that removes any divine constraints on liberated individuals, who as the neo-Protagorean measure of all things can in principle thus exercise their wills as they please. This is what the formal ethics of rights protected by the modern liberal state allows individuals to do within its laws. And the Western symbiosis of consumerism and capitalism since the industrious revolution has provided increasingly unencumbered, self-constructing selves with a never-ending array of stuff to fuel constantly reinforced acquisitiveness as they go about their business.

Once Newtonianism had triumphed even in most continental universities by the 1750s, theologians were more vulnerable than ever. The "leading figures of the Enlightenment, Newtonians to a man" were undiscriminating despisers of Aristotle and scholasticism.[169] Yet even theologians who appreciated Newtonianism could not clearly articulate why it was so problematic to try to explain human morality, politics, and social life on the basis of empirical observation and efficient causality alone. They could not see clearly that once intentionality and linguistically mediated meanings are extruded from human actions they cease to be intelligible as *human* actions at all, and thus cannot in principle be understood on the model of the natural sciences.[170] Not that the anti-Aristotelian pioneers would have been persuaded even if such critiques had been forthcoming and they had attended to them. As the previous chapter argued, theorists such as Hume and Adam Smith, uncritically innocent of the difference between historically constructed desires and putatively universal human nature, thought they were advancing Enlightened reason when in fact they were legitimating acquisitive ideologies on the basis of introspection and the observation of northwestern Europeans amid the industrious revolution. Very few confessional theologians were in a position to make substantive critiques, their place in universities having long afforded them safe harbor from the turbulent waters of early modern knowledge-making. Perhaps this made some of them readier to accept others' ground rules. "Utility" and "usefulness" were everywhere invoked to justify moral ideas and social practices, including by those French Catholic writers, for example, who embraced "Christian utilitarian apologetics" in their desire to remain *au courant* with Enlightenment discourse after 1760.[171] But this simply begged the real questions: useful for what, and by whom? University theologians, however, had in general long been kept from having seriously to inquire how so much new knowledge might fit together with their respective doctrinal truth claims. Instead, they were mocked by Voltaire, jeered by the *encyclopédistes,* and ridiculed as a type by almost everyone who was anyone in the Enlightened world of European learning. Nothing symbolizes the rejection of Christian theology better than the progressive exclusion of the Jesuits—the religious order that had epitomized Catholic erudition and teaching for more than two centuries—from Europe's Catholic countries beginning with Pombal's Portugal in 1759 and concluding with Pope Clement XIV's suppression of the order in 1773.[172] The rejection of theology was also symbolized in the anti-Catholic destruction wrought by the French Revolution itself, and in the suppression and seizure of monasteries by political leaders in France and elsewhere in Catholic Europe, which decimated the earlier post-Tridentine recovery of the contemplative female and male religious orders and the Christian experiential knowledge that they had continued to cultivate.[173]

THE FRENCH REVOLUTION and Napoleonic era were devastating for European higher education: where there had been 143 universities in 1789, there were only 83 in 1815.[174] These years mark a major caesura in the history of universities with respect to their relationship to religious truth claims, theology, knowledge-making, the state, and individual human desires, even though all the major elements in the subsequent secularization of knowledge were already present by the beginning of the nineteenth century. To be sure, they unfolded in a wide range of highly contingent ways in the particular institutions of different European countries as well as in North America. With the exception of Catholic universities, which followed suit later, by the early twentieth century universities both in Europe and North America had arrived in more or less the same place, with substantive religious truth claims excluded in principle from the pursuit and transmission of knowledge in the secularized academy.

The founding of the University of Berlin in 1809–1810 is widely regarded as inaugurating the era of the modern research university. Although Napoleon's own centralized system of state-controlled professional schools was established just before this in order to take the place of the French universities abolished in the Revolution, Berlin became the most influential model for the reform of existing and the establishment of new universities in Germany.[175] German research universities in turn, adapted in diverse ways, became from the second half of the nineteenth century the most important model for universities in other countries in Europe, North America, and eventually around the world.[176] But Berlin in the 1810s was as different from research universities a century later as it was from the confessional universities of early modern Europe. Much indebted to eighteenth-century Halle and Göttingen as well as to the coterie of philosophical idealists at Jena in the 1790s, the particular amalgam of priorities and projects at Berlin during the 1810s in what might be called the Romantic research university "was doomed virtually at the moment it came into existence."[177] But "the new Romantic university" at Berlin in its early years intensified certain institutional structures and ideological emphases that would endure, and whose transformation, in combination with other historical realities, would produce the secularization of knowledge that is largely taken for granted today.[178] The most consequential among these structures and emphases were the sequestration of theology, a commitment to research, an emphasis on the self, and a reliance on the state.

Most obviously, Berlin differed from confessional universities in the definitive dethroning of theology from its place of privilege. Extending a pattern pioneered by Leiden and Göttingen, theology retained its own faculty but was given no influence on other academic subjects in the philosophy faculty (the ancestor of modern university schools of arts/humanities and sciences). This quarantining of theology institutionalized Kant's argument in his *Conflict of the Faculties* (1798) that philosophy—as the expression of autonomous reason and human freedom—should be liberated from the confining constraints of dogmatic theology.[179] In the long term, this move contributed importantly to the secularization of knowledge by allowing other disciplines to ignore religious questions entirely as they conducted their respective inquiries. More radically than in the conflict at Leiden between Calvinists and Arminians in the early seventeenth century, theological concerns and disputes would remain internal matters for theologians and theology students, of little (and eventually no) consequence for the university's many other pursuers and purveyors of knowledge.

In the immediate term, at least in principle, there was little danger of theology being dogmatic in Berlin or elsewhere in Germany where the university's model was imitated. Undergirded by univocal metaphysical assumptions, both black-hole historicism and the academic Bible had in effect replaced scripture with what Jonathan Sheehan has called the "cultural Bible," an ancient set of texts to be studied *only* in historical context.[180] Meanwhile, the post-Pietist Schleiermacher, who played such an important role in shaping Berlin's early agenda, had freed religion altogether from texts, dogmas, and churches no less than from philosophy, science, and ethics. "That person does not have religion who believes in a holy writing," Schleiermacher had declared in 1799, "but only someone who needs none, and could probably make one for himself."[181] Thus was deconfessionalized, liberal Protestantism as ineffable, sublime, subjective feeling fitted with the guiding rationale for Berlin's original emphasis on research. The aim was not simply knowledge for knowledge's sake, nor to advance discoveries that would contribute to the sum of all knowledge, nor the Baconian pursuit of useful scientific knowledge, but rather *Wissenschaft* oriented to *Bildung*: the full self-development of the individual student's interests, capacities, and personality as the subjective realization of his unfettered freedom and autonomy.[182] The modern university was originally hatched from a Romantic vision of research as an adjunct to student self-realization.

Like the Göttingen-trained philologist Friedrich August Wolf (1759–1824), who came to Berlin after Napoleon's armies forced the closing of the University of Halle, Humboldt and his fellow philhellenists believed that relentless attention to the texts, objects, and culture of ancient Greece—what Suzanne Marchand has called a "peculiarly ascetic obsession"—would be the best historical mirror in which young men could begin to glimpse and then develop their own distinctive individual selves as modern Germans.[183] This neo-humanistic, post-confessional substitute for existing forms of Protestantism, which variously adapted would find adherents among educated elites in Britain and elsewhere in the nineteenth century,[184] explains why the experimental natural sciences were not part of Humboldt's original vision for the research university. With their technical demands, impersonal character, and pragmatic aims, what could they have contributed to *Bildung?* Indeed, *Wissenschaft* at Berlin in the early 1810s little resembled what it would become by the end of the century, whether in Germany, other European countries, or the United States. Not the pursuit of specialized knowledge within an academic discipline, research in the Romantic university concerned "the inculcation of unified principles of scientific inquiry" that retained an emphatic commitment to the unity of all knowledge in a manner formally analogous to the same in medieval Christianity.[185] But in fact this enterprise resembled medieval Christian theology as little as the Romantic cult of the self-directing individual concerned habituation in Christian virtues within a shared way of life. In the Romantic research university, the unity of knowledge did not mean Christian theology as the relationship of God to all things. It meant rather the subjective vision of the autonomous individual within the sublime whole of the cosmos conceived as *Naturphilosophie* in the manner of Schelling, with which men such as Humboldt and his brother, the naturalist explorer, Alexander, had replaced creation understood in traditional Christian terms.[186] This was far from Weberian disenchantment. That would come only after the nineteenth century had made its progress.

The Romantic research university was not only philosophically idealist; it remained largely an ideal. Much to the frustration of Fichte—an idealist in more than one sense—the university depended on the state for its sustainability, as indeed financially impoverished German universities had increasingly had to do during the eighteenth century (when the large majority nonetheless remained underfunded).[187] Prussia's overseers were no more likely to leave universities alone than their early modern confessional or Hanoverian predecessors at Göttingen had been. In Charles McClelland's estimate, "the central weakness in Humboldt's own thought was the assumption that the state is a moral force rather than merely the expression of the will of the king and a few hundred arbitrary central bureaucrats."[188] Even after the Karlsbad Decrees of 1819 increased governmental oversight of German universities, Hegel regarded the rational state not as a mere moral force, but as "the reality of the ethical Idea [*die Wirklichkeit der sittlichen Idee*]," which "has supreme right against individuals, whose supreme duty is to be members of the state."[189] An "organicist nationalism" helped the German professoriate to settle into a largely comfortable relationship with the state that began in the early nineteenth century and continued after Prussian unification in 1871.[190] Liberated from the constraints of confessional churches, the relationship of research universities—and thus of modern knowledge-making and higher education—to sovereign states would have far-reaching implications once research in philosophy and philology seminars yielded their primacy to physics and physiology institutes. This was so not only in Germany or in France, where the state maintained such tight control over the Grand Écoles and other institutions in its system of higher education, but also in the United States, where the federal government's formal control of colleges had always been much less, even after the Morrill Act in 1862 provided for the creation of land-grant institutions.[191] "Princeton in the Nation's Service," Woodrow Wilson entitled a famous address in 1896, well before putting the nation in what he took to be the world's service via Wilsonian interventionism as the twenty-eighth American president.[192]

LIKE ROMANTICISM AS a worldview, the Romantic research university disappeared from Germany during the nineteenth century, but important aspects of it migrated to the United States, where they hybridized with enthusiasm for Emersonian individualism and transcendentalism.[193] The transformation of the Romantic research university together with concurrent historical realities furthered the secularization of knowledge that had begun with the Reformation. By the end of the nineteenth century, the principal purpose of research had changed dramatically and had taken root in the transplantation and adaptation of universities inspired by the German model in countries on both sides of the North Atlantic. No longer focused on the self-realization of the individual student, the aim of research had become the increase of new knowledge per se as the defining, prestige-garnering activity especially of professionalizing scientists. Regardless of one's field, more new knowledge inevitably fostered increased specialization, because there was ever more to master. This in turn necessitated greater concentration in a smaller domain before one could reach the frontiers of knowledge and try to push them further. Beginning in the 1870s, that newfangled American adaptation of the German system, the "graduate school," expressly dedicated to the pursuit of specialized knowledge, was either grafted on to "undergraduate" colleges in the case of existing institutions such as Harvard under Charles Eliot, or was made the centerpiece of new institutions such as Johns Hopkins under Daniel Coit Gilman.[194] Greater specialization was reflected in the formation of increasingly distinct academic disciplines, including many familiar now in the tripartite division of the natural sciences, social sciences, and humanities.[195] The disciplines established their own professional organizations and specialized academic journals: already in 1887 there were almost 900 scholarly societies in Germany, and in 1900 nearly 1,300 journals in mathematics and the natural sciences.[196]

After the demonstration of the pedagogical utility and real-life applicability of laboratory chemistry by Justus von Liebig (1803–1873) in a university setting at Giessen in 1824, universities began increasingly to emphasize the natural sciences and medicine. Within a few decades they overshadowed philology and philosophy, the disciplines that had animated the Romantic research university.[197] By the end of the nineteenth century, on both sides of the Atlantic, the cumulative character of new natural-scientific knowledge and its demonstrably successful applications had secured the dominance of the natural sciences in research universities that they have held ever since. Engineering and technology were beginning to facilitate the more systematic application of scientific discoveries that fostered capitalist production, increased state military power, stimulated agricultural yields, and fed consumer acquisitiveness during the second industrial revolution of the late nineteenth century. In variations on a theme, all these intertwined developments were brought on board the bandwagon of nationalist progress, civilizing colonialism, and material prosperity in Imperial Germany, late Victorian Britain, Third Republic France, or the Gilded Age United States. Darwin's theories of natural selection and evolution not only began to revolutionize biology after *The Origin of Species* (1859), but were widely taken to provide a scientific underpinning for belief in Western domination of the world as tantamount to human progress and the spread of civilization as such.[198]

Through observation, measurement, quantification, and experiment centered on specific areas of investigation, natural scientists sought data that could be used to formulate theories in the quest to discover the invariable laws characteristic of natural regularities, which could be used to make predictions capable of verification. Then their findings could be applied through instrumental rationality in the service of human desires. The sciences worked; in the end, this rendered beside the point all abstruse questions about the epistemological status of their findings.[199] Their fundamental methods owed nothing to authoritative texts or authorities as such, and verifiable scientific findings were separable from investigators' particular beliefs and behaviors, including whatever religious or moral commitments they might or might not have. Despite the importance of national traditions in nineteenth-century science, knowledge in the natural sciences was in this sense objective and universal. The natural sciences demonstrated that methodological naturalism was a fruitful assumption and evidentiary empiricism the necessary method in the attempt to understand the regularities of the natural world, whether in Pasteur's microbiology or Helmholtz's physics.

In referring to natural scientists in 1896, Woodrow Wilson stated that "their work has been so stupendous that all other men of all other studies have been set staring at their methods, imitating their ways of thought, ogling their results."[200] Because the natural sciences were so successful, the nascent social sciences sought to imitate them. If social scientists were to make similar progress in their inquiries, they reasoned, they should adopt the same methodological naturalism and empiricism, so as to seek to discover the objective, universal laws that govern human behavior, social life, political relations, and economic activity. Thus might they realize the Enlightenment aspiration to apply Newtonianism to human life, albeit with a rigorous empiricism, the fulfillment of what Auguste Comte called a "social physics"—for as one of sociology's founding figures, Émile Durkheim, put it, society "is part of nature and nature's highest expression. The social realm is a natural realm that differs from others only in its greater complexity."[201] Indeed, the implications of new social sciences such as sociology and psychology were far from purely theoretical, because if their practitioners could discover invariable laws, human behavior could be accurately predicted and closely managed.[202] So too, social scientists could be enlisted by governments to furnish experts to help remedy the social disruptions and dislocations wrought by rapid industrialization and urbanization, indeed even "to lay the foundation for true human happiness, ethical advance, the overcoming of evil, and the salvation of humanity and society."[203] Just as application of the natural sciences in manufacturing processes and the transformation of the built environment had helped to create these modern problems, the social sciences would be applied to help fix them. Both would thus serve the onward march of progress and civilization.

At the end of the nineteenth century, the success of the natural sciences had made their epistemology the paradigm for knowledge as such—in Daniel Coit Gilman's phrase, the university's goal was science, "another name for truth."[204] Knowledge was universal, objective, and not dependent on the divergent, personal, individual beliefs of its practitioners—in sharp contrast to Protestantism as an empirical, social reality. The fact of Protestant pluralism had been a constant reality from the early 1520s. But its intellectual implications had been minimized in early modern Europe because only Lutheran and Reformed Protestant regimes, including the Church of England, had universities. The confessional character of magisterial Protestant universities had permitted politically privileged theologians within a given regime largely to ignore the fact of Protestant pluralism derived from *sola scriptura,* and to defer the confrontation with much of the early modern knowledge-making that went on outside universities. By design and from the time of its founding the United States was never a confessional country. Yet the widespread adoption of Scottish Common Sense philosophy and of deliberately nonconfessional natural theology in divergently Protestant American colleges not only served as a shared intellectual scaffolding analogous to Aristotelianism in the Reformation era, but also *functioned* in crypto-confessional ways. It veiled the implications of Protestant doctrinal disagreements. Despite the extraordinary proliferation of different Protestant groups and claims in the "democratization of American Christianity" during the first half of the nineteenth century, Protestant professors at American colleges continued to rely on inductive, fact-gathering, Baconian science refracted through Scottish Enlightenment moral philosophy and epistemology to sustain their commitment to the unity of knowledge.[205]

In 1871, the Presbyterian theologian Charles Hodge (1797–1878) famously proclaimed that "the Bible is to the theologian what nature is to the man of science. It is his storehouse of facts; and his method of ascertaining what the Bible teaches, is the same as that which the natural philosopher adopts to ascertain what nature teaches."[206] Hodge's insouciant confidence reflected an intellectual complacency about religio-social and historical realities born of decades of Protestant cultural hegemony in the United States, when "colleges typically functioned as the intellectual arm of American Protestantism."[207] After 1870 or so, the epistemological mirage that Hodge shared with so many of his contemporaries was exposed in American universities newly dedicated to knowledge-making. American Protestant theologians were as little equipped to handle the intellectual challenges of Darwinism, German biblical criticism, and historicism as Aristotelian natural philosophers had been prepared to accommodate Newtonianism in the eighteenth century.[208] Even more fundamentally, they had no answer when confronted with the principle of noncontradiction concerning their rival truth claims, beyond either redoubled proclamations of the correctness of their respective views (which only underscored the problem),[209] or an attempt to determine, as some sort of lowest common denominator, what it was that all Protestants shared in common and then to promote it. As had been true since the 1520s, it turned out that they shared only their rejection of the authority of the Roman Catholic Church. Those in higher education, public life, and industry who desired the secularization of knowledge seized their opportunity. Through deliberate, self-conscious efforts from the 1870s through the 1920s they changed (although not all at once) the status quo of higher education in what Christian Smith has called "the secular revolution," George Marsden has analyzed as the incremental institutionalization of nonbelief, and Julie Reuben has shown coincided with the increasing elimination of substantive moral aims from higher education.[210] Not fortuitously, a Who's Who of Gilded Age American industrialists hugely funded universities that "self-consciously pioneered functionally secular education and scholarship," including Ezra Cornell, Johns Hopkins, Leland Stanford, Andrew Carnegie, Andrew Mellon, Cornelius Vanderbilt, James Duke, and John D. Rockefeller (at the University of Chicago).[211]

In the end, knowledge-making and teaching in leading American universities were secularized because the de facto diversity and individualism of Protestant truth claims could not be reconciled with the epistemological demands of science for universality and objectivity.[212] In this sense knowledge did not merely *happen* to be secularized because American Protestant theologians lacked the wherewithal to handle new intellectual challenges— it *had* to be because of the unintended and unwanted consequences of the Reformation itself. What did the Bible say? *That* was the question, and there had never been anything remotely resembling a consensual answer despite centuries of Protestant claims about scripture's perspicuity. The institutionalization of individual religious freedom, pioneered in the United States, was the definitive beginning of the end of the magisterial Reformation. It revealed what the Reformation as such produced absent the power of political authorities standing behind hermeneutic authorities: the aggregate of whatever individuals happened to prefer. This fit perfectly with the ideology of American individualism that so struck Tocqueville and other nineteenth-century European visitors to the United States. But it did not fit at all with knowledge-making, once research on the German model with the natural sciences as the epistemological standard became the aspiration for leading American universities in the decades after the Civil War. The fissiparous particularity of Protestant truth claims, theology, and experiential knowledge was an insuperable problem. So knowledge had to be secularized and religious truth claims excluded from nascent academic disciplines just as religious convictions had to be privatized, indeed regarded as subjective beliefs and individual opinions no matter their content or the religious tradition in question. The secularization of knowledge and its institutionalization in research universities thus radicalized the way in which controversial theological issues had been bracketed in the early modern Republic of Letters.

Still, the most influential late nineteenth-century response in American universities did not secularize knowledge outright when confronted with new intellectual challenges and the realities of Protestant doctrinal diversity. Rather, following in the footsteps of Schleiermacher, Emerson, and others, it created what turned out to be a bridge to the secularization of knowledge by redefining Protantism. Divisive "denominational sects" (which made truth claims) were distinguished from laudable "nonsectarian Christianity" (which made none that were binding), and "theology" (which was objectionably particular) was disdained whereas "religion" (which was ostensibly universal) was embraced.[213] "Theological commitments and faith practices became 'Christian principles and values,' the coming kingdom of God, then 'broad principles of revealed religion,' then piety and morals, and eventually civilization, science, and reason."[214] And then finally, "whatever." If Christianity's fundamental principles were thought to be individualism, democracy, and modern freedom, if a church's goals and society's objectives were viewed as identical, and if God's providence was considered tantamount to prosperity and progress, then Christianity, church, and providence were superfluous. According to the sociologist of religion N. Jay Demerath, the sharp decline in liberal Protestant churchgoing since the 1960s—and the presence of a parallel "liberal Protestantism without Protestantism" in universities—is the paradoxical result of liberal Protestantism's hegemonic triumph in the wider culture.[215] Relatedly, with the rise of the Religious Right and militant Islamism, the way was cleared for a hugely expanded referential range for the term "fundamentalism": shedding its original, limited connotations of post-Darwinian biblicist literalism, the term is now widely used in the media and by many academics to refer to (and to deride) *any* firmly held religious belief. Viewed from the secularist side of the "culture wars," simply to be a religious believer who actually believes anything of substance is considered objectionable. Thus the cultural charge of "fundamentalism" in the early twenty-first century resembles that of "sect" in the late nineteenth, with "sectarian" still routinely used to discount and dismiss any religious views with identifiable content that one happens not to like.

The curricular slack created from the American demise of Scottish moral philosophy in the later nineteenth century was taken up by the humanities. Something was needed to counterbalance the impersonal, objective, and disciplinarily specialized natural sciences, and the supposedly impersonal and allegedly objective social sciences that wanted to be like them. The civilizing formation of students would be provided by literature, philosophy, and the arts—an ersatz *Bildung* for young Americans seeking to discover whatever it turned out they wanted to believe about the Life Questions—by teaching them "liberal culture" focused on beauty and which sought "to broaden sympathies, to deepen understanding of the human condition, to infuse ideals," sometimes with an explicit exposure to that new invention, "the great books."[216] In Anthony Kronman's estimate, this pedagogical dedication to "secular humanism" as the primary role of the humanities in higher education was just as things should have been, until humanities professors started to wreck it in the 1960s. Rather than continuing to lead students to embrace whatever they wanted to believe about life, they too increasingly got the idea that research should be their primary professional objective, which in combination with the advent of political correctness and the colonization of scholarship by ideology has led to "education's end" that has "given up on the meaning of life" in colleges and universities.[217] What Kronman overlooks is that the ideological fissiparity of the contemporary academy and its buyers'-market hyperpluralism is simply a secularized outgrowth and recapitulation of the irresolvable Protestant pluralism that had set the stage for the secular revolution in the first place. That is why professors in colleges and universities rarely talk about the meaning of life or morality, just as John Mearsheimer says they ought not.[218] How could they? Like Kronman, Harry Lewis laments that "colleges feed students candy rather than tougher stuff that will strengthen their ethical bones," and they "offer students neither a coherent view of the point of a college education nor any guidance on how they might discover for themselves some larger purpose in life."[219] But on what basis could they do so?

In the second half of the nineteenth century, Scottish Common Sense philosophy in Protestant colleges passed the baton to liberal Protestantism and secular humanism in research universities, which largely endured into the 1960s. Then secular humanism began to be exposed as a tendentious stopgap that had been concocted without coherent foundations in order to deal with the breakdown of Scottish moral philosophy that had in turn masked the incompatibilities among rival Protestant truth claims. Deliberately constructed so as to accommodate a wide range of individual answers to questions about human morality, meaning, value, and purpose, secular humanism lacked both any shared criteria for deciding among the rival truth claims and preferences that resulted, and any nonarbitrary means for choosing among competing, second-order criteria of evaluation. So epistemological constructivists under the influence of French poststructuralism called the bluff in the name of "theory" and started adding truth claims of their own (even while sometimes self-contradictorily claiming to reject the notion of truth).[220] They continue to do so, contributing to contemporary hyperpluralism in the academy. Postmodern constructivism and antifoundationalism since the 1960s is not the repudiation of higher education's secular humanism, as Kronman imagines, but rather the continuation and further extension of the de facto arbitrariness it was designed to permit.[221]

The nineteenth-century demise of Humboldtian science and Romantic *Naturphilosophie* left a void. Purportedly scientific, it was abandoned as a sentimental expression of post-Christian meaning seekers. So too, the dissipation of Scottish moral philosophy wedded to Baconian science and post-Newtonian natural theology left a void. With theology banished from knowledge-making in research universities on both sides of the Atlantic, no successor enterprise sought to understand how knowledge in all disciplines might fit together. Only increasingly specialized and segmented knowledge remained. By the early twentieth century, rigorous positivism and careful scientific experiments in countless specific disciplinary domains had produced mountains of data and constantly new prospects for fresh research. No empirically obvious, ineffable, holistic meaning was apparent in the masses of specialized data, though. Nor were there any disciplines both adequately equipped to discern how all knowledge might fit together and also concerned with connecting it to the Life Questions. So in some people, such as Max Weber, science produced feelings of disenchantment, and prompted a claim that science, knowledge, and objectivity were entirely distinct from religion, beliefs, and subjectivity.[222] Weber's fact-value distinction or its equivalent has dominated subsequent knowledge-making, with all religious truth claims and theology excluded from the first half of the distinction. Fittingly, a young Karl Barth, utterly disenchanted with liberal Protestantism, published his *Epistle to the Romans* in 1919, the same year that Weber's "Science as a Vocation" appeared. By the end of the Great War there were plenty of reasons for disenchantment that had nothing to do with science per se. Without question, knowledge-making as such had progressed mightily, especially in the natural sciences, their findings wholly distinct from how they might be used. Chemistry as an academic discipline, for example, was wholly separable from the nearly 90,000 deaths and more than 1.2 million casualties that its application in lethal gases had caused during the Great War.[223] Scientific knowledge was one thing, its deployment another. Weber died in 1920 and so did not live to see the much more efficient uses to which chemistry could be put when the leaders of the Third Reich called on Zyklon B.[224]

NOT IN THEMSELVES, but *given the assumptions of metaphysical univocity and Occam's razor,* the methodological naturalism and evidentiary empiricism that define knowledge as secular also mask the ideological alchemy by which methodological precept became metaphysical assertion. The story of the secularization of knowledge is usually told—by those who believe that metaphysical univocity and black-hole historicism are true—as though it were the rational unfolding of an intellectual inevitability. In fact, it has been and remains the imposition of an ideological imperialism in which academic "freedom," to all intents and purposes, now excludes the freedom to pursue in most universities the possibility that some religious truth claims might actually be what they claim to be. There is real irony here, given the failure of classic secularization theory correctly to predict the putatively inevitable "withering away" of religion in society at large. The secularization of knowledge in research universities, along with the consideration of religious traditions strictly as objects of study rather than as potential sources of knowledge, has eliminated the most important forum in Western society for the consideration of religious truth claims on their own terms in relationship to the rest of knowledge. It is quite possible that it has thereby indirectly helped to foster unthinking, anti-intellectual religion outside the academy, where religion is often much more than merely academic and sometimes destructively violent.

Yet the inculcation among students of the academy's secular ideology in its current configuration, as Chapter 4 suggested, is carefully calibrated because it rests on nothing but the pragmatist relativism required to serve the sociocultural and political realities of modern liberal states. Its aim is not the pursuit of truth—or rather, "truth"—with respect to any of the Life Questions, but rather indoctrination in the conviction that there are no definitive answers. Given the pressures exerted by fractious diversity in the hyperpluralistic wider society, higher education must on the whole instill *enough* skepticism to divest students of any substantive truth claims—especially religious ones—that could disrupt the demands of the most important social virtue, namely open-ended toleration. Students must minimally be brought to relativize their religious views, demoting them to the level of subjective beliefs, which is one of the things that a book such as Jeffrey Stout's *Democracy and Tradition* is designed to do.[225] Simply by dint of cultural osmosis, most Americans already have done their duty in this respect by the time they reach their late teens. But if not, exposure to the dominance of scientistic naturalism along with historical and cultural pluralism, plus reading some Nietzsche and Rawls in approved ways, usually does the trick, especially when backed by the professorial authority that makes college classrooms the site of such vast disparities in power. And the undergraduate conversion imperative of subjectivizing and relativizing one's own commitments is reinforced by the absence of any guidance, discipline, or courses for students about how even to begin to think through all the countervailing ideas and claims to which they are exposed. With theology "altogether absent from the mainstream academic enterprise" and philosophy nearly always a highly technical, specialized discipline as ideologically secular as any other, students have essentially no chance of sorting through the claims and evidence they encounter, or of stumbling on some measure of coherence.[226] Hence they can concentrate on having a good time and getting good enough grades to get a good job and to pursue the goods life.

But higher education must not encourage students to be *too* skeptical, to follow Nietzsche to the end, to transfer the implications of the reigning ideological scientism and metaphysical naturalism into the domain of morality and human life. Because then, quite plainly, they might see that there is in fact no more basis for (critically important) human rights or convictions about equality than there is evidence for (silly and superstitious) human souls or God, and indeed, no scientific evidence for any objective values, meaning, or purpose whatsoever. And if enough people started to see this, the behavioral outcomes could make Peter Singer's advocacy for the legitimacy of infanticide—"*we* can see that the grounds for not killing persons do not apply to newborn infants"—look like child's play.[227] So higher education must aim to instill a carefully calibrated—and on the terms of scientistic naturalism, completely baseless—skepticism. That is why, even though he seems to recognize that there is no natural basis for human rights if naturalism is true, Ronald Dworkin, despite his intellectual sophistication, in the end responds to the question about the truth of the objective existence of rights like a flummoxed clergyman pressed by an impertinent layperson: "You'd better believe it."[228]

In the past two centuries the secularization of knowledge has been overwhelmingly a phenomenon born of Protestantism, from Romantic research universities to the leading American institutions, which, after the blows inflicted on German universities from the Great War through Hitler's Reich, have become the world's pacesetting institutions of higher education. Catholic universities in Europe, already weakened and on the defensive after the suppression of the Jesuits, were devastated by the French Revolution and the Napoleonic wars. With Catholic universities eviscerated in France and embattled in Italy, a handful of German universities harbored what vitality there was in early nineteenth-century Catholic theology. Even though it was viewed with reactionary suspicion if not hostility by Rome and was penetrated by Wolffian rationalism and German idealism, theology in these institutions was not ideologically sequestered in the manner of the Romantic research university modeled by Berlin.[229] Rather, the overriding curricular weakness of Catholic theology throughout the era of ultramontanism from the aftermath of the French Revolution to the Second Vatican Council in the 1960s was both institutional and intellectual: its isolation in seminaries, and its narrow focus on philosophical issues at the expense of attempting to understand the church's teachings in relationship to the exponential increase in new knowledge. Still, the emergence of neo-Thomism in the mid-nineteenth century brought with it a critique and rejection of post-Cartesian epistemological assumptions in ways that partly adumbrated the thought of the later Wittgenstein, whereas other German theologians (and some French theologians, such as Louis

Bautain) had in the manner of a handful of German Benedictines beginning in the 1780s accepted the terms of post-Kantian philosophy as setting
supposedly inescapable intellectual boundaries for Catholic theology.[230]

The intellectual achievements of twentieth-century philosophers and
theologians diversely inspired by Aquinas, from Marie-Dominique Chenu
and Jacques Maritain to G. E. M. Anscombe and Alasdair MacIntyre,
should be distinguished from the ways in which neo-Thomism was institutionalized in Catholic higher education following Leo XIII's call for the
revival of Aquinas in *Aeterni Patris* (1879). The institutionalization proved
capable—especially among the Catholic immigrant minority in the United
States—of training clergy and sustaining an extensive educational subculture from primary schools through seminaries and universities. But it
downplayed knowledge-making in other disciplines and kept research in
them at a distance from the Aristotelian and Thomistic philosophical categories that underpinned the theology. This distancing was reinforced by
papal encyclicals such as *Pascendi Dominici Gregis* (1907) and *Humani
Generis* (1950), which, as a symptomatic reflection *of* Catholic theology's
long-standing insulation from the wider world of knowledge-making, blithely
lumped together many-stranded and complex intellectual issues under conflationary labels such as "Modernism."[231] Partly for this reason, with the
possible exception of Louvain in Belgium, no Catholic institutions were
among the world's leading research universities in the early or mid-twentieth
century.[232] This fact helped to make Catholicism's truth claims seem all the
more hollow to non-Catholics, who were more likely to concur with George
Bernard Shaw's dictum that ideological restrictions and a lack of academic
freedom made the idea of a Catholic university a contradiction in terms. If
Protestantism enriched by the Scottish or German Enlightenments could
not stand up to historicist scholarship, critical philosophy, and the findings
of science, how could intellectually retrograde, papally dominated, superstitious Catholicism possibly hope to?

The neo-Thomist curriculum of Catholic higher education essentially
evaporated within a decade beginning in the 1960s. This was not simply
because Catholics were eager to "embrace the modern world" in the wake
of Vatican II's *aggiornamento*. It was also because of the papally reinforced gap between what Catholicism purported to be on the one hand,
and cutting-edge knowledge-making in leading research universities on the
other.[233] Popes themselves had unintentionally helped to set up for implo-
sion the very intellectual framework on which they had insisted. Ironically,
the inadequate understanding of Catholic theology's *relationship* to research in academic disciplines was bound to follow from papal suspicion
of scientific and historical knowledge-making, and it lay behind comically

simplistic papal diagnoses and remedies for the problems of modernity—as if the intellectual cure were as easy as "Scholasticism." Quite obviously, one could not seek to understand how Catholic truth claims related to the findings of any given academic discipline unless one had knowledge of both. But one could not become an expert in particle physics, evolutionary biology, ancient Near Eastern archaeology, or any other discipline unless one were trained in a genuine research university. Doubly ironically, however, by denouncing without unpacking and adequately analyzing complex realities such as "Modernism," "Rationalism," and "Historicism," popes from Leo XIII through Pius XII unintentionally laid the foundation for an equally simplistic reaction. They created the conditions for the no less intellectually dubious, binary sociological division between "conservatives" and "liberals" in European and North American Catholicism since the Second Vatican Council, which tends simply to mirror the ideological divisions dictated by secular politics in the wider society.

Through their actions popes also unwittingly contributed to the secularization of Catholic universities. Beginning in the 1960s newly and understandably self-critical Catholic universities had a lot of intellectual catching up to do amid a swirl of much wider, dramatic social changes and political turmoil. But in "accepting modernity" with scarcely less eagerness than preceding popes had denounced it, their leaders tended uncritically to embrace many tangled, hidden assumptions embedded in the history of the secularized institutions whose structures and practices they adopted.[234] Even when refracted through certain Catholic lenses, these assumptions fostered the secularization of knowledge. If a particular (and quite common mis)reading of Aquinas on faith and reason, for example, was thought to model the institutional relationship between theology and all other disciplines—theology is to faith, revelation, and supernatural grace as all other disciplines are to knowledge, reason, and the natural world—then one not only risked but rendered likely the sequestration of Catholic truth claims from the rest of knowledge-making in a manner similar to theology's demotion in the nineteenth-century Romantic research university, but in a different idiom. Even among Catholic institutions that did not make the inherently relativizing and secularizing move of replacing theology with religious studies departments, theology's integrative potential would be lost if it was simply regarded as one, self-contained discipline among others. The same was true of philosophy, if it was thought that the solution to the problem of intellectually staid neo-Thomism in the curriculum as taught from textbooks was simply the imitation of philosophy as it was done in secular universities. So too, with so many tendentious moral and metaphysical assumptions in so many disciplines interwoven with academic research, much of knowledge-making was bound to conflict with Catholic truth claims. In a rush to "make up for lost time" and to pursue "excellence" in order to narrow the embarrassing gap between the level of knowledge-making in Catholic institutions and in leading research universities, Catholic university leaders unwittingly invited in an intellectual Trojan horse bearing a load of subversive assumptions. No wonder American Catholic universities have been in a perpetual state of hand-wringing and endless debates about "Catholic identity" ever since. Most Catholic institutions rapidly secularized the "academic part" of their universities in the 1960s and 1970s—as if it were separable from the other parts, like nature was supposedly separable from grace—and then wondered why everything else changed, too.

The greatest Catholic thinker of the nineteenth century, John Henry Newman (1801–1890), was a convert whose conversion long antedated *Aeterni Patris* and owed nothing to neo-Thomism. Rather, Newman struggled his way to Roman Catholicism by mastering both the Greek and Latin church fathers as well as the history of theology, and by working for years through questions about history and Christians' conflicting doctrinal claims. His conversion in 1845 cost him his position at Oriel College, Oxford, as both of England's venerable universities were still confessionally Anglican institutions (and remained such until the 1870s).[235] Newman's distance from neo-scholasticism and his relentless inquiry as an outsider gave him a deeper sense than any other nineteenth-century Catholic intellectual of the interconnectedness of all knowledge in relationship to theology. In his *Idea of a University* (1852), he conceptualized the relationship among theology, philosophy, and the legitimate investigative autonomy of all other academic disciplines, and thus of Christianity's widest intellectual aspiration to understand the relationship between God and all things.[236] But Newman's idea and ideal for the Catholic University in Dublin was not for a *research* university dedicated to the pursuit of new knowledge any more than had been true of the Oxford he had known from the late 1810s into the early 1840s, a university's purpose being "the diffusion and extension of knowledge rather than the advancement."[237]

Despite its timidity in the face of knowledge-making by secularizing research universities, the neo-Thomist subculture had understood, whether intuitively or explicitly, the extent to which Christianity in Roman Catholicism is first and foremost a shared way of life. Its fundamental mode is not propositional but participatory, not scholarly but sacramental, not individualistic but interactive. Accordingly, compartmentalized lives devoted to consumerism not only are idolatrously antithetical to Catholicism but are bound to erode the experiential knowledge acquired in its communities of faith, and thereby to render Catholicism's truth claims implausible, objectionable, and/or seemingly irrelevant (as they do in a parallel way with liturgy). When this happens, theology—as the rational endeavor to understand the interrelatedness of the faith's truth claims, and more broadly God in relationship to all things—loses its traditional point because it loses its connectedness to the practices of a shared way of life and the experiential knowledge associated with them. Instead, the intellectual default becomes the secularized and specialized knowledge produced in academic disciplines and applied via technology in order to cater to the self-determined desires of dechristianized, Humean individuals. In sum, the hegemonic features of modern, liberal Western states—the political protection of the individual rights of autonomous consumers to construct themselves as they please amid wall-to-Walmart, post-Fordist capitalism—contribute powerfully albeit indirectly to the secularization of knowledge by sapping the taproot of Catholic theology: the shared practice of the virtues that constitutes communities of faith and is the source of its experiential knowledge.

The Protestant reformers of the sixteenth century sought to address serious problems besetting late medieval Christendom. They would doubtless be shocked if they could see where their insistence on scripture alone has unintentionally led, so radically at odds to their deepest hopes for the renewal of Christian faith and life. Yet unwanted disagreements about the Bible's meaning coupled with the enthronement of theology in the confessionalized universities of early modern Europe set the stage for the secularization of knowledge. Not only did it institutionalize doctrinal disagreements, but by pushing so much knowledge-making outside universities, it weakened theology and enfeebled the intellectual courage of Lutherans, Reformed Protestants, and Roman Catholics alike. When the deferred reckoning came it was diversely ruinous. In conjunction with the burgeoning individual acquisitiveness fed by the industrious revolution, and the understandable desire to avoid religio-political violence, religious conviction was privatized and theology sequestered so that the world could be made safe for Baconian knowledge-making in the service of human desires, whatever they happened to be. What started on this score in the seventeenth century is going stronger than ever today.

# Against Nostalgia

JUDGED ON their own terms and with respect to the objectives of their own leading protagonists, medieval Christendom failed, the Reformation failed, confessionalized Europe failed, and Western modernity is failing, but each in different ways and with different consequences, and each in ways that continue to remain important in the present. This sums up the argument of the book. To be sure, the genealogical method employed is expandable, and more comprehensive accounts are possible. Additional domains of human life have scarcely been mentioned that could have been analyzed in the same manner—sex, marriage, and families, for example, or forms of communication—by tracing their long-term transformations over time from the late Middle Ages to the present, with particular attention paid to the impact of the Reformation era. Nevertheless, the six chapters as they stand explain much about how the contemporary Western world came about, and how the Reformation era continues to influence it. As was stated in the Introduction, my intent in treating the subjects of the respective chapters discretely was strictly analytical. No domain of life was lived in isolation from the others. Along the way, I have referred to some of their points of overlap and intersection while trying to avoid burdening the exposition with too many cross-references. Still, the work's structure and method risk leaving a mistaken impression that these are six separate stories, rather than an analysis of human realities that were lived together in a tangled, temporal succession by historical protagonists frequently unaware of where their actions would lead. That is how all human life is lived. The principal aim of this conclusion is to sketch briefly a narrative picture of the whole based on the six chapters taken together, to note some of its implications, and to make a suggestion about contemporary academic discourse.

Alexandra Walsham has recently written that because of the manner in which long-standing paradigms for understanding the Reformation "were themselves partly a deliberate product of [protagonists'] own propaganda, polemic, and retrospective, mythologizing rhetoric . . . the task of writing a history of Protestantism with the notion of 'progress' left out remains a formidable one."[1] This book about the unintended Reformation and its multifarious, long-term influences over half a millennium would seem to qualify as such a history, even though it is much more than a conventional history of Protestantism.

Despite contrary claims by those who espouse supersessionist conceptions of history or hold alternative beliefs about reality, the failure of medieval Christendom was not a function of the demonstrated or demonstrable falsity of central doctrinal truth claims of the Christian faith as promulgated by the Roman Catholic Church. Over the course of more than a millennium the church had gradually and unsystematically institutionalized throughout Latin Europe a comprehensive, sacramental worldview based on truth claims about God's actions in history, centered on the incarnation, life, teachings, death, and resurrection of Jesus of Nazareth. Intellectual life on the eve of the Reformation was vibrant if sometimes contentious, variously institutionalized not only in universities but also in monasteries, at princely courts and among participants in the "religious Republic of Letters."[2] Nor was the failure of medieval Christendom the result of the wide diversity of ways in which the faith was expressed from Scandinavia and Scotland to Sicily and Spain. An enforced uniformity of piety and religious practice was neither a medieval social fact nor even an ecclesiastical ideal. Much was left to lay discretion and initiative in the unprecedentedly devout fifteenth century.

The failure of medieval Christendom derived rather from the pervasive, long-standing, and undeniable failure of so many Christians, including members of the clergy both high and low, to live by the church's own prescriptions and exhortations based on its truth claims about the Life Questions. It was at root a botching of moral execution, a failure to practice what was preached. Judged by the church's own criteria—the extent to which Christians were holy and pursuing greater holiness by imitating Christ via the shared practice of the virtues in communities of faith—the concrete realities of late medieval Christendom as a whole were far from what Jesus had preached and distant from the church's own ideals. Sins were everywhere. In one way or another, this is precisely what exercised so many committed reformers within the church from the eleventh into the early sixteenth century. How could the gulf between prescriptions and practices be narrowed, and human life be made more genuinely Christian? Late medieval Christianity was an institutionalized worldview, but one that by its own standards fell gravely short of having realized its own constantly repeated ideals, despite the self-flattering claims of those theologians who identified the church with the kingdom of God. Every domain of human life was adversely affected. Communities were hampered in their capacity to foster habituation into the virtues on which the individual good, the common good, and eternal salvation depended. In the fifteenth century, secular authorities from civic magistrates to royal sovereigns increasingly took ecclesiastical reform into their own hands in the absence of serious interest or initiative by most churchmen, and in light of the difficulties encountered by those ecclesiastical leaders who did take action.

No less consequential than myriad sins by members of the clergy and laity were the widespread failures of secular and ecclesiastical authorities to find nonoppressive ways of exercising power consistent with *caritas*. The challenge was to use power in a manner that sought not simply to safeguard the common good (by maintaining and enforcing rules that are indeed necessary for the existence of moral communities), but also to foster within those communities the individual flourishing of the women and men who were created in God's image and likeness. To the extent that *caritas* was indiscernible in the exercise of power, Christianity might well have seemed simply a noxious ideology wielded for the purpose of ensuring order in a hierarchical society of ranks and stations. This awareness among the church's late medieval critics did not have to wait for the modern invention of sociology or political science as academic disciplines. The naturalization of socioeconomic hierarchy in a preindustrial but monetized economy of relative scarcity, an economy increasingly permeated by market practices, was taken to justify enormous discrepancies between rich and poor in ways that highlighted medieval Christianity's central moral blindness. Without this obliviousness, the early Reformation's most conspicuous and disruptive popular manifestation, the Peasants' War of the mid-1520s, might never have happened. In the later Middle Ages and into the sixteenth century, not only oligarchic, aristocratic, and royal secular authorities but also the highest-ranking ecclesiastical authorities enjoyed power, privilege, possessions, and money, which seem only rarely to have been used in genuinely self-denying ways that expressed the virtues and sought the good of those beyond families and friends.

Many of those who rejected the authority of the Roman church in the sixteenth century were moved by the same problems, but they proposed a different diagnosis, one that various suppressed individuals and groups had in their respective ways proffered in preceding centuries. They thought that doctrinal error lay behind medieval Christendom's moral shortcomings. They believed that human life was so troubled not merely because of the manifest failure of so many sinful Christians to live up to the church's teachings, as so many medieval reformers had said. It was also that many of the church's teachings were themselves false, as those condemned for heresy in the Middle Ages had also claimed. Certain key doctrines were grave misunderstandings of the way God worked and misrepresentations of how he revealed himself in history. Only God's true teachings could ground a genuine renewal of human life, and they were to be found in the Bible alone liberated from the self-interested trappings and traditions of the Roman church. In order for Christianity to be the right *sort* of shared human life actually willed by God, it had to be based on the correct interpretation of God's word in scripture.

The Reformation succeeded in providing an alternative way of grounding Christian answers to the Life Questions and thus of providing the basis for the living of Christian lives ideologically and socially separated from the Roman Catholic Church. The history of Protestantism over the past five hundred years provides a great many examples. But the Reformation's putative solution to Christendom's problems turned out to be a simultaneous failure relative to its protagonists' intentions. In contrast to medieval Christendom, this was not in the first instance a moral failure (leaving aside the historical evidence for ways in which many Reformation-era Protestants also failed to live up to their respective ideals and teachings). Rather, the Reformation's failure derived directly from the patent infeasibility of successfully applying the reformers' own foundational principle. For even when highly educated, well-intentioned Christians interpreted the Bible, beginning in the early 1520s they did not and manifestly could not agree about its meaning or implications. Nor would anti-Roman Christians change or compromise their exegetical claims about the meaning of God's word on points they regarded as essential. Furthermore, what *was* essential rather than inessential and the criteria for distinguishing between them were themselves just additional things about which they could and did disagree. The unintended problem created by the Reformation was therefore not simply a perpetuation of the inherited and still-present challenge of how to make human life more genuinely Christian, but also the new and compounding problem of how to know what true Christianity was. "Scripture alone" was not a solution to this new problem, but its cause. It implied questions about the nature of knowledge and raised explicitly the specter of radical doctrinal skepticism and relativism already in the 1520s. Supplementary interpretive criteria such as illumination by the Holy Spirit or the exercise of discursive reason in the determination of true doctrine increased rather than resolved the disagreements they were intended to overcome, as did bolder claims of direct prophetic inspiration or new revelation from God. This was the case throughout the Reformation era and has remained so ever since.

Hence the Reformation is the most important distant historical source for contemporary Western hyperpluralism with respect to truth claims about meaning, morality, values, priorities, and purpose. Despite the hopes and dreams of Reformation protagonists, the result of their distinctive appeal to scripture alone was not a set of clear mandates for reforming human life according to "the Gospel," but an undesired, open-ended range of rival truth claims about answers to the Life Questions. Because what was at stake was so important, and because Christianity informed all of human life, exegetical disagreements were translated into doctrinal disagreements that were in turn expressed in socio-moral division and political contestation. Against the intentions of anti-Roman reformers but as a result of their actions, the church became the churches.

Most competing Protestant protagonists in the sixteenth century did not draw from their disagreements the conclusion that the Reformation's foundational principle or its adjuncts were themselves the source of the new problem. (Those who did so tended to return to the Roman church.)[3] Rather, they usually reasserted—and argued, in endless doctrinal controversies and sometimes with formidable erudition—that they were right and their rivals wrong. This settled nothing. Having rejected the authority of the Roman church, Protestants shared no institutions or authorities in common to which they could turn to resolve disputes among themselves. This was evident already in the 1520s and has remained the case ever since. Instead, their disagreements were themselves institutionalized most influentially in the only two Protestant traditions that, because their leaders secured lasting political protection from secular authorities, turned out to be the great exceptions among anti-Roman Christians in the Reformation era: Lutheranism and Reformed Protestantism (including the Church of England). Especially after the Peasants' War of 1524–1526 and the Anabaptist Kingdom of Münster a decade later, the large majority of anti-Roman answers to the Life Questions were suppressed, and socially or politically challenging expressions of Protestantism were curtailed until they emerged again in England in the early 1640s. This control was an imperative in the eyes of those committed to maintaining a traditional sociopolitical order, because some Christians wanted radically to remake socioeconomic and political realities according to their very different understandings of the Gospel. The largely successful suppression of radical Protestantism in the century between the Kingdom of Münster in 1534–1535 and the English Revolution also helped to minimize the implications of the Reformation's practical failure, because the predominance of Lutheranism and Reformed Protestantism made it seem as though Christians who had rejected Rome exhibited more doctrinal coherence than in fact they did. Nearly all radical and magisterial Protestants agreed, though, with the traditional condemnation of the avarice that was so obviously present in the Roman church, so corruptive of the rest of human life, and so contrary to biblical condemnations of greed.

The late medieval Christianity that Protestant reformers sought to fix was not something called "religion," separate from the rest of life. It was an institutionalized worldview on which eternal life depended, with ramifications for all of human life lived in certain ways rather than others. Regardless of the particular forms taken by their respective ambitions, magisterial Protestant reformers shared this assumption plus many other biblically based beliefs with their late medieval predecessors and Catholic contemporaries. Accordingly, Lutheran, Reformed Protestant, and Catholic leaders (especially after the Council of Trent) embarked on the arduous work of confessionalization in their respective territories. Secular authorities oversaw the churches they controlled and together with ecclesiastical leaders sought to create a better-informed, better-behaved, more-disciplined and self-disciplined laity compared to the laypeople of pre-Reformation Christendom. Better-educated, more-conscientious clergy led worship, supervised lay piety, catechized, preached, explained, exhorted, encouraged, threatened, and consoled, reinforcing repeatedly the newly central virtue of obedience in every domain of human life. The threat of heterodoxy necessitated vigilance because dissenters subverted the very conditions of the moral communities that authorities sought to forge. Secular rulers also oversaw their respective institutions of higher education, politically privileging theology and seeking to ensure that the transmission of knowledge in the training of bureaucratic officials was shielded from threats to orthodoxy. Outside of confessionalized universities, the same rulers were patronizing the pursuit of new knowledge, especially the observation-based knowledge about material things in the natural world that could be used to serve human desires. In a divided and confessionalizing Christendom, sovereign secular authorities exercised all public political power, ceding to the control of their respective churches only what seemed to serve their own desires and perceived interests. Encouraged oftentimes by clerical advisers convinced that they saw clearly the particular paths of God's providence, conscientious rulers sometimes took advantage of the new opportunities for the military defense and proactive promotion of Christian truth as they respectively understood it. They made war on each other, off and on, from the late 1520s through the 1640s, with confessional hostilities persisting much longer.

In terms of what its respective protagonists hoped to achieve, the failure of confessional Europe was twofold: they failed politically and militarily, just as they failed to create moral communities free of religious dissent. In the first instance, none of the leaders in the religio-political conflicts during the Reformation era achieved their principal military or political goals in any enduring ways. Unlike the medieval heresies that secular and ecclesiastical authorities had largely managed to suppress and control, Lutheranism and Reformed Protestantism, including the Church of England, demonstrated their institutionalized staying power. Sustained political support from secular authorities made them in this respect parallel to Catholic regimes and distinguished them from marginalized and persecuted radical Protestants who collectively manifested a much wider range of claims about true Christianity. At the same time, despite the apocalyptic expectations of many Protestant reformers about the demise of the papal Antichrist, Catholicism not only persisted but its leaders regrouped, reenergized, and spread the faith around the world from Brazil and New France to the Philippines. By the mid-seventeenth century the religio-political conflicts of the Reformation era, capped by the Thirty Years War and the English civil wars, had proved ruinously destructive, extremely expensive, and frequently subversive of rulers' own desires to serve God as they shored up their political authority. In various forms confessional regimes endured in most European states throughout the eighteenth century, but partly because of the failure of bellicose confessionalism, some monarchical authorities began experimenting more robustly with modifications and accommodations in the direction of religious toleration. Some of them began to look with particular interest on a new nation, the Dutch Republic, whose political leaders and mercantile elite supported a Reformed Protestant public church but eschewed confessionalization in the interests of promoting commercial profits and pursuing lives increasingly devoted to the acquisition of things that money could buy. This was an alternative to assumptions about the relationship among Christianity, morality, the exercise of power, and economic prosperity that ignored the biblical condemnation of avarice but looked as though it might be able to overcome the vexing problem of confessional antagonisms.

In the second instance, early modern confessional regimes failed within their respective polities to rid their moral communities of religious dissent.

This was true in Puritan New England no less than in Europe. Confession-alizing efforts to secure subjects' obedience echoed in geographically more circumscribed but politically more demanding, more narrowly prescribed ways the ambitions of medieval Christian authorities at least to ensure conformity through the threat of punishment wherever persuasion or per-sonal enthusiasm failed to produce desired behavior and piety. This was not a problem for everyone: the willingly devout seem largely to have welcomed the confessionalizing efforts of the early modern period, whether manifest in the efflorescence of Catholic Marian and eucharistic piety, the spread of in-dividual Bible reading among Lutherans and Reformed Protestants, or the astonishing demand for devotional literature among all confessions. Indeed, eager practitioners were likely to think that authorities were not doing enough to foster the formation of godly fellow Christians. The willingly de-vout helped to make confessionalization a partial success, marking the Ref-ormation era as one of fervent religiosity among Catholics and Protestants alike. Committed believers who agreed with authorities' truth claims in confessional regimes did not resent their demands of obedience per se, be-cause whatever else it entails Christianity is, like Judaism, most fundamen-tally and ineradicably a matter of obedience to God, the faith's sine qua non.

The real questions, then, were whether subjects thought that secular and ecclesiastical authorities had the truth claims right, and whether they thought those in charge acted in ways that Christian rulers and pastors should act. If so, then obedience was not a problem, but merely an obvi-ous, almost trivial condition for the pursuit of substantive Christian life in community. Those subjects that disagreed, however, were bound to resent the same requirements that others willingly embraced as a minimal prereq-uisite for shared Christian life. And now there were many different non-Roman versions of God's truth from which to choose, including whatever one might come up with oneself. More than a few Protestants pleased to have thrown off the Roman yoke were frustrated to find themselves under much more restrictive forms of "new popery." Confessional authorities sought to compel obedience among the unwilling by exercising coercive power, which tended to cause discontent in proportion to their efforts pre-cisely among those whose conformity was sought. Objectors resented as in-vasively obnoxious or presumptuously tyrannical the heavy-handed mea-sures of confessional regimes from Catholic Spain to Presbyterian Scotland, most dramatically manifest in judicial executions for heterodoxy. Some ad-vocates of toleration argued that even if authorities were seeking to create and protect a Christian community, such actions were unchristian attacks on human beings who were ostensibly supposed to be part of that commu-nity and whom God had created in his image. This createdness in God's

image was why and how human beings had individual rights, as canon lawyers had begun to argue in the twelfth century. Now the inherited discourse
of individual rights was being appropriated in novel ways, against Catholic
as well as magisterial Protestant confessional regimes.

Experience demonstrated that grudging conformity was simply incompatible with joy, was not the truth that made one free, and did not conduce
to one's flourishing. In order for Christianity to thrive as shared life in
Christ rather than to be experienced as an ideology of coercive oppression,
faith had to be adopted freely and practiced willingly. But this was antithetical to the ambitions of confessional authorities, secular and ecclesiastical alike, and it was unlikely to be spontaneously pursued by individuals
left to their own devices, because Jesus's commands grated sharply against
ordinary human inclinations. Hence the importance of communities of faith
through which the virtues could be inculcated and in which joy would be
apparent, communities to which Christians would *want* to belong. But how
could those communities be fashioned without at least some exercise of
force, when necessary, given the recalcitrant desires of selfish individuals to
seek their own advantage and have their own way? It was the same medieval conundrum of *caritas* and coercion, but now in the context of a divided
Christendom among much more resolute confessionalizing regimes. Those
for whom Christianity seemed little more than obeying hated rules and
committing catechetical propositions to memory understandably hoped for
something better, a way of life that would dispense with resented impositions. Thus was the stage set for Enlightenment emancipation and the postu-
lation of Western modernity's autonomous individual selves. But how much
of the rest of Christianity, and in what forms, would be retained? By the
mid-seventeenth century, amid deadlocked doctrinal controversies and revivified Pyrrhonian skepticism, new options were being pursued that sought
to transcend disputed religious truth claims by endeavoring to base answers
to the Life Questions entirely on reason.

Western modernity was forged in the context of the unintended persistence of Christian pluralism and the failures of confessional rulers to
achieve their goals. Its central problem at the outset was different from that
of medieval Christendom, the Reformation, or confessional Europe: how
might human life be structured such that human beings could coexist in
peaceful stability and security even though they disagreed about God's
truth and were frequently hostile toward one another? The answer would
apparently have to include some (at least implicit) definition of "religion"
and a stipulation of this new thing's relationship to the rest of human life.
In the first half of the seventeenth century that strange neo-medieval polity,
the Dutch Republic, was to a significant extent practicing what would

become the modern answer before it was theorized. Especially in the maritime and mercantile province of Holland, a distinction was in effect being drawn between public and private life, and "religion"—understood largely as a matter of belief, worship, and devotion—was being individualized, privatized, and separated from political and economic life. So long as one obeyed the laws that provided for common security and stability, one could believe whatever one wished and worship in private however one pleased. Attracted by prospects of peace and a better life that contrasted so starkly with persecution for their faith, religious refugees poured into the Dutch Republic and contributed to its economic prosperity. In circumstances of relative religious toleration, the consequences of the Reformation's failed foundational principle grew clearer: without political authorities seeking to enforce specifically Reformed Protestant or Lutheran interpretations of scripture, the open-ended arbitrariness generated by *sola scriptura* and its supplements became more apparent, just as it was in England in the 1640s and had been in Germany and Switzerland in the 1520s. The same relatively tolerant Dutch attitude and latitude extended into higher education. Keeping its other faculties from being dominated by theology, the Dutch Republic's new institution in Leiden dispensed with confessional oaths, attracted star scholars, and within a generation of its founding in 1575 had become one of Europe's leading universities. Across confessional lines, most Dutch Christians understandably preferred the prospect of greater material prosperity to religio-political hostilities and their disruptions of human life, even if the pursuit of the goods life as though it were the good life was antithetical to the Gospel. Nevertheless, here was something about which, it seemed, nearly all people could agree notwithstanding their theological differences.

What the Dutch adumbrated was first institutionalized in the United States near the end of the eighteenth century among men and women more thoroughly inculturated to regard material acquisitiveness not as sinful avarice, but as benign self-interest and the providentially sanctioned path to individual happiness, societal prosperity, and national strength. By then the Dutch innovations had been well theorized. Self-consciously and institutionally, the American federal government would neither support nor permit an established church, but rather begin to undo the magisterial Reformation altogether. Provided they were politically quiescent and compliant, citizens could believe and proselytize for anything, at least within the limits that were in effect prescribed by the new nation's Protestant "moral establishment."[4] A politically protected individual right to freedom of religious belief and practice within the state's laws solved the European problem of confessional coercion, in part because of widely shared agreement about what "religion" was. It also provided a template for the articulation of other individual rights, which, when enforced, similarly protected specified human beings from abusive mistreatment. But only since the 1970s, nearly two centuries after the American and French Revolutions and more than two decades after the United Nations Universal Declaration of Human Rights, has the self-conscious protection of human beings via *human* rights *against* oppressive states spread around the world on the ruins of failed socialist revolutions, the demise of territorially imperialist Western colonialism, and the decolonization that followed the Second World War.[5] Nevertheless, considered as such and despite its restrictive intertwining with nationalist states for most of its history since the late eighteenth century, this spread of protective individual rights is perhaps the greatest outcome of modern Western liberalism, notwithstanding the still incomplete extension of human rights to women, children, ethnic minorities, and post-colonial peoples. Other impressive modern Western triumphs include the extraordinary progress of the natural sciences and their applications in medicine and manufacturing technologies that have made possible the flourishing of literally billions of human beings. These are great achievements, particularly when compared to Western modernity's fascist and communist regimes of the brutal twentieth century and the many millions of human lives that they destroyed.

Y ET THE SAME institutional arrangements that solved the central problem posed by the failure of confessional Europe created the conditions for the failure of Western modernity itself, which is now well under way in different respects. In order to see this, we have not only to consider simply and narrowly the problems that modern liberalism solved, but also what its institutional arrangements have facilitated in combination with other historical developments. A centrally important, paradoxical characteristic of modern liberalism is that it does not prescribe what citizens should believe, how they should live, or what they should care about, but it nonetheless depends for the social cohesion and political vitality of the regimes it informs on the voluntary acceptance of widely shared beliefs, values, and priorities that motivate people's actions. Otherwise liberal states have to become more legalistic and coercive in order to insure stability and security. In the West, many of those basic beliefs, values, and priorities—including self-discipline, self-denial, self-sacrifice, ethical responsibility for others, duty to one's community, commitment to one's spouse and children—derive most influentially in the modern Western world from Christianity and were shared across confessional lines in early modern Europe. Advanced secularization, precipitated partly by the capitalism and consumerism encouraged by liberal states, has considerably eroded them in the past several decades and thus placed increasing pressures on public life through the social frag-mentation and political apathy of increasing numbers of citizens who ex-ercise their rights to live for themselves and to ignore politics. This is one way in which modernity's failure is under way, a symptom of which is the constant stream of (thus far, ineffectual) proposals about how to reinvigo-rate democracy, restore public civility, get citizens to care about politics, and so forth. More abstractly but important in different ways, the ideo-logical secularism of the public sphere and the naturalist metaphysical as-sumptions of academic life, combined with the state of philosophy and the explanatory successes of the natural sciences, prevent the articulation of any intellectually persuasive warrant for believing in the realities presup-posed by liberal political discourse and the institutional arrangements of modernity: that there are such things as persons, and that they have such things as rights. Secularization and scientism are thus subverting moder-nity's most fundamental assumptions from within, developments that are facilitated by the same institutional arrangements of liberalism that solved early modern Europe's problem of religious coexistence.

Despite the political, military, and socio-moral failures of confessional Europe, neither Roman Catholicism nor Protestantism went away, whether in the eighteenth century or at any point since. Instead, they have persisted alongside and in complex interactions with secular ideologies, social reali-ties, and economic developments up to the present within the institutional protection afforded (and the control exercised) by modern liberal states. At the same time, the literally endless, back-and-forth non-dialogue of theological controversialists in the Reformation era was the springboard for the secularization of public discourse. Enduring doctrinal disagree-ments also problematized the epistemological status of theology compared to other sorts of knowledge, notwithstanding its privileged status in Reformation-era universities, academies, and seminaries. Thus were the seeds also sown, with the failures of confessional rulers to achieve their goals, for the eventual marginalization of theology, secularization of knowledge, and relativization of religious truth claims as such in public life. If any solutions to the issues about which Christians disagreed were going to be found, whether intellectually or institutionally, it seemed that they would have to be built on bases other than the ones in dispute among Christians. Otherwise one would still be caught in the maelstrom of doc-trinal controversy, arguing about the sacraments, the nature of the church, the interpretation of scripture, and so forth. Ironically, even the many be-liefs about which Catholics and the large majority of Protestants agreed—the trinitarian nature of the transcendent creator-God, the natural world as creation, the divinity of Jesus, his bodily resurrection, the reality of the

Holy Spirit, original sin, the necessity of faith for salvation, eternal judgment by God, scripture as the revealed word of God, and many aspects of Christian morality—were thereby set up for an exclusion from public discourse and a segregation from the realm of knowledge-making. A major reason for this secularizing exclusion was the tendency of early modern Protestants and Catholics to emphasize their points of difference rather than of commonality, precisely the opposite of what has characterized ecumenical efforts in the past half-century. Early modern doctrinal controversy seemed to dictate that reason alone, not scripture or the Holy Spirit or ecclesiastical authority, not God's actions in history however understood, would have to provide answers to the Life Questions, in an intellectual parallel to the ways in which Christianity was being disembedded from political and economic life beginning in the Dutch Republic. What other plausible options were there? Ever since the later seventeenth century, and seeking to transcend the problems of the Reformation era, Western modernity has banked intellectually on reason to deliver the goods.

The two most influential expressions of modern Western rationality have been foundationalist philosophy and the natural sciences, which were more closely related in the seventeenth century than they subsequently became. Modernity is failing partly because reason alone in modern philosophy has proven no more capable than scripture alone of discerning or devising consensually persuasive answers to the Life Questions. The natural sciences, on the other hand, have been an extraordinary success; but because of the self-imposed limitations that have *made* them so successful, by definition they can offer no answers to any of the Life Questions.

What remains in the absence of shared answers to the Life Questions is a hyperpluralism of divergent secular and religious truth claims in contemporary Western states, and of individuals pursuing their desires whatever they happen to be. The world in which all Europeans and North Americans are living today is a combination of hegemonic and hyperpluralistic realities, the former safeguarding and permitting the latter. Highly bureaucratized sovereign states wield a monopoly of public power in enforcing laws. The hegemonic cultural glue comes especially from all-pervasive capitalism and consumerism: scientific findings are applied in manufacturing technologies to make the stuff consumers want, whatever they want, heirs to the early modern Christians who made the industrious revolution that preceded and prepared the way for the Industrial Revolution. There is no shared, substantive common good, nor are there any realistic prospects for devising one (at least in the immediately foreseeable future). Nor does secular discourse offer any realistic prospects for rationally resolving any of the many contested moral or political issues that emerge from the increasingly wide range of ways in which individuals self-determine the good for themselves within liberalism's politically protected formal ethics of rights. Appeals to a Rawlsian "overlapping consensus" are akin to reminders of the fact that antagonistic Christians nevertheless continued to share many beliefs in common in the sixteenth century. Indeed they did. But it hardly conduced to their moral agreement or political cooperation.

As a result, public life today, perhaps especially in the United States, is increasingly riven by angry, uncivil rivals with incompatible views about what is good, true, and right. Many of these views and values are increasingly distant from substantive beliefs that derived most influentially from Christianity and that in the eighteenth and nineteenth centuries remained much more widely shared, notwithstanding inherited early modern confessional antagonisms. But the rejection of such answers to the Life Questions has led to the current Kingdom of Whatever partly because of the dissolution of the social relationships and communities that make more plausible those beliefs and their related human practices. Most visibly in recent decades, this dissolution owed and continues to owe much to the liquefying effects of capitalism and consumerism on the politically protected individuals within liberal states, as men and women in larger numbers prioritize the fulfillment of their self-chosen, acquisitive, individual desires above any social (including familial) solidarities except those they also happen to choose, and only for as long as they happen to choose them. Which means, of course, that the solidity of these social "solidarities" is better understood as liquidity, if not vaporosity. Nevertheless, these same liberal states continue to *depend* on the widely embraced pursuit of consumerist acquisitiveness to hold together the ideological hyperpluralism within their polities. Hence modernity is failing, too, because having accepted the redefinition of avarice as benign self-interest—a latter-day extension of early modern Christians' self-colonization by capitalism—it relies for cohesion on a naturalized acquisitiveness that simultaneously undermines *other* shared beliefs, common values, and social relationships on which the sustainability of liberal states also depends. And this cultural contradiction of capitalism stands quite apart from what else seems very likely: that ever greater levels of consumption are contributing to global climate change in potentially dangerous ways, another unintended consequence of the political protection of individual rights within modern liberal states (and of burgeoning consumption by citizens in illiberal states, too, as in the case now of China).

But is philosophy really failing with respect to the Life Questions? In ways analogous to Protestantism and on its own terms, the evidence suggests that it has already failed. Those who dispute this might revisit the historical evidence and survey the state of contemporary philosophy. Considering the practical problems posed by deadlocked doctrinal controversy in the Reformation era, modern philosophers beginning with Descartes understandably sought to articulate universal truths based on reason alone, without reference to authority or tradition. By the late twentieth century, there was every indication that this ambition had been a long-lived albeit profoundly influential washout. Instead of discovering or devising rationally demonstrated answers to questions about God, metaphysics, morality, human nature, or human priorities, or even offering any evidence of convergence toward such answers, modern philosophers replicated in a rationalist key the unintended, open-ended, apparently irresolvable pluralism of Protestantism. Those who carry on in the same tradition continue to do so. There is nothing remotely resembling agreement or convergence among contemporary philosophers about what is true, what reason prescribes, what their discipline's starting point or assumptions ought to be, what philosophy's most important problems are and priorities should be, or by what methods philosophers should or could try to resolve their disagreements. Based on the evidence of the past four centuries and the state of contemporary philosophy, the rational conclusion is that reason alone has failed as a means by which to discover or devise the truth about the nature of reality, morality, what human beings should care about, and how they should live. Despite high hopes for its success since the seventeenth century, modern philosophy has foundered in its central ambition. It sought universal, rationally demonstrable truth, but has produced instead an open-ended welter of preferential, ultimately arbitrary truth claims. The implications extend much further than philosophy as such because of the pervasive influence of modern philosophical ideas about human nature and reality, often uncritically taken for granted, throughout the social scientific and humanistic disciplines. At the same time, the demise of modern philosophy has left considerable skeptical detritus in its wake, with many academics inferring relativism from pluralism and asserting the truth claim that all "truths" about matters of morality and meaning are contingent and constructed. After a centuries-long modern interlude, this is a postmodern reappearance of the early modern skepticism that Descartes and other thinkers sought to overcome: Montaigne *redivivus,* but now without recourse to custom in the Kingdom of Whatever.

The modern natural sciences, on the other hand, have been and continue to be an astonishing success, nowhere more obviously than in their technological applications and never more so than in the past half century. From Copernicus through Galileo to Newton and beyond, most early modern investigators of nature's regularities understood themselves to be discovering the rationality with which God had imbued his creation. But it turned out that whether the natural world was God's creation or not, the explanation of those regularities did not depend on theology or morality and was intellectually separable from them via amoral methodological naturalism. By deliberately setting aside the Life Questions and any questions of value, meaning, morality, purpose, or teleology strictly in favor of efforts to explain natural phenomena, scientists have produced and continue to produce ever greater, cumulative, specialized knowledge of the natural world in their respective domains of inquiry, Kuhnian protestations notwithstanding. Besides its countless contributions to human flourishing, the application of scientific findings has also contributed to untold destruction and human suffering, especially in the past century. Nor is this surprising, because science itself does not prescribe nor can it even suggest whether, how, or to what ends its findings should be applied. These are moral issues, about which the findings of science per se can say nothing. But moral questions are vigorously contested and incapable of rational resolution not only within the narrow scope of modern moral philosophy, but more broadly within the wider society's hyperpluralism that is protected and incubated by modern liberal states. Science enables human beings to do increasingly extraordinary things in manipulating the natural world, but says nothing and can say nothing about what we should do or why we should do it. It is definitionally amoral. Yet power is overwhelmingly concentrated in the hands of political leaders and the wealthy, who are thus in a position to enact their moral preferences through the technological applications of science in disproportionately influential ways.

Modern reason in its two most influential expressions is therefore a schizophrenically mixed bag: philosophy has dramatically failed, but science has spectacularly succeeded. One consequence is that the ever-expanding technological capacities afforded by scientific advances are set within an increasingly rancorous culture of moral disagreement and political contestation. If not necessarily a failure of modernity per se, this fact certainly contributes to its volatility and potential for man-made catastrophes on scales inconceivable in the preindustrial world. Another consequence of modern reason's schizophrenia goes to the root of modernity's inability to justify intellectually some of its most basic moral, political, and legal assumptions. Not that this inability has yet been widely recognized. But the exclusion in the secularized academy of any religious claims or metaphysical assumptions besides naturalism has eliminated any possibility of justifying the belief that members of the species *Homo sapiens* are persons, or that rights are real. There are certainly no grounds for thinking that rights are *natural,* rooted in nature as many Enlightenment theorists claimed, given all that biological and medical research has disclosed about human bodies. Never in any anatomical investigation or surgical procedure or lab test on any human being has any evidence for any rights been discovered. Nor has a shred of dignity been detected or any value been measured. Nor indeed has a person ever been observed. The persistent, even adamant, positing of rights has no evidentiary basis given the metaphysical assumptions and epistemological demands that govern not only the natural sciences, but knowledge-making across the disciplines in the academy. Thus the fundamental categories at the basis of Western modernity's most influentially institutionalized philosophy—liberalism—cannot be rationally legitimated on the terms of the scientistic naturalism that prevails in research universities and in the public sphere. Those who regard this as a pseudo-problem easily resolved by reference to an allegedly shared, intuitive, commonsensical understanding of what it means to be a person should consider more carefully the unresolved disagreements about abortion. Transhumanists, with their biogenetic aspirations to hasten a post-human future for today's descendants of *Homo sapiens,* understand much more clearly that "persons" and "rights" no less than "dignity" are fictions if metaphysical naturalism is true.

Rights and dignity can be real only if human beings are more than biological matter. The modern secular discourse on human rights depends on retaining in some fashion—but without acknowledging—the belief that every human being is created in the image and likeness of God, a notion that could be rooted in nature so long as nature was regarded as creation, whether overtly recognized as such or not. But if nature is not creation, then there are no creatures, and human beings are just one more species that happened randomly to evolve, no more "endowed by their creator with certain unalienable rights" than is any other bit of matter-energy. Then there simply are no rights, just as there are no persons, and no theorizing can conjure them into existence. The intellectual foundations of modernity are failing because its governing metaphysical assumptions in combination with the findings of the natural sciences offer no warrant for believing its most basic moral, political, and legal claims.

I WISH THIS BOOK could have had a happier ending. But that would have happened only if the world in which we are living today were different. And our present world would be different only if the past had not been what it was, because the past made the present what it is. At the outset of the twentieth century Lenin asked, "What is to be done?" His answers turned out to be disastrous. I am not among those who believe in comprehensive blueprints for human social engineering backed by political power. That has tended not to go so well, especially in the past century.

Nor do I have any illusions about what academic books can achieve in light of the powers that rule the world. Intellectuals per se have only their arguments, not billions of dollars in capital or arsenals of sophisticated military weaponry. Still, if the analysis of this book is near the mark, some things might be done in the small world of higher education and research universities, on its terms and yet in ways that could (and in terms of what is intellectually justified, should) shift some of its assumptions.

Zygmunt Bauman has recently written that "for the past two or three centuries since that great leap to human autonomy and self-management variously called 'Enlightenment' or 'the advent of the modern era,' history has run in a direction no one planned, no one anticipated, and no one wished it to take." That seems incontestable. He adds: "What makes this course so astonishing and such a challenge to our understanding is that these two to three centuries started with the human resolve to take history under human administration and control—deploying for that purpose reason, believed to be the most powerful among human weapons (indeed, a flawless human facility to know, to predict, to calculate, and so to raise the 'is' to the level of the 'ought')—and were filled throughout with zealous and ingenious human effort to act on that resolve."[6] But what if that faith in reason alone, however it appeared to many protagonists in the Enlightenment, was actually a major misstep rather than the progressive panacea it appeared to be? If this were true, it might change one's historical perspective considerably. Rather than being astonished and confronted with "such a challenge to our understanding," we might instead have discovered something that would explain much about the course of Western history since the mid-seventeenth century. Yet by itself such a hypothesis, even if it were true, would still be incomplete, because its chronological compass would be insufficient to explain the character of the present world in which we are living.

Not only present-day champions of the Enlightenment and its legacy but also the large majority of postmodern critics of modernity and the Enlightenment assume a supersessionist notion of history. They presume we can account for the Western world as it is today by largely ignoring the Reformation era and the Middle Ages, which belong, so they think, to a premodern past that was ostensibly transcended and left behind beginning in the seventeenth and eighteenth centuries. Enlightenment reason having now failed, so the thinking goes among its postmodern critics, we are left only with skeptical shards and individualistic *bricolage*. This book has sought to show both that such supersessionist assumptions are mistaken and that their correlative, allegedly unavoidable skeptical conclusions are by no means necessary. It has also sought to show something of why this is so. The world Westerners are living in today cannot be understood without seeing the deep ways in which it is an unintended extension and continuation of late medieval and Reformation-era developments that are not dead and gone, but remain influential in the early twenty-first century. Nor are the only intellectually viable options today the rationalist or skeptical ones circumscribed by metaphysical naturalism. But these are the only sorts permitted in the secularized academy.

The genealogical analysis presented here provides the intellectual basis for an interpretation of Western modernity and the ways in which it is failing that differs from the diagnoses of postmodern secular critics. It also differs from the ongoing efforts of those secular believers who seek to defend and somehow salvage Enlightened modernity's beleaguered presuppositions. To be sure, modern Western liberalism solved the serious problem of religio-political disruption in early modern Europe, and modern Western states extended religious liberty and other individual rights in ways that were not true of early modern confessional regimes. But the failure of modern philosophy to provide a convincing rational substitute for religion with respect to the Life Questions suggests that there is no reason to believe modern claims about the supersessionist triumph of secular reason over religion per se. On the contrary, the failure strongly implies that philosophical efforts to contrive a universal, self-sufficient, rational replacement for religion, for all their historical intelligibility and desirability in the context of early modern Christian doctrinal controversies, were self-deceived from the outset, and that those intellectuals who continue today to carry on likewise are engaged in a similarly self-deceived enterprise. At the same time, the rejection of historical supersessionism as a mistaken view of Western history since the Middle Ages permits a candid recognition of the fact that intellectually sophisticated expressions of religious worldviews exist today as part of Western hyperpluralism. They have not been "left behind" or "overturned" by "modernity" or "reason." They have been institutionally excluded and ideologically denounced, not disproven. Their dismissal out of hand by most scholars seems less a function of familiarity with relevant intellectual realities than of the fact that secular research universities have banished theology from among the academic disciplines, permitting most scholars to pretend as though intellectually serious theology, philosophy of religion, and nonskeptical yet historicist biblical scholarship do not exist. But they do. And perhaps some religious truth claims really are true, and maybe their rejection helps to explain both why Western history has unfolded as it has in the past half millennium and why modernity is now failing. Perhaps the baby of religion, once invented to cope with the unwanted and unintended effects of the Reformation, has been rashly thrown out with the bathwater of its past political perversions and social failures.

The natural world investigated by the sciences has always been and continues to be understood by Jews, Christians, and Muslims as God's creation. Modern science is widely thought to have falsified this notion or at least made it utterly implausible to the well educated. But as the contemporary social fact of intellectually sophisticated religious believers demonstrates, it has not, it need not, and this is not what happened historically. Rather, Reformation-era theological disagreements rendered newly important in the seventeenth century the widespread metaphysical univocity inherited from the late Middle Ages, which reinforced the default influence of ordinary linguistic grammar on discourse about God. Neo-Scotist univocity plus Occam's razor as it was applied to an either-or understanding of "natural" and "supernatural" are still widely (if unself-consciously) assumed and taken for granted today. This explains the common category mistake among the theologically ill-informed that God, if real, must be some sort of entity "out there" in the universe and must be discoverable through the empirical methods of scientific investigation. Most of those who unknowingly conflate their metaphysical assumptions with the findings of the natural sciences regard the relationship between science and religion as a competitive, zero-sum game. Thus they confuse success in explaining natural regularities with the allegedly diminished plausibility of the claims of any and all revealed religions. In fact, any and all possible discoveries of the natural sciences are compatible with the reality of a transcendent creator-God understood in non-univocal terms, whether in Judaism, Christianity, or Islam. It is unsurprising that this recognition is not widely understood, given the sociological fact that most scholars and scientists tend to be notably (but explicably) lacking in theological sophistication and self-awareness of their own metaphysical beliefs.

Contrary to widespread assumptions, the findings of the natural sciences accordingly provide no legitimate intellectual grounds for an a priori exclusion of all religious truth claims from academic discourse. It all depends on what the claims are. In practical moral terms, however, eliminating any consideration of a creator-God who will judge human beings means unburdening human life of restrictions on human desires. *That* is important. It protects our hyperpluralism from the unbearably invasive claim that some widely held beliefs and widely enacted behaviors might be objectively detrimental to human flourishing as such, indeed from the similarly outrageous implication that there is such a thing as "human flourishing as such" to which anything could be "objectively detrimental." Such notions are intolerable. So "God" (for those who choose to be religious believers) can only be what individuals individually want "God" to be. That way, "God" cannot cause trouble and we can each individually get on with our lives as we please within the state's institutions and legal stipulations. This line of thought suggests one important reason for wanting to keep religious discourse out of the public sphere and the secularized academy: it protects one sort of substantive challenge to late Western modernity's core ideology of the liberated and autonomous self. No matter what, each neo-Protagorean individual must be the sovereign of his or her own Cartesianized universe, determining his or her own truths, making his or her own meanings, and following his or her own desires. This is a non-negotiable sine qua non of Western modernity in its current forms. It is also a major reason why it is failing.

The processes by which theology and the consideration of religious truth claims were excluded from universities between the late eighteenth and the early twentieth centuries made sense at the time. Few theologians possessed the intellectual wherewithal to engage with the burgeoning findings of the emergent academic disciplines within modern research universities, and those who did tended to assume uncritically the unavoidability of a post-Kantian philosophical framework, itself premised on a strictly deterministic Newtonian universe of invariable natural laws from which the possibility of miracles had been excluded. In addition, many religious claims *were* made in nineteenth-century academic settings with nonchalant complacency, and thus deserved to be excluded from institutions devoted to the pursuit of knowledge in the absence of serious arguments about why such claims belonged. Moreover, in the nineteenth century it seemed to many learned observers not only that the natural sciences *and* philosophy were progressive, but that both were helping progressively to pave the high road to human happiness through the beneficent spread of global civilization with a colonizing Western face. Then came the twentieth century.

Our situation now is different, with the intellectual tables turned. Now some intellectually sophisticated postmodern critics who are religious believers have gotten behind and underneath modernity's secularist assumptions and offered explanatorily powerful interpretations of their implications. The governing modern ideology of liberalism is failing in multiple respects. It lacks the intellectual resources to resolve any real-life moral disagreements, to provide any substantive social cohesion, or even to justify its most basic assumptions. In a reversal of the situation common in the nineteenth century, now it is many secular academics who tend to be uncritically complacent about the historical genesis of and intellectual grounds for their beliefs, oblivious of what Steven Smith has recently exposed as their "smuggling" of premises and assumptions insupportable within naturalist assumptions.[7] Therefore, consistent with the academy's commitments to the open pursuit of intellectual inquiry without ideological restrictions, to critical rationality, to the importance of rethinking and reconsidering, to the questioning of assumptions, to academic freedom, and motivated by the desire to shed light on our current problems and to seek more fruitful ways to address them, the contemporary academy should unsecularize itself. It should become less ideologically narrow and closed-minded, opening up the Weberian "iron cage of secular discourse."[8] Those who bring religious perspectives to bear must be prepared to argue for their claims in intellectually coherent ways and based on knowledge of the assumptions and findings of the academic disciplines with which they engage. But the a priori exclusion of religious truth claims from research universities is no longer intellectually justifiable and might well be closing off potentially important avenues for addressing some of our many contemporary problems.

Unsecularizing the academy would require, of course, an intellectual openness on the part of scholars and scientists sufficient to end the long-standing modern charade in which naturalism has been assumed to be demonstrated, evident, self-evident, ideologically neutral, or something arrived at on the basis of impartial inquiry. It would require all academics—not only those with religious commitments—to acknowledge their metaphysical beliefs as beliefs rather than to keep pretending that naturalist beliefs are something more or skeptical beliefs are something else. The secularization of knowledge was a historically contingent process that derives from the religious disagreements of the Reformation era, even though it has been for a century or so an ideological imperialism masquerading as an intellectual inevitability. Future scholars and scientists are socialized into its assumptions as they pass through its institutionalized portal in the graduate schools of research universities. Facing up to these things is bound to be unnerving and is sure to be resisted, because confronting challenges to cherished beliefs and seemingly settled assumptions is rarely a cause for comfort.

Preferential "usable pasts" aside, the actual past made the real present in which we are living. It continues to affect us whether or not we understand how. And the abiding influence of the Reformation era on the real present cannot be understood unless supersessionist conceptions of history are corrected and conventional historical periodization is challenged. For all the putative encouragement of original thought in the academy, in fact we are generally expected to accept the scholarly division of labor we have inherited and the assumptions that govern it. Subversive ideas and unsettling research that threaten seemingly settled foundational assumptions are just as likely to be welcomed now as they were in the late Middle Ages—that is, not at all. Along with other scholars in their respective disciplines and specializations, we are supposed to stick to established genres, cleave to discretely circumscribed intellectual goals, and follow well-established methods. These are different things: to study the distant past, to show how the distant past continues to inform the present, to explore the intellectual formation of the assumptions that govern historical inquiry, to analyze central problems of the contemporary Western world, and to critique the presuppositions within which modern knowledge across the disciplines is pursued and transmitted. But aren't all these things parts of a single complex story?

# Abbreviations

| | |
|---|---|
| CO | John Calvin. *Joannis Calvini opera quae supersunt omnia* |
| CR | *Corpus Reformatorum* |
| HUE | *History of the University in Europe* |
| MQR | *Mennonite Quarterly Review* |
| ODNB | *Oxford Dictionary of National Biography* |
| QGT | *Quellen zur Geschichte der Täufer* |
| QGTS | *Quellen zur Geschichte der Täufer in der Schweiz* |
| STC, 1475–1640 | *A Short Title Catalogue of Books Printed in England, Ireland, Scotland, and Wales, 1475–1640.* 2nd ed. 3 vols. Ed. A. W. Pollard, G. R. Redgrave, et al. London: Bibliographical Society, 1976–1991 |
| WA | Martin Luther. *D. Martin Luthers Werke. Kritische Gesamtausgabe* |
| ZW | Huldrych Zwingli. *Huldreich Zwinglis Sämtliche Werke* |

# Notes

## Introduction

1. William Faulkner, *Requiem for a Nun* (New York: Random House, 1950), p. 92.
2. One medieval historian whose notice this history did not escape is Philippe Buc, who has seen the importance of Reformation-era Protestant critiques of Catholic sacramentality and ritual for twentieth-century anthropological theories of religion. See pt. 2 of Buc, *The Dangers of Ritual: Between Early Medieval Texts and Social Scientific Theory* (Princeton, N.J.: Princeton University Press, 2001), pp. 161–261.
3. Brad S. Gregory, *Salvation at Stake: Christian Martyrdom in Early Modern Europe* (Cambridge, Mass., and London: Harvard University Press, 1999), p. 352.
4. Daniel Lord Smail, Introduction to "History and the Telescoping of Time: A Disciplinary Forum," *French Historical Studies* 34:1 (2011): 5.
5. I am grateful to Kerrie McCaw for suggesting this analogy.
6. Friedrich Nietzsche, *Der Antichrist* [1895], in Nietzsche, *Werke: Kritische Gesamtausgabe*, ed. Giorgio Colli and Mazzino Montinari, pt. 6, vol. 3 (Berlin: Walter de Gruyter, 1969), p. 177/12–13 (emphasis in original). Nietzsche wrote the work in late 1888.
7. Albert O. Hirschman, *The Passions and the Interests: Political Arguments for Capitalism before Its Triumph* (Princeton, N.J.: Princeton University Press, 1977).
8. Alasdair MacIntyre, *After Virtue: A Study in Moral Theory*, 3rd ed. (Notre Dame, Ind.: University of Notre Dame Press, 2006).

9. Amos Funkenstein, *Theology and the Scientific Imagination from the Middle Ages to the Seventeenth Century* (Princeton, N.J.: Princeton University Press, 1986). Because the so-called New Atheists see no connection, they fail to understand the source or character of their own metaphysical commitments. As Richard Dawkins has recently pronounced, oblivious of the irony of his own words: "I would happily have forgone bestsellerdom if there had been the slightest hope of Duns Scotus illuminating my central question of whether God exists." Dawkins, *The God Delusion* (2006; Boston and New York: Mariner Books, 2008), p. 14. For a critique of the New Atheists' unawareness of how their antireligious beliefs depend on metaphysical univocity, see Brad S. Gregory, "Science versus Religion? The Insights and Oversights of the 'New Atheists,'" *Logos: A Journal of Catholic Thought and Culture* 12:4 (2009): 31–36.

10. Funkenstein, *Theology*, pp. 25–31.

11. Another innovative analysis that to some extent resembles their approach is Buc's *longue-durée* intellectual history of ritual in part 2 of his *Dangers of Ritual*.

12. Michel Foucault, *Discipline and Punish: The Birth of the Prison*, trans. Alan Sheridan (1977; Harmondsworth, U.K.: Penguin, 1979), p. 31.

13. Max Weber, *Die protestantische Ethik und der "Geist" des Kapitalismus* [1904/5], ed. Klaus Lichtblau and Johannes Weiß, 3rd ed. (1993; Weinheim: Beltz Athenäum, 2000).

14. Smail, Introduction to "History and the Telescoping of Time," pp. 1–2.

15. Peter Laslett, *The World We Have Lost: England before the Industrial Age*, 3rd ed. (New York: Scribner's, 1984).

16. Peter Fritzsche, *Stranded in the Present: Modern Time and the Melancholy of History* (Cambridge, Mass., and London: Harvard University Press, 2004). A similar conception of a sharp caesura is common among Americans and some American historians, prone to accepting too readily a discourse about the extent to which the United States constituted in the late eighteenth century a dramatic departure from its British (and more broadly, European) past, a discourse that began in the 1770s and has never disappeared.

17. Max Weber, "Wissenschaft als Beruf" [1919], in Weber, *Gesamtausgabe*, Abteilung I: *Schriften und Reden*, vol. 17, ed. Wolfgang J. Mommsen and Wolfgang Schluchter with Birgitt Morgenbrod (Tübingen: J. C. B. Mohr, 1992), p. 80/15–17.

18. "Specialists read manuscripts in advance of publication. They review books, comment on conference sessions, and provide external tenure and promotion evaluations. Scholars have learned how important it is to appease their specialist colleagues. In this way, the inflationary spiral of research overproduction is joined by a different sort of spiral, one that screws in toward ever smaller subjects. Thanks to the geochronological fields by which history has been framed since the rise of nations, this has meant increasingly narrow time bands." Smail, Introduction to "History and the Telescoping of Time," pp. 5–6.

19. Charles Taylor, *A Secular Age* (Cambridge, Mass., and London: Belknap Press of Harvard University Press, 2007), p. 29.

20. For the insight that "*Chronos* is not *Zeitgeist*," see the introduction to Candida R. Moss, *Ancient Christian Martyrdom: Diverse Practices, Theologies, and Traditions* (New Haven, Conn., and London: Yale University Press, forthcoming). I am grateful to Professor Moss for discussion on this and many related issues, and for sharing her manuscript with me in advance of its publication.

21. Hans Blumenberg, *The Legitimacy of the Modern Age*, trans. Robert M. Wallace (Cambridge, Mass., and London: MIT Press, 1985). For a concise analysis of Blumenberg's (and Reinhart Koselleck's) efforts to defend the ideological and historical autonomy of modernity over against the Middle Ages, religion, and theology, in opposition to the arguments of Carl Schmitt, Walter Benjamin, and Karl Löwith, see Kathleen Davis, *Periodization and Sovereignty: How Ideas of Feudalism and Secularization Govern the Politics of Time* (Philadelphia: University of Pennsylvania Press, 2008), pp. 77–95.

22. Jacques Barzun, *From Dawn to Decadence: 500 Years of Western Cultural Life, 1500 to the Present* (New York: HarperCollins, 2000), pp. 773–802, quotation on 798; for a list of the four parts, see the table of contents on p. [vii].

23. Andrew Delbanco, *The Real American Dream: A Meditation on Hope* (Cambridge, Mass., and London: Harvard University Press, 1999), pp. 107, 114. Suggestively and commendably, however, Delbanco cautions against overly sharp schemes of periodization, noting in particular that "the history of ideas is usually better understood as a process of incorporation and transformation than as a series of successive movements discrete and distinct from one another." Ibid., 111–112, quotation on 112.

24. Taylor, *Secular Age*, pp. 19–21, 37–42. The implicit view of history and historical change in *A Secular Age* seems to reflect Taylor's earlier work on Hegel. See Taylor, *Hegel* (Cambridge: Cambridge University Press, 1975).

25. Friedrich Nietzsche, *Götzen-Dämmerung* [1889], in Nietzsche, *Werke*, ed. Colli and Montinari, pt. 6, vol. 3, p. 80/30–32.

26. See, for example, John Rawls, *Political Liberalism*, expanded ed. (1993; New York: Columbia University Press, 2005); Amy Gutmann and Dennis Thompson, *Democracy and Disagreement* (Cambridge, Mass., and London: Belknap Press of Harvard University Press, 1996); Frances Moore Lappé, *Democracy's Edge: Choosing to Save Our Country by Bringing Democracy to Life* (San Francisco: Jossey Bass, 2006); Ronald Dworkin, *Is Democracy Possible Here? Principles for a New Political Debate* (Princeton, N.J.: Princeton University Press, 2006); Alan Wolfe, *The Future of Liberalism* (New York: Knopf, 2009).

27. Taylor, *Secular Age*, p. 14 (my emphasis). For a critique of Taylor's philosophical presuppositions and the ways in which they adversely affect his conceptualization of historical change and characterization of the present, see Peter E. Gordon, "The Place of the Sacred in the Absence of God: Charles Taylor's *A Secular Age*," *Journal of the History of Ideas* 69 (2008): 647–673, esp. 666–673.

28. Karl Marx, *Der achtzehnte Brumaire des Louis Bonaparte* [1852], in Karl Marx and Friedrich Engels, *Gesamtausgabe*, Abteilung I: *Texte*, vol. 11 (Berlin:

Dietz Verlag, 1985), pp. 96/23–97/1: "Die menschen machen ihre eigene Geschichte, aber sie machen sie nicht aus freien Stücken unter selbstgewählten, sondern unter unmittelbar vorhandenen, gegebenen und überlieferten Umständen."

29. On the inherently ideological and political character of historical periodization, especially the deeply ingrained contrast between "medieval/religious/feudal and modern/secular/capitalist," see Davis, *Periodization and Sovereignty* (quotation on p. 2).

30. For the second quoted phrase, see Glenn W. Olsen, *The Turn to Transcendence: The Role of Religion in the Twenty-First Century* (Washington, D.C.: Catholic University of America Press, 2010), p. 34.

31. For Stein's philosophical education prior to her conversion, see Alasdair MacIntyre, *Edith Stein: A Philosophical Prologue, 1913–1922* (Lanham, Md.: Rowman & Littlefield, 2006); for Anscombe, see Jenny Teichman, "Anscombe, (Gertrude) Elizabeth Margaret (1919–2001)," in *ODNB*, online ed., ed. Lawrence Goldman (Oxford: Oxford University Press, 2005), http://www.oxforddnb.com/view/article/75032 (accessed 18 March 2010); for the exchange between Habermas and Ratzinger, see Jürgen Habermas and Joseph Ratzinger, *The Dialectics of Secularization: On Reason and Religion,* ed. Florian Schuller, trans. Brian McNeil (San Francisco: Ignatius Press, 2006).

32. For "lumpers" and "splitters," see J. H. Hexter, "The Historical Method of Christopher Hill," in Hexter, *On Historians: Reappraisals of Some of the Masters of Modern History* (Cambridge, Mass.: Harvard University Press, 1979), pp. 241–251. Having sought and been unable to locate the source of Le Roy Ladurie's well-known contrast between these two sorts of historians, I take heart from this remark by John Elliott: "After searching through Professor Le Roy Ladurie's writings for this reference, and failing to find the hoped-for truffle, I eventually appealed to the author for help. He, too, does not know where he published it, but assures me that I can safely attribute it to him." Elliott, "Reconstructing the Past," in *Useful Knowledge: The American Philosophical Society Millennium Program,* ed. Alexander G. Bearn (Philadelphia: American Philosophical Society, 1999), p. 191 n. 9.

33. For some recent contributions to the debate about whether the disagreements and divisions are aptly described as a "culture war," including the distinction between the rhetoric of politicians and pundits in contrast to the attitudes and behaviors of most Americans, see *Cultural Wars in American Politics: Critical Reviews of a Popular Myth,* ed. Rhys H. Williams (New York: Aldine de Gruyter, 1997); Nolan T. McCarty, Keith T. Poole, and Howard Rosenthal, *Polarized America: The Dance of Ideology and Riches* (Cambridge, Mass., and London: MIT Press, 2006); James Davison Hunter and Alan Wolfe, *Is There a Culture War? A Dialogue on Values and American Public Life* (Washington, D.C.: Brookings Institution Press, 2006); and Morris P. Fiorina with Samuel J. Abrams and Jeremy C. Pope, *Culture War? The Myth of a Polarized America,* 3rd ed. (Boston: Longman/Pearson, 2011).

34. Daniel Bell, "Afterword: 1996," in *The Cultural Contradictions of Capitalism* (1976; New York: Basic Books, 1996), p. 315.

35. Anthony Grafton, "A Sketch Map of a Lost Continent: The Republic of Letters," in Grafton, *Worlds Made of Words: Scholarship and Community in the Modern West* (Cambridge, Mass., and London: Harvard University Press, 2009), p. 16.

36. Jürgen Habermas, *The Theory of Communicative Action,* trans. Thomas McCarthy, 2 vols. (Boston: Beacon Press, 1984); Rawls, *Political Liberalism;* Amy Gutmann and Dennis Thompson, *Why Deliberative Democracy?* (Princeton, N.J.: Princeton University Press, 2004).

37. Diana Mutz, *Hearing the Other Side: Deliberative versus Participatory Democracy* (Cambridge: Cambridge University Press, 2006), p. 3.

38. Bill Bishop, *The Big Sort: Why the Clustering of Like-Minded Americans Is Tearing Us Apart* (Boston: Houghton Mifflin, 2008).

39. Peter W. Cookson Jr. and Caroline Hodges Persell, *Preparing for Power: America's Elite Boarding Schools* (New York: Basic Books, 1985); Jonathan Kozol, *The Shame of the Nation: The Restoration of Apartheid Schooling in America* (New York: Crown Publishers, 2005); Michael W. Apple, "The Cultural Politics of Home Schooling," *Peabody Journal of Education* 75 (2000): 256–271; Kurt J. Bauman, *Home Schooling in the United States: Trends and Characteristics,* Working Papers Series 53 (Washington, D.C.: U.S. Census Bureau, Population Division, 2001).

40. On the latter point, see the essays in *A Republic Divided,* ed. Annenberg Democracy Project (Oxford: Oxford University Press, 2007).

41. See Mary Ann Glendon, *Rights Talk: The Impoverishment of Political Discourse* (New York: Free Press, 1991).

42. Among numerous studies, see the huge compilation of data by the Intergovernmental Panel on Climate Change, *Climate Change 2007: The Physical Science Basis* (Cambridge: Cambridge University Press, 2007); Ross Gelbspan, *Boiling Point: How Politicians, Big Oil and Coal, Journalists, and Activists Have Fueled a Climate Crisis—And What We Can Do to Avert Disaster* (New York: Basic Books, 2004); Elizabeth Kolbert, *Field Notes from a Catastrophe: Man, Nature, and Climate Change* (New York: Bloomsbury, 2006); John Houghton, *Global Warming: The Complete Briefing,* 4th ed. (Cambridge: Cambridge University Press, 2009). For a historical perspective on the gradually emergent realization of global warming over the past century, see Spencer R. Weart, *The Discovery of Global Warming* (Cambridge, Mass., and London: Harvard University Press, 2004).

43. N. Gregory Mankiw, *Principles of Economics,* 5th ed. (Mason, Ohio: Cengage Learning, 2008), pp. 12–13. "In 1900, per capita income (in 1999 dollars) was $4,200; it was about $33,700 in 1999." Donald M. Fisk, "American Labor in the 20th Century," Compensation and Working Conditions (Fall 2001), Bureau of Labor Statistics, U.S. Bureau of Labor, http://www.bls.gov/opub/cwc/cm20030124ar02p1.htm, citing U.S. Council of Economic Advisors, 2000, *Economic Report to the President, 2000* (Washington, D.C.: U.S. Government

Printing Office, 2000), p. 279 (accessed 21 January 2010). For a broader discussion, see also Stanley Lebergott, *Pursuing Happiness: American Consumers in the Twentieth Century* (Princeton, N.J.: Princeton University Press, 1993).

44. On the relationship between consumerism and individual identity in "liquid modern" society, see Zygmunt Bauman, *Does Ethics Have a Chance in a World of Consumers?* (Cambridge, Mass., and London: Harvard University Press, 2008), pp. 157–188.

45. For a few examples of the lifestyle among the richest 1 percent of Americans (who own approximately 40 percent of the country's financial wealth), see Christopher Tennant, *The Official Filthy Rich Handbook* (New York: Workman Publishing, 2008); Robert Frank, *Richistan: A Journey through the American Wealth Boom and the Lives of the New Rich* (New York: Three Rivers Press, 2008); George Irvin, *Super Rich: The Rise of Income Inequality in Britain and the United States* (Cambridge: Polity Press, 2008).

46. Candace Jackson, "The $60 Million Dream House," *Wall Street Journal*, 7 January 2011, pp. D1–D2.

47. See, for example, Gary S. Becker, *The Economic Approach to Human Behavior* (Chicago: University of Chicago Press, 1978), pp. 5–14.

48. See Richard Layard, *Happiness: Lessons from a New Science* (New York: Penguin, 2005); Peter C. Whybrow, *American Mania: When More Is Not Enough* (New York: W. W. Norton, 2005); Tim Kasser, *The High Price of Materialism* (Cambridge, Mass., and London: MIT Press, 2002), esp. pp. 5–22; David G. Myers, *The American Paradox: Spiritual Hunger in an Age of Plenty* (New Haven, Conn., and London: Yale University Press, 2000), pp. 126–160; James B. Twitchell, *Living It Up: America's Love Affair with Luxury* (New York: Simon & Schuster, 2002).

49. For a more optimistic view about the ways in which global warming will supposedly force a radical change in human consumption and usher in an environmentally sustainable, better future, see Paul Gilding, *The Great Disruption: Why the Climate Crisis Will Bring On the End of Shopping and the Birth of a New World* (New York: Bloomsbury Press, 2011).

50. Jan de Vries, *The Industrious Revolution: Consumer Behavior and the Household Economy, 1650 to the Present* (Cambridge: Cambridge University Press, 2008), p. ix.

51. Steven Weinberg, *Facing Up: Science and Its Cultural Adversaries* (Cambridge, Mass., and London: Harvard University Press, 2001), pp. 120, 47.

52. See, for example, Simon Young, *Designer Evolution: A Transhumanist Manifesto* (New York: Prometheus, 2006).

53. For a penetrating analysis of the wide-ranging implications of the reduction of all moral assertions to human preferences and conventions, see John M. Rist, *Real Ethics: Rethinking the Foundations of Morality* (Cambridge: Cambridge University Press, 2002).

54. John T. Noonan Jr., *Persons and Masks of the Law: Cardozo, Holmes, Jefferson, and Wythe as Makers of the Masks* (New York: Farrar, Straus and Giroux, 1976), p. 28.

## 1. Excluding God

1. Max Weber, "Wissenschaft als Beruf" [1919], in Weber, *Gesamtausgabe, Abteilung I: Schriften und Reden,* vol. 17, ed. Wolfgang J. Mommsen and Wolfgang Schluchter with Birgitt Morgenbrod (Tübingen: J. C. B. Mohr, 1992), pp. 86/21–23, 87/4–7, 91/11–12, 92/4–15, 93/2–3, 107–110. On the (controversy concerning the) dating of the work's composition, see ibid., "Einleitung," pp. 43–46.

2. Edward Larson and Larry Witham, "Leading Scientists Still Reject God," *Nature* 394 (1998): 313. Although Neil Gross and Solon Simmons found that 51.5 percent of American professors across twenty disciplines in institutions of higher education from community colleges to elite universities believe in God—a percentage much lower than in the American population at large—this percentage was lower among research scholars, a finding consistent with a study by Elaine Howard Ecklund and Christopher P. Scheitle of the religious beliefs and practices of natural and social scientists at twenty leading American research universities. See Gross and Simmons, "The Religiosity of American College and University Professors," *Sociology of Religion* 70:2 (2009): 101–129; Ecklund and Scheitle, "Religion among Academic Scientists: Distinctions, Disciplines, and Demographics," *Social Problems* 54:2 (2007): 289–307. I thank Christian Smith for calling my attention to these studies. Ecklund, in her more recent book based on more than 1,600 surveys and 275 interviews with natural and social scientists at twenty-one elite American research universities, notes that "about 36 percent of scientists have *some form* of a belief in God." Ecklund, *Science vs. Religion: What Scientists Really Think* (New York: Oxford University Press, 2010), p. 35 (my emphasis).

3. Brad S. Gregory, "The Other Confessional History: On Secular Bias in the Study of Religion," *History and Theory, Theme Issue* 45 (2006): 132–149.

4. John R. Searle, *The Rediscovery of the Mind* (Cambridge, Mass., and London: MIT Press, 1992), pp. 90–91.

5. See, for example, Sam Harris, *The End of Faith: Religion, Terror, and the Future of Reason* (New York and London: W. W. Norton, 2004); Richard Dawkins, *The God Delusion* (2006; Boston and New York: Mariner Books, 2008); Daniel Dennett, *Breaking the Spell: Religion as a Natural Phenomenon* (New York: Penguin, 2006); Christopher Hitchens, *God Is Not Great: How Religion Poisons Everything* (New York: Twelve, 2007); Michel Onfray, *Atheist Manifesto: The Case against Christianity, Judaism, and Islam,* trans. Jeremy Leggatt (New York: Arcade, 2007); John Allen Paulos, *Irreligion: A Mathematician Explains Why the Arguments for God Just Don't Add Up* (New York: Hill & Wang, 2008).

6. See, for example, John Polkinghorne, *Quantum Physics and Theology: An Unexpected Kinship* (New Haven, Conn., and London: Yale University Press, 2007); Robert John Russell, *Cosmology from Alpha to Omega: The Creative Mutual Interaction of Theology and Science* (Minneapolis: Fortress Press, 2008); Kenneth R. Miller, *Finding Darwin's God: A Scientist's Search for*

*Common Ground between God and Evolution* (New York: Harper, 1999); Francis Collins, *The Language of God: A Scientist Presents Evidence for Belief* (New York: Free Press, 2006); Michael J. Buckley, *At the Origins of Modern Atheism* (New Haven, Conn., and London: Yale University Press, 1987); David B. Burrell, *Aquinas: God and Action* (Notre Dame, Ind.: University of Notre Dame Press, 1979); Alasdair MacIntyre, "Epistemological Crises, Dramatic Narrative, and the Philosophy of Science," in *Selected Essays,* vol. 1, *The Tasks of Philosophy* (Cambridge: Cambridge University Press, 2006), pp. 3–23; Alvin Plantinga, *Warranted Christian Belief* (Oxford: Oxford University Press, 2000); John M. Rist, *What Is Truth? From the Academy to the Vatican* (Cambridge: Cambridge University Press, 2008); David Bentley Hart, *The Beauty of the Infinite: The Aesthetics of Christian Truth* (Grand Rapids, Mich.: Eerdmans, 2003); John F. Haught, *Deeper Than Darwin: The Prospect for Religion in the Age of Evolution* (Boulder, Colo.: Westview Press, 2003); Christopher C. Knight, *The God of Nature: Incarnation and Contemporary Science* (Minneapolis: Fortress Press, 2007); Joseph Ratzinger, *Introduction to Christianity,* trans. J. R. Foster (1969; San Francisco: Ignatius Press, 2004); and Christoph Schönborn, *Chance or Purpose? Creation, Evolution, and a Rational Faith,* ed. Hubert Philip Weber, trans. Henry Taylor (San Francisco: Ignatius Press, 2007).

7. For a recent synthetic overview of the complexities of oral and textual transmission in the formation of the Christian Bible, see Lee Martin McDonald, *The Biblical Canon: Its Origin, Transmission, and Authority* (Peabody, Mass.: Hendrickson, 2007). On the coherence of those New Testament writings that by no later than the late second century had been deliberately shaped as a canonical collection of texts, see Brevard S. Childs, *The New Testament as Canon: An Introduction* (1984; Valley Forge, Pa.: Trinity Press International, 1994).

8. On the distinctiveness of the Christian doctrine of creation compared to other ancient accounts, see Robert Sokolowski, *The God of Faith and Reason: Foundations of Christian Theology* (Notre Dame, Ind.: University of Notre Dame Press, 1982), pp. 12–40. I am well aware of the issues pertaining to gender inclusiveness and discourse about God, but find none of the alternatives proposed thus far to be theologically and stylistically adequate, or preferable to the use of "he" and "his." Throughout this book I have therefore used "he" and "his" when referring to God in conjunction with those traditions that refer to God in this way, including Christianity. Although in some religious traditions, such as Mormonism, God is conceived as explicitly male, in traditional Christianity God not only has no sex or gender, but as transcendent and entirely nonspatial he cannot be (as we shall see) the straightforward bearer of any predicates in the same ways in which they belong to creatures.

9. For the likely pseudonymous authorship and dating of Paul's pastoral epistles (1 Tm, 2 Tm, and Ti) as "somewhat before or around AD 100," see Robert A. Wild, "The Pastoral Letters," in *The New Jerome Biblical Commentary,* ed. Raymond E. Brown, Joseph A. Fitzmyer, and Roland E. Murphy (Up-

per Saddle River, N.J.: Prentice Hall, 1990), pp. 892–893, quotation on 893.

10. Augustine, *Confessiones*, 1.4, in *Corpus Augustinianum Gissense*, ed. Cornelius Mayer, electronic edition (Charlottesville, Va.: Intelex, 2000).

11. Anselm of Canterbury, *Proslogion*, in *S. Anselmi Cantuariensis Archepiscopi opera omnia*, vol. 1, ed. Francis Schmitt (Edinburgh: Thomas Nelson, 1946), chap. 16, p. 113/4.

12. Hildegard of Bingen, *Scivias*, ed. Adelgundis Führkötter and Angela Carlevaris, vol. 43a in *Corpus Christianorum. Continuatio Mediaevalis* (Turnhout: Brepols, 1978), 3.1.1., pp. 330–331, quotation at 331/143–147.

13. "Et ex hoc patet quod non habet genus neque differentias, neque est definitio ipsius neque demonstratio nisi per effectum, quia definitio est ex genere et differentia, demonstrationis autem medium est definitio." Thomas Aquinas, *Summa Theologiae*, Blackfriars ed., vol. 2, trans. Timothy McDermott (London: Eyre & Spottiswoode; New York: McGraw-Hill, 1964), I, q. 3, a. 5, p. 36. See also I, q. 1, a. 7, in which Aquinas says that "de Deo non *possimus* scire quid est" (my emphasis); ibid., vol. 1, trans. Thomas Gilby (London: Eyre & Spottiswoode; New York: McGraw-Hill, 1973), p. 26. For an understanding of Aquinas along these lines informed by Lonergan, Wittgenstein, and analytical philosophy, and antithetical to claims that his view of God is of a conceptually continuous capstone of a "great chain of being," see David Burrell, *Analogy and Philosophical Language* (New Haven, Conn., and London: Yale University Press, 1973), with "improperly knowable" as the interpretation of "ana-logical" at p. 126, and Burrell, *Aquinas: God and Action*. See also Fergus Kerr, *After Aquinas: Varieties of Thomism* (Malden, Mass., and Oxford: Blackwell, 2002), pp. 35–51. The phrase "otherly other" in reference to this understanding of God is from Robert Barron, *The Priority of Christ: Toward a Postliberal Catholicism* (Grand Rapids, Mich.: Brazos Press, 2007), p. 55. My understanding of this view of God and creation is indebted in general to Barron, as well as to Sokolowski and Burrell.

14. John of the Cross, *The Ascent of Mt. Carmel* [1579–1585], in *The Collected Works of St. John of the Cross*, trans. Kieran Kavanaugh and Otilio Rodriguez (Washington, D.C.: Institute of Carmelite Studies, 1979), 2.4.4, p. 113.

15. John Henry Newman, "Mysteries of Nature and of Grace," in *Discourses Addressed to Mixed Congregations* [1849] (London: Longmans, Green & Co., 1913), p. 264.

16. William Stacy Johnson, *The Mystery of God: Karl Barth and the Postmodern Foundations of Theology* (Louisville, Ky.: Westminster John Knox Press, 1997), p. 20. "Barth thought of God as *other* than being. The mystery of God cannot be reduced to the being of the world as it is." Ibid. (italics in original).

17. Flannery O'Connor, letter to Alfred Corn, 30 May 1962, in *The Habit of Being*, ed. Sally Fitzgerald (New York: Farrar, Straus and Giroux, 1979), p. 477 (my emphasis).

18. Charles Larmore, *The Morals of Modernity* (Cambridge: Cambridge University Press, 1996), p. 41.

19. On the complex history of the emergence of the term "supernatural," which was not conceived technically and consistently as a contrast to the "natural" until Aquinas, see part 3 of Henri de Lubac, *Surnaturel: Études historiques* (Paris: Aubier, 1946), pp. 323–428.

20. Dante Alighieri, *La commedia secondo l'antica vulgata*, ed. Giorgio Pettrochi, vol. 2, *Inferno* (Florence: Casa Editrice Le Lettere, 1994), 4.131, p. 73: " 'l maestro di color che sanno." On the translation of most of the Aristotelian corpus in the twelfth century, its increasing importance from the mid-thirteenth, the fact that most translations were done from Greek rather than Arabic, and the particular importance of William of Moerbeke's improved translations of the 1260s and early 1270s, see Bernard G. Dod, "Aristoteles latinus," in *The Cambridge History of Later Medieval Philosophy: From the Rediscovery of Aristotle to the Disintegration of Scholasticism, 1100–1600*, ed. Norman Kretzmann, Anthony Kenny, and Jan Pinborg (Cambridge: Cambridge University Press, 1982), pp. 46–53, 74–78.

21. It is more than a little ironic that Aquinas not only used Aristotelian categories to preserve the traditional, radical distinction between God and creation, but also to formulate technically the distinction between "natural" and "supernatural." As we shall see, the latter categories were pitted against one another by later thinkers within a different metaphysics, in ways that were especially consequential following the advent of deadlocked doctrinal controversies in the Reformation era.

22. For Aquinas's exposition, see *Summa Theologiae*, Blackfriars ed., vol. 58, trans. William Barden (London: Eyre & Spottiswoode; New York: McGraw-Hill, 1965), III, q. 75, a. 5, pp. 72–76.

23. On Henry of Ghent's analogical view and its differences from Aquinas's, see Stephen Dumont, "Henry of Ghent and Duns Scotus," in *Medieval Philosophy*, vol. 3 in *Routledge History of Philosophy*, ed. John Marenbon (London and New York: Routledge, 1998), pp. 298–307; Burrell, *Analogy*, pp. 96–98, 104. On Scotus's univocity, see also Peter King, "Scotus on Metaphysics," in *The Cambridge Companion to Duns Scotus*, ed. Thomas Williams (Cambridge: Cambridge University Press, 2003), pp. 18–21; William E. Mann, "Duns Scotus on Natural and Supernatural Knowledge of God," in ibid., pp. 245–247; and Cyril L. Shircel, *The Univocity of the Concept of Being in the Philosophy of John Duns Scotus* (Washington, D.C.: Catholic University of America Press, 1942), esp. pp. 127–170.

24. Dumont, "Henry of Ghent and Duns Scotus," in *Medieval Philosophy*, ed. Marenbon, p. 297.

25. On Avicenna's metaphysical views in relationship to those of Scotus, see Etienne Gilson, "Avicenne et le point de départ de Duns Scot," *Archives d'Histoire Doctrinale et Litteraire du Moyen Âge* 2 (1927): 89–149, noted in David B. Burrell, "Avicenna," in *A Companion to Philosophy in the Middle Ages*, ed. Jorge J. E. Garcia and Timothy B. Noone (Malden, Mass.: Blackwell, 2003), p. 207; see also Burrell, *Analogy*, pp. 96–97, 100, 179.

26. The so-called Radical Orthodoxy theologians (including John Milbank, Catherine Pickstock, and Graham Ward) have emphasized the importance of

Scotist univocity in the formation of modern ideologies, but they take their cues from postmodern philosophical perspectivalism. The most important and influential among their works is Milbank's *Theology and Social Theory: Beyond Secular Reason* (Oxford: Blackwell, 1990), to some of the critical aspects of which I am indebted. For a critique of their philosophical problems and insufficient historical awareness, see *Deconstructing Radical Orthodoxy*, ed. Wayne Hankey and Douglas Hedley (Burlington, Vt.: Ashgate, 2005).

27. Barron, *Priority of Christ*, p. 193. "By admitting a simple and univocal concept of being, Scotus provided a true conceptual community between God and creature and placed the project of natural knowledge of the divine nature on a firm epistemological footing." Dumont, "Henry of Ghent and Duns Scotus," in *Medieval Philosophy*, ed. Marenbon, p. 313. It was exactly this "firmness" that would turn out to have enormous consequences by providing for the assimilation of God to the natural world.

28. On the three university faculties of theology until the foundations at Prague and in Italy during the 1340s, see Monika Asztalos, "The Faculty of Theology," in *HUE*, vol. 1, *Universities in the Middle Ages*, ed. Hilde de Ridder-Symoens (Cambridge: Cambridge University Press, 1992), pp. 414, 433.

29. "Aquinas is perhaps best known for his theory of analogy. On closer inspection it turns out that he never had one." Burrell, *Aquinas: God and Action*, p. 55. For the ways in which Tommaso de Vio (Cajetan; 1468–1538) and Francisco Suárez (1548–1617) transformed Aquinas's analogical views into a systematic theory of proportionality, which influenced the understanding and teaching of Thomism in Catholic theology into the twentieth century, see William C. Placher, *The Domestication of Transcendence: How Modern Thinking about God Went Wrong* (Louisville, Ky.: Westminster John Knox Press, 1996), pp. 71–76. It was this domesticated Thomism of proportional analogy with God atop a "great chain of being" to which Barth objected so vehemently in *Der Romerbrief* (1919). See Johnson, *Mystery of God*, p. 20. Ironically, in contrast to the Thomism of proportionality against which Barth reacted, Aquinas's view was closer to his own than he thought. See Kerr, *After Aquinas*, pp. 35–37, 42, 60, 62–63. On Occam's univocity as a continuation of Scotus's, see Burrell, *Analogy*, pp. 185–193; on Occam's univocity in general, see Armand Maurer, *The Philosophy of William of Ockham in the Light of Its Principles* (Toronto: Pontifical Institute of Mediaeval Studies, 1999), pp. 277–292.

30. On the centrality of the distinction between the *potentia Dei absoluta* and the *potentia Dei ordinata* for Occam and subsequent medieval nominalism, see Heiko A. Oberman, *The Harvest of Medieval Theology: Gabriel Biel and Late Medieval Nominalism* (Cambridge, Mass.: Harvard University Press, 1963), pp. 30–56, 90–103. It seems clear that Oberman disdained Thomism in ways analogous to Barth, and dedicated much of his early scholarly career to the resuscitation of medieval nominalism, because he mistakenly accepted as Aquinas's thought the later Thomism of proportional analogy that predominated in Roman Catholic theology from the time of Cajetan and Suárez into the twentieth century.

31. This best known articulation of Occam's razor is not found in his writings but rather was formulated in 1639 by the Irish Franciscan John Ponce in a note to Scotus's *Opera omnia* that Ponce coedited with Luke Wadding. Arthur Gibson, "Ockham's World and Future," in *Medieval Philosophy*, ed. Marenbon, pp. 346, 359 n. 33. On Ponce (Punch), see Terry Clavin, "Punch, John (1599–1672/3)," in *ODNB*, online ed., ed. Lawrence Goldman (Oxford: Oxford University Press, 2004), http://www.oxforddnb.com/view/article/22487 (accessed 19 August 2010).

32. Heiko A. Oberman, "Fourteenth-Century Religious Thought: A Premature Profile," in *The Dawn of the Reformation: Essays in Late Medieval and Early Reformation Thought* (Edinburgh: T. & T. Clark, 1986), pp. 4–8, and Oberman, "The Shape of Late Medieval Thought: The Birthpangs of the Modern Era," in ibid., p. 26; William J. Courtenay, "The Role of English Thought in the Transformation of University Education in the Late Middle Ages," in *Rebirth, Reform, and Resilience: Universities in Transition, 1300–1700*, ed. James M. Kittelson and Pamela J. Transue (Columbus: Ohio State University Press, 1984), pp. 103–162; Francis Rapp, *L'Église et la vie religieuse en Occident à la fin du Moyen Âge*, 6th ed. (Paris: Presses Universitaires de France, 1999), pp. 112–113. On the new universities established or reopened from the beginning of the schism through 1500, see Jacques Verger, "Patterns," in *HUE*, vol. 1, ed. de Ridder-Symoens, pp. 57–59, 64–65, [73], and Rapp, *L'Église*, pp. 102–103; and on the large increase in the number of universities with theology faculties, see Verger, "Patterns," pp. 59–60, Asztalos, "Faculty of Theology," in *HUE*, vol. 1, ed. de Ridder-Symoens, pp. 435–440, and John Van Engen, "Multiple Options: The World of the Fifteenth-Century Church," *Church History* 77:2 (2008): 279.

33. Amos Funkenstein, *Theology and the Scientific Imagination from the Middle Ages to the Seventeenth Century* (Princeton, N.J.: Princeton University Press, 1986), pp. 30–35, 37–41.

34. The application of mathematics to experiments beginning in fourteenth-century universities required an abrogation of Aristotelian disciplinary and intellectual distinctions between mathematics and natural philosophy. Viewed in these terms, Galileo's achievements in the mathematization of mechanics and his statement in *Il saggiatore* (1623) that God has written the book of nature in the language of mathematics represented the clearing of a higher conceptual hurdle than did Copernicus's positing of heliocentrism, because mathematics and astronomy had been more closely associated to begin with in the ancient world and the medieval scholastic curriculum. See Edward Grant, *Physical Science in the Middle Ages* (New York: John Wiley & Sons, 1971), pp. 36–59; Peter Dear, *Revolutionizing the Sciences: European Knowledge and Its Ambitions, 1500–1700* (Princeton, N.J.: Princeton University Press, 2001), pp. 15–18.

35. See Joel Kaye, *Economy and Nature in the Fourteenth Century: Money, Market Exchange, and the Emergence of Scientific Thought* (Cambridge: Cambridge University Press, 1998).

36. The deterministic causality of the pneuma throughout homogeneous matter contradicted entirely the Aristotelian conception of reality as heterogeneous,

an ordered hierarchy of diverse forms with ontologically distinct essences that were in turn reflected in the disciplinary distinctions and curricula of universities. A universe composed of essentially different natural kinds lent itself much more readily to the traditional distinction between God and creation than did the Stoic universe, in which spirit and matter were identified. A univocal metaphysics within Christianity, however, could (and did) provide an intellectual bridge from the traditional conception to a neo-Stoic view of the relationship between God and creation.

37. Jill Kraye, "Moral Philosophy," in *The Cambridge History of Renaissance Philosophy,* ed. Charles B. Schmitt and Quentin Skinner (Cambridge: Cambridge University Press, 1988), pp. 367–370.

38. For Gassendi, who "had little difficulty in reconciling the basic tenets of Catholic Christianity with his modified brand of Epicurean metaphysics," see Daniel Garber et al., "New Doctrines of Body and Its Powers, Place, and Space," in *The Cambridge History of Seventeenth-Century Philosophy,* ed. Garber and Michael Ayers, vol. 1 (Cambridge: Cambridge University Press, 1998), pp. 569–573, quotation on 573; for Mersenne's Platonizing Epicureanism, see Buckley, *Atheism,* pp. 56–64.

39. John Calvin, *Institutio Christianae religionis* [1559], in *CO,* vol. 2, ed. G. Baum, E. Cunitz, and E. Reuss, vol. 30 in *CR* (Brunswick: C. A. Schwetschke & Sohn, 1864), 1.16.3, cols. 146, 147.

40. See Brad S. Gregory, *Salvation at Stake: Christian Martyrdom in Early Modern Europe* (Cambridge, Mass., and London: Harvard University Press, 1999), pp. 114–116, 121, 125, 201–212, 219–225; Gregory, "Anabaptist Martyrdom: Imperatives, Experience, and Memorialization," in *A Companion to Anabaptism and Spiritualism, 1521–1700,* ed. John D. Roth and James M. Stayer (Leiden: E. J. Brill, 2007), pp. 485–488.

41. Alexandra Walsham, *Providence in Early Modern England* (Oxford: Oxford University Press, 1999); see also Walsham, "The Reformation and 'The Disenchantment of the World' Reassessed," *Historical Journal* 51:2 (2008): 497–528, and, for Germany, Robert W. Scribner, "The Reformation, Popular Magic and the 'Disenchantment of the World,'" *Journal of Interdisciplinary History* 23 (1993): 475–494. The tendency of many historians indiscriminately to lump medieval Christian sacramentality together with "magic"—Keith Thomas's classic work being probably the best-known example—is itself a latter-day consequence of the historical processes traced in this chapter and in Chapter 6: scholars who adopt social scientific theories that presuppose the truth of metaphysical naturalism born of metaphysical univocity uncritically impose it on Christian truth claims within an evolutionary narrative of progressive secularization. See Thomas, *Religion and the Decline of Magic: Studies in Popular Beliefs in Sixteenth- and Seventeenth-Century England* (New York: Scribner's, 1971), esp. pp. 25–50.

42. On medieval skepticism about alleged miracles, see Steven Justice, "Did the Middle Ages Believe in Their Miracles?" *Representations* 103 (2008): 1–29.

43. See Francis Higman, *La diffusion de la Réforme en France, 1520–1565* (Geneva: Labor et Fides, 1992), pp. 63–78, with the text of Marcourt's placard at 72–75.

44. For the widespread implications of eucharistic controversy in the conflicts between French Catholics and Huguenots from the 1520s through the outbreak of the Wars of Religion, see Christopher Elwood, *The Body Broken: The Calvinist Doctrine of the Eucharist and the Symbolization of Power in Sixteenth-Century France* (New York: Oxford University Press, 1999); for a learned account of the traditional theology of the sacrifice of the Mass on the eve of the Reformation, and the attacks on and misunderstandings of it among Protestant reformers on the Continent and especially in England, see Francis Clark, *Eucharistic Sacrifice and the Reformation*, 2nd ed. (Oxford: Blackwell, 1960).

45. Menno Simons, *Fundament en klare aenwysinghe van de salighmakende leere Jesu Christi* [1558], repr. in Simons, *Opera omnia theologica, of Alle de godtgeleerde wercken van Menno Symons* (Amsterdam: Johannes van Veen, 1681), p. 29. Throughout this 1558 edition, Menno not only expanded the exposition but also intensified his anti-Roman rhetoric in comparison to the first edition of the same work. The latter quoted passage, for example, in the first edition reads simply "a sinful, ungodly priest with a bit of bread [*eenen sondighen, ongodlicke pape met eenen bete broots*]." Menno Simons, *Dat Fundament des Christelycken Leers* [1539–40], ed. H. W. Meihuizen (The Hague: Martinus Nijhoff, 1967), p. 92.

46. Huldrych Zwingli, *Eine klare Underrichtung vom Nachtmahl Christi* [1526], in *ZW*, vol. 4, ed. Emil Egli et al., vol. 91 in *CR* (Leipzig: M. Heinsius Nachfolger, 1927), pp. 827–830, quotation at 830/22–24: "er zur grechten des vatters sitzt, die welt verlassen hab, nit me by uns sye; und nebend denen nit bston mag, das imm sacrament fleisch und blüt sye."

47. *Lumen Gentium (Dogmatic Constitution on the Church)*, 21 November 1964, in *Documents of Vatican II*, ed. Austin P. Flannery (Grand Rapids, Mich.: Eerdmans, 1975), 1.11, p. 362; *Catechism of the Catholic Church* (1994; New York: Image, 1995), para. 1324, p. 368; John Paul II, introduction to *Ecclesia de Eucharistia*, encyclical letter, 17 April 2003, para. 1, http://www.vatican.va/holy_father/special_features/ encyclicals/documents/ hf_jp-ii_enc_20030417_ecclesia_eucharistia_en.html (accessed 9 March 2010).

48. Erika Rummel, *The Humanist-Scholastic Debate in the Renaissance and Reformation* (Cambridge, Mass., and London: Harvard University Press, 1995), pp. 2–6, 16–18; Paul F. Grendler, *The Universities of the Italian Renaissance* (Baltimore and London: Johns Hopkins University Press, 2002), pp. 209–222, 247–248, 353–392; Paul Oskar Kristeller, "Humanism," in *Cambridge History of Renaissance Philosophy*, ed. Schmitt and Skinner, pp. 115, 133–136. See also James H. Overfield, *Humanism and Scholasticism in Late Medieval Germany* (Princeton, N.J.: Princeton University Press, 1984), and Walter Rüegg, "Epilogue: The Rise of Humanism," in *HUE*, vol. 1, ed. de Ridder-Symoens, pp. 442–468.

49. On Cisneros and the College of San Ildefonso at the University of Alcalá, see Lu Ann Homza, *Religious Authority in the Spanish Renaissance* (Baltimore and London: Johns Hopkins University Press, 2000), pp. 1–3, and Erika Rummel, *Jiménez de Cisneros: On the Threshold of Spain's Golden Age* (Tempe, Ariz.: Arizona Center for Medieval and Renaissance Studies, 1999), pp. 53–65; on Fisher's scholasticism and humanism and his support of both at Cambridge, see Richard Rex, *The Theology of John Fisher* (Cambridge: Cambridge University Press, 1991), pp. 28–29, 50–64; and for a brief treatment of the Busleydens and Erasmus with respect to Louvain's *Collegium trilingue*, see *Contemporaries of Erasmus: A Biographical Register of the Renaissance and Reformation*, vol. 1, ed. Peter G. Bietenholz (Toronto: University of Toronto Press, 1985), pp. 235–236. The magisterial study of the institution's establishment and early history is Henry de Vocht, *History of the Foundation and Rise of the Collegium Trilingue Lovaniense, 1517–1550*, 4 vols. (Louvain: Bibliothèque de l'Université, 1951–1955); see also Walter Rüegg, "Themes," in *HUE*, vol. 1, ed. de Ridder-Symoens, pp. 35–36.

50. For the persistence of religious violence among Catholics and Protestants into the early eighteenth century, see Benjamin J. Kaplan, *Divided by Faith: Religious Conflict and the Practice of Toleration in Early Modern Europe* (Cambridge, Mass., and London: Belknap Press of Harvard University Press, 2007), pp. 336–343.

51. See Erika Rummel, *The Confessionalization of Humanism in Reformation Germany* (Oxford: Oxford University Press, 2000); Pontien Polman, *L'Élément historique dans la controverse religieuse du XVIe siècle* (Gembloux: J. Duculot, 1932); Irena Backus, *Historical Method and Confessional Identity in the Era of the Reformation (1378–1615)* (Leiden: E. J. Brill, 2003).

52. Richard Popkin, *The History of Scepticism from Savonarola to Bayle*, 3rd ed. (Oxford: Oxford University Press, 2003), esp. pp. 65–74; see also Susan E. Schreiner, *Are You Alone Wise? The Search for Certainty in the Early Modern Era* (New York: Oxford University Press, 2011).

53. For an overview of the improved relations and increased cooperation between Roman Catholics and evangelical Protestants since the 1950s, especially in the United States, see Mark A. Noll and Carolyn Nystrom, *Is the Reformation Over? An Evangelical Assessment of Contemporary Roman Catholicism* (Grand Rapids, Mich.: Baker Academic, 2005).

54. Quoted in Marcus Hellyer, *Catholic Physics: Jesuit Natural Philosophy in Early Modern Germany* (Notre Dame, Ind.: University of Notre Dame Press, 2005), p. 178. On Boscovich's understudied, post-Newtonian, unified theory of a single attraction-repulsion force that anticipated developments in chemistry, optics, magnetism, thermodynamics, and electricity between 1780 and 1820, see Ugo Baldini, "The Reception of a Theory: A Provisional Syllabus of Boscovich Literature, 1746–1800," in *The Jesuits II: Cultures, Sciences, and the Arts, 1540–1773*, ed. John O'Malley et al. (Toronto: University of Toronto Press, 2006), pp. 405–450. The insistence on Aristotelianism hampered the wide range of Jesuit scientific inquiry and experiment into the eighteenth

century; after the profound disruptions and widespread closings of universities in the Napoleonic period, the adoption of neo-scholasticism in the late nineteenth century tended to isolate Catholic higher education from wider intellectual trends until the 1960s, as we shall see in Chapter 6. On the influence of the Roman Inquisition's censorship on Jesuit science, which was real but less important in practice than has often been supposed, and which diminished over the course of the seventeenth and eighteenth centuries, see Hellyer, *Catholic Physics*, pp. 35–52, 173–177. Writing a year before the condemnation of Copernicanism, Galileo noted the wisdom of "the holiest Fathers" in the past who "knew how harmful and how contrary to the primary function of the Catholic church it would be to want to use scriptural passages to establish conclusions about nature, when by means of observation and necessary demonstrations one could at some point demonstrate the contrary of what the words literally say." "Galileo's Letter to the Grand Duchess Christina (1615)," in *The Galileo Affair: A Documentary History*, ed. and trans. Maurice A. Finocchiaro (Berkeley and Los Angeles: University of California Press, 1989), p. 110.

55. My argument here intersects with that of Michael Buckley, who argues that insofar as religion was regarded as "bankrupt" by the beginning of the seventeenth century because of the disruptions and violence linked to the Reformation and its attempted suppression, Catholic theologians such as Leonard Lessius (1554–1623) and Mersenne argued against atheism strictly as philosophers rather than as theologians. See Buckley, *Atheism*, esp. pp. 38–39, 47, 54–55, 64–67. See also Wilhelm Schmidt-Biggemann, "New Structures of Knowledge," in *HUE*, vol. 2, *Universities in Early Modern Europe (1500–1800)*, ed. Hilde de Ridder-Symoens (Cambridge: Cambridge University Press, 1996), pp. 507–509, 517–518. The fact and nature of doctrinal controversy explains *why* "the fundamental reality of Jesus as the embodied presence and witness of the reality of god [sic] within human history was never brought into the critical struggle of Christianity in the next three hundred years." Buckley, *Atheism*, p. 67. Or rather, and more precisely, all the efforts that *were* made in this regard immediately marked an endeavor as controversial (because controverted) theology—because in fundamental ways, what Catholics and Protestants were arguing over in so many domains (sacraments, ecclesiology, exegesis, ministry, and so forth) were subsidiary adjuncts to belief about God's incarnation in Jesus and what it entailed for human life.

56. On Leibniz's persistent efforts at ecclesiastical reunification, see Maria Rosa Antognazza, *Leibniz: An Intellectual Biography* (Cambridge: Cambridge University Press, 2009), pp. 99, 121, 202–203, 218–221, 256–259, 278 n. 295, 285, 294, 309, 338–342, 361, 366–367, 390, 398–406, 462–463, 471, 480–481, 528–529. Leibniz developed his theodicy, for example, in conjunction with his efforts to reunify the magisterial Protestant churches. Ibid., pp. 480–481.

57. See Michael Hunter, *Science and Society in Restoration England* (Cambridge: Cambridge University Press, 1981), pp. 27–31, 35–39; Barbara J. Shapiro, *A Culture of Fact: England, 1550–1720* (Ithaca, N.Y., and London: Cornell University Press, 2000), pp. 112–114, 163–164; and Michael Heyd, *"Be So-*

*ber and Reasonable": The Critique of Enthusiasm in the Seventeenth and Early Eighteenth Centuries* (Leiden: E. J. Brill, 1995).

58. On the emergence of Galileo's mechanics in context, see William A. Wallace, *Galileo and His Sources: The Heritage of the Collegio Romano in Galileo's Science* (Princeton, N.J.: Princeton University Press, 1984); on the circle of descriptive naturalists around Federico Cesi to which Galileo belonged in Rome, see David Freedberg, *The Eye of the Lynx: Galileo, His Friends, and the Beginnings of Modern Natural History* (Chicago: University of Chicago Press, 2002); and on the realities of court patronage and their relevance for an adequate understanding of Galileo, see Mario Biagioli, *Galileo, Courtier: The Practice of Science in the Age of Absolutism* (Chicago: University of Chicago Press, 1993).

59. René Descartes, *Meditationes de prima philosophia* [1641], in Descartes, *Oeuvres,* ed. Charles Adam and Paul Tannery, vol. 7 (Paris: J. Vrin, 1964); Daniel Garber, *Descartes's Metaphysical Physics* (Chicago: University of Chicago Press, 1992); Buckley, *Atheism,* pp. 68–99.

60. Baruch Spinoza, *Ethica* [1677], in Spinoza, *Opera,* ed. Carl Gebhardt, vol. 2 (Heidelberg: C. Winter, 1925); Edwin Curley, *Behind the Geometrical Method: A Reading of Spinoza's Ethics* (Princeton, N.J.: Princeton University Press, 1988); Steven Nadler, *Spinoza's Ethics: An Introduction* (Cambridge: Cambridge University Press, 2006).

61. Thomas Hobbes, *Leviathan* [1651], ed. Richard Tuck (1991; Cambridge: Cambridge University Press, 1996), 1.1–5, pp. 13–37; Yves Charles Zarka, "First Philosophy and the Foundations of Knowledge," in *The Cambridge Companion to Thomas Hobbes,* ed. Tom Sorell (Cambridge: Cambridge University Press, 1996), pp. 62–85.

62. Isaac Newton, *The Principia: Mathematical Principles of Natural Philosophy* [1687], ed. and trans. I. Bernard Cohen and Anne Whitman (Berkeley and Los Angeles: University of California Press, 1999); see especially Cohen's lengthy introduction and commentary, "A Guide to Newton's *Principia,*" in ibid., pp. 1–370, and for a more compressed overview, see Cohen, "Newton's Concepts of Force and Mass, with Notes on the Laws of Motion," in *The Cambridge Companion to Newton,* ed. I. Bernard Cohen and George E. Smith (Cambridge: Cambridge University Press, 2002), pp. 57–84, in combination with Curtis Wilson, "Newton and Celestial Mechanics," in ibid., pp. 202–226; see also Buckley, *Atheism,* pp. 99–144.

63. Schmidt-Biggemann, "New Structures of Knowledge," in *HUE,* vol. 2, ed. de Ridder-Symoens, pp. 507–509.

64. Funkenstein, *Theology,* p. 27.

65. Augustine, *Sermones,* pt. 1, sermon 52.16, in *Corpus Augustinianum Gissense,* ed. Mayer, electronic ed. Augustine's word choice, from *capere,* implies the would-be ability to take hold of, seize, possess, or grasp God intellectually.

66. See the careful analysis in Zbigniew Janowski, *Augustinian-Cartesian Index: Texts and Commentary* (South Bend, Ind.: St. Augustine's Press, 2004).

67. Descartes, *Meditationes,* in *Oeuvres,* ed. Adam and Tannery, vol. 7, pp. 35–52.

68. Funkenstein, *Theology,* pp. 77–80.

69. Hobbes, *Leviathan,* 1.12, p. 77.

70. Funkenstein, *Theology,* pp. 89–97; Buckley, *Origins,* p. 138; Howard Stein, "Newton's Metaphysics," in *Cambridge Companion to Newton,* ed. Cohen and Smith, pp. 266–275.

71. Funkenstein, *Theology,* pp. 80–86; for the comparison between the clarity of the ideas of God and of a triangle, see Spinoza's 1674 letter to Hugo Boxel in Spinoza, *Opera,* ed. Gephardt, vol. 4, letter 56, p. 261/7–11.

72. Leibniz, *Discours de métaphysique* [1686], ed. H. Lestienne (Paris: Félix Alcan, 1907), pp. 89, 90. Matthew Stewart's lively account of the sharp contrast between Spinoza and Leibniz mentions neither their shared metaphysical univocity, nor the fact that a traditional Christian conception of God remained a viable intellectual option in the seventeenth century and beyond. Stewart, *The Courtier and the Heretic: Leibniz, Spinoza, and the Fate of God in the Modern World* (New York: W. W. Norton, 2006).

73. See John W. Cooper, *Panentheism: The Other God of the Philosophers, from Plato to the Present* (Grand Rapids, Mich.: Baker Academic, 2006), which devotes most of its attention to the nineteenth and twentieth centuries. For Whitehead and Hartshorne, see ibid., pp. 166–185. For an overview by the most prominent Continental process philosopher of the late twentieth century, see Jan Van der Veken, *Proces-denken: Een oriëntatie,* 2nd ed. (Leuven: Centrum voor Metafysica en Wijsgerige Godsleer, 1986).

74. "Ratio enim humana in rebus divinis est multum deficiens, cujus signum est quia philosophi de rebus humanis naturali investigatione perscrutantes in multis erraverunt et sibi ipsis contraria senserunt." Aquinas, *Summa Theologiae,* Blackfriars ed., vol. 31, trans. T. C. O'Brien (London: Eyre & Spottiswoode; New York: McGraw-Hill, 1974), II–II, q. 2, a. 4, p. 76.

75. Blaise Pascal, *Pensées* [1670] in Pascal, *Oeuvres complètes,* ed. Louis Lafuma (Paris: Éditions du Seuil, 1963), no. 417, p. 550, electronic edition (Charlottesville, Va.: Intelex, 2006).

76. On Pomponazzi, see Martin Pine, *Pietro Pomponazzi, Radical Philosopher of the Renaissance* (Padua: Antenore, 1986); on Cardano, see Anthony Grafton, *Cardano's Cosmos: The Worlds and Works of a Renaissance Astrologer* (Cambridge, Mass., and London: Harvard University Press, 1999); on Bruno, see Ingrid D. Rowland, *Giordano Bruno: Philosopher/Heretic* (New York: Farrar, Straus and Giroux, 2008); on Kircher, see the contributions in *Athanasius Kircher: The Last Man Who Knew Everything,* ed. Paula Findlen (New York: Routledge, 2004).

77. "Lagrange and Laplace demanded a physics like Descartes' in its autonomy, while at the same time denying the need to found its fundamental assertions on the nature or actions of god [*sic*]. Physics was to be theological neither in its final reaches, as in Newton, nor in its foundational moments, as in Descartes." Buckley, *Atheism,* p. 326. On Newton's theological interests and biblical interpretation, see, for example, Scott Mandelbrote, "'A Duty of the Greatest Moment': Isaac Newton and the Writing of Biblical Criticism," *British Journal for the History of Science* 26 (1993): 281–302; see also the

magisterial work by Richard M. Westfall, *Never at Rest: A Biography of Isaac Newton* (Cambridge: Cambridge University Press, 1980); and for an example of Newton's exegesis of biblical prophecies, see *Isaac Newton's Observations on the Prophecies of Daniel and the Apocalypse of St. John: A Critical Edition*, ed. Stephen J. Barnett (Lewiston, N.Y.: Edwin Mellen Press, 1999).

78. William Derham, *Physico-Theology: or, A Demonstration of the Being and Attributes of God, from His Works of Creation* (London: for W. Innys, 1713); William Paley, *Natural Theology* [1802], ed. Matthew D. Eddy and David Knight (Oxford: Oxford University Press, 2006). Derham's work was translated into German and French and was reprinted numerous times in the eighteenth century; the thirteenth English edition appeared in 1768. On physico-theology, see also Jonathan I. Israel, *Radical Enlightenment: Philosophy and the Making of Modernity, 1650–1750* (Oxford: Oxford University Press, 2001), pp. 456–464; Israel, *Enlightenment Contested: Philosophy, Modernity, and the Emancipation of Man, 1670–1752* (Oxford: Oxford University Press, 2006), pp. 201–214. For Samuel Clarke's use of Newtonian mechanics in his natural theology, see Buckley, *Atheism*, pp. 168–193.

79. See Israel, *Radical Enlightenment*, pp. 565–574, 609–614, 619–622, 704–713; Israel, *Enlightenment Contested*, pp. 712–722, 751–762, 781–803.

80. For the United States prior to 1870 or so, see Jon H. Roberts and James Turner, *The Sacred and the Secular University*, intro. John F. Wilson (Princeton, N.J.: Princeton University Press, 2000), pp. 20–28.

81. Buckley tells the well-known story in *Atheism*, p. 325, with reference to Roger Hahn, "Laplace and the Vanishing Role of God in the Physical Universe," in *The Analytic Spirit: Essays in the History of Science in Honor of Henry Guerlac*, ed. Harry Woolf (Ithaca, N.Y.: Cornell University Press, 1981), pp. 85–86.

82. Israel, *Radical Enlightenment*, and *Enlightenment Contested*.

83. Mark Lilla, *The Stillborn God: Religion, Politics, and the Modern West* (New York: Knopf, 2007), pp. 58–59.

84. Placher, *Domestication of Transcendence*, pp. 74–76, quotation on 75.

85. On this "metaphysics of uniformity" that discredited not only miracle claims but also ignored the anomalous natural wonders that had captivated Europeans for centuries, see Lorraine Daston and Katharine Park, *Wonders and the Order of Nature, 1150–1750* (New York: Zone Books, 1998), pp. 329–363, quotation on 355. Daston and Park do not refer in their study to Scotus or metaphysical univocity, but they rightly note the presuppositions that were meant to exclude miracles and marvels: "Nature was governed by immutable laws, *and* these laws insured that natural phenomena were always regular and uniform" (p. 351, italics in original).

86. Funkenstein, *Theology*, p. 116.

87. Ronald Dworkin, "Objectivity and Truth: You'd Better Believe It," *Philosophy and Public Affairs* 25 (Spring 1996): 120.

88. See Tom Sorell, *Scientism: Philosophy and the Infatuation with Science* (London and New York: Routledge and Kegan Paul, 1991).

89. Dawkins, *God Delusion.* For a critique of Dawkins and the other "New Atheists" on this point, see Brad S. Gregory, "Science Versus Religion? The Insights and Oversights of the 'New Atheists,'" *Logos: A Journal of Catholic Thought and Culture* 12:4 (2009): 31–36.

90. See the ramifying remarks of Sokolowski, *God of Faith and Reason,* pp. 35–38.

91. John Locke, *An Essay Concerning Human Understanding* [1689], ed. Peter H. Nidditch (Oxford: Clarendon Press, 1975), 2.8, pp. 132–143.

92. Dear, *Revolutionizing the Sciences,* p. 9 (italics in original). See also Steven Shapin, *The Scientific Revolution* (Chicago and London: University of Chicago Press, 1996), pp. 13, 161–165; and Daston and Park, *Wonders,* p. 354: "In order to be made useful, nature had to be made uniform."

93. In Leszek Kołakowski's words, "even if Descartes did not deny providence, his philosophy did." Kołakowski, *God Owes Us Nothing: A Brief Remark on Pascal's Religion and on the Spirit of Jansenism* (Chicago and London: University of Chicago Press, 1995), p. 136. As Buckley puts it, "Descartes's world was secular, but not his total system." Buckley, *Atheism,* p. 350; on Descartes and Bérulle, see ibid., pp. 71–73, 75.

94. Bertrand Russell, *Religion and Science* (1935; Oxford: Oxford University Press, 1997); Jacques Monod, *Le hazard et la nécessité: Essai sur la philosophie naturelle de la biologie moderne* (Paris: Éditions de Seuil, 1970).

95. Francis Bacon, *Instauratio magna,* in *Novum organum* (London: [Bonham Norton and] John Bill, 1620), pp. 25, 26. On Bacon's interest in ecclesiastical history, and the likely influence of Matthias Flacius Illyricus's *Magdeburg Centuries* on his collaborative conception of knowledge in his *New Atlantis,* see Anthony Grafton, "Where Was Salomon's House? Ecclesiastical History and the Intellectual Origins of Bacon's *New Atlantis,*" in *Worlds Made of Words: Scholarship and Community in the Modern West* (Cambridge, Mass., and London: Harvard University Press, 2009), pp. 98–113.

96. Peter Pesic, "Wrestling with Proteus: Francis Bacon and the 'Torture' of Nature," *Isis* 90 (1999): 81–94.

97. Harold Cook, *Matters of Exchange: Commerce, Medicine, and Science in the Dutch Golden Age* (New Haven, Conn., and London: Yale University Press, 2007), pp. 1–73, quotation on 41.

98. Joel Mokyr, *The Gifts of Athena: Historical Origins of the Knowledge Economy* (Princeton, N.J.: Princeton University Press, 2002), p. 3. Seventeenth-century England's many economic "projects" shared the same fundamental aspiration: "A project was a practical scheme for exploiting material things; it was capable of being realized through industry and ingenuity." Joan Thirsk, *Economic Policy and Projects: The Development of a Consumer Society in Early Modern England* (Oxford: Clarendon Press, 1978), p. 1.

99. David Bentley Hart, *Atheist Delusions: The Christian Revolution and Its Fashionable Enemies* (New Haven, Conn., and London: Yale University Press, 2009), pp. 81–82, 232–233, quotation on 233.

100. Christopher Marlowe, *Doctor Faustus: With the English Faust Book,* ed. David Wootton (Indianapolis: Hackett, 2005), 1.1.83–93, p. 6. The play was

first performed in late 1588 or 1589; the earliest reliable text was published in 1604. Ibid., "Introduction," p. xii.

101. Carl Becker, *The Heavenly City of the Eighteenth-Century Philosophers* (New Haven, Conn., and London: Yale University Press, 1932), p. 42.

102. Quoted in Peter Gay, *Voltaire's Politics: The Poet as Realist* (1959; New Haven, Conn., and London, 1988), pp. 262, 265.

103. Baruch Spinoza, *Tractatus Theologico-Politicus* [1670], in Spinoza, *Opera*, ed. Gebhardt, vol. 3, pp. 81–96, quotations at 82/13–14, 87/2–4. For other references to the natural order as fixed and immutable, see ibid., pp. 84/22–23, 85/9, 86/20–21. See also Brad S. Gregory, "Faith in Reason: Spinoza's *Tractatus Theologico-Politicus* in an Historical Context," unpublished licentiate thesis, Institute of Philosophy (Hooger Instituut voor Wijsbegeerte), Catholic University of Louvain, Louvain, Belgium, 1987.

104. Friedrich Nietzsche, *Jenseits von Gut und Böse* [1886], in Nietzsche, *Werke: Kritische Gesamtausgabe*, ed. Giorgio Colli and Mazzino Montinari, pt. 6, vol. 2 (Berlin: Walter de Gruyter, 1968), p. 13/20–21 (emphasis in original). Spinoza's fans offer diametrically opposite assessments of his method and the form of his philosophy. Edwin Curley, for example, suggests "that Spinoza's choice of the axiomatic method represents nothing more, and nothing less, than an awesome commitment to intellectual honesty and clarity." In *The Collected Works of Spinoza,* ed. and trans. Curley, vol. 1 (Princeton, N.J.: Princeton University Press, 1985), p. 402.

105. R. M. Burns, *The Great Debate on Miracles: From Joseph Glanvill to David Hume* (Lewisburg, Pa.: Bucknell University Press, 1981).

106. David Hume, *An Enquiry Concerning Human Understanding* [1748], ed. Stephen Buckle (Cambridge: Cambridge University Press, 2007), with section 10, "Of Miracles," at pp. 96–116. Hume's work was originally entitled *Philosophical Essays Concerning Human Understanding;* it was subsequently republished as *An Enquiry Concerning Human Understanding* and is conventionally known as the *First Enquiry* in order to distinguish it from Hume's *Enquiry Concerning the Principles of Morals* (1751).

107. Hume, *First Enquiry,* ed. Buckle, p. 97.

108. Ibid., pp. 97, 100, 101.

109. Ibid., p. 101 (my emphasis).

110. See Jacalyn Duffin, *Medical Miracles: Doctors, Saints, and Healing in the Modern World* (New York: Oxford University Press, 2007), pp. 25–33. Referring to her analysis of over 1,400 purported miracles across more than four centuries, the non-Catholic hematologist and medical historian Duffin shows that far from credulously accepting testimony, the ecclesiastical officials of the Congregation of Rites (and since 1969, the Congregation for the Cause of the Canonization of Saints) have since the late sixteenth century actively sought the expert testimony of (usually) physicians (because most alleged miracles by would-be saints involve allegedly inexplicable healings) whose explicit charge is to explain the putative miracles in naturalistic terms, in accord with the best available scientific knowledge. In other words, since the late sixteenth century, at least until the recent relaxation in the stringency

of canonization proceedings under John Paul II, the Roman Catholic Church's presumptive goal in canonization proceedings has been to disprove alleged miracle claims. On Bassi, see also Paula Findlen, "Science as a Career in Enlightenment Italy: The Strategies of Laura Bassi," *Isis* 84 (1993): 441–469. In 1750, Benedict XIV's patronage led to the appointment at the University of Bologna of another brilliant woman, Maria Gaetana Agnesi (1718–1799), whom the university's academic senate named as *lectrice honoraria* in mathematics. See Massimo Mazzotti, *The World of Maria Gaetana Agnesi, Mathematician of God* (Baltimore: Johns Hopkins University Press, 2007), p. 122.

111. J. Houston, *Reported Miracles: A Critique of Hume* (Cambridge: Cambridge University Press, 1994), esp. pp. 121–207; C. Stephen Evans, *The Historical Christ and the Jesus of Faith: The Incarnational Narrative as History* (Oxford: Clarendon Press, 1996), esp. pp. 153–156; David Johnson, *Hume, Holism, and Miracles* (Ithaca, N.Y.: Cornell University Press, 1999); John Earman, *Hume's Abject Failure: The Argument against Miracles* (New York: Oxford University Press, 2000). In seeking to defend Hume's argument against Johnson's and Earman's critiques, Robert Fogelin rightly notes that "Hume's attitude toward miracles is of a piece with some of his most fundamental philosophical commitments," including his commitment to Newtonianism and desire to apply it to an understanding of human nature, and "his general commitment to the methods of natural science. Any event or activity whose causes lie outside the natural order represents a limitation on natural science." Robert J. Fogelin, *A Defense of Hume on Miracles* (Princeton, N.J.: Princeton University Press, 2003), pp. 55, 58, 61, quotations on 55, 61. Like so many commentators, Fogelin takes Hume's commitment to "natural science" as though it were metaphysically straightforward. Fogelin also correctly—and tellingly—notes that "to the extent that such miraculous interventions are acknowledged, history and the science of politics could not be pursued in the naturalistic spirit that Hume adopts." Ibid., p. 61. That is, their acknowledgment would have constrained human desires in ways Hume would have found undesirable—hence the denial of miracles was ideologically crucial for Hume.

112. Perhaps best known in the twentieth century are Rudolf Bultmann's claims that because "all our thinking to-day is shaped irrevocably by modern science," and modern science renders "senseless and impossible" any belief in the "mythical view of the world" with which the New Testament is inextricably linked, "it is impossible to use electric light and the wireless and to avail ourselves of modern medical and surgical discoveries, and at the same time to believe in the New Testament world of spirits and miracles." Bultmann, *Kerygma and Myth: A Theological Debate* [1948], ed. and trans. Reginald H. Fuller (1953; New York: Harper & Row, 1961), pp. 3–5. The same view is foundational in Van Harvey, *The Historian and the Believer: The Morality of Historical Knowledge and Christian Belief* (1966; Champaign-Urbana: University of Illinois Press, 1996), a work heavily based on assumptions drawn from Ernst Troeltsch and F. H. Bradley, among others, including Bradley's

well-known essay, "The Presuppositions of Critical History" [1874]. See F. H. Bradley, *The Presuppositions of Critical History, and Aphorisms,* ed. Guy Stock (Bristol, U.K.: Thoemmes Press, 1993). For a critique of such an approach and its assumptions, see Evans, *Historical Christ,* pp. 137–202, and the discussion of miracles and history in Michael R. Lincona, *The Resurrection of Jesus: A New Historiographical Approach* (Downers Grove, Ill.: IVP Academic, 2010), pp. 133–198.

113. I am grateful to Steve Heaney for discussion about these issues.

114. For this same idea developed in a different context, see Brad S. Gregory, "No Room for God? History, Science, Metaphysics, and the Study of Religion," *History and Theory* 47 (2008): 504–507.

115. Significantly, with the exception of Thomas Reid, nearly all Enlightenment thinkers contrasted the reliability of rational demonstration or sense perception by the individual epistemological subject with the supposedly inherent unreliability of testimony by others, and with what Reid called the "social operations of mind." On testimony as a fundamental and irreducible source of human knowledge that is interwoven with sense perception, memory, and inference, see the seminal study by C. A. J. Coady, *Testimony: A Philosophical Study* (Oxford: Clarendon Press, 1992). For an example of the significance of Coady's work in current New Testament scholarship, including the ways in which the reported miracles of Jesus are regarded, see Richard Bauckham, *Jesus and the Eyewitnesses: The Gospels as Eyewitness Testimony* (Grand Rapids, Mich.: Eerdmans, 2006).

116. Any adequate assessment of the history of modern biblical criticism, from Hobbes and Spinoza in the seventeenth century through Protestant and Catholic exegesis up to the present, must be aware of the extent to which not only the empirical findings of science have been conflated with metaphysical naturalism, but also the extent to which historical-critical textual criticism has uncritically assumed naturalism as a *dogma* rather than as a merely abstractive methodological assumption of scientific inquiry. As this chapter has sought to show, the deeper context for this sort of dogmatic naturalism is metaphysical univocity (as we shall see again in Chapter 6). The "overthrow of humanist criticism" of the Bible beginning in the later seventeenth century, as Jonathan Israel correctly states, was "a historical-critical and linguistic exercise anchored in a wider naturalistic philosophical standpoint" in which "historical" meant *"in fact conceptually impossible until, philosophically, all supernatural agency and magical forces are consciously eliminated from the perceived historical process."* Israel, *Enlightenment Contested,* pp. 409, 411 (my emphasis); see also Israel, *Radical Enlightenment,* pp. 447–451. The critical point, unmentioned by Israel, is that there was and is no logical connection between historicism and naturalism. Textual biblical criticism per se *did not and could not* have demonstrated that miracles had not or could not have happened. It is clear as well that the same assumption of dogmatic naturalism as a latter-day outgrowth of metaphysical univocity transformed by the theological controversies of the Reformation era was pervasive in the eighteenth and nineteenth centuries, when Protestant exegetes in England

and Germany solidified the dominant ground rules of modern biblical interpretation. See Hans Frei, *The Eclipse of Biblical Narrative: A Study in Eighteenth and Nineteenth Century Hermeneutics* (New Haven, Conn., and London: Yale University Press, 1974); Jonathan Sheehan, *The Enlightenment Bible: Translation, Scholarship, Culture* (Princeton, N.J.: Princeton University Press, 2005); Michael C. Legaspi, *The Death of Scripture and the Rise of Biblical Studies* (New York: Oxford University Press, 2010). Although Sheehan does not discuss it, the Bible's reconstitution as a culturally central rather than a religiously authoritative text in eighteenth-century Germany and nineteenth-century England presupposed metaphysical naturalism or its functional equivalent, a thoroughgoing epistemological skepticism about all alleged miracles.

117. In 1989, 82 percent of Americans polled agreed with the proposition that "even today, miracles are still performed by the power of God," and only 6 percent disagreed completely with the proposition. George Gallup Jr. and Jim Castelli, *The People's Religion: American Faith in the 90's* (New York: Macmillan; London: Collier, 1989), p. 58, cited in John P. Meier, *A Marginal Jew: Rethinking the Historical Jesus*, vol. 2, *Mentor, Message, and Miracles* (New York: Doubleday, 1994), pp. 520–521. Against Rudolf Bultmann and the many contemporary intellectuals who agree with him, Meier rightly infers from this data that "the academic creed of 'no modern person can believe in miracles' should be consigned to the dustbin of empirically falsified hypotheses." Ibid., p. 521.

118. Funkenstein, *Theology*, pp. 116, 360–363; Buckley, *Origins*, pp. 322–363.

119. The scholarship of Hugh McLeod has been especially important in building on the earlier work by Owen Chadwick, *The Secularization of the European Mind in the Nineteenth Century* (Cambridge: Cambridge University Press, 1975). See McLeod, *Secularisation in Western Europe, 1848–1914* (New York: St. Martin's Press, 2000), and *The Decline of Christendom in Western Europe*, ed. McLeod and Werner Ustorf (Cambridge: Cambridge University Press, 2003). On the importance of the acceleration of the process since the 1960s, see Callum G. Brown, *The Death of Christian Britain* (London and New York: Routledge, 2001), and McLeod, *The Religious Crisis of the 1960s* (New York: Oxford University Press, 2008).

120. On nineteenth-century irreligion and atheism among intellectual and cultural elites, see James Turner, *Without God, without Creed: The Origins of Unbelief in America* (Baltimore and London: Johns Hopkins University Press, 1985); A. N. Wilson, *God's Funeral* (New York: W. W. Norton, 1999); Richard Olson, *Science and Scientism in Nineteenth-Century Europe* (Champaign-Urbana: University of Illinois Press, 2007).

121. Immanuel Kant, *Die Religion innerhalb der Grenzen der blossen Vernunft* [1793], in Kant, *Gesammelte Schriften*, ed. Königlich Preußischen Akademie der Wissenschaften, vol. 6 (Berlin: Georg Reimer, 1914). For an important recent study of Kant's conception of divine providence along these lines, see Ulrich L. Lehner, *Kants Vorsehungskonzept auf dem Hintergrund der deutschen Schulphilosophie und -theologie* (Leiden: E. J. Brill, 2007).

122. Friedrich Daniel Ernst Schleiermacher, *Über die Religion: Reden an die Gebildeten unter ihren Verächtern* [1799], in Schleiermacher, *Kritische Gesamtausgabe*, Erste Abteilung: *Schriften und Entwürfe*, vol. 2, *Schriften aus der Berliner Zeit 1796–1799*, ed. Günter Meckenstock (Berlin: Walter de Gruyter, 1984), pp. 212/16–18, 211/32–33.

123. For example, he asserts that in Christianity "the Being of God gets Interpreted ontologically by means of the ancient ontology." Martin Heidegger, *Being and Time* [1927], trans. John Macquarrie and Edward Robinson (1962; Oxford: Blackwell, 1980), p. 74.

124. This last point is an extrapolation based on Sokolowski, *God of Faith and Reason*, pp. 21–23, 31–34, 46–51. In the introduction to *Being and Time*, Heidegger says that " 'Being' cannot indeed be conceived as an entity; *enti non additur aliqua natura:* nor can it acquire such a character as to have the term 'entity' applied to it. . . . Thus we cannot apply to Being the concept of 'definition' as presented in traditional logic, which itself has its foundations in ancient ontology and which, within certain limits, provides a quite justifiable way of defining 'entities.' " Heidegger, *Being and Time*, p. 23. On Heidegger's early work, *Duns Scotus's Doctrine of Categories and Meanings* (1915), see Herbert Spiegelberg, *The Phenomenological Movement*, 3rd ed. (The Hague: Martinus Nijhoff, 1982), pp. 355–358.

125. See, for example, Daniel C. Dennett, *Darwin's Dangerous Idea: Evolution and the Meanings of Life* (New York: Simon & Schuster, 1996). For a superb recent account of the discovery of the mechanism of genetic inheritance, see James Schwartz, *In Pursuit of the Gene: From Darwin to DNA* (Cambridge, Mass., and London: Harvard University Press, 2008).

126. On the late nineteenth and twentieth centuries, see James R. Moore, *The Post-Darwinian Controversies: A Study of the Protestant Struggle to Come to Terms with Darwin in Great Britain and America, 1870–1900* (Cambridge: Cambridge University Press, 1979); Alfred Kelly, *The Descent of Darwin: The Popularization of Darwinism in Germany, 1860–1914* (Chapel Hill: University of North Carolina Press, 1981); Ronald L. Numbers, *Darwinism Comes to America* (Cambridge, Mass., and London: Harvard University Press, 1998). For the reactions to Darwinism in Roman Catholicism, see Don O'Leary, *Roman Catholicism and Modern Science: A History* (New York and London: Continuum, 2006). Edward J. Larson treats the educational and legal history of the relationship between evolution and creationism in the United States through the 1990s in *Trial and Error: The American Controversy over Creation and Evolution*, 3rd ed. (Oxford: Oxford University Press, 2003).

127. For this process of secularization in American universities, see George M. Marsden, *The Soul of the American University: From Protestant Establishment to Established Nonbelief* (New York: Oxford University Press, 1994); Julie A. Reuben, *The Making of the Modern University: Intellectual Transformation and the Marginalization of Morality* (Chicago and London: University of Chicago Press, 1996); Roberts and Turner, *Sacred and Secular University;* and Christian Smith, "Secularizing American Higher Education: The

Case of Early American Sociology," in *The Secular Revolution: Power, Interests, and Conflict in the Secularization of American Public Life,* ed. Christian Smith (Berkeley and Los Angeles: University of California Press, 2003), pp. 97–159.

128. In the late nineteenth century, John Zahm, an American Catholic priest and professor of chemistry and physics at the University of Notre Dame, implicitly recognized this in his bestselling book, *Evolution and Dogma* (1896). See R. Scott Appleby, "Between Americanism and Modernism: John Zahm and Theistic Evolution," *Church History* 56 (1987): 476–483. Many contemporary "intelligent design" (ID) protagonists share with their neo-Darwinian opponents the same univocal metaphysics and the assumption that natural causality and supernatural influence are mutually exclusive. Advocates of ID posit that ordinary biological processes of natural selection and genetic mutation can account for much but not everything in the evolution of species, the remainder requiring recourse to God's intervention. Advances in the explanatory power of evolutionary theory send ID protagonists scrambling to find remaining sites for supernatural intervention; their opponents claim that none are left. Sharing notions of metaphysical univocity, both assume that God needs "room" to be God—which is precisely what traditional Christian theology says that God does not need, as a corollary of his radical transcendence and distinctness from creation. On this point, see also Gregory, "Insights," pp. 40–41.

129. For many examples, see the texts collected in *The Patristic Understanding of Creation: An Anthology of Writings from the Church Fathers on Creation and Design,* ed. William A. Dembski, Wayne J. Downs, and Justin B. A. Frederick (Riesel, Tex.: Erasmus Press, 2008); see also, especially for Basil of Caesarea and Gregory of Nyssa, Robert Louis Wilken, *The Spirit of Early Christian Thought: Seeking the Face of God* (New Haven, Conn., and London: Yale University Press, 2003), pp. 136–161.

130. Dennett, *Breaking the Spell,* pp. 245, 243, with the second quotation from Dennett, *Darwin's Dangerous Idea,* pp. 184–185. For a critique of a few of the many problems with Dennett's *Breaking the Spell,* see David Bentley Hart, "Daniel Dennett Hunts the Snark," *First Things* 169 (January 2007): 30–38.

131. Dennett, *Breaking the Spell,* pp. 210–217, 232–233, quotation on 233. The closest Dennett comes to entertaining a non-univocal Christian notion of God is in the following passage: "Professor Faith wants to teach me a new word, 'apophatic,' " which means, Dennett alleges, that "God is a Something that is Wonderful. He is an appropriate recipient of prayers, and that's about all we can say about Him. My concept of God is *apophatic!* What, you may ask, does that mean? It means that I *define* God as ineffable, unknowable, something beyond all human ken." Ibid., p. 232 (italics in original). Dennett might have deigned to learn something about the Cappadocian church fathers, with whom apophatic, negative theology is associated in early Christianity. He might also have explored the ways in which divine transcendence is related to divine immanence, creation to incarnation, in their writings, and to have followed their influence through subsequent Eastern and Western Chris-

tian mysticism and theology. But this would have required some work—which, were the scholarly engagement serious, would also have exposed the subjective contingency of Dennett's own assumptions and atheistic beliefs.

132. Brian Greene, *The Elegant Universe: Superstrings, Hidden Dimensions, and the Quest for the Ultimate Theory* (1999; New York: Vintage Books, 2003), p. 3 (italics in original).

133. See Lee Smolin, *The Trouble with Physics: The Rise of String Theory, the Fall of a Science, and What Comes Next* (Boston and New York: Mariner Books, 2007), and even more forcefully, Peter Woit, *Not Even Wrong: The Failure of String Theory and the Search for Unity in Physical Law* (New York: Basic Books, 2006).

134. In the words of theoretical physicist Freeman Dyson, "In fact, science is not a collection of truths. It is a continuing exploration of mysteries. Wherever we go exploring in the world around us, we find mysteries. Our planet is covered by continents and oceans whose origin we cannot explain. Our atmosphere is constantly stirred by poorly understood disturbances that we call weather and climate. The visible matter in the universe is outweighed by a much larger quantity of dark invisible matter that we do not understand at all. The origin of life is a total mystery, and so is the existence of human consciousness. We have no clear idea how the electrical discharges occurring in nerve cells in our brains are connected with our feelings and desires and actions. . . . Science is the sum total of a great multitude of mysteries. It is an unending argument between a great multitude of voices." Dyson, "How We Know," *New York Review of Books* 58:4, 10 March 2011, p. 10.

135. For just a few examples of Christian intellectuals who in sophisticated ways have in recent decades taken the findings of science as the basis for theological reflection, see Stanley Jaki, *The Road of Science and the Ways to God* (Edinburgh: Scottish Academic Press, 1978); Joachim Illies, *Schöpfung oder Evolution: Ein Naturwissenschaftler zur Menschenwerdung* (Zurich: Edition Interform, 1979); R. Jastrow, *God and the Astronomers* (New York: W. W. Norton, 1992); Keith Ward, *Religion and Revelation: A Theology of Revelation in the World's Religions* (Oxford: Clarendon Press, 1994), esp. pp. 283–343; Mark W. Worthing, *God, Creation, and Contemporary Physics* (Minneapolis: Fortress Press, 1996); N. H. Gregersen and J. W. Van Huyssteen, *Rethinking Theology and Science: Six Models for the Current Dialogue* (Grand Rapids, Mich.: Eerdmans, 1998); Miller, *Finding Darwin's God*; Haught, *Deeper Than Darwin*; Arthur R. Peacocke, *Evolution: The Disguised Friend of Faith? Selected Essays* (Philadelphia and London: Templeton Foundation Press, 2004); Collins, *Language of God*; Knight, *God of Nature*; Schönborn, *Chance or Purpose*; John Polkinghorne, *Exploring Reality: The Intertwining of Science and Religion* (New Haven, Conn., and London: Yale University Press, 2007), *Belief in God in an Age of Science* (New Haven, Conn., and London: Yale University Press, 2003), and *Quantum Physics and Theology*; Russell, *Cosmology from Alpha to Omega*; and *Creation and Evolution: A Conference with Pope Benedict XVI in Castel Gondolfo*, trans. Michael J. Miller (San Francisco: Ignatius Press, 2008).

136. Dyson, "How We Know," pp. 10–12.

137. Edward O. Wilson, *On Human Nature*, with a new preface (1978; Cambridge, Mass., and London: Harvard University Press, 2004), p. 1.

138. For Plantinga's argument, criticisms of it, and his rejoinders, see *Naturalism Defeated? Essays on Plantinga's Evolutionary Argument against Naturalism*, ed. James K. Beilby (Ithaca, N.Y.: Cornell University Press, 2002). Hart, *Atheist Delusions*, p. 103: "Even the simplest of things, and even the most basic of principles, must first of all *be*, and nothing within the universe of contingent things (nor even the universe itself, even if it were somehow 'eternal') can be intelligibly conceived of as the source or explanation of its own being" (italics in original). Hart is of course here restating in a compressed way Aquinas's third *via* in the *Summa Theologiae* I, q. 2, a. 3, based on ontological contingency. Despite the protestations of atheistic materialists to the contrary, "the universe" or "eternal matter-energy" cannot take the place of God (or some ontologically adequate substitute) here precisely because neither does nor can account for its own existence. "But where did God come from?" is a question that demonstrates an incomprehension of what Aquinas meant when he wrote, in accounting for ontological contingency, "hoc dicimus Deum"—"this we call God." Aquinas, *Summa Theologiae*, vol. 2, trans. McDermott, I, q. 2, a. 3, p. 16. To proclaim the universe as "just there" is not an answer to the question of ontological contingency, but a refusal to pursue it or an inability to see what the question means. I am grateful to John O'Callaghan for discussion about these issues.

139. Skeptics who are skeptical of their own views, and therefore open to new ideas and alternative truth claims, differ from fundamentalist skeptics who are sure of their skepticism and thus, it would seem, not skeptics but rather dogmatists.

## 2. Relativizing Doctrines

1. On the recent global spread of (especially evangelical Protestant) Christianity, see, for example, Mark A. Noll, *The New Shape of World Christianity: How American Experience Reflects Global Faith* (Downers Grove, Ill.: IVP Academic, 2009); see also Philip Jenkins, *The Next Christendom: The Coming of Global Christianity* (New York: Oxford University Press, 2002).

2. Max Weber, "Wissenschaft als Beruf" [1919], in Weber, *Gesamtausgabe*, Abteilung I: *Schriften und Reden*, vol. 17, ed. Wolfgang J. Mommsen and Wolfgang Schluchter with Birgitt Morgenbrod (Tübingen: J. C. B. Mohr, 1992), pp. 97–98, 99/13–15, 104/35–37.

3. Jeffrey Stout, *Democracy and Tradition* (Princeton, N.J.: Princeton University Press, 2004), p. 32. Chapters 2 and 3 of the present book answer his question with respect to Western Christianity since the Reformation.

4. Brad S. Gregory, "The Other Confessional History: On Secular Bias in the Study of Religion," *History and Theory, Theme Issue* 45 (2006): 132–149.

5. See, for example, Callum G. Brown, *The Death of Christian Britain* (London and New York: Routledge, 2001), and Hugh McLeod, *The Religious Crisis of the 1960s* (New York: Oxford University Press, 2008).

6. *Planned Parenthood v. Casey,* 505 U.S. 833 (1992) §2.

7. Lisa Jardine, *Worldly Goods: A New History of the Renaissance* (New York and London: W. W. Norton, 1996), p. 34.

8. Kwame Anthony Appiah, *Cosmopolitanism: Ethics in a World of Strangers* (New York and London: W. W. Norton, 2006), p. 10.

9. In the latter category see, for example, Donald Black, "Dreams of Pure Sociology," *Sociological Theory* 18:3 (2000): 343–367, and Stephan Fuchs, *Against Essentialism: A Theory of Culture and Society* (Cambridge, Mass., and London: Harvard University Press, 2001).

10. John Searle, *The Construction of Social Reality* (New York: Free Press, 1995), pp. 1–3, 27–29, 190–194; see also the critique by Christian Smith of the failure to maintain this distinction, in Smith, *What Is a Person? Rethinking Humanity, Social Life, and the Common Good from the Person Up* (Chicago: University of Chicago Press, 2010), especially the treatment of what Smith calls "strong constructionism" at pp. 123–149. Searle's distinction is in turn derived from G. E. M. Anscombe's distinction between "brute facts" and "institutional facts," in Anscombe, "On Brute Facts," *Analysis* 18:3 (1958): 69–72.

11. Michel Foucault, *Les mots et les choses* (Paris: Gallimard, 1966).

12. For trenchant observations on this point, see Steve Jones, *Darwin's Ghost: "The Origin of Species" Updated* (1999; New York: Ballantine Books, 2001), pp. 326–330.

13. On radical, anticonsumerist environmentalism of this sort, see for example David Pepper, *Communes and the Green Vision: Counterculture, Lifestyle, and the New Age* (London: Green Print, 1991); for a specific example of such a community, see the Web site for the Dancing Rabbit Ecovillage in Missouri, at http://www.dancingrabbit.org; for intentional communities related to environmentalism more broadly, see the Web site of the Fellowship for Intentional Community, at http://www.ic.org.

14. John J. Mearsheimer, "Mearsheimer's Response: 'Teaching Morality at the Margins,'" *Philosophy and Literature* 22 (1998): 195. Mearsheimer was responding to those who had questioned his characterization of the University of Chicago as "a remarkably amoral institution" along with "all other major colleges and universities in this country." Mearsheimer, "The Aims of Education," *Philosophy and Literature* 22 (1998): 149.

15. Mearsheimer, "Mearsheimer's Response," p. 196.

16. John Van Engen, "Multiple Options: The World of the Fifteenth-Century Church," *Church History* 77:2 (2008): 257–284; R. N. Swanson, *Religion and Devotion in Europe, c. 1215–c. 1515* (Cambridge: Cambridge University Press, 1995); Richard Kieckhefer, *Unquiet Souls: Fourteenth-Century Saints and Their Religious Milieu* (Chicago: University of Chicago Press, 1984).

17. Malcolm Lambert, *Medieval Heresy: Popular Movements from the Gregorian Reform to the Reformation,* 3rd ed. (Oxford: Blackwell, 2002); Euan Cameron, *Waldenses: Rejections of Holy Church in Medieval Europe* (Oxford: Blackwell, 2000); Anne Hudson, *The Premature Reformation: Wycliffite Texts and Lollard History* (Oxford: Clarendon Press, 1988); Thomas A. Fudge,

*The Magnificent Ride: The First Reformation in Hussite Bohemia* (Aldershot, U.K.: Ashgate, 1998).

18. Van Engen, "Multiple Options," and "The Future of Medieval Church History," *Church History* 71:3 (2002): 492–522; Swanson, *Religion and Devotion*; Eamon Duffy, *The Stripping of the Altars: Traditional Religion in England, c. 1400–c. 1580*, 2nd ed. (New Haven, Conn., and London: Yale University Press, 2005); Thomas A. Brady Jr., *German Histories in the Age of Reformations, 1400–1650* (Cambridge: Cambridge University Press, 2009), pp. 49–68.

19. Besides listening to and comparing the music for its stylistic and compositional differences, see Allan W. Atlas, *Renaissance Music: Music in Western Europe, 1400–1600* (New York: W. W. Norton, 1997), pp. 112–134, 145–167, 293–324, 407–413, 536–541; the respective contributions on the composition and characteristics of Josquin's Masses by Bonnie J. Blackburn, Alejandro Enrique Planchart, M. Jennifer Bloxam, and Richard Sherr, in *The Josquin Companion*, ed. Sherr (Oxford: Oxford University Press, 2000), pp. 51–247; Christopher A. Reynolds, *Papal Patronage and the Music of St. Peter's, 1380–1513* (Berkeley and Los Angeles: University of California Press, 1996); and Andrew Kirkman, *The Cultural Life of the Early Polyphonic Mass: Medieval Context to Modern Revival* (Cambridge: Cambridge University Press, 2010).

20. Besides comparing paintings, many of which are now in major art museums, see, for example, James Snyder, Larry Silver, and Henry Luttikhuizen, *Northern Renaissance Art: Painting, Sculpture, the Graphic Arts from 1350 to 1575*, rev. ed. (Upper Saddle River, N.J.: Pearson/Prentice-Hall, 2005); Susie Nash, *Northern Renaissance Art* (New York: Oxford University Press, 2009); Richard Marks, *Image and Devotion in Late Medieval England* (Stroud, U.K.: Sutton, 2004); Émile Mâle, *L'art religieux de la fin du Moyen Âge en France: Étude sur l'iconographie du Moyen Âge et sur ses sources d'inspiration*, 7th ed. (Paris: A. Colin, 1995); Michael Baxandall, *Painting and Experience in Fifteenth-Century Italy: A Primer in the History of Pictorial Style*, 2nd ed. (Oxford: Oxford University Press, 1988); Diana Norman, *Painting in Late Medieval and Renaissance Siena, 1260–1555* (New Haven, Conn., and London: Yale University Press, 2003); Richard Viladesau, *The Triumph of the Cross: The Passion of Christ in Theology and the Arts from the Renaissance to the Counter-Reformation* (New York: Oxford University Press, 2008), pp. 11–102.

21. See Heiko A. Oberman, *The Harvest of Medieval Theology: Gabriel Biel and Late Medieval Nominalism* (Cambridge, Mass.: Harvard University Press, 1963); Oberman, "The Shape of Late Medieval Thought: The Birthpangs of the Modern Era," in *The Dawn of the Reformation: Essays in Late Medieval and Early Reformation Thought* (Edinburgh: T. & T. Clark, 1986), pp. 26–29; Paul Oskar Kristeller, *Le thomisme et la pensée italienne de la renaissance* (Montreal: Institut d'Études Médiévales; Paris: J. Vrin, 1967); James K. Farge, *Orthodoxy and Reform in Early Reformation France: The Faculty of Theology of Paris, 1500–1543* (Leiden: E. J. Brill, 1985), pp. 13–18, 33–37; Adolar Zumkeller, *Theology and History of the Augustinian School in the Middle Ages*, ed. John E. Rotelle (Philadelphia: Augustinian Press, 1996); Eric Leland

Saak, *High Way to Heaven: The Augustinian Platform between Reform and Reformation, 1292–1524* (Leiden: E. J. Brill, 2002). For Fisher, see Malcolm Underwood, "John Fisher and the Promotion of Learning," in *Humanism, Reform and the Reformation: The Career of Bishop John Fisher,* ed. Brendan Bradshaw and Eamon Duffy (Cambridge: Cambridge University Press, 1989), pp. 25–46; Duffy, "The Spirituality of John Fisher," in ibid., pp. 222–225; and Richard Rex, *The Theology of John Fisher* (Cambridge: Cambridge University Press, 1991), pp. 28–29, 50–64; for Eck, see Erwin Iserloh, *Johannes Eck (1486–1543): Scholastiker, Humanist, Kontroverstheologe* (Münster: Aschendorff, 1981).

22. Johan Huizinga, *The Autumn of the Middle Ages,* trans. Rodney J. Payton and Ulrich Mammitzsch (Chicago: University of Chicago Press, 1996). Huizinga's classic work is much better known in English by the (misleading) title *The Waning of the Middle Ages,* which was (loosely) translated, adapted, and abridged by Fritz Hopman, first published in 1924, and many times reprinted; Huizinga's *Herfsttij der Middeleeuwen* first appeared in 1919. See Rodney J. Payton, "Translator's Introduction," in Huizinga, *Autumn,* trans. Payton and Mammitzsch, pp. ix–xviii. In his work on Gabriel Biel, Heiko Oberman noted the same misleading translation of Huizinga's work: "Deeply indebted as we are to Johan Huizinga's *The Waning of the Middle Ages,* the image of 'harvest' in our title is intentionally opposed to the connotations of 'decline' carried by the French and English translations of the Dutch 'Herfsttij,' which literally means 'harvest-tide.' " Oberman, *Harvest,* p. 5.

23. Duffy, *Stripping of the Altars;* Duffy, *Marking the Hours: English People and their Prayers, 1240–1570* (New Haven, Conn., and London: Yale University Press, 2006); Bernd Moeller, "Religious Life in Germany on the Eve of the Reformation," in *Pre-Reformation Germany,* ed. Gerald Strauss (New York: Harper & Row, 1972), pp. 13–42, originally published as "Frömmigkeit in Deutschland um 1500," *Archiv für Reformationsgeschichte* 56 (1965): 3–31; Anne Winston-Allen, *Stories of the Rose: The Making of the Rosary in the Middle Ages* (University Park: Pennsylvania State University Press, 1997); Ellen Ross, *The Grief of God: Images of the Suffering Jesus in Late Medieval England* (New York: Oxford University Press, 1997); Christopher F. Black, *Italian Confraternities in the Sixteenth Century* (Cambridge: Cambridge University Press, 1989); *Christianity and the Renaissance: Image and Religious Imagination in the Quattrocento,* ed. Timothy Verdon and John Henderson (Syracuse, N.Y.: Syracuse University Press, 1990), pp. 229–404; Berndt Hamm, "Normative Centering in the Fifteenth and Sixteenth Centuries: Observations on Religiosity, Theology, and Iconology," trans. John Frymire, in Hamm, *The Reformation of Faith in the Context of Late Medieval Theology and Piety,* ed. Robert J. Bast (Leiden: E. J. Brill, 2004), pp. 1–49, originally published as "Normative Zentrierung im 15. und 16. Jahrhundert. Beobachtungen zu Religiosität, Theologie und Ikonologie," *Zeitschrift für Historische Forschung* 26 (1999): 163–202; Caroline Walker Bynum, *Wonderful Blood: Theology and Practice in Late Medieval Northern Germany and Beyond* (Philadelphia: University of Pennsylvania Press, 2007).

24. See, for example, the documents in *Manifestations of Discontent in Germany on the Eve of the Reformation,* ed. and trans. Gerald Strauss (1971; Bloomington: University of Indiana Press, 1985); on anticlericalism, see Kaspar Elm, "Antiklerikalismus im deutschen Mittelalter," in *Anticlericalism in Late Medieval and Early Modern Europe,* ed. Peter A. Dykema and Heiko A. Oberman (Leiden: E. J. Brill, 1993), pp. 3–18, and the other articles on the late Middle Ages in this collection.

25. Francis Oakley, *The Western Church in the Later Middle Ages* (Ithaca, N.Y., and London: Cornell University Press, 1979), pp. 213–259; Gerald Strauss, "Ideas of *Reformatio* and *Renovatio* from the Middle Ages to the Reformation," in *Handbook of European History, 1400–1600: Late Middle Ages, Renaissance, and Reformation,* ed. Thomas A. Brady Jr., Heiko A. Oberman, and James D. Tracy, vol. 2 (Leiden: E. J. Brill, 1995), pp. 1–30; Michael A. Mullett, *The Catholic Reformation* (London and New York: Routledge, 1999), pp. 1–28. On Gerson, see Brian Patrick McGuire, *Jean Gerson and the Last Medieval Reformation* (University Park: Pennsylvania State University Press, 2005); on Bernardino, see Cynthia L. Polecritti, *Preaching Peace in Renaissance Italy: Bernardino of Siena and His Audience* (Washington, D.C.: Catholic University of America Press, 2000); on Antonino, see Peter Francis Howard, *Beyond the Written Word: Preaching and Theology in the Florence of Archbishop Antoninus, 1427–1459* ([Florence:] Leo S. Olschki, 1995).

26. John Van Engen, *Sisters and Brothers of the Common Life: The Devotio Moderna and the World of the Late Middle Ages* (Philadelphia: University of Pennsylvania Press, 2008); R. R. Post, *The Modern Devotion: Confrontation with Reformation and Humanism* (Leiden: E. J. Brill, 1968); Eric Cochrane, *Italy 1530–1630,* ed. Julius Kirshner (London and New York: Longman, 1988), pp. 106–123; Barry M. Collett, *Italian Benedictine Scholars and the Reformation: The Congregation of Santa Giustina of Padua* (Oxford: Clarendon Press, 1985); *Reformbemühungen und Observanzbestrebungen im spätmittelalterlichen Ordenswesen,* ed. Kaspar Elm (Berlin: Duncker & Humblot, 1989); Jean-Marie Le Gall, *Les moines au temps des Réformes: France (1480–1560)* (Seyssel: Champ Vallon, 2001); Lewis W. Spitz, *The Religious Renaissance of the German Humanists* (Cambridge, Mass.: Harvard University Press, 1963); John B. Gleason, *John Colet* (Berkeley and Los Angeles: University of California Press, 1989); *Erasmus' Vision of the Church,* ed. Hilmar Pabel (Kirksville, Mo.: Sixteenth Century Journal Publishers, 1995); James D. Tracy, *Erasmus of the Low Countries* (Berkeley and Los Angeles: University of California Press, 1996); Cornelis Augustijn, *Erasmus: Der Humanist als Theologe und Kirchenreformer* (Leiden: E. J. Brill, 1997).

27. Euan Cameron, *The European Reformation* (Oxford: Clarendon Press, 1991), pp. 38–41.

28. Ibid., pp. 40–41, 44–45. On curial cardinals' concern for their own and their family members' property and money, see Barbara McClung Hallman, *Italian Cardinals, Reform, and the Church as Property, 1492–1563* (Berkeley and Los Angeles: University of California Press, 1985); for the late medieval imperial episcopacy and anti-episcopal sentiment, see Thomas A. Brady Jr.,

"The Holy Roman Empire's Bishops on the Eve of the Reformation," in *Continuity and Change: The Harvest of Late Medieval and Reformation History: Essays Presented to Heiko Oberman on His 70th Birthday*, ed. Robert J. Bast and Andrew C. Gow (Leiden: E. J. Brill, 2000), pp. 21–47, and F. R. H. Du Boulay, *Germany in the Later Middle Ages* (London: Athlone Press, 1983), pp. 187–195.

29. Heiko A. Oberman, *Forerunners of the Reformation: The Shape of Late Medieval Thought, Illustrated by Key Documents* (New York: Holt, Rinehart and Winston, 1966); Erika Rummel, "Voices of Reform from Hus to Erasmus," in *Handbook*, ed. Brady et al., vol. 2, pp. 61–91.

30. On the concordats and the character of jurisdictionally "national" or "regional" churches in the fifteenth and early sixteenth centuries, see Van Engen, "The Church in the Fifteenth Century," in *Handbook*, ed. Brady et al., vol. 1, pp. 318–319; Cameron, *European Reformation*, pp. 53–55; Oakley, *Western Church*, pp. 72–74; Du Boulay, *Germany*, pp. 187–195; Brady, *German Histories*, pp. 135–139.

31. Francis Rapp, *Réformes et réformation à Strasbourg: Église et société dans le diocèse de Strasbourg (1450–1525)* (Paris: Éditions Ophrys, 1974), pp. 410–419; Manfred Schulze, *Fürsten und Reformation: Geistliche Reformpolitik weltlicher Fürsten vor der Reformation* (Tübingen: Mohr, 1991); Ronald K. Rittgers, *The Reformation of the Keys: Confession, Conscience, and Authority in Sixteenth-Century Germany* (Cambridge, Mass., and London: Harvard University Press, 2004), pp. 18–21; William Bradford Smith, *Reformation and the German Territorial State: Upper Franconia, 1300–1630* (Rochester, N.Y.: University of Rochester Press, 2008), pp. 17–58. Nor did the expulsion of bishops as civic rulers betoken changes in doctrine or alterations in prescriptions of proper religious practice. See J. Jeffrey Tyler, *Lord of the Sacred City: The "Episcopus exclusus" in Late Medieval and Early Modern Germany* (Leiden: E. J. Brill, 1999).

32. Referring to major Lutheran and Reformed Protestant theologians from the 1520s through the 1540s, Cameron rightly notes "the essential novelty and destructive power of the reformers' beliefs about human salvation" and "the devastating force of their logic": "At every critical point they challenged, redefined, and rearranged the very building-blocks of medieval belief: sin, law, faith, justification, the Church, in explicit defiance not only of the 'Occamist school', but of a much broader medieval consensus." Cameron, *European Reformation*, pp. 111–167, 191–193, quotations on 192, 111.

33. Heiko A. Oberman, *Luther: Man between God and the Devil*, trans. Eileen Walliser-Schwarzbart (New Haven, Conn., and London: Yale University Press, 1989), pp. 59–74; Walter Klaassen, *Living at the End of the Ages: Apocalyptic Expectation in the Radical Reformation* (Lanham, Md.: University Press of America, 1992). On medieval apocalypticism, see Bernard McGinn, *Visions of the End: Apocalyptic Traditions in the Middle Ages* (New York: Columbia University Press, 1979), and Curtis V. Bostick, *The Antichrist and the Lollards: Apocalypticism in Late Medieval and Reformation England* (Leiden: E. J. Brill, 1998); and on apocalyptic preaching in Italy in

the early sixteenth century, see Ottavia Niccoli, *Prophecy and the People in Renaissance Italy*, trans. Lydia G. Cochrane (Princeton, N.J.: Princeton University Press, 1990), pp. 89–120.

34. Donald Weinstein, *Savonarola and Florence: Prophecy and Patriotism in the Renaissance* (Princeton, N.J.: Princeton University Press, 1970); Lauro Martines, *Fire in the City: Savonarola and the Struggle for the Soul of Renaissance Florence* (New York: Oxford University Press, 2006); Berndt Hamm, "Between Severity and Mercy. Three Models of Pre-Reformation Urban Reform Preaching: Savonarola—Staupitz—Geiler," in *Reformation of Faith*, ed. Bast, pp. 55–65.

35. Martin Luther, *Disputatio excellentium . . . Iohannis Eccii et D. Martini Lutheri Augustiniani* [1519], in *WA*, vol. 2 (Weimar: Hermann Böhlau, 1884), p. 279/23–28.

36. "Fallitur quisquis aliunde christianismi formam petit, quam e scriptura canonica." Philipp Melanchthon, *Loci communes rerum theologicarum, seu hypotyposes theologicae* [1521], in *CR*, vol. 21 (Braunschweig: C. A. Schwetschke & Sohn, 1854), cols. 82–83.

37. Andreas Bodenstein von Karlstadt, *Predig oder homilien uber den propheten Malachiam gnant* [1522], sig. B3v, quoted in Ronald J. Sider, *Andreas Bodenstein von Karlstadt: The Development of His Thought, 1517–1525* (Leiden: E. J. Brill, 1974), p. 164 (Sider's trans.).

38. Huldrych Zwingli, *Von Clarheit vnnd gewüsse oder vnbetrogliche des worts gottes* [1522], in *ZW*, vol. 1, ed. Emil Egli and Georg Finsler, in *CR*, vol. 88 (Leipzig: M. Heinsius, 1905), p. 382/20–26, quotation at lines 24–26.

39. "Die Akten der zweiten Disputation vom 26.–28. Oktober 1523," in *ZW*, vol. 2, ed. Egli and Finsler, in *CR*, vol. 89 (Leipzig: M. Heinsius Nachfolger, 1908), p. 717/9–11, 26–28.

40. "Die Mühlhauser Artikel" [1524], in *Flugschriften der Bauernkriegszeit*, ed. Adolf Laube and Hans Werner Seiffert (Berlin: Akademie-Verlag, 1975), p. 80/13–14, 3–4.

41. Argula von Grumbach, *Wye ein Christliche fraw des adels, in Bayern dürch iren, in Gottlicher schrifft, wolgegrundtenn Sendbrieffe, die hohenschul zu Ingoldstadt. . . .* ([Erfurt: Matthes Maler,] 1523), sig. [A4]. On Zell, see Elsie Anne McKee, *Katharina Schütz Zell*, 2 vols. (Leiden: E. J. Brill, 1999).

42. Karlstadt, *Ob man gemach faren, und des ergernüssen der schwachen verschonen soll, in sachen so gottis willen angehn* [1524], repr. in *Karlstadts Schriften aus den Jahren 1523–25*, ed. Erich Hertzsch, vol. 1 (Halle: Max Niemeyer Verlag, 1956), p. 75/17–18.

43. Zwingli, *Clarheit*, in *ZW*, vol. 1, p. 360/7–10.

44. Luther, *Von anbeten des Sacraments des heyligen leychnams Christi* [1523] in *WA*, vol. 11 (Weimar: Hermann Böhlaus Nachfolger, 1900), p. 438/12–14.

45. "Darauß aber volget, dz wir an die schrifft angehenckt seyn, das sich keiner nach seines hertzen gutduncken richten dörfft. . . ." Karlstadt, *Ob man gemach*, in *Karlstadts Schriften*, ed. Hertzsch, vol. 1, p. 75/31–33.

46. ". . . uß eignem gütdunken nit ein einigs stuk erfinden, leren und uffrichten." Conrad Grebel to Thomas Müntzer, 5 September 1524, in *QGTS*, vol. 1, ed.

Leonhard von Muralt and Walter Schmid (Zurich: S. Hirzel-Verlag, 1952), p. 17.

47. Hans Hut, "Von dem geheimnus der tauf. . . ." [1527], repr. in *QGT,* vol. 3, *Glaubenszeugnisse oberdeutscher Taufgesinnter,* pt. 1, ed. Lydia Müller (Leipzig: Heinsius, 1938), p. 15.

48. Luther, *Tractatus de libertate Christiana* [1520], in *WA,* vol. 7 (Weimar: Hermann Böhlaus Nachfolger, 1897), p. 51/12–13: "Quaeres autem, 'Quod nam est verbum hoc, aut qua arte utendum est eo, cum tam multa sint verba dei?'" Luther's own German translation of his Latin is significantly different, and for a wider audience avoided any reference to "so many words of God": "Fragistu aber 'wilchs ist denn das wort, das solch grosse gnad gibt, Und wie sol ichs gebrauchen?'" Luther, *Von der Freiheit eines Christenmenschen* [1520], in ibid., p. 22/23–24.

49. For the Old Testament, eucharistic practices, and oral confession, see Sider, *Karlstadt,* pp. 108–112, 143–146; for images, see Karlstadt, *Von abtuhung der Bylder, Vnd das keyn Betdler vnther den Christen seyn soll* [1522], repr. in *Flugschriften der frühen Reformationsbewegung (1518–1524),* vol. 1, ed. Adolf Laube et al. (Verduz: Topos Verlag, 1983), pp. 105–127. Karlstadt refused to change his views, so his preaching was restricted and a treatise that he had written (in a veiled manner) against Luther was confiscated and destroyed. See James S. Preus, *Carlstadt's "Ordinaciones" and Luther's Liberty: A Study of the Wittenberg Movement, 1521–22* (Cambridge, Mass.: Harvard University Press, 1974), pp. 73–77.

50. See the list of the treatises in *Luther's Works,* vol. 37, ed. Robert H. Fischer (Philadelphia: Fortress Press, 1961), pp. 8–11; see also G. R. Potter, *Zwingli* (Cambridge: Cambridge University Press, 1976), p. 296. The classic, magisterial work on the theological controversy is Walther Köhler, *Zwingli und Luther: Ihr Streit über das Abendmahl nach seinen politischen und religiösen Beziehungen,* 2 vols. (1924, 1953; New York and London: Johnson, 1971).

51. For an overview of the early conflict between Luther and Zwingli and its consequences, see Philip Benedict, *Christ's Churches Purely Reformed: A Social History of Calvinism* (New Haven, Conn., and London: Yale University Press, 2002), pp. 15–48. On the Marburg Colloquy itself, see also G. R. Potter, *Zwingli* (Cambridge: Cambridge University Press, 1976), pp. 316–331; Heinrich Bornkamm, *Luther in Mid-Career, 1521–1530,* ed. Karin Bornkamm, trans. E. Theodore Bachmann (Philadelphia: Fortress Press, 1983), pp. 633–652; Martin Brecht, *Martin Luther,* vol. 2, *Shaping and Defining the Reformation, 1521–1532,* trans. James L. Schaaf (Minneapolis: Fortress Press, 1990), pp. 325–334. In Oberman's words, "Marburg marked a profound, painful turning point in Reformation history, as the joy of having discovered the Bible to be the conclusive foundation of Evangelical faith could not remain undiminished when the reformers came to disagree over the 'clear' text of the Scriptures." Oberman, *Luther,* p. 244.

52. On Zwingli and the earliest Swiss Anabaptists, see Potter, *Zwingli,* pp. 160–197; for a recent overview of the origins of Swiss Anabaptism, see C. Arnold Snyder, "Swiss Anabaptism: The Beginnings, 1523–1525," in *A Companion*

*to Anabaptism and Spiritualism, 1521–1700,* ed. John D. Roth and James M. Stayer (Leiden: E. J. Brill, 2007), pp. 45–81. For the city council's mandate of 7 March 1526 sentencing obstinate Anabaptists to death by drowning, see *QGTS,* vol. 1, pp. 180–181; see also Snyder, *Anabaptist History and Theology: An Introduction* (Kitchener, Ont.: Pandora Press, 1995), p. 60.

53. Grebel to Müntzer, in *QGTS,* vol. 1, p. 18; [Felix Mantz], "Protestation und Schutzschrift [an den Rat von Zürich]," in ibid., p. 26; Hut, "Geheimnus der Tauf," in *QGT,* vol. 3, p. 27; Michael Sattler, *Brüderlich vereynigung etzlicher kinder Gottes, sieben Artickel betreffend. . . ."* [1533], ed. Walter Köhler, in *Flugschriften aus den ersten Jahren der Reformation,* ed. Otto Clemen, vol. 2 (Leipzig and New York: Rudolf Haupt, 1908), p. 307.

54. Huldrych Zwingli, *Von dem Touff, vom Widertouff und vom Kindertouff* [1525], in *ZW,* vol. 4, ed. Emil Egli et al., vol. 91 in *CR* (Leipzig: M. Heinsius Nachfolger, 1927), p. 216/14–16, 22–25.

55. On the Peasants' War, see Peter Blickle, *The Revolution of 1525: The German Peasants' War from a New Perspective,* trans. Thomas A. Brady Jr. and H. C. Erik Midelfort (Baltimore and London: Johns Hopkins University Press, 1981), and *The German Peasants' War: A History in Documents,* ed. and trans. Tom Scott and Bob Scribner (Atlantic Highlands, N.J., and London: Humanities Press International, 1991); on Müntzer, see Hans-Jürgen Goertz, *Thomas Müntzer: Apocalyptic, Mystic, and Revolutionary,* trans. Jocelyn Jaquiery, ed. Peter Matheson (Edinburgh: T. & T. Clark, 1993), and Abraham Friesen, *Thomas Muentzer, a Destroyer of the Godless: The Making of a Sixteenth-Century Religious Revolutionary* (Berkeley and Los Angeles: University of California Press, 1990). For Hergot and Gaismair, see "Michael Gaismairs Tiroler Landesordnung" [1526], and Hans Hergot, *Von der neuen Wandlung eines christlichen Lebens* [1527], in *Flugschriften der Bauernkriegszeit,* ed. Laube and Seiffert, pp. 139–143, 547–557; Blickle, *Revolution of 1525,* pp. 145–154; Walter Klaassen, *Michael Gaismair: Revolutionary and Reformer* (Leiden: E. J. Brill, 1978).

56. See Claus-Peter Clasen, *Anabaptism: A Social History, 1525–1618. Switzerland, Austria, Moravia, and South and Central Germany* (Ithaca, N.Y., and London: Cornell University Press, 1972), pp. 30–48; Snyder, *Anabaptist History and Theology;* Werner O. Packull, *Hutterite Beginnings: Communitarian Experiments during the Reformation* (Baltimore and London: Johns Hopkins University Press, 1995); and the contributions on Anabaptism in *Companion to Anabaptism and Spiritualism,* ed. Roth and Stayer.

57. See James M. Stayer, *Anabaptists and the Sword,* 2nd ed. (Lawrence, Kans.: Coronado Press, 1976), pp. 93–131, 141–146; Snyder, *Anabaptist History and Theology,* pp. 51–59, 191–193.

58. See Packull, *Hutterite Beginnings;* John S. Oyer, *Lutheran Reformers against Anabaptists: Luther, Melanchthon and Menius and the Anabaptists of Central Germany* (The Hague: Martinus Nijhoff, 1964). On Pilgram Marpeck's indebtedness to and origins among the Austerlitz Brethren, see James A. Stayer, "Pilgram Marpeck and the Austerlitz Brethren: A 'Disappeared' Anabaptist Denomination," *Mennonite Life* 64 (Summer 2010), online edition,

http://www.bethelks.edu/mennonitelife/2010/pilgram.php (accessed 5 February 2011). I am grateful to Professor Stayer for discussion on this point and for drawing my attention to his article. On Marpeck, see also Stephen Boyd, *Pilgram Marpeck: His Life and Social Theology* (Mainz: Verlag Philipp von Zabern, 1992).

59. For the division between Gnesio-Lutherans and Philippists prior to the Formula of Concord, see Irene Dingel, "The Culture of conflict in the Controversies Leading to the Formula of Concord (1548–1580)," in *Lutheran Ecclesiastical Culture, 1550–1675,* ed. Robert Kolb (Leiden: E. J. Brill, 2008), pp. 15–64; for the multiple Dutch Anabaptist groups and the schisms among them, see S. Zijlstra, *Om de ware gemeente en de oude gronden: Geschiedenis van de dopersen in de Nederlanden, 1531–1675* (Hilversum: Verloren; Leeuwarden: Fryske Akademy, 2000), pp. 148–169, 197–210, 270–315, 381–401; on conflicts between Calvinists and Arminians in the Dutch Republic and England, see Benedict, *Christ's Churches,* pp. 305–316; for the enormous range of radical Protestants to c. 1580, see George Hunston Williams, *The Radical Reformation,* 3rd ed. (Kirksville, Mo.: Sixteenth Century Studies Publishers, 1992); for the same heterogeneity in the seventeenth century, see Leszek Kołakowski, *Chrétiens sans église: La conscience religieuse et le lien confessional au XVIIe siècle,* trans. Anna Posner (Paris: Gallimard, 1969).

60. Benjamin J. Kaplan, *Divided by Faith: Religious Conflict and the Practice of Toleration in Early Modern Europe* (Cambridge, Mass., and London: Belknap Press of Harvard University Press, 2007), p. 3.

61. For Calvin's conversion, see the account in Bruce Gordon's recent biography, *Calvin* (New Haven, Conn., and London: Yale University Press, 2009), pp. 33–35; see also the analysis of the events of autumn 1533 in the classic study by Alexandre Ganoczy, *The Young Calvin,* trans. David Foxgrover and Wade Provo (Philadelphia: Westminster Press, 1987), pp. 76–83.

62. For a concise overview, see Richard C. Gamble, "Calvin's Controversies," in *The Cambridge Companion to John Calvin,* ed. Donald K. McKim (Cambridge: Cambridge University Press, 2004), pp. 188–203; see also Jean-François Gilmont, *John Calvin and the Printed Book,* trans. Karin Maag (Kirksville, Mo.: Truman State University Press, 2005), pp. 69–73, 93–107. On Luther's doctrinal conflicts with magisterial and radical Protestants, see Mark U. Edwards Jr., *Luther and the False Brethren* (Stanford, Calif.: Stanford University Press, 1975).

63. William Chillingworth, *The Religion of Protestants a Safe Way to Salvation. . . .* (Oxford: Leonard Lichfield, 1638), p. 375.

64. Kaplan, *Divided by Faith,* p. 142.

65. See Jerzy Kłoczowski, "The Polish Church," in *Church and Society in Catholic Europe of the Eighteenth Century,* ed. William J. Callahan and David Higgs (1979; Cambridge: Cambridge University Press, 2008), pp. 122–137; Magda Teter, *Jews and Heretics in Catholic Poland: A Beleaguered Church in the Post-Reformation Era* (Cambridge: Cambridge University Press, 2006); John McManners, *Church and Society in Eighteenth-Century France,* 2 vols. (Oxford: Clarendon Press, 1998); William B. Taylor, *Magistrates of the Sa-*

cred: *Priests and Parishioners in Eighteenth-Century Mexico* (Stanford, Calif.: Stanford University Press, 1996); Arturo C. Jemolo, *Church and State in Italy, 1850–1950,* trans. David Moore (Oxford: Blackwell, 1960); *The Churches and Social Order in Nineteenth- and Twentieth-Century Canada,* ed. Michael Gauvreau and Ollivier Hubert (Montreal: McGill–Queen's University Press, 2006); Kees de Groot, *Brazilian Catholicism and the Ultramontane Reform* (West Lafayette, Ind.: Purdue University Press, 2003).

66. The post-Reformation proliferation and transformation of Protestantism includes, for example, seventeenth- and eighteenth-century German Pietism, General and Particular Baptists in early seventeenth-century England, Methodism beginning in eighteenth-century Britain, and the First and Second Great Awakenings in Anglophone North America. Colonial North America was characterized by all sorts of divergent Protestant truth claims and correlative established churches, dissenter denominations, millenarian expectations, and prophetic assertions. See, for example, David D. Hall, *Worlds of Wonder, Days of Judgment: Popular Religious Belief in Early New England* (New York: Knopf, 1989); Jon Butler, *Awash in a Sea of Faith: Christianizing the American People* (Cambridge, Mass., and London: Harvard University Press, 1990); and Erik R. Seeman, *Pious Persuasions: Laity and Clergy in Eighteenth-Century New England* (Baltimore and London: Johns Hopkins University Press, 1999), who notes (p. 204) that "in the last decades of the eighteenth century New England's religious culture consisted of a bounteous and almost bewildering variety of beliefs and practices," apart from the even greater variety when the mid-Atlantic and southern states are considered. The "democratization" of American Protestantism in the first third of the nineteenth century "produced not just pluralism but also striking diversity. The flexibility and innovation of religious organizations made it possible for an American to find an amenable group no matter what his or her preference in belief, practice, or institutional structure." Nathan O. Hatch, *The Democratization of American Christianity* (New Haven, Conn., and London: Yale University Press, 1989), p. 65. The same American Protestant pluralism is confirmed more broadly in the work of scholars such as George Marsden and Mark Noll, the latter of whom notes that in the United States, "by one recent count, there are now nineteen separate Presbyterian denominations, thirty-two Lutheran, thirty-six Methodist, thirty-seven Episcopal or Anglican, sixty Baptist, and 241 Pentecostal." Mark A. Noll, *The Work We Have to Do: A History of Protestants in America* (New York: Oxford University Press, 2000), p. 124. Such a count leaves aside all the churches and congregations that trace their roots to sixteenth-century Anabaptism and other expressions of the radical Reformation, not to mention the myriad independent "evangelical" and other Protestant churches with more-recent historical origins.

67. Martin Luther, *An den christlichen Adel deutscher Nation von des christlichen Standes Besserung* [1520], in *WA,* vol. 6 (Weimar: Hermann Böhlau, 1888), p. 450/13; Karlstadt, *Ob man gemach faren* [1524], in *Karlstadts Schriften,* ed. Hertzsch, vol. 1, p. 75/17–18.

68. For small-scale exceptions of a kind, see Michael D. Driedger, *Obedient Heretics: Mennonite Identities in Lutheran Hamburg and Altona during the Confessional Age* (Aldershot, U.K.: Ashgate, 2002). See also reference to "microconfessionalization" among Dutch Anabaptists in the late sixteenth century in Brad S. Gregory, *Salvation at Stake: Christian Martyrdom in Early Modern Europe* (Cambridge, Mass., and London: Harvard University Press, 1999), pp. 231–235. The enforcement of a religious minority's shared Christian identity by its ecclesiastical leaders should not be conflated with confessionalization understood as the attempted creation of a shared Christian identity across a population as a whole, backed by secular political power.

69. See, for example, Alister McGrath, *Reformation Thought: An Introduction* (Oxford: Basil Blackwell, 1988), pp. 106–109; Heiko A. Oberman, "'*Quo vadis, Petre?*' Tradition from Irenaeus to *Humani Generis*," in Oberman, *Dawn of the Reformation*, pp. 284–286; Susan E. Schreiner, *Are You Alone Wise? The Search for Certainty in the Early Modern Era* (New York: Oxford University Press, 2011), pp. 80–82.

70. Luther, *Disputatio inter Ioannem Eccium et Martinum Lutherum* [1519], in *WA*, vol. 59, p. 465/1004–1006, quoted in Manfred Schulze, "Martin Luther and the Church Fathers," in *The Reception of the Church Fathers in the West: From the Carolingians to the Maurists*, ed. Irena Backus, vol. 2 (Leiden: E. J. Brill, 1997), p. 621 (Schulze's trans.); see also ibid., pp. 601, 612.

71. See Irena Backus, "Ulrich Zwingli, Martin Bucer and the Church Fathers," in *Reception*, ed. Backus, vol. 2, pp. 644, 650; Johannes van Oort, "John Calvin and the Church Fathers," in ibid., p. 690; Anthony N. S. Lane, *John Calvin: Student of the Church Fathers* (Edinburgh: T. & T. Clark, 1999), pp. 35–40, 53–54. As Schreiner rightly observes, all Protestant claims that acknowledged patristic interpretations insofar as they were consistent with scripture "left the exegete with the task of deciding when the fathers conformed to Scripture and when they did not." Schreiner, *Wise?*, p. 82.

72. For a few works that only hint at the extent of this literature, see Peter Milward, *Religious Controversies of the Elizabethan Age: A Survey of Printed Sources* (London: Scolar Press, 1977); Milward, *Religious Controversies of the Jacobean Age: A Survey of Printed Sources* (Lincoln, Neb., and London: University of Nebraska Press, 1978); *Katholische Kontroverstheologen und Reformer des 16. Jahrhunderts*, ed. Wilbirgis Klaiber (Münster: Aschendorff, 1978); Louis Desgraves, *Répertoire des ouvrages de controverse entre Catholiques et Protestants en France* (1598–1685), 2 vols. (Geneva: Droz, 1984).

73. *Tyndale's New Testament* [1534 ed.], trans. William Tyndale, ed. David Daniell (New Haven, Conn., and London: Yale University Press, 1989), p. 244.

74. Zwingli, *Clarheit*, in *ZW*, vol. 1, p. 365/34–35.

75. William Tyndale, *An Answere Vnto Sir Thomas Mores Dialoge* [1531], ed. Anne M. O'Donnell and Jared Wicks, vol. 3 in *The Independent Works of William Tyndale* (Washington, D.C.: Catholic University of America Press, 2000), p. 48/28–29, and more generally pp. 48–49.

76. Grumbach, *Sendbrieffe*, sig. B1v.

77. Hubmaier, *Ein Christennliche Leertafel, die ein yedlicher mensch, ee vnd er im Wasser getaufft wirdt, vor wissenn solle* [1526/7], in Hubmaier, *Schriften,* ed. Gunnar Westin and Torsten Bergsten, in *QGT,* vol. 9 (Gütersloh: Gerd Mohn, 1962), p. 324. Cf. Zwingli, *Clarheit,* in *ZW,* vol. 1, 375/31–376/5.

78. Hans Denck, "Protestation und bekantnuß etlicher puncten" [1528], in Clarence Bauman, *The Spiritual Legacy of Hans Denck: Interpretation and Translation of Key Texts* (Leiden: E. J. Brill, 1991), p. 250/3–5.

79. John Calvin, *Institutio Christianae religionis* [1559], in *CO,* vol. 2, ed. G. Baum, E. Cunitz, and E. Reuss, vol. 30 in *CR* (Brunswick: C. A. Schwetschke & Sohn, 1864), 1.7.5, col. 60.

80. *Tyndale's New Testament* [1534 ed.], ed. Daniell, pp. 245–246, 284.

81. For an extensive recent treatment of the inextricability of rival claims about the authenticating testimony of the Holy Spirit from the doctrinal controversies of the sixteenth century, see Schreiner, *Wise?*

82. Desiderius Erasmus, *De libero arbitrio diatribe, sive collatio* (Basel: Johannes Froben, 1524), sig. b1.

83. Zwingli, *Clarheit,* in *ZW,* vol. 1, p. 379/18–19; Luther, *Vom Abendmahl Christi, Bekenntnis* [1528], in *WA,* vol. 26 (Weimar: Hermann Böhlaus Nachfolger, 1909), p. 317/20–22.

84. On the disputes between humanists and scholastics prior to the Reformation (which is considered further in Chapter 6), see Erika Rummel, *The Humanist-Scholastic Debate in the Renaissance and Reformation* (Cambridge, Mass., and London: Harvard University Press, 1995), pp. 63–125.

85. See Gregory, *Salvation at Stake;* for Anabaptists specifically, see also Gregory, "Anabaptist Martyrdom: Imperatives, Experience, and Memorialization," in *Companion to Anabaptism and Spiritualism,* ed. Roth and Stayer, pp. 467–506.

86. Allan Anderson, *An Introduction to Pentecostalism: Global Charismatic Christianity* (Cambridge: Cambridge University Press, 2004), pp. 45–57.

87. On the ways in which this verse in particular was intertwined with sixteenth-century contestation about the discernment of spirits as divine or diabolical, see Schreiner, *Wise?,* pp. 261–321.

88. Guy de Brès, *La racine, source et fondement des Anabaptistes ou rebaptisez de nostre temps. . . .* ([Rouen]: chez Abel Clémence, 1565), sigs. a4v–[a7].

89. See Gregory, *Salvation at Stake,* pp. 137, 139, 340–341, 344–347.

90. R. Emmet McLaughlin, "Spiritualism: Schwenckfeld and Franck and Their Early Modern Resonances," in *Companion to Anabaptism and Spiritualism,* ed. Roth and Stayer, pp. 119–161; Andrew C. Fix, *Prophecy and Reason: The Dutch Collegiants in the Early Enlightenment* (Princeton, N.J.: Princeton University Press, 1991); H. Larry Ingle, *First among Friends: George Fox and the Creation of Quakerism* (New York: Oxford University Press, 1994); Leo Damrosch, *The Sorrows of the Quaker Jesus: James Nayler and the Puritan Crackdown on the Free Spirit* (Cambridge, Mass., and London: Harvard University Press, 1996).

91. For the contemporary United States, see Wade Clark Roof, *Spiritual Marketplace: Baby Boomers and the Remaking of American Religion* (Princeton, N.J.:

Princeton University Press, 1999); Robert Wuthnow, *The Restructuring of American Religion* (Princeton, N.J.: Princeton University Press, 1988), *After Heaven: Spirituality in America since the 1950s* (Berkeley and Los Angeles: University of California Press, 1998), and *After the Baby Boomers: How Twenty- and Thirty-Somethings Are Shaping the Future of American Religion* (Princeton, N.J.: Princeton University Press, 2007). See also the recent sociological study of American teenagers by Christian Smith with Melina Lundquist Denton, *Soul Searching: The Religious and Spiritual Lives of American Teenagers* (New York: Oxford University Press, 2005); and Smith with Patricia Snell, *Souls in Transition: The Religious and Spiritual Lives of Emerging Adults* (New York: Oxford University Press, 2009), which deals with Americans in their twenties.

92. John O'Malley, *The First Jesuits* (Cambridge, Mass., and London: Harvard University Press, 1993), pp. 25–28.

93. Thomas Müntzer, "Prager Manifest" [1520], in Müntzer, *Schriften und Briefe: Kritische Gesamtausgabe,* ed. Günther Franz (Gütersloh: Gerd Mohn, 1968), p. 503/8–11.

94. Lois Y. Barrett, "Ursula Jost and Barbara Rebstock of Strasbourg," in *Profiles of Anabaptist Women: Sixteenth-Century Reforming Pioneers,* ed. C. Arnold Snyder and Linda A. Huebert Hecht (Waterloo, Ont.: Wilfred Laurier University Press, 1996), pp. 273–287; Klaus Deppermann, *Melchior Hoffman: Social Unrest and Apocalyptic Visions in the Age of Reformation,* trans. Malcolm Wren, ed. Benjamin Drewery (Edinburgh: T. & T. Clark, 1987); Ralf Klötzer, "The Melchiorites and Münster," in *Companion to Anabaptism and Spiritualism,* ed. Roth and Stayer, pp. 217–256.

95. Gary K. Waite, *David Joris and Dutch Anabaptism, 1524–1543* (Waterloo, Ont.: Wilfred Laurier University Press, 1990); Alastair Hamilton, *The Family of Love* (Cambridge: James Clarke and Co., 1981), pp. 24–64.

96. On Hacket and other Elizabethan figures, as well as Davis, see Keith Thomas, *Religion and the Decline of Magic* (Oxford: Oxford University Press, 1971), pp. 133–134, 137–138; on Traske, see David Como, *Blown by the Spirit: The Emergence of an Antinomian Underground in Pre–Civil-War England* (Stanford, Calif.: Stanford University Press, 2004), pp. 138–175; on Familism in England, see Christopher W. Marsh, *The Family of Love in English Society, 1550–1630* (Cambridge: Cambridge University Press, 1994).

97. On prophecies in particular, see Thomas, *Religion and Decline of Magic,* pp. 136–140; Christopher Hill, *The World Turned Upside Down: Radical Ideas during the English Revolution* (Harmondsworth, U.K.: Penguin, 1972), pp. 89–92, 278–279, 287–291. On the Revolution's religious radicals more generally, see Hill, ibid.; *Radical Religion in the English Revolution,* ed. J. F. McGregor and Barry Reay (London and New York: Oxford University Press, 1984); Nicholas McDowell, *The English Radical Imagination: Culture, Religion, and Revolution, 1630–1660* (Oxford: Clarendon Press, 2003); and Ann Hughes, *Gangraena and the Struggle for the English Revolution* (Oxford: Oxford University Press, 2004).

98. One historian who has traced striking similarities between certain Reformation-era radical Protestant ideas and those of Joseph Smith is John L. Brooke, in

*The Refiner's Fire: The Making of Mormon Cosmology, 1644–1844* (Cambridge: Cambridge University Press, 1994). The most recent major biography of Smith is Richard L. Bushman, *Joseph Smith: Rough Stone Rolling* (New York: Knopf, 2005). On Smith's place among many other Americans who claimed and/or expected new revelation in the early nineteenth century, see David F. Holland, "Ongoing Revelation: An Idea and Its Contexts in Early America," unpublished Ph.D. dissertation, Stanford University, 2005.

99. Compare *A Journal or Historical Account of the Life, Travels, Sufferings, Christian Experiences and Labour of Love in the Work of the Ministry of that Ancient, Eminent, and Faithful Servant of Jesus Christ, George Fox, . . . ,* vol. 1 (London: Thomas Northcott, 1694), pp. 5–9, with *History of Joseph Smith, the Prophet by Himself,* ed. B. H. Roberts, vol. 1 in *History of the Church of Jesus Christ of Latter Day Saints* (Salt Lake City, Utah: Deseret News, 1902), pp. 2–6. On Smith's dictation of his first-person account beginning in 1839, see Dean C. Jessee, "The Writing of Joseph Smith's History," *BYU Studies* 11 (1971): 439–473, with a helpful chart of Smith's many scribes on 441 and the reproduction of James Mulholland's holograph of the first page of the *History* on 451.

100. David Chidester, *Salvation and Suicide: Jim Jones, the Peoples Temple, and Jonestown,* 2nd ed. (1988; Bloomington: Indiana University Press, 2003); Kenneth G. C. Newport, *The Branch Davidians of Waco: The History and Beliefs of an Apocalyptic Sect* (New York: Oxford University Press, 2006).

101. Joseph Smith's conception of God the Father as literally an exalted, spatio-temporal, Caucasian human male on a distant planet is not only a radical departure from the traditional Christian view of God, but also an extreme manifestation of a metaphysically univocal view of God as a highest being among others within the universe. In a sense the Mormon conception of God represents a sort of parallel to Spinoza's: whereas he alleged that the universe was literally God's body considered under one of the humanly accessible modes of the one substance, LDS doctrine claims that God the Father has a divinized human body and dwells near the star Kolob. According to *Doctrine and Covenants* 130:22, "the Father has a body of flesh and bones as tangible as man's"; see http://scriptures.lds.org/dc/130/22#22. On God's spatial location, see the commentary on chapter 3 of the "Book of Abraham" (part of the *Pearl of Great Price*), at http://institute.lds. org/manuals/pearl-of-great-price-student-manual/pgp-3-a3-01.asp.

102. Jan Shipps, *Mormonism: The Story of a New Religious Tradition* (Champaign-Urbana: University of Illinois Press, 1985).

103. Steven L. Shields, *Divergent Paths of the Restoration: A History of the Latter Day Saint Movement,* 3rd ed. (Bountiful, Utah: Restoration Research, 1982); for the RLDS church in particular, see Inez Smith Davis, *The Story of the Church: A History of the Church of Jesus Christ of Latter Day Saints, and of Its Legal Successor, the Reorganized Church of Jesus Christ of Latter Day Saints,* 13th ed. (Independence, Mo.: Herald Publishing House, 1989).

104. Huldrych Zwingli, *Ein klare Unterrichtung vom Nachtmal Christi. . . .* [1526], in *ZW,* vol. 4, pp. 789–862.

105. Jerome Friedman, *Michael Servetus: A Case Study in Total Heresy* (Geneva: Droz, 1978).

106. Williams, *Radical Reformation,* 3rd ed., pp. 401–404, 459–477, 956–959, 965–990, 1103–1133, 1162–1174, 1196–1197, 1229–1236; Jean Pierre Osier, *Faust Socin, ou, Le christianisme sans sacrifice* (Paris: Cerf, 1996); *Reformation und Frühaufklärung in Polen: Studien über den Sozinianismus und seinen Einfluß auf das westeuropäische Denken im 17. Jahrhundert,* ed. Paul Wrzecionko (Göttingen: Vandenhoeck & Ruprecht, 1977); *Socinianism and Its Role in the Culture of XVIth to XVIIIth Centuries,* ed. Lech Szczucki (Warsaw: Polish Academy of Sciences, 1983); W. J. Kühler, *Het Socinianisme in Nederland,* intro. Aart de Groot (1912; Leeuwarden: De Tille, 1980); Earl Morse Wilbur, *A History of Unitarianism,* 2 vols. (Cambridge, Mass.: Harvard University Press, 1945, 1952).

107. W. M. Spellman, *The Latitudinarians and the Church of England, 1660–1700* (Athens and London: University of Georgia Press, 1993), pp. 33–47, 72–88.

108. McLaughlin, "Spiritualism," in *Companion to Anabaptism and Spiritualism,* ed. Roth and Stayer, p. 136; Williams, *Radical Reformation,* p. 700.

109. Samuel Fisher, *Rusticos ad Academicos in Exercitationibus Expostulatoriis, Apologeticis Quatuor. The Rustick's Alarm to the Rabbies. . . .* (London: for Robert Wilson, 1660), sigs. [(a4)v]–(B1) (original italics and roman type reversed). On the Oxford-educated Fisher, who in 1658 traveled as far as Rome and Venice, where he preached to Catholics and Jews, see Stefano Villani, "Fisher, Samuel (*bap.* 1604, *d.* 1665)," in *ODNB,* online ed., ed. Lawrence Goldman (Oxford: Oxford University Press, 2004), http://www.oxforddnb.com/view/article/9507 (accessed 5 July 2010).

110. Fix, *Prophecy and Reason,* pp. 192–214; Jonathan I. Israel, *Radical Enlightenment: Philosophy and the Making of Modernity, 1650–1750* (Oxford: Oxford University Press, 2001), pp. 203–205, 342–358; for Fisher's influence on Spinoza, see Richard H. Popkin, "Spinoza and Samuel Fisher," *Philosophia: Philosophical Quarterly of Israel* 15 (1985): 219–236.

111. Jeremy Taylor, *Ductor Dubitantium, or The Rule of Conscience. . . .* (London: James Flesher for Richard Royston, 1660), 1.2.51, p. 56.

112. Luther, *Von anbeten,* in *WA,* vol. 11, p. 434/30–34.

113. Calvin, *Institutio,* in *CO,* vol. 2, 1.13.21, col. 107.

114. John Toland, *Christianity not Mysterious. Or, A Treatise Shewing, That there is nothing in the Gospel Contrary to Reason, Nor Above it: And that no Christian Doctrine can be properly call'd a Mystery* (London: n.p., 1696), p. 6 (italics in original).

115. Spellman, *Latitudinarians,* pp. 83–88.

116. Ibid., pp. 148–150.

117. Thomas Sprat, *The History of the Royal Society* [1667], quoted in John Spurr, "'Rational Religion' in Restoration England," *Journal of the History of Ideas* 49 (1988): 563.

118. Thomas Edwards, *Gangraena, or, A Catalogue and Discovery of many of the Errours, Heresies, Blasphemies and pernicious Practices of the Sectaries of this time, vented and acted in* England *in these four last years.* . . . (London: T. R. and E. M. for Ralph Smith, 1646). For a recent analysis of Edwards's work in context, see Hughes, *Gangraena;* on the rationalist criticism of Christian prophetic and spiritualist claims in the later seventeenth and early eighteenth centuries, see Michael Heyd, *"Be Sober and Reasonable": The Critique of Enthusiasm in the Seventeenth and Early Eighteenth Centuries* (Leiden: E. J. Brill, 1995).

119. Quoted in Steven E. Ozment, *Mysticism and Dissent: Religious Ideology and Social Protest in the Sixteenth Century* (New Haven, Conn., and London: Yale University Press, 1973), p. 196 (Ozment's trans.).

120. Israel, *Radical Enlightenment,* pp. 197–217.

121. Charles Blount, *Miracles No Violation of the Laws of Nature* (London: for Robert Sollers, 1683), pp. 21, 6 (italics in original).

122. For an expository overview of Ritschl's theology that makes clear his indebtedness to post-Kantian philosophical assumptions, see Albert Temple Swing, *The Theology of Albrecht Ritschl* (New York: Longman, 1901); on Troeltsch in context, see Mark D. Chapman, *Ernst Troeltsch and Liberal Theology: Religion and Cultural Synthesis in Wilhelmine Germany* (New York: Oxford University Press, 2002); for an example of Bultmann's assumptions in play, see Bultmann, *Kerygma and Myth: A Theological Debate* [1948], ed. and trans. Reginald H. Fuller (1953; New York: Harper & Row, 1961); for Jefferson, see *The Jefferson Bible,* intro. F. Forrester Church (Boston: Beacon Press, 1989). Jaroslav Pelikan's helpful afterword mentions Reimarus's scholarship, extracts from which Lessing had published in 1777, in relationship to Jefferson's project. See Pelikan, "Jefferson and His Contemporaries," in ibid., pp. 157–160. For Lessing, his relationship to Reimarus's work, and the *Fragmentenstreit* after 1777, see also H. B. Nisbet, "Introduction" to Gotthold Ephraim Lessing, *Philosophical and Theological Writings,* ed. and trans. Nisbet (Cambridge: Cambridge University Press, 2005), pp. 6–12.

123. See, for example, Newman's critique of "liberalism" understood as "false liberty of thought" in note A to Newman, *Apologia Pro Vita Sua* [1864], ed. David J. DeLaura (New York and London: W. W. Norton, 1968), pp. 218, 223.

124. See, for example, Robert Bellah et al., *Habits of the Heart: Individualism and Commitment in American Life,* updated ed. (Berkeley and Los Angeles: University of California Press, 1996), pp. 219–249; Suzanne Strempek Shea, *Sundays in America: A Yearlong Road Trip in Search of Christian Faith* (Boston: Beacon Press, 2008).

125. Philip Rieff, *The Triumph of the Therapeutic: Uses of Faith after Freud,* intro. Elisabeth Lasch-Quinn (1966; Wilmington, Del.: ISI Books, 2006), p. 10. On the widespread sense of religion understood in terms of subjective, individualistic preference in the United States, see Smith with Denton, *Soul Searching,* pp. 118–171, and Smith with Snell, *Souls in Transition,* pp. 143–165, 286–289.

126. Stout, *Democracy and Tradition*, p. 32.

127. "Wer des glaubens gefeilet hat, der mag darnach glewben was er wil, gilt eben gleich." Luther, *Sermon Von dem Sacrament des leibs vnd bluts Christi, widder die Schwarmgeister* [1526], in *WA*, vol. 19 (Weimar: Hermann Böhlaus Nachfolger, 1897), p. 484/19–20.

128. Michel de Montaigne, "Apologie de Raimond Sebond," in Montaigne, *Essais II* [1580], ed. Emmanuel Naya, Delphine Reguig-Naya, and Alexandre Tarrête ([Paris:] Gallimard, 2009), pp. 159–399; Richard H. Popkin, *The History of Scepticism from Savonarola to Bayle*, 3rd ed. (Oxford: Oxford University Press, 2003), pp. 18, 36, 44–56. The first edition of Popkin's work, entitled *The History of Scepticism from Erasmus to Descartes*, appeared in 1960. See also the analysis of Montaigne's confrontation with and accommodation of skepticism and relativism in Zachary Sayre Schiffman, *On the Threshold of Modernity: Relativism in the French Renaissance* (Baltimore and London: Johns Hopkins University Press, 1991), pp. 53–77. Whatever may have been the case for Montaigne in particular, Schiffman's argument that the methods and pedagogical techniques of humanism led inherently to skepticism is unsustainable, given the large numbers of humanistically educated nonskeptics in the sixteenth and seventeenth centuries. Like Popkin, Schiffman situates Descartes's foundationalist aspirations in the context of the problems posed by skepticism and relativism; ibid., pp. 103–128. Before his death in 1592, Montaigne published a revised and expanded edition of his *Essais* in 1588; a posthumous edition, with his further revisions and additions, appeared in 1595. See M. A. Screech, "Introduction" to Michel de Montaigne, *The Complete Essays*, ed. and trans. Screech (1987; Harmondsworth, U.K.: Penguin, 1991), pp. xv–xvi, liii. On the presence of Sextus manuscripts in a handful of the leading Italian humanist libraries in the quattrocento, combined with the lack of any significant spread then of Pyrrhonian skeptical ideas, see the meticulous article by Gian Mario Cao, "The Prehistory of Modern Scepticism: Sextus Empiricus in Fifteenth-Century Italy," *Journal of the Warburg and Courtauld Institutes* 64 (2001): 229–280. "In relation to Sextus, it is true to say that the fifteenth century witnessed a revival not of sceptical philosophy but of sceptical texts." Ibid., p. 263.

129. On Descartes's stint as a soldier under Maurice of Nassau, see Geneviève Rodis-Lewis, "Descartes' Life and the Development of His Philosophy," in *The Cambridge Companion to Descartes*, ed. John Cottingham (Cambridge: Cambridge University Press, 1992), pp. 29–32, and Stephen Gaukroger, *Descartes: An Intellectual Biography* (Oxford: Clarendon Press, 1995), pp. 65–67; on Hobbes's exile in Paris, see Noel Malcolm, "A Summary Biography of Hobbes," in *The Cambridge Companion to Hobbes*, ed. Tom Sorrell (Cambridge: Cambridge University Press, 1996), pp. 28–33.

130. On the Republic of Letters and its transformation between the early sixteenth and the late eighteenth centuries, see Anthony Grafton, "A Sketch Map of a Lost Continent: The Republic of Letters," in Grafton, *Worlds Made by Words: Scholarship and Community in the Modern West* (Cambridge,

Mass., and London: Harvard University Press, 2009), pp. 9–34; Constance M. Furey, *Erasmus, Contarini, and the Religious Republic of Letters* (Cambridge: Cambridge University Press, 2006); Peter N. Miller, *Peiresc's Europe: Learning and Virtue in the Seventeenth Century* (New Haven, Conn., and London: Yale University Press, 2000); Anne Goldgar, *Impolite Learning: Conduct and Community in the Republic of Letters, 1680–1750* (New Haven, Conn., and London: Yale University Press, 1995); and Dena Goodman, *The Republic of Letters: A Cultural History of the French Enlightenment* (Ithaca, N.Y.: Cornell University Press, 1994).

131. Giordano Bruno, *One Hundred and Twenty Articles against Mathematicians and Philosophers* [1588], quoted in Ingrid D. Rowland, *Giordano Bruno: Philosopher/Heretic* (New York: Farrar, Straus and Giroux, 2008), p. 208 (Rowland's trans.).

132. Michel de Montaigne, "De la solitude," in Montaigne, *Essais I* [1580], ed. Emmanuel Naya, Delphine Reguig-Naya, and Alexandre Tarrête ([Paris:] Gallimard, 2009), p. 445.

133. On Montaigne's political thought and substantive aspirations as an ethical theorist, see Biancamaria Fontana, *Montaigne's Politics: Authority and Governance in the "Essais"* (Princeton, N.J.: Princeton University Press, 2008), and David Quint, *Montaigne and the Quality of Mercy: Ethical and Political Themes in the "Essais"* (Princeton: Princeton University Press, 1998).

134. Fox, *Journal*, p. 3 (italics in original).

135. René Descartes, *Meditationes de prima philosophia* [1641], in Descartes, *Oeuvres*, ed. Charles Adam and Paul Tannery, vol. 7 (Paris: J. Vrin, 1964), p. 17/2–8.

136. Ibid., pp. 17/13–18/2.

137. Thomas Hobbes, *Leviathan* [1651], ed. Richard Tuck (1991; Cambridge: Cambridge University Press, 1996), 1.4, pp. 24–31, quotations at 28, 29 (italics in original).

138. Baruch de Spinoza to Albert Burgh [after 11 September 1675], in Spinoza, *Opera*, ed. Carl Gebhardt, vol. 4 (Heidelberg: C. Winter, 1925), letter 76, p. 320/3–4.

139. Spinoza, *Tractatus de intellectus emendatione* [1677], in Spinoza, *Opera*, ed. Gebhardt, vol. 2, p. 14/3–7. Although this work was not published until after his death, on the basis of Spinoza's correspondence Edwin Curley argues that it "must have been written before September 1661." Curley, "General Preface" in *The Collected Works of Spinoza*, vol. 1, ed. and trans. Curley (Princeton, N.J.: Princeton University Press, 1985), p. xiii.

140. Spinoza, *Tractatus de intellectus emendatione*, in Spinoza, *Opera*, ed. Gebhardt, vol. 2, pp. 14–15, 8/16–17. For the formal demonstration in the *Ethics* of the determined necessity of all things in nature, see Spinoza, *Ethica* [1677], in *Opera*, vol. 2, pt. 1, proposition 29, pp. 70–71, the scholium of which includes the distinction between *natura naturans* and *natura naturata;* for the fixed and immutable character of the natural order as articulated in the *Tractatus Theologico-Politicus* [1670], see *Opera*, ed. Gebhardt, vol. 3, pp. 82/13–14, 84/22–23, 85/9, 86/20–21.

141. Spinoza, *Ethica*, in Spinoza, *Opera*, ed. Gebhardt, vol. 2, pt. 1, pp. 45–47; pt. 2, proposition 7, scholium, pp. 89–90.

142. David Hume, "Introduction" to *A Treatise of Human Nature* [1739–1740], ed. L. A. Selby-Bigge, 2nd ed., rev. P. H. Nidditch (Oxford: Clarendon Press, 1978), p. xiii.

143. Hume, "Introduction" to *Treatise*, ed. Selby-Bigge, p. xvii; Hume, *Treatise*, 1.4.5, p. 241 (my emphases).

144. Hume, "Introduction" to *Treatise*, ed. Selby-Bigge, p. xvi; Hume, *Treatise*, 1.1.1, p. 1.

145. Jean-Jacques Rousseau, *Les rêveries du promeneur solitaire* [1782], in Rousseau, *Oeuvres complètes*, ed. Bernard Gagnebin and Marcel Raymond, vol. 1 (Paris: Gallimard, 1959), p. 1016.

146. Ibid., pp. 1013, 1014, 1015, 1015, 1017, 1017, 1017, 1018, 1018. For the "Profession de foi du vicaire savoyard," see Rousseau, *Émile, ou, de l'éducation* [1762], in Rousseau, *Oeuvres complètes*, ed. Gagnebin and Raymond, vol. 4 (Paris: Gallimard, 1969), pp. 565–635.

147. Immanuel Kant, "Beantwortung der Frage: Was ist Aufklärung?" [1784], in Kant, *Gesammelte Schriften*, ed. Königlich Preußischen Akademie der Wissenschaften, vol. 8, *Abhandlungen nach 1781* (Berlin and Leipzig: Walter de Gruyter, 1923), p. 35/1–3, 7–9 (emphasis in original).

148. Immanuel Kant, "Vorrede zur ersten Auflage," *Kritik der reinen Vernunft* [1781], in Kant, *Gesammelte Schriften*, ed. Königlich Preußischen Akademie der Wissenschaften, vol. 4 (Berlin: Georg Reimer, 1911), pp. 9/33–38, 7/20–21, 8/4–5, 9/5–10, 10/9–11.

149. Immanuel Kant, *Kritik der praktischen Vernunft* [1788], in Kant, *Gesammelte Schriften*, ed. Königlich Preußischen Akademie der Wissenschaften, vol. 5 (Berlin: Georg Reimer, 1913), 1.1.1, pp. 19–21.

150. Georg Wilhelm Friedrich Hegel, "Vorrede" to *Phänomenologie des Geistes* [1807], in Hegel, *Gesammelte Werke*, vol. 9, ed. Wolfgang Bonsiepen and Reinhard Heede (Hamburg: Felix Meiner, 1980), pp. 11/33–34, 14–15, 48/25–28.

151. Ibid., p. 14/23–25.

152. Georg Wilhelm Friedrich Hegel, "Vorrede" to *Grundlinien der Philosophie des Rechts* [1820], in Hegel, *Gesammelte Werke*, vol. 14/1, ed. Klaus Grotsch and Elisabeth Weisser-Lohmann (Hamburg: Felix Meiner, 2009), pp. 9/15–17, 6/30–31, 11/14–16, 13/10–12, 6/11–12. Although the original title page indicates 1821, the work first appeared in 1820.

153. Georg Wilhelm Friedrich Hegel, "Vorrede," to *Wissenschaft der Logik. Erster Band: Die Objektive Logik (1812–1813)*, in Hegel, *Gesammelte Werke*, vol. 7, ed. Friedrich Hogemann and Walter Jaeschke (Hamburg: Felix Meiner, 1978), p. 7/15–20.

154. Ralph Waldo Emerson, "Self-Reliance," in *Essays: First Series* [1841], in Emerson, *Essays and Lectures*, ed. Joel Porte (New York: Library of America, 1983), pp. 271, 261, 262, 269, 265, 276, 267, 276–277.

155. Karl Marx, ["Thesen über Feuerbach,"] in Karl Marx and Friedrich Engels, *Werke*, vol. 3 (Berlin: Dietz, 1962), thesis 11, p. 7 (italics in original).

156. The monumental intellectual history of Marxism, from the eighteenth-century precursors and early nineteenth-century influences on Marx himself, to the New Left and Maoism in the 1950s and 1960s, is Leszek Kołakowski, *Main Currents of Marxism: Its Rise, Growth, and Dissolution,* 3 vols., trans. P. S. Falla (Oxford: Clarendon Press, 1978). On the concrete fortunes of Marxism and Marxist movements in a global context during the short twentieth century, see Eric Hobsbawm, *The Age of Extremes: A History of the World, 1914–1991* (New York: Pantheon, 1994).

157. Marx (in Kreuznach) to Arnold Ruge, September 1843, printed in *Deutsch-Französische Jahrbücher,* 1844, repr. in "Ein Briefwechsel von 1843," in Karl Marx and Friedrich Engels, *Gesamtausgabe,* Abteilung I: *Texte,* vol. 2 (Berlin: Akademie Verlag, 2009), pp. 487/7–8, 487/34, 488/27–29 (italics in original).

158. Hegel, "Vorrede" to *Philosophie des Rechts,* in Hegel, *Gesammelte Werke,* vol. 14/1, ed. Grotsch and Weisser-Lohmann, p. 15/14–24, quotation at lines 15–16.

159. Marx, "Briefwechsel von 1843," in Marx and Engels, *Gesamtausgabe,* Abteilung I: *Texte,* vol. 2, pp. 486/38–487/2.

160. John Stuart Mill, *Utilitarianism* [1861], in *On Liberty and Other Essays,* ed. John Gray (1991; Oxford: Oxford University Press, 1998), pp. 131, 133, 131, 133, 137, 149, 156.

161. Edmund Husserl to Franz Brentano, 15 October 1904, quoted in Herbert Spiegelberg, *The Phenomenological Movement,* 3rd ed. (The Hague: Martinus Nijhoff, 1982), p. 82 (Spiegelberg's trans.).

162. See not only Martin Heidegger, *Being and Time* [1927], trans. John Macquarrie and Edward Robinson (1962; Oxford: Blackwell, 1980), but also the way in which Heidegger had been developing ideas that would be central to *Sein und Zeit* in his summer-semester lectures of 1925 at the University of Marburg, in Heidegger, *History of the Concept of Time: Prolegomena,* trans. Theodore Kisiel (Bloomington: Indiana University Press, 1999).

163. See especially Emmanuel Levinas, *Totalité et infini: essai sur l'extériorité* (The Hague: Martinus Nijhoff, 1961), and Levinas, *Autrement qu'être: Ou au-delà de l'essence* (The Hague: Martinus Nijhoff, 1974).

164. Hume, "Introduction" to *Treatise,* ed. Selby-Bigge, p. xiv.

165. Frederick C. Beiser, *German Idealism: The Struggle against Subjectivism, 1781–1801* (Cambridge, Mass., and London: Harvard University Press, 2002), pp. 6–9.

166. For a critique of Kuhn's antirealist claims and tendency to take the transition from Aristotelian to Newtonian physics as paradigmatic of all major shifts in scientific understanding, see Steven Weinberg, *Facing Up: Science and Its Cultural Adversaries* (Cambridge, Mass., and London: Harvard University Press, 2001), pp. 85–86, 104, 187–209, 268–269. The seminal work to which Weinberg was responding, and which has had such a wide influence not only in the history and philosophy of science but much more broadly, is Thomas S. Kuhn, *The Structure of Scientific Revolutions,* 2nd ed. (Chicago: University of Chicago Press, 1970), the first edition of which appeared in 1962.

167. Taylor, *Ductor Dubitantium,* 2.1.31, p. 231; 2.1.33, p. 232.

168. Alasdair MacIntyre, *Three Rival Versions of Moral Inquiry: Encyclopedia, Genealogy, and Tradition* (Notre Dame, Ind.: University of Notre Dame Press, 1990), pp. 6–8; see also MacIntyre, "First Principles, Final Ends, and Contemporary Philosophical Issues," in *The Tasks of Philosophy*, vol. 1 in *Selected Essays* (Cambridge: Cambridge University Press, 2006), pp. 143–178.

169. John R. Betz, *After Enlightenment: The Post-Secular Vision of J. G. Hamann* (Malden, Mass., and Oxford: Wiley-Blackwell, 2009).

170. John Stuart Mill, *On Liberty* [1859], in *On Liberty and Other Essays*, ed. Gray, p. 25.

171. Hegel, "Vorrede" to *Philosophie des Rechts*, in Hegel, *Gesammelte Werke*, vol. 14/1, ed. Grotsch and Weisser-Lohmann, p. 7/23–26.

172. For these quotations, on Spinoza, see Friedrich Nietzsche, *Götzen-Dämmerung* [1889], in Nietzsche, *Werke: Kritische Gesamtausgabe*, ed. Giorgio Colli and Mazzino Montinari, pt. 6, vol. 3 (Berlin: Walter de Gruyter, 1969), p. 120/11, and Nietzsche, *Jenseits von Gut und Böse* [1886], in ibid., pt. 6, vol. 2 (Berlin: Walter de Gruyter, 1968), p. 13/20–21 (emphasis in original); on Kant, see *Götzen-Dämmerung*, pp. 73/3 (emphasis in original), 104/2–3.

173. Hubert L. Dreyfus and Paul Rabinow, *Michel Foucault: Beyond Structuralism and Hermeneutics*, 2nd ed. (Chicago: University of Chicago Press, 1983), pp. 104–107.

174. Among numerous symptoms of this phenomenon is the attention by medieval historians and literary scholars to medieval heresy and its attempted suppression in ways disproportionate to its historical influence. The same applies to the imbalanced concentration on the Roman Inquisition and its activities in early modern Italian religious history, especially among Italian scholars who are ideologically among the *laici*. I am grateful to Emanuele Colombo for discussions on the latter point.

### 3. Controlling the Churches

1. Mark Lilla, *The Stillborn God: Religion, Politics, and the Modern West* (New York: Knopf, 2007), p. 55; John T. Noonan Jr., *The Lustre of Our Country: The American Experience of Religious Freedom* (Berkeley and Los Angeles: University of California Press, 1998), pp. 8, 9.

2. Unless otherwise apparent from the context, throughout this chapter the term "secular" has the institutional and jurisdictional meaning of nonecclesiastical, not the intellectual or ideological meaning of non- or antireligious. Thus "secular authorities" throughout most of European history have been nonecclesiastical, lay Christian authorities who exercised power in the public sphere, not atheistic or unbelieving authorities.

3. On the extension of the wars of the Reformation era into the early eighteenth century, as well as the multiple ways in which religious toleration was concretely practiced among Protestants and Catholics beginning in the sixteenth century, see Benjamin J. Kaplan, *Divided by Faith: Religious Conflict and the Practice of Toleration in Early Modern Europe* (Cambridge, Mass., and London: Belknap Press of Harvard University Press, 2007).

4. Perez Zagorin, *How the Idea of Religious Toleration Came to the West* (Princeton, N.J.: Princeton University Press, 2003); Thomas Hobbes, *Leviathan* [1651], ed. Richard Tuck (1991; Cambridge: Cambridge University Press, 1996).

5. Zagorin, *Idea of Religious Toleration.*

6. On the centrality to Jesus's preaching of "the kingdom of God"—a phrase not found in the Hebrew Old Testament and either "rare or nonexistent" in the deuterocanonical and apocryphal books of the Old Testament, the Old Testament pseudepigraphia, the Qumran sources, Philo of Alexandria, Josephus, and most of the targums—see John P. Meier, *A Marginal Jew: Rethinking the Historical Jesus,* vol. 2, *Mentor, Message, and Miracles* (New York: Doubleday, 1994), pp. 237–506, with quotations and references to these sources on 238. On the centrality as well as the polyvalent complexity of "the kingdom of God" in Jesus's sayings and parables, see also E. P. Sanders, *The Historical Figure of Jesus* (1993; Harmondsworth, U.K.: Penguin, 1995), pp. 169–204, and James D. G. Dunn, *Jesus Remembered,* vol. 1 in *Christianity in the Making* (Grand Rapids, Mich., and Cambridge, U.K.: Eerdmans, 2003), pp. 383–487.

7. This particular saying, with variant wording, also appears two times each in Matthew and Luke: see Mt 10:39, 16:25; Lk 9:24, 17:33.

8. On the complex, fragmentary, and unsystematic character of the relationship between Jesus's legal judgments within first-century Jewish rabbinic tradition, and his moral pronouncements that sometimes reinforced and at other times dismissed them, see John P. Meier, *A Marginal Jew,* vol. 4, *Law and Love* (New Haven, Conn., and London: Yale University Press, 2009). The fourth volume of Meier's ongoing study, building on the work of scholars such as Gaza Vermes, Jacob Neusner, and E. P. Sanders, makes clear that the shared way of life that Jesus commanded was one manifestly rooted in the Torah—which he nevertheless sometimes abrogated with a shocking boldness on his own authority. "It is Torah and Torah alone that puts flesh and bones on the spectral figure of 'Jesus the Jew.' No halakic Jesus, no historical Jesus." Ibid., p. 648.

9. On the inextricably reciprocal relationship between Christian morality and social practices in early Christian communities, see the ethnographic analysis in Wayne A. Meeks, *The Origins of Christian Morality: The First Two Centuries* (New Haven, Conn., and London: Yale University Press, 1993).

10. See Peter Brown, *Poverty and Leadership in the Later Roman Empire* (Hanover, N.H.: University Press of New England, 2001). Because of its focus on the poor, "in the period of late antiquity, then, Christian and Jewish charity was not simply one accustomed form of generosity among others, practiced with greater zeal than previously but not otherwise remarkable. It was a new departure." Ibid., p. 6.

11. Eusebius, *The History of the Church,* trans. G. A. Williamson, rev. and ed. Andrew Louth (Harmondsworth, U.K.: Penguin, 1989), bk. 10, pp. 303–333.

12. Peter Brown, *The Rise of Western Christendom: Triumph and Diversity,* A.D. 200–1000 (Cambridge, Mass., and Oxford: Blackwell, 1996), pp. 140–141.

Brown's remarks refer to Gregory the Great, whose views were to exercise such a major influence on subsequent medieval political and moral thought and practice, but Gregory was building on ideas found in Augustine and other patristic writers. In the second edition of his work, Brown phrases somewhat differently the same idea with reference to Gregory: "this power should be wielded, with humility and unflinching self-awareness, for the good of others." Brown, *Rise of Western Christendom,* 2nd ed. (Malden, Mass., and Oxford: Blackwell, 2003), p. 209.

13. On the early spread of Christianity via urban social networks, see Rodney Stark, *Cities of God: The Real Story of How Christianity Became an Urban Movement and Conquered Rome* (San Francisco: HarperCollins, 2006); see also Wayne A. Meeks, *The First Urban Christians: The Social World of the Apostle Paul* (New Haven, Conn., and London: Yale University Press, 1983), esp. pp. 40–50.

14. Eamon Duffy, *Saints and Sinners: A History of the Popes* (New Haven, Conn., and London: Yale University Press, 1997), pp. 37–85; Thomas F. X. Noble, *The Republic of St. Peter: The Birth of the Papal State, 680–825* (Philadelphia: University of Pennsylvania Press, 1984).

15. On this point see, for example, Euan Cameron, *The European Reformation* (Oxford: Clarendon Press, 1991), pp. 21–23, 27–28.

16. "Though usually a bishop, a clergyman or an abbot, the *rector,* the ruler of souls, envisaged by Gregory [the Great] might be any holy lay person, any pious local magnate, any Christian king. Each, in a different but strictly homologous manner, did the same thing: each had been given by God the opportunity to exercise persuasive power in the interests of the one, true goal of a Christian society, the salvation of souls." Brown, *Rise of Western Christendom,* 1st ed., p. 143. On the eve of the Reformation, Erasmus told the teenage prince Charles, soon to be elected Holy Roman emperor, the same thing: "Neither should the prince flatter himself thus: 'These things are applicable to bishops, not to me.' On the contrary, they do apply to you, if you are a Christian; if you are not a Christian, they do not at all apply to you." Desiderius Erasmus, *Institutio principis Christiani.* . . . [1516], ed. O. Herding, in Erasmus, *Opera omnia,* series 4, vol. 1 (Amsterdam: North-Holland Publishing Co., 1974), p. 159/705–707.

17. Brian Tierney, *The Crisis of Church and State, 1050–1300* (1964; Toronto: University of Toronto Press, 1988), pp. 18–19.

18. For two valuable collections of primary sources in translation with analysis, see *From Irenaeus to Grotius: A Sourcebook in Christian Political Thought,* ed. Oliver O'Donovan and Joan Lockwood O'Donovan (Grand Rapids, Mich.: Eerdmans, 1999), and Tierney, *Crisis of Church and State.*

19. It is an anachronism (following Huizinga) to claim that "in the later Middle Ages the integrity and autonomy of the secular world was firmly established; the spiritual became truly spiritual, and the profane ceased to be merely profane." Steven Ozment, *The Age of Reform, 1250–1550: An Intellectual and Religious History of Late Medieval and Reformation Europe* (New Haven, Conn., and London: Yale University Press, 1980), p. 181. Similarly, Bernd

Moeller in a classic essay claimed that in late medieval free imperial cities "the civil community was confused with the religious" in a manner "so strange to our modern way of thinking." Moeller, "Imperial Cities and the Reformation," in Moeller, *Imperial Cities and the Reformation: Three Essays*, ed. and trans. H. C. Erik Midelfort and Mark U. Edwards Jr. (1972; Durham, N.C.: Labyrinth Press, 1982), p. 46. Moeller's last phrase is the salient one and undermines his putatively descriptive claim, because the "modern way of thinking" to which he refers is itself a product of the historical process analyzed in this chapter. The alleged confusion between religion and other domains of human life is only possible once they have been conceptualized as discrete and separable, which begins in the Reformation era as an unintended consequence of religious disagreements and their associated disruptions. For an important recent analysis of the historical process by which "religion" was differentiated from the rest of life, and the implications of this process for contemporary discourse about the relationship between politics and religion, see William T. Cavanaugh, *The Myth of Religious Violence: Secular Ideology and the Roots of Modern Conflict* (New York: Oxford University Press, 2009), esp. pp. 57–122.

20. On Philip IV and Boniface VIII, see Tierney, *Crisis of Church and State*, pp. 172–175; O'Donovan and O'Donovan, *Irenaeus to Grotius*, pp. 389–390.

21. John Van Engen, "The Future of Medieval Church History," *Church History* 71 (2002): 492.

22. John A. Scott, *Understanding Dante* (Notre Dame, Ind.: University of Notre Dame Press, 2004), pp. 143–166; Cary J. Nederman, *Community and Consent: The Secular Political Theory of Marsiglio of Padua's "Defensor Pacis"* (Lanham, Md.: Rowman & Littlefield, 1995); O'Donovan and O'Donovan, *Irenaeus to Grotius*, pp. 413–452.

23. O'Donovan and O'Donovan, *Irenaeus to Grotius*, pp. 482–513; Matthew Spinka, *John Hus' Concept of the Church* (Princeton, N.J.: Princeton University Press, 1966); Malcolm Lambert, *Medieval Heresy: Popular Movements from the Gregorian Reform to the Reformation*, 3rd ed. (Oxford: Blackwell, 2002), pp. 254–257, 329–330; Francis Oakley, *The Western Church in the Later Middle Ages* (Ithaca, N.Y.: Cornell University Press, 1979), pp. 193–200.

24. John Van Engen, *Sisters and Brothers of the Common Life: The Devotio Moderna and the World of the Late Middle Ages* (Philadelphia: University of Pennsylvania Press, 2008).

25. Bernard Guillemain, *La politique bénéficiale du Pape Benoît XII, 1334–1342* (Paris: H. Champion, 1952). The curial staff at Avignon more than tripled in size, to over six hundred, in comparison to its size during the pontificate of Nicholas III (1277–1280). Oakley, *Western Church*, p. 46.

26. Gerd Tellenbach, *The Church in Western Europe from the Tenth to the Early Twelfth Century*, trans. Timothy Reuter (Cambridge: Cambridge University Press, 1993), pp. 69–72; Duffy, *Saints and Sinners*, pp. 103–111.

27. Niccolò Machiavelli, *The Prince*, trans. and ed. David Wootton (Indianapolis: Hackett, 1995), with esteem for Alexander and especially Cesare Borgia at pp. 14, 22, 24–27, 29–30, 37, 43, 51, 66–67.

28. On Julius II, see Christine Shaw, *Julius II: The Warrior Pope* (Oxford: Blackwell, 1993); for Erasmus's anonymous treatise, written c. 1513–1514 and published in early 1517, see *The "Julius Exclusus" of Erasmus*, trans. Paul Pascal, intro. J. Kelley Sowards (Bloomington: Indiana University Press, 1968).

29. R. W. Southern, *Western Society and the Church in the Middle Ages* (Harmondsworth, U.K.: Penguin, 1970), pp. 159–165. For Petrarch's attacks on the Avignonese papacy, see *Petrarch's Book without a Name: A Translation of the "Liber sine nomine,"* trans. Norman P. Zacour (Toronto: Pontifical Institute of Mediaeval Studies, 1973), quotation on 108.

30. David Burr, *The Spiritual Franciscans: From Protest to Persecution in the Century after Saint Francis* (University Park: Pennsylvania State University Press, 2001), pp. 196–200; Bernard McGinn, *Antichrist: Two Thousand Years of the Human Fascination with Evil* (New York: HarperCollins, 1994), pp. 172–176; Robert E. Lerner, "The Black Death and Western European Eschatological Mentalities," *American Historical Review* 86 (1981): 533–552.

31. For conciliarism from the mid-twelfth to the late fourteenth century, see the classic work by Brian Tierney, *Foundations of the Conciliar Theory: The Contribution of Medieval Canonists from Gratian to the Great Schism,* enlarged ed. (Leiden: E. J. Brill, 1998).

32. This paragraph is based on Oakley, *Western Church,* pp. 223–231; Thomas M. Izbicki, *Protector of the Faith: Cardinal Johannes de Turrecremata and the Defense of the Institutional Church* (Washington, D.C.: Catholic University of America Press, 1981), pp. 1–18; John Van Engen, "The Church in the Fifteenth Century," in *Handbook of European History, 1400–1600: Late Middle Ages, Renaissance, and Reformation,* ed. Thomas A. Brady Jr., Heiko A. Oberman, and James D. Tracy, vol. 1 (Leiden: E. J. Brill, 1995), pp. 318–319; Duffy, *Saints and Sinners,* pp. 170–176; Michael A. Mullett, *The Catholic Reformation* (London and New York: Routledge, 1999), p. 9; Thomas A. Brady Jr., *German Histories in the Age of Reformations, 1400–1650* (Cambridge: Cambridge University Press, 2009), pp. 80–86, 92–93; J. N. D. Kelly, *The Oxford Dictionary of the Popes* (Oxford and New York: Oxford University Press, 1986), pp. 239–240, 241–243.

33. Paul E. Sigmund, *Nicholas of Cusa and Medieval Political Thought* (Cambridge, Mass.: Harvard University Press, 1963), pp. 220–221, cited in Ozment, *Age of Reform,* p. 174.

34. Barbara McClung Hallman, *Italian Cardinals, Reform, and the Church as Property, 1492–1563* (Berkeley and Los Angeles: University of California Press, 1985), p. 130.

35. Van Engen, "Church in the Fifteenth Century," in *Handbook of European History,* ed. Brady, Oberman, and Tracy, pp. 318–319.

36. John Edwards, *The Spain of the Catholic Monarchs, 1474–1520* (Oxford: Blackwell, 2000), pp. 213–217.

37. On princely initiatives, see Manfred Schulze, *Fürsten und Reformation: Geistliche Reformpolitik weltlicher Fürsten vor der Reformation* (Tübingen:

Mohr, 1991); Peter A. Dykema, "The Reforms of Count Eberhard of Württemberg: 'Confessionalization' in the Fifteenth Century," in *Reformations Old and New: Essays on the Socio-economic Impact of Religious Change, c. 1470–1630*, ed. Beat A. Kümin (Aldershot, U.K.: Scolar Press, 1996), pp. 39–56; William Bradford Smith, *Reformation and the German Territorial State: Upper Franconia, 1300–1630* (Rochester, N.Y.: University of Rochester Press, 2008), pp. 17–58; on episcopal inertia, see Thomas A. Brady Jr., "The Holy Roman Empire's Bishops on the Eve of the Reformation," in *Continuity and Change: The Harvest of Late Medieval and Reformation History: Essays Presented to Heiko Oberman on his 70th Birthday*, ed. Robert J. Bast and Andrew C. Gow (Leiden: E. J. Brill, 2000), pp. 21–47, and F. R. H. Du Boulay, *Germany in the Later Middle Ages* (London: Athlone Press, 1983), pp. 187–195.

38. Moeller, "Imperial Cities." in Moeller, *Imperial Cities and the Reformation*, ed. and trans. Midelfort and Edwards.

39. On cities' exclusion of bishops, see J. Jeffrey Tyler, *Lord of the Sacred City: The "Episcopus exclusus" in Late Medieval and Early Modern Germany* (Leiden: E. J. Brill, 1999). On cities' control of religious life in general, see Francis Rapp, *Réformes et réformation à Strasbourg: Église et société dans le diocèse de Strasbourg (1450–1525)* (Paris: Éditions Ophrys, 1974), esp. pp. 410–419; *Kirche und Gesellschaft im Heiligen Römischen Reich des 15. und 16. Jahrhunderts*, ed. Hartmut Boockmann (Göttingen: Vandenhoeck & Ruprecht, 1994); Ronald K. Rittgers, *The Reformation of the Keys: Confession, Conscience, and Authority in Sixteenth-Century Germany* (Cambridge, Mass., and London: Harvard University Press, 2004), pp. 18–21. On pre-Reformation endowed preacherships in particular, see Bernhard Neidiger, "Wortgottesdienst vor der Reformation: Die Stiftung eigener Predigtpfründen für Weltkleriker im späten Mittelalter," *Rheinische Vierteljahrsblätter* 66 (2002): 142–189.

40. Bernd Moeller, "Religious Life in Germany on the Eve of the Reformation," in *Pre-Reformation Germany*, ed. Gerald Strauss (New York: Harper & Row, 1972), pp. 13–42, originally published as "Frömmigkeit in Deutschland um 1500," *Archiv für Reformationsgeschichte* 56 (1965): 3–31; Berndt Hamm, "Normative Centering in the Fifteenth and Sixteenth Centuries: Observations on Religiosity, Theology, and Iconology," trans. John Frymire, in Hamm, *The Reformation of Faith in the Context of Late Medieval Theology and Piety*, ed. Robert J. Bast (Leiden: E. J. Brill, 2004), pp. 1–49; Eamon Duffy, *The Stripping of the Altars: Traditional Religion in England c. 1400–c. 1580*, 2nd ed. (New Haven, Conn., and London: Yale University Press, 2005).

41. As Moeller put it, "they certainly wanted to remain Catholic and members of the church, both in faith as well as in ordinary life." Moeller, "Imperial Cities," in Moeller, *Imperial Cities and the Reformation*, ed. and trans. Midelfort and Edwards, p. 49.

42. Egidio de Viterbo, in *Sacrorum conciliorum nova et amplissima collectio*, ed. Giovan Domenico Mansi et al., vol. 32 (Paris: H. Welter, 1901), col. 669D; on Giles of Viterbo more broadly, see John W. O'Malley, *Giles of Viterbo on*

*Church and Reform: A Study in Renaissance Thought* (Leiden: E. J. Brill, 1968).

43. Hamm's category of *normative Zentrierung* refers broadly to "the alignment of both religion and society towards a standardizing, authoritative, regulating and legitimizing focal point" and is intended to facilitate the analysis of continuity and change from the fourteenth through the seventeenth century. For fifteenth-century *Frömmigkeitstheologie* it was "'normative,' in that it involved standards, rules, and orientation aids for leading a Christian life" and it involved "'centering,' in that a reduction of themes and concepts occurred at the pivotal discursive level of what ensured salvation, a reduction that emphasized above all else the Passion of Christ and the co-redeemer Mary, the mercy of God and the repentance of man." Hamm, "Normative Centering," in Hamm, *Reformation of Faith*, pp. 2–43, quotations at 3, 21–22.

44. On the reunion reached at the Council of Ferrara-Florence in 1439, see Izbicki, *Protector*, pp. 10–12.

45. Lambert, *Medieval Heresy*, pp. 124–126, 284–287, 323–370.

46. Luther, *An den christlichen Adel deutscher Nation von des christlichen Standes Besserung* [1520], in *WA*, vol. 6 (Weimar: Hermann Böhlau, 1888), p. 417/24 (Luther's wordplay is "gewurm und geschwurm"); Luther, *Ein Sendbrief an den Papst Leo X* [1520], in *WA*, vol. 7 (Weimar: Hermann Böhlaus Nachfolger, 1897), p. 5/10–11, 27–29. On the process between October 1517 and May 1521 whereby Luther came to repudiate the papacy and reject papal authority, see Scott H. Hendrix, *Luther and the Papacy: Stages in a Reformation Conflict* (Philadelphia: Fortress Press, 1981), pp. 22–136.

47. Luther, *An den christlichen Adel*, in *WA*, vol. 6, p. 412/26–31.

48. Ibid., pp. 439–441, 441/13–14 (quotation), 445–446, 447–448, 451–452. Luther's rejection of papal authority pervades the entire treatise.

49. On Luther's apocalypticism and conviction that in the End Times of the early sixteenth century Satan was more active than ever, see Heiko A. Oberman, *Luther: Man between God and the Devil*, trans. Eileen Walliser-Schwartzbart (New Haven, Conn., and London: Yale University Press, 1989), esp. pp. 102–109.

50. This is a major theme in Luther, *Von der Freiheit eines Christenmenschen* [1520], in *WA*, vol. 7 (Weimar: Hermann Böhlaus Nachfolger, 1897), pp. 20–38.

51. Luther, *Von weltlicher Oberkeit, wie weit man ihr gehorsam Schuldig sei* [1523], in *WA*, vol. 11 (Weimar: Hermann Böhlaus Nachfolger, 1900), p. 262/12, 7–10. The two complete quoted sentences (lines 7–10): "Das welltlich regiment hatt gesetz, die sich nicht weytter strecken denn uber leyb und güt und was eußerlich ist auff erden. Denn uber die seele kan und will Gott niemant lassen regirn denn sich selbs alleyne."

52. On this point with respect to social ethics broadly understood, see R. H. Tawney, *Religion and the Rise of Capitalism*, intro. Adam B. Seligman (1926; New Brunswick, N.J.: Transaction, 1998), pp. 99–102.

53. Larissa Taylor, *Soldiers of Christ: Preaching in Late Medieval and Reformation France* (New York: Oxford University Press, 1992), p. 91.

54. "Das man in die bibel ader das helig worte Gotes bevel, darnach gerechtig-
keit und urtell fellen, ursach, auf das man dem armen tu wie dem reichen."
"Die Mühlhäuser Artikel" [1524], in *Flugschriften der Bauernkriegszeit*, ed.
Adolf Laube and Hans Werner Seiffert (Berlin: Akademie-Verlag, 1978),
p. 80/1–4, 13–16 (quotation at lines 13–15). Six biblical citations immediately follow the quoted passage; the eleven brief articles include dozens of
others.
55. "Die Zwölf Artikel," in *Flugschriften der Bauernkriegszeit*, ed. Laube and
Seiffert, p. 28/13–18.
56. Thomas Müntzer, *Hoch verursachte Schutzrede vnd antwwort wider das
Gaistloße Sanfft lebende fleysch zü Wittenberg*. . . . [1524], "Michael Gaismairs Tiroler Landesordnung" [1526], and Hans Hergot, *Von der neuen
Wandlung eines christlichen Lebens* [1527], in *Flugschriften der Bauernkriegszeit*, ed. Laube and Seiffert, pp. 83–98, 139–143, 547–557; Peter Blickle, *The
Revolution of 1525: The German Peasants' War from a New Perspective*,
trans. Thomas A. Brady Jr. and H. C. Erik Midelfort (Baltimore and London:
Johns Hopkins University Press, 1981), pp. 145–154; Walter Klaassen, *Mi-
chael Gaismair: Revolutionary and Reformer* (Leiden: E. J. Brill, 1978); Tom
Scott, "Hubmaier, Schappeler and Hergot on Social Revolution," in *The Impact of the European Reformation: Princes, Clergy and People*, ed. Bridget
Heal and Ole Peter Grell (Aldershot, U.K.: Ashgate, 2008), pp. 17, 32–36.
Müntzer explicitly refused exactly the separation of inner and outer, soul and
body, that was central to Luther. See Hans-Jürgen Goertz, *Innere und äussere
Ordnung in der Theologie Thomas Müntzers* (Leiden: E. J. Brill, 1967),
pp. 133–149.
57. Hans-Jürgen Goertz in particular has argued that anticlericalism was the
heart of the early German Reformation; see esp. Goertz, *Pfaffenhaß und groß
Geschrei: Die reformatorischen Bewegungen in Deutschland 1517 bis 1529*
(Munich: Beck, 1987). See also the articles on the early German Reformation
in *Anticlericalism in Late Medieval and Early Modern Europe*, ed. Peter A.
Dykema and Heiko A. Oberman (Leiden: E. J. Brill, 1993), and for particular
attention to the relationship between the social standing and the divergent
views of reform among lay writers in the early evangelical movement, see
Miriam Usher Chrisman, *Conflicting Visions of Reform: German Lay Propaganda Pamphlets, 1519–1530* (Atlantic Highlands, N.J., and London: Humanities Press, 1996).
58. Indispensable here is Peter Blickle's classic work, which argues that the peasants' understanding of Christian freedom in the early Reformation was the
crucial element differentiating the scale and urgency of the uprisings in the
mid-1520s from the *Bundschuh* peasant rebellions of previous decades.
Blickle, *Revolution of 1525*, esp. pp. 155–161. See also Blickle, *Communal
Reformation: The Quest for Salvation in Sixteenth-Century Germany*, trans.
Thomas Dunlap (Atlantic Highlands, N.J., and London: Humanities Press,
1992); Heiko A. Oberman, "The Gospel of Social Unrest," in *The Dawn of
the Reformation: Essays in Late Medieval and Early Reformation Thought*
(Edinburgh: T. & T. Clark, 1986), esp. pp. 170–173; Tom Scott and Bob

Scribner, "Introduction" to *The German Peasants' War: A History in Documents* (Atlantic Highlands, N.J., and London: Humanities Press, 1991), pp. 1–64; Peter Matheson, *The Imaginative World of the Reformation* (Minneapolis: Fortress Press, 2001), esp. pp. 65–76; Hans-Jürgen Goertz, "Karlstadt, Müntzer and the Reformation of the Commoners, 1521–1525," in *A Companion to Anabaptism and Spiritualism, 1521–1700*, ed. John D. Roth and James M. Stayer (Leiden: E. J. Brill, 2007), pp. 1–44.

59. On imperial cities and territories in general, see especially Christopher Ocker, *Church Robbers and Reformers in Germany, 1525–1547: Confiscation and Religious Purpose in the Holy Roman Empire* (Leiden: E. J. Brill, 2006); see also Henry J. Cohn, "Church Property in the German Protestant Principalities," in *Politics and Society in Reformation Europe: Essays for Sir Geoffrey Elton on His Sixty-Fifth Birthday*, ed. E. I. Kouri and Tom Scott (London: Macmillan, 1987), pp. 158–187; and Walter Ziegler, "Reformation und Klosterauflösung: Ein ordensgeschichtlicher Vergleich," in *Reformbemühungen und Observanzbestrebungen im spätmittelalterlichen Ordenswesen*, ed. Kaspar Elm (Berlin: Duncker & Humblot, 1989), pp. 585–614; on Strasbourg in particular, see Thomas A. Brady Jr., *Protestant Politics: Jacob Sturm (1489–1553) and the German Reformation* (Atlantic Highlands, N.J.: Humanities Press, 1995), pp. 170–174.

60. The classic study of the Henrician suppression of the monasteries is David Knowles, *The Religious Orders in England*, vol. 3, *The Tudor Age* (Cambridge: Cambridge University Press, 1959), pp. 268–417; see also Joyce Youings, *The Dissolution of the Monasteries* (London: Allen & Unwin, 1971); Ethan H. Shagan, *Popular Politics and the English Reformation* (Cambridge: Cambridge University Press, 2003), pp. 162–196; Richard Rex, *Henry VIII and the English Reformation*, 2nd ed. (Houndmills, U.K.: Palgrave, 2006), pp. 45–55; and most recently, Geoffrey Moorhouse, *The Last Divine Office: Henry VIII and the Dissolution of the Monasteries* (New York: BlueBridge, 2009).

61. For a recent overview, see Ralf Klötzer, "The Melchiorites and Münster," in *Companion to Anabaptism and Spiritualism*, ed. Roth and Stayer, pp. 217–256; on the immediate reactions to Münster by both Catholics and magisterial Protestants, see Sigrun Haude, *In the Shadow of "Savage Wolves": Anabaptist Münster and the German Reformation during the 1530s* (Boston: Humanities Press, 2000).

62. Werner O. Packull, *Hutterite Beginnings: Communitarian Experiments during the Reformation* (Baltimore and London: Johns Hopkins University Press, 1995); John S. Oyer, *Lutheran Reformers against Anabaptists: Luther, Melanchthon and Menius and the Anabaptists of Central Germany* (The Hague: Martinus Nijhoff, 1964); S. Zijlstra, *Om de ware gemeente en de oude gronden: Geschiedenis van de dopersen in de Nederlanden, 1531–1675* (Hilversum: Verloren; Leeuwarden: Fryske Akademy, 2000); James A. Stayer, "Pilgram Marpeck and the Austerlitz Brethren: A 'Disappeared' Anabaptist Denomination," *Mennonite Life* 64 (Summer 2010), online edition, http://www.bethelks.edu/mennonitelife/2010/pilgram.php (accessed 5 February 2011); *Companion to Anabaptism and Spiritualism*, ed. Roth and Stayer.

63. Swiss villages in which a majority of citizens were baptized as Anabaptists in 1525 include Hallau and Waldshut; following his expulsion from the region, Balthasar Hubmaier was the leading figure behind the establishment of Anabaptism in Nikolsburg in 1526–1527, before the suppression of religious dissent in the region under Ferdinand I. See James A. Stayer, *The German Peasants' War and Anabaptist Community of Goods* (Montreal and Kingston, Ont.: McGill–Queen's University Press, 1991), pp. 63–64, 139–141.

64. For the period up to 1580 or so, easily the most comprehensive work is George Hunston Williams, *The Radical Reformation,* 3rd ed. (Kirksville, Mo.: Sixteenth Century Studies Publishers, 1992); for the seventeenth century, see Leszek Kołakowski, *Chrétiens sans église: La conscience religieuse et le lien confessional au XVIIe siècle,* trans. Anna Posner (Paris: Gallimard, 1969).

65. For Calvin's influence on politics in Geneva, see especially William G. Naphy, *Calvin and the Consolidation of the Genevan Reformation,* 2nd ed. (Louisville, Ky.: Westminster John Knox Press, 2003).

66. See, for example, Alain Tallon, *Conscience nationale et sentiment religieux en France au XVIe siècle: Essai sur la vision gallicane du monde* (Paris: Presses Universitaires de France, 2002), and Jotham Parsons, *The Church in the Republic: Gallicanism and Political Ideology in Renaissance France* (Washington, D.C.: Catholic University of America Press, 2004).

67. Quoted in Robert Bireley, *The Refashioning of Catholicism, 1450–1700: A Reassessment of the Counter Reformation* (Washington, D.C.: Catholic University of America Press, 1999), p. 83.

68. Quoted in Patrick Williams, *Philip II* (Houndmills, U.K.: Palgrave, 2001), p. 73. "He genuinely did regard the pope as a junior partner where the affairs of the Spanish Church were concerned." On Philip's attitude and actions regarding Trent and oversight of Spanish ecclesiastical affairs, see Helen Rawlings, *Church, Religion and Society in Early Modern Spain* (Houndmills, U.K.: Palgrave, 2002), pp. 55–77, and Henry Kamen, *Philip II of Spain* (New Haven, Conn., and London: Yale University Press, 1997), pp. 103–105.

69. On the "territorialization" of the Catholic Church under secular rulers during the Reformation era and the efforts of Jesuit thinkers to address it through the papal *potestas indirecta,* see Harro Höpfl, *Jesuit Political Thought: The Society of Jesus and the State, c. 1540–1630* (Cambridge: Cambridge University Press, 2004), pp. 339–365.

70. The papal brief *Zelo domus Dei* protested against the terms of the Peace of Westphalia on 20 August 1650, but was backdated to 26 November 1648 so as to leave a juridical open door without jeopardizing the war's political conclusion that the papacy desired. See Robert Bireley, *The Jesuits and the Thirty Years War: Kings, Courts, and Confessors* (Cambridge: Cambridge University Press, 2003), pp. 255–256; see also Peter H. Wilson, *The Thirty Years War: Europe's Tragedy* (Cambridge, Mass., and London: Belknap Press of Harvard University Press, 2009), p. 754. For a brief overview of the suppression of the Society of Jesus in the absence of an adequate scholarly monograph, see Jonathan Wright, "The Suppression and Restoration," in *The*

Cambridge Companion to the Jesuits, ed. Thomas Worcester (Cambridge: Cambridge University Press, 2008), pp. 263–272, as well as the relevant articles in part 6 of *The Jesuits II: Cultures, Sciences, and the Arts, 1540–1773*, ed. John W. O'Malley et al. (Toronto: University of Toronto Press, 2006).

71. For one example, see Joseph Leo Koerner, *The Reformation of the Image* (Chicago: University of Chicago Press, 2004); another example, considerably more influential in medieval history since its initial publication in 1987, is R. I. Moore, *The Formation of a Persecuting Society: Authority and Deviance in Western Europe, 950–1250*, 2nd ed. (Malden, Mass., and Oxford: Blackwell, 2007).

72. Patrick Collinson, *The Elizabethan Puritan Movement* (1967; Oxford: Clarendon Press, 1990), pp. 177–207, 385–467.

73. John Bossy, *Christianity in the West, 1400–1700* (Oxford: Oxford University Press, 1987), pp. 153–161.

74. On the Gunpowder Plot, see Mark Nicholls, *Investigating Gunpowder Plot* (Manchester: Manchester University Press, 1991). James Sharpe provides a readable narrative of the plot and its discovery in his *Remember, Remember: A Cultural History of Guy Fawkes Day* (Cambridge, Mass., and London: Harvard University Press, 2005), pp. 38–69, and the plot is discussed and contextualized by Michael Questier in the most extensive and sophisticated study of the politics of later sixteenth- and early seventeenth-century English recusants; see Questier, *Catholicism and Community in Early Modern England: Politics, Aristocratic Patronage and Religion, c. 1550–1640* (Cambridge: Cambridge University Press, 2006), pp. 279–286.

75. Mack P. Holt, *The French Wars of Religion, 1562–1629*, 2nd ed. (Cambridge: Cambridge University Press, 2005), pp. 182–194.

76. For a recent magisterial synthesis, see Austin Woolrych, *Britain in Revolution, 1625–1660* (Oxford: Oxford University Press, 2002); on religious radicalism during the English Revolution, see Christopher Hill, *The World Turned Upside Down: Radical Ideas during the English Revolution* (Harmondsworth, U.K.: Penguin, 1972); *Radical Religion in the English Revolution*, ed. J. F. McGregor and Barry Reay (London and New York: Oxford University Press, 1984); Nicholas McDowell, *The English Radical Imagination: Culture, Religion, and Revolution, 1630–1660* (Oxford: Clarendon Press, 2003); and Ann Hughes, *Gangraena and the Struggle for the English Revolution* (Oxford: Oxford University Press, 2004).

77. On England's religio-political changes during these decades, see Christopher Haigh, *English Reformations: Religion, Politics, and Society under the Tudors* (Oxford: Clarendon Press, 1993), and Peter Marshall, *Reformation England, 1480–1642* (London: Hodder Arnold, 2003), pp. 35–119; the phrase "Tudor church militant" is from Diarmaid MacCulloch, *Tudor Church Militant: Edward VI and the Protestant Reformation* (London: Allen Lane, 1999).

78. Ignatius Loyola's views in the *Constitutions* of the Society of Jesus were an extension of the traditional idea that hierarchically well-positioned secular authorities, like ecclesiastical authorities, contributed to the salvation of

Christians body and soul. Because powerful rulers could achieve so much more for the salvation of embodied souls than could ordinary men and women, Ignatius thought the Jesuits' attention should be properly focused especially on them: "The spiritual aid which is given to important and public persons ought to be regarded as more important, since it is a more universal good. This is true whether these persons are laymen such as princes, lords, magistrates, or ministers of justice, or whether they are clerics such as prelates." Ignatius Loyola, *The Constitutions of the Society of Jesus* [1558], trans. George E. Ganss (St. Louis: Institute of Jesuit Resources, 1970), 7.2, p. 275. This idea and the actions it inspired are crucial to understanding the Jesuits' involvements in political affairs in early modern Europe. On the relationship between their political ideas and these involvements, see Höpfl, *Jesuit Political Thought.*

79. See sessions 6 (justification) and 7.1 (sacraments in general), in *Canons and Decrees of the Council of Trent* [1564], trans. H. J. Schroeder (St. Louis: Herder, 1941), pp. 308–324, 329–331 (Latin); 29–46, 51–53 (English).

80. This point is missed by scholars who think that a de facto, more-or-less tolerant Christianity of the sort fairly common in the seventeenth-century Dutch Republic constituted a "nonconfessional" or "a-confessional" Christianity. See, for example, Benjamin J. Kaplan, *Divided by Faith,* and *Calvinists and Libertines: Confession and Community in Utrecht, 1578–1620* (Oxford: Oxford University Press, 1995), pp. 261–304, and Willem Frijhoff, "Dimensions de la coexistence confessionnelle," in *The Emergence of Tolerance in the Dutch Republic,* ed. C. Berkvens-Stevelinck, J. Israel, and G. H. M. Posthumus Meyjes (Leiden: E. J. Brill, 1997), pp. 213–237.

81. For the argument that most Anabaptist separatism was a consequence of the failure of the attempted revolution of 1525, in which many Anabaptists and future Anabaptists were involved, rather than a principled pacifist stance in the manner of Conrad Grebel, see James A. Stayer, "Anabaptists and Future Anabaptists in the Peasants' War," in Stayer, *German Peasants' War,* pp. 61–92; C. Arnold Snyder, *Anabaptist History and Theology: An Introduction* (Kitchener, Ont.: Pandora Press, 1995), pp. 58–63.

82. For examples of such accommodation, see John Oyer, "Nicodemites among Württemberg Anabaptists," *MQR* 71 (1997): 487–514; Mark Furner, "Lay Casuistry and the Survival of Later Anabaptists in Bern," *MQR* 75 (2001): 429–470; Hans-Jürgen Goertz, "Nonconformists on the Elbe River: Pious, Rich, and Perplexed. Four Hundred Years of Mennonites in Hamburg and Altona," *MQR* 76 (2002): 413–430; John D. Roth, "Marpeck and the Later Swiss Brethren, 1540–1700," in *Companion to Anabaptism and Spiritualism,* ed. Roth and Stayer, pp. 347–388; and Michael Driedger, "Anabaptists and the Early Modern State: A Long-Term View," in ibid., pp. 507–544.

83. I am grateful to David Luthy, John Roth, and Arnold Snyder for conversations about this point.

84. Mullett, *Catholic Reformation,* p. 8; for an introductory commentary and English translation of both Leo X's reforming bull issued during the Fifth Lateran Council, *Supernae dispositionis arbitrio* (1514), and of the *Consil-*

*ium de emendanda ecclesia,* see John C. Olin, *The Catholic Reformation: Savonarola to Ignatius Loyola. Reform in the Church, 1495–1540* (New York: Harper & Row, 1969), pp. 54–64, 182–197.

85. Martin Bucer, *De regno Christi Iesu servatoris nostri, libri II.* . . . (Basel: Johannes Oporinus, 1557), bk. 2, chap. 57, p. 227. On Bucer's period of exile in England from April 1549, following the Schmalkaldic War and the imposition of the Augsburg Interim, until his death on 28 February 1551, see Martin Greschat, *Martin Bucer: A Reformer and His Times,* trans. Stephen E. Buckwalter (Louisville, Ky.: Westminster John Knox Press, 2004), pp. 227–249, with discussion of *De regno Christi* at 239–245.

86. For a few examples, see Geoffrey Parker, "Success and Failure in the First Century of the Reformation," *Past and Present* 136 (1992): 69–77; Simon Ditchfield, "'In Search of Local Knowledge': Rewriting Early Modern Italian Religious History," *Cristianesimo nella storia* 19:2 (1998): 255–296; Marc Forster, *Catholic Revival in the Age of the Baroque: Religious Identity in Southwest Germany* (Cambridge: Cambridge University Press, 2001); Charles H. Parker, *Faith on the Margins: Catholics and Catholicism in the Dutch Golden Age* (Cambridge, Mass., and London: Harvard University Press, 2008). These examples pertain only to Europe, but of course an enormous range of complex interactions between indigenous traditions and Catholicism is characteristic of the regions in Asia and especially the Americas where the Roman church was established along with Spanish and Portuguese colonies and/or trading posts during the sixteenth century.

87. Brown, *Rise of Western Christendom,* 2nd ed., pp. 207–213.

88. *Tyndale's New Testament* [1534 ed.], trans. William Tyndale, ed. David Daniell (New Haven, Conn., and London: Yale University Press, 1989), p. 244.

89. On the theory and practice of the suppression of Christian heterodoxy in the Reformation era, see Brad S. Gregory, *Salvation at Stake: Christian Martyrdom in Early Modern Europe* (Cambridge, Mass., and London: Harvard University Press, 1999), pp. 74–96. For a broad overview from late antiquity through the Middle Ages, see also Zagorin, *Idea of Religious Toleration,* pp. 14–45, and for early modern England, see Alexandra Walsham's analysis of "fraternal correction and holy violence" in her *Charitable Hatred: Tolerance and Intolerance in England, 1500–1700* (Manchester and New York: Manchester University Press, 2006), pp. 39–105, quotation on 39.

90. See Bruce Gordon, *The Swiss Reformation* (Manchester: Manchester University Press, 2002), pp. 122–140; Brady, *Protestant Politics,* pp. 292–370, and *German Histories,* pp. 220–228; Holt, *French Wars of Religion;* Robert J. Knecht, *The French Civil Wars* (Harlow, U.K.: Longman, 2000); Geoffrey Parker, *The Dutch Revolt* (1977; Harmondsworth, U.K.: Penguin, 1981); *The Origins and Development of the Dutch Revolt,* ed. Graham Darby (London and New York: Routledge, 2001); Wilson, *Thirty Years War;* and Woolrych, *Britain in Revolution.*

91. Blaise Pascal, *Pensées* [1670], in Pascal, *Oeuvres complètes,* ed. Louis Lafuma (Paris: Éditions du Seuil, 1963), no. 172, p. 523, electronic edition (Charlottesville, Va.: Intelex, 2006).

92. Peter Brown, "St. Augustine's Attitude to Religious Coercion," *Journal of Roman Studies* 54 (1964): 107–116; Brown, *Rise of Western Christendom,* 2nd ed., pp. 207–213.

93. Parker, *Dutch Revolt,* pp. 154–155; Kaplan, *Divided by Faith,* p. 242. For the same phenomenon across the border in the Holy Roman Empire, see Nicole Grochowina, "Confessional Indifference in East Frisia," *Reformation and Renaissance Review* 17:1 (2005): 111–124; Grochowina, "Grenzen der Konfessionalisierung—Dissidentum und konfessionelle Indifferenz im Ostfriesland des 16. und 17. Jahrhunderts," in *Interkonfessionalität—Transkonfessionalität—binnenkonfessionelle Pluralität,* ed. Kaspar von Greyerz et al. (Gütersloh: Gütersloher Verlagshaus, 2003), pp. 48–72.

94. On the institutions and religious culture of eighteenth-century French Catholicism, see the magisterial study by John McManners, *Church and Society in Eighteenth-Century France,* 2 vols. (Oxford: Clarendon Press, 1998).

95. Eamon Duffy, *Fires of Faith: Catholic England under Mary Tudor* (New Haven, Conn., and London: Yale University Press, 2009), pp. 7, 79.

96. Gregory, *Salvation at Stake;* see also *Martyrdom in an Ecumenical Perspective: A Mennonite-Catholic Conversation,* ed. Peter C. Erb (Kitchener, Ont.: Pandora Press, 2007).

97. See Balthasar Hubmaier, *Von ketzern und iren verbrennern.* . . . [1524], in Hubmaier, *Schriften,* ed. Gunnar Westin and Torsten Bergsten, vol. 9 in *QGT* (Gütersloh: Gerd Mohn, 1962), pp. 95–100; and Roland H. Bainton, "The Parable of the Tares as the Proof Text for Religious Liberty to the End of the Sixteenth Century," *Church History* 1 (1932): 67–89.

98. The most extensive intellectual history on religious toleration in the Reformation era remains Joseph Lecler, *Histoire de la tolérance au siècle de la Réforme,* 2 vols. ([Paris:] Aubier, 1955), but see also Zagorin, *Idea of Religious Toleration;* Henry Kamen, *The Rise of Toleration* (New York: McGraw-Hill, 1967); and the essays in *Tolerance and Intolerance in the European Reformation,* ed. Ole Peter Grell and Bob Scribner (Cambridge: Cambridge University Press, 1996). In Roman Catholicism, the crucial Vatican II document is *Dignitatis humanae;* see *Documents of Vatican II,* ed. Austin P. Flannery (Grand Rapids, Mich.: Eerdmans, 1975), pp. 799–812.

99. For the insults against the scribes and Pharisees, see Mt 3:7; Mt 12:34; Mt 15:7; Mt 22:18; Mt 23:13–17, 19, 23–29, 33; Mk 7:6; for the driving of the money changers from the temple, see Mt 21:12–13; Mk 11:15–17; Lk 19:45–46; and Jn 2:15–16.

100. On the approximate number of judicial executions for heresy or religious treason in the Reformation era, see Gregory, *Salvation at Stake,* p. 6.

101. *Moderate Voices in the European Reformation,* ed. Luc Racaut and Alec Ryrie (Aldershot, U.K.: Ashgate, 2005); see also the articles in *Conciliation and Confession: The Struggle for Unity in the Age of Reform, 1415–1648,* ed. Howard P. Louthan and Randall C. Zachman (Notre Dame, Ind.: University of Notre Dame Press, 2004).

102. Cavanaugh, *Myth of Religious Violence,* pp. 130–141, 183–194.

103. Ibid., esp. pp. 123–180. In his argument about the importance of the "creation myth of the wars of religion" in the construction of modern liberalism's

"myth of religious violence," Cavanaugh acknowledges that the Reformation era's violence included those acting in ways that were intertwined with their religious commitments, but shows that only anachronistically can "religion" be singled out and blamed for it—as if "religion" was something separate and separable from political power, social relationships, and culture *during the sixteenth century,* as opposed to gradually separated from them beginning in and as a *consequence* of the Reformation era. Cavanaugh argues that by blaming "religion" for the violence of the Reformation era, modern liberal political ideology recycles its foundation myth in order to cast the modern, secular state in the role of societal savior and to deflect attention away from its own—ostensibly legitimate and supposedly peacemaking—violence.

104. On the draining, wide-ranging effects of especially the Thirty Years War, see Theodore K. Rabb, *The Struggle for Stability in Early Modern Europe* (New York: Oxford University Press, 1975), pp. 116–145.

105. J. C. D. Clark, *English Society, 1660–1832: Religion, Ideology and Politics during the Ancien Regime,* 2nd ed. (Cambridge: Cambridge University Press, 2000); McManners, *Church and Society;* on Carlos III, see Nigel Aston, *Christianity and Revolutionary Europe, c. 1750–1830* (Cambridge: Cambridge University Press, 2002), pp. 156, 165–167. On eighteenth-century measures that sought to create a more nationalist German Catholic Church doctrinally loyal to but jurisdictionally more independent of Rome, see Michael Printy, *Enlightenment and the Creation of German Catholicism* (Cambridge: Cambridge University Press, 2009).

106. John Brewer, *The Sinews of Power: War, Money and the English State, 1688–1783* (New York: Knopf, 1989).

107. Henry D. Rack, *Reasonable Enthusiast: John Wesley and the Rise of Methodism,* 3rd ed. (London: Epworth Press, 2002); Adrian Burdon, *Authority and Order: John Wesley and His Preachers* (Aldershot, U.K.: Ashgate, 2005). On the explosive growth of Methodism in the United States after 1790, see Mark A. Noll, *America's God: From Jonathan Edwards to Abraham Lincoln* (New York: Oxford University Press, 2002), pp. 168–170, 180–181, 330–341, and Nathan O. Hatch, *The Democratization of American Christianity* (New Haven, Conn., and London: Yale University Press, 1989), pp. 81–93.

108. R. R. Palmer, *Catholics and Unbelievers in Eighteenth-Century France* (Princeton, N.J.: Princeton University Press, 1947), p. 225, with reference to Albert Monod, *De Pascal à Chateaubriand: Les défenseurs français du christianisme de 1670 à 1802* (Paris: F. Alcan, 1916).

109. See Aston, *Christianity and Revolutionary Europe,* pp. 134–171.

110. *Emergence of Tolerance,* ed. Berkvens-Stevelinck et al.; *Calvinism and Religious Toleration in the Dutch Golden Age,* ed. R. Po-chia Hsia and H. F. K. van Nierop (Cambridge: Cambridge University Press, 2002); Zijlstra, *Ware gemeente;* Parker, *Faith on the Margins;* Miriam Bodian, *Hebrews of the Portuguese Nation: Conversos and Community in Early Modern Amsterdam* (Bloomington: Indiana University Press, 1997); Kaplan, *Divided by Faith,* pp. 172–176, 237–239, 241–243, 321–324.

111. William Temple, *Observations upon the United Provinces of the Netherlands* (London: A. Maxwell for Sa. Gellibrand, 1673), p. 181.

112. On the extent to which Dutch confessional coexistence depended on political authorities who were "highly authoritarian" in exercising religious policies that comprised "a rather strict disciplinarian regime and a considerable amount of social engineering," see Joke Spaans, "Religious Policies in the Seventeenth-Century Dutch Republic," in *Calvinism and Religious Toleration,* ed. Po-chia Hsia and van Nierop, pp. 72–86, quotations on 86. Temple described the surveillant oversight by magistrates who granted sects the right to worship publicly, "with the condition, That one or more Commissioners shall be appointed, who shall have free admission at all their meetings, shall be both the Observers and Witnesses of all that is acted or preached among them, and whose testimony shall be received concerning any thing that passes there to the prejudice of the State; In which case the Laws and Executions are as severe as against any Civil Crimes." Ibid., pp. 178–179.

113. Temple, *Observations,* p. 183.

114. On the creation of "religion" as an abstract, analytical category in late seventeenth- and eighteenth-century England, see Peter Harrison, *"Religion" and the Religions in the English Enlightenment* (Cambridge: Cambridge University Press, 1990); Harrison builds on the classic work by William Cantwell Smith, *The Meaning and End of Religion: A New Approach to the Religious Traditions of Mankind* (New York: Macmillan, 1963). Both Harrison and Smith are important to the argument in Cavanaugh, *Myth of Religious Violence.*

115. John Rawls, *Political Liberalism,* expanded ed. (1993; New York: Columbia University Press, 2005), pp. 13, 175.

116. For the United States, see James B. Twitchell, *Shopping for God: How Christianity Went from in Your Heart to in Your Face* (New York: Simon & Schuster, 2007); see also Wade Clark Roof, *Spiritual Marketplace: Baby Boomers and the Remaking of American Religion* (Princeton, N.J.: Princeton University Press, 1999), as well as the work of Robert Wuthnow, including *The Restructuring of American Religion* (Princeton, N.J.: Princeton University Press, 1988), *After Heaven: Spirituality in America since the 1950s* (Berkeley and Los Angeles: University of California Press, 1998), and *After the Baby Boomers: How Twenty- and Thirty-Somethings Are Shaping the Future of American Religion* (Princeton, N.J.: Princeton University Press, 2007). On the eclectic, consumerist character of the religious choices of college-age students and other young adults in their twenties, see Christian Smith with Patricia Snell, *Souls in Transition: The Religious and Spiritual Lives of Emerging Adults* (New York: Oxford University Press, 2009). For an example of the deliberate advocacy of marketing strategies to attract church members, see Richard L. Reising, *Church Marketing 101: Preparing Your Church for Greater Growth* (Grand Rapids, Mich.: Baker Books, 2006).

117. Kaplan, *Divided by Faith,* pp. 171–197; for *schuilkerken* among Dutch Catholics in particular, see Parker, *Faith on the Margins,* pp. 51–53.

118. Thomas Jefferson, *Notes on the State of Virginia* [1781], ed. William Peden (1954; Chapel Hill: University of North Carolina Press, 1982), p. 159.

119. John Locke, "An Essay on Toleration" [1667], in Locke, *Political Essays,* ed. Mark Goldie (Cambridge: Cambridge University Press, 1997), pp. 137, 136.

120. Locke, *A Letter Concerning Toleration* [1689], ed. James H. Tully (Indianapolis: Hackett, 1983), pp. 26, 28.

121. Jan de Vries and Ad van der Woude, *The First Modern Economy: Success, Failure, and Perseverance of the Dutch Economy, 1500–1815* (Cambridge: Cambridge University Press, 1997). For a critique of their argument based on the decline of the Golden Age Dutch economy and the lack of an early modern Dutch national identity comparable to England's, see Liah Greenfeld, *The Spirit of Capitalism: Nationalism and Economic Growth* (Cambridge, Mass., and London: Harvard University Press, 2001), pp. 59–104.

122. Simon Schama, *The Embarrassment of Riches: An Interpretation of Dutch Culture in the Golden Age* (New York: Knopf, 1987); de Vries and van der Woude, *First Modern Economy*; Harold J. Cook, *Matters of Exchange: Commerce, Medicine, and Science in the Dutch Golden Age* (New Haven, Conn., and London: Yale University Press, 2007).

123. *Consumption and the World of Goods*, ed. John Brewer and Roy Porter (London and New York: Routledge, 1993); John Brewer, *The Pleasures of the Imagination: English Culture in the Eighteenth Century* (Chicago: University of Chicago Press, 1997); Jan de Vries, *The Industrious Revolution: Consumer Behavior and the Household Economy, 1650 to the Present* (Cambridge: Cambridge University Press, 2008); Colin Campbell, *The Romantic Ethic and the Spirit of Modern Consumerism* (Oxford: Blackwell, 1987); James Twitchell, *Lead Us into Temptation: The Triumph of American Materialism* (New York: Columbia University Press, 1999).

124. On Madison's views of religious toleration, see Noonan, *Lustre of Our Country*, pp. 61–91, and Garrett Ward Sheldon, *The Political Philosophy of James Madison* (Baltimore and London: Johns Hopkins University Press, 2001), pp. 27–36. For Madison's famous and influential "Memorial and Remonstrance Against Religious Assessments," submitted to Virginia's General Assembly around 20 June 1785, see James Madison, *Writings*, ed. Jack N. Rakove (New York: Library of America, 1999), pp. 29–36. Steven Waldman considers Madison along with Franklin, Adams, Jefferson, and Washington in *Founding Faith: Providence, Politics, and the Birth of Religious Freedom in America* (New York: Random House, 2008).

125. For the text of Jefferson's bill, see Thomas Jefferson, *Writings*, ed. Merrill D. Peterson (New York: Library of America, 1984), pp. 346–348. On the complexities and deep ideological divisions that lay behind the debate over the First Amendment, and the extent to which Madison was displeased by the form in which it was eventually approved, see David Sehat, *The Myth of American Religious Freedom* (New York: Oxford University Press, 2011), pp. 45–50.

126. Quoted in Noonan, *Lustre of Our Country*, pp. 61–62 (italics in original). "Although eighteenth-century American religious pluralism most likely did not exceed that found throughout Europe as a whole, by 1760 it probably had no equal in any single European society." Jon Butler, *Awash in a Sea of Faith: Christianizing the American People* (Cambridge, Mass., and London: Harvard University Press, 1990), p. 174.

127. Sehat, *Myth of American Religious Freedom,* pp. 15–29.
128. Steven D. Smith, *Foreordained Failure: The Quest for a Constitutional Principle of Religious Freedom* (New York: Oxford University Press, 1995), pp. 17–34; Philip Hamburger, *Separation of Church and State* (Cambridge, Mass., and London: Harvard University Press, 2002), p. 213. In fact, "when Congress sent the Bill of Rights to the states in 1789, six states [Massachusetts, Connecticut, Maryland, New Hampshire, South Carolina, and Vermont] still paid churches and were able to continue to do so under the provisions of the First Amendment." Sehat, *Myth of American Religious Freedom,* p. 49; see also p. 20, where the six states are listed. On the varied trajectories of the individual states with respect to disestablishment during the Revolutionary period and into the early nineteenth century, see Thomas S. Kidd, *God of Liberty: A Religious History of the American Revolution* (New York: Basic Books, 2010), pp. 167–186, as well as Sehat, *Myth of American Religious Freedom,* pp. 15–29.
129. Butler, *Awash in a Sea of Faith;* Noll, *America's God,* pp. 156 (quotation), 161–165.
130. As Mark Noll notes, "by the mid-nineteenth century, the force of the biblical proslavery argument had weakened everywhere except the United States." Noll, *The Civil War as a Theological Crisis* (Chapel Hill: University of North Carolina Press, 2006), pp. 33–35 (quotation on 34).
131. Quoted (from 1819) in Noonan, *Lustre of Our Country,* p. 88.
132. Alexis de Tocqueville, *Democracy in America,* ed. J. P. Mayer, trans. George Lawrence, vol. 1 [1835] (1966; New York: HarperCollins, 2000), 2.9, pp. 290, 292. On the enormous variety within American Protestantism in the first third of the nineteenth century, see Hatch, *Democratization of American Christianity.*
133. Sehat, *Myth of American Religious Freedom.*
134. Tocqueville, *Democracy in America,* vol. 2 [1840], 1.1, p. 432. For the broader historical sweep within which Tocqueville's observation fits, as well as the historical consequences and contemporary implications of American evangelical Protestant anti-intellectualism, see Mark A. Noll, *The Scandal of the Evangelical Mind* (Grand Rapids, Mich.: Eerdmans, 1994).
135. Henry F. May, *The Enlightenment in America* (Oxford: Oxford University Press, 1976), pp. 337–358; see also Noll, *America's God,* pp. 93–113, 233–238, and Eva Marie Garroutte, "The Positivist Attack on Baconian Science and Religious Knowledge in the 1870s," in *The Secular Revolution: Power, Interests, and Conflict in the Secularization of American Public Life,* ed. Christian Smith (Berkeley and Los Angeles: University of California Press, 2003), pp. 197–200.
136. Christian Smith with Melinda Lundquist Denton, *Soul Searching: The Religious and Spiritual Lives of American Teenagers* (New York: Oxford University Press, 2005), pp. 6, 118–171, quotations on 164, 147, 164, 165.
137. Madison, "Memorial and Remonstrance," in Madison, *Writings,* ed. Rakove, p. 30.
138. Thomas Paine, *The Age of Reason* [1794], in Paine, *Political Writings,* ed. Bruce Kuklick (Cambridge: Cambridge University Press, 2000), p. 268.

139. Tocqueville, *Democracy in America*, vol. 2, 1.1, p. 429. According to Tocqueville, Catholics in the United States shared many of the same sensibilities and attitudes with the Protestant majority in ways that distinguished them from Catholics in Europe. Ibid., p. 449.

140. See Noll, *America's God*, and Hatch, *Democratization*. I am also grateful to Mark Noll for discussion on this point.

141. Hobbes, *Leviathan* [1651], ed. Tuck, esp. 1.11, pp. 70–71; David Hume, *A Treatise of Human Nature* [1739–1740], ed. L. A. Selby-Bigge, 2nd ed., ed. P. H. Nidditch (Oxford: Clarendon Press, 1978), 3.2.2, pp. 491–492; Adam Smith, *The Theory of Moral Sentiments* [1759], ed. Knud Haakonssen (Cambridge: Cambridge University Press, 2002), 1.3.2.1, p. 61; Erving Goffman, *The Presentation of Self in Everyday Life* (Garden City, N.Y.: Doubleday, 1959).

142. On American capitalism in the nineteenth and early twentieth centuries, including its relationship to Christianity, see *God and Mammon: Protestants, Money, and the Market, 1790–1860*, ed. Mark A. Noll (New York: Oxford University Press, 2001); Charles Sellers, *The Market Revolution: Jacksonian America, 1815–1846* (New York: Oxford University Press, 1991); Stewart Davenport, *Friends of the Unrighteous Mammon: Northern Christians and Market Capitalism, 1815–1860* (Chicago and London: University of Chicago Press, 2008); Jack Beatty, *Age of Betrayal: The Triumph of Money in America, 1865–1900* (New York: Vintage Books, 2008); and William Leach, *Land of Desire: Merchants, Power, and the Rise of a New American Culture* (New York: Vintage Books, 1994).

143. Charles Taylor, *A Secular Age* (Cambridge, Mass., and London: Belknap Press of Harvard University Press, 2007).

144. Tocqueville, *Democracy in America*, vol. 1, 2.9, p. 290. For example, Dorothy Day's Catholic Workers are antistate, politically radical pacifists on the left, with no discernible influence on national or state politics in the United States.

145. Noonan, *Lustre of Our Country*, pp. 226–231, quotation on 231.

146. Smith, *Foreordained Failure*; Noonan, *Lustre of Our Country*, pp. 181–210 (on "free exercise"); Winnifred Fallers Sullivan, *The Impossibility of Religious Freedom* (Princeton, N.J.: Princeton University Press, 2002).

147. I am grateful to Robert Sullivan for this image as a characterization of contemporary American Christianity. In the words of Stanley Hauerwas, "America, though oftentimes identified as one of the more religious cultures still in existence, is much more determined by the secular than is Italian culture. I know that sounds extremely odd, but in Italy, Christianity is in the stones, and in America, we have no stones. The Christianity in America is not thick in practices that actually form bodies to understand better what it means to be Christian." Hauerwas, interview in *Traces* 5:5 (May 2003): 22, quoted in Glenn W. Olsen, *The Turn to Transcendence: The Role of Religion in the Twenty-First Century* (Washington, D.C.: Catholic University of America Press, 2010), p. 37.

148. Smith, *Soul Searching*, p. 171. Smith's analysis would seem to be confirmed in a somewhat different way and with a more positive valence in the recent sociological description of religion in the United States by Robert Putnam

and David Campbell, who emphasize its fluidity and diversity, and the ways in which social relationships (including intermarriages) with those of different religious backgrounds lead most Americans to value religious individualism and diversity and to de-emphasize particular doctrinal truth claims. See Robert D. Putnam and David E. Campbell, *American Grace: How Religion Divides and Unites Us* (New York: Simon & Schuster, 2010), esp. pp. 516–550.

149. For a sampling of the contemporary range of American Protestant beliefs and practices conveyed anecdotally, see Suzanne Strempek Shea, *Sundays in America: A Yearlong Road Trip in Search of Christian Faith* (Boston: Beacon Press, 2008).

150. "Dissent from freedom, choice, and diversity is suppressed informally at virtually every turn, and this as much as anything else demonstrates that our society has already organized itself around new principles." Loren J. Samons II, *What's Wrong with Democracy? From Athenian Practice to American Worship* (Berkeley and Los Angeles: University of California Press, 2004), p. 185. See more generally pp. 175–186, on unencumbered, individual freedom to choose as itself the American "religion of democracy." For a trenchant analysis of the ways in which the countercultural movements of the 1960s represented not a reversal but rather a perpetuation in different guises of more fundamental assumptions about individual autonomy from the 1950s, see Christopher Shannon, *A World Made Safe for Differences: Cold War Intellectuals and the Politics of Identity* (Lanham, Md.: Rowman & Littlefield, 2001).

151. Dominick McGoldrick, *Human Rights and Religion: The Islamic Headscarf Debate in Europe* (Oxford: Hart Publishing, 2006).

152. On England, see Callum G. Brown, *The Death of Christian Britain* (London and New York: Routledge, 2001); on Germany, see Barbara Theriault, *"Conservative Revolutionaries": Protestant and Catholic Churches in Germany after Radical Political Change in the 1990s* (New York: Berghahn Books, 2004).

153. Grace Davie, *Religion in Britain since 1945: Believing without Belonging* (Oxford: Blackwell, 1994) and *Religion in Modern Europe: A Memory Mutates* (New York: Oxford University Press, 2000); *Identités religieuses en Europe*, ed. Grace Davie and Danièle Hervieu-Léger (Paris: Découverte, 1996); *The Cultural Diversity of European Unity: Findings, Explanations and Reflections from the European Values Study*, ed. Wil Arts, Jacques Hagenaars, and Loek Halman (Leiden: E. J. Brill, 2003), pp. 371–400.

154. Jean-Jacques Rousseau, *Du contrat social* [1762], intro. Maurice Halbwachs (1943; Paris: Aubier, 1967), 1.7, p. 108.

155. James J. Sheehan, *Where Have All the Soldiers Gone? The Transformation of Modern Europe* (Boston: Houghton Mifflin, 2008).

156. Thomas Pakenham, *The Scramble for Africa: White Man's Conquest of the Dark Continent from 1876–1912* (New York: Random House, 1991); Adam Hochschild, *King Leopold's Ghost: A Story of Greed, Terror, and Heroism in Colonial Africa* (Boston: Houghton Mifflin, 1998); and more generally, C. A.

Bayly, *The Birth of the Modern World, 1780–1914* (Oxford: Blackwell, 2004).

157. From among a massive scholarly literature, see, for example, Raul Hilberg, *The Destruction of the European Jews*, 3 vols. (1961; New Haven, Conn., and London: Yale University Press, 2003); Omer Bartov, *Murder in Our Midst: The Holocaust, Industrial Killing, and Representation* (New York: Oxford University Press, 1996); *The Holocaust: Origins, Implementation, Aftermath*, ed. Omer Bartov (New York and London: Routledge, 2000).

158. Frances Lannon, *Privilege, Persecution, and Prophecy: The Catholic Church in Spain, 1875–1975* (Oxford and New York: Clarendon Press, 1987); Alfonso Botti, *Nazionalcattolicesimo e Spagna nuova (1881–1975)* (Milan: Franco Angeli, 1992).

159. Daniel Peris, *Storming the Heavens: The Soviet League of the Militant Godless* (Ithaca, N.Y.: Cornell University Press, 1998). On the Soviet suppression of religion I am also indebted to conversations with Amir Weiner and Richard Hernandez.

160. Timothy Snyder, *Bloodlands: Europe between Hitler and Stalin* (New York: Basic Books, 2010).

161. On the church's relationship with Napoleon, including the Concordat of 1801 and its aftermath, see William Roberts, "Napoleon, the Concordat of 1801, and Its Consequences," in *Controversial Concordats: The Vatican's Relations with Napoleon, Mussolini, and Hitler* (Washington, D.C.: Catholic University of America Press, 1999), pp. 34–80, and Nicholas Atkin and Frank Tallett, *Priests, Prelates and People: A History of European Catholicism since 1750* (New York: Oxford University Press, 2003), pp. 71–84. On the anti-Catholic violence and suppression of the church in the French Revolution, which peaked in 1793–1794, see Michelle Vovelle, *The Revolution against the Church,* trans. Alan José (Columbus: Ohio State University Press, 1991), and Nigel Aston, *Religion and Revolution in France, 1780–1804* (Washington, D.C.: Catholic University of America Press, 2000), pp. 179–195.

162. Benedict XVI, *God Is Love: Deus Caritas Est* (San Francisco: Ignatius Press, 2006).

## 4. Subjectivizing Morality

1. Christian Smith, *Moral, Believing Animals: Human Personhood and Culture* (New York: Oxford University Press, 2003).

2. Alasdair MacIntyre, *After Virtue: A Study in Moral Theory,* 3rd ed. (Notre Dame, Ind.: University of Notre Dame Press, 2006), pp. 6–11; MacIntyre, *Whose Justice? Which Rationality?* (Notre Dame, Ind.: University of Notre Dame Press, 1988), pp. 1–3; MacIntyre, *Three Rival Versions of Moral Inquiry: Encyclopedia, Genealogy, and Tradition* (Notre Dame, Ind.: University of Notre Dame Press, 1990), pp. 5–7. In important respects, MacIntyre's critique of modern moral philosophy develops the arguments in the influential article by G. E. M. Anscombe, "Modern Moral Philosophy," *Philosophy*

53 (1958): 1–18. Although some thinkers distinguish in various ways between "morality" and "ethics," in this chapter I use them and their adjuncts
interchangeably.

3. MacIntyre, *After Virtue,* pp. 52–55.

4. J. L. Mackie, *Ethics: Inventing Right and Wrong* (1977; Harmondsworth,
   U.K.: Penguin, 1980), p. 15; David Gauthier, *Morals by Agreement* (Oxford:
   Clarendon Press, 1986).

5. MacIntyre, *After Virtue,* pp. 11–22.

6. On the modern liberal harm principle as being "without any intrinsic content, into which adept advocates can pour whatever substantive views and
   values they happen to favor," see the critique of John Stuart Mill and Joel
   Feinberg in Steven D. Smith, *The Disenchantment of Secular Discourse* (Cambridge, Mass., and London: Harvard University Press, 2010), pp. 70–106,
   quotation on 72.

7. Philip Rieff, *The Triumph of the Therapeutic: Uses of Faith after Freud,* intro.
   Elisabeth Lasch-Quinn (1966; Wilmington, Del.: ISI Books, 2006).

8. John Rawls, in criticizing the way in which both Thomas Aquinas and Ignatius Loyola advocated the rational ordering and coordinated subordination
   of all human goods to the desire for salvation and vision of God, wrote that
   "human good is heterogeneous because the aims of the self are heterogeneous. Although to subordinate all our aims to one end does not strictly
   speaking violate the principles of rational choice (not the counting principles
   anyway), it still strikes *us* as irrational, or more likely as mad. The self is dis-
   figured and put in the service of one of its ends for the sake of system." John
   Rawls, *A Theory of Justice* (Cambridge, Mass.: Belknap Press of Harvard
   University Press, 1971), pp. 553–554, quotation on 554 (my emphasis). Rawls's
   "us" remains unspecified, but obviously it does not encompass those who
   reject his notion of rationality, conception of the self, and opinion that this
   sort of participation in religious life constitutes a disfigurement of the self for
   the sake of "system."

9. The quoted phrase refers to the title of J. B. Schneewind, *The Invention of
   Autonomy: A History of Modern Moral Philosophy* (Cambridge: Cambridge
   University Press, 1998), an analysis that sees as the central narrative of moral
   philosophy in the seventeenth and eighteenth centuries the transformation of
   an ethics of obedience into an ethics of self-governance in which "*we* came
   to a distinctively modern way of understanding ourselves as moral agents"
   (p. 5, my emphasis).

10. See, for example, Amy Gutmann and Dennis Thompson, *Democracy and
    Disagreement: Why Moral Conflict Cannot Be Avoided in Politics, and What
    Should Be Done about It* (Cambridge, Mass., and London: Belknap Press of
    Harvard University Press, 1996); *Deliberative Politics: Essays on "Democ-
    racy and Disagreement,"* ed. Stephen Macedo (New York: Oxford University
    Press, 1999).

11. John Stuart Mill, *On Liberty* [1859], in Mill, *On Liberty and Other Essays,*
    ed. Jonathan Gray (Oxford: Oxford University Press, 1991), p. 17.

12. Rieff, *Triumph,* p. 20.

13. See, for example, Charles Larmore, *The Morals of Modernity* (Cambridge: Cambridge University Press, 1996), p. 54; Thomas L. Haskell, "The Curious Persistence of Rights Talk in the Age of Interpretation," in *Objectivity Is Not Neutrality: Explanatory Schemes in History* (Baltimore and London: Johns Hopkins University Press, 1998), pp. 126–133.

14. Alan Wolfe, *The Future of Liberalism* (New York: Knopf, 2009), p. 4.

15. See, for example, John Rawls, "Introduction" to *Political Liberalism*, expanded ed. (1993; New York: Columbia University Press, 2003), pp. xxii–xxvii; Schneewind, *Invention of Autonomy*, p. 7; Jeffrey Stout, *Democracy and Tradition* (Princeton, N.J.: Princeton University Press, 2004), pp. 93–97; Mark Lilla, *The Stillborn God: Religion, Politics, and the Modern West* (New York: Knopf, 2007), pp. 52–53. For the inseparability of "religion" from the rest of human life in the sixteenth century, and for a trenchant critique of the "myth of the wars of religion" as typically employed by liberal political theorists (as well as U.S. Supreme Court justices since the 1940s), see William T. Cavanaugh, *The Myth of Religious Violence: Secular Ideology and the Roots of Modern Conflict* (New York: Oxford University Press, 2009), pp. 130–141, 151–160, 183–194.

16. On the last point about Lutherans, Reformed Protestants, and Jansenists, see Jennifer Herdt, *Putting On Virtue: The Legacy of the Splendid Vices* (Chicago: University of Chicago Press, 2008), which underestimates the importance of the persistence of Aristotelian virtue ethics in post-Reformation Roman Catholicism, which was of course a religious tradition much broader than the handful of seventeenth-century Jesuits whom she analyzes in her study at pp. 128–164, 227–234. For MacIntyre's assessment of changes in late medieval universities (an issue considered below in Chapter 6), see MacIntyre, *Three Rival Versions*, pp. 156–165. In none of the three major works that are regarded as MacIntyre's trilogy does the Reformation era play a substantive role. *After Virtue* mentions Luther and Calvin in passing as anti-Aristotelians (pp. 53–54, 95, 165, 167), for example, and *Whose Justice? Which Rationality?* notes (p. 209) the "continued flourishing in Protestant as well as in Catholic circles during the seventeenth century" of "Aristotelian modes of thought and action," without even having previously mentioned the Reformation. Most recently, MacIntyre has ranked "the remaking of the everyday life of the social and political order" as "much the most important" of the "series of disruptive and transformative events" that undermined traditional, teleological ethics in the sixteenth and seventeenth centuries, but he does not connect this remaking to the upheavals derived from the religious disagreements of the Reformation. MacIntyre, "Intractable Moral Disagreements," in *Intractable Disputes about the Natural Law: Alasdair MacIntyre and His Critics,* ed. Lawrence S. Cunningham (Notre Dame, Ind.: University of Notre Dame Press, 2009), p. 40.

17. On this last point, see Cavanaugh, *Myth of Religious Violence*, pp. 160–177; see also Bruce D. Porter, *War and the Rise of the Modern State* (New York: Free Press, 1994), pp. 23–61. On state-building prior to the Reformation in general, see, for example, Hendrik Spruyt, *The Sovereign State and Its Competitors*

(Princeton, N.J.: Princeton University Press, 1994), and John Watts, *The Making of Polities: Europe, 1300–1500* (Cambridge: Cambridge University Press, 2009). For a specific, recent case study of a territory within the Holy Roman Empire, see William Bradford Smith, *Reformation and the German Territorial State: Upper Franconia, 1300–1630* (Rochester, N.Y.: University of Rochester Press, 2008), pp. 9–58.

18. One scholar who has seen the intertwined relationship between political thought and moral philosophy in the early modern period is Richard Tuck; see his *Philosophy and Government, 1572–1651* (Cambridge: Cambridge University Press, 1993).

19. Smith, *Disenchantment*, pp. 85–86, quotation on 86.

20. Hence the nervousness of Jeffrey Stout and other defenders of liberalism about the recent influence of MacIntyre, not to mention the influence of even more radical critics of secularism and liberal democracy such as John Milbank and Stanley Hauerwas. Unless such critics can be refuted and those sympathetic to their arguments persuaded (following thinkers such as Emerson and Dewey) to subordinate their individual goods to the alleged higher good of a commitment to formal rights and democratic institutions—Wolfe's "best way of life"—their critiques might become more socially significant and politically influential, which would risk the inciting of disaffection that would force liberal democratic states to become more oppressive. See Stout, *Democracy and Tradition*, pp. 92–179. Stout's alternative, pragmatist conception of American democratic tradition is premised on skepticism; for a critique of it, see Jeanne Heffernan Schindler, "Democracy and Tradition: A Catholic Alternative to American Pragmatism," *Logos: A Journal of Catholic Thought and Culture* 11:2 (2008): 18–29.

21. Mill, *On Liberty*, in *On Liberty and Other Essays*, ed. Gray, p. 49.

22. For the quotations, see respectively Smith, *Disenchantment*, p. 221, and Wolfe, *Future of Liberalism*, p. 4.

23. In Glenn W. Olsen's words, "those who believe in general progress cannot take seriously those who, if not rejecting modernity root and branch, believe we have gone seriously astray. It is simply impossible to believe that other ways of life and thought, especially earlier ways, might have been better than what we know now." Olsen, *The Turn to Transcendence: The Role of Religion in the Twenty-First Century* (Washington, D.C.: Catholic University of America Press, 2010), p. 64.

24. For the quotations, see respectively John M. Rist, *Real Ethics: Rethinking the Foundations of Morality* (Cambridge: Cambridge University Press, 2002), p. 179, and Don S. Browning, "The United Nations Convention on the Rights of the Child: Should It Be Ratified and Why?" *Emory International Law Review* 20 (2006): 172–173, quoted in John Witte Jr., *The Reformation of Rights: Law, Religion, and Human Rights in Early Modern Calvinism* (Cambridge: Cambridge University Press, 2007), pp. 334–335.

25. On the importance of Reformed Protestantism in the advent of the modern emergence of rights long before the Enlightenment, and its influence on the Enlightenment discourse concerning rights, see Witte, *Reformation of Rights*.

26. Larmore, *Morals of Modernity*, p. 40.

27. On this point I am indebted to Rist, *Real Ethics,* esp. pp. 178–204, as well as to David Bentley Hart, *Atheist Delusions: The Christian Revolution and Its Fashionable Enemies* (New Haven. Conn., and London: Yale University Press. 2009), esp. pp. 19–26. See also Christopher Shannon, *A World Made Safe for Differences: Cold War Intellectuals and the Politics of Identity* (Lanham, Md.: Rowman & Littlefield, 2001).

28. Olsen, *Turn to Transcendence,* p. 62.

29. For an overview of the Aristotelianism of moral philosophy and political thought in late medieval universities, see Jill Kraye, "Moral Philosophy," in *The Cambridge History of Renaissance Philosophy,* ed. Charles B. Schmitt and Quentin Skinner (Cambridge: Cambridge University Press, 1988), pp. 325–348.

30. For an extensive index of visual representations from the fifth through the fifteenth century, see *Virtue and Vice: The Personifications in the Index of Christian Art,* ed. Colum Hourihane (Princeton, N.J.: Princeton University Press, 2000); for an index with more than six thousand items (including variants) of medieval works on the virtues and vices, see *Incipits of Latin Works on the Virtues and Vices, 1100–1500 A.D., Including a Section of Incipits of Works on the Pater Noster,* ed. Morton W. Bloomfield et al. (Cambridge, Mass.: Medieval Academy of America, 1979).

31. See *Magistri Petri Lombardi Parisiensis episcopi Sententiae in IV libris distinctae* [c. 1150], 3rd ed., vol. 2 (Grottaferrata [Rome]: Collegii S. Bonaventurae ad Claras Aquas, 1981), bk. 3, dist. 23–36, pp. 141–206; Monika Asztalos, "The Faculty of Theology," in *HUE,* vol. 1, *Universities in the Middle Ages,* ed. Hilde de Ridder-Symoens (Cambridge: Cambridge University Press, 1992), p. 418; *Medieval Commentaries on the "Sentences" of Peter Lombard,* vol. 1, ed. G. R. Evans (Leiden: E. J. Brill, 2002), and vol. 2, ed. Philipp W. Rosemann (Leiden: E. J. Brill, 2010).

32. See the broadly ramifying remarks (applicable to much more than Aquinas) in Thomas Hibbs, "The Fearful Thoughts of Mortals: Aquinas on Conflict, Self-Knowledge, and the Virtues of Practical Reasoning," in *Intractable Disputes,* ed. Cunningham, pp. 273–312, esp. at 276–282.

33. Thomas Hemerken à Kempis, *De imitatione Christi* [c. 1420], in à Kempis, *Opera omnia,* vol. 2, ed. Michael J. Pohl (Freiburg im Breisgau: Herder, 1904), 1.4, p. 12/6–8.

34. À Kempis, *Imitatione Christi,* in à Kempis, *Opera,* vol. 2, ed. Pohl, 1.3, p. 9/26–27.

35. On Grosseteste's translation, see Bernard G. Dod, "Aristoteles latinus," in *The Cambridge History of Later Medieval Philosophy: From the Rediscovery of Aristotle to the Disintegration of Scholasticism, 1100–1600,* ed. Norman Kretzmann, Anthony Kenny, and Jan Pinborg (Cambridge: Cambridge University Press, 1982), pp. 61, 77.

36. The painting is now in the Rijksmuseum, Amsterdam, object number SK-A-2815.

37. Augustin de Backer, *Essai bibliographique sur le livre "De imitatione Christi"* (1864; reprint, Amsterdam: Desclée de Brouwer, 1966), pp. 1–9, 34–35, 107–111, 127–129, 149, 155–156, 174. For the pervasive emphasis on the imitation

of Christ in ancient Christianity, see Candida R. Moss, *The Other Christs: Imitating Jesus in Ancient Christian Ideologies of Martyrdom* (New York: Oxford University Press, 2010), esp. pp. 19–44.

38. John Van Engen, *Sisters and Brothers of the Common Life: The Devotio Moderna and the World of the Later Middle Ages* (Philadelphia: University of Pennsylvania Press, 2008), p. 267. See more generally Van Engen's reconstruction of their community-based, virtue-driven, prayerful religious life at pp. 266–304.

39. [John Mirk,] *The festyvall* ([London: Wynkyn de Worde,] 1508), fol. 157. For the number of editions, see *STC 1475–1640,* vol. 2, pp. 156–157.

40. Kraye, "Moral Philosophy," in *Renaissance Philosophy,* ed. Schmitt and Skinner, p. 309.

41. Augustine, *In epistulam Iohannis ad Parthos tractatus decem,* 7.8, in *Corpus Augustinianum Gissense,* ed. Cornelius Mayer, electronic edition, pt. 8 (Charlottesville, Va.: Intelex, 2000).

42. Hadewijch of Brabant, *Brieven,* ed. J. van Mierlo, vol. 1, *Tekst en commentar* (Antwerp: Standaard Boekhandel, [1947]), letter 26, pp. 217/1–218/9.

43. Thomas Aquinas, *Summa Theologiae,* Blackfriars ed., vol. 34, trans. R. J. Batten (London: Eyre & Spottiswoode; New York: McGraw-Hill, 1975), II–II, q. 23, a. 6, 8, pp. 22–26, 30–32.

44. Wayne A. Meeks, *The Origins of Christian Morality: The First Two Centuries* (New Haven, Conn., and London: Yale University Press, 1993), p. 103. My general understanding of early Christian ethics and its relationship to the creation and maintenance of moral communities is indebted to Meeks's study.

45. For a brief overview of the likely deutero-Pauline authorship of Ephesians and its composition probably in the late first century, see Paul J. Kobelski, "The Letter to the Ephesians," in *The New Jerome Biblical Commentary,* ed. Raymond E. Brown, Joseph A. Fitzmyer, and Roland E. Murphy (Upper Saddle River, N.J.: Prentice Hall, 1990), pp. 883–885.

46. Outside the Gospels, see, for example, Rom 12:4–21, Rom 13:12–14, 1 Cor 5:11, 1 Cor 6:18–20, Gal 5:19–26, Eph 4:11–5:20, Phil 2:1–4, Col 3:5–15, Ti 3:1–8, Heb 13:1–16, Jas 3:13–18, 1 Pt 1:13–16, 1 Pt 2:1, 1 Pt 2:11, 1 Pt 3:8, 2 Pt 1:5–7.

47. à Kempis, *Imitatione Christi,* in à Kempis, *Opera,* vol. 2, ed. Pohl, 2.8, p. 72/25–26.

48. David Herlihy notes the deleterious impact of the Black Death on the quality of recruits to the religious orders after 1350. See Herlihy, *The Black Death and the Transformation of the West,* ed. Samuel K. Cohn Jr. (Cambridge, Mass., and London: Harvard University Press, 1997), pp. 45–46.

49. Brian Tierney, *The Idea of Natural Rights: Studies on Natural Rights, Natural Law and Church Law, 1150–1625* (Atlanta: Scholars Press, 1997), pp. 54–68.

50. Tierney discusses this example in *Idea,* pp. 69–74.

51. The quoted phrase is Samuel Moyn's from his important recent study, *The Last Utopia: Human Rights in History* (Cambridge, Mass., and London: Belknap Press of Harvard University Press, 2010), p. 22. Moyn rightly regards the modern idea of natural rights, in its departure from medieval Chris-

tian conceptions of natural rights associated with natural law, as "so different in its intentions and implications as to be a different concept": "Natural law was originally one rule given from above, where natural rights came to be a list of separate items" (p. 21). But Moyn is so intent on criticizing dubious historical continuities (especially between the Enlightenment and the present), and in emphasizing the recent emergence and historical contingency "of contemporary human rights as a set of global political norms providing the creed of a transnational social movement" (p. 11), that he neglects the complexity of multiple influences related to rights over the *longue durée,* without which the particular phenomenon in which he is interested would have been inconceivable. Moyn's critique superbly delineates the extent to which the contemporary secular discourse and movement of universal human rights depended on *separating* them from "the politics of the state to which even the most naturalistic of rights assertions were closely tethered from the beginning" of the modern era (p. 31), but narratives centered on radical historical discontinuities in ways that downplay abiding historical influences tend to be as partial and misleading as narratives of continuities that neglect genuine ruptures and major transformations. Almost never is the human past one to the exclusion of the other, and ignoring either is bound to cause problems in attempts to understand the relationship between past and present.

52. Tierney, *Idea,* pp. 83–88, 118–130, 157–203, 207–238. See also A. S. Brett, *Liberty, Right, and Nature: Individual Rights in Later Scholastic Thought* (Cambridge: Cambridge University Press, 1997).

53. Francisco de Vitoria, "On the American Indians" [1539], in Vitoria, *Political Writings,* ed. and trans. Anthony Pagden and Jeremy Lawrence (Cambridge: Cambridge University Press, 1991), pp. 231–292.

54. This point is well seen by Herdt in *Putting on Virtue,* pp. 107–127.

55. See David J. Collins, *Reforming Saints: Saints' Lives and Their Authors in Germany, 1470–1530* (New York: Oxford University Press, 2008), esp. pp. 19–50.

56. See Alison Knowles Frazier, *Possible Lives: Authors and Saints in Renaissance Italy* (New York: Columbia University Press, 2005), pp. 30–35, and the extensive, annotated hand list of quattrocento Italian humanist authors and their hagiographical compositions at pp. 327–494.

57. The quoted phrase is from Thomas More; see Brian Gogan, *The Common Corps of Christendom: Ecclesiological Themes in the Writings of Sir Thomas More* (Leiden: E. J. Brill, 1982). In my view, Constance Furey overestimates the extent to which erudite Christian humanists from the 1510s through the 1530s sought to fashion a moral community among themselves that was separate from their membership in the Roman church to which they continued to belong. See Furey, *Erasmus, Contarini, and the Religious Republic of Letters* (Cambridge: Cambridge University Press, 2006).

58. *The Prefatory Epistles of Jacques Lefèvre d'Etaples and Related Texts,* ed. Eugene F. Rice Jr. (New York and London: Columbia University Press, 1972), pp. 23–25, 41–45; Philip Edgcumbe Hughes, *Lefèvre: Pioneer of Ecclesiastical Renewal in France* (Grand Rapids, Mich.: Eerdmans, 1984), pp. 3, 5;

Kraye, "Moral Philosophy," in *Renaissance Philosophy,* ed. Schmitt and Skinner, p. 348; Anthony Grafton, "The Availability of Ancient Works," in ibid., p. 778. On Bruni's and subsequent humanist translators' assumption about Aristotle's original literary eloquence in the *Nicomachean Ethics* and other works, and the effects of their assumption on their translations, see Luca Bianchi, "Continuity and Change in the Aristotelian Tradition," in *The Cambridge Companion to Renaissance Philosophy,* ed. James Hankins (Cambridge: Cambridge University Press, 2007), pp. 52–53. On the debate sparked by Bruni's translations of Aristotle about the objectives of *eloquentia* in Ciceronian Latin translations from ancient Greek texts, see Paul Botley, *Latin Translation in the Renaissance: The Theory and Practice of Leonardo Bruni, Giannozzo Manetti, Erasmus* (Cambridge: Cambridge University Press, 2004), pp. 41–62.

59. Desiderius Erasmus, "Paraclesis ad lectorem pium," in *Novum instrumentum.* . . . (Basel: Johannes Froben, 1516), sigs. [aaa6], bbb1.

60. See Andrew Colin Gow, "The Contested History of a Book: The German Bible of the Later Middle Ages and Reformation in Legend, Ideology, and Scholarship," *Journal of Hebrew Scriptures* 9:13 (2009): 1–37; Gow, "Challenging the Protestant Paradigm: Bible Reading in Lay and Urban Contexts of the Later Middle Ages," in *Scripture and Pluralism: Reading the Bible in the Religiously Plural Worlds of the Middle Ages and the Renaissance,* ed. Thomas J. Heffernan and Thomas E. Burman (Leiden: E. J. Brill, 2006), pp. 161–191; Thomas Kaufmann, "Vorreformatorische Laienbibel und reformatorisches Evangelium," *Zeitschrift für Theologie und Kirche* 101 (2004): 138–174.

61. Niccolò Machiavelli, *The Prince,* trans. and ed. David Wootton (Indianapolis: Hackett, 1995), p. 48.

62. On Savonarola, see Donald Weinstein, *Savonarola and Florence: Prophecy and Patriotism in the Renaissance* (Princeton, N.J.: Princeton University Press, 1970); Lauro Martines, *Fire in the City: Savonarola and the Struggle for the Soul of Renaissance Florence* (New York: Oxford University Press, 2006).

63. Machiavelli, *Prince,* trans. and ed. Wootton, pp. 20, 54, 52. In his advice to Prince Charles before the latter's election as Holy Roman emperor, for example, Erasmus warned him that "for the most part human nature inclines toward evil [*plaeraque mortalium ingenia vergant in malum*]." Desiderius Erasmus, *Institutio principis Christiani.* . . . [1516], ed. O. Herding, in Erasmus, *Opera omnia,* series 4, vol. 1 (Amsterdam: North-Holland Publishing Co., 1974), p. 139/101.

64. Machiavelli, *Prince,* trans. and ed. Wootton, p. 55; see also pp. 48–49, 54.

65. Machiavelli, *The Discourses,* ed. Bernard Crick, trans. Leslie L. Walker (1970; Harmondsworth, U.K.: Penguin, 1986), 2.2, p. 278.

66. Ibid., 1.12, p. 144.

67. Sebastian de Grazia, *Machiavelli in Hell* (Princeton, N.J.: Princeton University Press, 1989), pp. 114–121, 376–385.

68. "The historic responsibility of Machiavelli consists in having accepted, recognized, endorsed as a rule the fact of political immorality, and in having

stated that good politics, politics conformable to its true nature and to its genuine aims, is by essence non-moral politics." Jacques Maritain, "The End of Machiavellianism" [1942], in *The Crisis of Modern Times: Perspectives from "The Review of Politics,"* ed. A. James McAdams (Notre Dame, Ind.: University of Notre Dame Press, 2007), esp. pp. 99–104 (quotation on 99).

69. On anti-Machiavellian Catholic political theorists in the sixteenth and early seventeenth centuries, see Robert Bireley, *The Counter-Reformation Prince: Anti-Machiavellianism or Catholic Statecraft in Early Modern Europe* (Chapel Hill: University of North Carolina Press, 1990). For Machiavelli's phrase, see *Prince*, trans. and ed. Wootton, p. 48.

70. Antonio Blado published the first edition of *I Discorsi* in Rome in 1531, as well as the first of the two editions of *Il principe* that appeared in 1532, the second of which was published in Florence by Bernardo di Giunta. See Sydney Anglo, *Machiavelli: The First Century* (Oxford: Oxford University Press, 2005), pp. 85, 166, 705, 706.

71. Tierney, *Idea of Natural Rights*, pp. 170–194, 200–203; Heiko A. Oberman, *Luther: Man between God and the Devil*, trans. Eileen Walliser-Schwartzbart (New Haven, Conn., and London: Yale University Press, 1989), p. 186; Martin Brecht, *Martin Luther*, vol. 1, *His Road to Reformation, 1483–1521*, trans. James L. Schaaf (Minneapolis: Fortress Press, 1985), pp. 423–424; Martin Luther, *An den christlichen Adel deutscher Nation von des christlichen Standes Besserung* [1520], in *WA*, vol. 6 (Weimar: Hermann Böhlau, 1888), pp. 441/13–14, 459.

72. Michael Sattler, *Brüderlich vereynigung etzlicher kinder Gottes, sieben Artickel betreffend. . . .* [1533], ed. Walter Köhler, in *Flugschriften aus den ersten Jahren der Reformation*, ed. Otto Clemen, vol. 2 (Leipzig and New York: Rudolf Haupt, 1908), p. 309. On the significance of Sattler's life as a Benedictine monk and its relationship to his later Anabaptist ideas, see C. Arnold Snyder, *The Life and Thought of Michael Sattler* (Scottdale, Pa., and Kitchener, Ont.: Herald Press, 1984), esp. pp. 30–65.

73. Thomas Müntzer, *Hoch verursachte Schutzrede und antwwort, wider das Gaistloße Sanft lebende fleysch zü Wittenberg. . . .* [1524], in Müntzer, *Schriften und Briefe: Kritische Gesamtausgabe*, ed. Günther Franz (Gütersloh: Gerd Mohn, 1968), pp. 322/1, 323/5.

74. Balthasar Hubmaier, *Von der Freyheit des Willens. . . .* [1527], in Hubmaier, *Schriften*, ed. Gunnar Westin and Torsten Bergsten, vol. 9 in *QGT* (Gütersloh: Gerd Mohn, 1968), p. 381.

75. See R. Emmet McLauglin, "Spiritualism: Schwenckfeld and Franck and Their Early Modern Resonances," in *A Companion to Anabaptism and Spiritualism, 1521–1700*, ed. John D. Roth and James M. Stayer (Leiden: E. J. Brill, 2007), pp. 124–140.

76. See Werner O. Packull, *Hutterite Beginnings: Communitarian Experiments during the Reformation* (Baltimore and London: Johns Hopkins University Press, 1995); James M. Stayer, *The German Peasants' War and Anabaptist Community of Goods* (Montreal and Kingston, Ont.: McGill–Queen's University Press, 1991), pp. 139–159.

77. This legacy of the Reformation would become clearer only in the nineteenth and twentieth centuries, above all in the United States, when divergent Protestant churches and groups grew in unprecedented numbers. Yet paradoxically, in part because increasingly powerful nineteenth- and twentieth-century states continued better than ever to control their churches, and partly because increasing numbers of Christians across confessional lines were eager participants in the material acquisitiveness characteristic of the industrious revolution, the disruptive social consequences of proliferating Protestant moral communities diminished even though Protestant pluralism increased. At the same time, from the end of the eighteenth into the early twentieth century a legally enforced Protestant "moral establishment" compensated for the American institutional disestablishment of churches. On the expansive growth in the number of Protestant groups in the United States during the first decades of the nineteenth century, see Nathan O. Hatch, *The Democratization of American Christianity* (New Haven, Conn., and London: Yale University Press, 1989); on the industrious revolution, see Jan de Vries, *The Industrious Revolution: Consumer Behavior and the Household Economy, 1650 to the Present* (Cambridge: Cambridge University Press, 2008); and on the ways in which formal institutional disestablishment in the United States was sustained by a Protestant legal moral establishment throughout the nineteenth century, see David Sehat, *The Myth of American Religious Freedom* (New York: Oxford, 2011).

78. Claus-Peter Clasen, "Executions of Anabaptists, 1525–1618: A Research Report," *MQR* 47 (1973): 118–119.

79. For two examples, see Mark U. Edwards Jr., *Luther and the False Brethren* (Stanford, Calif.: Stanford University Press, 1975), p. 197, and Elsie Anne McKee, *Katharina Schütz Zell* (Leiden: E. J. Brill, 1999), vol. 1, pp. 265, 273. Edwards distinguishes between "central reformation principles" and "issues such as acceptable ceremonial practice, the real presence in the Lord's Supper, the separation of secular and spiritual authority, and the relation between law and gospel," and McKee contrasts "the Reformation basics" with "the secondary issues which were debated among Protestants," relegating to the latter category the boundaries between different groups, the toleration of those with different views, the Lord's Supper, baptism, and church order (vol. 1, p. 265). The same problem characterizes the entire conceptualization of the Reformation era in Scott Hendrix, *Recultivating the Vineyard: The Reformation Agendas of Christianization* (Louisville, Ky., and London: Westminster John Knox Press, 2004).

80. On the Marburg Colloquy, see G. R. Potter, *Zwingli* (Cambridge: Cambridge University Press, 1976), pp. 316–331; Heinrich Bornkamm, *Luther in Mid-Career, 1521–1530*, ed. Karin Bornkamm, trans. E. Theodore Bachmann (Philadelphia: Fortress Press, 1983), pp. 633–652; Martin Brecht, *Martin Luther*, vol. 2, *Shaping and Defining the Reformation, 1521–1532*, trans. James L. Schaaf (Minneapolis: Fortress Press, 1990), pp. 325–334; Oberman, *Luther*, pp. 236–237; and Bruce Gordon, *The Swiss Reformation* (Manchester and New York: Manchester University Press, 2002), pp. 75–76.

81. Potter, *Zwingli,* p. 329; see also Oberman, *Luther*, pp. 238–244.

82. Schneewind, *Invention of Autonomy,* p. 5.

83. John Calvin, *Institutio Christianae religionis* [1559], in *CO,* vol. 2, ed. G. Baum, E. Cunitz, and E. Reuss, vol. 30 in *CR* (Brunswick: C. A. Schwetschke & Sohn, 1864), 4.12.1, col. 905: "quemadmodum salvifica Christi doctrina anima est ecclesiae, ita illic disciplina pro nervis est." On the development of Calvin's political thought in relationship to his theology as a whole, see Harro Höpfl, *The Christian Polity of John Calvin* (Cambridge: Cambridge University Press, 1982).

84. Huldrych Zwingli, *Ußlegen und gründ der schlußreden oder Articklen....* [1523], in *ZW,* vol. 2, ed. Emil Egli and Georg Finsler, in *CR,* vol. 89 (Leipzig: M. Heinsius Nachfolger, 1908), pp. 330/22–23, 332/6–7.

85. For an overview of the extensive scholarship on confessionalization, especially in the Holy Roman Empire and including Lutheranism, see Thomas A. Brady Jr., "Confessionalization—The Career of a Concept," in *Confessionalization in Europe, 1555–1700: Essays in Honor and Memory of Bodo Nischan,* ed. John M. Headley, Hans J. Hillerbrand, and Anthony J. Papalas (Aldershot, U.K.: Ashgate, 2004), pp. 1–20; on the centrality of hymns and hymn singing in contributing to the formation of the German Lutheran moral communities, see Christopher Boyd Brown, *Singing the Gospel: Lutheran Hymns and the Success of the Reformation* (Cambridge, Mass., and London: Harvard University Press, 2005); for the Scandinavian countries, see *The Scandinavian Reformation: From Evangelical Movement to Institutionalisation of Reform,* ed. Ole Peter Grell (Cambridge: Cambridge University Press, 1995); and for the early Scandinavian Reformation, see James L. Larson, *Reforming the North: The Kingdoms and Churches of Scandinavia, 1520–1545* (Cambridge: Cambridge University Press, 2010).

86. Calvin, *Institutio,* in *CO,* vol. 2, 2.2.25, col. 206.

87. Ibid., 2.1.8, col. 183.

88. Ibid., 2.8.1, col. 266. See also, for example, Luther, *De servo arbitrio* [1525], in *WA,* vol. 18 (Weimar: Hermann Böhlaus Nachfolger, 1908), pp. 632/29–633/5, esp. 632/33–36: "Siquidem, quam diu persuasus fuerit, sese vel tantulum posse pro salute sua, manet in fiducia sui, nec de se penitus desperat, ideo non humiliatur coram Deo, sed locum, tempus, opus aliquod sibi praesumit vel sperat vel optat saltem, quo tandem perveniat ad salutem."

89. Luther, *An den christlichen Adel,* in *WA,* vol. 6, p. 458/4–5, 14–15. For a recent overview of Luther's ethics and its relationship to justification, Law and Gospel, ecclesiology, and his political ideas, see Max Josef Suda, *Die Ethik Martin Luthers* (Göttingen: Vandenhoeck & Ruprecht, 2006).

90. Luther, *De servo arbitrio,* in *WA,* vol. 18, pp. 635/17–22, with *"Noluntas"* at line 14.

91. Sachiko Kusukawa, *The Transformation of Natural Philosophy: The Case of Philip Melanchthon* (Cambridge: Cambridge University Press, 1995), pp. 62–74. "Natural philosophy could not teach the message of the Gospel, but, as Law, it could provide theoretical grounding of a moral philosophy of civil obedience, which in turn was necessary to defend Luther's cause." Ibid., p. 204.

92. Kraye, "Moral Philosophy," in *Renaissance Philosophy,* ed. Schmitt and Skinner (Cambridge: Cambridge University Press, 1988), p. 323 (quotation); see also Richard A. Muller, *Post-Reformation Reformed Dogmatics: The Rise and Development of Reformed Orthodoxy, ca. 1520 to ca. 1725,* 2nd ed., vol. 1, *Prolegomena to Theology* (Grand Rapids, Mich.: Baker Academic, 2003), p. 364.

93. Luther, *Von Kaufshandlung und Wucher* [1524], in *WA,* vol. 15 (Weimar: Hermann Böhlaus Nachfolger, 1899), p. 302/25–28.

94. David A. Weir, *The Origins of the Federal Theology in Sixteenth-Century Reformation Thought* (Oxford: Clarendon Press; New York: Oxford University Press, 1990); Charles S. McCoy and J. Wayne Baker, *Fountainhead of Federalism: Heinrich Bullinger and the Covenantal Tradition* (Louisville, Ky.: Westminster John Knox Press, 1991), pp. 34–39; William K. B. Stoever, *"A Faire and Easie Way to Heaven": Covenant Theology and Antinomianism in Early Massachusetts* (Middletown, Conn.: Wesleyan University Press, 1978); E. Brooks Holifield, *Theology in America: Christian Thought from the Age of the Puritans to the Civil War* (New Haven, Conn., and London: Yale University Press, 2003), pp. 39–42.

95. Servais Pinckaers, *The Sources of Christian Ethics,* 3rd ed., trans. Mary Thomas Noble (Washington, D.C.: Catholic University of America Press, 1995), pp. 266–273, 277–279, 298–300.

96. See Albert R. Jonson and Stephen Toulmin, *The Abuse of Casuistry: A History of Moral Reasoning* (Berkeley and Los Angeles: University of California Press, 1990), pp. 142–171; John O'Malley, *The First Jesuits* (Cambridge, Mass., and London: Harvard University Press, 1993), pp. 144–147; and more broadly, Johann Theiner, *Die Entwicklung der Moraltheologie zur eigenständigen Disziplin* (Regensburg: F. Pustet, 1970). On the importance of casuistry in the Jesuits' political thought and in their practical advice to rulers in the late sixteenth and early seventeenth centuries, as well as for the Jesuits' emphasis on the virtue of obedience, see Harro Höpfl, *Jesuit Political Thought: The Society of Jesus and the State, c. 1540–1630* (Cambridge: Cambridge University Press, 2004).

97. For a twentieth-century example of this manualist genre, see the first two volumes of the frequently reprinted work by Henry Davis, *Moral and Pastoral Theology,* 6th rev. ed., 4 vols. (London and New York: Sheed & Ward, 1949), as well as the overview in the section on moral theology by Augustinus Lehmkuhl in the article "Theology," *The Catholic Encyclopedia,* vol. 14 (New York: Encyclopedia Press, 1912), pp. 601–611, esp. 606–611.

98. François de Sales, *Introduction à la vie dévote* [1609], in de Sales, *Oeuvres,* vol. 3 (Annecy: J. Niérat, 1893), pp. 123–287, quotation on 123.

99. Blaise Pascal, *Pensées* [1670], in Pascal, *Oeuvres complètes,* ed. Louis Lafuma (Paris: Éditions du Seuil, 1963), no. 418, p. 551, electronic edition (Charlottesville, Va.: Intelex, 2006). Pascal's verb, *abêtir,* literally means "to make like an animal"—that is, to neutralize the distinctively human faculty of reason that obstructs faith in the case of a doubting skeptic or rationalist.

100. For a nuanced assessment of the war's effects, which varied enormously over time and by region, see Peter H. Wilson, *The Thirty Years War: Europe's*

*Tragedy* (Cambridge, Mass., and London: Belknap Press of Harvard University Press, 2009), pp. 779–851.

101. Philip F. Riley, *A Lust for Virtue: Louis XIV's Attack on Sin in Seventeenth-Century France* (Westport, Conn.: Greenwood Press, 2001).

102. On the extent to which a Protestant "moral establishment" enforced by law compensated for the American institutional disestablishment of churches, see Sehat, *Myth of American Religious Freedom.*

103. Thomas Jefferson, "A Declaration by the Representatives of the United States of America, in General Congress Assembled," in *Writings,* ed. Merrill D. Peterson (New York: Library of America, 1984), p. 19. Jefferson had written "by their Creator with inherent and inalienable rights" rather than "with certain inalienable rights," and the printed version of the Declaration read "unalienable" rather than "inalienable." Pauline Maier, *American Scripture: Making the Declaration of Independence* (1997; New York: Vintage, 1998), pp. 135, 144, 236.

104. On the diversity of Christian affiliations among the representatives in the Continental Congress, see Steven Waldman, *Founding Faith: Providence, Politics, and the Birth of Religious Freedom* (New York: Random House, 2008), pp. 90–91.

105. Pauline Maier notes that the ideas about natural rights endowed by a creator from the Declaration's preamble "had become, in the generalized form captured by Jefferson, a political orthodoxy whose basic principles colonists could pick up from sermons or newspapers or even schoolbooks without ever reading a systematic work of political theory," but she does not connect this to the fact that "Americans held strong religious beliefs in 1776, and the Declaration was meant to state the convictions of the country's 'good people.'" Maier, *American Scripture,* pp. 135, 149.

106. On the importance of the 1970s and the relative unimportance of the 1940s in the internationalization of human rights, including the insignificant short-term impact of the Holocaust and the United Nations Universal Declaration of Human Rights (1948), see Moyn, *Last Utopia.*

107. Witte, *Reformation of Rights,* pp. 106–122; see also Quentin Skinner, *The Foundations of Modern Political Thought,* vol. 2, *The Age of Reformation* (Cambridge: Cambridge University Press, 1978), pp. 199–238; on the Magdeburg Confession, see also David M. Whitford, *Tyranny and Resistance: The Magdeburg Confession and the Lutheran Tradition* (St. Louis: Concordia, 2001).

108. See, for example, Perez Zagorin, *Ways of Lying: Dissimulation, Persecution, and Conformity in Early Modern Europe* (Cambridge, Mass., and London: Harvard University Press, 1990), pp. 94–99, 111–130; John S. Oyer, "Nicodemites among Württemberg Anabaptists," *MQR* 71 (1997): 487–514; Mark Furner, "Lay Casuistry and the Survival of Later Anabaptists in Bern," *MQR* 75 (2001): 429–470; Hans-Jürgen Goertz, "Nonconformists on the Elbe River: Pious, Rich, and Perplexed. Four Hundred Years of Mennonites in Hamburg and Altona," *MQR* 76 (2002): 413–430; John D. Roth, "Marpeck and the Later Swiss Brethren, 1540–1700," in *Companion to Anabaptism,* ed. Roth and Stayer, pp. 347–388; and Michael Driedger, "Anabaptists and the Early Modern State: A Long-Term View," in ibid., pp. 520–531.

109. J[ohn] M[ilton], *A Treatise of Civil power in Ecclesiastical causes Shewing That it is not lawfull for any power on earth to compell in matters of religion* (London: Tho[mas] Newcomb, 1659), pp. 7–8, 9.

110. John Locke, *A Letter Concerning Toleration* [1689], ed. James H. Tully (Indianapolis: Hackett, 1983), p. 28.

111. William Temple, *Observations upon the United Provinces of the Netherlands* (London: A. Maxwell for Sa. Gellibrand, 1673), pp. 178–184, quotations on 179, 182.

112. Charles-Louis de Secondat, Baron de Montesquieu, "Author's Foreword" in *The Spirit of the Laws,* ed. and trans. Anne M. Cohler, Basia C. Miller, and Harold S. Stone (Cambridge: Cambridge University Press, 1989), p. xli (italics in original).

113. The quoted term is Richard Tuck's; on the new popularity of Tacitus as opposed to Cicero among the neo-Stoic skeptics, see Tuck, *Philosophy and Government,* pp. 31–64.

114. This is the major theme of Tuck's *Philosophy and Government* and the broad intellectual and political context in which he interprets Grotius and Hobbes.

115. Knud Haakonssen, *Natural Law and Moral Philosophy: From Grotius to the Scottish Enlightenment* (Cambridge: Cambridge University Press, 1996), pp. 24–25; see also Schneewind, *Invention of Autonomy,* pp. 66–81, and Tuck, *Philosophy and Government,* pp. 154–201.

116. On the two most important Jesuit advisers—Adam Contzen for Maximilian and William Lamormaini for Ferdinand—in the context of the complexities of imperial Catholic ambitions and actions from 1618 through the Edict of Restitution in 1629, see Robert Bireley, *The Jesuits and the Thirty Years War: Kings, Courts, and Confessors* (Cambridge: Cambridge University Press, 2003), pp. 33–99, as well as Bireley's earlier monographs, *Maximilian von Bayern, Adam von Contzen S. J. und die Gegenreformation in Deutschland, 1624–1635* (Göttingen: Vandenhoeck & Ruprecht, 1975), and Bireley, *Religion and Politics in the Age of the Counterreformation: Emperor Ferdinand II, William Lamormaini, S.J., and the Formation of Imperial Policy* (Chapel Hill: University of North Carolina Press, 1981). See also Wilson, *Thirty Years War,* pp. 357–361, 446–448. On English Protestant disaffection with Laud and Charles in the 1630s and its consequences after the opening of the Long Parliament in November 1640, see Austin Woolrych, *Britain in Revolution* (Oxford: Oxford University Press, 2002), pp. 75–83, 156–188.

117. See, for example, T. H. Breen, *The Marketplace of Revolution: How Consumer Politics Shaped American Independence* (New York: Oxford University Press, 2004); Joyce Appleby, *Capitalism and a New Social Order: The Republican Vision of the 1790s* (New York: New York University Press, 1984); Richard L. Bushman, *The Refinement of America: Persons, Houses, Cities* (New York: Vintage, 1992). On the household-based increase in levels of production and consumption of the "long eighteenth century" prior to the Industrial Revolution, see de Vries, *Industrious Revolution;* and on the extent to which rural Virginia was marked by highly developed consumer practices and sensibilities by the 1760s, see Ann Smart Martin, *Buying into the World*

of Goods: Early Consumers in Backcountry Virginia (Baltimore and London: Johns Hopkins University Press, 2008).

118. On the importance of a cultural synthesis comprising Protestant evangelicalism, political republicanism, and Scottish-Enlightenment Common Sense moral philosophy in providing cohesion among white Americans from the 1790s through the Civil War, see Mark A. Noll, America's God: From Jonathan Edwards to Abraham Lincoln (New York: Oxford University Press, 2002).

119. John T. McGreevy, Catholicism and American Freedom: A History (New York and London: W. W. Norton, 2003), pp. 43–49.

120. Dwight D. Eisenhower, address at the Freedoms Foundation, Waldorf Astoria Hotel, New York, 22 December 1952. On 10 January 1957, Eisenhower explicitly gestured to Genesis 1:26–27 in his State of the Union Address: "Our country and its government have made mistakes—human mistakes. They have been of the head—not of the heart. And it is still true that the great concept of the dignity of all men, alike created in the image of the Almighty, has been the compass by which we have tried and are trying to steer our course." For both quotations, see http://www.eisenhower.archives.gov/All_About_Ike/Quotes/Quotes.html, accessed 25 November 2009. That in his 1952 remark Eisenhower was not appealing vaguely to any American "civil religion" but was rather referring specifically to the Jewish and Christian notion of human beings' createdness in God's image, and for a marvelous application of the tools of biblical and patristic scholarship to the use of Eisenhower's phrase, see Patrick Henry, "'And I Don't Care What It Is': The Tradition-History of a Civil-Religion Proof Text," Journal of the American Academy of Religion 49 (1981): 35–48 at p. 41. I thank Mark Noll for calling this article to my attention.

121. Richard J. Ellis, To the Flag: The Unlikely History of the Pledge of Allegiance (Lawrence: University Press of Kansas, 2005), pp. 126, 129–137.

122. Albert O. Hirschman, The Passions and the Interests: Political Arguments for Capitalism before Its Triumph (Princeton, N.J.: Princeton University Press, 1977), p. 129.

123. The unacknowledged, self-deceived importation of Christian moral and metaphysical assumptions by eighteenth-century philosophes is a major theme in Carl Becker's classic set of essays, The Heavenly City of the Eighteenth-Century Philosophers (New Haven, Conn., and London: Yale University Press, 1932). Steven Smith has recently made analytical use of Becker's point in his argument for opening up "the iron cage of secular rationalism" that characterizes official public and academic discourse in the United States. Smith, Disenchantment, pp. 61 (quotation), 151–186.

124. Sam Harris, The End of Faith: Religion, Terror, and the Future of Reason (New York and London: W. W. Norton, 2004), pp. 170–171.

125. C. A. J. Coady, Testimony: A Philosophical Study (Oxford: Clarendon Press, 1992), p. 75.

126. This is the common theme running through the linked essays in Haakonssen, Natural Law and Moral Philosophy. See also Becker, Heavenly City, pp. 44–70.

127. Jefferson, "Declaration," in *Writings*, ed. Peterson, p. 19, and "A Bill for Establishing Religious Freedom," in ibid., pp. 348, 346; *Jefferson and Madison on Separation of Church and State: Writings on Religion and Secularism*, ed. Lenni Brenner (Fort Lee, N.J.: Barricade, 2004), p. 48. However Jefferson's personal beliefs are assessed, certain passages in his writings clearly suggest that the God in whom he believed was more than the noninterventionist God of deism. In a much-quoted passage pertaining to slavery from the *Notes on the State of Virginia*, for example, part of which is inscribed on the wall of the Jefferson Memorial in Washington, D.C., he wrote: "And can the liberties of a nation be thought secure when we have removed their only firm basis, a conviction in the minds of the people that these liberties are of the gift of God? That they are not to be violated but with his wrath? Indeed I tremble for my country when I reflect that God is just: that his justice cannot sleep for ever: that considering numbers, nature and natural means only, a revolution of the wheel of fortune, an exchange of situation, is among possible events: that it may become probable by supernatural interference! The Almighty has no attribute which can take side with us in such a contest." Jefferson, *Notes on the State of Virginia* [1781], in *Writings*, ed. Peterson, p. 289.

128. Compare Thomas Hobbes, *Leviathan* [1651], ed. Richard Tuck (1991; Cambridge: Cambridge University Press, 1996), 1.13, pp. 86–90; John Locke, *Second Treatise of Government* [1689], in *Two Treatises of Government*, ed. Peter Laslett (Cambridge: Cambridge University Press, 1988), 2.4–15, pp. 269–278; and Jean-Jacques Rousseau, *Discours sur l'origine et les fondements de l'inégalité parmi les hommes* [1755], in Rousseau, *Oeuvres complètes*, vol. 3, ed. Bernard Gagnebin and Marcel Raymond (Paris: Gallimard, 1964), pt. 1. For early fourteenth-century discussions about the state of nature in relationship to the controversy surrounding Franciscan poverty and property, see Tierney, *Idea of Natural Rights*, pp. 148–163.

129. Hobbes, *Leviathan*, ed. Tuck, 1.11, p. 70.

130. Augustine, *Confessiones*, 1.1, in *Corpus Augustinianum Gissense*, ed. Cornelius Mayer, electronic edition, pt. 2 (Charlottesville, Va.: Intelex, 2000).

131. Hobbes, *Leviathan*, 1.6, p. 39. As Spinoza put it, "as far as good and evil are concerned, they denote nothing positive in things considered in themselves [*nihil etiam positivum in rebus*], nor are they anything other than modes of thinking, or notions that we form accordingly insofar as we compare things with each other"; indeed, "by good I will understand what we know with certainty to be useful to us [*certò scimus nobis esse utile*]." Baruch de Spinoza, *Ethica* [1677], in Spinoza, *Opera*, ed. Carl Gebhardt, vol. 2 (Heidelberg: Carl Winters, 1925), pt. 4, preface and def. 1, pp. 208/8–11, 209/12–13.

132. Lawrence Stone, *The Family, Sex, and Marriage in England, 1500–1800*, abr. ed. (New York: Harper & Row, 1979), p. 159 (my emphasis). See also Keith Thomas, *The Ends of Life: Roads to Fulfilment in Early Modern England* (Oxford: Oxford University Press, 2009), and for the Dutch Republic, Simon Schama: *The Embarrassment of Riches: An Interpretation of Dutch Culture in the Golden Age* (New York: Knopf, 1987).

133. Schneewind, *Invention of Autonomy,* pp. 424–427; see also John Phillips, *The Marquis de Sade: A Very Short Introduction* (Oxford: Oxford University Press, 2005).

134. David Hume, *A Treatise of Human Nature* [1739–1740], ed. L. A. Selby-Bigge, 2nd ed., ed. P. H. Nidditch (Oxford: Clarendon Press, 1978), 2.3.3, p. 415.

135. Rawls, *Theory of Justice,* pp. 432–433.

136. Moyn, *Last Utopia.*

137. Hume, *Treatise,* ed. Selby-Bigge and Nidditch, 2.3.4, pp. 418–419.

138. "The modern liberal will proclaim his social sympathy and strike a militant posture in defense of rights, but he can no longer explain why that biped who conjugates verbs should be the bearer of 'rights.' " Hadley Arkes, *Natural Rights and the Right to Choose* (Cambridge: Cambridge University Press, 2002), p. 2.

139. Jeremy Bentham, "Anarchical Fallacies," in *Complete Works,* ed. John Bowring, vol. 2 (1843; Adamant, Vt.: Adamant Press, 2001), p. 501 (italics in original).

140. This is a different way of understanding MacIntyre's (in)famous dismissal of universal human rights in *After Virtue* as akin to belief in unicorns and witches. Ibid., pp. 69–70. If metaphysical naturalism is true, he is right; but if there is an objective metaphysical basis for human rights (for example, that all human beings really are created in God's image and likeness), then his claim is mistaken, even though it would not be refutable on the basis of secular reason, including the empirical findings of science, alone. On the eliminationist implications of metaphysical naturalism for human rights, see also Christian Smith, "Does Naturalism Warrant a Moral Belief in Universal Benevolence and Human Rights?" in *The Believing Primate: Scientific, Philosophical, and Theological Reflections on the Origin of Religion,* ed. Jeffrey Schloss and Michael J. Murray (New York: Oxford University Press, 2009), pp. 292–317. See also Steven Smith's critique of Martha Nussbaum's attempt to defend universal human rights without recourse to metaphysics or religion as an extension of the same attempt (and failure) among eighteenth-century *philosophes,* in Smith, *Disenchantment,* pp. 162–186.

141. Ronald Dworkin, *Taking Rights Seriously* (Cambridge, Mass.: Harvard University Press, 1977). "Once deprived of its normative dimension, how could 'nature' or 'natural law' serve as sources of evaluative criteria or judgments? How could one squeeze moral values, or judgments about justice, or interpretations of the 'meaning' of it all, out of brute empirical facts?" Smith, *Disenchantment,* p. 153.

142. Richard B. Carter, *Descartes' Medical Philosophy: The Organic Solution to the Mind-Body Problem* (Baltimore and London: Johns Hopkins University Press, 1983), pp. 44–47, 121, 123–129, 133, 167–168, 185.

143. To their credit, moral philosophers such as Charles Larmore and Russ Shafer-Landau have seen that a skeptical, pragmatist "ethics without ontology" cannot circumvent the problems presented by metaphysical naturalism and moral relativism for human rights, though it may be doubted whether their

post-Christian neo-neo-Platonisms could suffice to settle any moral disagreements or could be prevented from collapsing into emotivism. See Larmore, *Morals of Modernity*, p. 116: "Basically, Plato was right. Either we must admit that the world is more than the natural world and that it comprises not only physical and psychological reality, but normative reality as well, or, like the Sophists, we must abandon reason for persuasion." See also Russ Shafer-Landau, *Whatever Happened to Good and Evil?* (New York: Oxford University Press, 2004) and *The Fundamentals of Ethics* (New York: Oxford University Press, 2010). This recognition by Larmore and Shafer-Landau directly contradicts the expressivist moral view of Allan Gibbard, according to whom a Platonism of objective moral claims as being "among the facts of the world" is "fantastic" and to be rejected in favor of his own version of non-cognitive morality. Gibbard, *Wise Choices, Apt Feelings: A Theory of Normative Judgment* (Cambridge, Mass.: Harvard University Press, 1990), p. 154. For two skeptical, pragmatist examples of attempts to sustain defenses of human rights and morality without any ontological grounding, see Stout, *Democracy and Tradition*, and Hilary Putnam, *Ethics without Ontology* (Cambridge, Mass.: Harvard University Press, 2004). In his most recent major study, Ronald Dworkin clearly sees the same problem as Larmore and Shafer-Landau, endeavoring his own sort of escape from the naturalist cul-de-sac by trying to defend objective morality through an appropriation of Hume and Kant without recourse to metaphysics in any traditional sense; see Dworkin, *Justice for Hedgehogs* (Cambridge, Mass., and London: Belknap Press of Harvard University Press, 2011). Rejecting what he calls the "totalitarian metaphysics" of modern philosophy and the "establishment metaphysics" it sought to overcome, he writes that "we need a cleaner break, a new revolution. . . . But we must find our conceptions of truth and falsity, responsibility and irresponsibility, facts and realism, within the realm of value itself—on as clean a sheet as possible. We must abandon colonial metaphysics." Ibid., pp. 417–418. Whatever their assumptions and starting points, the endeavor to find such conceptions that are convincing is what modern philosophers have been trying to do, unsuccessfully, for centuries. And who are "we"? Or perhaps Dworkin only means actually to speak for himself and those who agree with his assumptions.

144. Smith, *Disenchantment*, pp. 26–39, 105–106, 170, 177, 185, 212, 215, 221.
145. Quoted in Smith, *Disenchantment*, p. 179.
146. An attempt to justify this calibration, with a nervousness about the inferences that some have drawn from the combination of scientistic naturalism and cultural relativism, informs the argument in Ronald Dworkin, "Objectivity and Truth: You'd Better Believe It," *Philosophy and Public Affairs* 25 (Spring 1996): 87–139, an article that was the beginning of the line of thinking that has led recently to *Justice for Hedgehogs*. Like everyone except those who are pathological, Dworkin writes in his article that he could not imagine relinquishing the belief that human beings have a distinctive moral faculty in favor of the belief that genocide or torturing a child in front of its mother are acceptable, but in the end, given the constraints of naturalism, he offers no

reason beyond his conviction itself: "If you can't help believing something, steadily and wholeheartedly, you'd better believe it. Not, as I just said, because the fact of your belief argues for its own truth, but because you cannot think any argument a decisive refutation of a belief it does not even dent. In the beginning, and in the end, is the conviction" (pp. 117–118, quotation on 118). But there are arguments that not only can dent but entirely undermine such a belief, one of which is the belief that science alone can tell us anything true about reality, and it reveals no basis whatsoever for thinking that human rights are real; therefore matter-energy is as it does, in human bodies as elsewhere. Consequently, with this belief there would be no warrant for Dworkin's quasi-Kantian conviction that "morality is a distinct, independent dimension of our experience, and it exercises its own sovereignty" (p. 128), however convinced of it he or anyone else happens to be. The same conclusion applies to the argument in his recent book.

147. Becker, *Heavenly City;* Smith, *Disenchantment,* pp. 151–186.

148. Jonathan Israel, *Enlightenment Contested: Philosophy, Modernity, and the Emancipation of Man, 1650–1752* (Oxford: Oxford University Press, 2006), quotations on p. 809, 869 (italics in original). Israel's argument in this work complements and extends that in his earlier *Radical Enlightenment: Philosophy and the Making of Modernity, 1650–1750* (Oxford: Oxford University Press, 2001); the continuation of the Radical Enlightenment in the later eighteenth century is addressed in briefer compass in Israel's *A Revolution of the Mind: Radical Enlightenment and the Intellectual Origins of Modern Democracy* (Princeton, N.J.: Princeton University Press, 2010), which is a prelude to the forthcoming, full-length work that will complete his trilogy on the Enlightenment.

149. Smith, "Naturalism," in *Believing Primate,* ed. Schloss and Murray, p. 307.

150. Ralph Waldo Emerson, "Self-Reliance," in *Essays: First Series* [1841], in Emerson, *Essays and Lectures,* ed. Joel Porte (New York: Library of America, 1983), esp. pp. 261–262; Mill, *On Liberty,* in *On Liberty and Other Essays,* ed. Gray, pp. 74–82.

151. Mary Ann Glendon, *Rights Talk: The Impoverishment of Political Discourse* (New York: Free Press, 1991). Glendon's plea for the recovery of alternative languages of morality anchored in duties or the good is insufficiently aware of the way in which disputes about the good that began in the early Reformation, and that have persisted ever since, led to the modern ethics of rights, which, through political protection of preferential individual goods, facilitates the emergence of the public friction that provides the impetus for her book. Many scholars who study the United States operate within a supersessionist historical and institutional framework that prevents them from seeing how the Reformation era continues critically to influence the issues in which they are interested.

152. The same assumption of metaphysical univocity and the use of Occam's razor that, combined with the findings of the natural sciences, leave no "room" for God, also leave no "room" for the soul; both presuppose a rejection of a traditional Christian metaphysics and theology of creation, from the perspective of

which it is mistaken to construe either God or the soul in spatial or quasi-spatial terms. The findings of science present no more difficulty for the reality of the soul than for the reality of God within a traditional Christian world-view, nor could any empirical investigation confirm or disprove the soul's reality—a point lost on scholars who mistakenly think that empirical investigation of the natural world, including the investigation of the human body, somehow tends against belief in the reality of the human soul. This is so only if one makes neo-Scotist metaphysical assumptions, pits the natural and supernatural against each other, and believes that only science can tell us anything true about reality. For an example of the way in which the conflation of the findings of science with such beliefs leads in this direction, see Owen Flanagan, *The Problem of the Soul: Two Visions of Mind and How to Reconcile Them* (New York: Basic Books, 2002) and *The Really Hard Problem: Meaning in a Material World* (Cambridge, Mass., and London: MIT Press, 2007). The same conflation is also unwittingly made in the supersessionist account of the history of personal identity from the ancient world to the present in Raymond Martin and John Barresi, *The Rise and Fall of Soul and Self: An Intellectual History of Personal Identity* (New York: Columbia University Press, 2006). The difficulty of keeping clear about these issues, and their importance for one's view of human beings, are apparent even in a scholar as sophisticated as James O'Donnell, who thinks that advances in neuroscience threaten to undermine traditional Christian psychology centered on the soul: "Whatever becomes of 'soul' will determine what becomes of Augustine." James D. O'Donnell, *Augustine: A New Biography* (New York: Harper, 2006), p. 326.

153. "Large sections of a half-educated public, flattered as 'sophisticated,' may be ready for the death of God; they are not (yet) ready for the death of public (or private) morality." Rist, *Real Ethics*, p. 239.

154. Quotation from "evildeddy," 28 July 2009 on http://www.datehookup.com/Thread-314402.htm, accessed 9 November 2009.

155. Hugo Grotius, *The Rights of War and Peace* [1625], ed. Richard Tuck, bk. 1 (Indianapolis: Liberty Fund, 2005), p. 89. Although still frequently regarded by some scholars as a daring phrase that supposedly heralded a new, modern, secular discourse on natural law, the phrase "was a rather common topos of late scholastic discourse" that Grotius could have gotten "from Suarez or from any one of half a dozen sixteenth-century authors." Tierney, *Idea of Natural Rights*, pp. 319–320, with reference to James St. Ledger, *The "Etiamsi daremus" of Hugo Grotius: A Study in the Origins of International Law* (Rome: Pontificium Athenaeum Internationale Angelicum, 1962), and L. Besselink, "The Impious Hypothesis Revisited," *Grotiana*, n.s., 9 (1988), 3–63.

156. Friedrich Nietzsche, *Götzen-Dämmerung* [1889], in Nietzsche, *Werke: Kritische Gesamtausgabe*, ed. Giorgio Colli and Mazzino Montinari, pt. 6, vol. 3 (Berlin: Walter de Gruyter, 1969), p. 92/7–15 (emphasis in original).

157. This point has been made in various ways not only by MacIntyre and Steven Smith, but also by Christian Smith, John Rist, and David Bentley Hart. See Hart's *Atheist Delusions* as well as his *Beauty of the Infinite: The Aesthetics*

*of Christian Truth* (Grand Rapids, Mich.: Eerdmans, 2003); MacIntyre, *After Virtue;* Steven Smith, *Disenchantment;* Christian Smith, "Naturalism," in *Believing Primate,* ed. Schloss and Murray; Rist, *Real Ethics.* Jonathan Israel, for example, in the conclusion of *Enlightenment Contested,* waxes eloquent about the alleged, Radical Enlightenment, rational foundations of contemporary human rights without any substantive mention of Nietzsche in his book.

158. MacIntyre, *After Virtue,* p. 71.

159. See Walter Isaacson's interview of Woody Allen, entitled "The Heart Wants What It Wants," *Time,* 31 August 1992, accessed 16 November 2009 at http://www.time.com/time/magazine/article/0,9171,976345-5,00.html.

160. Johann Wolfgang von Goethe, *The Sorrows of Young Werther* [1774], in *The Sorrows of Young Werther and Novella,* trans. Elizabeth Mayer and Louise Bogan (New York: Vintage, 1971), p. 99.

161. See, for example, Ray Kurzweil, *The Singularity Is Near: When Humans Transcend Biology* (New York: Penguin, 2005); Joel Garreau, *Radical Evolution: The Promise and Peril of Enhancing Our Minds, Our Bodies—and What It Means to Be Human* (New York: Broadway Books, 2005); Simon Young, *Designer Evolution: A Transhumanist Manifesto* (New York: Prometheus, 2006).

162. Nikolas Rose, *The Politics of Life Itself: Biomedicine, Power, and Subjectivity in the Twenty-First Century* (Princeton, N.J.: Princeton University Press, 2007), p. 4 (my emphasis).

163. On the problems that ensue for legal theory (including legal positivism) if a transcendent foundation for laws and justice is rejected, see Steven D. Smith, *Law's Quandary* (Cambridge, Mass., and London: Harvard University Press, 2004); see also Arkes, *Natural Rights and the Right to Choose.*

164. Young, *Transhumanist Manifesto,* p. 45.

165. Kurzweil, *Singularity,* p. 486.

166. Christopher Marlowe, *Doctor Faustus: With the English Faust Book,* ed. David Wootton (Indianapolis: Hackett, 2005), 1.1.92, p. 6.

167. Mill, *On Liberty,* in *On Liberty and Other Essays,* ed. Gray, p. 76.

168. Ibid., p. 91; Wolfe, *Future of Liberalism,* p. 4.

169. Talal Asad, *Formations of the Secular: Christianity, Islam, Modernity* (Stanford, Calif.: Stanford University Press, 2003), p. 6. Asad continues: "Consider what happens when the parties to a dispute are unwilling to compromise on what for them is a matter of principle (a principle that articulates action and being, not a principle that is justifiable by statements of belief). If citizens are not reasoned around in a matter deemed nationally important by the government and the majority that supports it, the threat of legal action (and the violence this implies) may be used." Ibid.

170. In his different way, Charles Taylor is preoccupied with this same process of attenuation over the past half millennium in *A Secular Age* (Cambridge, Mass., and London: Belknap Press of Harvard University Press, 2007).

## 5. Manufacturing the Goods Life

1. See the essays in *Post-Fordism: A Reader*, ed. Ash Amin (Oxford: Blackwell, 1993), esp. Amin, "Post-Fordism: Models, Fantasies and Phantoms of Transition," pp. 1–39.

2. Zygmunt Bauman, *Does Ethics Have a Chance in a World of Consumers?* (Cambridge, Mass., and London: Harvard University Press, 2008), p. 72. Bauman here echoes Marx's famous maxim, of course, in *The Eighteenth Brumaire of Louis Bonaparte* [1852], about human beings making history but not under circumstances of their choosing.

3. See, for example, Pun Ngai, *Made in China: Women Factory Workers in a Global Workplace* (Durham, N.C.: Duke University Press, 2005); Robert J. S. Ross, *Slaves to Fashion: Poverty and Abuse in the New Sweatshops* (Ann Arbor: University of Michigan Press, 2004); Leslie Salzinger, *Genders in Production: Making Workers in Mexico's Global Factories* (Berkeley and Los Angeles: University of California Press, 2003); Ellen Israel Rosen, *Making Sweatshops: The Globalization of the U.S. Apparel Industry* (Berkeley and Los Angeles: University of California Press, 2002).

4. Katherine S. Newman and Victor Tan Chen, *The Missing Class: Portraits of the Near Poor in America* (Boston: Beacon Press, 2008); David K. Shipler, *The Working Poor: Invisible in America* (New York: Knopf, 2004); Mark Robert Rank, *One Nation, Underprivileged: Why American Poverty Affects Us All* (New York: Oxford University Press, 2004); William Julius Wilson, *When Work Disappears: The World of the New Urban Poor* (New York: Knopf, 1996); Douglas Massey and Nancy Denton, *American Apartheid: Segregation and the Making of the Underclass* (Cambridge, Mass.: Harvard University Press, 1993); Katherine S. Newman, *Declining Fortunes: The Withering of the American Dream* (New York: Basic Books, 1993).

5. Karl Marx and Friedrich Engels, *Manifest der Kommunistischen Partei* [1848], in Marx and Engels, *Werke*, vol. 4 (Berlin: Dietz, 1964), p. 465: "Alles Ständische und Stehende verdampft." Marshall Berman made the more poetic translation of this phrase the title of his well-known work on modernity, modernism, and modernization, *All That Is Solid Melts into Air: The Experience of Modernity* (1982; New York: Penguin, 1988).

6. Bauman, *Ethics*, pp. 42–55, 157–172.

7. Arlie Russell Hochschild, *The Commercialization of Intimate Life: Notes from Home and Work* (Berkeley and Los Angeles: University of California Press, 2003), p. 8. See also Jean Kilbourne, *Can't Buy Me Love: How Advertising Changes the Way We Think and Feel* (New York: Free Press, 2000). On the extent to which already by the early 1990s corporations were gathering extensive information about the personal lives of potential consumers for marketing purposes, see also Erik Larson, *The Naked Consumer: How Our Private Lives Become Public Commodities* (New York: Henry Holt, 1992).

8. On religion, see Vincent J. Miller, *Consuming Religion: Christian Faith and Practice in a Consumer Culture* (New York and London: Continuum, 2003); James B. Twitchell, *Shopping for God: How Christianity Went from in Your*

*Heart to in Your Face* (New York: Simon & Schuster, 2007); and William T. Cavanaugh, *Being Consumed: Economics and Christian Desire* (Grand Rapids, Mich.: Eerdmans, 2008). For weddings in Britain, see Sharon Boden, *Consumerism, Romance, and the Wedding Experience* (New York: Palgrave Macmillan, 2003); for weddings in the United States, see Vicki Howard, *Brides, Inc.: American Weddings and the Business of Tradition* (Philadelphia: University of Pennsylvania Press, 2006), and Rebecca Mead, *One Perfect Day: The Selling of the American Wedding* (New York: Penguin, 2007). On the conceptualization of bodies in terms of parts and organs, see the essays in *Commodifying Bodies,* ed. Nancy Scheper-Hughes and Loïc Wacquant (London and Thousand Oaks, Calif.: Sage Publications, 2002), and for the black-market trade in body parts in the United States, see Annie Cheney, *Body Brokers: Inside America's Underground Trade in Human Remains* (New York: Broadway Books, 2006). See also Steph Wilkinson, *Bodies for Sale: Ethics and Exploitation in the Human Body Trade* (New York: Routledge, 2003). On advertising and marketing to children, see Juliet B. Schor, *Born to Buy: The Commercialized Child and the New Consumer Culture* (New York: Scribner, 2004).

9. David Brooks, *Bobos in Paradise: The New Upper Class and How They Got There* (New York: Simon & Schuster, 2001); Jean M. Twenge, *Generation Me: Why Today's Young Americans Are More Confident, Assertive, Entitled—and More Miserable Than Ever Before* (New York: Free Press, 2006).

10. Amanda Ford, *Retail Therapy: Life Lessons Learned While Shopping* (York Beach, Me.: Conari Press, 2002); Amy Elliott, *A Girl's Guide to Retail Therapy: Unleash the Healing Power of Shopping* (New York: Barnes & Noble, 2006), which "treats the concept of feel-good shopping with the reverence it deserves" (p. 6).

11. Herbert Marcuse, *One-Dimensional Man: Studies in the Ideology of Advanced Industrial Society* (1964; London: ARK Paperbacks, 1986).

12. For the most influential works themselves, see Milton Friedman, *Capitalism and Freedom* (Chicago: University of Chicago Press, 1962), and Friedrich A. Hayek, *The Road to Serfdom: Text and Documents. The Definitive Edition,* ed. Bruce Caldwell (Chicago: University of Chicago Press, 2007). Hayek's text was first published in 1944.

13. David Landes, *The Unbound Prometheus: Technological Change and Industrial Development in Western Europe from 1750 to the Present,* 2nd ed. (Cambridge: Cambridge University Press, 2003), pp. xi, 19. The first quoted phrase, and the preface to the second edition from which it is taken, reflect the consistency of Landes's views since the work was originally published in 1969. For a more strident argument about the historical primacy and superiority specifically of British technological and capitalist innovation, see Landes, *The Wealth and Poverty of Nations: Why Some Are So Rich and Some So Poor* (New York: W. W. Norton, 1999).

14. For only a few examples, see Thomas Koulopoulos, *Smartsourcing: Driving Innovation and Growth through Outsourcing* (Avon, Mass.: Platinum Press, 2006); Atul Vashistha and Avinash Vashistha, *The Offshore Nation: Strategies for Success in Outsourcing and Offshoring* (New York: McGraw-Hill,

2006); Erran Carmel and Paul Tija, *Offshoring Information Technology: Sourcing and Outsourcing to a Global Workforce* (Cambridge: Cambridge University Press, 2006); Douglas Brown and Scott Wilson, *The Black Book of Outsourcing: How to Manage the Changes, Challenges, and Opportunities* (Hoboken, N.J.: Wiley, 2005); Mark J. Power, Kevin C. Desouza, and Carlo Bonifazi, *The Outsourcing Handbook: How to Implement a Successful Outsourcing Process* (London and Philadelphia: Kogan Page, 2006).

15. Daniel Acuff and Robert H. Reiher, *What Kids Buy: The Psychology of Marketing to Kids* (New York: Free Press, 1997), p. 17; see also Gene Del Vecchio, *Creating Ever-Cool: A Marketer's Guide to a Kid's Heart* (Gretna, La.: Pelican Publishing, 1997).

16. James Twitchell, "Two Cheers for Materialism," in *The Consumer Society Reader*, ed. Juliet B. Schor and Douglas B. Holt (New York: Free Press, 2000), pp. 283, 289, 282 (italics in original), repr. from *Wilson Quarterly* 23:2 (1999): 16–26. Twitchell has pursued multiple aspects of this line of argument in a series of books. See his *Adcult USA: The Triumph of Advertising in American Culture* (New York: Columbia University Press, 1997); *Lead Us into Temptation: The Triumph of American Materialism* (New York: Columbia University Press, 1999), with the same passage quoted above at p. 23; *Living It Up: America's Love Affair with Luxury* (New York: Simon & Schuster, 2002); and most recently, *Branded Nation: The Marketing of Megachurch, College Inc., and Museumworld* (New York: Simon & Schuster, 2004).

17. Stanley Lebergott, *Pursuing Happiness: American Consumers in the Twentieth Century* (Princeton, N.J.: Princeton University Press, 1993), p. 13.

18. Twitchell, "Two Cheers," in *Reader*, ed. Schor and Holt, p. 282.

19. For the massive compilation of scientific data by the Intergovernmental Panel on Climate Change, see *Climate Change 2007: The Physical Science Basis* (Cambridge: Cambridge University Press, 2007); for an astute analysis of the character of the debate in light of the burgeoning data, see Andrew E. Dessler and Andrew A. Parson, *The Science and Politics of Global Climate Change* (Cambridge: Cambridge University Press, 2006). See also, for example, Ross Gelbspan, *Boiling Point: How Politicians, Big Oil and Coal, Journalists, and Activists Have Fueled a Climate Crisis—And What We Can Do to Avert Disaster* (New York: Basic Books, 2004); Elizabeth Kolbert, *Field Notes from a Catastrophe: Man, Nature, and Climate Change* (New York: Bloomsbury, 2006); John Houghton, *Global Warming: The Complete Briefing*, 4th ed. (Cambridge: Cambridge University Press, 2009).

20. For some examples of works in this genre, see Christopher C. Horner, *The Politically Incorrect Guide to Global Warming and Environmentalism* (Washington, D.C.: Regnery Publishing, 2007); S. Fred Singer and Dennis T. Avery, *Unstoppable Global Warming Every 1,500 Years*, exp. ed. (Lanham, Md.: Rowman & Littlefield, 2008); Roy Spencer, *Climate Confusion: How Global Warming Hysteria Leads to Bad Science, Pandering Politicians, and Misguided Policies That Hurt the Poor* (New York: Encounter Books, 2008); Christopher

Booker, *The Real Global Warming Disaster: Is the Obsession with "Climate Change" Turning Out to Be the Most Costly Scientific Blunder in History?* (London: Continuum, 2009); Ian Plimer, *Heaven and Earth: Global Warming, the Missing Science* (Lanham, Md.: Taylor Trade Publishing, 2009).

21. Max Weber, *Die protestantische Ethik und der "Geist" des Kapitalismus* [1904–1905], ed. Klaus Lichtblau and Johannes Weiß, 3rd ed. (1993; Weinheim: Beltz Athenäum, 2000), pp. 154, 153. The well-known English translation by Talcott Parsons (1930) is based on Weber's revised version of the work published in 1920. On the differences and relationship between the 1904–1905 and 1920 editions, see the introduction by Peter Baehr and Gordon C. Wells in Weber, *The Protestant Ethic and the "Spirit" of Capitalism* [1904–1905], in *The Protestant Ethic and the "Spirit" of Capitalism and Other Writings*, ed. and trans. Baehr and Wells (Harmondsworth, U.K.: Penguin, 2002), pp. xxxiii–xlii.

22. For two collections of relevant essays, see *Weber's Protestant Ethic: Origins, Evidence, Contexts,* ed. Hartmut Lehmann and Guenther Roth (1987; Cambridge: Cambridge University Press, 1993), and *The Protestant Ethic Turns 100: Essays on the Centenary of the Weber Thesis,* ed. William H. Swatos Jr. and Lutz Kaelber (Boulder, Colo.: Paradigm Publishers, 2005).

23. Lisa Jardine, *Worldly Goods: A New History of the Renaissance* (New York: W. W. Norton, 1996), p. 436.

24. Ibid., p. 12.

25. For a study in which the discontinuity and differences between Renaissance and contemporary consumerism are more evident than in Jardine's treatment, see Evelyn Welch, *Shopping in the Renaissance* (New Haven, Conn., and London: Yale University Press, 2005).

26. For the United States see, for example, Mark R. Warren, *Dry Bones Rattling: Community Building to Revitalize American Democracy* (Princeton, N.J.: Princeton University Press, 2001); William Greider, *The Soul of Capitalism: Opening Paths to a Moral Economy* (New York: Simon & Schuster, 2003); Theda Skocpol, *Diminished Democracy: From Membership to Management in American Civic Life* (Norman: University of Oklahoma Press, 2004); Frances Moore Lappé, *Democracy's Edge: Choosing to Save Our Country by Bringing Democracy to Life* (San Francisco: Jossey Bass, 2006); Ronald Dworkin, *Is Democracy Possible Here? Principles for a New Political Debate* (Princeton, N.J.: Princeton University Press, 2006); Tony Judt, *Ill Fares the Land* (New York: Penguin, 2010).

27. Jan de Vries, *The Industrious Revolution: Consumer Behavior and the Household Economy, 1650 to the Present* (Cambridge: Cambridge University Press, 2008), p. ix. On the anything-but-inevitable or natural emergence of modern capitalism in the Western world, and the extent to which it constitutes a sharp departure from most of human history and most human cultures, see the recent synthetic narrative by Joyce Appleby, *The Relentless Revolution: A History of Capitalism* (New York: W. W. Norton, 2010).

28. Appleby, *Relentless Revolution.*

29. Albert O. Hirschman, *The Passions and the Interests: Political Arguments for Capitalism before Its Triumph* (Princeton, N.J.: Princeton University Press, 1977).

30. For the distinction between capitalist practices and capitalist society understood in this way, I am indebted to Amintore Fanfani, *Catholicism, Protestantism, and Capitalism* [1935] (New York: Sheed & Ward, 1955). It is related to Weber's careful distinction, in one of the most important paragraphs in his classic work, between capitalist forms (which existed in the Middle Ages) and a capitalist spirit (which is distinctive of the modern era). Weber, *Protestantische Ethik*, ed. Lichtblau and Weiß, pp. 50–51. Although some aspects of my argument in this chapter bear comparison to those of Daniel Bell in *The Cultural Contradictions of Capitalism*, his argument relies on Weber's Protestant ethic and on a supersessionist, epochal conception of historical change. Bell, *The Cultural Contradictions of Capitalism* (1976; New York: Basic Books, 1996). Modern Western capitalism is less an outgrowth of either Reformation-era Protestantism or Catholicism than it is an alternative to and rejection of both.

31. Jardine, *Worldly Goods*, p. 34; de Vries, *Industrious Revolution*, pp. 44–70.

32. See de Vries, *Industrious Revolution*.

33. Joel Mokyr, *The Gifts of Athena: Historical Origins of the Knowledge Economy* (Princeton, N.J.: Princeton University Press, 2002).

34. Although I do not use the terms in just the same way as Karl Polanyi, I am indebted in general to his conceptions of embeddedness and disembedding in the changes wrought by the shift from a premodern to a modern economy, in Polanyi, *The Great Transformation: The Political and Economic Origins of Our Time*, foreword by Joseph E. Stiglitz, introduction by Fred Block (1944; Boston: Beacon Press, 2001).

35. On Schumpeter, see the recent biography by Thomas K. McCraw, *Prophet of Innovation: Joseph Schumpeter and Creative Destruction* (Cambridge, Mass., and London: Belknap Press of Harvard University Press, 2007).

36. For an overview of patristic ideas, see Justo L. González, *Faith and Wealth: A History of Early Christian Ideas on the Origin, Significance, and Use of Money* (Eugene, Ore.: Wipf and Stock Publishers, 1990).

37. On Ambrose, see ibid., pp. 187–193, and on Ambrose in the context of the significant upturn in the denunciation of *avaritia* among northern Italian bishops in the late fourth and fifth centuries, see Richard Newhauser, *The Early History of Greed: The Sin of Avarice in Early Medieval Thought and Literature* (Cambridge: Cambridge University Press, 2000), pp. 70–75.

38. Bernard of Clairvaux, *Sermones super cantica canticorum*, ed. J. Leclercq, C. H. Talbot, and H. M. Rochais, vol. 2 in *Sancti Bernardi opera* (Rome: Editiones Cistercienses, 1958), sermon 50.3, pp. 79/27–80/1.

39. Peter Damian, *De contemptu saeculi*, 6, quoted in Newhauser, *Early History of Greed*, p. 127 (Newhauser's trans.). Throughout the Middle Ages Paul was regarded as the author of both Ephesians and Colossians.

40. *Fasciculus Morum: A Fourteenth-Century Preachers' Handbook*, ed. and trans. Siegfried Wenzel (University Park: Pennsylvania State University Press,

1989), 4.2, p. 315, quoted in Diana Wood, *Medieval Economic Thought* (Cambridge: Cambridge University Press, 2002), p. 54 (Wood's trans.).

41. González, *Faith and Wealth;* see also Newhauser, *Early History of Greed.*

42. M. I. Finley's argument about the nature of the ancient economy remains basically intact despite the criticisms leveled against it since the 1980s. See Finley, *The Ancient Economy,* 2nd ed., foreword by Ian Morris (Berkeley and Los Angeles: University of California Press, 1999). The first edition appeared in 1973. For Aristotle's reflections on money and his economic ideas in general I am indebted in this paragraph to the analysis by Scott Meikle, *Aristotle's Economic Thought* (Cambridge: Cambridge University Press, 1995), which supersedes all modern interpretations that allege the incoherence or superficiality of Aristotle's discussions of economic issues in *Nicomachean Ethics* 5.5 and *Politics* 1.8–10.

43. Meikle, *Aristotle's Economic Thought,* pp. 43–67.

44. On economics for Aristotle as strictly and merely a subdivision of ethics, see M. I. Finley, "Aristotle and Economic Analysis," *Past and Present* 47 (1970): 3–25. Meikle justly criticizes Finley and other interpreters for underestimating the insight and implications of the genuinely *economic* (although not *modern* economic) analysis in *Nicomachean Ethics* 5.5 and *Politics* 1.8–10, but agrees with Finley that Aristotle entirely subordinates economics to his teleological ethics and its integral relationship to shared political life as the human good. Meikle, *Aristotle's Economic Thought,* pp. 169–172, 196–198.

45. The first complete Latin translation of the *Nicomachean Ethics* was Robert Grosseteste's, probably made in 1246–1247, whereas William of Moerbeke translated the *Politics* around 1260. Bernard G. Dod, "Aristoteles latinus," in *The Cambridge History of Later Medieval Philosophy: From the Rediscovery of Aristotle to the Disintegration of Scholasticism, 1100–1600,* ed. Norman Kretzmann, Anthony Kenny, and Jan Pinborg (Cambridge: Cambridge University Press, 1982), pp. 63, 78.

46. See the deft analysis of the ways in which Aquinas's economic thought both relies on and departs from Aristotle's, in Christopher A. Franks, *He Became Poor: The Poverty of Christ and Aquinas's Economic Teachings* (Grand Rapids, Mich.: Eerdmans, 2009). Joel Kaye's otherwise impressive study of the relationship between scholastic economic analysis and proto-scientific natural philosophy mischaracterizes Aristotle's economic thought by neglecting its subordination to his ethics and politics, and by contrasting rather than seeing (as Meikle does) the coherence of the respective discussions in the *Nicomachean Ethics* and *Politics.* Kaye, *Economy and Nature in the Fourteenth Century: Money, Market Exchange, and the Emergence of Scientific Thought* (Cambridge: Cambridge University Press, 1998), pp. 37–55.

47. Leon Battista Alberti, *The Family in Renaissance Florence, Books One–Four: I libri della famiglia* [c. 1434–1441], trans. Renée Neu Watkins (1969; Long Grove, Ill.: Waveland Press, 2004), p. 162 (Watkins's trans.). For the Italian, see Alberti, *I libri della famiglia,* ed. Ruggiero Romano, Alberto Tenenti, and Francesco Furlan (Turin: Einaudi, 1994), p. 175, as well as p. 173, where one

of the dialogue's protagonists, Giannozzo, lauds the virtue of efficient household management by exclaiming, "Santa cosa la masserizia!" On Alberti's complex and somewhat conflicted Christian and classical attitudes toward the accumulation of wealth and the use of money in the wider context of fifteenth-century Florentine society, see Anthony Grafton, *Leon Battista Alberti: Master Builder of the Italian Renaissance* (2000; Cambridge, Mass.: Harvard University Press, 2002), pp. 59–60, 68, 158, 176–180.

48. On Omobono of Cremona, whom Innocent III canonized in 1199 and who "took care of abandoned children, fed poor people, and otherwise offered help to those who did not know where else to turn" even as he "never ceased to be a merchant," see Lester K. Little, *Religious Poverty and the Profit Economy in Medieval Europe* (Ithaca, N.Y.: Cornell University Press, 1978), p. 215. On harsher attitudes, more surveillant practices, and greater civic control of the poor in the fifteenth and early sixteenth centuries, including the spread of a distinction between the deserving and undeserving poor, see Michel Mollat, *The Poor in the Middle Ages: An Essay in Social History,* trans. Arthur Goldhammer (New Haven, Conn., and London: Yale University Press, 1986). pp. 251–288.

49. *La Chiesa e il Convento di San Marco a Firenze* ([Florence]: Cassa di Risparmio di Firenze, 1989), pp. 14–21.

50. The other three corporal works of mercy—welcoming the stranger, caring for the sick, and visiting the imprisoned—need not have involved money directly, depending on the form they took, although they likely would have implied it indirectly (to welcome a stranger by offering hospitality, for example, presupposed a dwelling the sustenance of which, at least in an urban setting, required money). So too, to speak in the terms of neoclassical economists, all the corporal and spiritual works of mercy involved the opportunity cost of forgoing whatever one might otherwise have done with one's time. On the year-round circulation of money in medieval cities, as opposed to its distinctive seasonal pattern of circulation in the countryside, see Peter Spufford, *Money and Its Use in Medieval Europe* (Cambridge: Cambridge University Press, 1988), pp. 382–386. All the corporal acts of mercy are derived from Mt 25:31–46 except for burying the dead, which is based on Tb 1:17, 4:3–4, and 6:15.

51. Michael McCormick, *Origins of the European Economy: Communications and Commerce, AD 300–900* (Cambridge: Cambridge University Press, 2001), with a summary of these points at pp. 791–798.

52. On the overwhelmingly agricultural economy of the early Middle Ages and the importance of landed, aristocratic demand in shaping what by the ninth century was "a world of regional and sub-regional economies," see the final chapter of Chris Wickham, *Framing the Early Middle Ages: Europe and the Mediterranean, 400–800* (Oxford: Oxford University Press, 2005), pp. 693–824, quotation on 820. The same basic picture was true of the ninth and tenth centuries, when an increase in levels of economic exchange was dependent above all on intensified extraction of agricultural produce by landlords who exercised greater control over their peasants. See Wickham, *The Inheri-*

*tance of Rome: Illuminating the Dark Ages* (New York: Viking, 2009), pp. 371, 529–551.

53. Robert S. Lopez, *The Commercial Revolution of the Middle Ages, 950–1350* (1971; Cambridge: Cambridge University Press, 1976); Little, *Religious Poverty*, pp. 3–18. On the increased economic activity in Western Europe in the tenth century, see Wickham, *Inheritance of Rome*, pp. 543–551. "From the 1160s onwards there were renewed supplies of silver available in Europe and on the basis of these a total transformation took place of practically every facet of the economy and of society in which money was involved." Spufford, *Money*, p. 99; see more generally part 2, pp. 109–263.

54. Little, *Religious Poverty*, pp. 11–12; Spufford, *Money*, pp. 139–142; and more broadly on the fairs in Champagne, see Spufford, *Power and Profit: The Merchant in Medieval Europe* (New York: Thames & Hudson, 2002), pp. 143–152, and Steven A. Epstein, *An Economic and Social History of Later Medieval Europe, 1000–1500* (Cambridge: Cambridge University Press, 2009), pp. 82–83.

55. For an interpretation of twelfth- and thirteenth-century medieval Italian communes along these lines, see Augustine Thompson, *Cities of God: The Religion of the Italian Communes, 1125–1325* (University Park: Pennsylvania State University Press, 2005).

56. On these sermons by Albert in Augsburg, see Little, *Religious Poverty*, pp. 213–214.

57. Kaye, *Economy and Nature*, p. 54. In Richard Britnell's apt words, "Complex personal ties and responsibilities between members of a small group are discouraging to the development of regular exchanges founded on the idea of money values. Market relationships depend upon a degree of impersonality more easily maintained between strangers than between neighbours and relatives." Britnell, *The Commercialisation of English Society, 1000–1500*, 2nd ed. (Cambridge: Cambridge University Press, 1996), p. 7.

58. On the eremitical revival as well as the reformed monastic orders in relationship to the growth of cities and the monetization of the economy, see Little, *Religious Poverty*, pp. 70–96, as well as C. H. Lawrence, *Medieval Monasticism*, 3rd ed. (Harlow, U.K.: Longman, 2001), pp. 146–198. On the rapid growth of the Cistercians, which peaked in the 1130s and 1140s, see also Louis J. Lekai, *The Cistercians: Ideals and Reality* ([Kent, Ohio]: Kent State University Press, 1977), pp. 33–51, as well as the important revisionist account by Constance Hoffman Berman that stresses the incorporation of previously existing monastic communities: Berman, *The Cistercian Evolution: The Invention of a Religious Order in Twelfth-Century Europe* (Philadelphia: University of Pennsylvania Press, 2000).

59. Little, *Religious Poverty*, pp. 113–120, 128–134. On the Humiliati, see also Frances Andrews, *The Early Humiliati* (Cambridge: Cambridge University Press, 1999); on the beguines in the Low Countries, see Walter Simons, *Cities of Ladies: The Beguines in the Medieval Low Countries, 1200–1565* (Philadelphia: University of Pennsylvania Press, 2001).

60. Richard Pynson published the first edition in London in 1493. On the provenance of the work, see the critical edition, *Dives and Pauper*, vol. 1, pt. 1, ed.

Priscilla Heath Barnum, vol. 275 in Early English Text Society (London: Oxford University Press, 1976), pp. ix–x.

61. John T. Noonan Jr., *The Scholastic Analysis of Usury* (Cambridge, Mass.: Harvard University Press, 1957), pp. 100–132; Wood, *Medieval Economic Thought*, pp. 181–205; Kaye, *Economy and Nature*, pp. 83–87; Franks, *He Became Poor*, pp. 80–83; Odd Langholm, *Economics in the Medieval Schools* (Leiden: E. J. Brill, 1992), pp. 51, 318–320, 370, 416, 476–477, 523–527.

62. For a penetrating critique of Noonan's analysis of just price and usury as a conflation of what were fundamentally different concerns, with particular reference to Aquinas, see Franks, *He Became Poor*, pp. 92–104; cf. Noonan, *Scholastic Analysis*, pp. 82–99. Franks adds considerable nuance to de Roover's seminal article (largely followed by Kaye) that noted the ways in which, basing their arguments on Roman law, scholastic writers tended to equate just price with market price. See Raymond de Roover, "The Concept of the Just Price: Theory and Economic Policy," *Journal of Economic History* 18 (1958): 418–434; Kaye, *Economy and Nature*, pp. 87–101.

63. Kaye, *Economy and Nature*, p. 89.

64. More insightful than Wood's overview of the relationship between private property and the common good (*Medieval Economic Thought*, pp. 17–41) is Franks, *He Became Poor*, pp. 53–66.

65. Quoted in Wood, *Medieval Economic Thought*, p. 3, from Jean Gerson, who was in turn quoting from chapter 12 of Henry's *De contractibus*, in Gerson's *Opera omnia*, vol. 4 (Cologne, 1484), fol. 191 (Wood's trans.). R. H. Tawney quoted the same sentence in *Religion and the Rise of Capitalism*, intro. Adam B. Seligman (1926; New Brunswick, N.J., and London: Transaction, 1998), p. 36.

66. Tawney, *Religion*, p. 62.

67. On the financial dealings of the papacy in particular, from the Gregorian reform to the eve of the Reformation, see the magisterial study by Philippe Simonnot, *Les papes, l'église et l'argent: Histoire économique du christianisme des origines à nos jours* (Paris: Bayard, 2005), pp. 365–554. On criticisms of Rome and the papacy that began even before the advent of the profit economy, see Josef Benzinger, *Invectiva in Romam: Romkritik im Mittelalter vom 9. bis zum 12. Jahrhundert* (Lübeck and Hamburg: Matthiesen, 1968). For an attempt by economists to model the medieval Latin church as a whole as a monopolistic, maximizing, profit-seeking corporation, see Robert B. Ekelund et al., *Sacred Trust: The Medieval Church as an Economic Firm* (New York: Oxford University Press, 1996).

68. See David Burr, *The Spiritual Franciscans: From Protest to Persecution in the Century after Saint Francis* (University Park: Pennsylvania State University Press, 2001); Brian Tierney, *The Idea of Natural Rights: Studies on Natural Rights, Natural Law and Church Law, 1150–1625* (Athens, Ga.: Scholars Press, 1997), pp. 93–169.

69. Little refers to the incident in *Religious Poverty*, p. 160. For the text, see Thomas de Celano, *Vita secunda S. Francisci*, in *Analecta Franciscana*, vol. 10 (Quaracchi: S. Bonaventura, 1941), 2.28, p. 166/3–10. On the early phase

of the construction of Santa Croce, see *Il complesso monumentale di Santa Croce: La basilica, le cappelle, i chiostri, il museo,* ed. Umberto Baldini and Bruno Nardini (Florence: Nardini, 1983), pp. 14–15.

70. John Colet, *Oratio habita a D. Ioanne Colet Decano Sancti Pauli ad Clerum in Conuocatione* ([London:] Richard Pynson, [1512]), p. 7. For the dating of this sermon to January 1510 instead of its traditional date of 6 February 1512, see John B. Gleason, *John Colet* (Berkeley and Los Angeles: University of California Press, 1989), pp. 181, 184, 370 n. 33.

71. *Dives et pauper* (Westminster: Wynkyn de Worde, 1496), sig. a1.

72. John T. Noonan Jr., *A Church That Can and Cannot Change: The Development of Catholic Moral Teaching* (Notre Dame, Ind.: University of Notre Dame Press, 2005), with ownership of slaves by popes and religious orders at pp. 36–41, 79, 87–93; see also George Huppert, *After the Black Death: A Social History of Early Modern Europe,* 2nd ed. (Bloomington and Indianapolis: Indiana University Press, 1998), pp. 112–116.

73. J. G. A. Pocock, *The Machiavellian Moment: Florentine Political Thought and the Atlantic Republican Tradition,* rev. ed. (Princeton, N.J.: Princeton University Press, 2003). The work was first published in 1975.

74. *Dives et pauper* (1496), sig. a4. The same view was shared, for example, by the fifteenth-century, anti-Lollard, Welsh bishop of Chichester, Reginald Pecock; see Tawney, *Religion,* p. 301 n. 106. On Pecock more generally, see Wendy Scase, "Pecock, Reginald (*b. c.* 1392, *d.* in or after 1459)," in *ODNB,* ed. H. C. G. Matthew and Brian Harrison (Oxford: Oxford University Press, 2004), online ed., ed. Lawrence Goldman, http://www.oxforddnb.com/view/article/21749 (accessed 23 January 2010).

75. Thomas Hemerken à Kempis, *De imitatione Christi* [c. 1420], in à Kempis, *Opera omnia,* vol. 2, ed. Michael J. Pohl (Freiburg im Breisgau: Herder, 1904), 1.25, p. 54/3–5. On canons and canonesses involved with the Modern Devout, including the Windesheim Congregation, see John Van Engen, *Sisters and Brothers of the Common Life: The Devotio Moderna and the World of the Later Middle Ages* (Philadelphia: University of Pennsylvania Press, 2008), pp. 56, 93–94, 125, 154–161.

76. On this relationship among the Black Death, labor scarcity, higher wages, and more ambitious consumption, see David Herlihy, *The Black Death and the Transformation of the West,* ed. and intro. Samuel K. Cohn Jr. (Cambridge, Mass., and London: Harvard University Press, 1997), pp. 47–51; Christopher Dyer, *Standards of Living in the Middle Ages: Social Change in England, c. 1200–1520,* rev. ed. (Cambridge: Cambridge University Press, 1998), pp. 88, 176–177, 207, 216, 218–219, 221, 298–301, 311; Mollat, *Poor,* pp. 198–201, 211; Werner Rösener, "The Agrarian Economy, 1300–1600," in *Germany: A New Economic and Social History, 1450–1630,* ed. Bob Scribner (London: Arnold, 1996), pp. 63–66; and Epstein, *Economic and Social History,* pp. 215–221. On sumptuary legislation, see Alan Hunt, *Governance of the Consuming Passions: A History of Sumptuary Law* (New York: St. Martin's Press, 1996); Carole Collier Frick, *Dressing Renaissance Florence: Families, Fortunes, and Fine Clothing* (Baltimore and London:

Johns Hopkins University Press, 2002), pp. 3, 95, 179–200; and Tom Scott, *Society and Economy in Germany, 1300–1600* (Houndmills, U.K., and New York: Palgrave, 2002), pp. 204–205.

77. Jardine, *Worldly Goods.*

78. On the relationship between the Black Death and the invention of the printing press, see Herlihy, *Black Death,* p. 50; on books as luxury objects, see Jardine, *Worldly Goods,* pp. 135–180; on humanism as a self-conscious cultural ideology, see the introduction to Anthony Grafton and Lisa Jardine, *From Humanism to the Humanities: Education and the Liberal Arts in Fifteenth- and Sixteenth-Century Europe* (Cambridge, Mass.: Harvard University Press, 1986), pp. xi–xvi.

79. Thomas A. Brady Jr., "The Rise of Merchant Empires, 1400–1700: A European Counterpoint," in *The Political Economy of Merchant Empires: State Power and World Trade, 1350–1750,* ed. James D. Tracy (Cambridge: Cambridge University Press, 1991), p. 132.

80. See Edwin S. Hunt and James M. Murray, *A History of Business in Medieval Europe, 1200–1520* (Cambridge: Cambridge University Press, 1999), pp. 62–67, 109–112, 209–218; Richard A. Goldthwaite, *The Economy of Renaissance Florence* (Baltimore: Johns Hopkins University Press, 2009); Raymond de Roover, *The Rise and Decline of the Medici Bank, 1397–1494* (Cambridge, Mass.: Harvard University Press, 1963); de Roover, *Money, Banking and Credit in Medieval Bruges: Italian Merchant Bankers, Lombards and Money Changers: A Study in the Origins of Banking* (Cambridge, Mass.: Medieval Academy of America, 1948).

81. See Richard A. Goldthwaite, *Wealth and the Demand for Art in Italy, 1300–1600* (Baltimore and London: Johns Hopkins University Press, 1993).

82. Mollat, *Poor,* pp. 233–237.

83. *Complesso di Santa Croce,* ed. Baldini and Nardini, p. 15.

84. Odd Langholm, *The Merchant in the Confessional: Trade and Price in the Pre-Reformation Penitential Handbooks* (Leiden: E. J. Brill, 2003), esp. pp. 256–271.

85. On the pervasive theme of God's mercy and forgiveness in preaching, piety, and pastoral care in the decades prior to the Reformation, an emphasis that failed to convince or console Luther, see Berndt Hamm, "Normative Centering in the Fifteenth and Sixteenth Centuries: Observations on Religiosity, Theology, and Iconology," trans. John Frymire, in Hamm, *The Reformation of Faith in the Context of Late Medieval Theology and Piety,* ed. Robert J. Bast (Leiden: E. J. Brill, 2004), pp. 1–49.

86. Quoted in Jardine, *Worldly Goods,* p. 126.

87. On the absence of central, stable *political* institutions in the creation of the medieval Mediterranean and European trading network, and the implications of this fact for the "new institutional history" among social scientists, see Avner Greif, *Institutions and the Path to the Modern Economy: Lessons from Medieval Trade* (Cambridge: Cambridge University Press, 2006).

88. On sociological downward causation, a notion adapted from the philosophy of biology and belonging to the open causal systems characteristic of human

relationships and institutions rather than the closed causal systems character-
istic of natural phenomena as studied in the natural sciences, see Christian
Smith, *What Is a Person? Rethinking Humanity, Social Life, and the Moral
Good from the Person Up* (Chicago and London: University of Chicago
Press, 2010), pp. 40–42, 95–97, 292–295.

89. On the New Devout's deliberate manual labor and their understanding of its
religious significance, see Van Engen, *Sisters and Brothers*, pp. 188–193.

90. "In the all-important area of foodstuffs, a market sensitive to the interplay of
supply and common need and operating independently of external control
both existed and, by the fourteenth century, was commonly understood to
exist." Kaye, *Economy and Nature*, pp. 24–26, quotation on 26. On agricultural production for the market by some ecclesiastical houses and aristocratic
households in England by the late thirteenth century, see Dyer, *Standards of
Living*, p. 68.

91. This paragraph is indebted to Fanfani, *Catholicism, Protestantism, and Capitalism*, pp. 32–33, 44–45, 78–79, 138, 177.

92. Keith Wrightson, *Earthly Necessities: Economic and Social Lives in Early
Modern Britain* (New Haven, Conn., and London: Yale University Press,
2000), p. 29; see also pp. 57, 111.

93. Again, for this distinction between capitalist practices and capitalist society
I am indebted to Fanfani, *Catholicism, Protestantism, and Capitalism*, as
well as to Weber's distinction between the forms and spirit of capitalism. For a
few examples of the punishment of economic crimes by ecclesiastical and secular courts, see Tawney, *Religion*, pp. 50–53. Concerned to curtail infractions,
civic officials revised the statutes of sumptuary legislation thirty-four times in
fifteenth-century Florence. Frick, *Dressing Renaissance Florence*, p. 95.

94. Goldthwaite, *Economy*, p. 590.

95. Poggio Bracciolini, *De avaritia* [1429], in *Opera omnia*, ed. Riccardo Fubini,
vol. 1 (Turin: Bottega d'Erasmo, 1964), pp. 10–17, 17–29. On the context for
the composition of Poggio's dialogue, and his hostility toward the mendicant
friars, including the Observant Franciscans and Bernardino of Siena in particular, see John W. Oppel, "Poggio, San Bernardino of Siena, and the Dialogue *On Avarice*," *Studies in the Renaissance* [*Renaissance Quarterly*] 30:4,
(1977): 564–587.

96. Cynthia L. Polecritti, *Preaching Peace in Renaissance Italy: Bernardino of
Siena and His Audience* (Washington, D.C.: Catholic University of America
Press, 2000); Noonan, *Scholastic Analysis*, pp. 71–77; Grafton, *Alberti*,
pp. 176–177. See also Raymond de Roover, *San Bernardino of Siena and
Sant' Antonino of Florence: The Two Great Economic Thinkers of the Mid-
dle Ages* (Boston: Baker Library, Harvard Graduate School of Business
Administration, 1967).

97. Frick, *Dressing Renaissance Florence*, pp. 110–113, 180.

98. See the translated sources in *Selected Writings of Girolamo Savonarola: Religion and Politics, 1490–1498*, trans. and ed. Anne Borelli and Maria Pastore
Passaro, intro. Alison Brown (New Haven, Conn., and London: Yale University Press, 2006), esp. pp. 244–258, 315–348.

99. Tawney, *Religion,* p. 61.

100. Goldthwaite, *Economy,* p. 592 (quotation); Grafton, *Alberti,* pp. 180–181.

101. H. M. Robertson, *Aspects of the Rise of Economic Individualism: A Criticism of Max Weber and His School* (Cambridge: Cambridge University Press, 1933).

102. Because protagonists in the Peasants' War had been reared in a world in which Christianity was an institutionalized worldview, the very notion of seeking to distinguish their "religious" from their "economic" motives makes little sense, whether or not they explicitly adverted to scripture or an overtly religious rationale to support their claims and behaviors. For them as for their medieval predecessors, nothing lay outside God's creation or was beyond his concern and justice. Like the endeavor to distinguish "religious" from "political" motives in the Reformation, the distinction between "religion" and "economics" is an anachronistic retrojection of what subsequently became separated only as an outcome of the conflicts of the Reformation era and has consequently characterized Western modernity.

103. Jakob Strauss, *Haüptstück vnd artickel christenlicher leer wider den vnchrystenlyche[n] wuecher, darumb etlych pfaffen tzue Eyssenach so gar vnrywig vnd bemyet sint* [Erfurt: Wolfgang Stürmer, 1523], repr. in *Flugschriften der frühen Reformationsbewegung,* ed. Adolf Laube, vol. 2 (Berlin: Akademie-Verlag, 1983), p. 1074/20–21. Strauss followed this in 1524 with another, longer pamphlet against usury: *Das wucher zu nehmen vnd gebe[n] vnserm Christlichem glauben vnd brüderlich lieb . . . entgegen yst. . . .* ([Erfurt: Johann Loersfeld], 1524), repr. in *Flugschriften der Bauernkriegszeit,* ed. Adolf Laube and Hans Werner Seiffert (Berlin: Akademie-Verlag, 1978), pp. 178–189, 589–590.

104. Thomas Müntzer, *Hoch verursachte Schutzrede und antwwort, wider das Gaistloße Sanfftlebende fleysch zü Wittenberg. . . .* [1524], repr. in Müntzer, *Schriften und Briefe: Kritische Gesamtausgabe,* ed. Günther Franz (Gütersloh: Gerd Mohn, 1968), p. 329/9–10.

105. "Die 24 Artickel gemeiner Landschaft Salzburg" (May–June 1525), in *Quellen zur Geschichte des Bauernkrieges,* ed. Günther Franz (Munich: R. Oldenbourg, 1963), no. 94, p. 296/13–16.

106. *An die versamlung gemayner Pawerschafft so in Hochdeütscher Nation vnd vil anderer ort. . . .* [Nuremberg: Hieronymus Höltzel, 1525], repr. in *Flugschriften der Bauernkriegszeit,* ed. Laube and Seiffert, pp. 117/27–118/8, 582–585, at 117/27–29, 117/35–38, 118/6–8.

107. [Hans Hergot], *Von der newen wandlung eynes Christenlichen lebens* [Leipzig: Michael Blum, 1526/27], repr. in *Flugschriften der Bauernkriegszeit,* ed. Laube and Seiffert, pp. 547–557, 642–643 at p. 547/9–18. For "secten" at p. 547/14 as a misprint for "stedt," see p. 642 n. 2.

108. On Winstanley and other socioeconomically radical Protestants during the English Revolution, see Christopher Hill, *The English Bible and the Seventeenth-Century Revolution* (London: Allen Lane, 1993) and *The World Turned Upside Down: Radical Ideas during the English Revolution* (1972; Harmondsworth, U.K.: Penguin, 1975). See also Winstanley's extensive cor-

pus of writings, collected in *The Complete Works of Gerrard Winstanley*, 2 vols., ed. Thomas N. Corn, Ann Hughes, and David Loewenstein (Oxford: Oxford University Press, 2009).

109. Thomas Müntzer, *Außlegung des andern vnterschyds Danielis deß propheten gepredigt auffm schlos zu Alstet.* . . . (Allstedt: [Müntzer's press], 1524), repr. in *Flugschriften der frühen Reformationsbewegung*, ed. Laube, vol. 2, p. 985/7.

110. James M. Stayer, *The German Peasants' War and Anabaptist Community of Goods* (Montreal and Kingston, Ont.: McGill–Queen's University Press, 1991). Stayer has overturned an earlier historiography in which social history and Mennonite confessional history had convergently claimed a sharp separation between rebellious commoners and pacifist Anabaptists in the mid-1520s. For an example of this older picture from social-historical and confessional perspectives, see respectively Claus-Peter Clasen, *Anabaptism: A Social History, 1525–1618: Switzerland, Austria, Moravia, South and Central Germany* (Ithaca, N.Y., and London: Cornell University Press, 1972), pp. 152–157, and Harold S. Bender, *The Anabaptist Vision* (Scottdale, Pa., and Waterloo, Ont.: Herald Press, 1944), pp. 10–11.

111. Stayer, *German Peasants' War*; see also C. Arnold Snyder, *Anabaptist History and Theology: An Introduction* (Kitchener, Ont.: Pandora Press, 1995), pp. 225–252, quotation on 228. Snyder is explicit about the inseparability of salvation from concrete, economic realities among Anabaptists on pp. 227, 247. Werner Packull has extended Stayer's paradigm in his important study of the Anabaptist communities (including the Austerlitz Brethren, Gabrielites, and Philipites) that in addition to the Hutterites practiced communal ownership of goods before their expulsion from Moravia in 1535. See Werner O. Packull, *Hutterite Beginnings: Communitarian Experiments during the Reformation* (Baltimore and London: Johns Hopkins University Press, 1995). On the flourishing of the Hutterites under the leadership of Leonhard Lanzenstil, Pieter Riedemann, Leonhard Dax, and especially Peter Walpot from the 1550s until Walpot's death in 1578, and indeed into the early 1590s, see Leonard Gross, *The Golden Years of the Hutterites: The Witness and Thought of the Communal Moravian Anabaptists during the Walpot Era, 1565–1578*, rev. ed. (Kitchener, Ont.: Pandora Press; Scottdale, Pa.: Herald Press, 1998).

112. Menno Simons, *Van het rechte christen gheloove.* . . . ([Franeker: Jan Hendricksz], 1556), sigs. J5r–v, K2. The first edition appeared around 1542, published in Antwerp by Henrick Peetersen van Middelborch. For both printers, see Paul Valkema Blouw, "Drukkers voor Menno Simons en Dirk Philips," *Doopsgezinde Bijdragen*, n.s., 17 (1991), 73.

113. Snyder, *Anabaptist History and Theology*, p. 248.

114. Anne Goldgar, *Tulipmania: Money, Honor, and Knowledge in the Dutch Golden Age* (Chicago: University of Chicago Press, 2007), pp. 132, 149–151, 152. On the socioeconomic assimilation of Mennonites in the Dutch Republic, see Mary Sprunger, "Hoe rijke mennisten de hemel verdienden: Een eerste verkenning van de betrokkenheid van aanzienlijke doopsgezinden bij het

Amsterdamse zakenleven in de Goude Eeuw," *Doopsgezinde Bijdragen,* n.s., 18 (1992), 39–52; Sprunger, "Waterlanders and the Dutch Golden Age: A Case Study on Mennonite Involvement in Seventeenth-Century Dutch Trade and Industry as One of the Earliest Examples of Socio-Economic Assimilation," in *From Martyr to Muppy: A Historical Introduction to Cultural Assimilation Processes of a Religious Minority in the Netherlands; The Mennonites,* ed. Alastair Hamilton, Sjouke Voolstra, and Piet Visser (Amsterdam: Amsterdam University Press, 1994), pp. 133–148.

115. Martin Luther, *Von Kaufshandlung und Wucher* [1524], in WA, vol. 15 (Weimar: Hermann Böhlaus Nachfolger, 1899), pp. 294–295, quotations at 294/22–23, 295/26–27; cf. Luther, *(Großer) Sermon von dem Wucher* [1520], in WA, vol. 6 (Weimar: Hermann Böhlau, 1888), pp. 33–60. See also Luther's *(Kleiner) Sermon von dem Wucher* [1519], in WA, vol. 6, pp. 1–8; *Eyn Sermon von dem unrechten Mammon* [1522], in WA, vol. 10/3 (Weimar: Hermann Böhlaus Nachfolger, 1905), pp. 283–292; and *An die Pfarrherrn, wider den Wucher zu predigen* [1540], in WA, vol. 51 (Weimar: Hermann Böhlaus Nachfolger, 1914), pp. 325–424. For Luther's view that avarice contradicted faith, see Ricardo Willy Reith, "Luther on Greed," *Lutheran Quarterly* 15 (2001): 336–351, which draws on a wider range of sources than Luther's sermons and treatises pertaining explicitly to usury and commerce; and see also, much more extensively, Hans-Jürgen Prien, *Luthers Wirtschaftsethik* (Göttingen: Vandenhoeck & Ruprecht, 1992).

116. Huldrych Zwingli, *Von göttlicher und menschlicher grechtigheit. . . .* [1523], in ZW, vol. 2, ed. Emil Egli and Georg Finsler, in CR, vol. 89 (Leipzig: M. Heinsius Nachfolger, 1908), p. 516/10–13.

117. Martin Bucer, *De regno Christi Iesu servatoris nostri, libri II. . . .* (Basel: Johannes Oporinus, 1557), bk. 2, chap. 57, p. 229; see also bk. 2, chap. 50, pp. 203–205, on the reform of commerce ("De reformanda mercatura"), as well as Tawney, *Religion,* p. 142. On the sale of monastic lands as well as chantry holdings, see Wrightson, *Earthly Necessities,* pp. 141–145.

118. Robert Crowley, *An informacion and Peticion agaynst the oppressours of the poore Commons of thys Realme. . . .* (London: John Daye, [1548]), sig. A4v. Wrightson quotes part of this passage in *Earthly Necessities,* p. 151, and discusses the Commonwealthsmen at pp. 149–152; see also Tawney, *Religion,* pp. 144–150.

119. John Calvin, *Institutio Christianae religionis* [1559], in CO, vol. 2, ed. G. Baum, E. Cunitz, and E. Reuss, vol. 30 in CR (Brunswick: C. A. Schwetschke & Sohn, 1864), 3.10.2, col. 529; 3.7.1, col. 506; 3.10.3, col. 530.

120. See Jeannine E. Olson, *Calvin and Social Welfare: Deacons and the Bourse française* (Selinsgrove, Pa.: Susquehanna University Press, 1989).

121. Mark Valeri, "Religion, Discipline, and the Economy in Calvin's Geneva," *Sixteenth Century Journal* 28:1 (1997): 128 (quotation), 131.

122. See in general the classic work by André Biéler, *La pensée économique et sociale de Calvin* (Geneva: Librairie de l'Université, 1959), as well as a more condensed reprise of some of the same themes in Biéler, *The Social Humanism of Calvin,* trans. Paul T. Fuhrmann (Richmond, Va.: John Knox Press,

1964). See also François Dermange, "Calvin's View of Property: A Duty Rather Than a Right," in *John Calvin Rediscovered: The Impact of His Social and Economic Thought*, ed. Edward Dommen and James D. Bratt (Louisville, Ky., and London: Westminster John Knox Press, 2007), pp. 33–51.

123. Calvin, *Institutio*, in *CO*, vol. 2, 3.7.8, col. 512. On the distinction between usury and production loans, see Biéler, *Social Humanism*, p. 56.

124. Robertson, *Aspects*, pp. 135–136; see also Jardine, *Worldly Goods*, pp. 328–329; and for a detailed study, see Johann Peter Wurm, *Johannes Eck und der oberdeutsche Zinsstreit, 1513–1515* (Münster: Aschendorff, 1997).

125. On the Jesuits' involvement in economic theorizing in the later sixteenth century, see Robertson, *Aspects*, pp. 103–110, 136–160.

126. Mark Valeri, *Heavenly Merchandize: How Religion Shaped Commerce in Puritan America* (Princeton, N.J.: Princeton University Press, 2010), pp. 26–35, 50–67.

127. See Philip Benedict, "The Historiography of Continental Calvinism," in *Weber's Protestant Ethic*, ed. Lehmann and Roth, pp. 312–318; Robert S. DuPlessis, *Transitions to Capitalism in Early Modern Europe* (Cambridge: Cambridge University Press, 1997), pp. 135–136; Jelle C. Riemersma, *Religious Factors in Early Dutch Capitalism, 1550–1650* (The Hague: Mouton, 1967); Simon Schama, *The Embarrassment of Riches: An Interpretation of Dutch Culture in the Golden Age* (New York: Knopf, 1987), pp. 329–341; Gordon Marshall, *Presbyteries and Profits: Calvinism and the Development of Capitalism in Scotland, 1560–1707* (Oxford: Clarendon Press, 1980); Bernard Bailyn, *The New England Merchants in the Seventeenth Century* (Cambridge, Mass.: Harvard University Press, 1955), pp. 16–111; James A. Henretta, "The Protestant Ethic and the Reality of Capitalism in Colonial America," in *Weber's Protestant Ethic*, ed. Lehmann and Roth, pp. 327–346; Mark Valeri, "Religious Discipline and the Market: Puritans and the Issue of Usury," *William and Mary Quarterly* 54:4 (1997): 747–751, 762–766. Valeri's article shows the rootedness of the Great Migration Puritans' economic views in the English Puritanism of the preceding half century and rightly notes their (and Calvin's) emphasis on a corporate, social ethics, as opposed to Henretta's following of Weber's erroneous emphasis on anxiety-ridden Calvinist individuals. See also Valeri, *Heavenly Merchandize*.

128. Valeri, *Heavenly Merchandize*, p. 233.

129. John Bossy, *Christianity in the West, 1400–1700* (Oxford: Oxford University Press, 1987), pp. 153–161.

130. "...assertam et defensam oporteat per mortem quoque, etiam si mundus totus non solum conflictari et tumultuari debeat, verum etiam in unum cahos ruere et in nihilum redigi." Luther, *De servo arbitrio* [1525], in *WA*, vol. 18 (Weimar: Hermann Böhlaus Nachfolger, 1908), p. 625/15–17.

131. On the conditions among German laborers in the late nineteenth and early twentieth centuries, see the introduction to *The German Worker: Working-Class Autobiographies from the Age of Industrialization*, ed. and trans. Alfred Kelly (Berkeley and Los Angeles: University of California Press, 1989),

pp. 1–45, as well as the excerpts in this collection from the male and female workers themselves.

132. Philipp Melanchthon, *Loci communes rerum theologicarum, seu hypotyposes theologicae* [1521], in *CR,* vol. 21, ed. H. E. Bindseil (Braunschweig: C. A. Schwetschke & Sohn, 1854), cols. 90, 92.

133. Thomas Hobbes, *Leviathan* [1651], ed. Richard Tuck (1991; Cambridge: Cambridge University Press, 1996), 1.11, p. 70.

134. "A la espada y el compass / Más y más y más y más." Quoted in J. H. Elliott, *The Old World and the New, 1492–1650* (Cambridge: Cambridge University Press, 1970), p. 53.

135. The first quoted phrase is Huizinga's, quoted in Maarten Prak, *The Dutch Republic in the Seventeenth Century* (Cambridge: Cambridge University Press, 2005), p. 3; the second quoted phrase is Prak's, ibid., p. 4. On the Dutch Republic's successful war financing, see ibid., pp. 75–84, and Harold Cook, *Matters of Exchange: Commerce, Medicine, and Science in the Dutch Golden Age* (New Haven, Conn., and London: Yale University Press, 2007), pp. 59–60.

136. Jan de Vries and Ad van der Woude, *The First Modern Economy: Success, Failure, and Perseverance of the Dutch Economy, 1500–1815* (Cambridge: Cambridge University Press, 1997), pp. 279–285, 362–369, quotation on 364.

137. On the publications and disruptions associated with the disagreements between Remonstrants and Counter-Remonstrants from 1616–1618, see Jonathan I. Israel, *The Dutch Republic: Its Rise, Greatness, and Fall, 1477–1806* (Oxford: Clarendon Press, 1995), pp. 433–444; on the relationship between the Amsterdam *beurs* and *wisselbank,* see Schama, *Embarrassment of Riches,* pp. 346–350.

138. Cook, *Matters of Exchange,* p. 60.

139. Rembrandt's painting is reproduced and discussed in Benjamin J. Kaplan, *Divided by Faith: Religious Conflict and the Practice of Toleration in Early Modern Europe* (Cambridge, Mass., and London: Belknap Press of Harvard University Press, 2007), pp. 237–238, and in S. Zijlstra, *Om de ware gemeente en de oude gronden: Geschiedenis van de dopersen in de Nederlanden, 1531–1675* (Hilversum: Verloren; Leeuwarden: Fryske Akademy, 2000), p. 481. For Temple's observations, discussed in Chapter 3, see William Temple, *Observations upon the United Provinces of the Netherlands* (London: A. Maxwell for Sa. Gellibrand, 1673), pp. 181–184. Schama, *Embarrassment of Riches.*

140. Thieleman Jans van Braght, *Het Bloedigh Tooneel der Doops-gesinde, en Weereloose Christenen.* . . . (Dordrecht: Jacob Braat, 1660), sigs. [(\*)4v]–(\*\*)2, quotations on [(\*)4v], (\*\*)1v. Van Braght's massive work, the culmination of the Dutch Mennonite martyrological tradition, was republished in two luxurious, illustrated folio volumes in Amsterdam in 1685. See Brad S. Gregory, "Anabaptist Martyrdom: Imperatives, Experience, and Memorialization," in *A Companion to Anabaptism and Spiritualism, 1521–1700,* ed. John D. Roth and James M. Stayer (Leiden: E. J. Brill, 2007), pp. 467–468,

492–502; Gregory, *Salvation at Stake: Christian Martyrdom in Early Modern Europe* (Cambridge, Mass., and London: Harvard University Press, 1999), pp. 231–249.

141. Van Braght, *Bloedigh Tooneel*, sig. (**)2.

142. Cook, *Matters of Exchange*, pp. 68–73.

143. On Dutch religious choice and the complex combination of religious tolerance and intolerance in the United Provinces in the seventeenth century, see the nuanced study by Judith Pollmann, *Religious Choice in the Dutch Republic: The Reformation of Arnoldus Buchelius, 1565–1641* (Manchester: Manchester University Press; New York: St. Martin's Press, 1999); on the large numbers of Dutch Christians who deliberately opted for no formal church affiliation, see Geoffrey Parker, *The Dutch Revolt* (1977; Harmondsworth, U.K.: Penguin, 1981), pp. 154–155; Kaplan, *Divided by Faith*, p. 242.

144. Prak, *Dutch Republic*, pp. 87–89, 122; Goldgar, *Tulipmania*, pp. 203–204.

145. Goldgar, *Tulipmania*, pp. 2, 133–134, 187, 229–230.

146. Prak, *Dutch Republic*, p. 89.

147. "What is taste, after all, but one way of transforming physical objects into high culture, thereby rationalizing the feeling of possessiveness, the sense of attachment to physical objects? And it was with taste that one established social credentials." Goldthwaite, *Wealth*, p. 249.

148. Hobbes, *Leviathan*, ed. Tuck, 1.15, p. 105; 1.10, p. 63 (italics and capitals in original).

149. Temple, *Observations*, pp. 183–184 (italics in original).

150. Kaplan, *Divided by Faith*.

151. On military suppliers, see Geoffrey Parker, *The Military Revolution: Military Innovation and the Rise of the West, 1500–1800* (Cambridge: Cambridge University Press, 1988), pp. 64–65; for the example of Elias Trip, whose activities as a munitions supplier during the Eighty Years War with Spain contributed to his rise from the son of a barge captain to one of the wealthiest men in Amsterdam, see Prak, *Dutch Republic*, pp. 122–123.

152. On the pioneering theoreticians of religious toleration in the early modern period, see Perez Zagorin, *How the Idea of Religious Toleration Came to the West* (Princeton, N.J.: Princeton University Press, 2003).

153. Mokyr, *Gifts of Athena*, and Mokyr, *The Enlightened Economy: An Economic History of Britain, 1700–1850* (New Haven, Conn., and London: Yale University Press, 2010).

154. For households rather than autonomous individuals as the key to reciprocally related, rising production and consumption in the industrious revolution, see de Vries, *Industrious Revolution*, pp. 73–185.

155. See Woodruff D. Smith, *Consumption and the Making of Respectability, 1600–1800* (New York and London: Routledge, 2002); see also Linda Levy Peck, *Consuming Splendor: Society and Culture in Seventeenth-Century England* (Cambridge: Cambridge University Press, 2005); John Brewer, *The Pleasures of the Imagination: English Culture in the Eighteenth Century* (Chicago: University of Chicago Press, 1997); Daniel Roche, *A History of*

*Everyday Things: The Birth of Consumption in France, 1600–1800*, trans. Brian Pearce (Cambridge: Cambridge University Press, 2000).

156. For the Vincentians, see Luigi Mezzadri and José María Román, *The Vincentians: A General History of the Congregation of the Mission*, vol. 1, *From the Foundation to the End of the Seventeenth Century, 1625–1697*, ed. John E. Rybolt and Joseph E. Dunne, trans. Robert Cummings (Hyde Park, N.Y.: New City Press, 2009).

157. Joyce Appleby, "Consumption in Early Modern Social Thought," in *Consumption and the World of Goods*, ed. John Brewer and Roy Porter (New York and London: Routledge, 1993), p. 169. Similarly and more assertively, referring to Americans in the 1820s and 1830s, Charles Sellers writes that "only by headlong flight into domesticity, benevolence, and feeling could they tolerate the market's calculating egotism." Sellers, *The Market Revolution: Jacksonian America, 1815–1846* (New York: Oxford University Press, 1991), p. 202.

158. N[icholas] B[arbon], *A Discourse of Trade* (London: Tho. Milbourn, 1690), pp. 15, 35 (my emphases). On Barbon, who became wealthy as a real estate developer in London after the fire of 1666, see R. D. Sheldon, "Barbon, Nicholas (1637/1640–1698/9)," in *ODNB*, ed. H. C. G. Matthew and Brian Harrison (Oxford: Oxford University Press, 2004); online ed., ed. Lawrence Goldman, January 2008, http://www.oxforddnb.com/view/article/1334 (accessed 23 February 2010).

159. Valeri, *Heavenly Merchandize*, pp. 126–137, 143–145, 152–157, 164–165, 167–168, 171–176.

160. Barbon astutely remarked that "Fashion or the alteration of Dress, is a great Promoter of *Trade*, because it occasions the Expence of Cloaths, before the Old ones are worn out: It is the Spirit and Life of *Trade*; It makes a Circulation, and gives a Value by Turns, to all sorts of Commodities; keeps the great Body of *Trade* in Motion." Barbon, *Discourse*, p. 65 (italics in original).

161. Adam Smith, *The Theory of Moral Sentiments* [1759], ed. Knud Haakonssen (Cambridge: Cambridge University Press, 2002), 1.3.2.1, p. 62.

162. Cook, *Matters of Exchange*, pp. 53–54.

163. De Vries, *Industrious Revolution*, p. 55; Schama, *Embarrassment of Riches*, pp. 310–313.

164. Cook, *Matters of Exchange*, p. 53.

165. See, for example, Michael North, *Art and Commerce in the Dutch Golden Age*, trans. Catherine Hill (New Haven, Conn., and London: Yale University Press, 1997); Mariët Westermann, *A Worldly Art: The Dutch Republic, 1585–1718* (New York: Abrams, 1996); de Vries, *Industrious Revolution*, pp. 55–56; Schama, *Embarrassment of Riches*, pp. 313, 318–319.

166. Schama, *Embarrassment of Riches*, p. 314, with the household items on 313–314. On "splendor" as the interior, domestic parallel to the Aristotelian virtue of magnificence, see Goldthwaite, *Wealth*, p. 249.

167. See Brady, "Rise of Merchant Empires," in *Political Economy*, ed. Tracy, pp. 148–155.

168. Hirschman, *Passions*, p. 62.

169. This is the principal argument of Liah Greenfeld, *The Spirit of Capitalism: Nationalism and Economic Growth* (Cambridge, Mass., and London: Harvard University Press, 2000); see also Fanfani, *Catholicism, Protestantism, and Capitalism,* pp. 87–118. Speaking of the English in the mid-eighteenth century, Wrightson notes that "as with the Dutch a century earlier, the pursuit of profit and the pursuit of power seem to have gone hand in hand." Wrightson, *Earthly Necessities,* p. 260; and more generally for the relationship between the British state and economic ambition between 1650 and 1750, see ibid., pp. 249–268.

170. For a detailed analysis of the religious and political aspects of the first two wars, see Steven C. A. Pincus, *Protestantism and Patriotism: Ideologies and the Making of English Foreign Policy, 1650–1668* (Cambridge: Cambridge University Press, 1996); see also J. R. Jones, *The Anglo-Dutch Wars of the Seventeenth Century* (London and New York: Longman, 1996); and for the wars from the Dutch side, see Israel, *Dutch Republic,* pp. 713–717, 766–774, 812–813.

171. Philip S. Gorski, "The Little Divergence: The Protestant Reformation and Economic Hegemony in Early Modern Europe," in *Protestant Ethic,* ed. Swatos and Kaelber, pp. 180–181. The phrase "fiscal-military state" to describe eighteenth-century Britain is John Brewer's; see Brewer, *The Sinews of Power: War, Money and the English State, 1688–1783* (New York: Knopf, 1989), with discussion of the navy at pp. 9–12, 33–37. Brewer notes that "only after 1650 did the government have both the desire and the capacity to pursue a bellicose policy of commercial development." Ibid., p. 11.

172. De Vries and van der Woude, *First Modern Economy,* pp. 673–683. Liah Greenfeld has argued, against de Vries and van der Woude, that the Dutch Republic's lack of *sustained* economic growth disqualifies it as the "first modern economy," which was rather England because of the latter's combination of continuous economic growth and overt nationalism. Greenfeld, *Spirit of Capitalism,* pp. 59–104. What different historians regard or do not regard as "modern" does not, of course, affect the extent to which Dutch economic behaviors in the first half of the seventeenth century were taken up by the English.

173. Brady, "Rise of Merchant Empires," in *Political Economy,* ed. Tracy, pp. 151–152; see also Valeri, *Heavenly Merchandize.*

174. Hirschman, *Passions,* pp. 48–56, 81–93, 100–113.

175. Smith, *Theory of Moral Sentiments* [1759], ed. Haakonssen, 1.3.2.1, p. 61.

176. See Carole Shammas, *The Pre-Industrial Consumer in England and America* (1990; Los Angeles: Figueroa Press, 2008); Ann Smart Martin, *Buying into the World of Goods: Early Consumers in Backcountry Virginia* (Baltimore and London: Johns Hopkins University Press, 2008); Richard Bushman, *The Refinement of America: Persons, Houses, Cities* (1993; New York: Vintage, 1994); T. H. Breen, *The Marketplace of Revolution: How Consumer Politics Shaped American Independence* (New York: Oxford University Press, 2004), which argues that American colonists' common experience as consumers precipitated their concerted rebellion against British taxation in the early

1770s; Joyce Appleby, *Capitalism and a New Social Order: The Republican Vision of the 1790s* (New York: NYU Press, 1984); *God and Mammon: Protestants, Money, and the Market, 1790–1860,* ed. Mark A. Noll (New York: Oxford University Press, 2001); Sellers, *Market Revolution;* Stewart Davenport, *Friends of the Unrighteous Mammon: Northern Christians and Market Capitalism, 1815–1860* (Chicago and London: University of Chicago Press, 2008).

177. For the 1880s through the 1920s, see William Leach, *Land of Desire: Merchants, Power, and the Rise of a New American Culture* (New York: Vintage Books, 1994); on the advent of modern, mass-culture advertising in the 1920s, see Stuart Ewen, *Captains of Consciousness: Advertising and the Social Roots of the Consumer Culture* (1976; New York: Basic Books, 2001); on the twentieth century, see Lebergott, *Pursuing Happiness;* and for consumer culture after World War II, see Lizabeth Cohen, *A Consumer's Republic: The Politics of Mass Consumption in Postwar America* (New York: Vintage Books, 2004).

178. See Victoria de Grazia, *Irresistible Empire: America's Advance through 20th-Century Europe* (Cambridge, Mass., and London: Belknap Press of Harvard University Press, 2005).

179. Charles-Louis de Secondat, Baron de Montesquieu, *The Spirit of the Laws* [1748], ed. and trans. Anne M. Cohler, Basia Carolyn Miller, and Harold Samuel Stone (Cambridge: Cambridge University Press, 1989), 4.20.4, p. 340.

180. "The medieval theorist condemned as a sin precisely that effort to achieve a continuous and unlimited increase in material wealth which modern societies applaud as a quality, and the vices for which he reserved his most merciless denunciations were the more refined and subtle of the economic virtues." Tawney, *Religion,* pp. 35–36.

181. Valeri, *Heavenly Merchandize,* pp. 234–235, 240–248. On the same point, de Vries notes that "by the 1740s, the Quakers of Pennsylvania were as much in need of a Great Awakening as were the Calvinists of New England. In neither case did a new-found spirituality slow the refinement and enlargement of their material cultures." De Vries, *Industrious Revolution,* p. 172.

182. "The dignity of the national identity—which is a distinctive characteristic of the national experience—lies at the basis of the commitment to the nation, that is, to the common good, among the member population. . . . The general good, and specifically the prestige, of the nation is the ultimate value that justifies, and renders *both ethical and rational,* the unending striving for ever-increasing wealth." Greenfeld, *Spirit of Capitalism,* p. 96 (my emphasis).

183. On utilitarianism as the de facto morality of modern economics, and its incompatibility with Aristotle's economic views and Aristotelian moral philosophy, see Meikle, *Aristotle's Economic Thought,* pp. 38–42, 106–108, 177, 180, 189–196.

184. David Hume, "Of the Rise and Progress of the Arts and Sciences" [1742], in *Essays Moral, Political, and Literary,* ed. Eugene F. Miller, rev. ed. (Indianapolis: Liberty Fund, 1987), p. 113; Hume, *A Treatise of Human Nature* [1739–1740], ed. L. A. Selby-Bigge, 2nd ed., ed. P. H. Nidditch (Oxford: Clarendon Press, 1978), 2.3.3, p. 415; 3.2.2, pp. 491–492.

185. Despite the significant growth in English trade in the first four decades of the seventeenth century, the English "still played second fiddle to their Dutch competitors in most of the markets they had entered." Wrightson, *Earthly Necessities,* pp. 180–181, quotation on 181; see also pp. 199, 228, 242, 252, 260. On the English "quickly learning from Dutch success" in economic matters in the seventeenth century, see Steve Pincus, *1688: The First Modern Revolution* (New Haven, Conn., and London: Yale University Press, 2009), pp. 50–59, 81–87, quotation on 51. For the Dutch envy that Sir Walter Raleigh articulated in 1605, see Greenfeld, *Spirit of Capitalism,* pp. 42–43. On the English competition with and surpassing of the Dutch by the end of the seventeenth century, see de Vries and van der Woude, *First Modern Economy,* pp. 287–289, 484–486. For the Dutch influence on England more broadly in the seventeenth and eighteenth centuries, see also Lisa Jardine, *Going Dutch: How England Plundered Holland's Glory* (New York: HarperCollins, 2009). On the protectionist character of British commerce and early industry before the 1850s, see Ha-Joon Chang, *Kicking Away the Ladder: Development Strategy in Historical Perspective* (London: Anthem Press, 2003), pp. 19–24, 60–61.

186. For the pioneering developments in French papermaking that made use of late seventeenth-century Dutch technology, see Leonard N. Rosenband, *Papermaking in Eighteenth-Century France: Management, Labor, and Revolution at the Montgolfier Mill, 1761–1805* (Baltimore and London: Johns Hopkins University Press, 2000); see also Rosenband, "Becoming Competitive: England's Papermaking Apprenticeship, 1700–1800," in *The Mindful Hand: Inquiry and Invention from the Late Renaissance to Early Industrialisation,* ed. Lissa Roberts, Simon Shaffer, and Peter Dear (Amsterdam: Koninklijke Nederlandse Akademie van Wetenschappen, 2007), pp. 379–401.

187. See Mokyr, *Industrial Enlightenment* and *Enlightened Economy;* Landes, *Unbound Prometheus* and *Wealth and Poverty;* Appleby, *Relentless Revolution.*

188. Hayek, *Road to Serfdom,* ed. Caldwell, p. 57. Acton's remark originally appeared in his "Review of Sir Erskine May's Democracy in Europe" [1878].

189. De Vries's consideration of confessionalization as the consistent expression of the industrious revolution is problematic, in part because he frames the latter's emergence as an expansion of classical and aristocratic ideals of leisure rather than in relationship to the Reformation era and the traditional embeddedness of economics within Christian ethics. De Vries, *Industrious Revolution,* pp. 40–58, with the discussion of confessionalization on 56–57.

190. For a few examples that embody the conviction that God wants you to be rich, see Derek Prince, *God's Plan for Your Money* (New Kensington, Pa.: Whitaker House, 1995); Dwight Nichols, *God's Plan for Your Finances* (New Kensington, Pa.: Whitaker House, 1998); and a work that has sold over 150,000 copies, is in its nineteenth printing, and has been translated into nine other languages, Jack Hartman, *Trust God for Your Finances* (Dunedin, Fla.: Lamplight Publications, 1993).

191. Alexis de Tocqueville, *Democracy in America,* vol. 2 [1840], ed. J. P. Mayer, trans. George Lawrence (New York: HarperCollins, 2000), 2.11, p. 534.

192. On the American consumerist conquest of Europe that began in the early twentieth century and gained much momentum after World War II until it

had become largely hegemonic by the 1970s, see de Grazia, *Irresistible Empire,* with the specific point about the reversal at pp. 4–5, quotation on p. 3. On contemporary European secularism and its relationship to affluence, see Phil Zuckerman, *Society without God: What the Least Religious Nations Can Tell Us about Contentment* (New York: NYU Press, 2008), a sociological study of two of Europe's most secularized countries, Denmark and Sweden.

193. De Grazia, *Irresistible Empire,* quotation on p. 11.

194. See the essays in *Does Technology Drive History? The Dilemma of Technological Determinism,* ed. Merritt Roe Smith and Leo Marx (Cambridge, Mass.: MIT Press, 1994), especially Robert Heilbroner's classic essay, "Do Machines Make History?" at pp. 53–66, originally published in *Technology and Culture* 8 (July 1967): 335–345. I thank Len Rosenband for calling this collection to my attention, and for countless discussions about the relationship among economic history, society, and morality. The primacy of consumer demand over the production traditionally emphasized by economists and economic historians has been an important feature of the scholarship on the history of consumerism for several decades. Significant early contributions in what has become a historiographical flood since the early 1990s include Elizabeth Waterman Gilboy, "Demand as a Factor in the Industrial Revolution," in *The Causes of the Industrial Revolution in England,* ed. R. M. Hartwell (London: Methuen, 1967), pp. 121–138, and Eric L. Jones, "The Fashion Manipulators: Consumer Tastes and British Industries, 1660–1800," in *Business Enterprise and Economic Change,* ed. Louis P. Cain and Paul J. Uselding (Kent State, Ohio: Kent State University Press, 1973), pp. 198–226.

195. That the pressures faced by industrial working-class families antedated the Industrial Revolution and were already faced by their predecessors as a result of the industrious revolution, as de Vries notes, helps to correct a historiography that endeavors to trace modern familial dysfunction to the effects of industrialization. De Vries, *Industrious Revolution,* pp. 186–187. But had nineteenth-century working-class family members been aware of the fact noted by de Vries, it is hard to see what amelioration or consolation it would have afforded. De Vries understatedly concedes that "the industrious household had both its positive and negative features, and industrial society added a new dimension to these features." Ibid., p. 187. De Vries's critique of analyses of twentieth-century consumerism is structurally analogous, correcting the historiography with reference to much longer-term historical trajectories, but not denying the reality of the phenomena under discussion. Ibid., pp. 242–243.

196. Davenport, *Friends,* pp. 35–84; for Chalmers, see Boyd Hilton, *The Age of Atonement: The Influence of Evangelicalism on Social and Economic Thought, 1785–1865* (Oxford: Clarendon Press, 1988).

197. For Müntzer's influence on Hut, see the magisterial study by Gottfried Seebaß, *Müntzers Erbe: Werk, Leben und Theologie des Hans Hut* (Gütersloh: Gütersloher Verlagshaus, 2002). The work was originally Seebaß's *Habilitationsschrift* (1972).

198. "From the mid-eighteenth century onward, the striking fact of American colonial material culture was not its self-sufficient rusticity but its market dependence." De Vries, *Industrious Revolution*, p. 172. For the penetration of consumer practices into rural Virginia, see Martin, *Buying into the World of Goods*; see also, more broadly, David Jaffee, *A New Nation of Goods: The Material Culture of Early America* (Philadelphia and Oxford: University of Pennsylvania Press, 2010).

199. Tocqueville, *Democracy in America*, vol. 2, ed. Mayer, 2.10, p. 532. Similarly, "one usually finds that love of money is either the chief or a secondary motive at the bottom of everything the Americans do. This gives a family likeness to all their passions and soon makes them wearisome to contemplate." Ibid., 3.17, p. 615.

200. On the persistent yet malleable and contested variations in Americans' understanding of themselves as providentially favored by God, see Nicholas Guyatt, *Providence and the Invention of the United States, 1607–1876* (Cambridge: Cambridge University Press, 2007).

201. On the "breadwinner-homemaker household" that superseded the industrious household and predominated in northwestern Europe and North America from c. 1850 into the 1950s, see de Vries, *Industrious Revolution*, pp. 186–237. Against arguments that contend that wives were forced from market labor into the domestic sphere by a resurgent patriarchy and/or the (abstract) demands of capitalism, de Vries contends that the new household arrangement was driven by "the attractive power of the new consumer clusters" to all family members, which included greater domestic comfort, better health, and a concern for respectability. Ibid., pp. 189–199, 210–237, quotation on 237. The new familial pattern presupposed and "sought to exploit the new opportunities and parry the new risks generated by the market economy unfolding beyond its doors," which supported "the standard of living to which people aspired," made possible above all by higher industrial wages for male heads of households. Ibid., p. 237.

202. Colin Campbell, *The Romantic Ethic and the Spirit of Modern Consumerism* (Oxford: Blackwell, 1987), esp. pp. 77–95, 190–201. Campbell's attempt to link seventeenth- and eighteenth-century English Protestantism to later Romantic consumerism is problematic; ibid., pp. 99–137.

203. In Twitchell's estimation, "opuluxe *is* one dimensional, shallow, ahistorical, without memory, and expendable. But it is also strangely democratic and unifying. If what you want is peace on earth, a unifying system that transcends religious, cultural, and caste differences, well, whoops! here it is.... Forget happiness; if decreasing pain and discomfort is a goal, consumption of the 'finer things' has indeed done what governments, churches, schools, and even laws have promised. Far more than these other systems, betterment through consumption has delivered the goods.... We have made consuming stuff, most of it unnecessary stuff, the dominant prerequisite of organized society." Twitchell, *Living It Up*, pp. 274–275, 285, 288 (italics in original). Bauman is rather less sanguine: "The greater our individual freedom, the less it is relevant to the world in which we practice it. The more tolerant the world becomes of the choices we make, the less the game, our playing it, and

the way we play it are open to our choice. No longer does the world appear amenable to kneading and molding; instead, it seems to tower above us— heavy, thick, and inert, opaque, impenetrable and impregnable, stubborn and insensitive to any of our intentions, resistant to our attempts to render it more hospitable to human coexistence." Bauman, *Ethics,* pp. 110–111.

204. John Maynard Keynes, "Economic Possibilities for Our Grandchildren" [1930], in *Essays in Persuasion* (1931; New York: W. W. Norton, 1963), p. 369. A generation before, even the steel magnate Andrew Carnegie, at the time one of the wealthiest men in the world, had made less strident but similar, self-deceived predictions about the United States: "We are yet as a nation in the heyday of youth. In time we shall tone down and live simpler lives and create different standards. Wealth will be dethroned as higher tastes prevail, its pursuit becoming less absorbing and less esteemed. . . . The making of money as an aim will then be rated as an ignoble ambition." Andrew Carnegie, "The Gospel of Wealth II" [1906], in *The "Gospel of Wealth" Essays and Other Writings,* ed. David Nasaw (New York: Penguin, 2006), pp. 66–67.

205. On "liquid modernity" as associated with a consumerist society, as opposed to "solid modernity" as characteristic of industrial society, see Bauman, *Ethics,* pp. 138–139, 184–188; see also, among Bauman's many other works, *Liquid Modernity* (Cambridge: Polity Press; Malden, Mass.: Blackwell, 2000).

206. Charles Taylor, *A Secular Age* (Cambridge, Mass., and London: Belknap Press of Harvard University Press, 2007).

207. Neil Postman, *Amusing Ourselves to Death: Public Discourse in the Age of Show Business* (New York: Viking, 1985).

208. See *Catholic Social Thought: The Documentary Heritage,* ed. David O'Brien and Thomas A. Shannon (Maryknoll, N.Y.: Orbis Books, 1992); Benedict XVI, *Charity in Truth (Caritas in Veritate)* (San Francisco: Ignatius Press, 2009). The official condemnation of certain elements of liberation theology in 1984 by the Roman Catholic Church's Congregation for the Doctrine of the Faith, then under the secretaryship of Joseph Ratzinger, represent not a repudiation of the traditional Christian concern for the poor, but rather a recognition of the incompatibility between certain basic Marxist assumptions and the church's truth claims about reality, human nature, and human flourishing. See "Instruction on Certain Aspects of the 'Theology of Liberation,'" at http://www.vatican.va/roman_curia/congregations/cfaith/documents/ rc_con_cfaith_doc_19840806_theology-liberation_en.html (accessed 25 February 2010). Although material things are indispensable to human flourishing in Catholic Christianity, they are to be always subordinated to the shared life of faith, practice of the virtues, and love of God and neighbor in light of the hope of eternal salvation; according to Catholic teaching, the acquisitive goods life is not the good life, but its most common modern substitute and simulacrum.

## 6. Secularizing Knowledge

1. Nor do research laboratories usually concern themselves with the social sciences or (especially) the humanistic disciplines that are ensconced alongside the natural sciences and engineering in research universities (even though governments and private organizations also fund some university research in the social sciences and humanities).

2. Clark Kerr, "Preface, 1963," in *The Uses of the University*, 5th ed. (Cambridge, Mass., and London: Harvard University Press, 2001), p. xii. The original chapters were first delivered as the Godkin Lectures at Harvard in April 1963. Ibid., p. xi.

3. See David John Frank and Jay Gabler, *Reconstructing the University: Worldwide Shifts in Academia in the 20th Century* (Stanford, Calif.: Stanford University Press, 2006).

4. Even in Catholic universities, knowledge in each of the academic disciplines tends to be treated no differently than it is in secular universities, and the truth claims of Catholicism and other religious traditions are usually regarded as candidates for knowledge only in theology departments—as if one and the same thing could be true in theology but not in physics or psychology, or vice versa.

5. James Turner, "Catholicism and Modern Knowledge: A Historical Sketch," in Turner, *Language, Religion, Knowledge: Past and Present* (Notre Dame, Ind.: University of Notre Dame Press, 2003), p. 120.

6. Alasdair MacIntyre, *God, Philosophy, Universities: A Selective History of the Catholic Philosophical Tradition* (Lanham, Md.: Rowman & Littlefield, 2009), p. 135.

7. Kerr, *Uses*, pp. 5, 31.

8. For this specific point and on this issue more broadly I am indebted to MacIntyre, *God, Philosophy, Universities*, pp. 15–18, 174–176.

9. Louis Menand, *The Marketplace of Ideas: Reform and Resistance in the American University* (New York and London: W. W. Norton, 2010), pp. 119–121, quotation on 119.

10. On the latter point I am indebted to discussions with James Turner, and grateful to him for sharing with me a draft of his forthcoming book on philology and the historical formation of the modern humanistic disciplines.

11. Mark Noll, *The Scandal of the Evangelical Mind* (Grand Rapids, Mich.: Eerdmans, 1994), p. 109.

12. For a recent, extremely erudite version of this narrative, see the two works by Jonathan I. Israel, *Radical Enlightenment: Philosophy and the Making of Modernity, 1650–1750* (Oxford: Oxford University Press, 2001) and *Enlightenment Contested: Philosophy, Modernity, and the Emancipation of Man, 1670–1752* (Oxford: Oxford University Press, 2006). Israel has recently condensed his encyclopedic learning about what he calls the Radical Enlightenment and carried the story into the late eighteenth century in *A Revolution of the Mind: Radical Enlightenment and the Intellectual Origins of Modern Democracy* (Princeton, N.J.: Princeton University Press, 2010).

13. Indeed, one might characterize the underestimations of the complexities of the natural world and the historical past as a series of self-congratulatory misperceptions, self-deceptions, and exercises in unjustified overconfidence from the Middle Ages until well into the twentieth century. At least now, some scientists and scholars are willing honestly to admit how much we simply do not know about the universe and the human past, despite (and *because of*) the enormous and undeniable growth of knowledge since the Middle Ages.

14. I use the term "scientific" here somewhat anachronistically but for the sake of analytical clarity to denote the pursuit of knowledge of the natural world based on observation, description, and experiment rather than on syllogistic demonstration from premises to conclusions as derived from texts regarded as authoritative.

15. Benedict of Nursia, *RB 1980: The Rule of St. Benedict in Latin and English with Notes,* ed. and trans. Timothy Fry et al. (Collegeville, Minn.: Liturgical Press, 1981), p. 164. My remarks in this and the following paragraph about the relationship between knowledge and Christian life in medieval monasticism are indebted to the classic work of Jean Leclercq, *The Love of Learning and the Desire for God: A Study of Monastic Culture,* trans. Catherine Misrahi (New York: Fordham University Press, 1982), the original lectures for which were delivered in Rome in 1955–1956. For an overview of medieval monastic life, see C. H. Lawrence, *Medieval Monasticism: Forms of Religious Life in Western Europe in the Middle Ages,* 3rd ed. (New York and London: Longman, 2000), which includes the mendicant orders.

16. On the monastic divine office and its adaptation by the secular clergy, see John Harper, *The Forms and Order of the Western Liturgy from the Tenth to the Eighteenth Century: A Historical Introduction and Guide for Students and Musicians* (Oxford: Clarendon Press, 1991), pp. 73–108.

17. Leclercq, *Love of Learning;* for an overview of the schedule of Psalms repeated each week in the monastic and secular divine office, respectively, see Harper, *Western Liturgy,* pp. 258–259.

18. Benedict, *RB 1980,* ed. and trans. Fry et al., pp. 180–186.

19. Augustine, *De doctrina Christiana,* in *Corpus Augustinianum Gissense,* ed. Cornelius Mayer, electronic edition, pt. 2 (Charlottesville, Va.: Intelex, 2000). Augustine apparently began this work sometime in the mid-390s but set it aside and did not complete it until 426/7. R. P. H. Green, "Introduction" to Augustine, *On Christian Teaching,* trans. Green (Oxford: Oxford University Press, 1997), pp. ix–xi, [xxvi]. On the work's extensive influence throughout the Middle Ages in the West, see *Reading and Wisdom: The "De doctrina Christiana" of Augustine in the Middle Ages,* ed. E. D. English (Notre Dame, Ind.: University of Notre Dame Press, 1995).

20. Faith Wallis, "Introduction" to *Bede: The Reckoning of Time* [725], trans. Wallis (Liverpool: Liverpool University Press, 1999), pp. xviii–xxxiv.

21. On early monasticism from Egyptian eremitism through Benedict to early medieval Benedictine communities in Ireland and England, see Marilyn Dunn, *The Emergence of Monasticism: From the Desert Fathers to the Early Middle*

*Ages* (Oxford: Blackwell, 2000); for the twelfth-century monastic revival in the context of wider religious currents in the wake of the Gregorian reforms, see Giles Constable, *The Reformation of the Twelfth Century* (Cambridge: Cambridge University Press, 1996); on the Cistercians in particular, see the important revisionist account by Constance Hoffman Berman, *The Cistercian Evolution: The Invention of a Religious Order in Twelfth-Century Europe* (Philadelphia: University of Pennsylvania Press, 2000).

22. See John Van Engen, *Sisters and Brothers of the Common Life: The Devotio Moderna and the World of the Later Middle Ages* (Philadelphia: University of Pennsylvania Press, 2008).

23. Ibid., pp. 80–81, 154–157. After receiving papal approval in 1395, "the Congregation of Windesheim proved arguably the most successful new religious order in the fifteenth century." Ibid., pp. 154–155, quotation on 154.

24. Roger Lovatt, "The *Imitation of Christ* in Late Medieval England," *Transactions of the Royal Historical Society,* 5th ser., 18 (1968): 113; Augustin De Backer, *Essai bibliographique sur le livre "De imitatione Christi"* (1864; reprint, Amsterdam: Desclée de Brouwer, 1966), pp. 34–35, 107–111, 127–129, 149, 155–156, 174; *STC 1475–1640,* vol. 2, p. 303, nos. 23954.7–23958.

25. Franz Posset, *Renaissance Monks: Monastic Humanism in Six Biographical Sketches* (Leiden: E. J. Brill, 2005), p. 20, which refers to Richard Newald, "Beiträge zur Geschichte des Humanismus in Oberösterreich," *Jahrbuch des oberösterreichischen Musealvereins* 81 (1926): 155–223.

26. W. B. Lockwood, "Vernacular Scriptures in Germany and the Low Countries before 1500," in *The Cambridge History of the Bible,* vol. 2, *The West from the Fathers to the Reformation,* ed. G. W. H. Lampe (Cambridge: Cambridge University Press, 1969), pp. 428–434; C. A. Robson, "Vernacular Scriptures in France," in ibid., pp. 436, 448–451; Kenelm Foster, "Vernacular Scriptures in Italy," in ibid., pp. 452–465; Margherita Morreale, "Vernacular Scriptures in Spain," in ibid., pp. 465–474. See also Andrew Colin Gow, "Challenging the Protestant Paradigm: Bible Reading in Lay and Urban Contexts of the Later Middle Ages," in *Scripture and Pluralism: Reading the Bible in the Religiously Plural Worlds of the Middle Ages and the Renaissance,* ed. Thomas Heffernan and Thomas E. Burman (Leiden: E. J. Brill, 2006), pp. 161–191, and Thomas Kaufmann, "Vorreformatorische Laienbibel und reformatorisches Evangelium," *Zeitschrift für Theologie und Kirche* 101 (2004): 138–174.

27. On printed editions of Books of Hours, which frequently combined vernacular with Latin prayers, see Eamon Duffy, *Marking the Hours: English People and Their Prayers, 1240–1570* (New Haven, Conn., and London: Yale University Press, 2006), pp. 121–146; Albert Labarre, "Heures (Livres d'Heures)," in *Dictionnaire de spiritualité ascétique et mystique,* vol. 7, pt. 1 (Paris: Beauchesne, 1969), cols. 420–423. Both Duffy and Paul Saenger have argued that familiarity with the liturgy would have enabled the use of Latin prayers by more laypeople than had had formal training in the language. See Duffy, *The Stripping of the Altars: Traditional Religion in England, c. 1400–c. 1580,* 2nd ed. (New Haven, Conn., and London: Yale University Press, 2005),

pp. 221–222, and *Marking the Hours,* pp. 59–60; Paul Saenger, "Books of Hours and the Reading Habits of the Later Middle Ages," in *The Culture of Print: Power and the Uses of Print in Early Modern Europe,* ed. Roger Chartier, trans. Lydia G. Cochrane (Princeton, N.J.: Princeton University Press, 1989), pp. 142, 148, 149.

28. On the complex, diverse emergence of the rosary between the twelfth and fifteenth centuries, see Anne Winston-Allen, *Stories of the Rose: The Making of the Rosary in the Middle Ages* (University Park: Pennsylvania State University Press, 1997), pp. 13–30. The addition of life-of-Christ meditations to the repetitive foundation of Ave Marias and Paternosters "transformed the Ave Maria prayer into a Jesus prayer, a shift that reflects the popular impulse toward *imitatio Christi* piety. The new meditation technique corresponded to religious exercises made popular by the Devotio Moderna movement.... With the addition of the Creed and the Gloria, the rosary became a means of summarizing the doctrines of the faith. By rehearsing the mysteries of redemption, the worshiper also practiced the virtues." Ibid., p. 27.

29. For an overview of the early mendicant orders, including the Augustinians and Carmelites as well as the Franciscans and Dominicans, see C. H. Lawrence, *The Friars: The Impact of the Early Mendicant Movement on Western Society* (New York: Longman, 1994); on the Franciscans in the Middle Ages, see the classic work by John R. H. Moorman, *A History of the Franciscan Order from Its Origins to the Year 1517* (Oxford: Clarendon Press, 1968), as well as Michael Robson, *The Franciscans in the Middle Ages* (Woodbridge, U.K.: Boydell Press, 2009); on the Dominicans through the fifteenth century, see William A. Hinnebusch, *A History of the Dominican Order,* 2 vols. (Staten Island, N.Y.: Alba House, 1965).

30. See Luisa Valente, *Logique et théologie: Les écoles parisiennes entre 1150 et 1220* (Paris: Vrin, 2008).

31. Peter Abelard, *"Sic et non": A Critical Edition* [1121], ed. Blanche B. Boyer and Richard McKeon (Chicago: University of Chicago Press, 1977).

32. See Philipp W. Rosemann, *The Story of a Great Medieval Book: Peter Lombard's "Sentences"* (Toronto: University of Toronto Press, 2007).

33. On Bernard *contra* Abelard, see Gillian R. Evans, *Bernard of Clairvaux* (New York: Oxford University Press, 2000), pp. 47, 104–106, 111–125, as well as the broader contextualization of their opposition in Peter Godman, *The Silent Masters: Latin Literature and Its Censors in the High Middle Ages* (Princeton, N.J.: Princeton University Press, 2000).

34. *Medieval Latin: An Introduction and Bibliographical Guide,* ed. F. A. C. Mantello and A. G. Rigg (Washington, D.C.: Catholic University of America Press, 1996), pp. 269–270. Leery of the potential misuse of discursive rationality when applied to the mysteries of the faith, Bernard used *theologia* pejoratively, joining it with *stultilogia*—"stupidology." Evans, *Bernard,* p. 48.

35. A *universitas* was so called not because it purported to include all subjects of study (a notion more nearly akin to the term *studium generale*), but because like analogous organizations in medieval cities it included all the members of

a group dedicated to some purpose. In this case, it was masters and students who had constituted themselves as a corporation, were devoted to the *studium* of higher education, and had received papal approbation. Jacques Verger, "Patterns," in *HUE*, vol. 1, *Universities in the Middle Ages*, ed. Hilde de Ridder-Symoens (Cambridge: Cambridge University Press, 1992), pp. 35–38.

36. Verger, "Teachers," in *HUE*, vol. 1, ed. de Ridder-Symoens, p. 163.

37. For the quotation, see Verger, "Teachers," in ibid., p. 163; for the students failing, see Rainer Christopher Schwinges, "Student Education, Student Life," in ibid., p. 235.

38. Gordon Leff, "The Trivium and the Three Philosophies," in ibid., pp. 307–308. Orléans was an example of a university without a faculty of arts; it had only a faculty of law. Verger, "Patterns" in ibid., p. 42; Antonio García y García, "The Faculties of Law," in ibid., p. 401.

39. Verger, "Patterns" in ibid., p. 42; Verger, "Teachers," in ibid., pp. 163–164. Paris lacked the teaching of Roman law beginning in 1219, however, after its prohibition by Pope Honorius III, which in turn opened the way for the teaching of Roman law at Orléans at the behest of Pope Gregory IX. García y García, "Faculties of Law," in ibid., p. 389; Paolo Nardi, "Relations with Authority," in ibid., pp. 89–90.

40. Monika Asztalos, "Faculty of Theology," in ibid., pp. 414, 433.

41. On the suspicion and condemnations of Aristotle's natural philosophy and metaphysics at the University of Paris in the early thirteenth century, see Asztalos, "Faculty of Theology," in ibid., pp. 420–423; for the chronology of the availability of Aristotle's works in Latin translations, see Bernard G. Dod, "Aristoteles latinus," in *The Cambridge History of Later Medieval Philosophy: From the Rediscovery of Aristotle to the Disintegration of Scholasticism, 1100–1600*, ed. Norman Kretzmann, Anthony Kenny, and Jan Pinborg (Cambridge: Cambridge University Press, 1982), pp. 45–79.

42. For a penetrating comparative study of the crucial differences between the Aristotelian notion of the eternity of the universe and neo-Platonic ideas of emanation on the one hand, and Jewish, Christian, and Islamic notions of free creation by a transcendent creator-God on the other, see David B. Burrell, *Freedom and Creation in Three Traditions* (Notre Dame, Ind.: University of Notre Dame Press, 1993).

43. On the complex, multistranded character of Bonaventure's relationship to Aristotelianism in light of his selective appropriation of Joachite ideas, see Joseph Ratzinger, *The Theology of History in St. Bonaventure*, trans. Zachary Hayes (1971; Chicago: Franciscan Herald Press, 1989), pp. 119–163.

44. For the increase after 1378, see Verger, "Patterns," in *HUE*, vol. 1, ed. de Ridder-Symoens, pp. 57, 64–65, [70]; on the founding of the University of Wittenberg, see Heinz Kathe, *Die Wittenberger philosophische Fakultät, 1502–1817* (Cologne: Böhlau, 2002), pp. 1–2.

45. Thomas Aquinas, *Summa Theologiae*, Blackfriars ed., vol. 1, trans. Thomas Gilby (London: Eyre & Spottiswoode; New York: McGraw-Hill, 1973), I, q. 1, a. 8, p. 30.

46. On lectures and disputations, see Verger, "Teachers," in *HUE,* vol. 1, ed. de Ridder-Symoens, pp. 154–156; Anthony Kenny and Jan Pinborg, "Medieval Philosophical Literature," in *Cambridge History of Later Medieval Philosophy,* ed. Kretzmann, Kenny, and Pinborg, pp. 19–29.

47. Schwinges, "Student Education, Student Life," in *HUE,* vol. 1, ed. de Ridder-Symoens, p. 231, which also stresses the stability and continuity of the form and content of university teaching from the thirteenth through the fifteenth century, and from Iberia to Scandinavia.

48. P. Glorieux, *La littérature quodlibétique de 1260 à 1320* (Lille: Desclée de Brouwer, 1925), pp. 18–35, 62–66; Kenny and Pinborg, "Medieval Philosophical Literature," in *Cambridge History of Later Medieval Philosophy,* ed. Kretzmann, Kenny, and Pinborg, p. 22.

49. For general remarks and specific case studies that illuminate the intertwined character of classical scholarship and the pursuit of natural-historical knowledge beginning among fifteenth-century Italian humanists, see Anthony Grafton, *Defenders of the Text: The Traditions of Scholarship in an Age of Science, 1450–1800* (Cambridge, Mass., and London: Harvard University Press, 1991), pp. 1–5, 11–12, 178–203; Grafton, *Bring Out Your Dead: The Past as Revelation* (Cambridge, Mass., and London: Harvard University Press, 2001), pp. 1–10, 97–137. On the extent to which most of the major figures of the seventeenth-century scientific revolution were indebted to problems that arose from grappling with Aristotelian texts and scholastic methods in universities, see Roy Porter, "The Scientific Revolution and Universities," in *HUE,* vol. 2, *Universities in Early Modern Europe (1500–1800),* ed. Hilde de Ridder-Symoens (Cambridge: Cambridge University Press, 1996), pp. 531–562. "The great scientific revolutionaries rejected Aristotle; but it was their academic grounding in Aristotle that gave them the ability to do it." Ibid., p. 551.

50. As Francis Bacon would say of alchemy at the outset of the seventeenth century, "assuredly the search and stir to make gold hath brought to light a great number of good and fruitful inventions and experiments, as well for the disclosing of nature as for the use of man's life." Bacon, "The Advancement of Learning" [1605], in Bacon, *Major Works,* ed. Brian Vickers (Oxford: Oxford University Press, 1996), p. 143. On late medieval magic, see the analysis in Richard Kieckhefer, *Forbidden Rites: A Necromancer's Manual of the Fifteenth Century* (University Park: Pennsylvania State University Press, 1997); for a brief overview of Renaissance magic, see Brian P. Copenhaver, "Magic," in *The Cambridge History of Science,* vol. 3, *Early Modern Science,* ed. Katharine Park and Lorraine Daston (Cambridge: Cambridge University Press, 2006), pp. 518–540; on late medieval astrology, see Laura Ackerman Smoller, *History, Prophecy, and the Stars: The Christian Astrology of Pierre d'Ailly, 1350–1420* (Princeton, N.J.: Princeton University Press, 1994); on Renaissance astrology, see Anthony Grafton, *Cardano's Cosmos: The Worlds and Works of a Renaissance Astrologer* (Cambridge, Mass., and London: Harvard University Press, 1999); for a brief overview of late medieval and early modern alchemy, see William R. Newman, "From Alchemy to 'Chymis-

try,'" in *Cambridge History of Science,* vol. 3, ed. Park and Daston, pp. 497–517, which broaches some of the issues treated in much more detail in Newman's *Atoms and Alchemy: Chymistry and the Experimental Origins of the Scientific Revolution* (Chicago and London: University of Chicago Press, 2006).

51. Olaf Pedersen, "Tradition and Innovation," in *HUE,* vol. 2, ed. de Ridder-Symoens, pp. 470–471, quotation on 471.

52. Desiderius Erasmus, *Moriae encomium, id est stultitiae laus* [1511], in Erasmus, *Opera omnia,* ser. 4, vol. 3, ed. Clarence H. Miller (Amsterdam and Oxford: North-Holland Publishing Co., 1979), pp. 144–158; [Crotus Rubeanus and Ulrich von Hutten], *Epistolae obscurorum virorum* [1515], ed. Aloys Bömer (Aalen: Scientia Verlag, 1978). On Rubeanus's and especially Hutten's atypical, anticlerical and antischolastic sarcasm in the *Letters* among the humanists involved in the Reuchlin Affair, see James H. Overfield, *Scholasticism and Humanism in Late Medieval Germany* (Princeton, N.J.: Princeton University Press, 1984), pp. 291, 293–297.

53. See Heiko A. Oberman, *The Harvest of Medieval Theology: Gabriel Biel and Late Medieval Nominalism* (Cambridge, Mass.: Harvard University Press, 1963); Alexander Broadie, "Mair, John (*c.* 1467–1550)," in *ODNB,* ed. H. C. G. Matthew and Brian Harrison (Oxford: Oxford University Press, 2004); online ed., ed. Lawrence Goldman, May 2006, http://www.oxforddnb.com/view/article/17843 (accessed 5 May 2010); Alexandre Ganoczy, "Jean Major, exegete gallican," *Recherches de science religieuse* 56 (1968): 457–495; Erwin Iserloh, *Johannes Eck (1486–1543): Scholastiker, Humanist, Kontroverstheologe* (Münster: Aschendorff, 1981). On the vitality of scholasticism in the fifteenth and early sixteenth centuries, see also Anthony Grafton and Lisa Jardine, *From Humanism to the Humanities: The Institutionalizing of the Liberal Arts in Fifteenth- and Sixteenth-Century Europe* (Cambridge, Mass.: Harvard University Press, 1987), pp. xii–xiii; and for Germany in particular, with reference to Biel, Conrad Summenhart, Conrad Wimpina, Eck, Jacob Trutvetter, and Jacob von Hochstraten, see Overfield, *Scholasticism and Humanism,* pp. 46–47, 99–100.

54. See the recent study by Guillaume de Tanoüarn, *Cajétan: Le personnalisme intégral* (Paris: Cerf, 2009).

55. James K. Farge, *Orthodoxy and Reform in Early Reformation France: The Faculty of Theology of Paris, 1500–1543* (Leiden: E. J. Brill, 1985).

56. See Alasdair MacIntyre, *Three Rival Versions of Moral Inquiry: Encyclopedia, Genealogy, and Tradition* (Notre Dame, Ind.: University of Notre Dame Press, 1990), pp. 156–162. I am also grateful to Tobias Hoffman for conversation on this point. Nominalists, of course, made a point to distinguish between reason and faith, philosophy and theology, in ways that shaped their entire intellectual enterprise, and in effect denied the possibility of the integral unicity of truth. See, for example, Oberman, *Harvest,* pp. 30–56.

57. Alasdair MacIntyre notes a parallel in this respect between late medieval philosophy and contemporary analytical philosophy. The technical specialization of late medieval philosophy is *itself* reflected, for example, in the

"forty-six essays by forty-one authors" in the topically and encyclopedically arranged *Cambridge History of Later Medieval Philosophy* (1982), in whose specialized essays "the relationship of individual theses and arguments as parts to wholes never appears." MacIntyre, *Three Rival Versions,* pp. 160–162, quotations on 160, 161.

58. On logic, see the contributions in *Cambridge History of Later Medieval Philosophy,* ed. Kretzmann, Kenny, and Pinborg, pp. 254–269, 273–381; on the vibrant, innovative vitality of logic in Scotland's universities at the end of the fifteenth and in the early sixteenth century, see Alexander Broadie, *The Circle of John Mair: Logic and Logicians in Pre-Reformation Scotland* (Oxford: Clarendon Press, 1985). On the importance of the natural philosophers at Merton College, Oxford, in the fourteenth century, see Edith Dudley Sylla, "The Oxford Calculators," in *Cambridge History of Later Medieval Philosophy,* ed. Kretzmann et al., pp. 540–563; for the *calculatores* and their influence on Parisian masters such as Buridan and Oresme in the kinematics of terrestrial motion, see Edward Grant, *The Foundations of Modern Science in the Middle Ages: Their Religious, Institutional, and Intellectual Contexts* (Cambridge: Cambridge University Press, 1996), pp. 99–103; and for the influence of Western Europe's monetizing economy on the *calculatores* and Parisian masters, which moved in the direction of a measurable, relativistic, and mechanical conception of the natural world, see Joel Kaye, *Economy and Nature in the Fourteenth Century: Money, Market Exchange, and the Emergence of Scientific Thought* (Cambridge: Cambridge University Press, 1998).

59. See Brian Patrick McGuire, *Jean Gerson and the Last Medieval Reformation* (Philadelphia: University of Pennsylvania Press, 2005).

60. Thomas Hemerken à Kempis, *De imitatione Christi* [c. 1420], in à Kempis, *Opera omnia,* vol. 2, ed. Michael J. Pohl (Freiburg im Breisgau: Herder, 1904), 1.1, p. 6/2–8; 1.2, p. 7/5–10. Very shortly thereafter, à Kempis drives home the point again: "What concern should *genera* and *species* be to us? The one to whom the eternal Word speaks is liberated [*expeditur*] from many opinions." Ibid., 1.3, p. 9/1–5. Or again, emphasizing the priority of the virtues and experiential knowledge over erudition: "First of all, remain at peace yourself, and then you will be able to make peace with others. A peaceful man does more good than a highly learned man." Ibid., 2.3, p. 64/3–5. On the centrality in general of the cultivation of the virtues and shared spiritual life among members of the communities dedicated to the *devotio moderna,* see Van Engen, *Sisters and Brothers,* pp. 266–304. Aristotle begins his *Metaphysics* with the famous line, "All men by nature desire to know." In *The Complete Works of Aristotle,* ed. Julian Barnes, vol. 2 (Princeton, N.J.: Princeton University Press, 1984), 980a22, p. 1552.

61. For overviews, see Charles G. Nauert Jr., *Humanism and the Culture of Renaissance Europe,* 2nd ed. (Cambridge: Cambridge University Press, 2006); *The Cambridge Companion to Renaissance Humanism,* ed. Jill Kraye (Cambridge: Cambridge University Press, 1996); *Renaissance Humanism: Foundations, Forms, and Legacy,* 3 vols., ed. Albert Rabil Jr. (Philadelphia: University of Pennsylvania Press, 1988).

62. See Michael D. Reeve, "Classical Scholarship," in *Cambridge Companion to Renaissance Humanism*, ed. Kraye, pp. 20–46; Martin Davies, "Humanism in Script and Print in the Fifteenth Century," in ibid., pp. 47–62; L. D. Reynolds and N. G. Wilson, *Scribes and Scholars: A Guide to the Transmission of Greek and Latin Literature*, 2nd ed. (Oxford: Clarendon Press, 1974), pp. 120–142; Anthony Grafton, "The Availability of Ancient Works," in *The Cambridge History of Renaissance Philosophy*, ed. Charles B. Schmitt and Quentin Skinner (Cambridge: Cambridge University Press, 1988), pp. 767–791; Grafton, *Defenders of the Text*.

63. The magisterial work on the reception and interpretation of Plato's dialogues in fifteenth-century Italy is James Hankins, *Plato in the Italian Renaissance*, 2 vols. (Leiden: E. J. Brill, 1990); for an overview, see Christopher S. Celenza, "The Revival of Platonic Philosophy," in *The Cambridge Companion to Renaissance Philosophy*, ed. James Hankins (Cambridge: Cambridge University Press, 2007), pp. 72–96.

64. See Grafton, "Renaissance Readers and Ancient Texts," in *Defenders*, pp. 23–46, who even when he is analyzing humanists who held both these attitudes, juxtaposes the contrast between classicism and historicism as ultimately incompatible, without considering the relationship of this alleged antinomy to Christianity's truth claims. On the early humanists' historical sense in general, see also Donald R. Kelley, *Faces of History: Historical Inquiry from Herodotus to Herder* (New Haven, Conn., and London: Yale University Press, 1998), pp. 130–141.

65. For Italy, see Paul F. Grendler, *The Universities of the Italian Renaissance* (Baltimore and London: Johns Hopkins University Press, 2002), pp. 209–214; for the second half of the fifteenth century in central Europe, where the University of Vienna was preeminent in this respect, see Overfield, *Humanism and Scholasticism*, pp. 102–120; for England, where the first instructors were Italians, see Richard Rex, *The Theology of John Fisher* (Cambridge: Cambridge University Press, 1991), pp. 15–16.

66. On the academies, see Robert Black, "The Philosopher and Renaissance Culture," in *Cambridge Companion to Renaissance Philosophy*, ed. Hankins, pp. 20–26; on humanists as print shop correctors, see Grafton, "Printers' Correctors and the Publication of Classical Texts," in Grafton, *Bring Out Your Dead*, pp. 141–155.

67. Grendler, *Universities*, pp. 247–248, 353–366, 389–390.

68. Erika Rummel, *The Humanist-Scholastic Debate in the Renaissance and Reformation* (Cambridge, Mass., and London: Harvard University Press, 1995).

69. On humanists' criticism of scholastic demonstration in favor of epideictic dialogues, especially before the late fifteenth century, see Rummel, *Humanist-Scholastic Debate*, pp. 41–62. If anything, such accusations intensified with the advent of the Reformation, when the scholastic criticism of humanists' skepticism was heightened as a result of doctrinal disagreement. See Erika Rummel, *The Confessionalization of Humanism in Reformation Germany* (New York: Oxford University Press, 2000), pp. 50–74.

70. On the impact of the New World on learned European culture, including humanism, see Anthony Grafton with April Shelford and Nancy Siraisi, *New Worlds, Ancient Texts: The Power of Tradition and the Shock of Discovery* (Cambridge, Mass., and London: Belknap Press of Harvard University Press, 1992).

71. For an overview, see Anthony Grafton, "A Sketch Map of a Lost Continent: The Republic of Letters," in Grafton, *Worlds Made of Words: Scholarship and Community in the Modern West* (Cambridge, Mass., and London: Harvard University Press, 2009), pp. 9–34.

72. See Constance M. Furey, *Erasmus, Contarini, and the Religious Republic of Letters* (Cambridge: Cambridge University Press, 2006).

73. Erika Rummel, *Erasmus and His Catholic Critics*, vol. 1, *1515–1522* (Nieuwkoop: De Graaf, 1989), pp. 2, 34–38; see also Jerry Bentley, *Humanists and Holy Writ: New Testament Scholarship in the Renaissance* (Princeton, N.J.: Princeton University Press, 1983), pp. 112, 115–121, and Allan K. Jenkins and Patrick Preston, *Biblical Scholarship and the Church: A Sixteenth-Century Crisis of Authority* (Aldershot, U.K.: Ashgate, 2007), pp. 27–52.

74. On Manetti, see Paul Botley, *Latin Translation in the Renaissance: The Theory and Practice of Leonardo Bruni, Giannozzo Manetti, Erasmus* (Cambridge: Cambridge University Press, 2004), pp. 83–98, quotation on 85. Botley notes that "Manetti was certainly well aware that translating the Scriptures was a controversial undertaking." Ibid., p. 87. Yet it can hardly have been viewed as inherently subversive or troubling to Nicholas V, who according to Manetti requested that he undertake the work and who patronized not only him but also the philological biblical scholarship of Valla at the papal court. See John Monfasani, "Criticism of Biblical Humanists in Quattrocento Italy," in *Biblical Humanism and Scholasticism in the Age of Erasmus*, ed. Erika Rummel (Leiden: E. J. Brill, 2008), pp. 15–17, 20–21, 26, 31, 32. On the controversy over Erasmus's 1516 and 1519 editions, from his prepublication exchange in 1514–1515 with Louvain's Maarten van Dorp through 1522, when the third edition of his New Testament appeared, see Rummel, *Erasmus and His Catholic Critics*, vol. 1. For Erasmus's controversies with Dorp, Jacobus Stunica, Jacques Masson, Noël Beda, and Pierre Cousturier concerning various aspects of his New Testament, see Jenkins and Preston, *Biblical Scholarship*, pp. 53–80; see also Alejandro Coroleu, "Anti-Erasmianism in Spain," in *Biblical Humanism and Scholasticism*, ed. Rummel, pp. 74–83 (for the controversies with Stunica and Sancho Carranza de Miranda); James K. Farge, "Noël Beda and the Defense of Tradition," in ibid., pp. 152–161 (for the exchanges with Beda); Cecilia Asso, "Martin Dorp and Edward Lee," in ibid., pp. 167–195; and Marcel Gielis, "Leuven Theologians as Opponents of Erasmus and of Humanistic Theology," in ibid., pp. 197–214 (with discussion of Masson at 204–208).

75. Monfasani, "Criticism of Biblical Humanists," in *Biblical Humanism and Scholasticism*, ed. Rummel, pp. 19–20. "It is quite wrong to suppose, as is sometimes implied, that the medieval church and scholars opposed corrections to the Vulgate. Making such corrections was precisely why medieval

Hebraists stressed the *Hebraica veritas*. Furthermore, the substantial lists of variants and alternate readings found in the medieval Bible *Correctoria* become pointless unless they were collected to correct the received Latin text." Ibid., p. 20, with reference to Heinrich Denifle, "Die Handschriften der Bibel-Correctorien des 13. Jahrhunderts," *Archiv für Literatur- und Kirchengeschichte des Mittelalters* 4 (1888): 485–597.

76. On papal humanist patronage in the fifteenth and early sixteenth centuries, see John F. D'Amico, *Renaissance Humanism in Papal Rome: Humanists and Churchmen on the Eve of the Reformation* (Baltimore and London: Johns Hopkins University Press, 1983); see also (especially for the pontificate of Nicholas V) Monfasani, "Criticism of Biblical Humanists," in *Biblical Humanism and Scholasticism*, ed. Rummel, pp. 31–32.

77. Desiderius Erasmus, "Paraclesis ad lectorem pium," in *Novum instrumentum. . . .* (Basel: Johannes Froben, 1516), sigs. aaa4v, bbb1.

78. Augustine, *De doctrina Christiana*, 1.43, in *Corpus Augustiniana Gissense*, ed. Mayer, electronic ed., pt. 2: "Homo itaque fide et spe et caritate subnixus eaque inconcusse retinens non indiget scripturis nisi ad alios instruendos."

79. Rummel, *Confessionalization of Humanism*, p. 46. Quite inconsistently, and neglecting the relationship between practices and doctrines, Rummel also asserts that "the moral teachings of earlier [i.e., pre-Reformation] humanists had lacked a doctrinal cast." On the contrary, their teachings presupposed the doctrines of medieval Christianity—which is why "there had been no need for precision as long as Christendom was undivided." Ibid., p. 49.

80. Dirk Wassermann, *Dionysius der Kartäuser: Einführung in Werk und Gedankenwelt* (Salzburg: Institut für Anglistik und Amerikanistik, 1996); Stefan Podlech, *Discretio: Zur Hermeneutik der religiösen Erfahrung bei Dionysius dem Kartäuser* (Salzburg: Institut für Anglistik und Amerikanistik, 2002).

81. Augustin Renaudet, "Jean Standonck, un réformateur catholique avant la Réforme," in Renaudet, *Humanisme et Renaissance* (1958; Geneva: Slatkine Reprints, 1981), pp. 114–161; James K. Farge, "Jan Standonck," in *Contemporaries of Erasmus: A Biographical Register of the Renaissance and Reformation*, vol. 3, ed. Peter G. Bietenholz and Thomas B. Deutscher (Toronto: University of Toronto Press, 1987), pp. 281–282. Standonck also established the students of the Collège de Montaigu as a religious Congregation imbued with *devotio moderna* piety and Carthusian discipline, with daughter houses in Cambrai, Valenciennes, Mechelen, and Leuven. Paolo Sartori, "Frans Titelmans, the Congregation of Montaigu, and Biblical Scholarship," in *Biblical Humanism and Scholasticism*, ed. Rummel, pp. 215–218.

82. Posset, *Renaissance Monks*, pp. 16–17.

83. For the Cistercians in Germany, see Posset, *Renaissance Monks*, pp. 23–24; for England, see R. B. Dobson, "The Religious Orders, 1370–1540," in *The History of the University of Oxford*, vol. 2, *Late Medieval Oxford*, ed. J. I. Catto and T. A. R. Evans (Oxford: Clarendon Press, 1992), pp. 537–579, and P. Cunich, "Benedictine Monks at the University of Oxford and the Dissolution of the Monasteries," in *The Benedictines in Oxford*, ed. H. Wansborough and A. Marrett Crosby (London: Darton, Longman, and Todd, 1997), p. 165,

both cited in James G. Clark, "Print and Pre-Reformation Religion: The Benedictines and the Press, c. 1470–c. 1550," in *The Uses of Script and Print, 1300–1700,* ed. Julia Crick and Alexandra Walsham (Cambridge: Cambridge University Press, 2004), p. 78.

84. Posset, *Renaissance Monks,* p. 16; *Caritas Pirckheimer: Ordensfrau und Humanistin—ein Vorbild für den Öcumene: Festschrift zum 450. Todestag,* ed. Georg Diechstetter (Cologne: Wienand, 1982).

85. Erasmus, *Moriae encomium,* in *Opera,* ser. 4, vol. 3, ed. Miller, pp. 158–168.

86. Barry Collett, *Italian Benedictine Scholars and the Reformation: The Congregation of Santa Giustina of Padua* (Oxford: Clarendon Press, 1985).

87. Posset, *Renaissance Monks,* esp. the introductory overview on pp. 14–28 (which includes mention of the six case studies on which the book concentrates); on Trithemius specifically, see Noel L. Brann, *The Abbot Trithemius (1462–1516): The Renaissance of Monastic Humanism* (Leiden: E. J. Brill, 1981). On the printed scholarly editions of classical Latin and Greek authors in many English Benedictine houses by the 1520s, see Clark, "Print," in *Uses of Script and Print,* ed. Crick and Walsham, p. 80. German Dominicans, too, such as Johannes Cuno in Nuremberg, were receptive to humanism. See Martin Sicherl, *Johannes Cuno, ein Wegbereiter des Griechischen in Deutschland: Eine biographisch-kodikologische Studie* (Heidelberg: Winter, 1978).

88. David J. Collins, *Reforming Saints: Saints' Lives and Their Authors in Germany, 1470–1530* (New York: Oxford University Press, 2008), p. 55.

89. On the Reuchlin Affair, as well as less spectacular conflicts among German humanists and scholastics in the first decade of the century, see Overfield, *Humanism and Scholasticism,* pp. 173–207, 247–297; see also Erika Rummel, *The Case against Johann Reuchlin: Religious and Social Controversy in Sixteenth-Century Germany* (Toronto: University of Toronto Press, 2002).

90. E. Jane Dempsey Douglas, *Justification in Late Medieval Preaching: A Study of John Geiler of Keisersberg* (Leiden: E. J. Brill, 1966), pp. 6–7, 18, 68, 103–105, 206–207 (on Wimpfeling as well as Geiler); Rex, *Theology of John Fisher;* de Tanoüarn, *Cajétan;* Paul F. Grendler, "Italian Biblical Humanism and the Papacy, 1515–1535," in *Biblical Humanism and Scholasticism,* ed. Rummel, pp. 251–263 (on Cajetan); Iserloh, *Johannes Eck;* J. M. Miskuly, *Thomas Murner and the Eucharist* (St. Bonaventure, N.Y.: Franciscan Institute, 1990), pp. 7–18; Ilse Guenther, "Hieronymous Emser," in *Contemporaries of Erasmus,* vol. 1, ed. Bietenholz and Deutscher (Toronto: University of Toronto Press, 1985), pp. 429–430; Collins, *Reforming Saints,* p. 7 (on Emser); Monique Samuel-Scheyder, *Johannes Cochlaeus: Humaniste et adversaire de Luther* (Nancy: Presses Universitaires de Nancy, 1993).

91. Erika Rummel, *Jiménez de Cisneros: On the Threshold of Spain's Golden Age* (Tempe, Ariz.: Arizona Center for Medieval and Renaissance Studies, 1999), pp. 53–65; Basil Hall, "Biblical Scholarship: Editions and Controversies," in *Cambridge History of the Bible,* vol. 3, *From the Reformation to the Present Day,* ed. Hall (Cambridge: Cambridge University Press, 1963), pp. 50–52, 56–57; Lu Ann Homza, *Religious Authority in the Spanish Renaissance* (Baltimore and London: Johns Hopkins University Press, 2000), pp. 2–3.

92. Ironically, Francis Bacon, writing retrospectively in the first decade of the seventeenth century, seems to have agreed: "If those schoolmen to their great thirst of truth and unwearied travail of wit had joined variety and universality of reading and contemplation, they had proved excellent lights, to the great advancement of all learning and knowledge." Bacon, "Advancement of Learning," in Bacon, *Major Works,* ed. Vickers, p. 141.

93. On the Renaissance humanists' emphasis on moving the will to virtuous civility and good manners to the preclusion of producing serious, original philosophy, see James Hankins, "Humanism, Scholasticism, and Renaissance Philosophy," in *Cambridge Companion to Renaissance Philosophy,* ed. Hankins, pp. 30–48, esp. at 39–46. Speaking of Italian humanists, Ronald Witt notes that "encoded in the fiber of the [Latin] language for them was a strenuous moral code and the clearsighted vision of reality that they claimed to impart in their instruction." Ronald G. Witt, *In the Footsteps of the Ancients: The Origins of the Humanists from Lovato to Bruni* (Leiden: E. J. Brill, 2003), p. 506.

94. The remark by Manetti's teacher, the Camaldolese monk and humanist Ambrogio Traversari (1386–1439), cut both ways: "holiness is one thing, and learning another [*Aliud enim sanctitas est, atque aliud eruditio*]." Quoted in Botley, *Latin Translation,* p. 83.

95. In the absence of a recent monograph, see David L. Wykes, "The Contribution of the Dissenting Academy to the Emergence of Rational Dissent," in *Enlightenment and Religion: Rational Dissent in Eighteenth-Century Britain,* ed. Knud Haakonssen (Cambridge: Cambridge University Press, 1996), pp. 99–139, as well as older scholarship by J. W. Ashley Smith, *The Birth of Modern Education: The Contribution of the Dissenting Academies, 1660–1800* (London: Independent Press, 1954); Herbert McLachlan, *English Education under the Test Acts: Being the History of the Nonconformist Academies, 1662–1820* (Manchester: Manchester University Press, 1931); and Irene Parker, *Dissenting Academies in England: Their Rise and Progress and Their Place among the Educational Systems of the Country* (Cambridge: Cambridge University Press, 1914).

96. Maria Rosa di Simone, "Admission," in *HUE,* vol. 2, ed. de Ridder-Symoens, p. 303; see also Rummel, *Confessionalization of Humanism,* pp. 30, 34.

97. For Lutheran Germany, see Kenneth G. Appold, "Academic Life and Teaching in Post-Reformation Lutheranism," in *Lutheran Ecclesiastical Culture, 1550–1675,* ed. Robert Kolb (Leiden: E. J. Brill, 2008), pp. 65–115; on the increased emphasis on religious instruction in Italian schools in the sixteenth century, see Paul F. Grendler, *Schooling in Renaissance Italy: Literacy and Learning, 1300–1600* (Baltimore and London: Johns Hopkins University Press, 1989), pp. 333–399; for two recent, comparative, cross-confessional overviews of broader attempts to instill discipline by authorities, see Philip S. Gorski, *The Disciplinary Revolution: Calvinism and the Rise of the State in Early Modern Europe* (Chicago and London: University of Chicago Press, 2003), pp. 114–137, and Ute Lotz-Heumann, "Imposing Church and Social Discipline," in *The Cambridge History of Christianity,* vol. 6, *Reform and*

*Expansion, 1500–1660,* ed. R. Po-chia Hsia (Cambridge: Cambridge University Press, 2007), pp. 244–260.

98. On confessional control of higher education in the Reformation era, see Notker Hammerstein, "Relations with Authorities," in *HUE,* vol. 2, ed. de Ridder-Symoens, pp. 117–121, 125–129, 130–131, 132–133, 134–137, 139, 140, 143, 147–148, 150–151; Peter A. Vandermeersch, "Teachers," in ibid., pp. 226–227; Rosa di Simone, "Admission," in ibid., 293; Hilde de Ridder-Symoens, "Mobility," in ibid., 419–421, 424–425, 429, 446; and Pedersen, "Tradition and Innovation," in ibid., pp. 478–480.

99. Rainer A. Müller, "Student Education, Student Life," in ibid., pp. 338–343.

100. Indeed, for most universities this concern extended throughout the early modern period; see Laurence Brockliss, "Curricula," in ibid., p. 586.

101. Rummel, *Confessionalization of Humanism,* pp. 44–49; John O'Malley, *The First Jesuits* (Cambridge, Mass., and London: Harvard University Press, 1993), pp. 208–216, 253–256; Grendler, *Schooling,* pp. 377–379; Marc Fumaroli, *L'âge de l'éloquence: Rhétorique et "res literaria" de la Renaissance au seuil de l'époque classique* (1980; Geneva: Droz, 2009), pp. 233–256; on the teaching and study of Arabic from Guillaume Postel through Joseph Scaliger, see J. Fück, *Die arabischen Studien in Europa bis in den Anfängen des 20. Jahrhunderts* (Leipzig: Otto Harrassowitz, 1955), pp. 36–53.

102. Charles B. Schmitt, *Aristotle and the Renaissance* (Cambridge, Mass.: Harvard University Press, 1983); Schmitt, "The Rise of the Philosophical Textbook," in *Cambridge History of Renaissance Philosophy,* ed. Schmitt and Skinner, pp. 796–804. On Melanchthon's appropriation of Aristotle in fashioning a distinctively Lutheran natural philosophy with respect to ethics, the soul, and divine providence, see Sachiko Kusukawa, *The Transformation of Natural Philosophy: The Case of Philip Melanchthon* (Cambridge: Cambridge University Press, 1995); on the variegated appropriation of Aristotelian ideas in Reformed Protestant and Lutheran theology, see Richard Muller, *Post-Reformation Reformed Dogmatics: The Rise and Development of Reformed Orthodoxy, ca. 1520 to ca. 1725,* 2nd ed., vol. 1, *Prolegomena to Theology* (Grand Rapids, Mich.: Baker Academic, 2003), pp. 360–382.

103. Walter J. Ong, *Ramus, Method, and the Decay of Dialogue: From the Art of Discourse to the Art of Reason* (1958; Chicago and London: University of Chicago Press, 2004), pp. 295–307; Brockliss, "Curricula," in *HUE,* vol. 2, ed. de Ridder-Symoens, p. 582.

104. Peter Dear, *Discipline and Experience: The Mathematical Way in the Scientific Revolution* (Chicago and London: University of Chicago Press, 1995), pp. 32–62; Rivka Feldhay, "The Cultural Field of Jesuit Science," in *The Jesuits: Cultures, Sciences, and the Arts, 1540–1773,* ed. John W. O'Malley et al. (Toronto: University of Toronto Press, 1999), pp. 116–126; William A. Wallace, *Galileo and His Sources: The Heritage of the Collegio Romano in Galileo's Science* (Princeton, N.J.: Princeton University Press, 1984), pp. 136–148.

105. On the early Jesuit schools and the emergence of education from the late 1540s as their principal ministry in their desire "to help souls," see O'Malley, *First Jesuits,* pp. 200–242; on the worldwide Jesuit correspondence network

and its importance for natural-historical knowledge, see Steven J. Harris, "Mapping Jesuit Science: The Role of Travel in the Geography of Knowledge," in *Jesuits*, ed. O'Malley et al., pp. 212–240. The Jesuits' global network and its importance for knowledge-making are also implied in many of the other articles in this collection and in its sequel, *The Jesuits II: Cultures, Sciences, and the Arts, 1540–1773*, ed. John W. O'Malley et al. (Toronto: University of Toronto Press, 2006).

106. Anthony Grafton, "Where Was Salomon's House? Ecclesiastical History and the Intellectual Origins of Bacon's *New Atlantis*," in Grafton, *Worlds Made of Words*, pp. 102–108; see also Pontien Polman, *L'élément historique dans la controverse religieuse du XVIe siècle* (Gembloux: J. Duculot, 1932), and Irena Backus, *Historical Method and Confessional Identity in the Era of the Reformation (1378–1615)* (Leiden: E. J. Brill, 2003). Despite their genuine contributions to the advance of historical knowledge, these ecclesiastical historians were not above manipulating or ignoring evidence when it suited their purposes; for some examples of Baronio doing so, see Cyriac K. Pullapilly, *Caesar Baronius: Counter-Reformation Historian* (Notre Dame, Ind., and London: University of Notre Dame Press), pp. 166–170. On the use of ecclesiastical history by "local Baronios" to legitimate local liturgical and hagiographical traditions, see Simon Ditchfield, *Liturgy, Sanctity and History in Tridentine Italy: Pietro Maria Campi and the Preservation of the Particular* (Cambridge: Cambridge University Press, 1995).

107. Anthony Grafton, "Protestant versus Prophet: Isaac Casaubon on Hermes Trismegistus," in Grafton, *Defenders of the Text*, pp. 145–161; on Ficino's resuscitation of the Hermetic corpus, see Grafton, "Availability," in *Cambridge History of Renaissance Philosophy*, ed. Schmitt and Skinner, p. 783. Casaubon also pilloried Baronio for mistakes in his use of Hebrew, subpar knowledge of Jewish rituals, institutions, and scholarship, and inadequacies in his mastery of technical chronology. See Grafton and Joanna Weinberg, *"I have always loved the Holy Tongue": Isaac Casaubon, the Jews, and a Forgotten Chapter in Renaissance Scholarship* (Cambridge, Mass., and London: Harvard University Press, 2011), pp. 164–169, 182–184, 190–196, 209–214.

108. There were some instances in which a ruler's religious commitments diverged from the confessional affiliation of universities in his territories, such as Brandenburg (after 1618, Brandenburg-Prussia) after the conversion to Calvinism of the Elector Johann Sigismund in 1613, which made for friction with the Lutheran universities of Frankfurt an der Oder, Königsberg, and Duisberg. See Thomas Albert Howard, *Protestant Theology and the Making of the Modern German University* (Oxford: Oxford University Press, 2006), p. 89.

109. Bruce M. Metzger and Bart D. Ehrman, *The Text of the New Testament: Its Transmission, Corruption, and Restoration*, 4th ed. (Oxford and New York: Oxford University Press, 2004), pp. 149–154. On Mill, and the even more accomplished philologist Richard Bentley, both of whom sought to shield scripture from deists and other detractors, see also Jonathan Sheehan, *The Enlightenment Bible: Translation, Scholarship, Culture* (Princeton, N.J.: Princeton University Press, 2005), pp. 44–50. Theodore Beza's stance captures the

attitude of the most learned and influential Protestant theologians of the late sixteenth century: he deliberately made little use of his oldest (and best) Greek manuscripts during decades of meticulous attention to the text of the New Testament, *because* they diverged so much from Estienne's *Editio Regia.* Metzger and Ehrman, *Text,* p. 151. On the character of Erasmus's edition and its closeness to the *textus receptus,* as well as the influence of the latter into the nineteenth century, see also Kurt Aland and Barbara Aland, *The Text of the New Testament: An Introduction to the Critical Editions and to the Theory and Practice of Modern Textual Criticism,* 2nd ed., trans. Erroll F. Rhodes (Grand Rapids, Mich.: Eerdmans, 1989), pp. 3–19.

110. For this reason, the relationship between scripture and doctrinal truth claims for the Roman church was asymmetrical in comparison to the same relationship for the wide range of different Protestants who championed *sola scriptura.* Protestant charges prompted post-Reformation Catholic biblical scholars to engage in a wide range of research they likely would not otherwise have undertaken, but not in ways that entailed what Michael Legaspi calls the "textualization" of the Bible that led to the "death of scripture," because the Bible was never outside the church. Protestants rejected the Roman church's authority, but this never turned the Bible for Catholics into "a disputed book in a confessional no-man's-land," any more than had been the case when medieval heretics rejected the church's authority. Michael C. Legaspi, *The Death of Scripture and the Rise of Biblical Studies* (New York: Oxford University Press, 2010), pp. 18–26, last quotation on 21.

111. *Canons and Decrees of the Council of Trent,* ed. and trans. H. J. Schroeder (St. Louis: Herder, 1941), session 4, pp. 297 (Latin), 18 (English).

112. On the Vulgate at Trent as well as the Sixtine and Clementine editions, see Guy Bedouelle, "La Réforme catholique," in *Le temps des Réformes et la Bible,* ed. Bedouelle and Bernard Roussel (Paris: Beauchesne, 1989), pp. 342–354. For the Tridentine debates in the spring of 1546 about the study of scripture and the bishops' decision not to prioritize humanistic methods above scholasticism, see Louis B. Pascoe, "The Council of Trent and Bible Study: Humanism and Scripture," *Catholic Historical Review* 52 (1966): 18–38. Contrary to misconceptions, Catholic biblical scholarship persisted in the late sixteenth century despite the realities of (inconsistent) censorship and the controversies such scholarship continued to provoke among scholars and prelates within the Roman church, for "scholarship and censorship went hand-in-hand." Peter Godman, *The Saint as Censor: Robert Bellarmine between Inquisition and Index* (Leiden: E. J. Brill, 2000), p. 79. Robert J. Wilkinson has recently given some suggestion of just how complex and enduring were the intellectual strands of sixteenth-century Catholic biblical scholarship: it included both humanistic philology and Christian-kabbalistic hermeneutics from the era of the Fifth Lateran Council and Complutensian Polyglot Bible before the Reformation, through the first published edition of the Syriac New Testament in 1555, to the controversial Antwerp Polyglot Bible of 1571 that was printed by Christophe Plantin (a Familist), inspired in significant measure by the messianic and mystical apocalyticism of Guil-

laume Postel, and overseen at the end by the great Spanish biblical scholar with Christian-kabbalistic leanings, Benito Arias Montano (1527–1598), a participant in the late sessions of the Council of Trent and an ecclesiastical censor whose own work was censored after his death. Robert J. Wilkinson, *Orientalism, Aramaic, and Kabbalah in the Catholic Reformation: The First Printing of the Syriac New Testament* (Leiden: E. J. Brill, 2007), and Wilkinson, *The Kabbalistic Scholars of the Antwerp Polyglot Bible* (Leiden: E. J. Brill, 2007). See also Alastair Hamilton, *The Family of Love* (Cambridge: James Clarke and Co., 1981), pp. 74–82; Bernard Roussel, "Des Auteurs," in *Temps des Réformes et la Bible,* ed. Bedouelle and Roussel, pp. 262–269; and John A. Jones, "The Censor Censored: The Case of Benito Arias Montano," *Romance Studies* 13:1 (1995): 19–29. Other achievements of late sixteenth-century Catholic biblical scholarship were less controversial than the Antwerp Polyglot. Referring to the Sixtine edition of the Septuagint of 1587, for example, the first edition "to be based on an extensive uncial manuscript" (Vaticanus graecus 1209, later known as Vatican B), Basil Hall wrote that it is "by modern standards perhaps the only satisfactory achievement in the editing of a biblical text obtained in the sixteenth century, and the editors could rightly claim that by diligent correction it had been restored to its former splendour." Hall, "Biblical Scholarship," in *Cambridge History of the Bible,* vol. 3, p. 58. The fourth-century Vatican B (or Codex Vaticanus, as it is also known) remains along with the Codex Sinaiticus one of the two best, most complete early Greek manuscripts of the New Testament. On post-Tridentine biblical scholarship among the Jesuits, including at the Collegio Romano, see O'Malley, *First Jesuits,* p. 259; and on post-Tridentine Catholic biblical scholarship more generally, see Bedouelle, "Réforme catholique," in *Temps des Réformes et la Bible,* ed. Bedouelle and Roussel, pp. 361–368.

113. Brother Lawrence of the Resurrection, *L'Expérience de la présence de Dieu* (Paris: Seuil, 1998); see also Conrad de Meester, *Vie et pensées du Frère Laurent de la Résurrection* (Paris: Cerf, 1992).

114. On Morin and his relationship with the Reformed Protestant scholar Louis Cappel, see Legaspi, *Death of Scripture,* pp. 19, 20–21. On Simon, see Jean Steinmann, *Richard Simon et les origines de l'exégèse Biblique* (Paris: Desclée de Brouwer, 1960), and more recently the study by Sascha Müller, *Kritik und Theologie: Christliche Glaubens- und Schrifthermeneutik nach Richard Simons (1638–1712)* (St. Ottilien: EOS, 2004).

115. "Galileo's Letter to the Grand Duchess Christina (1615)," in *The Galileo Affair: A Documentary History,* ed. and trans. Maurice A. Finocciaro (Berkeley and Los Angeles: University of California Press, 1989), pp. 87–118, quotation on 96.

116. Robert Bellarmine to Paolo Antonio Foscarini, 12 April 1615, in *Galileo Affair,* ed. and trans. Finocchiaro, p. 68. For the condemnation by the Roman Inquisition of 5 March 1616, see ibid., pp. 148–150. For a careful assessment of the proceedings of 1615–1616 and Bellarmine's judgment in the condemnation of Copernicanism, see Godman, *Saint as Censor,* pp. 214–221.

117. Furey, *Religious Republic of Letters.*

118. Grafton, "Republic of Letters," in Grafton, *Worlds Made of Words,* pp. 16–32.

119. Grafton and Weinberg, *Isaac Casaubon,* p. 174.

120. Harris, "Mapping Jesuit Science," in *Jesuits,* ed. O'Malley et al.; for the Jesuits' missionary efforts as an integrated global endeavor with particular reference to Germany, Mexico, and China, see Luke Clossey, *Salvation and Globalization in the Early Jesuit Missions* (Cambridge: Cambridge University Press, 2008).

121. See the still far from complete critical editions of their letters in *Melanchthons Briefwechsel: Kritische und kommentierte Gesamtausgabe,* ed. Heinz Scheible et al. (Stuttgart: Frommann-Holzboog, 1977–), which will eventually include over 9,000 letters, fewer than one-third of which have been edited; Heinrich Bullinger, *Briefwechsel,* ed. Fritz Büsser, vols. 1–13 (Zurich: Theologischer Verlag, 1972–), which extends only to 1543 (Bullinger died in 1575); and *Correspondance de Théodore de Bèze,* ed. Hippolyte Aubert, Fernand Aubert, Henri Meylan et al., 33 vols. (Geneva: Droz, 1960–), which covers from 1539–1592 (Beza died in 1605).

122. Grafton, "Republic of Letters," in Grafton, *Worlds Made of Words,* and Anne Goldgar, *Impolite Learning: Conduct and Community in the Republic of Letters, 1680–1750* (New Haven, Conn., and London: Yale University Press, 1995).

123. Pedersen, "Tradition and Innovation," in *HUE,* vol. 2, ed. de Ridder-Symoens, p. 481; Bruce T. Moran, "Courts and Academies," in *Cambridge History of Science,* vol. 3, ed. Park and Daston, p. 269.

124. On Peiresc, see Peter N. Miller, *Peiresc's Europe: Learning and Virtue in the Seventeenth Century* (New Haven, Conn., and London: Yale University Press, 2000); on Vesalius and Hevelius, see Alix Cooper, "Homes and Households," in *Cambridge History of Science,* vol. 3, ed. Park and Daston, pp. 226, 227; on Vesalius, see also Harold J. Cook, *Matters of Exchange: Commerce, Medicine, and Science in the Dutch Golden Age* (New Haven, Conn., and London: Yale University Press, 2007), pp. 37–39; on Aldrovandi, see Paula Findlen, *Possessing Nature: Museums, Collecting, and Scientific Culture in Early Modern Italy* (Berkeley and Los Angeles: University of California Press, 1994).

125. On alchemical laboratories, see Pamela Smith, "Laboratories," in *Cambridge History of Science,* vol. 3, ed. Park and Daston, pp. 299–301, and more extensively see Smith, *The Business of Alchemy: Science and Culture in the Holy Roman Empire* (Princeton, N.J.: Princeton University Press, 1994); for mention of female alchemists in the Holy Roman Empire, see Tara Nummedal, *Alchemy and Authority in the Holy Roman Empire* (Chicago and London: University of Chicago Press, 2007), pp. 2, 18, as well as her forthcoming book on the female alchemist Anna Maria Zieglerin; for Mildmay, see Cooper, "Homes and Households," in *Cambridge History of Science,* vol. 3, ed. Park and Daston, p. 227.

126. See Pedersen, "Tradition and Innovation," in *HUE,* vol. 2, ed. de Ridder-Symoens, pp. 468–469; Grafton, *Defenders of the Text,* pp. 114, 115, 129–

130, 236; Gerhard Oestreich, *Neostoicism and the Early Modern State,* ed. Brigitta Oestreich and H. G. Koenigsberger, trans. David McLintock (Cambridge: Cambridge University Press, 1982), pp. 77–79; Geoffrey Parker, *The Military Revolution: Military Innovation and the Rise of the West, 1500–1800* (Cambridge: Cambridge University Press, 1988), pp. 18–23.

127. Grafton, *New Worlds, Ancient Texts;* Klaus A. Vogel, "European Expansion and Self-Definition," in *Cambridge History of Science,* vol. 3, ed. Park and Daston, pp. 818–839.

128. Cook, *Matters of Exchange;* Steven J. Harris, "Networks of Travel, Correspondence, and Exchange," in *Cambridge History of Science,* vol. 3, ed. Park and Daston, pp. 341–362.

129. See the diverse case studies in *Patronage and Institutions: Science, Technology, and Medicine at the European Court, 1500–1750,* ed. Bruce T. Moran (Woodbridge, U.K.: Boydell Press, 1991).

130. Moran, "Courts and Academies," in *Cambridge History of Science,* vol. 3, ed. Park and Daston, p. 271.

131. On Galileo, see Mario Biagioli, *Galileo, Courtier: The Practice of Science in the Age of Absolutism* (Chicago and London: University of Chicago Press, 1993); on Brahe and Kepler, see R. J. W. Evans, *Rudolf II and His World: A Study in Intellectual History, 1576–1612* (Oxford: Clarendon Press, 1973), pp. 136–138, 152–153, 187–190, 245–247, 279–280; on the "exodus of the scientists" from early modern universities, see Pedersen, *HUE,* vol. 2, ed. de Ridder-Symoens, pp. 470–474.

132. Steven Shapin, "The Man of Science," in *Cambridge History of Science,* vol. 3, ed. Park and Daston, pp. 181–183; for Leibniz, see Maria Rossa Antognazza, *Leibniz: An Intellectual Biography* (Cambridge: Cambridge University Press, 2008), pp. 67, 80.

133. Brockliss, "Curricula," in *HUE,* vol. 2, p. 583.

134. Bacon, *New Atlantis* [1627], in Bacon, *Major Works,* ed. Vickers, pp. 480–486.

135. Grafton, "Republic of Letters," in Grafton, *Worlds Made of Words,* p. 27.

136. See Paula Findlen, "Sites of Anatomy, Botany, and Natural History," in *Cambridge History of Science,* vol. 3, ed. Park and Daston, pp. 277, 278–279, 282, including the respective tables for both sorts of facilities.

137. Carl Bangs, *Arminius: A Study in the Dutch Reformation* (Nashville, Tenn.: Abingdon Press, 1971), pp. 231–331; Jonathan I. Israel, *The Dutch Republic: Its Rise, Greatness, and Fall, 1477–1806* (Oxford: Clarendon Press, 1995), pp. 393–395, 422–465. On the theology students and professors in the university's early years, see Karin Maag, *Seminary or University? The Genevan Academy and Reformed Higher Education, 1560–1620* (Aldershot, U.K.: Scolar Press; Brookfield, Vt.: Ashgate, 1995), pp. 174–178.

138. For the appointment of Catholics at Leiden in the university's early years, see Hamilton, *Family of Love,* pp. 99–100; on the elimination of the Reformed confessional oath for students in 1578, see Maag, *Seminary or University?* p. 175.

139. Anthony Grafton, "Humanism and Scholarship at Leiden," in Grafton, *Bring Out Your Dead,* pp. 125, 126; on the establishment of these two institutions,

the States College (1592) and Walloon College (1606), and their effects on theology instruction at Leiden, see Maag, *Seminary or University?* pp. 178–182.

140. Glasgow and Edinburgh did not require a profession of faith in the Church of Scotland. De Ridder-Symoens, "Mobility," in *HUE*, vol. 2, ed. de Ridder-Symoens, p. 438.

141. See *The humble advice of the Assembly of Divines, now by authority of Parliament sitting at Westminster, concerning a confession of faith. . . .* (London: Stationers' Company, 1647); T. L. Underwood, "Denne, Henry (1605/6?–1666)," in *ODNB*, ed. H. C. G. Matthew and Brian Harrison (Oxford: Oxford University Press, 2004); online ed., ed. Lawrence Goldman, January 2008, http://www.oxforddnb.com/view/article/7497 (accessed 17 May 2010); *The Complete Works of Gerrard Winstanley*, 2 vols., ed. Thomas N. Corn, Ann Hughes, and David Loewenstein (Oxford: Oxford University Press, 2009); Leo Damrosch, *The Sorrows of the Quaker Jesus: James Nayler and the Puritan Crackdown on the Free Spirit* (Cambridge, Mass., and London: Harvard University Press, 1996).

142. Richard Popkin, *The History of Scepticism from Savonarola to Bayle,* 3rd ed. (Oxford: Oxford University Press, 2003); Zachary Sayre Schiffman, *On the Threshold of Modernity: Relativism in the French Renaissance* (Baltimore and London: Johns Hopkins University Press, 1991). For some seventeenth-century English examples of religious skepticism born of interpretative individualism and doctrinal pluralism, see Christopher Hill, *The English Bible and the Seventeenth-Century Revolution* (London: Penguin, 1993), pp. 225–238.

143. Thomas Hobbes, *Leviathan* [1651], ed. Richard Tuck (1991; Cambridge: Cambridge University Press, 1996), 1.7, pp. 47–49, and 3.33, p. 267; for Wilkins, see Barbara Shapiro, *John Wilkins, 1614–1672: An Intellectual Biography* (Berkeley and Los Angeles: University of California Press, 1969), pp. 228–234; John Locke, *An Essay Concerning Human Understanding* [1689], ed. Peter H. Nidditch (Oxford: Clarendon Press, 1975), 4.1–3, 16–18, pp. 525–562, 657–696.

144. John Milton, *Areopagitica* [1644], in *Areopagitica and Other Political Writings of John Milton,* foreword by John Alvis (Indianapolis: Liberty Fund, 1999), p. 34 (my emphasis).

145. Francis Bacon, "Of Tribute; or, Giving That Which is Due" [c. 1592], in Bacon, *Major Works,* ed. Vickers, p. 34.

146. Jan de Vries, *The Industrious Revolution: Consumer Behavior and the Household Economy, 1650 to the Present* (Cambridge: Cambridge University Press, 2008).

147. Wilhelm Schmidt-Biggemann, "New Structures of Knowledge," in *HUE,* vol. 2, ed. de Ridder-Symoens, p. 523.

148. James McClellan III, "Scientific Institutions and the Organization of Science," in *Cambridge History of Science,* vol. 4, *Eighteenth-Century Science,* ed. Roy Porter (Cambridge: Cambridge University Press, 2003), p. 90; on Göttingen's Societät (later Akademie) der Wissenschaften, see Howard, *Protestant Theology,* p. 112.

149. Pedersen, "Tradition and Innovation," in *HUE*, vol. 2, ed. de Ridder-Symoens, p. 486; Brockliss, "Curricula," in ibid., p. 617 (quotation); Findlen, "Sites of Anatomy," in *Cambridge History of Science*, vol. 3, ed. Park and Daston, p. 289.

150. On the advent and rapid spread of scientific journals associated with the academies beginning with the French *Journal des sçavans* and the Royal Society's *Philosophical Transactions*, see Rüegg, "Themes," in *HUE*, vol. 2, ed. de Ridder-Symoens, pp. 16–17; Pedersen, "Tradition and Innovation" in ibid., pp. 485–486.

151. On Francke and the University of Halle in the context of the efflorescence of German Pietism at the beginning of the eighteenth century, see Sheehan, *Enlightenment Bible*, pp. 55–62; on the political circumstances of its founding and the transformation of its religious character after 1740, see Howard, *Protestant Theology*, pp. 88–94, 98–104; on Wolff and his expulsion, see Israel, *Enlightenment Contested*, pp. 654–656, and Howard, *Protestant Theology*, pp. 95–98. For the three Enlightenments—natural-legal under Christian Thomasius, Pietist under Francke, and rationalist under Wolff—in the early decades at Halle, see also Legaspi, *Death of Scripture*, pp. 38–40, who draws on Ian Hunter, "Multiple Enlightenments: Rival *Aufklärer* at the University of Halle, 1690–1730," in *The Enlightenment World*, ed. Martin Fitzpatrick et al. (London: Routledge, 2007), pp. 576–595. In contrast to Halle, James Jakob Fehr has shown the ways in which Pietism and Wolffian rationalism were combined from the late 1710s to the mid-1750s at the University of Königsberg (where Kant was a student beginning in 1740 and began lecturing in 1755), in Fehr, *"Ein wunderlicher nexus rerum": Aufklärung und Pietismus in Königsberg unter Franz Albert Schultz* (Hildesheim and New York: G. Olms, 2005). I thank Ulrich Lehner for calling Fehr's work to my attention.

152. On the founding, character, course offerings, and pedagogy of Göttingen, see Legaspi, *Death of Scripture*, pp. 27–28, 33–51, quotation on 33; Charles E. McClelland, *State, Society, and University in Germany, 1700–1914* (Cambridge: Cambridge University Press, 1980), pp. 35–57; and Howard, *Protestant Theology*, pp. 104–121, with reference to the journal and academy in relationship to the university at pp. 113, 114–116.

153. Legaspi, *Death of Scripture*, pp. 45–50; Howard, *Protestant Theology*, pp. 106–112, 120–121.

154. There were exceptions. Especially in the 1730s and 1740s, significant numbers of Jesuits teaching in French universities, including those in Paris's faculty of theology, demonstrated an openness to Newtonianism along with ideas drawn from Malebranche and Locke. See Jeffrey D. Burson, "The Catholic Enlightenment in France from the *Fin de Siècle* Crisis of Consciousness to the Revolution, 1650–1789," in *A Companion to the Catholic Enlightenment in Europe*, ed. Ulrich L. Lehner and Michael Printy (Leiden: E. J. Brill, 2010), pp. 79–91. On enthusiasm for Newton, Locke, and Gassendi among learned Italian Catholics in the same decades, see Mario Rosa, "The Catholic *Aufklärung* in Italy," in ibid., pp. 222–223.

155. John R. Betz, *After Enlightenment: Hamann as Post-Secular Visionary* (Malden, Mass.: Wiley-Blackwell, 2009), pp. 230–257; Ulrich Lehner, *Enlightened Monks: The German Benedictines, 1740–1803* (Oxford: Oxford University Press, 2011), pp. 175–225, with discussion of Gerbert at 205–207. "Although he, along with many other enlightened theologians, emphasized a praxis-oriented theology, no traces of any Enlightenment influence can be found in Gerbert's writings. Rather, his work seems to stem from his monastic fervour, the ideals of the Tridentine Reform, scripture-based theology, and the Maurists, who had rediscovered patristic theology." Lehner, ibid., p. 206. For the influence of the Maurists' scholarship on Benedictines in central Europe, see ibid., pp. 11–26. I am grateful to Professor Lehner for discussions about monasticism and the Enlightenment, and for sharing with me his book manuscript on German Benedictines in advance of its publication.

156. Lehner, *Enlightened Monks*, pp. 171–174; see also Michael Printy, "Catholic Enlightenment and Reform Catholicism in the Holy Roman Empire," in *Companion to the Catholic Enlightenment,* ed. Lehner and Printy, pp. 179–180.

157. The combination of Enlightened and Reformed Protestant ideas in Edwards's thought is a theme that runs throughout the magisterial biography by George M. Marsden, *Jonathan Edwards: A Life* (New Haven, Conn., and London: Yale University Press, 2003), but see especially pp. 59–81. Mark Noll notes the paradox of Edwards having promoted the evangelical revivalism that "led to a decline of theology" because it "set up a style of faith with scant use for patient, comprehensive Christian thinking about the world and life as a whole." Noll, *Scandal,* p. 80. On Muratori, see Alphonse Dupront, *L. A. Muratori et la société européene des pré-Lumières* (Florence: L. S. Olschki, 1976), and Rosa, "Catholic *Aufklärung* in Italy," in *Companion to the Catholic Enlightenment,* ed. Lehner and Printy, pp. 218–222. On Boscovich, see Marcus Hellyer, *Catholic Physics: Jesuit Natural Philosophy in Early Modern Germany* (Notre Dame, Ind.: University of Notre Dame Press, 2005), pp. 177–178, 229–232, and Ugo Baldini, "The Reception of a Theory: A Provisional Syllabus of Boscovich Literature, 1746–1800," in *The Jesuits II,* ed. O'Malley et al., pp. 405–450. For the widespread and variegated engagement of Catholic intellectuals and political leaders with new ideas in the eighteenth century, see in general *Companion to the Catholic Enlightenment,* ed. Lehner and Printy; and for the Holy Roman Empire in particular, see Michael Printy, *Enlightenment and the Creation of German Catholicism* (Cambridge: Cambridge University Press, 2009).

158. Burson, "Catholic Enlightenment in France," in *Companion to the Catholic Enlightenment,* ed. Lehner and Printy, pp. 79–81; Lehner, *Enlightened Monks,* pp. 183–184, 189–191, 199–203, 208–209, 212–215.

159. Legaspi, *Death of Scripture,* pp. 46–47, quotation on 46.

160. For the quotation, see Legaspi, *Death of Scripture,* p. xi.

161. On the emergence of this notion of culture among the "Göttingen School" in the later 1770s, see Michael C. Carhart, *The Science of Culture in Enlightenment Germany* (Cambridge, Mass., and London: Harvard University Press, 2007); for the insulating effect of historicism in making the biblical past fit

for instrumental redeployment in the present, see Legaspi, *Death of Scripture,* which extends the arguments in Sheehan, *Enlightenment Bible.*

162. Gotthold Ephraim Lessing, "On the Proof of the Spirit and of Power" [1777], in *Philosophical and Theological Writings,* ed. and trans. H. B. Nisbet (Cambridge: Cambridge University Press, 2005), p. 87.

163. Baruch Spinoza, *Tractatus Theologico-Politicus* [1670], in Spinoza, *Opera,* ed. Carl Gebhardt, vol. 3 (Heidelberg: C. Winter, 1925). Legaspi sees this parallel in his *Death of Scripture,* pp. 4, 23–25, 132–134.

164. Peter Miller, for example, in referring to the work of early modern practitioners of *historia sacra* and biblical scholarship, alleges that "once the sacred was made fully and finally historical, it ceased to be sacred." Miller, "The 'Antiquarianization' of Biblical Scholarship and the London Polyglot Bible (1653–57)," *Journal of the History of Ideas* 62:3 (2001): 465. Among numerous counterexamples are the many Catholic biblical exegetes since the promulgation of the papal encyclical *Divino afflante spiritu* (1943) whose scholarship is fully historicist *and* consistent with robust Christian truth claims. See, for example, the contributions to *The New Jerome Biblical Commentary,* ed. Raymond E. Brown, Joseph A. Fitzmyer, and Roland E. Murphy (Upper Saddle River, N.J.: Prentice Hall, 1990). Summarizing the views of and then quoting Maurice-Dominique Chenu with respect to the historicization of Aquinas, in a way that applies no less to the Bible, Fergus Kerr writes: "We need not fear that, the deeper we get into the genesis and composition of a text, the more slippery will be the slope to relativism—just the opposite. 'The truth is no less true for being inscribed in time.'" Kerr, *Twentieth-Century Catholic Theologians* (Malden, Mass., and Oxford: Blackwell, 2007), p. 28. Many current or recent Protestant exegetes, too (including, for example, Brevard Childs, Richard Bauckham, Samuel Byrskog, N. T. Wright), are entirely historicist in their methodologies without being skeptical in their conclusions about Christian truth claims concerning, say, the bodily resurrection of Jesus. See also the recent study by Michael R. Licona, *The Resurrection of Jesus: A New Historiographical Approach* (Downers Grove, Ill.: IVP Academic, 2010). The denial of miracles as real events or more generally of a God who acts in history does not and cannot follow from critical historicism per se—unless "critical" is *defined* as metaphysically naturalist in the manner of Spinoza, which in fact has nothing to do with historicism as such and is logically distinct from it.

165. For the distinction between a "scriptural Bible" and an "academic Bible," see Legaspi, *Death of Scripture,* p. viii; Sheehan, *Enlightenment Bible.*

166. For multiple examples, see Lehner, *Enlightened Monks,* pp. 183–184, 189–191, 199–203, 208–209, 212–215.

167. For this point I am indebted to Robert Sokolowski, *The God of Faith and Reason: Foundations of Christian Theology* (Washington, D.C.: Catholic University of America Press, 1982), pp. 33–38.

168. On the denial of medieval Catholic sacramentality in modern cultural anthropology as a secularizing extension of Protestant conceptions of the sacraments, see Philippe Buc, *The Dangers of Ritual: Between Early Medieval*

Texts and Social Scientific Theory (Princeton, N.J.: Princeton University Press, 2001), pp. 164–168, 175–176, 194, 199–202. On the transformation of human beings with souls to human beings with minds in conjunction with the emergence of psychology as an intellectual discipline in the nineteenth century, see Edward S. Reed, *From Soul to Mind: The Emergence of Psychology, from Erasmus Darwin to William James* (New Haven, Conn., and London: Yale University Press, 1997); for a similar analysis of the eighteenth- and nineteenth-century transformation of the passions in the secularization of discourse about human beings, see Thomas Dixon, *From Passions to Emotions: The Creation of a Secular Psychological Category* (Cambridge: Cambridge University Press, 2003); and for the same authorial metaphysical commitments underpinning a survey that stretches from the ancient world to the present, see Raymond Martin and John Barresi, *The Rise and Fall of Soul and Self: An Intellectual History of Personal Identity* (New York: Columbia University Press, 2006).

169. On the triumph of Newtonianism in university arts faculties, see Brockliss, "Curricula," in *HUE*, vol. 2, ed. de Ridder-Symoens, pp. 586–587, quotation on 587; Porter, "Scientific Revolution and Universities," in ibid., pp. 538–539; Laurence Brockliss, "Science, Universities, and Other Public Spaces: Teaching Science in Europe and the Americas," in *Cambridge History of Science*, vol. 4, ed. Porter, pp. 60–68.

170. For two examples of arguments that human behavior cannot in principle be understood on the model of the natural sciences, which explains the social sciences' "absence of the discovery of any law-like generalizations whatsoever," see Peter Winch, *The Idea of a Social Science and Its Relation to Philosophy* (1958; London: Routledge and Kegan Paul, 1984), and Alasdair MacIntyre, *After Virtue: A Study in Moral Theory*, 3rd ed. (Notre Dame, Ind.: University of Notre Dame Press, 2006), pp. 79–108, quotation on 88. See also the argument about the importance of emergence in contrast to reductionism in understanding individual human beings and social life in Christian Smith, *What Is a Person? Rethinking Humanity, Social Life, and the Moral Good from the Person Up* (Chicago and London: University of Chicago Press, 2010), pp. 25–89.

171. Burson, "Catholic Enlightenment in France," in *Companion to Catholic Enlightenment*, ed. Lehner and Printy, pp. 111–114, quoted phrase on 112.

172. In the absence of a comprehensive modern monograph, see the brief overview in Jonathan Wright, "The Suppression and Restoration," in *The Cambridge Companion to the Jesuits*, ed. Thomas Worcester (Cambridge: Cambridge University Press, 2008), pp. 263–272, as well as the relevant articles in part 6 of *Jesuits II*, ed. O'Malley et al.

173. See Derek Beales, *Prosperity and Plunder: European Catholic Monasteries in the Age of Revolution, 1650–1815* (Cambridge: Cambridge University Press, 2003); on the secular seizure of nearly all monastic properties in Catholic German lands at the outset of the nineteenth century, see also Lehner, *Enlightened Monks*, pp. 227–228. On the vitality of the medieval contemplative orders after Trent, see, for example, Louis J. Lekai, *The Rise of the Cistercian*

*Strict Observance in Seventeenth Century France* (Washington, D.C.: Catholic University of America Press, 1968); Yves Chaussy, *Les Bénédictines et la réforme catholique en France au XVIIe siècle* (Paris: Éditions de la Source, 1975); Wolfgang Seibrich, *Gegenreformation als Restauration: Die restaurativen Bemühungen der alten Orden im deutschen Reich von 1580 bis 1648* (Münster: Aschendorff, 1991).

174. Walter Rüegg, "Themes," in *HUE,* vol. 3, *Universities in the Nineteenth and Early Twentieth Centuries (1800–1945),* ed. Rüegg (Cambridge: Cambridge University Press, 2004), p. 3.

175. On France, see Rüegg, "Themes," in *HUE,* vol. 3, ed. Rüegg, pp. 4–5, 6–10; Christophe Charle, "Patterns," in ibid., pp. 34–35; Paul Gerbod, "Relations with Authority," in ibid., pp. 85, 86, 93. On Berlin's founding, primacy, and influence, see McClelland, *State, Society, and University,* pp. 101–149; Howard, *Protestant Theology;* Rüegg, "Themes," in *HUE,* vol. 3, ed. Rüegg, pp. 5, 13–23; and Theodore Ziolkowski, *German Romanticism and Its Institutions* (Princeton, N.J.: Princeton University Press, 1990), pp. 286–308.

176. On the far from straightforward influence of the "German model" on American universities with particular reference to the University of Michigan from the 1850s into the 1890s, see James Turner and Paul Bernard, "The 'German Model' and the Graduate School: The University of Michigan and the Origin Myth of the American University," in Turner, *Language, Religion, Knowledge,* pp. 69–94.

177. Ziolkowski, *German Romanticism,* p. 286. On the importance of the Jena circle in the 1790s in providing the philosophical underpinnings, conception of the unity of knowledge, and institutional model for the University of Berlin, see ibid., pp. 218–308.

178. The quoted phrase is Ziolkowski's, in ibid., p. 293.

179. In this work, Kant devoted more attention to the relationship between philosophy and the theology faculty than to the relationship between philosophy and the law and medical faculties combined. Immanuel Kant, *Der Streit der Fakultäten* [1798], in Kant, *Gesammelte Schriften,* ed. Königlich Preußischen Akademie der Wissenschaften, vol. 7 (Berlin: Georg Reimer, 1917), pp. [13]–116. See also Thomas Albert Howard's well-contextualized discussion of the work in Howard, *Protestant Theology,* pp. 121–129, as well as the broader context of German university reform initiatives at Jena in the 1790s in Ziolkowski, *German Romanticism,* pp. 237–252.

180. Sheehan, *Enlightenment Bible,* pp. 219–240.

181. Friedrich Daniel Ernst Schleiermacher, *Über die Religion: Reden an die Gebildeten unter ihren Verächtern* [1799], in Schleiermacher, *Kritische Gesamtausgabe,* Erste Abteilung: *Schriften und Entwürfe,* vol. 2, *Schriften aus der Berliner Zeit 1796–1799,* ed. Günter Meckenstock (Berlin: Walter de Gruyter, 1984), p. 242/15–17. Schleiermacher's influence on the University of Berlin was at least as great as Humboldt's in its early years; see Howard, *Protestant Theology,* pp. 178–211.

182. McClelland, *State, Society, and University,* pp. 104, 110, 111–112, 118, 124–125; Howard, *Protestant Theology,* 131, 138, 141, 174, 181.

183. Suzanne L. Marchand, *Down from Olympus: Archaeology and Philhellenism in Germany, 1750–1970* (Princeton, N.J.: Princeton University Press, 1996), pp. 3–35, quotation on 35.

184. For a study of one influential example in Victorian Britain, see Robert E. Sullivan, *Macaulay: The Tragedy of Power* (Cambridge, Mass., and London: Harvard University Press, 2009), esp. pp. 128–133, 145, 169–171. I am also grateful to the author for discussion on this and many related points. On the transplantation of the German "cultural Bible" to England beginning around 1830, see Sheehan, *Enlightenment Bible,* pp. 247–258.

185. For the quotation, see McClelland, *State, Society, and University,* p. 132; on the importance of the unity of *Wissenschaft* in the Romantic university, see Ziolkowski, *German Romanticism,* pp. 239–240, 247–249, 251–252, 253–254, 288.

186. Richard G. Olson, *Science and Scientism in Nineteenth-Century Europe* (Urbana and Chicago: University of Illinois Press, 2008), pp. 87–121; Terry Pinkard, *German Philosophy, 1760–1860: The Legacy of Idealism* (Cambridge: Cambridge University Press, 2002), pp. 178–183; Charle, "Patterns," in *HUE,* vol. 3, ed. Rüegg, pp. 47–49.

187. McClelland, *State, Society, and University,* pp. 91–93, 126–127; on Fichte's subordination of theology to philosophy, see Howard, *Protestant Theology,* pp. 160–166. The subordination of nineteenth-century German research universities to the state, beginning with Berlin, is a major theme in Howard's study and for Berlin in the 1810s is also discussed by Ziolkowski, *German Romanticism,* pp. 299–308.

188. McClelland, *State, Society, and University,* p. 141.

189. Georg Wilhelm Friedrich Hegel, *Grundlinien der Philosophie des Rechts* [1820], in Hegel, *Gesammelte Werke,* vol. 14/1, ed. Klaus Grotsch and Elisabeth Weisser-Lohmann (Hamburg: Felix Meiner, 2009), p. 201/4, 21–22. Hegel's political philosophy, which echoed themes widespread in German Romanticism, is in itself nuanced and complex but lent itself nonetheless to frightening appropriations. For interpretations keen to separate Hegel's political thought from some of the uses to which it was put, see Charles Taylor, *Hegel* (Cambridge: Cambridge University Press, 1975), pp. 428–461, and Kenneth Westphal, "The Basic Context and Structure of Hegel's *Philosophy of Right,*" in *The Cambridge Companion to Hegel,* ed. Frederick C. Beiser (Cambridge: Cambridge University Press, 1993), pp. 234–269. On the Karlsbad Decrees and the close of the reform era of the German universities, which "ended in Prussia (and elsewhere) with a heightened degree of state power over the universities and all other aspects of public education," see McClelland, *State, Society, and University,* pp. 144–149, quotation on 144.

190. Olson, *Science and Scientism,* pp. 113–121, quotation on 121; McClelland, *State, Society, and University,* pp. 217–231, 238, 314–321, 326.

191. On nineteenth-century France, see Rüegg, "Themes," in *HUE,* vol. 3, ed. Rüegg, pp. 4–5, 6–10; Charle, "Patterns," in ibid., pp. 34–35; Paul Gerbod, "Relations with Authority," in ibid., pp. 85, 86, 93. On the United States, for the Morrill Act see John R. Thelin, *A History of American Higher Education*

(Baltimore and London: Johns Hopkins University Press, 2004), pp. 74–79, 104–105; for the beginning of steady federal support for American universities following the Hatch Act (1887) and the second Morrill Act (1890), see Roger L. Williams, *The Origins of Federal Support for Higher Education: George W. Atherton and the Land-Grant College Movement* (University Park: Pennsylvania State University Press, 1991); and for the enormous expansion in federal support for research in American universities from World War II through the 1980s, see Roger L. Geiger, *Research and Relevant Knowledge: American Research Universities since World War II* (New York: Oxford University Press, 1993).

192. Woodrow Wilson, "Princeton in the Nation's Service," 21 October 1896, in *The Papers of Woodrow Wilson,* vol. 10, 1896–1898, ed. Arthur S. Link (Princeton, N.J.: Princeton University Press, 1971), pp. 11–31; on Wilson's foreign policy and its enduring influence in American international affairs, see Lloyd E. Ambrosius, *Wilsonianism: Woodrow Wilson and His Legacy in American Foreign Relations* (New York: Palgrave Macmillan, 2002).

193. "Emerson provided an American version of the German idealist celebration of the self and creativity." George M. Marsden, *The Soul of the American University: From Protestant Establishment to Established Nonbelief* (New York: Oxford University Press, 1994), p. 187.

194. "The Germans invented the research ideal. The Americans invented an institution to house and perpetuate it. . . . The ever narrowing gyre of specialization was no accidental spinoff from the modern fragmentation of knowledge, but the flight plan of the graduate school from its launching." Turner and Bernard, "German Model," in Turner, *Language, Religion, Knowledge,* p. 94. On Gilman and the research emphasis at Johns Hopkins, see Marsden, *Soul,* pp. 153–156.

195. For Europe, see Konrad H. Jarausch, "Graduation and Careers," in *HUE,* vol. 3, ed. Rüegg, pp. 363–389. For the United States, see Dorothy Ross, *The Origins of American Social Science* (Cambridge: Cambridge University Press, 1991); Thomas L. Haskell, *The American Social Science Association and the Nineteenth-Century Crisis of Authority* (1977; Baltimore and London: Johns Hopkins University Press, 2000); Jon H. Roberts and James Turner, *The Sacred and the Secular University,* intro. John F. Wilson (Princeton, N.J.: Princeton University Press, 2000); Christian Smith, "Secularizing American Higher Education: The Case of Early American Sociology," in *The Secular Revolution: Power, Interests, and Conflict in the Secularization of American Public Life,* ed. Smith (Berkeley and Los Angeles: University of California Press, 2003), pp. 97–159.

196. Quoted from a 1906 work by Hermann Diels in L[orraine] Daston, "Die Akademien und die Einheit der Wissenschaften. Die Disziplinierung der Wissenschaften," in *Die Königlich Preussische Akademie der Wissenschaften zu Berlin im Kaiserreich,* ed. J. Kocka et al. (Berlin, 1999), pp. 73–74, as cited in Walter Rüegg, "Themes," in *HUE,* vol. 3, ed. Rüegg, p. 9 n. 17.

197. On Liebig, see William H. Brock, *Justus von Liebig: The Chemical Gatekeeper* (Cambridge: Cambridge University Press, 1997).

198. See Mike Hawkins, *Social Darwinism in European and American Thought, 1860–1945: Nature as Model and Nature as Threat* (Cambridge: Cambridge University Press, 1997), and Robert Bannister, *Social Darwinism: Science and Myth in Anglo-American Thought* (Philadelphia: Temple University Press, 1979).

199. This remains no less true today. Regardless of the character of their arguments, or how sophisticated their questioning of the relationship between natural-scientific truth claims and reality, philosophers and historians of science have no influence on the application of scientific findings by engineers, corporations, and governments. What matters for human beings' transformation of the world based on scientific findings is not the precise specification of their epistemological status, but simply that they work regardless of what that status might be.

200. Wilson, "Princeton," in *Papers*, vol. 10, ed. Link, p. 29.

201. On Comte set in a broad intellectual context, see Olson, *Science and Scientism*, pp. 62–84; Émile Durkheim, *The Elementary Forms of Religious Life* [1913], trans. Karen E. Fields (New York: Free Press, 1995), p. 17. Lester F. Ward, the founder of American academic sociology, held the same view as Durkheim on this point; see Roberts and Turner, *Sacred and Secular University*, p. 49. On the pervasive influence of Comte's positivism and the reception of his starkly supersessionist conception of history in the United States beginning in the 1850s, see Christian Smith, "Introduction: Rethinking the Secularization of American Public Life," in *Secular Revolution*, ed. Smith, pp. 54–55.

202. Christian Smith, "Sociology," in *Secular Revolution*, ed. Smith, esp. pp. 121–126, 147–149; see also MacIntyre, *After Virtue*, pp. 79–87, 106–108.

203. Smith, "Sociology," in *Secular Revolution*, ed. Smith, p. 122.

204. Daniel Coit Gilman, "Higher Education in the United States" [1893], in Gilman, *University Problems in the United States* (New York: Century Co., 1898), p. 298, quoted in Roberts and Turner, *Sacred and Secular University*, p. 64.

205. Nathan O. Hatch, *The Democratization of American Christianity* (New Haven, Conn., and London: Yale University Press, 1989); Marsden, *Soul*, pp. 90–93; Julie A. Reuben, *The Making of the Modern University: Intellectual Transformations and the Marginalization of Morality* (Chicago and London: University of Chicago Press, 1996), pp. 19–23.

206. Charles Hodge, *Systematic Theology*, vol. 1 (1872–1873; Grand Rapids, Mich.: Eerdmans, 1952), p. 10, quoted in Noll, *Scandal*, pp. 97–98, with discussion of the relationship between the Scottish Enlightenment and American Protestantism, as well as of the intellectual complacency it engendered, at pp. 83–107. See also Eva Marie Garroutte, "The Positivist Attack on Baconian Science and Religious Knowledge in the 1870s," in *Secular Revolution*, ed. Smith, pp. 197–215, where this same passage by Hodge is quoted on p. 199. On American Protestant intellectual complacency born of cultural hegemony, see also Smith, "Introduction," in *Secular Revolution*, pp. 62–64, 71–73.

207. For the quotation, see Roberts and Turner, *Sacred and Secular University,* p. 20; on the exercise of Protestant cultural hegemony throughout the nineteenth century via a legally institutionalized "moral establishment," see David Sehat, *The Myth of American Religious Freedom* (New York: Oxford University Press, 2011).

208. See especially Noll, *Scandal.* "When Christians turned to their intellectual resources for dealing with these matters, they found that the cupboard was nearly bare." Ibid., p. 106.

209. The same dynamic played out in Germany in the late nineteenth and early twentieth centuries. By the first decade of the twentieth century, "one has the phenomenon in Germany of a series of competing religious groups, each claiming to overcome the fragmentation and division of which they were in fact symptoms." George S. Williamson, "A Religious *Sonderweg?* Reflections on the Sacred and the Secular in the Historiography of Modern Germany," *Church History* 75:1 (2006): 152. On the tendency of many American Protestant colleges (including those run by Baptists, Methodists, and Presbyterians) to *emphasize* their denominational distinctiveness after the mid-nineteenth century, see David B. Potts, "American Colleges in the Nineteenth Century: From Localism to Denominationalism," *History of Education Quarterly* 11 (1971): 363–380.

210. *Secular Revolution,* ed. Smith; Marsden, *Soul;* Reuben, *Making.*

211. Smith, "Introduction," in *Secular Revolution,* ed. Smith, p. 75. The Standard Oil tycoon Rockefeller was himself "a pious Baptist layman of a traditional sort," but his first Baptist president at the University of Chicago, William Rainey Harper, held "ultra-low church principles" that essentially equated Christianity with American individualism and democracy, and regarded all the sciences as independent of any explicit theology or religious dogmas. See Marsden, *Soul,* pp. 236–251, quotations on 240, 248. The University of Chicago is thus fittingly grouped with these other institutions despite having been founded as a Baptist institution. Its imposing neo-Gothic Rockefeller Chapel, built in the 1920s, was "one of the clearest cases of a building erected in memory of a fading religious spirit." Ibid., p. 246.

212. Relatedly, John F. Wilson contrasts American Protestant pluralism and "centrifugal forces in the religious arena" with the centralizing tendencies in the study of law in American higher education after the Civil War. Wilson, "Introduction" to Roberts and Turner, *Sacred and Secular University,* pp. 8–9.

213. Reuben, *Making,* pp. 77–87; see also Marsden, *Soul.*

214. Smith, "Introduction," in *Secular Revolution,* ed. Smith, p. 71. In the formulation of Jon Roberts and James Turner, "morality elided into spirituality, and the elusory hybrid offered a kind of quasi transcendence if not pseudoreligion." *Sacred and Secular University,* p. 116.

215. N. Jay Demerath, "Cultural Victory and Organizational Defeat in the Paradoxical Decline of Liberal Protestantism," *Journal for the Scientific Study of Religion* 34:4 (1995): 458–469, as analyzed in Christian Smith with Patricia Snell, *Souls in Transition: The Religious and Spiritual Lives of Emerging Adults* (New York: Oxford University Press, 2009), pp. 287–289. Smith's interviews

with hundreds of young adults in the United States amply confirm that one "need not study liberal Protestant theology to be well inducted into its worldview, since it has simply become part of the cultural air that many Americans now breathe." Ibid., pp. 288–289. For the phrase "liberal Protestantism without Protestantism," see Marsden, *Soul,* p. 408.

216. On this substitutive role for philosophy, literature, and the arts in the late nineteenth century, see James Turner, "Secularization and Sacralization: Some Religious Origins of the Humanities Curriculum," in Turner, *Language, Religion, Knowledge,* pp. 50–68; see also Roberts and Turner, *Sacred and Secular University,* pp. 75–122, with the second quoted phrase on p. 105.

217. Anthony Kronman, *Education's End: Why Our Colleges and Universities Have Given Up on the Meaning of Life* (New Haven, Conn., and London: Yale University Press, 2007).

218. John J. Mearsheimer, "Mearsheimer's Response: 'Teaching Morality at the Margins,' " *Philosophy and Literature* 22 (1998): 194. See also and more generally Mearsheimer, "The Aims of Education," ibid., 137–155.

219. Harry R. Lewis, *Excellence without a Soul: Does Liberal Education Have a Future?* (New York: Public Affairs, 2006), pp. 5, 17.

220. For the same story from a rather different and more celebratory perspective, see François Cusset, *French Theory: How Foucault, Derrida, Deleuze, & Co. Transformed the Intellectual Life of the United States,* trans. Jeff Fort (Minneapolis and London: University of Minnesota Press, 2008).

221. In a related vein, Jon Roberts and James Turner state that "postmodern antifoundationalism is the natural child of philological historicism, bred up by the humanities." *Sacred and Secular University,* p. 118.

222. Max Weber, "Wissenschaft als Beruf" [1919], in Weber, *Gesamtausgabe,* Abteilung I: *Schriften und Reden,* vol. 17, ed. Wolfgang J. Mommsen and Wolfgang Schluchter with Birgitt Morgenbrod (Tübingen: J. C. B. Mohr, 1992), pp. 71–111.

223. For the figures and the discussion of chlorine, phosgene, and mustard gases in World War I, see Michael Duffy, "Weapons of War: Poison Gas," at http://www.firstworldwar.com/weaponry/gas.htm (accessed 25 May 2010).

224. Saul Friedlander, *The Years of Extermination: Nazi Germany and the Jews, 1939–1945* (New York: HarperCollins, 2007), pp. 236, 717 n. 147.

225. Jeffrey Stout, *Democracy and Tradition* (Princeton, N.J.: Princeton University Press, 2004).

226. For the quotation, see George M. Marsden, "Theology and the University: Newman's Ideas and Current Realities," in John Henry Newman, *The Idea of a University,* ed. Frank M. Turner (New Haven, Conn., and London: Yale University Press, 1996), p. 304. On this point in general, see also MacIntyre, *God, Philosophy, Universities,* pp. 15–18, 173–176.

227. Peter Singer, *Practical Ethics,* 3rd ed. (Cambridge: Cambridge University Press, 2011), p. 152 (my emphasis). Singer deserves credit for exposing the inconsistency of those who defend abortion rights but reject the permissibility of infanticide. What is unclear is why, if metaphysical naturalism is true, anyone *should* care about the "rights" Singer groundlessly imputes to ani-

mals or "persons," or why the reduction of suffering is a "good" thing in animals or "persons."

228. Ronald Dworkin, "Objectivity and Truth: You'd Better Believe It," *Philosophy and Public Affairs* 25 (Spring 1996): 87–139, esp. at pp. 117–118. The same problem (and attempt to overcome it) underlies his recent magnum opus; Dworkin, *Justice for Hedgehogs* (Cambridge, Mass., and London: Belknap Press of Harvard University Press, 2011).

229. Rüegg, "Themes," in *HUE*, vol. 3, ed. Rüegg, p. 6; Rüegg, "Theology and the Arts," in ibid., pp. 395–405; Gerald A. McCool, *Catholic Theology in the Nineteenth Century: The Quest for a Unitary Method* (New York: Seabury Press, 1977), pp. 17–32. After the French Revolution, most teaching of Catholic theology in Europe was limited to seminaries. Rüegg, "Theology and the Arts," in *HUE,* vol. 3, ed. Rüegg, pp. 396–397.

230. "The rise of modern Thomism is only fully intelligible as the Roman Catholic Church's repeated rejection of attempts by distinguished Catholic theologians to rethink Christian doctrine in terms of post-Cartesian philosophy." Fergus Kerr, *After Aquinas: Versions of Thomism* (Malden, Mass., and Oxford: Blackwell, 2002), p. 20. See also McCool, *Catholic Theology,* with discussion of Bautain at pp. 46–58. On the quasi-Thomistic character of the later Wittgenstein's thought, which influenced his students G. E. M. Anscombe and Peter Geach, see Kerr, *After Aquinas,* pp. 21–22, and Roger Pouivet, *After Wittgenstein, St. Thomas,* trans. Michael S. Sherwin (South Bend, Ind.: St. Augustine's Press, 2006).

231. On the central importance of neo-Thomism to American Catholic higher education in the late nineteenth and twentieth centuries, see Philip Gleason, *Contending with Modernity: Catholic Higher Education in the Twentieth Century* (New York: Oxford University Press, 1995), with discussion of *Pascendi Dominici Gregis* and *Humani Generis* at pp. 13–17 and 280–281, respectively.

232. Although the Catholic University of America was among the fourteen charter members of the Association of American Universities in 1900, it "failed to fulfill its promise of providing a national locus for advanced scholarship with a distinctive Catholic perspective." Thelin, *History,* pp. 110–112, quotation on 112.

233. Kathleen A. Mahoney, *Catholic Higher Education in Protestant America: The Jesuits and Harvard in the Age of the University* (Baltimore and London: Johns Hopkins University Press, 2003), pp. 243–247; on some of the internal intellectual and pedagogical reasons for the demise of neo-scholasticism, see Gleason, *Contending,* pp. 297–304.

234. The quoted phrase is Gleason's in *Contending,* p. 318.

235. On Newman's life, see Ian Ker, *John Henry Newman* (Oxford: Oxford University Press, 1988); on the opening of Oxford and Cambridge to non-Anglicans in the 1870s by acts of Parliament, see Charle, "Patterns," in *HUE,* vol. 3, ed. Rüegg, p. 61; more specifically, for the 1871 abolition of religious tests for fellowships and advanced degrees at Oxford and Cambridge, and for the Commission of 1877 and its influence on the continuing diminution

of the Anglican Church's role at Oxford, see A. J. Engel, *From Clergyman to Don: The Rise of the Academic Profession in Nineteenth-Century Oxford* (Oxford: Clarendon Press, 1983), pp. 77–81, 173–178.

236. Newman, *Idea of a University*, ed. Turner, especially Discourses 2–6, pp. 25–108.

237. Ibid., "Preface," p. 3. See also Martha McMackin Garland, "Newman in His Own Day," in Newman, *Idea of a University*, ed. Turner, p. 274, and Frank Turner, "Newman's University and Ours," in ibid., p. 284.

## Conclusion

1. Alexandra Walsham, "The Reformation and the 'Disenchantment of the World' Reassessed," *Historical Journal* 51 (2008): 528.

2. Constance M. Furey, *Erasmus, Contarini, and the Religious Republic of Letters* (Cambridge: Cambridge University Press, 2006).

3. For many examples of Reformation-era Protestant converts to Roman Catholicism, see Andreas Räß, *Die Convertiten seit der Reformation nach ihrem Leben und aus ihren Schriften,* 14 vols. (Freiburg im Breisgau: Herder, 1866–1880), which covers the period from the beginning of the Reformation through the eighteenth century. I thank John Frymire for calling my attention to this work.

4. David Sehat, *The Myth of American Religious Freedom* (New York: Oxford University Press, 2011).

5. Samuel Moyn, *The Last Utopia: Human Rights in History* (Cambridge, Mass., and London: Belknap Press of Harvard University Press, 2010).

6. Zygmunt Bauman, *Does Ethics Have a Chance in a World of Consumers?* (Cambridge, Mass., and London: Harvard University Press, 2008), p. 111.

7. Steven D. Smith, *The Disenchantment of Secular Discourse* (Cambridge, Mass., and London: Harvard University Press, 2010), pp. 26–39, 105–106, 170, 177, 185, 212, 215, 221.

8. Ibid., p. 25; see also pp. 23–24, 211–225.

# Acknowledgments

Without my awareness this book was gestating for more than twenty years before I started writing it. In this sense it is not only a book about the unintended Reformation, but also an unintended book. This protracted germination period means that a great many friends, colleagues, students, and institutions have had a role in its making and in making it better than it otherwise would have been. It gives me great pleasure to thank at least some of them here. It goes without saying that I remain solely responsible for all of the book's shortcomings.

I am grateful to John Frymire, Patrick Griffin, John O'Malley, Nathaniel Peters, Jim Sheehan, Christian Smith, and Bob Sullivan for their comments on and criticisms of an earlier version of the entire manuscript. Before that, Jim Sheehan, Peter Brown, and Tony Grafton graciously read and made suggestions on a very preliminary draft of the introduction and first three chapters. I am indebted to two first-rate philosophical theologians and colleagues at Notre Dame, David Burrell and Cyril O'Regan, for their astute comments on a draft of Chapter 1. In addition, Gary Anderson, Ulrich Lehner, Joe Nawrocki, Mark Noll, and Dan Philpott read and offered comments and suggestions on drafts of individual chapters. Candida Moss made valuable criticisms and suggestions on an earlier version of the Introduction plus other key passages in the text. I profited from the comments on Chapter 5 of the graduate students at Notre Dame who read it in draft in my graduate seminar in the fall of 2010. Alasdair Mac-Intyre provided feedback on an early overview of the undertaking. Without Tom Brady's criticisms several years ago of a paper distantly related to this project, the book itself probably would not have taken shape. Tom has my gratitude as well for his role as a reader of the manuscript for the press, as do Tony Grafton and the anonymous third reader. All three made valuable criticisms and suggestions.

My having taught at two quite different kinds of institutions, Stanford University and the University of Notre Dame, has influenced this project by prompting reflection on the relationship among religion, history, secularization, and knowledge. In Stanford's history department, where I taught from 1996 to 2003, Keith Baker, Paula Findlen, David Kennedy, Jack Rakove, Aron Rodrigue, Paul Seaver, Jim Sheehan, Amir Weiner, and above all Philippe Buc contributed importantly to discussions about issues relevant to this book. My current home institution, the University of Notre Dame, has a critical mass of superb scholars of religion in general and of Christianity in particular, from whose input I have benefited immensely. In the history department, I am grateful for discussions with Lauren Faulkner, Patrick Griffin, Tom Kselman, Sabine MacCormack, John McGreevy, George Marsden, Margaret Meserve, Tom Noble, Mark Noll, Deborah Tor, Jim Turner, John Van Engen, and especially Bob Sullivan, who has been a discerning interlocutor for years. I am also indebted to many colleagues in other departments of the university for conversations, input, inspiration, and feedback, among them Gary Anderson, Phil Bess, Paolo Carozza, John Cavadini, Brian Daley, Rick Garnett, Rob Gimello, Alasdair MacIntyre, Ed Maginn, John Meier, Susannah Monta, Candida Moss, John O'Callaghan, Cyril O'Regan, and Christian Smith.

In addition to so many fruitful discussions at Notre Dame, I am grateful to have delivered papers related to this project at the University of Wisconsin at Madison, the University of California at Berkeley, Stanford University, Yale University, the University of Chicago, Northwestern University, Rutgers University, Creighton University, DePaul University, Ohio University, Augustana College, and the University of Montana, all of which offered the occasion for valuable questions and discussion. I am especially thankful for tough questions from and good conversations with David Loewenstein, Ethan Shagan, Jonathan Sheehan, Bob Gregg, Carlos Eire, Bruce Gordon, Ward Holder, Richard Strier, Ed Muir, Regina Schwartz, John O'Keefe, Robert Ingram, Peter Marshall, LuAnn Homza, John Frymire, Paul Dietrich, and Dave Emmons. Leading the annual, weeklong summer faculty seminar in June 2010 at the University of St. Thomas in St. Paul, Minnesota, was invaluable for the revision of Chapter 6. Presentations abroad related to the material in the book also improved it, including talks at the State University of Milan, the University of Oslo, the University of St. Andrews, the Hebrew University in Jerusalem, and the National Taiwan University in Taipei. I owe special thanks to Emanuele Colombo, Tor Egil Førland, Andrew Pettegree, Bridget Heal, Emily Michelson, Haym Soloveitchik, Guy Stroumsa, Vivienne Westbrook, and Fiona Kao for their invitations and hospitality on these occasions.

The experience of regularly teaching a two-semester honors humanities seminar for first-year undergraduates at Notre Dame has contributed to this book in critical ways: not only does it regularly oblige me to read, reread, and discuss works from Homer to the present, but the course's exceptional students effectively do double duty as anthropological informants about the attitudes and assumptions of contemporary American eighteen- and nineteen-year-olds. I am deeply grateful to all of them. Other undergraduate students at Stanford and Notre Dame have over the years influenced me by the example of their lives; their impact on this book is indirect yet profound, and perhaps without their inspiration it would not have been written. These students include, among many others, Kyle Bertoli, Susan Bigelow, Kate Brubacher, MaryKate Conboy, Mary Crisham, Christina Dehan, Andy Hlabse, Andrew Hochstedler, Claire Hoipkemier, Meg Hunter-Kilmer, Kyle Karches, Caroline (Murphy) Lashutka, Keri Oxley, Aaron Sanders, Chris Scaperlanda, Alexa (Puscas) Sifuentes, Eva St. Clair, Laura (Scrafford) Slonkosky, and above all (and also for her music) Danielle Rose Skorich.

The book is dedicated to an unlikely pair: my first, longest-running, and most influential intellectual mentor and to the memory of my grandmother. Len Rosenband not only read the entire manuscript but, through our regular telephone conversations, has shared continuously in the project from my initial attempts to articulate what I was trying to do. He has been nothing but a blessing and bringer of *mitzvot* in my life since I walked into his Western civ class as an undergraduate, and I would not be who I am as a scholar or a person without his influence. My maternal grandmother, Helen Heider, was not a scholar; she had only an eighth-grade education, but was among the wisest people I have known in my life. She knew what mattered and why, and she too was nothing but a blessing in my life before her death at age ninety-five in 2009. Although this book is not officially dedicated to my wife, Kerrie McCaw, or our son, Sean McCaw-Gregory, words will always be inadequate to express how much I owe them and how grateful I am to them for everything.

# Index

Anabaptism *(continued)*
204; Dutch, 91, 103; and withdrawal
from politics, 99, 156, 450n81; civic, 151,
448n63; and rejection of magisterial
Protestantism, 151, 204; and accommo-
dation with confessional regimes, 156;
and Christianity as shared way of life,
156; on obedience to God rather than
men, 156; and inseparability of salvation
from economic realities, 264–265;
hostility to commercial life, 265. *See also*
Community of goods; Hutterites;
Mennonites; Münster, Anabaptist
Kingdom of; Reformation, radical; Swiss
Brethren
Anglican Church, 163, 167–168, 177
Anglo-Dutch wars, 283
Anscombe, G. E. M. (Elizabeth), 13–14, 361
Anselm of Canterbury, 30, 313, 314
Antonino of Florence, 85, 268
Antwerp, 261, 274
Antwerp Polyglot Bible, 520n112
Apocalypticism, 86, 140, 142, 202, 203,
371
Appiah, Kwame Anthony, 78
Appleby, Joyce, 242, 280
Aquinas, Thomas: conception of God,
30–31, 36, 38, 401n29; insufficiency of
reason concerning God, 50; on theologi-
cal virtues, 192; use of Aristotelian
(moral) philosophy, 192, 261, 315–316,
400n21; on *caritas*, 194; on authoritative
Christian tradition, 316; modern
influence of, 361; on faith and reason,
362; on ontological contingency,
418n138
Aristocracy, early modern, 267, 281, 282
Aristotelianism, early modern, 45–46, 53,
331. *See also* Universities, early modern
confessional
Aristotelianism, medieval: and Christian
theology, 34, 35–36, 39, 315–316; in
universities, 36–37, 44, 53, 308, 315–317,
325, 326; and transubstantiation, 36;
criticism by Protestant reformers, 40, 45;
cosmology undermined by modern
science, 53–54. *See also* Scholasticism,
medieval; Universities, medieval
Aristotelian moral tradition, 5, 180; as
teleological, 181; rejection of, 181, 183,
185; lack of shared replacement for, 182;
politics as integral to, 183, 201, 216; in
medieval Christianity, 189, 192; rejection

by Luther, 207; appropriation by
Melanchthon, 208; in early modern
Catholicism, 211, 461n16. *See also* Good,
substantive morality of the; Virtue ethics;
Virtues
Aristotle: medieval condemnations of, 39,
315, 321; *Nicomachean Ethics*, 192,
198–199, 207, 208, 247, 252; economic
analysis of, 246–247; on benefits and
dangers of money, 247; distinction
between use value and exchange value,
247; and condemnation of usury, 247;
and subordination of economics to
morality, 247; and insatiability of avarice,
247, 285
Arminianism, 208, 275, 338–339
Arminius, Jakob, 338
Art, 257–258, 281
Asceticism, Christian, 240–241, 245, 251
Astrology, medieval/Renaissance, 39, 317
Astronomy, medieval, 311, 317, 402n34
Atheism, modern: as allegedly inevitable,
13; as alleged consequence of science, 26,
28, 29, 33, 67, 69, 70; in eighteenth
century, 52; views of universe in, 57;
demographic spread of, 64, 77, 111;
dependence on belief, 71, 72; as entailing
nihilism, 229. *See also* Naturalism;
Scientism; Univocity, metaphysical
Augustine, 195: conception of God, 30, 49;
on exercise of power as moral duty, 136,
157; attitude toward pagan philosophy,
192; on *caritas*, 194; on human restlessness, 222; on human selfishness, 246; and
education, 310, 317; on non-necessity of
scripture except for teaching, 323, 334
Autonomy, individual: as modern philosophical ideal, 112–113, 113–122, 215;
as culmination of history, 127; as
liberating, 183, 226, 373, 384–385;
regarding morality, 205–206, 222–223,
225, 226, 378; of Christians, 215,
215–216; and consumption/consumerism,
235, 240, 364; and negligence of others,
172–173, 236, 294; rejected by magisterial Protestant reformers, 266–268; in
Romantic research university, 349, 350;
and failing of modernity, 385. *See also*
Freedom, individual; Liberalism; Rights,
individual
Avarice: transvaluation of, 5, 261, 262, 282,
285–287, 288, 291, 371, 378; as deadly
sin, 233, 245, 246, 252, 258, 260,